INTERPRETATIONS AND FORECASTS

Books by Lewis Mumford

LEWIS MUMFORD

Interpretations and Forecasts: 1922-1972

Studies in Literature, History, Biography, Technics, and Contemporary Society

A HARVEST/HBJ BOOK

HARCOURT BRACE JOVANOVICH   NEW YORK AND LONDON

"The Origins of the American Mind" and "The Golden Day" from *The Golden Day,* copyright 1926 by Boni & Liveright, Inc., © 1953 by Lewis Mumford, are used by permission of Dover Publications, Inc. "Morning Star: Emerson," Introduction to *Ralph Waldo Emerson: Essays and Journals,* selected and with an introduction by Lewis Mumford, copyright © 1968 by Nelson Doubleday, Inc. is reprinted by permission of the publisher, Nelson Doubleday, Inc. "The Brown Decades" from *The Brown Decades,* copyright © 1931 by Harcourt, Brace and Company, Inc., © 1959 by Lewis Mumford, is used by permission of Dover Publications, Inc. "Prelude to the Present," from the New York *Herald Tribune,* January 11, 1931, is reprinted by permission of the W.C.C. Publishing Company, Inc. "Utopia, the City, and the Machine," from *Daedalus,* XCIV (Spring 1965), 271–92, is reprinted by permission of the American Academy of Arts and Sciences. "Standardization and Choice," from *Art and Technics* by Lewis Mumford, pages 85–110, copyright © 1952 by Columbia University Press, is used by permission. "Post-Historic Man," "Animal into Human," "Archaic Man," and "World Culture," from *The Transformations of Man,* copyright © 1956 by Lewis Mumford, are reprinted by permission of Harper & Row, Publishers, Inc. "The Opening Future," from *Man's Role in Changing the Face of the Earth,* edited by William L. Thomas, © The University of Chicago, 1956, is reprinted by permission of The University of Chicago Press. "The Flowering of Plants and Men" is copyright © 1970 by Columbia University Press. "Revolt of the Demóns" appeared originally in *The New Yorker.*

Library of Congress Cataloging in Publication Data

Mumford, Lewis, 1895–
   Interpretations and forecasts, 1922–1972.
   (A Harvest/HBJ book)
   Includes bibliographical references.
   I. Title.
AC8.M78   1979   081   79-10266
ISBN 0-15-644903-X

First Harvest/HBJ edition 1979
A B C D E F G H I J

More than once in recent years I have been asked to bring together in a single volume a representative collection of my writings over the last half century. An early attempt at such a book, 'The Human Prospect,' came out indeed almost twenty years ago. But since it reflected solely the independent judgment of the editors, Professor Harry T. Moore and Professor Karl Deutsch, it has served as a challenge, rather than a deterrent to the present work. Only three of the twenty-nine selections in the earlier book have been used in the present more ample collection.

At first I hesitated to take on this task, since all my major books, with one exception, 'Green Memories,' are still actively in print, beginning with 'The Story of Utopias' in 1922. But Elmer Newman's recent bibliography of my writings made me realize how little even my later work is known to the present generation, since some of my more valuable contributions appeared in periodicals of limited circulation, now vanished or difficult to consult. In order to keep the present volume from being over-compressed or over-bulky, I have reserved for a future occasion a similar selection from my writings on architecture, urbanism, and regionalism.

By concentrating on five main themes I have warded off the temptation to present scattered, unrelated samples of my "best work" and have confined myself to those areas where I have had a fresh contribution to make. By observing these conditions, this closely interwoven collection has, I trust, turned out to be, not a mere mélange or anthology, but virtually an original work in its own right: all the more useful, perhaps, as a general introduction because my earliest thoughts and my latest often gain in significance by appearing side by side.

—L.M.

CONTENTS

PART ONE

New World Horizons

CHAPTER ONE

The Origins
of the American Mind

The settlement of America had its origins in the unsettlement of Europe. America came into existence when the European was already so distant in mind from the ancient ideas and ways of his birthplace that the whole span of the Atlantic did not materially widen the gulf. The dissociation, the displacement, and finally the disintegration of European culture became most apparent in the New World: but the process itself began in Europe, and the interests that eventually dominated the American scene all had their origin in the Old World.

The Protestant, the inventor, the politician, the explorer, the restless delocalized man—all these types appeared in Europe before they rallied together to form the composite American. If we can understand the forces that produced them, we shall fathom the origins of the American mind. The settlement of the Atlantic seaboard was the culmination of one process, the breakup of medieval culture, and the beginning of another. If the disintegration went farthest in America, the processes of renewal have, at intervals, been most active in the new country; and it is for the beginnings of a genuine culture, rather than for its relentless exploitation of materials, that the American adventure has been significant. To mark the points at which the culture of the Old World broke down, and to discover in what places a new one has arisen are the two poles of this study. Something of value disappeared with the colonization of America. Why did it disappear? Something of value was created. How did that come about? If I do not fully answer these questions, I propose, at least, to put them a little more sharply; by tracing them to their historic beginnings, and by putting them in their social context.

In the thirteenth century the European heritage of medieval culture was still intact. By the end of the seventeenth it had become only a heap of fragments, and men showed, in their actions if not by their professions, that it no longer had a hold over their minds. What had happened?

If one tries to sum up the world as it appeared to the contemporaries of Thomas Aquinas or Dante one is conscious of two main facts. The physical earth was bounded by a narrow strip of seas: it was limited: while above and beyond it stretched the golden canopy of heaven, infinite in all its invitations and promises. The medieval culture lived in the dream of eternity: within that dream, the visible world of cities and castles and caravans was little more than the forestage on which the prologue was spoken. The drama itself did not properly open until the curtains of Death rang down, to destroy the illusion of life and to introduce the main scene of the drama, in heaven itself. During the Middle Ages the visible world was definite and secure. The occupations of men were defined, their degree of excellence described, and their privileges and duties, though not without struggle, were set down. Over the daily life lay a whole tissue of meanings, derived from the Christian belief in eternity: the notion that existence was not a biological activity but a period of moral probation, the notion of an intermediate hierarchy of human beings that connected the lowest sinner with the august Ruler of Heaven, the idea that life was significant only on condition that it was prolonged, in beatitude or in despair, into the next world. The beliefs and symbols of the Christian Church had guided men, and partly modified their activities, for roughly a thousand years. Then, one by one, they began to crack; one by one they ceased to be "real" or interesting; and gradually the dream that held them all together started to dissolve. When the process ceased, the united order of Christendom had become an array of independent and sovereign States, and the Church itself had divided up into a host of repellent sects.

At what point did medieval culture begin to break down? The current answer to this, "With the Renaissance," is merely an evasion. When did it finally cease to exist? The answer is that a good part of it is still operative and has mingled with the customs and ideas that have succeeded it. But one can, perhaps, give an arbitrary beginning and an arbitrary end to the whole process. One may say that the first hint of change came in the thirteenth century, with the ringing of the bells, and that medieval culture ceased to dominate and direct the European community when it turned its back upon contemporary experience and failed at last to absorb the meanings of that experience, or to modify its nature. The Church's inability to control usury; her failure to reckon in time with the Protestant criticism of her internal administration; the unreadiness of the scholastics to adapt their methods to the new interests and criteria of science; the failure to prevent the absorption of the free cities, the feudal estates, and the monasteries by the central government—these are some of the stigmata of the decline. It is impossible to give a date to all of them; but it is pretty clear that by the end of the seventeenth century one or another had come to pass in every part of Europe. In countries like England, which were therefore "advanced," all of them had come to pass.

It is fairly easy to follow the general succession of events. First, the bells tolled, and the idea of time, or rather, temporality, resumed its hold over men's minds. All over Europe, beginning in the thirteenth century, the townsman erected campaniles and belfries, to record the passing hour. Immersed in traffic or handicraft, proud of his city or his guild, the citizen began to forget his awful fate in eternity; instead, he noted the succession of the minutes, and planned to make what he could of them. It was an innocent enjoyment, this regular tolling of the hour, but it had important consequences. Ingenious workmen in Italy and Southern Germany invented clocks, rigorous mechanical clocks: they adapted the principle of the woodman's lathe and applied it to metal. Here was the beginning of the exact arts. The craftsman began by measuring time; presently he could measure millimeters, too, and with the knowledge and technique introduced by the clockmaker, he was ready to make the telescope, the microscope, the theodolite—all of them instruments of a new order of spatial exploration and measurement.

The interests in time and space advanced side by side. In the fifteenth century the mapmakers devised new means of measuring and charting the earth's surface, and scarcely a generation before Columbus's voyages they began to cover their maps with imaginary lines of latitude and longitude. As soon as the mariner could calculate his position in time and space, the whole ocean was open to him; and henceforward even ordinary men, without the special skill and courage of a Marco Polo or a Leif Ericsson, could travel to distant lands. So time and space took possession of the European's mind. Why dream of heaven or eternity, while the world was still so wide, and each new tract that was opened up promised, if not riches, novelty, and if not novelty, well, a new place to breathe in? So the bells tolled, and the ships set sail. Secure in his newly acquired knowledge, the European traveled outward in space, and, losing that sense of the immediate present which went with his old belief in eternity, he traveled backward and forward in time. An interest in archaeology and utopias characterized the Renaissance. They provided images of purely earthly realizations in past and future: ancient Syracuse and The City of the Sun were equally credible.

The fall of Constantinople and the diffusion of Greek literature had not, perhaps, such a formative influence on this change as the historian once thought. But they accompanied it, and the image of historic Greece and Rome gave the mind a temporary dwelling-place. Plainly, the knowledge which once held it so firmly, the convictions that the good Christian once bought so cheaply and cheerfully, no longer sufficed: if they were not altogether thrown aside, the humanists began, with the aid of classic literature, to fill up the spaces they had left open. The European turned aside from his traditional cathedrals and began to build according to Vitruvius. He took a pagan interest in the human body, too, and Leonardo's Saint John was so lost to Christianity that be became Bacchus without changing a feature. The Virgin herself lost her old sanctity. Presto! the

Child disappeared, the responsibilities of motherhood were gone, and she was now Venus. What had Saint Thomas Aquinas to say about theology? One could read the 'Phaedo.' What had Aristotle to say about natural history? Leonardo, unaided, discovered fossils in the Tuscan hills and inferred that the ocean was once there. Simple peasants might cling to the Virgin, ask for the intercession of the saints, and kneel before the cross; but these images and ideas had lost their hold upon the more acute minds of Europe. They had broken, these intellectual adventurers, outside the tight little world of Here and Eternity: they were interested in Yonder and Yesterday; and since eternity was a long way off and we'll "be damnably moldy a hundred years hence," they accepted tomorrow as a substitute.

There were some who found it hard to shake off the medieval dream in its entirety; so they retained the dream and abandoned all the gracious practices that enthroned it in the daily life. As Protestants, they rejected the outcome of historic Christianity, but not its inception. They believed in the Eucharist, but they did not enjoy paintings of the Last Supper. They believed in the Virgin Mary, but they were not softened by the humanity of Her motherhood. They read, voraciously, the literature of the Ancient Jews, and the legends of that sect which grew up by the shores of Galilee, but, using their private judgment and taking the bare words as the sum and substance of their religion, they forgot the interpretations from the early Fathers to Thomas Aquinas which refined that literature and melted it into a comprehensible whole. When the Protestant renounced justification by works, he included under works all the arts which had flourished in the medieval church and created an independent realm of beauty and magnificence. What remained of the faith was perhaps intensified during the first few generations of the Protestant espousal—one cannot doubt the original intensity and vitality of the protest—but alas! so little remained!

In the bareness of the Protestant cathedral of Geneva one has the beginnings of that hard barracks architecture which formed the stone tenements of seventeenth century Edinburgh, set a pattern for the austere meeting-houses of New England, and finally deteriorated into the miserable shanties that line Main Street. The meagerness of the Protestant ritual began that general starvation of the spirit which finally breaks out, after long repression, in the absurd jamborees of Odd Fellows, Elks, Woodmen, and kindred fraternities. In short, all that was once made manifest in a Chartres, a Strasbourg, or a Durham minster, and in the mass, the pageant, the art gallery, the theater—all this the Protestant bleached out into the bare abstraction of the printed word. Did he suffer any hardship in moving to the New World? None at all. All that he wanted of the Old World he carried within the covers of a book. Fortunately for the original Protestants, that book was a whole literature; in this, at least, it differed from the later protestant canons, perpetrated by Joseph Smith or Mary Baker Eddy. Unfortunately, however, the practices of a civilized society cannot be put between two black covers. So, in some respects, Protestant society ceased to be civilized.

Our critical eyes are usually a little dimmed by the great release of energy during the early Renaissance: we forget that it quickly spent itself. For a little while the great humanists, such as More, Erasmus, Scaliger, and Rabelais, created a new home for the spirit out of the fragments of the past, and the new thoughts were cemented together by the old habits of medieval civilization, which persisted among the peasants and the craftsmen long after they had been undermined in the Church and the palace.

The revival of classic culture, however, did not give men any new power of command over the workaday routine of life, for the very ability to re-enter the past and have commerce with its great minds implied leisure and scholarship. Thus the great bulk of the community had no direct part in the revival, and if the tailor or the tinker abandoned the established church, it was only to espouse that segment called Protestantism. Tailors and tinkers, almost by definition, could *not* be humanists. Moreover, beyond a certain point, humanism did not make connections with the new experience of the Columbuses and the Newtons any better than did the medieval culture. If the criticism of the pagan scholars released a good many minds from Catholic theology, it did not orient them toward what was "new" and "practical" and "coming." The Renaissance was not, therefore, the launching out of a new epoch: it simply witnessed the breakdown and disruption of the existing science, myth, and fable. When the Royal Society was founded in London in the middle of the seventeenth century the humanities were deliberately excluded. 'Science' was indifferent to them.

Once the European, indeed, had abandoned the dream of medieval theology, he could not live very long on the memory of a classic culture: that, too, lost its meaning; that, too, failed to make connections with his new experiences in time and space. Leaving both behind him, he turned to what seemed to him a hard and patent reality: the external world. The old symbols, the old ways of living, had become a blank. Instead of them, he took refuge in abstractions, and reduced the rich actuality of things to a bare description of matter and motion. Along this path went the early scientists, or natural philosophers. By mathematical analysis and experiment, they extracted from the complicated totality of everyday experience just those phenomena which could be observed, measured, generalized, and, if necessary, repeated. Applying this exact methodology, they learned to predict more accurately the movements of the heavenly bodies, to describe more precisely the fall of a stone and the flight of a bullet, to determine the carrying load of a bridge, or the composition of a fragment of 'matter.' Rule, authority, precedent, general consent—these things were all subordinate in scientific procedure to the methods of observation and mathematical analysis: weighing, measuring, timing, decomposing, isolating—all operations that led to results.

At last knowledge could be tested and practice reformed; and if the scientists themselves were usually too busy to see the upshot of their investigations, one who stood on the sidelines, Francis Bacon, was quick to announce their conclusion: science tended to the relief of man's estate.

With the aid of this new procedure, the external world was quickly reduced to a semblance of order. But the meanings created by science did not lead into the core of human life: they applied only to 'matter,' and if they touched upon life at all, it was through a post-mortem analysis, or by following Descartes and arbitrarily treating the human organism as if it were automatic and externally determined under all conditions. For the scientists, these new abstractions were full of meaning and very helpful; they tunneled through whole continents of knowledge. For the great run of men, however, science had no meaning for itself; it transferred meaning from the creature proper to his estate, considered as an independent and external realm. In short, except to the scientist, the only consequences of science were practical ones. A new view of the universe developed, naturally, but it was accepted less because of any innate credibility than because it was accompanied by so many cogent proofs of science's power. Philosophy, religion, art, none of these activities had ever baked any bread: science was ready, not merely to bake the bread, but increase the yield of the wheat, grind the flour, and eliminate the baker. Even the plain man would appreciate consequences of this order. Seeing was believing. By the middle of the seventeenth century all the implications of the process had been imaginatively grasped. In 1661 Joseph Glanvill wrote:

"I doubt not posterity will find many things that are now but rumors, verified into practical realities. It may be that, some ages hence, a voyage to the Southern tracts, yea, possibly to the moon, will not be more strange than one to America. To them that come after us, it may be as ordinary to buy a pair of wings to fly to remotest regions, as now a pair of boots to ride a journey; and to confer at the distance of the Indies by sympathetic conveyances may be as usual in future times as by literary correspondence. The restoration of gray hairs to juvenility, and renewing the exhausted marrow, may at length be effected without a miracle; and the turning of the now comparatively desert world into a Paradise may not improbably be effected from late agriculture."

The process of abstraction began in the theology of Protestantism as an attempt to isolate, deform, and remove historic connections; it became habitual in the mental operations of the physical scientist; and it was carried over into other departments.

The extended use of money, to replace barter and service, likewise began during this same period of disintegration. Need I emphasize that

in their origin Protestantism, physical science, and finance were all liberating influences? They took the place of habits and institutions which,
plainly, were moribund, being incapable of renewal from within. Need I
also emphasize the close historic inter-connection of the three things? We
must not raise our eyebrows when we discover that a scientist like Newton in seventeenth century England, or Rittenhouse in eighteenth century
America, became master of the mint, nor must we pass by, as a quaint
coincidence, the fact that Geneva is celebrated both as the home of Jean
Calvin and as the great center of watches and clocks. These connections
are not mystical nor factitious. The new financial order was a direct out-
growth of the new theological and scientific views. First came a mechanical method of measuring time: then a method of measuring space: finally,
in money, men began more widely to apply an abstract way of measuring
power, and in money they achieved a calculus for all human activity.

This financial system of measurement released the European from his
old sense of social and economic limitations. No glutton can eat a hundred
pheasants; no drunkard can drink a hundred bottles of wine at a sitting;
and if any one schemed to have so much food and wine brought to his
table daily, he would be mad. Once he could exchange the potential
pheasants and Burgundy for marks or thalers, he could direct the labor
of his neighbors, and achieve the place of an aristocrat without being to
the manor born. Economic activity ceased to deal with the tangible realities of the medieval world—land and corn and houses and universities and
cities. It was transformed into the pursuit of an abstraction—money. Tangible goods were only a means to this supreme end. When some incipient
Rotarian finally coined the phrase "Time is money," he expressed philo-
sophically the equivalence of two ideas which could not possibly be combined, even in thought, so long as money meant houses, food, pictures,
and time meant only what it does in Bergson's *durée,* that is, the succession of organic experiences.

Does all this seem very remote from the common life? On the contrary, it goes to the roots of every activity. The difference between historical periods, as the late T. E. Hulme pointed out, is a difference between the categories of their thought. If we have got on the trail of their
essential categories, we have a thread which will lead outward into even
remote departments of life. The fact is that from the seventeenth century
onward, almost every field was invaded by this process of abstraction. The
people not affected were either survivals from an older epoch, like the
orthodox Jews and Roman Catholics in theology, or the humanists in
literature, or they were initiators, working through to a new order—men
like Lamarck, Wordsworth, Goethe, Comte.

Last and most plainly of all, the disintegration of medieval culture became apparent in politics. Just as "matter," when examined by the physicist, is abstracted from the esthetic matrix of our experience, so the 'individual' was abstracted by the political philosopher of the new order from

the bosom of human society. He ceased, this individual, to maintain his omnipresent relations with city, family, household, club, college, guild, and office: he became the new unit of political society. Having abstracted this purely conceptual person in thought—he had, of course, no more actual existence than an angel or a cherub—the great problem of political thinking in the eighteenth century became: How shall we restore him to society?—for somehow we always find man, as Rousseau grimly said, in chains, that is, in relations with other human beings. The solution that Rousseau and the dominant schools of the time offered was ingenious: each individual is endowed with natural rights, and he votes these political rights into society, as the shareholder votes his economic rights into a trading corporation. This principle of consent was necessary to the well-being of a civil society; and assent was achieved, in free political states, through the operation of the ballot, and the delivery of the general will by a parliament.

The doctrine broke the weakening chain of historical continuity in Europe. It challenged the vested interests; it was ready to declare the existing corporations bankrupt; it was prepared to wipe away the traditional associations and nests of privileges which maintained the clergy, the nobility, the guilds. On its destructive side, the movement for political liberty, like that for free contract, free association, and free investigation, was sane and reasonable; for the abuses of the past were genuine and the grievances usually had more than a small touch of justice. We must not, however, be blind to the consequences of all these displacements and dissociations. Perhaps the briefest way of characterizing them is to say that they made America inevitable. To those who were engaged in political criticism, it seemed that a genuine political order had been created in the setting up of free institutions; but we can see now that the process was an inevitable bit of surgery, rather than the beginning of a more organic form of political association. By 1852 Henry James, Sr., was keen enough to see what had happened: "Democracy," he observed, "is not so much a new form of political life as a dissolution and disorganization of the old forms. It is simply a resolution of government into the hands of the people, a taking down of that which has before existed, and a recommitment of it to its original sources, but it is by no means the substitution of anything else in its place."

Now we begin to see a little more clearly the state of mind out of which the great migrations to the New World became possible. The physical causes have been dwelt on often enough; it is important to recognize that a cultural necessity was at work at the same time. The old culture of the Middle Ages had broken down; the old heritage lingered on only in the "backward" and "unprogressive" countries like Italy and Spain, which drifted outside the main currents of the European mind. Men's interests became externalized; externalized and abstract. They fixed their attention on some narrow aspect of experience, and they pushed that to the limit. Intelligent people were forced to choose between the fossilized shell of an old and complete culture, and the new culture, which in origin was thin, partial, abstract, and deliberately indifferent to man's proper interests. Choosing the second, our Europeans already had one foot in America. Let them suffer persecution, let the times get hard, let them fall out with their governments, let them dream of worldly success—and they will come swarming over the ocean. The groups that had most completely shaken off the old symbolisms were those that were most ready for the American adventure: they turned themselves easily to the mastery of the external environment. To them matter alone mattered.

The ultimate results of this disintegration of European culture did not come out, in America, until the nineteenth century. But its immediate consequence became visible, step by step, in the first hundred and fifty years or so of the American settlement. Between the landing of the first colonists in Massachusetts, the New Netherlands, Virginia, and Maryland, and the first thin trickle of hunters that passed over the Alleghenies, beginning figuratively with Daniel Boone in 1775, the communities of the Atlantic seaboard were outposts of Europe: they carried their own moral and intellectual climate with them.

During this period, the limitations in the thought of the intellectual classes had not yet wrought themselves out into defects and malformations in the community itself: the house, the town, the farm were still modeled after patterns formed in Europe. It was not a great age, perhaps, but it had found its form. Walking through the lanes of Boston, or passing over the wide lawns to a manor house in Maryland, one would have had no sense of a great wilderness beckoning in the beyond. To tell the truth, the wilderness did not beckon: these solid townsmen, these freeholders, these planters, were content with their civil habits; and if they thought of expansion, it was only over the ocean, in search of Palladian designs for their houses, or of tea and sperm-oil for their personal comfort. On the surface, people lived as they had lived in Europe for many a year.

In the first century of colonization, this life left scarcely any deposit in the mind. There was no literature but a handful of verses, no music except the hymn or some surviving Elizabethan ballad, no ideas except those that circled around the dogmas of Protestantism. But, with the eighteenth century, these American communities stepped fully into the sphere of European ideas, and there was an American equivalent for every new European type. It is amusing to follow the leading biographies of the time. Distinguished American figures step onto the stage, in turn, as if the Muse of History had prepared their entrances and exits. Their arrangement is almost diagrammatic: they form a résumé of the European mind. In fact, these Edwardses and Franklins seem scarcely living characters: they were Protestantism, Science, Finance, Politics.

The first on the stage was Jonathan Edwards: he figured in American thought as the last great expositor of Calvinism. Edwards wrote like a man in a trance, who at bottom is aware that he is talking nonsense; for he was in love with beauty of the soul, like Plato before him, and it was only because he was caught in the premises of determinism that, with a heavy conscience, he followed his dire train of thought to its destination. After Edwards, Protestantism lost its intellectual backbone. It developed into the bloodless Unitarianism of the early nineteenth century, which is a sort of humanism without courage, or it got caught in orgies of revivalism, and, under the name of evangelical Christianity, threw itself under the hoofs of more than one muddy satyr. There were great Protestant preachers after Edwards, no doubt: but the triumph of a Channing or a Beecher rested upon personal qualities; and they no longer drew their thoughts from any deep well of conviction.

All the habits that Protestantism developed, its emphasis upon industry, upon self-help, upon thrift, upon the evils of 'idleness' and 'pleasure,' upon the worldliness and wickedness of the arts, were so many gratuitous contributions to the Industrial Revolution. When Professor Morse, the inventor of the telegraph, was still a painter, traveling in Italy, he recorded in one of his letters the animus that pervaded his religious creed: the testimony loses nothing by being a little belated. "I looked around the church," he wrote, "to ascertain what was the effect upon the multitude, assembled. . . . Everything around them, instead of aiding devotion, was entirely calculated to destroy it. The imagination was addressed by every avenue; music and painting pressed into the service of —not religion but the contrary—led the mind away from the contemplation of all that is practical in religion to the charms of mere sense. No instruction was imparted; none ever seems to be intended."

It is but a short step from this attitude to hiring revivalist mountebanks to promote factory morale; nor are these thoughts far from that fine combination of commercial zeal and pious effort which characterize such auxiliaries as the Y.M.C.A. The fictions of poetry and the delusions of feeling were the bugbears of Gradgrind, Bounderby, and M'Choakumchild in Dickens's classic picture of industrialism: for the shapes and images they called forth made those which were familiar to the Protestant mind a little dreary and futile. It was not merely that Protestantism and science had killed the old symbols: they must prevent new ones from developing: they must abolish the contemplative attitude in which art and myth grow up, and create new forms for man's activities. Hence the fury of effort by which the leaders of the new day diverted energies to quantitative production. The capacity to do work, which the new methods in industry had so enormously increased, gave utilitarian objects an importance they had not hitherto possessed. Did not God's Word say: "Increase and multiply"? If babies, why not goods: if goods, why not dollars? Success was the Protestant miracle that justified man's ways to God.

The next figure that dominated the American scene stood even more completely for these new forces. He was, according to the pale lights of his time, a thoroughly cultivated man, and in his maturity he was welcomed in London and Paris as the equal of scientists like Priestley and Erasmus Darwin, and of scholars like d'Alembert and d'Holbach. As a citizen, by choice, of Philadelphia, Benjamin Franklin adopted the plain manners and simple thrifty ways of the Quakers. He went into business as a publisher, and with a sort of sweet acuteness in the pursuit of money, he imparted the secrets of his success in the collection of timely saws for which he became famous. The line from Franklin through Samuel Smiles to the latest advertisements for improving one's position and doubling one's income, in the paper that dates back to Franklin's ownership, is a pretty direct one. If one prefers Franklin's bourgeois qualities to those of his successors, it is only perhaps because his life was more fully rounded. If he was not without the usurious habits of the financier, he had also the dignity and freedom of the true scientist.

For Franklin was equally the money-maker, the scientist, the inventor, and the politician, and in science his fair boast was that he had not gained a penny by any of his discoveries. He experimented with electricity; he invented the lightning rod; he improved the draft of chimneys; in fact, on his last voyage home to America, shortly before his death, he was still improving the draft of chimneys. Finally he was a Deist: he had gotten rid of all the "gothick phantoms" that seemed so puerile and unworthy to the quick minds of the eighteenth century—which meant that he was completely absorbed in the dominant abstractions and myths of his own time, namely, matter, money, and political rights. He accepted the mechanical concept of time: time is money; the importance of space: space must be conquered; the desirability of money: money must be made; and he did not see that these, too, are phantoms, in preoccuption with which a man may lose most of the advantages of a civilized life. As a young man, Franklin even invented an elaborate system of moral-bookkeeping: utilitarianism can go no further.

Although Franklin's sagacity as a statesman can hardly be overrated, for he had both patience and principle, the political side of the American thought of his time is best summed up in the doctrines of a new immigrant, that excellent friend of humanity, Thomas Paine. Paine's name has served so many purposes in polemics that scarcely any one seems to take the trouble to read his books: and so more than one shallow judgment has found its way into our histories of literature, written by worthy men who were incapable of enjoying a sound English style, or of following, with any pleasure, an honest system of thought, clearly expressed. 'The Rights of Man' is as simple as a geometrical theorem; it contains, I think, most of what is valid in political libertarianism. I know of no other thinker who saw more clearly through the moral humbug that surrounds a good many theories of government. Said Paine:

"Almost everything appertaining to the circumstances of a nation has been absorbed and confounded under the general and mysterious word government. Though it avoids taking to its account the errors it commits and the mischiefs it occasions, it fails not to arrogate to itself whatever has the appearance of prosperity. It robs industry of its honors by pedantically making itself the cause of its effects; and purloins from the general character of man the merits that appertain to him as a social being."

Passage after passage in 'The Rights of Man' and 'The Age of Reason' is written with the same pithiness. Paine came to America as an adult, and saw the advantages of a fresh start. He believed that if first principles could be enunciated, here, and here alone, was a genuine opportunity to apply them. He summed up the hope in reason and in human contrivance that swelled through the eighteenth century. Without love for any particular country, and without that living sense of history which makes one accept the community's past, as one accepts the totality of one's own life, with all its lapses and mistakes, he was the vocal immigrant, justifying in his political and religious philosophy the complete break he had made with old ties, affections, allegiances.

Unfortunately, a man without a background is not more truly a man: he has merely lost the scenes and institutions which gave him his proper shape. If one studies him closely, one will find that he has secretly arranged another background, made up of shadows that linger in the memory, or he is uneasy and restless, settles down, moves on, comes home again, lives on hopeless tomorrows, or sinks back into mournful yesterdays. The immigrants who came to America after the War of Independence gave up their fatherland in exchange for a Constitution and a Bill of Rights: they forfeited all the habits and institutions which had made them men without getting anything in exchange except freedom from arbitrary misrule. That they made the exchange willingly, proves that the conditions behind them were intolerable; but that the balance was entirely in favor of the new country, is something that we may well doubt. When the new settlers migrated in bodies, like the Moravians, they sometimes managed to maintain an effective cultural life; when they came alone, as "free individuals," they gained little more than cheap land and the privileges of the ballot box. The land itself was all to the good; and no one minded the change, or felt any lack, so long as he did not stop to compare the platitudes of Fourth of July orations with the actualities of the Slave Trade, the Constitutional Conventions, Alien and Sedition Acts, and Fugitive Slave Laws.

It was possible for Paine, in the eighteenth century, to believe that culture was served merely by the absence of a church, a state, a social order such as those under which Europe labored. That was the error of his school, for the absence of these harmful or obsolete institutions left a vacancy in society, and that vacancy was filled by work, or more accurately speaking, by busy work, which fatigued the body and diverted the mind from the things which should have enriched it. Republican politics aided this externalism. People sought to live by politics alone; the National State became their religion. The flag, as Professor Carleton Hayes has shown, supplanted the cross, and the Fathers of the Constitution the Fathers of the Church.

The interaction of the dominant interests of industry and politics is illustrated in Paine's life as well as Franklin's. Paine was the inventor of the take-down iron bridge. Indeed, politics and invention recurred rhythmically in his life, and he turned aside from his experiments on the iron bridge to answer Edmund Burke's attack on the French Revolution. "The War of Independence," as he himself said, "energized invention and lessened the catalogue of impossibilities. . . . As one among thousands who had borne a share in that memorable revolution, I returned with them to the enjoyment of a quiet life, and that I might not be idle, undertook to construct a bridge of a single arch for this river [the Schuylkill]."

That I might not be idle! What a tale those words tell! While the aristocracy was in the ascendant, patient hirelings used to apply their knowledge of hydraulics to the working of fountains, as in Versailles, or they devised automatic chess-players, or they contrived elaborate clocks which struck the hour, jetted water, caused little birds to sing and wag their tails, and played selections from the operas. It was to such inane and harmless performances that the new skills in the exact arts were first put. The bored patron was amused; life plodded on; nothing was altered. But in the freedom of the new day, the common man, as indifferent to the symbols of the older culture as the great lords and ladies, innocent of anything to occupy his mind, except the notion of controlling matter and mastering the external world—the common man turned to inventions. Stupid folk drank heavily, ate gluttonously, and became libertines; intelligent, industrious men like Franklin and Paine turned their minds to increasing the comforts and conveniences of existence. Justification by faith: that was politics: the belief in a new heaven and a new earth to be established by regular elections and parliamentary debate. Justification by works: that was invention. No frivolities entered this new religion. The new devices all saved labor, decreased distances, and in one way or another multiplied riches.

With these inventors, the American, like his contemporary in Europe, began the utilitarian conquest of his environment. From this time on, men with an imaginative bias like Morse, the pupil of Benjamin West, men like Whitney, the schoolteacher, like Fulton, the miniature painter, turned to invention or at least the commercial exploitation of inventions without a qualm of distrust: to abandon the imaginative arts seemed natural and inevitable, and they no longer faced the situation, as the painters of the Renaissance had done, with a divided mind. Not that America began or monopolized the developments of the Industrial Revolution: the great outbreak of technical patents began, in fact, in England about 1760, and the first inklings of the movement were already jotted down in Leonardo da Vinci's notebooks. The point is that in Europe heavy layers of the old culture kept large sections of the directing classes in the old ways. Scholars, literary men, historians, artists still felt no need of justifying themselves by exclusive devotion to practical activities. In America, however, the old culture had worn thin, and in the rougher parts of the country it did not exist. No one in America was unaffected by the progress of invention; each improvement was quickly cashed in. When Stendhal wrote 'L'Amour' the American love of comfort had already become a by-word: he refers to it with contempt.

Given an old culture in ruins, and a new culture *in vacuo,* this externalizing of interest, this ruthless exploitation of the physical environment was, it would seem, inevitable. Protestantism, science, invention, political democracy, all of these institutions denied the old values; all of them, by denial or by precept or by actual absorption, furthered the new activities. Thus in America the new order of Europe came quickly into being. If the nineteenth century found us more raw and rude, it was not because we had settled in a new territory; it was rather because our minds were not buoyed up by all those memorials of a great past that floated over the surface of Europe. The American was thus a stripped European; and the colonization of America can, with justice, be called the dispersion of Europe—a movement carried on by people incapable of sharing or continuing its past. It was to America that the outcast Europeans turned, without a Moses to guide them, to wander in the wilderness; and here they have remained in exile, not without an occasional glimpse, perhaps, of the promised land.

(1926)

N O T E : To identify the original texts or the books reviewed see the list of Sources, page 497.

CHAPTER TWO

Morning Star: Emerson

"Why should we grope among the dry bones of the past, or put the living generation into masquerade out of its faded wardrobe? The sun shines today also. . . . There are new lands, new men, new thoughts. Let us demand our own works and laws and worship."

These words appeared in 1836 on the opening page of 'Nature,' the little book in which Ralph Waldo Emerson made his first public appearance as a writer. Two generations after the political Declaration of Independence, came this declaration of spiritual independence; and from that time on, the American scene has never looked quite the same as it did when our forefathers were still trying to think and feel, if not to act, as if the voyage across the Atlantic and the settlement in a new land had made no essential difference in their lives and prospects.

Not that Emerson was alone in making this bold demand, any more than Jefferson was alone when he drafted the document that justified the separation of the colonies from England. All up and down the Atlantic seaboard, and past the Alleghenies, along the Ohio and down the Mississippi, both the old settlers and the new immigrants, like Audubon, were beginning to think in this fashion. Noah Webster's preface to his 'Spelling Book' as early as 1783 uttered similar sentiments about the European past and the American future. James Fenimore Cooper's novels, especially the famous Leatherstocking series, were drafting a new outline of the American character, showing what it owed to the feral woodland, the oceanic space of the prairies, the teeming variety and tangled abundance of its vegetation, its fish, its game. Longfellow, while still a student at Bowdoin in the eighteen-twenties, had made the same demand for cultural autonomy in his Commencement Address on Our National Literature. But in Emerson this new attitude issued from the core of his being. To confirm and clinch this note of independence Emerson repeated it, a few years later, in 'The American Scholar,' and his whole life was an attempt to explore its implications, to profit by the energies it awakened, and in the end to correct its partialities and its deficiencies, in the light of further experience.

Whatever else Emerson was, he must be given a place similar to Washington's, as the father of American literature, for he made us conscious of those qualities native to the soil that distinguish it from the literature of other nations. Emerson, as I said long ago in 'The Golden Day,' was the glacier who became the white mountain torrent of Thoreau and expanded into the broad-bosomed lake of Whitman. Even the dark caverns and secret grottoes of Hawthorne and Melville, though they owed no open debt to Emerson, had their counterparts, as I shall show, in Emerson's own consciousness; while Mark Twain in his raciest moments was only following Emerson's prescription for good writing. Note what Emerson said in appreciation of Dante: "He knows how to throw the weight of his body into each act. . . . I find him full of the 'nobil volgare eloquenza,' that he knows 'God damn' and can be rowdy if he please, and he does please."

Emerson's fame and influence as a writer have gone through a number of stages. Even in his own native region, New England, this quintessential New Englander, this soaring steeple of the New World church, was at first rejected as an alien and heretical voice; and though he commanded lecture audiences all over the country in the middle years of the nineteenth century, his books won readers only slowly, and were often superciliously reviewed or contemptuously dismissed; though in England, thanks partly to Thomas Carlyle, Alexander Ireland, and Moncure Conway, he met a better fate. By the time of Emerson's death, it is true, the whole country knew, as well as his neighbors in Concord, that he was a commanding literary presence: yet even in the eighties, the impression he had made was still only a partial one, and in the very act of describing him, as an idealist, a transcendentalist, a neoplatonist, a romantic, a mystic, his critics overlooked the whole man who was at home not only in America but in Europe and the Orient, who was not merely a child of his own age, but a mature mind that gathered its ideas from many ancient sources not in the least American: from Plato, from Montaigne, from Shakespeare, from Goethe, from the Persian poets and the Hindu scriptures.

When the memory of the actual Emerson faded away, even as Emerson's mind itself had faded away during the last ten years of his life, an "ideal wraith" of Emerson took the place of the real man: a creature pallid, thin, impalpable, too pure, too starlike in his remoteness from this muddy world. Henry James, the novelist, who from his youth had known Emerson as a friend of the family, spoke of Emerson's "paleness" and the "white tint of his career," and repeated his father's mistaken judgment about Emerson's complete unconsciousness of evil. I shall not brush these descriptions away; for Emerson himself was partly responsible for them; but they are as far from doing justice to Emerson as was William James's description of Walt Whitman as a boisterous optimist, "indiscriminately hurrahing for the universe." Still Emerson was always humorously conscious of the physical impression he made: people would say, he noted, "Aren't you a little thinner than when I saw you last?"

Though Emerson continued to have his readers, sufficient to justify the twelve-volume collected edition of his works first published in 1883, and again in 1903, he became associated, in the mind of the generation that followed his death, with the lesser worthies of the genteel tradition; and the young writers who participated in the American literary renascence that began around 1910 treated him, as Van Wyck Brooks at first did, rather as a warning example to be shunned than as the prophet of the America that they were soon to be uncovering and rediscovering for themselves. Indeed, when Brooks first wrote about Emerson, in 'America's Coming of Age,' in 1915, he did so in a mood of "persistent spleen," as he himself confessed. At that moment, Emerson seemed to him only "The child of his age, and what he did was to give his Yankee instincts free play under the sanction of his Transcendental idealism."

Since that time, Emerson's reputation has been slowly rising; and the body of his attentive readers has been growing, stimulated perhaps by the fact that the America that has been coming into existence this last half century is the direct antithesis—in many respects a dismally dejected one—of the America that Emerson's thought embodied and transfigured. I myself carried a World's Classic edition of Emerson's 'Essays' in my middy blouse, while training in the Navy in 1918; and in the mid-twenties Brooks offset his first peevish disparagements by falling in love with Emerson and translating his life into a stream-of-consciousness biography, pieced together out of Emerson's own words—a method that was later to serve him in the writing of his path-breaking literary history, beginning with 'The Flowering of New England.' Though Brooks's portrait is remote from meeting the current academic standards for a reputable biography in the way Ralph Rusk's work does, it is in fact the most Emersonian biography conceivable: almost an autobiography.

Meanwhile, the scholarly resurrection of Emerson's reputation has gone on; first in F. O. Matthiessen's 'American Renascence,' and later in a succession of special studies, along with the first attempt by R. E. Spiller and S. E. Whicher to publish the remains of Emerson's early lectures, which had never been available. When the new edition of Emerson's Journals is completed, the ground will be laid for an even more comprehensive assessment of his life and work and thought than had ever been possible before. But it was not for professional scholars that Emerson wrote.

One of the reasons for the spotty and incomplete view of Emerson that persisted long past his death was the far too tardy publication of Emerson's Journals: for it is those Journals that one must explore from end to end to get the full range of Emerson's mind, and understand how little that mind can be reduced to any such simple formula as Protestantism, Transcendentalism, or Americanism—how, though it was touched by all of these things, it showed a score of other equally significant influences and projections as well. These Journals, published from 1909 to 1914 in ten volumes, never had the effect they should have exerted, for unfortunately the complete edition of the Journals was limited to five hundred copies; and in addition, because the editing, done in the discreet fashion of an older day, omitted many significant passages or revealing epithets —as if Emerson's own reserve even in the sancity of his private chamber was not sufficiently inhibited! This Bowdlerization is now being redressed in the *mange-tout* facsimile edition of the Journals now being published by the John Harvard Press.

Even the two one-volume selections from the Journals that followed —that by Bliss Perry in 1926 and that by Robert Linscott in 1960—did not suffice to alter the old popular estimate. So in choosing the essays for this edition, I have sought to paint a more balanced portrait of Emerson by giving fuller play to those parts of his work that complement or contradict the familiar emphasis on his transcendental idealism; and I have chosen the extracts from his Journals with this likewise in mind. For what Emerson said of Plato, his great exemplar, was equally true of himself: "Admirable texts can be quoted on both sides of every great question from him." And though Plato covered his manysidedness by using the form of the dialogue, Emerson's whole work, by its lack of organization, by its consistent disjointedness, says the same thing. Emerson had no doctrine, no dogma, no enveloping system. "Be an opener of doors for such as come after thee," he admonished himself in 1840, "and do not try to make the universe a blind alley." If he had any guiding principle, it might be reduced to a single sentence: Listen for the voice within and find out for yourself! But even this would pin Emerson down too tightly; for when the moment demanded, he had sage, experience-seasoned advice to give others, and he often set a fine practical example by his own timely actions, provided his readers were alert enough to take these words and examples to themselves.

Many of Emerson's best thoughts were re-phrased by Walt Whitman and Henry David Thoreau, sometimes obviously under Emerson's influence, at other times quite independently; and some of his ideas have passed into the language, as folksays, almost as proverbs. "Whoso would be a man must be a nonconformist." "An institution is but the lengthened shadow of a man." No one part of Emerson's thought should be taken as gospel, not even his most characteristic doctrines, until they are measured up against and corrected by still another contradictory idea. The damning criticisms of Emerson's ideas have come from those who have fastened on only a fragment of Emerson and have treated this as if it were a complete statement of his views. When one finds that two characters as radically different as Matthew Arnold and Friedrich Nietzsche both admired Emerson, it should be obvious that they had been reading two different Emersons—and that the Emerson Carlyle admired, though often grudgingly, was still a third.

These contradictions disclose the richness and amplitude of Emerson's mind, and the way to approach such richness is to follow his own example in drawing sustenance and energy from the writings of other men: not to read him too conscientiously and consecutively, but to dip into him frequently, almost at random, to find precisely the stimulus or the counter-statement, or even the irritation, that perhaps only he could give. We know that Herman Melville, for example, at least once listened to Emerson lecture, and read some of him; and it is very possible that in reacting scornfully to what seemed to him Emerson's spiritual blandness, or rather his blindness, he saw more clearly into his own black experience.

Before I discuss more specifically both the original ore out of which Emerson's thought was smelted, and those parts of it that were worked up by him into tools and weapons and jewels, into Yankee alarm clocks and Yankee 'notions,' into world-girdling cables and railroad systems and airways and space rockets—before this I must say a word about the man himself, his lineage and his habitat, his vocation and his general conduct of life. All of these colorful facts are present in his essays, his addresses, and his poems: but there they are fused into white light by his own incandescent mind. What belonged to eternity, and what belonged to the time, the place, the surrounding actors and institutions, all came together in the man himself.

Emerson was born in Boston, May 25, 1803, and died in Concord, April 27, 1882. Though he was a seafaring traveler, both in body and mind, these two communities gave him his social anchorage: the great seaport, trading and trafficking in every part of the world, accumulating capital to found cotton mills and railroad systems, schools and universities and art collections, and the modest, self-contained country village, whose citizens, like those of Lexington, were among the first to stand up, gun in hand, to preserve their hard-earned habits of communal self-government. By birth Emerson belonged to the clerical aristocracy, one might almost call them the rabbinate, which presided with dry moral rigor over the Protestant congregations; for a long line of ancestors, on both sides, were clergymen, as was his own father, who died in 1811 when Emerson was a boy of eight.

The first twenty-five years of Emerson's life were a struggle for bodily survival, for he was threatened with the lethal disease of his day, tuberculosis, which two of his three younger brothers succumbed to. The Emerson family, once the father died, lived in genteel penury, often close to starvation, so poor that Emerson was forced to share with a younger brother the greatcoat needed to face the grim Boston winter. Soon after marrying, his father had reported: "We are poor and cold and have little meal, and little wood, and little meat; but thank God, courage enough." Armed with this family fortitude, Emerson, like his younger brothers, got a university

education; and in the end the discipline of poverty underwrote his independence. By merely external pressures he could not be bullied or bribed.
The fact that the outer world gave him so little during his growing period
fostered his habit of living from within. But there his widowed mother
had set him a good example: even in their neediest days, she withdrew
for an hour after breakfast from the cares of the household, to meditate
behind a closed door.

"A man must thank his defects," Emerson wrote in 'Fate,' "and stand
in some terror of his talents." His original defects were a poor constitution, low vitality, shyness and awkwardness and diffidence in company,
a lack of outward warmth and responsiveness; and it took him half a
lifetime to compensate these defects, if not entirely to overcome them, in
acts of hospitality and friendly service and secret generosity. These acts
touched not only those he loved, like Carlyle, Thoreau, or Alcott, but
passing strangers, from Frederika Bremmer to Emma Lazarus. Happily
Emerson's courtly manners softened his remoteness; and to the very end,
as Walt Whitman noted on a final visit to him, he bore a notably cheerful
and intelligent face, such a face as Emerson regarded as the ultimate proof
and justification of culture.

If some of Emerson's essays, like those on Love and on Friendship,
seem a little too toplofty, a little too rarefied, this is perhaps because
during his early years he could survive only by keeping his actual environment—that bed of nails—at a distance, and countering it with ideal possibilities that existed only in his mind. His immunity to pain and grief, or at
least his reluctance to give vent to them, was not a mark of stolid optimism: it was rather a psychological nerve-block that enabled him to get
on with his true work: his daily reading of nature and culture and the
human soul, for the sake of catching some new illumination; for, as he
noted in 1861, "A rush of thoughts is the only conceivable prosperity that
can come to me." Fortunately, after his first marriage, Emerson's economic circumstances improved, though he never escaped the need for
earning a living sufficient to support a large household.

The dividing line in Emerson's intellectual development was his first
trip to Europe in 1833; for he returned from this adventure, despite its
physical ordeals, in robust health, with the old threat of tuberculosis overcome, and a kind of inner toughness that enabled him later, as a lecturer,
to endure the most grueling journeys into the West, in crowded canal
boats, sordid inhospitable taverns, over jolting icy roads: thrice crossing
the Mississippi on foot in dead of winter, sometimes reaching his destination more dead than alive. To have endured these vulgar indignities, to
have survived these misadventures, without a groan of self-pity, marks
Emerson's iron discipline. Such a character could afford to write "Whim"
over his door.

Now the trip to Europe was an attempt to overcome two great crises
in Emerson's life. The personal crisis was occasioned by the death (1831)

of his first wife, Ellen Tucker: a lovely, quietly impish, impassioned spirit, who had awakened an ardor and a love that he found himself unable adequately to express, though her going left an empty niche in his life that his second wife, .Lydia Jackson, a maturer woman, could never fill. It was surely with Ellen in mind that he wrote, in 1840: "I finish this morning transcribing my old essay on Love, but I see well its inadequateness. I, cold because I am hot—cold at the surface only, as a sort of guard and compensation for the fluid tenderness of the core—have much more experience than I have written there, more than I will, more than I can write."

Ellen's death was Emerson's first direct encounter with grief and desolation; and it was followed in a few years by the premature deaths of his two younger brothers, one of whom, Charles Chauncy, he always regarded as a talent superior to his own. Even before this, some sobering premonition had made him write, on being engaged to Ellen, that he was "now as happy as it is safe in life to be."

The other crisis was a religious one, occasioned by his abandoning the calling he had struggled during the twenties to fit himself for: that of a duly qualified clergyman in the Unitarian Church. He had approached the duties of a minister with some repulsion for the homely routines of visitation, comfort for the dying, moral suasion, with all their intrusive intimacies. But still more, he had come to realize that the God he had found in his consciousness had little need for either the dogmas or the rituals of an established Church: even the Christ that moved him was not a God come to earth, but a singular being who had demonstrated while on earth the secret by which any man might become godlike. Emerson broke with his congregation over a single issue: his unwillingness to celebrate the Lord's Supper. But that break widened, during the next decade, into a total rejection of the Church's whole institutional life and its claims to a unique revelation.

This parting of the ways removed the economic prop of Emerson's life, and made it necessary for him, within a few years, to find an alternative mode of getting a living: that of a lecturer at the new Lyceums that were springing up all over the country. For Emerson the lecture hall had become the living church of his day, spreading a many-tongued gospel that was destined to replace the "cant and snuffle of a dead Christianity." Emerson's lectures, in reality soliloquies spoken aloud, were little different in texture from the notes in his Journals, where many parts of them were first recorded as scattered items.

In shaking himself loose from the Unitarian Church, Emerson had found his true vocation: that of being Emerson. This new mode of preaching turned out to be another blessing in disguise, for without the direct face-to-face contact with mixed audiences of everyday people, in every part of the country except the South, Emerson would have lacked his sense of the more expansive and masculine America one associates with Audubon and Lincoln. New Englander that he was, he respected the uncouth vigor of the pioneers. And when Emerson met President Lincoln face to face, Lincoln reminded him of what he had said about Kentuckians in an Illinois lecture.

Emerson's difficulties did not come to an end with his marriage to Lydian —as he re-named his wife—in 1835, and his settling down in a commodious house, surrounded by a few acres of usable land at the edge of Concord: for if he had a good garden, productive pear trees, willing servants, a tender and devoted wife, he all too soon had the shattering experience of losing his five-year-old son through scarletina, that son whose angelic qualities had given him access to his father's otherwise inviolate study. Well had he written earlier to his spiritual monitor, Aunt Mary Moody Emerson: "He has seen but half the Universe who has never been shown the house of pain." Even in the serene years before little Waldo's death Emerson had faced, no less than Herman Melville did, the evils that dog the human condition: "Now, for near five years," he wrote in 1840, "I have been indulged by the gracious Heaven in my long holiday in this goodly house of mine, entertaining and entertained by so many worthy and gifted friends, and all this time poor Nancy Barron, the mad-woman, has been screaming herself hoarse at the Poor-house across the brook and I still can hear her whenever I open my window."

In the middle years between 1835 and 1865, Emerson did the bulk of his work: the little book on Nature, the two trenchant series of essays— in every way his central work—the book on English Traits, the sometimes crabbed but authentic poems, rough-skinned, tart, like his own winter pears, and those maturer reflections on the Conduct of Life, which at least one contemporary thought more "pungent and piercing" than anything he had written before. Despite Emerson's original need for solitude, despite his resolute effort to free his days for communion with nature and his own mind, he took on all the demands of daily life. On settling in Concord, he accepted the ancient office of Hog-Reeve; and as a husband and father, as a householder, a Lyceum lecturer, and an editor of 'The Dial,' he bore cheerfully, or if pressed, stoically, the duties of domestic and civic life. What he often characterized as his "indolence" was his need between whiles to recoup his energies for thought.

Whatever Emerson's reluctance to leave his study, his involvement in the political and social issues of his time, from the forties on, grew deeper: in the crises that culminated in the War Between the States, his moral commitment was not only firm but passionate. Witness his protest to President Martin Van Buren over the scandalous chicane practiced by the Federal government against the Cherokee Indians, the same sort of chronic official iniquity as the violation of our government's treaty with the Senecas that Edmund Wilson recently denounced. With this concern go Emerson's denunciation of slavery and the Fugitive Slave Law, his contemptuous dismissal of his one-time hero, Daniel Webster, the chief sponsor of that law; and not least his scalding attacks upon the infamous Mexican War, the Vietnam of his day, in his 'Ode' inscribed to W. H. Channing. Emerson's stand was not merely expressed in words: he told his children that no New England house was properly designed unless it held a secret chamber for hiding a runaway slave.

Well before the Civil War broke out, Emerson was alert to the heavy duties that lay before his generation. As early as 1838, in fact, he had written: "Our culture must . . . not omit the arming of the man. Let him hear in season that he is born into the state of war, and that the commonwealth and his own well being require that he should not go dancing in the weeds of peace." And as for peace, he knew well the price for it: "The peace principle [is not] to be carried into effect by fear. It can never be defended, it can never be executed by cowards. Everything great must be done in the spirit of greatness. The manhood that has been in war must be transferred to the cause of peace, before war can lose its charm and peace be venerable to men." In a single sentence, he had anticipated William James's 'The Moral Equivalent of War.'

In his mature years the aloof, self-contained, self-sufficient Emerson gave to society some of the allegiance he had once given too exclusively to solitude. For this was not only the period of his great friendships, with Carlyle, Arthur Hugh Clough, Bronson Alcott, Thoreau, Margaret Fuller, but also of the relaxing sociabilities of the Saturday Club, with its monthly luncheon meeting at the Parker House in Boston. There a more clubbable Emerson appeared, one who horrified the elder Henry James by drinking wine and covering his diffidence in company by smoking a cigar—as if a disembodied angel could enjoy a cigar!

"That only can we say which we have lived," Emerson had written in an early Journal. Those who go to his writing will not merely touch the man directly: they will find to what purpose he had lived. If in such a brief biographic summary as this, one must leave out much that is essential to the understanding of Emerson's life, those omissions will be sufficiently redressed by the reading of the essays and the journals. Even the chaste veils that cover private areas of his life will reveal something more of Emerson: the fact that he valued chastity and reserve. When he noted that "I like daylight, and hard clouds, hard expressions, and hard manners," he outlined his own character. But one must also remember that he wrote: "Give all to love; obey thy heart. . . . Let it have scope."

By 1865 Emerson's main written work, with the exception of a few poems, was done; and when the war was over, his lecturing tapered off too, though he would still at intervals struggle painfully through old lectures, handicapped by lapses of memory, but sustained by sympathetic and indulgent audiences. Ironically, one of the last lectures he gave was on Memory: a lecture in which he redressed his original over-emphasis upon the fresh and the new-born, while dismissing the past: "Life only avails, not the having lived." Now he realized, belatedly, that the American, in the raw confidence of youth, had forgotten too much: that memory was "the thread on which the beads of man are strung, making the personal identity which is necessary to moral action. Without it all life and thought are an unrelated succession." He had lived long enough to realize, at last, that the "having lived" availed too.

So much for Emerson the man: cold but fiery, pallid but intense, reticent but boldly outspoken, clear-headed but drunk with wine that "never grew in the belly of the grape." Since Emerson still has much to give us, not because his method or his mood reflects that of our own times, but because it is so defiantly the opposite, there is no need to gloze over his deficiencies. His coldness and remoteness were almost constitutional qualities: they are hardly more a subject for reproach than his sloping shoulders, his narrow frame, his long nose. He himself "thought it a good remark" that "I always seemed to be on stilts. . . . Most of the persons whom I see in my own house, I see across a gulf, I cannot go to them nor they come to me."

With this coldness went, it would seem, not a failure of love—far from it—but a lack of strong sexual ardor. As late as the age of thirty-one, he could dismiss Boccaccio because he represented only the pleasures of appetite, "which only at rare intervals, a few times in a lifetime, are intense." Even by the records of Puritan New England, that was a startling statement. The celebrations of sex in Whitman's 'Leaves of Grass' served, doubtless unconsciously, to fill in this omission in the master. But for all this quantitative deficiency in energy, Emerson had boxed the compass of life, in the sense that none of his great American contemporaries had done: even sexually he was more mature than the fastidious but adolescent Thoreau, or the amative but unmarried Whitman. The sweet Emersonian smile, as on an archaic Greek face, was the witness of a complete, fully manifested life: he was 'all there.' And his work, though seemingly in fragments, was equally complete.

Perhaps one of the reasons for the pallid impression that Emerson left on a later generation is that he himself in his last fifteen years gradually faded out of the picture, ceasing, after 1870, even to have the impulse to post in his Journals such stray thoughts as perhaps flickered through his mind. For the hardships of toil and travel, which he had endured so stoically under pressure, took their toll prematurely; and he himself, as early as 1866, listening to the voice within, wrote the poem 'Terminus': admonishing himself to take in sail, economize his energies, trim himself to "the storm of time." At almost the same moment, he pictured his own fate with wry humor: "In that country, a peculiarity is that after sixty years a certain mist or dimness, a sort of autumnal haze, settled on the figure, veiling especially all decays. Gradually, year by year, the outline became indistinct, and the halo gayer and brighter. At last, there was only left a sense of presence, and the virtue of personality, as if Gyges never turned his ring again. It was an immense social convenience."

Emerson wrote those lines, calmly foreseeing his own later years, at a time when his fame had spread widest and his position had become most assured. No one could have met the disturbances of senescence with more smiling tranquility, with more equable resignation. A little later, no longer able even to edit his unpublished papers, he left that task to his trusted friend, James Elliot Cabot, and his daughter, Ellen. Like a winter apple, still ruddy though mealy-ripe, he clung to the tree, safe from the worms and the wasps. When his thoughts no longer made sense, he had the sense to be silent. But the halo remained gay and bright; and today, against the addled counsels, the insensate threats, the artful, self-induced psychoses of our age, that halo has become gayer and brighter than ever, for it radiates from a poised and finely balanced personality. The sense of Emerson's luminous presence—that is what the reader will find on every page.

To understand the peculiar gifts of Emerson and the quality of his mind, one must realize that he was, primarily, neither a philosopher nor a didactic writer, still less a scholar or a scientist, but a poet: one who used the materials of other arts and disciplines to provide colors for his own palette. He did not regard himself as a great poet, but whatever he was, he told a friend, was of poet all through: yet he qualified this modestly, in another place, by saying that he was only half a poet. Yes: half a poet, if one thinks only of his verses: but what a half! Emerson nevertheless was a major poet, if one realizes that all his thought underwent a poetic transformation: an intensification, a distillation, a penetration that again and again would be crystallized in a perfect paragraph or poem. Though no poems are included in the present volume, Emerson the poet remains present everywhere, for all his thought is by its nature metaphoric and evocative, meant to excite a corresponding resonance directly in the reader's mind.

As a writer, Emerson stands on the level of the great essayists he admired—Michel de Montaigne and Francis Bacon: he has the same wide range of interests, the same sharp perceptions, the same gift for reducing a whole chapter of experience to a single sentence; and in addition, he has a crystalline freshness all his own, as of cool water bubbling upward from an underground spring. Though, like Montaigne, he ceaselessly read and often quoted old authors, he presents even old thoughts as if he were perceiving them for the first time and asking what, after all, they meant here and now.

If any one essay might be singled out to reveal Emerson's peculiar virtue and character as an American, it would probably be that on Self-Reliance; for there he spoke with the unmistakable voice of New World man, opening up and exploring a virgin continent of the mind, testing himself against nature, and finding out how much past knowledge and equipment he might need in order to survive and prosper. "We shall not always set so great a price on a few texts, a few lives," Emerson felt, since the ideas we now do reverence to were not the product of books, but of first-hand experience. "Nothing is at last sacred but the authority of your own mind." In this essay various other New World beliefs are either expressed or implied: the need for experiment, the virtue of self-government and independence, the poison of mechanically imitating ancient models which served another people, another place, and other circumstances.

In 'Self-Reliance' Emerson established, better than anyone else had yet done, the central trait of the American character, at the moment when it became conscious of its special nature and its potential destiny. This sense was expressed in art by the esthetic doctrines of Horatio Greenough, in the novel by Cooper, Hawthorne, Melville, in moral philosophy by Thoreau, in poetry by Whitman, as later in philosophy by William James and John Dewey; and it was not by accident that the most original of American architects, who bore indubitably the New World stamp, Frank Lloyd Wright, was more deeply devoted to Emerson than to any other writer. Emerson saw that if his country was to have free cultural intercourse with other countries, it must first have a character of its own. He realized that even the swagger and crudity of the Kentuckian or the Hoosier were better than a subservient colonialism that sought only to ape traditional Old World forms that had outlived their uses, or to keep up with the passing fashions of Paris and London.

This was the note Emerson struck repeatedly in 'Nature,' in 'Self-Reliance,' and again in 'The American Scholar.' But neither Emerson, nor those who were truly influenced by him, could be trapped for long by an in-growing provincial isolationism. If they had left Europe behind them, it was to take not only America but the whole world as their spiritual province. Before Whitman had composed his 'Salut au Monde' and his 'Passage to India,' Emerson had made that same salute and traced the same passage himself, the latter with the aid of a small library of Oriental classics that some English friends had brought over to Concord. So deeply did Emerson immerse himself in the religion and philosophy of that elder Old World that Hindus have taken his poem 'Brahma,' one of a half dozen perfect poems he had written, as a true expression of the essential Hindu spirit.

Because Emerson had so firmly established his own identity, rooted in his country and his region, he was able in 'English Traits' to take a cool and composed view of the institutions, the customs, and the character of the British people, without any sense of rivalry or subservience—neither undervaluing them, nor overpraising them, nor uncritically accepting them. And yet, in the end, he dispassionately pronounced the English "the best of all existing nations"—qualifying this favorable judgment by a single epithet: "Alas!" (Alas! that is, for the rest of us.) This effort to establish national identity, to achieve cultural self-reliance, was not for Emerson a final goal; for at the same time he noted in his Journals, as early as 1841, that "every nation, to emerge from barbarism, must have some foreign impulse, a graft on the world stock." If he began as a New World man, he ended as a One World man.

So, when Emerson had swept away all the battered furniture and dusty heirlooms of the past, it was not for the purpose of conducting a miserable existence in an empty, cold, desolate chamber, decorated only by a National Flag, but in order to make use of the space, and to provide it with more adequate furnishings. Once free to choose, some of the old belongings would come back again, not because they were old and respectable, but because they were still imperishably new. "Away with the Dead!" meant "Hail to the Living!" He knew better than most that by regrouping old words one brings forth new thoughts. Past, present, and future, near and far, fused in his consciousness. "A true man belongs to no other time and place, but is the center of things." By the same token, once self-reliance was established, one might give and take aid freely, profiting the more by society because one was no longer dependent upon it.

Partly as a result of his temperamental remoteness and insulation, Emerson was more at home with Plato or Shakespeare than with his own contemporaries. As a young man he was an over-captious critic even of those writers he admired like Wordsworth, Landor, or Goethe. Most current novels seemed to him trivial and superficial: Jane Austen, Dickens, Thackeray, even Hawthorne, did not engage him. But he realized that Thoreau wrote an even meatier prose than his own, and he alone dared at once to acclaim Whitman's 'Leaves of Grass' as the original work that it was. Yet it is not as a critic of literature that one turns to Emerson: he was primarily a critic of life, and he had a capacity to face bitter realities that his contemporaries flinched from.

"Great men, great nations," Emerson wrote, "have not been boasters and buffoons, but perceivers of the terror of life, and have manned themselves to face it." And again in the same essay on Fate he observed: "We must see that the world is rough and surly, and will not mind drowning a man or a woman, but swallows your ship like a grain of dust. . . . The diseases, the elements, fortune, gravity, lightning, respect no persons. The way of Providence is a little rude. . . . The forms of the shark, the *labrus,* the jaw of the sea-wolf paved with crushing teeth, the weapons of the grampus and other warriors hidden in the sea,—are hints of ferocity in the interiors of nature. Let us not deny it up and down. Providence has a wild, rough, incalculable road to its end, and it is of no use to try to whitewash its huge, mixed instrumentalities, or to dress up that terrific benefactor in the clean shirt and white neckcloth of a student in divinity." Did Melville ever indict the nature of things in harsher terms?

Yet there was a difference between Emerson and the Melville of 'Moby-Dick' and 'Pierre,' not only in their respective visions of evil, but in their attitude as to how it should be treated: a difference that was not resolved in Melville until he came to the final verses of 'Clarel.' "What can we do in dark hours?" Emerson asked. And he answered: "We can abstain. In the bright hours we can impart." This is perhaps Emerson's final justification for his reserves, his inhibitions, his silences: he did not deny the existence of evil and pain, still less hide them from himself: but he answered them as his father had done when facing starvation: "Thank God we have courage enough." If there is any central lesson to be learned from Emerson's thought, it is the lesson of Heroism: *Have courage!* And he might have drily added, looking around him at the screaming madwoman, the corrupt politicians, the whip-happy slave mongers—You will need it!

Despite the diffuseness of his message, Emerson was the bringer of new tidings, a modern gospel; but he himself would have been the first to point out that this gospel had always been in existence, since it was wrought into the very nature of man. For Emerson saw that man's mind was the focal point for the forces of the universe, and that experience was incomplete until it translated the dumb language of natural objects and events into the conscious language of the mind, while that language itself required further translation into action: "A thought which does not go to embody or externize itself is no thought." Had he been as presumptuous as Kant, he might have presented these intuitions as "prolegomena to all future systems of metaphysics," but for two characteristic reserves: he was no system maker, and no system follower, either; and his new faith, as he put it, must include the skepticisms as well as the affirmations of humanity.

Just because Emerson rejected none of the offices of the mind, he was, within the compass of his own experience, full of fresh perceptions, and he anticipated vividly, sometimes by a generation, sometimes by a whole century, the more studious efforts and discoveries of other men. As early as 1832 Emerson wrote: "Dreams and Beasts are two keys by which we are to find out the secrets of our own nature. All mystics use them. They are like comparative anatomy. They test objects; or we may say, that must be a good theory of the universe, that theory will bring a commanding claim to confidence, which explains these phenomena." The theory of Beasts is that of Darwin and evolution: the theory of Dreams is Freud and the unconscious. In Emerson, neither of these interests was haphazard or the result of a lucky stab. From the currents of evolutionary doctrine that flowed through the nineteenth century, after Buffon and Lamarck, Emerson realized in poetic phrase well before Darwin that, "striving to be man, the worm mounts through all the spires of form." For him man's life in nature included every aspect of nature, however formidable, not only those that flattered or comforted man; yet nature, coming into consciousness in man, disclosed purposes and ideal ends that transcend all previous evolutionary experience.

But if the theory of beasts, that is, man's linkages with all organic nature, was important, this was tied up in Emerson's mind with that other mystery still to be penetrated, the mystery of dreams; and in taking dreams seriously, not least his own, Emerson was well in advance of the thinkers of his own day who had, since the time of Descartes, regarded the inner life as the special province of religion, a province which would shrink steadily just to the extent that science opened up the outer world and derived all values from that world. In this matter, Emerson was a better naturalist than most of his scientific contemporaries: he accepted dreams as a natural phenomenon which had some significance for man's own development. The fact that Emerson regarded sex, too, as one of the mysteries that needed further investigation—though he confined this recognition to his Journals—only shows how central, and in a sense, how faithful to natural revelation, his essential thought was.

Emerson's attaching importance to Beasts, Dreams, and Sex was an example of his devotion to the truths available to him through self-revelations rather than books, and this was connected with an even more central faith in the reality of God's presence and influence, disclosed in every manifestation of life. He would have nothing of the doctrine that supposed that revelation was something that happened long ago, was "given and gone, as if God were dead." God was tremendously alive for Emerson, as were the soul and the over-soul, the first immediate and individual, the second general and universal. This god was not the God of the Churches; and it is only now, perhaps, that we can begin to see what Emerson was really talking about, when he used the orthodox term God to express his new perception.

"There is a power above and behind us," wrote Emerson, "and we are the channel of its communication." If I am not deceived, Emerson had discovered the unconscious, and had realized that a direct access to the unconscious was as important in opening one's eyes to reality as the pageant of the outer world—or even more important, since the unconscious bore within it the whole experience of the race, from the beginning of time before consciousness itself had emerged.

Emerson himself links the experience of God with the operation of the unconscious, sometimes in so many words, as when he observed: "Blessed is the child: the unconscious is ever the act of God himself. Nobody can reflect upon his unconscious period; or any particular word or act in it, with regret or contempt." Or again, "The central fact is the super-human intelligence, pouring into us from the unknown fountain, to be received with religious awe and defended from any mixture of our will." When Emerson says, "Dare to love God without mediator or veil," he is saying, dare to respect and embrace and live openly with your unconscious.

In this poetic discovery of the role of the unconscious Emerson was not alone: the same discovery was made by Hawthorne and Melville, and this served as a secret link between those two souls, though as yet there was no name for the unconscious except the ancient one that Emerson loyally clung to: God. But as more than one religion had testified, this God has an almost equal counterpart and antagonist, Satan, whose exalted energies Milton and Blake had discovered even before Melville had baptized Moby-Dick in the name of the Devil. Through the exploration of dreams, fantasies, and psychal disorders that has gone on for the last half century and more, we now realize that both versions of the unconscious are true: this polarity plays an essential role in human creativity. Emerson's unconscious is mainly the luminous one, out of which love and brotherhood and justice and truth are born; while Melville's is the dark one, from which comes forth murderous hate, satanic pride, insensate destruction—or demonic revelation. 'Uriel,' the poem of Emerson's Robert Frost most admired, expresses the alternating polarities of the creative and destructive energies: "Evil may bless and ice may burn." Neither is to be trusted as an expression of cosmic and human potentialities without the other: but only when the luminous god gains the upper hand can life prosper.

At first, Emerson did not realize this ambivalent quality of the unconscious: when he was young, his private revelations were, apparently, so angelic and so well-disciplined that he trusted them absolutely. Even in middle life he had said jauntily, in reply to an older friend who asked how he could be sure that his confident new revelation might not come from below rather than from above, "If I am the Devil's child, I will live then from the Devil." This was all very well as a youthful act of defiant integrity: but it is no answer if it happens that the Devil's disciple is not a staid, well-bred, firmly moralized young man, needing to discard his moral braces, but a Hitler or a Stalin, heeding every sadistic impulse and magnifying all the possibilities for human iniquity.

In later life, both Melville and Emerson corrected their youthful bias:. Melville went on the Pilgrimage to the Holy Land that resulted in 'Clarel,' while Emerson fervently blessed the yoke of men's opinions which he had once forsworn. In his poem 'Grace,' Emerson even thanked his "Preventing God" for the defenses he had set around him: "example, custom, fear, occasion slow"—"sworn bondmen that served as parapet," keeping him from falling "into depths of sin." This again is one of those occasions when those who gauge Emerson's mind by this or that isolated expression fail to correct the momentary aberration by the full report of his life. By the same token, Emerson's wary consciousness of Moby-Dick, in 'Fate,' from which I have quoted, offsets what seems the shrinking tendermindedness of some of his more youthful perceptions.

Because Emerson's sense of the unconscious was so quick and vivid, so constantly nourished by his own dreams, in all their tormenting confusion and ambivalence, I have taken care to include more than one paragraph from his Journals on this subject; and when the complete Journals are finally available, I have little doubt that the restoration of other relevant passages, on sex and dreams, will make Emerson's own commerce with the unconscious more explicit and vivid. It is this aspect of his thought that, when it is uncovered and correctly interpreted, links his original attitude toward life with the experiences of our own age, and with an inchoate philosophy that is still tò do justice to nature and man and 'God'—the God whose fumbling hand is visible in every evolutionary process of organization, self-transformation, and creative growth.

All this, and more, one will find in Emerson. But there is no use looking in his work for a closely ordered philosophic system; and to make Emerson into a mere Transcendentalist, as many have done, is to show little insight into either the scope or the depth of his thought, for he transcended Transcendentalism as decisively as he protested against Protestantism and dematerialized Materialism. The nearest Emerson ever came to presenting his philosophy as a unity was in his first work on Nature, where he laid out the four chief categories of his thought—commodity, beauty, language, and discipline: but if that were his sole credential as a seminal thinker, it hardly met his own criteria; for he kept on contemplating a more adequate expression of his metaphysics in a "natural history of the mind," a work whose belated publication did not fulfill the hopes he had long nourished.

The fact is that Emerson's efforts to produce a coherent philosophy were untrue to Emerson's own system-shattering openness. His mission was to examine crumbling foundations, to condemn unsound structures, to clear the site of lumber, to quarry new materials—not to instruct the would-be builders, nor to design a new structure. Repeatedly Emerson told Carlyle that he had no talent for construction. But what Emerson regarded as a defect was perhaps his essential virtue: his unwillingness to deny a truth because it was inconsistent in appearance or in logic with other equally reputable truths. What he retained, through this constitutional ineptitude, was a readiness to examine and even anticipate incredible new discoveries that system-mongers could not open the door to without acknowledging the insufficiency of their systems.

In a strange though not un-Emersonian way, the best summation of Emerson's philosophic position and method came from a scholar who rejected his thought, George Edward Woodberry. "By the features of this doctrine," Woodberry wrote, "its mingling of physics and being, its divorce from Christian mythology, its freedom from past civilization, its priority to science and logic, its truly primitive methods of thought in conducting the mind still untrained and still grasping knowledge imperfectly, one is reminded of the early sages of Greece." Precisely: for in both cases this originality and imperfection marked the embryonic expression of a new culture.

Such a description places Emerson's mind in its proper social setting: it does justice to his intellectual nakedness, his bright innocence, his sparkling richness of potentialities. Unburdened by past encrustations, untrammeled by future constraints, he was free to move in any direction. Emerson, in short, was the most liberated mind that the West had produced in many centuries: as liberated as Shakespeare's. If Emerson "has no philosophy" it is because, like Shakespeare, his philosophy is as large as life, and cannot be reduced to an articulated skeleton without forfeiting its life. But even Woodberry, who confessed his lack of intellectual sympathy with Emerson, nevertheless felt in his work "the presence of a great mind." Could one hope for more?

"The day will come," Emerson prophesied, "when no badge or uniform or star will be worn." That day has not yet dawned; indeed, in our status-conscious, caste-bound America it seems farther away now than ever. No such ungraded, fully individuated society as yet exists anywhere. So perhaps the chief value of Emerson's thought for the present generation lies not in the ways that it anticipated or marched ahead of the special discoveries of our time, as in the place he gave to the unconscious and the prerational processes of the mind, but even more in the way it radically differs from our current assumptions and challenges our practices: our conformity, our timidity, our docility—or those fashionable negative images of these same traits, our mindless anarchies, our drug-excited audacities, our aimless violence.

Certainly Emerson's America is not our present America: it is rather an older but more youthful America, part achieved reality, part hopeful ideal, which we have lost. It is in Emerson's mind, more fully even than in Jefferson's, Whitman's, Thoreau's, or Lincoln's mind, that we can measure all that we have disowned or buried, and may, if we go further in the same direction, lose forever. And it is by entering Emerson's mind once more that we may recover at least a portion of our lost heritage, and gain courage—"courage enough!"—to seek a better life.

(1968)

CHAPTER THREE

The Golden Day

Dawn: Thoreau

No one who was awake in the early part of the nineteenth century was unaware that in the practical arrangements of life men were on the brink of a great change. The rumble of the Industrial Revolution was heard in the distance long before the storm actually broke; and before American society was completely transformed through the work of the land pioneer and the industrial pioneer, there arose here and there over the land groups of people who anticipated the effects of this revolution and were in revolt against all its preoccupations. Some of these groups reverted to an archaic theocracy, like that of the Mormons, in which a grotesque body of beliefs was combined with an extraordinary amount of economic sagacity and statesmanship; some of them became disciples of Fourier and sought to live in co-operative colonies, which would foster men's various capacities more fully than the utilitarian community.

The air quivered with both hope and trepidation. In the new industrial cities, the slum made its appearance; great bodies of depauperate immigrants with strange traditions altered the balance of power; politics became the business of clever rapscallions who looted the public treasury; by the end of the fifties an editorial writer in 'Harper's Weekly' prayed for professional administrators who might bring a public conscience into the corrupt democracy of the big cities. In general, all the forces that blighted America after the Civil War existed in embryonic form between 1830 and 1860. At the same time, the older regions began to reap the fruits of two centuries of contact with the new soil and new customs. It is at the hour when the old ways are breaking up that men step outside them sufficiently to feel their beauty and significance: lovers are often closest at the moment of parting. In New England, the inherited medieval civilization had become a shell; but, drying up, it left behind a sweet acrid aroma, and for a brief day it had a more intense existence in the spirit. Before the life itself collapsed, men felt the full weight of it in their imagination. In the act of passing away, the Puritan begot the Transcendentalist, and the will-to-power, which had made him what he was, with his firm but forbidding character and his conscientious but narrow activity, gave way to the will-to-perfection.

The period from 1830 to 1860 was in America one of disintegration and fulfillment: the new and the old, the crude and the complete, the base and the noble mingled together. Puritan fanatics like Goodyear brought to the vulcanization of rubber the same intense passion that Thoreau brought to Nature: sharp mountebanks like Barnum grew out of the same sort of Connecticut village that nourished an inspired schoolmaster like Bronson Alcott: genuine statesmen like Brigham Young organized the colonization of Utah whilst nonentities like Pierce and Buchanan governed the whole country. During this period, the old culture of the seaboard settlement had its Golden Day in the mind; the America of the migrations, on the other hand, partly because of weaknesses developed in the pioneer, partly because of the one-sided interests of the industrialist, and partly because of the volcanic eruption of the Civil War, had up to 1890 little more than the boomtown optimism of the Gilded Age to justify its existence.

Despite the foreboding that every intelligent mind felt when it contemplated the barbarism of the industrial age, inimical to any culture except that which grew out of its own inhuman absorption in abstract matter and abstract power, the dominant note of the period was one of hope. Before the Civil War the promise of the westward march expanded the sense of achievement that came over the Eastern states; and men faced the world with a confidence that went beyond the complacent optimism of the British Utilitarians—tainted as that was by Carlyle's dire reminders of the palpable wreckage and jetsam that had been washed into the slums of London, Manchester, and Birmingham on the wave of "industrial prosperity."

There were no Carlyles or Ruskins in America during this period; they were almost unthinkable. One might live in this atmosphere, or one might grapple with the White Whale and die; but if one lived, one lived without distrust, without inner complaint, and even if one scorned the ways of one's fellows, as Thoreau did, one remained among them, and sought to remedy in oneself the abuses that existed in society. Transcendentalism might criticize a fossilized past; but no one imagined that the future could be equally fossilized. The testimony is unqualified. One breathed hope, as one might breathe the heady air of early autumn, pungent with the smell of hickory fires and baking bread, as one walked through the village street.

"One cannot look on the freedom of this country, in connection with its youth," wrote Emerson in 'The Young American,' "without a presentment that here shall laws and institutions exist in some proportion to the majesty of Nature. . . . It is a country of beginnings, of projects, of vast designs and expectations. It has no past: all has an onward and prospective look." The voice of Whitman echoed Emerson through a trumpet: but that of

Melville, writing in 1850, was no less sanguine and full-pulsed: "God has predestinated, mankind expects, great things from our race; and great things we feel in our souls. The rest of the nations must soon be in our rear. We are the pioneers of the world; the advance guard, sent on through the wilderness of untried things, to break a new path in the New World that is ours. In our youth is our strength; in our inexperience, our wisdom."

"Every institution is the lengthened shadow of a man." Here and there in America during its Golden Day grew up a man who cast a shadow over the landscape. They left no labor-saving machines, no discoveries, and no wealthy bequests to found a library or a hospital: what they left was something much less and much more than that—an heroic conception of life. They peopled the landscape with their own shapes. This period nourished men, as no other has done in America before or since. Up to that time, the American communities were provincial; when it was over, they had lost their base, and spreading all over the landscape, deluged with new-comers speaking strange languages and carrying on Old-World customs, they lost that essential likeness which is a necessary basis for intimate communication. The first settlement was complete: agricultural and indus-trial life were still in balance in the older parts of the country; and on the seas trade opened up activities for the adventurous. When Ticknor was pre-paring to go to Germany, in the first decade of the century, there was one German dictionary, apparently, in New England. Within a generation, Goethe was translated, selections from the European classics were pub-lished; and importations of the Indian, Chinese, and Persian classics widened the horizon of people who had known India only by its shawls, China only by its tea.

The traffic of the American merchantmen across the seas brought ideas with every load of goods. Living lustily in all these new experiences, the pushing back of the frontier, the intercourse with the Ancient East, the promises of science and invention—steamboats; railroads; telegraphs; rub-ber raincoats; reapers; Von Baer; Faraday; Darwin—living in these things, and believing in them, the capacity for philosophic exploration increased, too; and when an Emerson went into retreat, he retired with an armful of experiences and ideas comparable only to the treasuries that the Elizabe-thans grandly looted. Within the circle of the daily fact, the Transcen-dentalists might protest against the dull materialism which was beginning to dominate the period: but it needed only a little boldness to convert the materialism itself into a source of new potencies.

An imaginative New World came to birth during this period, a new hemisphere in the geography of the mind. That world was the climax of American experience. What preceded led up to it: what followed dwindled away from it; and we who think and write today are either continuing the first exploration, or we are disheartened, and relapse into some stale formula, or console ourselves with empty gestures of frivolity.

The American scene was a challenge; and men rose to it. The writers of this period were not alone; if they were outcasts in the company of the usual run of merchants, manufacturers, and politicians, they were at all events attended by a company of people who had shared their experience and moved on eagerly with it. When all is reckoned, however, there is nothing in the minor writers that is not pretty fully recorded by Emerson, Thoreau, Whitman, Melville, and Hawthorne. These men, as D. H. Lawrence has well said, reached a verge. They stood between two worlds. Part of their experience enabled them to bring the protestant movement to its conclusion: the critical examination of men, creeds, and institutions, which is the vital core of protestantism, could not go much further. But already, out of another part of their experience, that which arose out of free institutions planted in an unpre-empted soil, molded by fresh contact with forest and sea and the more ingenious works of man, already this experience pushed them beyond the pit Melville fell into, and led them toward new institutions, a new art, a new philosophy, formed on the basis of a wider past than the European, caught by his Mediterranean or Palestinian cultures, was capable of seizing.

It was the organic break with Europe's past that enabled the American to go on; just as the immigration of people to America came to include specimens from almost all the folk of the world, so the American past widened sufficiently to bring Eastern and Western cultures into a common focus. The American went on. Whereas, in their search for a new basis for culture, Nietzsche went back to pre-Socratic Greece, Carlyle to Abbot Samson, Tolstoi and Dostoevski to primitive Christianity, and Wagner to the early Germanic fables, Emerson, Thoreau, and Whitman went forward leaning on the experiences about them, using the past as the logger uses the corduroy road, to push further into the wilderness and still have a sound bottom under him. They fathomed the possibilities, these Americans, of a modern basis for culture, and fathoming it, were nearer to the sources of culture, nearer to the formative thinkers and poets of the past, than those who sought to restore the past. What is vital in the American writers of the Golden Day grew out of a life which opened up to them every part of their social heritage. And a thousand more experiences and fifty million more people have made us no wiser. The spiritual fact remains unalterable, as Emerson said, by many or few particulars. It is the spiritual fact of American experience that we shall examine during the period of its clearest expression.

The pioneer who broke the trail westward left scarcely a trace of his adventure in the mind: what remains are the tags of pioneer customs, and mere souvenirs of the past, like the Pittsburg stogy, which is our living connection today with the Conestoga wagon, whose drivers used to roll cigars as the first covered wagons plodded over the Alleghenies.

What the pioneer felt, if he felt anything, in the midst of these new solitudes; what he dreamt, if he dreamt anything; all these things we must surmise from a few snatches of song, from the commonplace reports issued as the trail was nearing its end, by the generation of Mark Twain and Hamlin Garland, or by the reflections of their sons and daughters, romantically eager, like John G. Neihardt's, critically reflective, like Susan Glaspell's, or wistfully sordid, like Edgar Lee Masters' 'Anthology.' Those who really faced the wilderness, and sought to make something out of it, remained in the East; in their reflection, one sees the reality that might have been.

Henry David Thoreau was perhaps the only man who paused to give a report of the full experience. In a period when men were on the move, he remained still; when men were on the make, he remained poor; when civil disobedience broke out in the lawlessness of the cattle thief and the mining town rowdy, by sheer neglect, Thoreau practiced civil disobedience as a principle, in protest against the Mexican War, the Fugitive Slave Law, and slavery itself. Thoreau in his life and letters shows what the pioneer movement might have come to if this great migration had sought culture rather than material conquest, and an intensity of life, rather than mere extension over the continent.

Born in Concord about half a generation after Emerson, Thoreau found himself without the preliminary searchings and reachings of the young clergyman. He started from the point that his fellow-townsman, Emerson, had reached; and where the first cleared out of his mind every idea that made no direct connections with his personal experience, Thoreau cleared out of his life itself every custom or physical apparatus, to boot, which could not stand up and justify its existence. "A native of the United States," De Tocqueville had observed, "clings to the world's goods as if he were certain never to die; and he is so hasty at grasping at all within his reach, that one would suppose he was constantly afraid of not living long enough to enjoy them. He clutches everything, he holds nothing fast, but soon loosens his grasp to pursue fresh gratifications." Thoreau completely reversed this process: it was because he wanted to live fully that he turned away from everything that did not serve toward this end. He prized the minutes for what they brought, and would not exercise his citizenship at the town meeting if a spring day by Walden Pond had greater promise; nor would he fill his hours with gainful practices, as a maker of pencils or a surveyor, beyond what was needed for the bare business of keeping his bodily self warm and active.

Thoreau seized the opportunity to consider what in its essentials a truly human life was; he sought, in Walden, to find out what degree of food, clothing, shelter, labor was necessary to sustain it. It was not animal hardihood or a merely tough physical regimen he was after; nor did he fancy, for all that he wrote in contempt of current civilization, that the condition of the woodcutter, the hunter, or the American Indian was in itself to be preferred. What he discovered was that people are so eager to get the ostentatious "necessaries" of a civil life that they lose the opportunity to profit by civilization itself: while their physical wants are complicated, their lives, culturally, are not enriched in proportion, but are rather pauperized and bleached.

Thoreau was completely oblivious to the dominant myths that had been bequeathed by the seventeenth century. Indifferent to the illusion of magnitude, he felt that Walden Pond, rightly viewed, was as vast as the ocean, and the woods and fields and swamps of Concord were as inexhaustible as the Dark Continent. In his study of Nature, he had recourse on occasion to the scientific botanists and zoölogists; but he himself had possession of a method that they were slow to arrive at; and it is easier for us today to understand the metaphysical distinction of Thoreau's kind of nature and study than it would have been for Gray or Agassiz. Like Wordsworth before him, like Bergson after him, he realized that in current science "we murder to dissect," and he passed beyond the artful dismemberments of contemporary science to the flower and the bird and the habitat themselves. "Not a single scientific term or distinction," he wrote once in his notebook, "is the least to the purpose. You would fain perceive something and you must approach the object totally unprejudiced. You must be aware that nothing is what you take it to be. . . . Your greatest success will be simply to perceive that such things are, and you will have no communication to make the Royal Society." In other words, Thoreau sought in nature all the manifold qualities of being; he was not merely in search of those likenesses or distinctions which help to create classified indexes and build up a system. The esthetic qualities of a fern were as important for his mode of apprehension as the number of spores on a frond; it was not that he disdained science, but that, like the old herbalists and naturalists he admired, he would not let the practical offices of science, its classification, its measurements, its numerations, take precedence over other forms of understanding. Science, practiced in this fashion, is truly part of a humane life, and a Darwin dancing for joy over a slide in his microscope, or a Pupin finding the path to physics through his contemplation of the stars he watched as a herd-boy through the night, are not poorer scientists but richer ones for these joys and delights: they merely bow to the bias of utilitarianism when they leave these things out of their reports. In his attitude toward scientific truth Thoreau was perhaps a prophetic figure; and a new age may do honor to his metaphysics as well as to his humanity.

The resolute acceptance of his immediate milieu as equal to the utmost that the earth could offer stood by Thoreau in his other activities, too. He captained huckleberry parties as he might have led a battle, and was just as much the leader in one as he would have been in the other. His courage he reserved for better occasions than the battlefield, for he was ready to go to jail for his principles, and to mock Emerson for remaining outside. As for his country, he loved the land too well to confuse it with the shifting territorial boundaries of the National State. In this, he had that vital regional consciousness which every New Englander shared: Hawthorne himself had said that New England was as large a piece of territory as could claim his allegiance. Thoreau was not deceived by the rascality of politicians, who were ready to wage war for a coveted patch of Mexico's land, nor did he side with those who, for the sake of the Union, were ready to give up the principles that alone had made the Union valuable. What he loved was the landscape, his friends, and his companions in the spirit: when the Political State presumed to exercise a brass counter-claim on these loyalties it might go to the devil.

Thoreau's attitude toward the State, one must note, was just the opposite to that of the progressive pioneer. The latter did not care what sort of landscape he "located" in, so long as he could salute the flag of his country and cast his vote: Thoreau, on the contrary, was far too religious a man to commit the idolatry of saluting a symbol of secular power; and he realized that the affairs controlled by the vote represented only a small fraction of an interesting life, while so far from being indifferent to the land itself, he absorbed it, as men have absorbed legends, and guarded it, as men preserve ceremonies. The things which his contemporaries took for the supreme realities of life, matter, money, and political rights, had only an instrumental use for Thoreau: they might contribute a little to the arrangement of a good life, but the good life itself was not contained, was not even implied in them. One might spend one's life pursuing them without having lived. "There is not one of my readers," he exclaimed, "who has yet lived a whole human life."

In Thoreau's time, industrialism had begun to puff itself up over its multiplication of goods and the increase of wants that it fostered in order to provide the machine with an outlet for its ever-too-plentiful supply. Thoreau simply asked: "Shall we always study to obtain more of these things, and not sometimes be content with less?" "If we do not get our sleepers and forge rails and devote long days and nights to work," he observed ironically, "but go tinkering with our lives to improve *them,* who will build the railroads?" Thoreau was not a penurious fanatic, who sought to practice bare living merely as a moral exercise: he wanted to obey Emerson's dictum to save on the low levels and spend on the high ones. It is this that distinguishes him from the tedious people whose whole existence is absorbed in the practice of living on beans, or breathing deeply, or wearing clothes of a vegetable origin; simplification did not lead in Thoreau to the cult of simplicity: it led to a higher civilization.

What drove Thoreau to the solitude of the woods was no cynical contempt for the things beyond his reach. "Before we can adorn our houses with beautiful objects, the walls must be stripped, and our lives must be stripped, and beautiful housekeeping and beautiful living be laid for a foundation: now, a taste for the beautiful is most cultivated out of doors, where there is no house, and no housekeeper." The primeval woods were a favorable beginning for the search; but Thoreau did not think they could be the end of it. The land itself, however, did stir his imagination; he wrote:

> All things invite the earth's inhabitants
> To rear their lives to an unheard of height,
> And meet the expectation of the land.

"The expectation of the land"! One comes upon that phrase, or its equivalent, in almost every valid piece of early American thought. One thinks of moorland pastures by the sea, dark with bayberries and sweet fern, breaking out among the lichened rocks; and the tidal rivers bringing their weedy tang to the low meadows, wide and open in the sun; the purple pine groves, where the needles, bedded deep, hum to the wind, or the knotted New England hills, where the mountain laurel in June seems like upland snow, left over, or where the marble breaks through into clusters of perpetual laurel and everlasting; one sees mountain lakes, giant aquamarines, sapphires, topazes, and upland pastures where the blue, purple, lavender, and green of the huckleberry bushes give way in autumn to the fringe of sumach by the roadside, volcanoes of reds and crimsons; the yellow of September cornfields, with intenser pumpkins lying between the shocks, or the naked breasts and flanks of the autumn landscape, quivering in uneasy sleep before the white blanket puts it to rest. To smell this, taste this, and feel and climb and walk over this landscape, once untouched, like an unopened letter or a lover unkissed—who would not rise to meet the expectation of the land? Partly, it was the challenge of babyhood: how will it grow up and what will become of it? Partly, it was the charm of innocence; or again, it was the sense of the mighty variety that the whole continent gives, as if between the two oceans every possible human habitat might be built, and every conceivable variety of experience fathomed.

What the aboriginal Indian had absorbed from the young earth, Thoreau absorbed; what the new settlers had given her, the combing of the plow, the cincture of the stone fence or the row of planted elms, these things he absorbed too; for Thoreau, having tasted the settled life of Concord, knew that the wilderness was not a permanent home for man: one might go there for fortification, for a quickening of the senses, for a tightening of all the muscles; but that, like any retreat, is a special exercise and wants a special occasion: one returned to Nature in order to become, in a deeper sense, more cultivated and civilized, not in order to return to crudities that men had already discarded. Looking ahead, Thoreau saw what was needed to preserve the valuable heritage of the American wilderness. He wrote:

"The kings of England formerly had their forests to hold the king's game, for sport or food, sometimes destroying villages to create and extend them; and I think that they were impelled by a true instinct. Why should not we, who have renounced the king's authority, have our national preserves, where no villages need be destroyed, in which the bear and panther, and some even of the hunter race, may still exist, and not be 'civilized off the face of the earth,'—our own forests, not to hold the king's game merely, but to hold and preserve the king himself also, the lord of creation,—and not in idle sport of food, but for inspiration and our own true recreation? or shall we, like the villains, grub them all up, poaching on our own national domain?"

These pregnant suggestions of Thoreau, which were to be embodied only after two generations in our National and State Parks, and in projects like Benton MacKaye's great conception of the Appalachian trail, make the comments of those who see in him only an arch-individualist, half-Diogenes, half-Rousseau, seem a little beside the point. The individualism of an Emerson or a Thoreau was the necessary complement of the thoroughly socialized existence of the New England town; it was what prevented these towns from becoming collections of yes-men, with never an opinion or an emotion that differed from their neighbors. He wrote for his fellow-townsmen; and his notion of the good life was one that should carry to a higher pitch the existing polity and culture of Concord itself. "As the nobleman of cultivated taste surrounds himself with whatever conduces to his culture—genius—learning—wit—books—paintings—statuary—music—philosophical instruments, and the like; so let the village do—not stop short at a pedagogue, a person, a sexton, a parish library, and three selectmen, because our pilgrim forefathers got through a cold winter once on a bleak rock with these. To act collectively is according to the spirit of our institutions; and I am confident that, as our circumstances are more flourishing, our means are greater than the nobleman's." Do not those sentences alter a little our stereotype of homespun New England, of individualistic America?

Just as Thoreau sought Nature, in order to arrive at a higher state of culture, so he practiced individualism, in order to create a better order of society. Taking America as it was, Thoreau conceived a form, a habitat, which would retain what was unique in the American contact with the virgin forest, the cultivated soil, and the renewed institutions of the New England town. He understood the precise thing that the pioneer lacked. The pioneer had exhausted himself in a senseless external activity, which answered no inner demands except those for oblivion. In his experiment at Walden Pond, Thoreau "learned this, at least . . . that if one advances confidently in the direction of his dreams, and endeavors to live the life which he has imagined, he will meet with success unexpected in the common hours. . . . In proportion as he simplifies his life, the laws of the universe will appear less complex, and solitude will not be solitude, nor poverty poverty, nor weakness weakness. If you have built castles in the air, your work need not be lost; that is where they should be. Now put the foundations under them."

In short, Thoreau lived in his desires; in rational and beautiful things that he imagined worth doing, and did. The pioneer lived only in extraneous necessities; and he vanished with their satisfaction: filling all the conditions of his environment, he never fulfilled himself. With the same common ground between them in their initial feeling towards Nature, Thoreau and the pioneer stood at opposite corners of the field. What Thoreau left behind is still precious; men may still go out and make over America in the image of Thoreau. What the pioneer left behind, alas! was only the burden of a vacant life.

High Noon: Whitman

"He that by me spreads a wider breast than my own proves the width of my own." So Walt Whitman chanted in the 'Song of Myself'; and in the greatness of Whitman the genius of Emerson was justified. Walt Whitman was a cosmos: he was inclusive where Emerson and Thoreau were restrictive: he was sensual and jolly where they were refined and taut: he identified himself with the mere bulk and vastness of the American continent, and, with a tremendous appetite for the actual, entered into the experience of the pioneer, the roadhand, the mechanic, the woodman, the soldier, the farmer. In some remote Dutch ancestor of Whitman's one figures the men and women of Franz Hals's portraiture, people large, lusty, loving, men who like their sweetheart and their steak, women who give themselves to love as the flower bows to the weight of the bee. With Emerson, to repeat the obvious, one surveys the world from a glacial summit: the air is rarefied, and at the distance even the treacherous places in the landscape seem orderly and innocent. With Whitman one sees the heights from the bosom of the valley: the "unseen is proved by the seen, till that becomes unseen, and receives proofs of its own."

Whitman absorbed so much of the America about him, that he is more than a single writer: he is almost a literature. Pushing his way like some larval creature through one husk after another, through the hard shell of Puritanism, in which he wrote Temperance Tracts, through the shell of republicanism in which he glorified all the new political institutions, through the flimsy casement of romantic poetry, iridescent with cheap colors and empty rhymes, Whitman finally achieved his own metamorphosis, and emerged, with dripping wings, into the untempered midday of the American scene. The stages of this metamorphosis have created contradictions in Whitman's work; and if we are to appreciate his full achievement, we must be ready to throw aside the vestiges of his larval state.

First, there was in Whitman a certain measure of the political religiosity of Joel Barlow and Philip Freneau. Political nationalism, in certain aspects of Whitman's thought, assumed a mystical beauty and centrality: he wrote about the United States as if they were the tissue of men's eternal desires—as if the robbery of Mexican territory, for example, could be justified to the Mexicans as well as the Americans by the inevitable drag of our Manifest Destiny. Here Whitman was confusing spiritual with temporal dominion. He had conceived new spiritual patterns, appropriate to the modern, which were to be fulfilled in the America of his dreams; and it was hard to resist identifying this hope of a wider America with the expansionist activities of political bandits. In this mood, to speak frankly, Whitman ranted.

Nevertheless, when one sums up Whitman's observations upon the Union and upon the political state of the country, no one surely ever ranted with so many reservations; and it is unfair to take the bombastic lines out of the context that perpetually qualifies them. The political reality that was so precious to Whitman was only a means of permitting the growth of "superb persons," and a life, "copious, vehement, spiritual, bold." Moreover, between the Walt Whitman who wrote the original 'Leaves of Grass,' and the defeated and paralyzed man who lingered on through the Gilded Age, there is a difference; and by 1879 Whitman had come to realize that his democracy was one that had been based on free land and equal opportunity to use it, and that failure was beginning to threaten the political structure. "If the United States," he wrote, "like the countries of the Old World, are also to grow vast crops of poor, desperate, dissatisfied, nomadic, miserably waged populations, such as we see looming upon us of late years—steadily, even if slowly, eating into them like a cancer of lungs or stomach—then our republican experiment, not withstanding all its surface-successes, is at heart an unhealthy failure. . . ." That was not all. "By the unprecedented open-up of humanity en masse in the United States in the last hundred years, under our institutions, not only the good qualities of the race, but just as much the bad ones, are predominantly brought forward. Man is about the same, in the main, whether with despotism or whether with freedom."

That saving and irrefragable common sense was what ballasted all of Whitman's hopes and expectations. He lived to see the America he dreamed of undermined and rotten: he saw the Kings of Iron and Oil and Cotton supplant not merely the older ones who ruled by divine right but the new one elected quadrennially by the people: he saw the diverse but well-mixed America of his youth give way to the America of the melting pot, which neither welded the old nationalities nor had the spiritual power to create a new one: he saw the sickly barbers and perfumers of the New York literary schools of the forties turn into the gentlemanly tailors who cut their stories and their thoughts to fit the fat paunches of the middle classes in the seventies: he saw all this, and denied nothing. No critic ferreted out the weaknesses and pettinesses of America with a surer nose than Whitman tracked them down in his 'Democratic Vistas': what could be said against his dream, Whitman said, with the staunch candor of a friend. But his thought and his vision were unshaken; the promise of America had not disappeared. If it was absent from the immediate scene, it had nevertheless taken form in his poems; and his poems were still waiting to shape a new America.

In 'Leaves of Grass' Whitman had fulfilled Emerson in more ways than either of them suspected. There are passages of Emerson's prose which have, potentially, the prosody of Whitman; but whereas Emerson's poems, at their best, remain fragmentary and broken, because the meaning was somehow always warping the metes and measures Emerson respected and clung to, in Whitman, at his best, these new thoughts find their own beat, and become poetry of the first rank. Whitman had discovered Emerson's inner form in creating his own. He himself had stammered and stuttered so long as he kept to the old metres: his early work was weak and sentimental because he had nothing to say within the bounds of those previous culture-molds which Whitman tagged as "feudal." New streams of thought and experience were confluent in Whitman: the *Weltanschauung* of Hegel, precursor of the evolutionists, who saw the world as a continual becoming, and both the bad and the good as part of the total meaning of the universe; the electric doctrine of Emerson, which bade every man find his own center and every institution to answer up for its results in one's own life; the unstratified society of America, where the bus driver was as good as the next man, and the private soldier as great as the statesman whose policies reduced him to a pawn; the cleansing operations of science, which confronted every variety in thought, and made no more distinction between the clean and the unclean, the minute and the immense, than some indifferent deity, for whom the fall of a gnat and the fall of an Empire are of precisely the same importance. Out of the discussions of the Fourierists, and the societies of Free Lovers, and women who pressed for the political and social emancipation of their sex, as well as out of his own capacious adventures, Whitman got the courage to deal with the varieties of sexual experience, too: in the 'Children of Adam' and 'Calamus' he brushed past the nice restraints of Emerson—who "held his nose" at its passages—and Thoreau, who, like Natty Bumppo and Paul Bunyan, averted himself from any passion more intense than friendship.

Whitman took in the quaker, the puritan, the cosmopolitan, the pioneer, the republican; and what came out in his poems was none of these things: it was a new essence; none of the ordinary labels described it. It had the smell of reality which was science; it had the largeness of comprehension which was philosophy; and it had the doubts, searchings, quests, achievements, and consummations which are the stuff of life itself. Whitman found no need to add an extra dimension to his experience; to transcribe for him was in the highest sense to *translate*. Whatever tended to create full-bodied and full-minded men and women tended toward enlarging the significance of every single activity, no matter how base or minute. The veil of appearance was as mysterious and beautiful as anything behind the veil. Perhaps it was all Maya, all illusion; or perhaps life was like a set of Chinese boxes: one removed the outer box of appearance, and discovered another box—appearance. What of it? A single blade of grass was enough to confound all the atheists; and whatever else the universe might hold, he reckoned that there was no sweeter meat than that which clung to his own bones. Such faith does not need external props and certitudes: it mocks at the testimony of bibles, for it is itself the source of such testimony.

People have hesitated to call Whitman's poems poetry; it is useless to deny that they belong to sacred literature. If the 'Leaves of Grass' are not poetry, it is only because not every generation endows us with such a poet.

Literature may be evocative or formative: one plays upon sentiments, emotions, ideas that already exist: the other changes the very attitude of the audience, and calls new ones forth. The common American of the Golden Day responded to Longfellow and Whittier; for these men caught his ordinary mood, measured off and rhymed; and even when Whittier and Lowell wrote on abolition themes, they were only touching strings which a Garrison or a Wendell Phillips had already set in motion. It is amusing to note the way in which ante-bellum America responded to Whitman. Emerson and Thoreau were quick to see his genius, even to proclaim it. Lesser people, however, like Moncure Conway, were a little disappointed with him: they expected to find in Whitman the common workman, grown vocal, someone who could be taken into society and patronized; someone who would bolster up their notion of a poet who had risen from the lowly ranks.

Whitman was not a democrat, in the sense of being a popular mediocrity; he was a man of genius; who, mid all his school teaching, editing, carpentering, type-setting, and what-not remained consecrated to the profession of letters: Jesus Son of Sirach was no more certain of his vocation. Whitman was Pygmalion to his own Galatea: he had formed himself, so that he might give a new model to America. The imperturbable landscape, the satisfaction and aplomb of animals, the ecstasy of hearty lovers, the meditations of one who sits withdrawn in the crowd, or on a mountain top—Whitman extracted from things a new shape, which was himself. Every poem of Whitman's is the man; every part of the man threw forth tendrils which clung to the objects of poems. One could not become a sympathetic reader of Whitman without re-forming oneself into an approximation of this new shape. Only commonplace works of art reflect the everyday personality of the reader: the supreme works always show or hint of the new shape the reader may become: they are prophetic, formative. One might remove Longfellow without changing a single possibility of American life; had Whitman died in the cradle, however, the possibilities of American life would have been definitely impoverished. He created a new pattern of experience and character. The work he conceived still remains to be done: the America he evoked does not as yet exist.

Whitman was a poet in the braid Scots sense of *makkar:* a maker or creator. He was conscious of the fact that the accumulated culture of Europe had lost a good part of its original meaning, through lack of direct contact with the new forces of discovery, science, democracy; the work of the old *makkars* was crumbling away; at best, it was repeated by rote, as in the churches, without any sense of the living reality, or the finer passages were rolled on the tongue, for sensation's sake, by an aristocratic minority. "Note today," Whitman observed in 'Democratic Vistas,' "a curious spectacle and conflict. . . . Science, testing absolutely all thoughts, all works, has already burst well upon the world—a sun, mounting, most illuminating, most glorious, surely never again to set. But against it, deeply entrenched, holding possession, yet remains (not only through the churches and schools but by imaginative literature and unregenerate poetry) the fossil theology of the mythic-materialistic superstitious, untaught and credulous, fable-loving primitive ages of humanity."

Whitman saw that the office of sacred literature was no longer being performed; or at all events, that those who were pursuing it were not fully conscious of either the need or the opportunity. Vulgar literature was, indeed, growing hugely. "Today, in books, in the rivalry of writers, especially novelists, success (so-called) is for him or her who strikes the mean flat average, the sensational appetite for stimulus, incident, persiflage, etc., and depicts to the common caliber, sensual, exterior life." What remained of sacred literature was insufficient to offset this. It was to establish a central point in literature, in terms of science and the modern, that Whitman created; American poetry was to do in our day what the Vedas, the Nackas, the Talmud, the Old Testament, the Gospel, Plato's works had done for their time: it was to crystallize our most precious experience and in turn to modify, by that act of crystallization, the daily routine.

What, in fact, were the active formative literatures when Whitman wrote? In the Western World the principal one was, without doubt, that great miscellany called the Old Testament, supplemented by the Gospels; and among the cultivated classes, Homer, Horace, Plutarch, Dante, Shakespeare, Goethe played a lively but minor part. The Romantic movement, which went back to the ballads and the folk-literature of the various regions of Europe, was a recognition of the fact that something was lacking in both the Hebrew and the classic traditions, and in the literature which was directly founded upon them. What was lacking was the direct historic connection with a people, a place, and a special way of life. It is true that all literature has certain common characters, and no great works of the spirit are foreign and remote; but, as Whitman pointed out, "something is rooted in the invisible roots, the profoundest meanings, of a place, race, or nationality," and the Romantic movement had cut loose from classic and Hebraic influences in order to absorb this more intimate order of meaning and find a nearer and fresher source of spiritual activity. Blake, Keats, Shelley, had partly achieved this; Wordsworth alone, however, had created new forms without relying on a mythic-materialistic past.

With what was universal in all these efforts, Whitman could sympathize: Homer and Shakespeare and the Bible had been his daily food. He sought to do for common men and women, for the contemporary and the ordinary-heroic, what Shakespeare had achieved in his great images of the artistocratic life. In America, in modern life, on the farm and in the laboratory, in the progress of souls along the grand roads of the Universe, in company with the Great Companions, the swift and majestic men, the capacious and broad-bosomed women—here was the stuff for new Vedas, Cycles, and Testaments. Whitman overvalued, if anything, the contrivances of political democracy; but that was only a first step; he overcountenanced, if anything, the absorption of America in materialistic effort; that, however, was only the second step. Neither political democracy nor industrial progress was for him anything but a prelude to the third stage, rising out of the two previous ones, and creating a "native expression spirit" and an abundance of rich personalities.

In his effort to keep ballasted and always find a landing place in contemporary existence, Whitman was perhaps too receptive and undiscriminating in his acknowledgement of current values and aims; in his old age, he accepted with child-like delight the evidence of material prosperity he found on his Western trip. His Hegelianism was dangerous stuff: it led him to identify the Real and the Ideal, instead of seeing, as William James put it, that they were dynamically continuous. But at the core, Whitman was never deceived: he knew that the meaning of all current activity lay only in the forms or symbols it created and the rational purposes it embodied; and so far from believing that the work of the poet or artist would be supplanted by science, he believed that "the highest and subtlest and broadest truths of modern science wait for their true assignment and last vivid flashes of light—as Democracy waits for its—through first-class metaphysicians and speculative philosophs—having the basements and foundations for these new, more expanded, more harmonious, more melodious, freer American poems." To indicate these new meanings, to open up these new relationships, Whitman wrote his poems. I can think of no one in whom the unconscious and the conscious worked more in harmony: the life and the doctrine were one. So far as Whitman went, he achieved his end.

So far as he went! Most people are unaware that the 'Leaves of Grass,' 'Calamus,' the 'Children of Adam,' are only a part of the vast canvas he projected; they do not realize that he was diverted from his original intention and never lived to complete it. The 'Leaves of Grass' were to deal chiefly with the palpable and the material; there was to be a complementary volume which would center mainly on the spiritual and the inactual

—upon death and immortality and final meanings—for he was the poet of the body and he was the poet of the soul. Alas! the Civil War came. He threw himself into it as a hospital visitor, giving his personality and his radiant health to the sick and wounded, as these men had given themselves in the camp and on the battlefield. Within a few years this ordeal exacted its revenge: he became paralyzed, and as he never fully recovered his physical powers, his mental powers diminished too: if they are still at their summit in 'Drum-Taps,' they recurred only fitfully in the later poems: and though he could outline his aspiration with a firm hand in 'Democratic Vistas,' published in 1871, he could no longer model it and round it out. What he meant to create is implied in all his poems; the whole of it was never, perhaps, expressed.

Whitman himself had felt that the War for the American Union was the Odyssey of his generation; but except for himself and Herman Melville, no one lived to write about it in those terms; the stories of Ambrose Bierce, Stephen Crane, and Upton Sinclair did not treat it in this vein. Whitman did not see that the great conflict might have a Punic ending. As it turned out, the war was a struggle between two forms of servitude, the slave and the machine. The machine won, and the human spirit was almost as much paralyzed by the victory as it would have been by the defeat. An industrial transformation took place overnight: machines were applied to agriculture; they produced new guns and armaments; the factory regime, growing tumultuously in the Eastern cities, steadily undermined the balanced regimen of agriculture and industry which characterized the East before the war.

The machines won; and the war kept on. Its casualties were not always buried at Antietam or Gettysburg; they moldered, too, in libraries, studies, offices. The justifiable ante-bellum optimism of Emerson turned into a waxen smile. Whitman lost his full powers in what should have been his prime. Among the young men, many a corpse was left, to go through the routine of living. But before the Golden Day was over, the American mind had lived through a somber and beautiful hour, the hour of Hawthorne and Melville. With them, the sun turned to a candle, and cast black shadows upon the wall, not the empty grotesque shadows of Poe, but the shapes of a magnified if distorted humanity.

(1926)

CHAPTER FOUR

Melville: 'Moby-Dick'

'Moby-Dick' is a story of the sea, and the sea is life, "whose waters of deep woe are brackish with the salt of human tears." 'Moby-Dick' is the story of the eternal Narcissus in man, gazing into all rivers and oceans to grasp the unfathomable phantom of life—perishing in the illusive waters. 'Moby-Dick' is a portrait of the whale and a presentation of the demonic energies in the universe that harass and frustrate and extinguish the spirit of man. We must gather our own strength together if we are to penetrate 'Moby-Dick': no other fable, except perhaps Dante's, demands that we open so many doors and turn so many secret keys; for, finally, 'Moby-Dick' is a labyrinth, and that labyrinth is the universe. . . .

It is absurdly ineffectual to summarize the contents of 'Moby-Dick,' or to quote, dismembered, some of its great passages. Like the paintings in the Ajanta caves, the beauty of 'Moby-Dick' can be known only to those who will make a pilgrimage to it, and stay within its dark confines until what is darkness has become light, and one can make out, with the help of an occasional torch, its grand design, its complicated arabesque, the minute significance of its parts. No feeble pencil sketch can convey a notion of 'Moby-Dick's' extravagant beauty; but at the same time, without a hint of its design and its manner of execution, all subsequent commentary must seem flatulent and disproportionate. For three-quarters of a century 'Moby-Dick' has suffered at the hands of the superficial critic: it has been condemned because to one man it seemed confused, to another it was not a novel, to a third the characters were not 'real,' and to a fourth it was merely a weird, mystical, impossible tale of dubious veracity, an example of Bedlam literature, while to a fifth, it was just a straightforward account of the whaling industry, marred by a crazy captain and an adventitious plot. The final answer to all these criticisms lies, of course, in the book itself.

Before we can take the measure of 'Moby-Dick' we must, however, throw aside our ordinary measuring-sticks: one does not measure Saturn with the aid of an opera-glass and a dressmaker's tape. The conventional critic has dismissed 'Moby-Dick' because it is "not a novel," or if it is a novel, its story is marred by all sorts of extraneous material, history, natural history, philosophy, mythological excursions, what not. This sort of criticism would belittle 'Moby-Dick' by showing that it does not respect canons of a much pettier nature than the work itself, or because its colossal bulk cannot be caught in the herring-net of the commonplace story or romance. Even John Freeman, one of the most sympathetic interpreters of Melville, falls into this error; for, while acknowledging the great qualities of 'Moby-Dick,' he refers to its "digressions and delays" as if they were in fact digressions and delays; that is, as if the 'action' in the common novelist's development of plot carried the thread of the story. By the same criteria the 'Iliad' would not be a poem.

The matter is very easily put to rights if we simply abandon these false categories altogether. 'Moby-Dick' stands by itself as completely as the 'Divine Comedy' or the 'Odyssey' stands by itself. Benedetto Croce has correctly taught us that every work of art is indeed in this same position: that it is uniquely what it is, and cannot be understood except in terms of its own purpose. If, for purely practical reasons, we ignore this in dealing with the ruck of novels and stories, because their inner purpose is so insignificant, we must respect it strictly when we confront a work that does not conspicuously conform to the established canons; for, needless to say, an imaginative work of the first rank will disclose itself through its differences and its departures, by what it originates, rather than by what it is derived from or akin to. Had Melville seriously sought in 'Moby-Dick' to rival the work of Trollope or Reade or Dickens, had he simply desired to amuse and edify the great bourgeois public that consumed its three-decker novels as it consumed its ten-course public dinners, and wanted no delay in the service, no hitch in the round of food, drink, toasts, speeches, and, above all, no unaccustomed victuals on such occasions, then 'Moby-Dick' would have been a mistake and failure.

But one cannot count as a failure what was never an attempt. 'Moby-Dick' does not belong to this comfortable bourgeois world, any more than horse-hair shirts or long fasts; it neither aids digestion nor increases the sense of warm drowsy good nature that leads finally to bed: and that is all there is to it.

The same criticism that disposes of the notion that 'Moby-Dick' is a bad novel, by admitting freely that it is not a novel at all, equally disposes of its lack of verisimilitude. Although Melville was at first challenged on his facts, such as the ramming of the *Pequod* by Moby-Dick, events were just as kind to his reputation here as they were in the case of 'Typee': for while 'Moby-Dick' was on the press, news came of the sinking of the whaler *Ann Alexander* by the ferocious attack of a whale. No one of authority has attempted to quarrel with Melville's descriptions of the life and habits of whalemen and the whale: the testimony of every observer is that Melville left very little for any one else to say about the subject. This does not, however, dispose of the charge; for those who are wisely captious of Melville here will confine themselves to saying that no such crew ever existed, no such words ever passed human mouth, and no such thoughts could enter the mind of a Nantucketer, as entered Ahab's.

Again, one is tempted to grant the objection; for it makes no difference in the value of 'Moby-Dick' as a work of art. In the realistic convention, 'Moby-Dick' would be a bad book: it happens that the story is projected on more than one plane, and a good part of it belongs to another, and equally valid, convention. Melville himself was aware of the difference, and early in the book he calls upon the Spirit of Equality, which has spread its royal mantle of humanity over all his kind, to defend him against all mortal critics "if, then, to the meanest mariners, and renegades, and cast-aways, I shall hereafter ascribe high qualities, though dark; weave round them tragic graces; if even the most mournful, perchance the most abased among them all shall at times lift himself to the exalted mounts; if I shall touch that workman's arm with some ethereal light; if I shall spread the rainbow over his disastrous set of sun." Now, the convention in which Melville cast this part of 'Moby-Dick' was foreign to the nineteenth century; obscure people, like Beddoes, alone essayed it: to create these idealized figures called for such reserves of power that only minor poets, for the most part, unconscious of their weaknesses, attempted the task.

The objections to Melville's use of this convention would be fair enough if, like the minor poets, he had failed; but, through his success, one sees that the limitations of naturalism are no closer to reality than the limitations of poetic tragedy; and, on the contrary, Melville's valiant use of this convention enabled him to present a much fuller picture of reality than the purely external suggestions of current realism would have permitted him to show. What we call realism is a limited method of approaching reality: an external picture of a Cowperwood or a Gantry may have as little human truth in it as a purely fanciful description of an elf: and the artist who can draw upon more than one convention is, at all events, free from the curious illusion, so common in the nineteenth century, alike in philosophy, with its pragmatism, in science, with its dogmatic materialism, and in imaginative writing, with its realism, that this convention is not limited, and so far arbitrary, but the very stuff and vitals of existence. The question to settle is not: Did an Ahab ever sail from Nantucket? The question is: Do Ahab and Stubb and Starbuck and Tashtego live within the sphere where we find them? The answer is that they are tremendously alive; for they are aspects of the spirit of man. At each utterance, one feels more keenly their imaginative embodiment: so that by the time Ahab breaks into his loftiest Titanisms, one accepts his molten language, as one accepts his pride: they belong to the fibre and essence of the man. Ahab is a reality in relation to Moby-Dick; and when Melville projects him, he ceases to be incredible, because he is alive.

We need not concern ourselves particularly with those who look upon 'Moby-Dick' solely as a sort of World's Almanac or Gazetteer of the Whaling Industry, unhappily marred by the highly seasoned enticements of the narrative. This criticism is, indeed, but the other side of the sort of objection I have disposed of; and it tells more about the limitations of the reader than it does about the quality of 'Moby-Dick.' For the fact is that this book is a challenge and affront to all the habits of mind that typically prevailed in the nineteenth century, and still remain, almost unabated, among us: it comes out of a different world, and presupposes, for its acceptance, a more integrated life and consciousness than we have known or experienced, for the most part, these last three centuries. 'Moby-Dick' is not Victorian; it is not Elizabethan; it is, rather, prophetic of another quality of life which Melville had experienced and had a fuller vision of in his own time—a quality that may again come into the world, when we seek to pass beyond the discordant specialisms that still hold and preoccupy so many of us. To fathom this quality of Melville's experience and imagination, we must look a little deeper into his myth and his manner of projecting it. What is its meaning? And first, in what manner is that meaning conveyed to us?

'Moby-Dick' is a poetic epic. Typographically, 'Moby-Dick' conforms to prose, and there are long passages, whole chapters, which are wholly in the mood of prose: but in spirit and in actual rhythm, 'Moby-Dick' again and again rises to polyphonic verse which resembles passages of Webster's in that it can either be considered as broken blank verse, or as cadenced prose. Percy Boynton has performed the interesting experiment of transposing a paragraph in 'Pierre' into excellent free verse, so strong and subtle are Melville's rhythms; and one might garner a whole book of verse from 'Moby-Dick.' Melville, in 'Moby-Dick,' unconsciously respects Poe's canon that all true poetry must be short in length, since the mood cannot be retained, unbroken or undiminished, over lengthy passages, and if the form itself is preserved, the content nevertheless is prose. But while Poe himself used this dictum as an excuse for writing only short lyrics, Melville sustained the poetic mood through a long narrative by dropping frankly into prose in the intervening while. As a result, he was under no necessity of clipping the emotions or of bleaching the imaginative colors of 'Moby-Dick': like a flying-boat, he rises from the water to the air and returns to the water again without losing control over either medium. His prose is prose: hard, sinewy, compact; and his poetry is poetry, vivid, surging, volcanic, creating its own form in the very pattern of the emotional state itself, soaring, towering, losing all respect for the smaller conventions of veracity, when the inner triumph itself must be announced. It is in the very rhythm of his language that Ahab's mood, and all the devious symbols of 'Moby-Dick' are sustained and made credible: by no other method could the deeper half of the tale have been written. In these poetic passages, the phrases are intensified, stylized, stripped of their habitual associations. If occasionally, as with Shakespeare, the thought itself is borne down by the weight of the gold that decorates it, this is only a similar proof of Melville's immense fecundity of expression.

Both Poe and Hawthorne share some of Melville's power, and both of them, with varying success, wrought ideality and actuality into the same figure: but one has only to compare the best of their work with 'Moby-Dick' to see wherein Melville's great distinction lies. 'The Scarlet Letter,' 'The House of the Seven Gables,' 'William Wilson,' like most other works of fiction, are melodic: a single instrument is sufficient to carry the whole theme; whereas 'Moby-Dick' is a symphony; every resource of language and thought, fantasy, description, philosophy, natural history, drama, broken rhythms, blank verse, imagery, symbol, is utilized to sustain and expand the great theme. The conception of 'Moby-Dick' organically demands the expressive interrelation, for a single total effect of a hundred different pieces: even in accessory matters, like the association of the Parsee, the fire-worshipper, with the death of Ahab, the fire-defier, or in the makeup of the crew, the officers white men, the harpooners the savage races, red, black, brown, and the crew a mixed lot from the separate islands of the earth, not a stroke is introduced that has not a meaning for the myth as a whole. Although the savage harpooners get nearest the whale, the savage universe, it is Ahab and the Parsee, the Westerner and the Asiatic, who carry the pursuit to its ultimate end—while a single American survives to tell the tale!

Melville's instrumentation is unsurpassed in the writing of the last century: one must go to a Beethoven or a Wagner for an exhibition of similar powers: one will not find it among the works of literature. Here are Webster's wild violin, Marlowe's cymbals, Browne's sonorous bass viol, Swift's brass, Smollett's castanets, Shelley's flute, brought together in a single orchestra, complementing each other in a grand symphony. Melville achieved a similar synthesis in thought; and that work has proved all the more credible because he achieved it in language, too. Small wonder that those who were used to elegant pianoforte solos or barrel-organ instrumentation, were deafened and surprised and repulsed.

What is the meaning of 'Moby-Dick'? There is not one meaning; there are many; but in its simplest terms, 'Moby-Dick' is, necessarily, a story of the sea and its ways, as the 'Odyssey' is a story of strange adventure, and 'War and Peace' a story of battles and domestic life. The characters are heightened and slightly distorted: Melville's quizzical comic sense, not un-akin to Thoreau's, is steadily at work on them, and only Ahab escapes: but they all have their recognizable counterparts in the actual world. Without any prolonged investigation one could still find a Starbuck on Nantucket or a Flask on Martha's Vineyard.

On this level, 'Moby-Dick' brings together and focuses in a single picture the long line of sketches and preliminary portraits Melville had assembled in 'Typee,' 'Omoo,' 'Redburn,' and 'White-Jacket.' As a story of the sea, 'Moby-Dick' will always have a call for those who wish to recapture the magic and terror and stress and calm delight of the sea and its ships; and not less so because it seizes on a particular kind of ship, the whaler, and a special occupation, whaling, at the moment when they were about to pass out of existence, or rather, were being transformed from a brutal but glorious battle into a methodical, somewhat banal industry. Melville had the singular fortune to pronounce a valedictory on many ways of life and scenes that were becoming extinct. He lived among the South Sea Islanders when they were still pretty much as Captain Cook found them, just before their perversion and decimation by our exotic Western civilization. He recorded life on a man-of-war half a generation before the sail gave place to steam, wood to armor-plate, and grappling-irons to long-range guns. He described life on a sailing-packet before steam had increased the speed, the safety, and the pleasant monotony of trans-atlantic travel: and finally, he recorded the last heroic days of whaling. 'Moby-Dick' would have value as first-hand testimony, even if it were negligible as literature. If this were all, the book would still be important.

But 'Moby-Dick,' admirable as it is as a narrative of maritime adventure, is far more than that: it is, fundamentally, a parable on the mystery of evil and the accidental malice of the universe. On one reading, the white whale stands for the brute energies of existence, blind, fatal, overpowering, while Ahab is the spirit of man, small and feeble, but purposeful, that pits its puniness against this might, and its purpose against the blank senseless-ness of power. The evil arises with the good: the white whale grows up among the milder whales which are caught and cut up and used: one hunts for the one—for a happy marriage, livelihood, offspring, social companion-ship and cheer—and suddenly heaving its white bulk out of the calm sea, one comes upon the other: illness, accident, treachery, jealousy, vengeful-ness, dull frustration. The South Sea savage did not know of the white whale: at least, like death, it played but a casual part in his consciousness. It is different with the European: his life is a torment of white whales: the Jobs, the Aeschyluses, the Dantes, the Shakespeares pursue him and grap-ple with him, as Ahab pursues his antagonist.

All our lesser literature, all our tales of Avalon or Heaven or ultimate redemption, or, in a later day, the Future, is an evasion of the white whale: it is a quest of that boyish beginning which we call a happy ending. But the old Norse myth told that Asgard itself would be consumed at last, and the very gods would be destroyed: the white whale is the symbol of that persistent force of destruction, that meaningless force, which now figures as the outpouring of a volcano or the atmospheric disruption of a tornado or again as the mere aimless dissipation of unused energy into an unavail-able void—that spectacle which so disheartened the learned Henry Adams. The whole tale of the West, in mind and action, in the moral wrestlings of the Jews, in the philosophy and art of the Greeks, in the organization and technique of the Romans, in the precise skills and unceasing spiritual quests of the modern man, is a tale of this effort to combat the whale—to ward off his blows, to counteract his aimless thrusts, to create a purpose that will offset the empty malice of Moby-Dick. Without such a purpose, without the belief in such a purpose, life is neither bearable nor significant: unless one is fortified by these central human energies and aims, one tends to become absorbed in Moby-Dick himself, and, becoming a part of his being, can only maim, slay, butcher, like the shark or the white whale or Alexander or Napoleon. If there is no God, exclaims Dostoevsky's hero, then we may commit murder: and in the sense that God represents the totality of human value, meaning, and transcendent possibility the conclusion is inevitable.

It is useless to reduce man's purposes to those of the id; he is a figure in the whole web of life. Except for such kindness and loyalty as the creatures man has domesticated show, there is, as far as one can now see, no concern except in man himself over the ceaseless motions and accidents that take place in nature. Love and chance, said Charles Peirce, rule the universe: but that love is fitful, and although in the very concept of chance, as both Peirce and Captain Ahab declare, there is some rough notion of fair play, of fifty-fifty, of an even break, that is small immediate consolation for the creature that may lose not the game, but his life, by an unlucky throw of the dice. Ahab has more humanity than the gods he defies: indeed, he has more power, because he is conscious of the power he wields, and applies it deliberately, whereas Moby-Dick's power only seems deliberate because it cuts across the directed aims of Ahab himself. And in one sense, Ahab achieves victory: he vanquishes in himself that which would retreat from Moby-Dick and acquiesce in his insensate energies and his brutal sway. His end is tragic: evil engulfs him. But in battling against evil, with power instead of love, Ahab himself, in A. E.'s phrase, becomes the image of the thing he hates: he has lost his humanity in the very act of vindicating it. By physical defiance, by physical combat, Ahab cannot rout and capture Moby-Dick: the odds are against him; and if his defiance is noble, his final aim is confessedly mad. Cultivation, order, art—these are proper means by which man displaces accident and subdues the vacant external powers in the universe: the way of growth is not to become more powerful but to become more human.

Here is a hard lesson to learn: it is easier to wage war than to conquer in oneself the tendency to be partial, vindictive, and unjust: it is easier to demolish one's enemy than to pit oneself against him in a spiritual combat which will disclose one's weaknesses and provincialities. And that shapeless evil Ahab seeks to strike is the sum of one's enemies. He does not bow down to it and accept it: therein lie his heroism and virtue: but he fights it with its own weapons and therein lies his madness. All the things that Ahab despises when he is about to attack the whale, the love and loyalty of Pip, the memory of his wife and child, the sextant of science, the inner sense of calm, which makes all external struggle futile, are the very things that would redeem him and make him victorious.

Man's ultimate defense against the Universe, against evil and accident and malice, is not by any fictitious resolution of these things into an Absolute which justifies them and utilizes them for its own ends: this is specious comfort, and Voltaire's answer to Leibniz in 'Candide' seems to me a final one. Man's defense lies within himself, not within the narrow, isolated ego, which may be overwhelmed, but in that social self which we share with our fellows and which assures us that, whatever happens to our own carcasses and hides, good men will remain, to carry on the work, to foster and protect the things man has recognized as excellent. To make that self more solid, one must advance positive science, produce formative ideas, and embody ideal forms in which all men may, to a greater or less degree, participate—in short must create a realm which is independent of the insensate forces in the universe and cannot be lightly shaken by their onslaught. Melville's method, that of writing 'Moby-Dick,' was correct: as correct as Ahab's method, taken literally, that of fighting Moby-Dick, was fallacious.

In the very creation of Moby-Dick, Melville conquered the white whale that threatened him: instead of horror there was significance, instead of aimless energy there was purpose, and instead of random power there was meaningful life. The universe *is* inscrutable, unfathomable, overwhelming —like the white whale and his element. Art in the broad sense of all humanizing effort is man's answer to this condition: for it is the means by which he circumvents or postpones his doom, transcends his creaturely limitations, and bravely meets his tragic destiny.

Here, it seems to me, is the plainest interpretation of Melville's fable, and the one he was partly conscious of in the writing of it. But a great book is more a part of its milieu than either the writer or his public knows; and there is more in Moby-Dick than the figure of man's heroic defiance of brute energy, and evil, and the high gods.

In another sense, the whale stands for the practical life. Mankind needs food and light and shelter, and, with a little daring and a little patience, it gains these things from its environment: the whale that we cut up, dissect, analyze, melt down, pour into casks, and distribute in cities and households is the whale of industry and science. The era of whaling which opened only in the late seventeeth century is timed with the era of modern industry; and in the very year Melville wrote 'Moby-Dick,' 1851, industry and science were announcing their triumphs in that great cock-crow of the Crystal Palace Exhibition in London. Side by side with this purpose, which secures man's material existence, is another set of purposes which, though they sometimes take advantage of the means offered by the practical life, as Ahab takes advantage of his sordid crew and ordinary whaling to carry out his private revenge, run counter to the usual flow of our daily efforts.

The white whale cannot be met and captured by the usual means; more than that: to fulfill man's own deeper purposes, the captains of the spirit must oppose the prudence of Starbuck and the common sense of Stubb. Material sustenance, home, comfort, though their pursuit occupy the greater part of the daily round of humanity, are sometimes best forgotten and set at naught: indeed, when nobler human purposes are uppermost, they must be set at naught. He who steadily seeks to preserve life and fortify it must be ready to give up his life at a moment's notice when a fellow creature is in danger: he who would provide others with daily bread must be prepared to go hungry if the wheat that would nourish him is needed for the planting. All the more does this hold in the affairs of the spirit. When the human spirit expands itself to the uttermost, to confront the white whale and hew meaning and form from the blank stone of experience, one must reverse all the practical maxims: earth's folly, as Melville says, is Heaven's wisdom, and earth's wisdom is Heaven's greatest disaster.

The crew of the vessel seek the ordinary whale: they are after comfort and contentment and a greater share of the "lay"; but the Ahabs seek danger and hardship and a lay that has no value in terms of material sustenance and magnificence. And the paradox, the hard paradox, is this: both purposes are essential: Ahab could not set out at all without the aid of Peleg and Bildad and Charity and his harpooners and sailors, and they, for their part, would never know anything except sluggish routine were they not at times stirred up to great efforts by purposes they do not easily understand or consciously accept. Yet: there is an Ahab in every man, and the meanest member of the crew can be awakened to the values that Ahab prizes: given a storm and a stove boat, and the worst rascal on shipboard may be as magnificent as Odysseus. All men live most intensely when they are molded by such a purpose—or even, wanting that, by an enterprise that counterfeits it. Art, religion, culture in general, all those intangible triumphs of the spirit that are embodied in forms and symbols, all that spells purpose as opposed to senseless energy, and significance as opposed to routine—these efforts develop human life to its fullest, even when they work contrary to the ordinary standards of the world.

There, it seems to me, is another meaning in Ahab's struggle with Moby-Dick. He represents, not as in the first parable, an heroic power that misconceives its mission and misapplies itself: here he rather stands for human purpose in its highest expression. His pursuit is "futile" because it wrecks the boat and brings home no oil and causes material loss and extinguishes many human lives; but in another sense, it is not futile at all, but is the only significant part of the voyage, since oil is burned and ships eventually break up and men die and even the towers of proud cities crumble away as the buildings sink beneath the sand or the jungle, while all that remains, all that perpetuates the life and the struggle, are their forms and symbols, their art, their literature, their science, as they have been incorporated in the social heritage of man. That which is useful for the moment eventually becomes useless: the mummy's food and drink shrivel away or evaporate: but that which is "useless," the graven image or the tomb itself, continues to nourish the spirit of man. Life, Life purposive, Life formative, Life expressive, is more than living, as living itself is more than the finding of a livelihood. There is no triumph so petty and evanescent as that involved in capturing the ordinary whale: the nineteenth century made this triumph the end and object of all endeavor; and it put the spirit in chains of comfort and material satisfaction, which were heavier than fetters and harder to bear than the stake. By the same token, there is no struggle so permanent and so humanly satisfactory as Ahab's struggle with the white whale. In that defeat, in that succession of defeats, is the only pledge of man's ultimate victory, and the only final preventive of emptiness, boredom, and suicide. Battles are lost, as Whitman cried, in the same spirit that they are won. Some day the physical powers of man may be commensurate with his utmost spirit, and he will meet Leviathan on even terms.

The epic and mythic quality of 'Moby-Dick' has been misunderstood because those who examined the book have thought of the epic in terms of Homer, and the myth itself in relation to some obvious hero of antiquity, or some modern folk-hero, a Washington, a Boone, raised to enormous dimensions. "The great mistake seems to be," as Melville said in his essay on Hawthorne, "that even with those Americans who look forward to the coming of a great literary genius among us, they somehow fancy he will come in the costume of Queen Elizabeth's day; be a writer of dramas founded upon old English history or the tales of Boccaccio. Whereas, great geniuses are parts of the times, they themselves are the times and possess a corresponding coloring."

Now, 'Moby-Dick' was written in the best spirit of the nineteenth century, and though it escaped most of the limitations of that period, it escaped with its finest qualities intact. Heroes and gods in the old sense, as Walt Whitman plainly saw, had had their day: they fitted into a simpler scheme of life and thought, and a more credulous sort of attitude; so far from representing the ultimate triumph of the human imagination, from which the scientific mode of thought was not merely a departure but a falling off, the old myths were but the product of a juvenile fantasy. One might still use these figures, as Milton used an Arcadian image to express the corruptions of the Established Church; but they stood for a mode of consciousness and feeling remote from our modern experience. Science did not, as has been foolishly believed, destroy the myth-making power of man, or reduce all his inner strivings to bleak impotence: this has been the accidental, temporary effect of a one-sided science, serving, consciously or not, a limited number of practical activities. What the scientific spirit has actually done has been to exercise the imagination in finer ways than the autistic wish— the wish of the infant possessed of the illusion of power and domination—

was able to express. Faraday's ability to conceive the lines of force in a magnetic field was quite as great a triumph as the ability to conceive fairies dancing in a ring: and, as A. N. Whitehead has shown, the poets who sympathized with this new sort of imagination, poets like Shelley, Words-worth, Whitman, Melville, did not feel themselves robbed of their specific powers, but rather found them enlarged and refreshed.

One of the finest love-poems of the nineteenth century, Whitman's 'Out of the Cradle Endlessly Rocking,' is expressed in such an image as Darwin or Audubon might have used, were the scientist as capable of expressing his inner feelings as of noting 'external' events: the poet haunting the sea-shore and observing the mating of the birds, day after day following their life, could scarcely have existed before the nineteenth century. In the seventeenth century, such a poet would have remained in the garden and written about a literary ghost, Philomel, and not about an actual pair of birds: in Pope's time, the poet would have remained in the library and written about the birds on a lady's fan. Almost all the important works of the nineteenth century were cast in this mode and expressed this new imaginative range: they respect the fact: they are replete with observation: they project an ideal realm in and through, not over, the landscape of actuality. 'Notre Dame' might have been written by an historian, 'War and Peace' by a sociologist, 'The Idiot' might have been created by a psychiatrist, and 'Salammbô' might have been the work of an archaeologist. I do not say that these books were scientific by intention, or that they might be replaced by a work of science without grave loss; far from it. I merely point out that they are conceived in the same spirit; that they belong to a similar plane of consciousness. Much as Melville was enriched by the Elizabethan writers, there is that in 'Moby-Dick' which separates him completely from the poets of that day—and if one wants a word to describe the element that makes the difference, one must call it briefly science.

Now, this respect for fact, as opposed to irresponsible fantasy, did not of course exist for the first time in the nineteenth century: Defoe had this habit of mind in quite as great a measure as Melville: what is important is that it was for the first time wedded—deliberately if not completely—to the imagination. It no longer means a restriction, a dried-up quality, an incompleteness; it no longer deifies the empirical and the practical at the expense of the ideal and the aesthetic: on the contrary, these qualities are now completely fused together, as an expression of life's integrated totality. The symbolism again becomes equal to the reality. Hercules no longer serves in this way: although originally he was doubtless as full of immediate relationships as whaling; and a more complex and diffuse symbol—like Kutuzov's army in 'War and Peace'—is necessary. Had Milton sought to tell this parable of Melville's, he would probably have recast the story of Jonah and the whale, making Jonah the hero; but in doing so he could not help losing all the great imaginative parallels Melville is able to work out, through using material hitherto untouched by previous myth or history.

For Ahab's hate and the pursuit of the whale is only one part of the total symbol: the physiological character of the whale, its feeding, its mating, its whole life, from whatever sources Melville drew the data, is equally a part of it. Indeed, the symbol of Moby-Dick is complete and rounded, expressive of our present relations to the universe, only through the passages that orthodox criticism, exercised on lesser works and more meagre traditions, regards as extraneous or unimportant!

'Moby-Dick,' then, is one of the first great mythologies to be created in the modern world, created, that is, out of the stuff of that world, its science, its exploration, its terrestrial daring, its concentration upon power and dominion over nature, and not out of ancient symbols, Prometheus, Endymion, Orestes, or medieval folk-legends, like Dr. Faustus. 'Moby-Dick' lives imaginatively in the newly broken soil of our own life: its symbols, unlike Blake's original but mysterious figures, are direct and explicit: if the story is bedded in facts, the facts themselves are not lost in the further interpretation. 'Moby-Dick' thus brings together the two dissevered halves of the modern world and the modern self—its positive, practical, scientific, externalized self, bent on conquest and knowledge, and its imaginative, ideal half, bent on the transposition of conflict into art, and power into humanity. This resolution is achieved in 'Moby-Dick' itself: it is as if a Shakespeare and a Bacon, or, to use a more local metaphor, as if an Eakins and a Ryder, had collaborated on a single work of art, with a heightening of their several powers. The best handbook on whaling is also—I say this scrupulously—the best tragic epic of modern times and one of the fine poetic works of all time.

That is an achievement; and it is also a promise. Whitman went as far in his best poems, particularly in the 'Song of Myself'; and, with quite another method, Tolstoy went as far in 'War and Peace,' Dostoevsky in 'The Brothers Karamazov'; Hardy, less perfectly, approximated it perhaps in 'The Dynasts'; but no one went further. It is one of the great peaks of the modern vision of life. "May God keep us," wrote Blake, "from single vision and Newton's sleep." We now perhaps see a little more clearly what Blake's enigmatic words mean. In 'Moby-Dick' Melville achieved the deep integrity of that double vision which sees with both eyes—the scientific eye of actuality, and the illumined eye of imagination and dream.

Each age, one may predict, will find its own symbols in 'Moby-Dick.' Over that ocean the clouds will pass and change, and the ocean itself will mirror back those changes from its own depths. All these conscious interpretations, however, though they serve the book by approaching its deeper purpose, do not, cannot, quite penetrate the core of its reality. 'Moby-Dick' has a meaning which cannot be derived or dissociated from the work itself. Like every great work of art, it summons up thoughts and feelings profounder than those to which it gives overt expression. It introduces one, sometimes by simple, bald means, to the depths of one's own experience.

The book is not an answer, but a clue that must be carried further and worked out. The Sermon on the Mount has this quality. It does not solve all the difficult problems of morality, but it suggests a new point of view in facing them: it leads one who is sufficiently moved to follow through all the recesses of conduct which can be influenced by mildness, understanding, and love, but not otherwise. So with 'Moby-Dick': the book itself is greater than the fable it embodies, it foreshadows more than it actually reflects. In these pages there are colors beyond those of the spectrum, hitherto unrecorded, though often present. These invisible ultraviolet and infra-red lights affect us, penetrating deep tissues, even if they do not register to the human eye. Through Melville's presentation of the demonic dark side of man, today so visible, he threw into stark relief the true nature of the Divine. Though momentarily he had sided with the Devil in this "wicked" fable, he would spend the rest of his life, not justifying Ahab's or Pierre's nihilism, but seeking and groping toward God. As a work of art, 'Moby-Dick' is part of a new integration of thought, a widening of the fringe of consciousness, a deepening of insight into life's ultimate mysteries.

The shadow cast by 'Moby-Dick' throws into obscurity not merely the sand-hills, but likewise some of the mountains, of the last three centuries. Noting the extent of that shadow, one begins to suspect how high the mountain itself is, and how great its bulk, how durable its rock.

(1929)

CHAPTER FIVE

Audubon:
Passionate Naturalist

The life of John James Audubon was full of ambiguities, contradictions, frustrations, alienations. With such attributes, his biography could easily meet the fashionable specifications of our own period. But he was also a man of heroic mold, and heroes for the moment are not fashionable. What is worse for his present fame, he was, within his strict avian limits, a skilled draughtsman, indeed a consummate artist; and that is a severe disqualification in an age populated by solemn popcorny jokesters who transfer nothingness to a canvas and sell it as art, or who crown such vacuous achievements by erasing nothingness and coyly signing their names to that double nonentity.

In order to characterize either the new edition of Audubon's 'The Birds of America' or the latest biography I find it necessary to outline Audubon's life, for I have fallen in love with the man and his work all over again, as Melville fell in love with Hawthorne's enchanting mind. The most charitable thing one can say about this new biography is that the writer found Audubon's character so disenchanting and his whole career so distasteful, that only the most severe moral discipline could have kept him at his self-imposed task. In retelling Audubon's story I shall do justice to both Audubon and his new biographer; for I shall show that each is—in quite contrasting ways—strictly for the birds.

Jean Jacques Fougère Rabin Audubon, also nicknamed La Forêt, was born it now seems clear in 1785. But every attempt to unravel the mystery of his parentage only makes a greater mystery of equally valid documents and reported events, including some of Audubon's own letters to his wife. His childhood memories, curiously, did not go back farther than when he was eight, as a boy in Nantes, supposedly brought to France at four by his sea-going merchant father, Jean Audubon. Whether Audubon's early memories were erased by shock or deliberately suppressed or confusedly interwoven with an improbable past, which he was bound under oath to his father to conceal, we shall never know. Supposing he was indeed, as rumor long hinted, the lost Dauphin of France whisked out of prison during the revolution in 1793, certain princely traits in Audubon's character would be easier to explain. If on the other hand, Audubon was actually the illegitimate son of the sea-captain and a Santo Domingan Creole woman, this would hardly account for his uncertainty about dates and birthplaces and his sometimes imperfect sense of reality. But if his life was actually based on a fiction, that might well be responsible for his free and loose way of dealing with other parts of it, as it were a fictitious incident in the same improbable fairy story of a stolen prince condemned to obscurity.

At all events the verifiable story of Audubon's life begins only at the late age of eleven. From then on it can be followed with confidence till he died, old before his time, his mind crumbling away during the last four years, in 1851.

From the outset, Audubon bore the unmistakable brand of his own genius, for even as a child he was a passionate lover of birds, and soon became an indefatigable egg-snatcher, hunter, collector, and limner of birds. Behind that impulse was a traumatic incident in his childhood, which he recognized as having an influence on his later life. He had witnessed a pet monkey coldbloodedly attack and kill a favorite talking parrot, himself agonized because his outraged screams did not move a servant to intervene. Though his own love for birds did not prevent him from killing them for closer observation or for food, even as the equally humane Alfred Russel Wallace did later, one may interpret his pictures, in the light of this early event, as so many zealous efforts to restore dead birds to life. That desire dominated his existence, and as far as art may ever truly preserve life, he marvelously succeeded.

Handsome, headstrong, volatile, foolhardy, as bored with book learning as was young Darwin, Audubon was cut out for life on the American frontier. This, as much as his father's wish to save him from becoming a Napoleonic conscript, perhaps led his watchful parent to ship the lad at eighteen off to the New World, to look after Mill Grove, a farm with a lead mine he had acquired in Pennsylvania. Audubon, brought up luxuriously by a doting stepmother, ever ready to spoil him, arrived in the United States in 1803, full of highfalutin airs and pretensions. He later laughed at himself for having gone hunting in silk stockings and the finest ruffled shirt he could buy in Philadelphia. He played the flute and the violin, was a daring skater, a famous dancer, an expert fencer, and a crack shot with the rifle. In short, the perfect old-style aristocrat, proud, hot-tempered, careless of danger, and even more gaily careless of money —the precise opposite of the canny, methodical, money-making philistine that his new biographer tirelessly reproaches him for not being.

With this heady combination of qualities, Audubon might easily have been slain in a duel or have turned into a good-for-nothing Don Juan, frittering away his life in aimless erotic adventures. But he was saved by his two lifelong loves: his love of birds and his love of Lucy Bakewell, a girl on a neighboring estate, Fatland Ford, whom he courted in a cave, where they watched the peewees that fascinated him. At the end of five years, the reserved girl and the exuberant French coxcomb married and started their lives afresh as pioneers in the newly settled land beyond the Alleghenies. Almost overnight, Audubon changed his silks for leather hunting clothes and let his hair grow down to his shoulders; and in the course of his life, he gradually turned into an archetypal American, who astonishingly combined in equal measure the virtues of George Washington, Daniel Boone, and Benjamin Franklin.

In the Ohio and Mississippi Valleys, from Cincinnati and Louisville to New Orleans, Audubon found a mode of life that fulfilled his deepest need, as deep as his love for Lucy: direct contact with nature in every aspect and above all with the teeming animal and bird life of river, swamp, and woodland, at a time when the passenger pigeons periodically blackened the skies, and many species of bird, now extinct, were still thriving. Years later, in recollection, Audubon still thrilled over this life, though he had encountered his share of the frontier's rapscallions, bullies, thieves, and cutthroats. "I shot, I drew, I looked on nature only; my days were happy beyond human conception. . . . The simplicity and wholeheartedness of those days I cannot describe: man was man, and each, one to another, a brother." So he remembered that early period; and even at the end of his career he sought to recover the wild gamey taste of this frontier existence in his last Missouri River expedition. He shared, too, the pioneer's love for tall stories, wild humor, practical jokes; and sometimes, as in the gulling of the visiting naturalist, Raffinesque, with drawings of wild creatures that existed only in his fantasy, he got himself into hot water as a reliable naturalist by forgetting how these backwoods jokes might look in print.

Only one part of this existence was repulsive to Audubon, though his obligations as a family man made him go erratically through the motions: the necessity of making a living by trade. His career as a business man was a most extravagant practical joke that he played on himself: a predestined butt and victim through his own impulsive, generous nature. His own words tell everything. "Merchants crowded to Louisville. . . . None of them were, as I was, intent on the study of birds, but all were deeply impressed by the value of dollars. I could not bear to give the attention required by my business." On more than one journey, he confessed, he would thoughtlessly leave his horses unguarded, though laden with goods and dollars, to watch the motions of a warbler.

While Audubon's knowledge of birds became steadily richer, his business ventures, culminating in a crazy investment in a steam mill, made him poorer. Finally, in 1819, a time of general economic crisis, everything went to smash. He was jailed for debt and was declared bankrupt. Audubon always blamed his own bad judgment for what happened; but the misery of finding himself down and out was intensified by the deaths of his two sickly little daughters; and he had to start life again from scratch, at thirty-four, with only his clothes, his drawing outfit, and his gun. But from that low point on, though one would hardly guess it from Mr. Adams's biography, the curve of his life went upward for the next quarter of a century.

Until Audubon made the decision that launched his four-volume work on 'The Birds of America,' he and his Lucy went through half-a-dozen grim years that might have broken and permanently embittered a less stable couple. Driven to turn his attention partly from birds to human faces, in order to make a living as a limner of quick portraits, Audubon lived a penurious, vagrant life, as drawing teacher, dancing master, taxidermist. Meanwhile Lucy was left to fend largely for herself, as governess and teacher, while rearing their two sons, Victor and John Woodhouse. These were bitter years for both Audubon and his wife: years of recurrent poverty, frequent separation, partial alienation, blank despair. Even after Audubon's fortunes began to mend, Lucy seems to have distrusted his buoyant faith in their future, and to have openly doubted his ability to support his family and make their marriage again become a reality. But, determined both to establish his work and salvage his marriage, Audubon drew from his love for his wife and his sons the strength he needed to overcome his recurrent depressions and to go on. The phrenologists who described Audubon as a strong and constant lover and an affectionate father guessed right about his nature.

None of Audubon's biographers is able to give a full account of this marriage: who for that matter has ever given an even half-way full account of *any* marriage? But enough letters have been preserved, in addition to some of Audubon's journals, to indicate that this couple furnish a classic example of the opposed temperamental types that Freud first defined as oral and anal: let us call them, on a less infantile level, the spenders and the hoarders. Lucy, her letters show, was a downright, matter-of-fact soul; and from the meager evidence that remains one suspects that there must have been reservations, tensions, dissatisfactions almost from the beginning; for Lucy, brought up in comfort, could not share the hunter's unfettered outdoor pleasures, and worse, she did not have any birds to fall back on.

Lucy, in her tight, watchful, realistic, 'practical,' anxious way was the kind of woman who so often, once the first glamor of sexual intimacy has faded, leads a man to seek the carefree sympathy or the more relaxed erotic play of another woman. Fortunately, as far as negative evidence may indicate, Audubon's mistresses were all birds; and whatever Lucy's doubts and inhibitions, he never lost faith in their common destiny. "If I were jealous," Lucy once remarked, "I should have a bitter time of it, for every bird is my rival." Not that this dashing, warmhearted man was ever insensitive to the charms of women, whether they were his seventeen-year-old pupil, Eliza Pirrie, or the unidentifiable New Orleans woman who raised an erotic storm in his bosom by commissioning him to do a portrait of her, naked, or even a neat plump serving maid, "tripping as briskly as a killdeer."

Yet this was a true marriage, as well as an enduring one; and if Lucy's sufferings had fewer immediate compensations, both in the end gained, for the achievement of Audubon's great work was possible only because he had in the throes of the crisis that separated them absorbed Lucy's virtues and made them his own. He never lost his impulsive generosity or his contempt for mere money; but in the last third of his life these traits were counter-balanced by a strict attention to irksome financial details, an unwavering fidelity to his dominant purpose, and a capacity to drive himself, day after day, at his work, often drawing from fourteen to seventeen hours at a stretch or endlessly tramping the streets of Manchester or London to find subscribers for his folios. Perhaps the best proof of his inner transformation is that, once he was committed to the publication of 'The Birds of America,' he resolutely turned his back on the life he loved most, as hunter, naturalist, explorer, bird-watcher, and bird-listener, and lived in exile, to carry through the project. To ensure the great success that soon came to him, he endured the oppressions and discomforts of formal civilized life in London and Paris, overcoming his shyness, his terror of polite society, his healthy puritanic distaste for tobacco and spirits and refined food. In the course of this effort the booney backwoodsman became a great man of the world, at home among princes and presidents, accepted as an equal by artists and scientists, able to endure stuffy dinners and even duller lectures in the many scientific societies that enrolled him as a member.

Such an inner transformation after a severe crisis, sexual or religious, has been described at length by William James. It needed Audubon's complete failure in business for him to discover what now must seem to everyone—except his latest biographer—perfectly obvious: that the only life possible for him was that of a naturalist and a painter of the wild creatures he loved and studied so intensely. That obsession proved his salvation. Once he had accepted as a conscious vocation what had hitherto blindly absorbed him in practice, he was ready not only to enjoy it but to transpose the results to the realm of mind. In that task, he proved himself a master of every relevant detail, and within less than four years succeeded in rehabilitating his marriage, while establishing himself as a unique source of firsthand knowledge about the lives and habitats of American birds: over four hundred species, many painted and described for the first time.

Before appraising Audubon's central achievement, 'The Birds of America,' let me pay my disrespects to the new biography, whose constant derogation and denigration of Audubon called forth this preliminary excursion into Audubon's character and career. This new book, with a painstaking and even exemplary attention to recorded facts, goes over the same general ground as that covered by Francis Hobart Herrick (1917), Constance Rourke (1936), and Alice Ford (1964). On the surface, the author, to judge by information provided by his publisher, would seem to have special qualifications for appreciating Audubon's work and influence; for he is a professional conservationist, a trustee of the National Conservancy, a Vice President of a local Audubon Society. But all these helpful interests seem to have been nullified by a temperamental aversion to Audubon himself, which causes him to present Audubon's character in the most unfavorable light possible, and to turn his great career into a series of dismal and depressing failures.

The author has skillfully marshalled the known facts about Audubon's life as if with a single purpose in view: to support his conviction that if Audubon had only during the early years of his marriage paid sufficient attention to business, instead of perpetually playing truant, hunting, birdwatching, making his laborious drawings, 'The Birds of America' need never have been painted or published. That is a highly original judgment, indeed a breathtaking one, but Audubon himself was in full accord with it. "We had marked Louisville," he noted in 1835 in the Memoir he wrote for his family, "as a spot designed by nature to be a place of great importance, and, had we been as wise as we now are, I might never have published 'The Birds of America,' for a few hundred dollars, laid out at that period in lands or town lots would, if left to grow over with grass to a date ten years past, have become an immense fortune. But young heads are on young shoulders; it was not to be, and who cares?"

Who cares? The answer is, Audubon's latest biographer cares. He cares so much in fact that he sedulously minimizes, or rather tosses aside, 'The Birds of America'—its completion he describes as "anti-climax"—in order to concentrate on Audubon's many early lapses and failures as a business man. He even so far departs from truth as to make Audubon's later enterprises seem virtual failures, too. To justify his carefully slanted thesis, the biographer utters a judgment that gives him completely away, a sentence I shall treat as final. "Yet for all his cavalier attitude toward his firm, John James was seriously interested in making money. What he wanted was to be a successful merchant, a man of wealth. Yet he would not work at it." This statement needs only one correction. It is Audubon's hostile critic who wants him to have been a successful merchant and a man of wealth; but his own meticulous citations prove that Audubon never cherished any such ambitions; for the overwhelming passion of his life, from earliest childhood on, was his love of birds. To that he was ready even to sacrifice his Lucy. The biographer who could ignore the massive evidence of Audubon's whole career in order to make this preposterous interpretation of Audubon's ambitions should have stopped in his tracks when he had written those words. But since he went on, we must ask Rufus Wilmot Griswold, the studious defamer of Poe, to move up and make room for Mr. Adams.

What Audubon's defamer steadfastly regards as a wanton miscarriage of Audubon's opportunities and a betrayal of his duties to his wife was in fact what ensured Audubon's final commitment to his true vocation. But in addition Audubon's passage to his life work was favored, at intervals, by a series of chance promptings that registered as deeply as those childhood traumas that sometimes mar a whole life. Though Audubon hated his father's American agent Dacosta, indeed once wanted to murder him, he recorded gratefully that Dacosta's praise of his drawings and his prediction of a great career as a naturalist helped set him on his road. So, too, a few years later in 1810, a chance visit of the Scots ornithologist, Alexander Wilson, fortified Audubon's confidence in both his own ambitions and his draughtsmanship. Finally, it was a remark by an English traveler, Leacock, in 1822, that helped crystallize Audubon's determination to seek publication and patrons in England.

The one incontrovertible fact about Audubon's life, then, is that his passion for birds absorbed and determined his whole life, even though he had talents and sensibilities that spread in many directions, including quadrupeds and butterflies. It was because this passion for birds was so engrossing, as unreasonably engrossing as Dmitri's obsession with Grushenka, that his work transcended his disabilities as a painter or a scholar. Apart from the occasional 'normal errors' that even painstaking observers make, Audubon, in the judgment of his peers, from Baron Cuvier to Robert Cushman Murphy, was a supremely good ornithologist. While still an amateur Audubon maintained the most exacting standards in observing the behavior of birds, making on-the-spot records, opening their stomachs to discover their feeding habits, even studiously sampling them as food, for the further light their taste or texture disclosed. Even the study of bird migrations begins with Audubon, for he was the first naturalist to band young birds, to find out if they returned to their original habitat. "Nature," Audubon said, "must be seen first alive and well studied before attempts are made at representing it." That practice separates him from Buffon and Linnaeus and brings him close not only to Gilbert White and Thoreau but to Darwin and Wallace.

Certainly one side of Audubon might tempt a shallow biographer to characterize him as the typical romantic personality: passionate, impulsive, willful, lonely, convention-breaking; but nothing would conceal the real significance of Audubon's life and work so easily as this cliché. Yet at first glance, he seems a figment of Chateaubriand's imagination; or even more, he seems a robuster version of Rousseau; for besides their common love for wild nature, there was a certain similarity in their delicate mobile features, their hypersensitive proud natures, their fine ability to make enemies and become the objects of real—not fancied—persecution, such as Audubon suffered from George Ord and Charles Waterton, who hounded him as wantonly as Cobbett hounded Dr. Benjamin Rush.

Audubon loved his life as a genuine American backwoodsman: he took to the buckskin costume of the Western hunter as Rousseau less appropriately did to that of the Corsican mountaineer; and he disciplined himself to a stoic indifference to rain, cold, fatigue, hardship, as Rousseau sought to discipline Emile. On Audubon's first trip to England, he proudly kept to the Western style of long hair reaching down to the shoulders, as Buffalo Bill did long after him. When Audubon finally, on the pleadings of his Scots friends, assented to being shorn before leaving Edinburgh for London, he recorded the event in a sorrowful epitaph, surrounded by a heavy black border. It reminded him "of the horrible times of the French Revolution, when the same operation was performed upon all the victims murdered at the guillotine."

But where birds were concerned there was nothing willful or romantically sentimental about Audubon: he never flinched from killing or dissecting them. He concentrated upon condensing in graphic form his hard-won observations, line by line, feather by feather, and was as interested in the vulture disemboweling his victim as in a male turtle dove feeding or showing fondness to his mate. Except for a brief period in his youth in the atelier of Jacques Louis David, and later instructions in oil from John Stein and Thomas Sully, Audubon was self-taught; and in the interests of accuracy used pencil, pastel, water-color, even oil on the same picture, to capture the sheen of plumage or the beady gleam of an eye. In his efforts to make his paintings faithful to the object, he was his own harshest critic, ruthlessly destroying or copying over work that did not satisfy him. His performance was not an emotional expression of the romantic ego; it was as self-effacing as the late Artur Schnabel's interpretations of Beethoven: the personality dissolved into the music.

The painting and the eventual engraving of 'The Birds of America' is a saga in itself. For it was one thing to make ready the great collection he took to England in 1826, and another to have them reproduced accurately and handsomely, while securing subscribers willing to pay £174 for the whole series of 435 plates—over a thousand birds. (In the United States the price was $1,000.)

Any conventional business man might have quailed before the task Audubon undertook. Arriving in a strange country, only his capacity to make friends and to work to the point of exhaustion enabled him to survive. So far from showing incompetence in his business affairs, as he had done in the absurd misfit role of shopkeeper, Audubon now mastered every detail of his job, pocketing his touchy pride, seeking introductions and subscribers in every corner of Britain, meeting many rebuffs but can-

nily using every opportunity. Within a year he had commenced publication, and within a dozen years, the eighty-seventh part of 'The Birds of
America,' which completed the fourth volume, was published.

By his own exertions Audubon had not merely launched his life-work
but had achieved a sufficient income to persuade his wife to join him in
1830. In a little while, he re-established his whole family and drew his
sons, who shared some of his talents, into the work; for Victor, the elder,
and more especially John Woodhouse, the younger, both trained themselves as his assistants—indeed even when fifteen John had shipped him
skins for sale or gift in Britain. In that sense, the whole work became a
mighty labor of love: one that makes mock, incidentally, of the oedipal
fixations of our own generation. And the fact that both sons married
daughters of Audubon's close friend and colleague, John Bachman, only
makes the joke on Freud a little more pointed. Once the birds took their
rightful place in Audubon's life, even his shaken marriage was redeemed.

The fact that Audubon heeded the lessons of adversity and completely
made over his life in order to fulfill his vocation and restore his marriage
is even more astonishing than his actual ornithological achievement and
widening influence as naturalist. Once embarked on the publication of
'The Birds of America,' he mastered every part of his formidable task. He
chose the right engraver, supervised the coloring of the plates—at one
time fifty painters were employed, and once they all struck because he had
criticized the sloppy work of one of them—he solicited subscriptions, appointed agents, saw that bills were collected. On top of all this he not
merely painted the many new pictures needed to make the work as complete as possible, but went on further explorations, in New Jersey and
Florida, and even chartered a ship to carry his search to Labrador. And
once Audubon had surrendered to the demands of his life-mission, even
his practical judgment proved shrewder than that of his professional ad-
visers. Against the warning of Bohn, the famous bookseller, he chose the
grand form of his first elephant-size folio and priced it at a "prohibitive"
cost a set, despite the competition of cheaper posthumous editions by his
able forerunner and rival Alexander Wilson. That daring decision to spare
no expense went flat against sober business judgment—and proved much
sounder.

The man who by his own exertions and his own ability could lift himself out of the financial morass into which he had sunk in 1819 was no
ordinary man, and certainly no flighty, self-indulgent romantic. To characterize such a life as a failure is to present a venomous travesty of the
truth. No one could have had a juster view of his own talents and limitations than Audubon himself. In 1830 he wrote in his journal: "I know
that I am a poor writer, that I can scarcely manage a tolerable English
letter, and not a much better French one, though that is easier to me. I
know I am not a scholar, but meantime I am aware that no man living
knows better than I do the habits of our birds; no man living has studied

them as much as I have done, and with the assistance of my old journals and memorandum books, which were written on the spot, I can at least put down plain truths which may be useful and interesting, so I shall set to at once. I cannot however give *scientific* descriptions, and here I must have assistance." Audubon's capacity for friendship served him well here. Where he was weak, William MacGillivray, the young Scots naturalist, and Bachman, of Charleston, South Carolina, a well-schooled American naturalist, supplied the missing scientific notations.

Audubon's actual life had an epic quality that the American poets of his time dreamed of: it prefigured, in the act of living, the message of 'Walden,' 'The Song of Myself,' and 'Moby-Dick,' dramatically uniting their themes and adding an essential element that was unfortunately lacking in all three: the presence and power of woman and the ascendancy of love. So far only Constance Rourke, with her insight into frontier life and its humor, and Van Wyck Brooks in 'The World of Washington Irving,' have in any degree captured the spirit or taken the measure of this man, though perhaps the quickest way to come close to him is through his few salvaged journals—most of them were destroyed, supposedly in the great New York fire of 1835—now published in a Dover edition.

When one views Audubon's personality and work as a whole, there is little that needs be apologized for or explained away. Even his large carefree gestures are merely those of a large soul, though they may irk those who do not understand his particular combination of humility and self-confidence, tenderness and toughness, loving care and ruthless neglect, his audacious high spirits and his "intemperate practice of temperance," as he himself put it. Even in his lifetime, the man was almost a myth; and that fact doubtless tempted some of his ornithological adversaries to treat his exact observations as if they, too, were falsified or inflated. But the real Audubon is even bigger than the myth.

What makes Audubon the important figure that he still is, now perhaps more than ever, is that his life and work brought together all the formative energies of his time, romanticism and utilitarianism, geographic exploration, mechanical invention, biological observation, esthetic naturalism, and transposed them into consummate works of art which, like the works of Turner, Constable, and Edward Lear, constantly transcended their own naturalistic premises. In the 'Ornithological Biography,' which he published as a companion to his Folio, and republished in the later "miniature" edition of 'The Birds of America,' his very absence of system enabled him to give a fuller account of natural processes and functions than any more abstract approach permitted: for he included the observer as well as the object observed. If, to later scientists, he seemed the last of the old-fashioned naturalists, he has now become the first of a new breed of ethologists, among whom Tinbergen, Lorenz, and Portmann are perhaps best known.

Similarly, Audubon was a practicing ecologist, long before the name and the science were established as such. For almost a century before museums of natural history showed their specimens in natural postures against their natural habitat, Audubon depicted them in this fashion. Even his passion for birds has a new significance, for since Rachel Carson's 'Silent Spring,' we realize as never before that the presence of birds is the most sensitive possible index of a well-balanced human habit, with sound practices of settlement and cultivation; while their absence indicates an organic imbalance, brought on by reckless deforestation, defoliation, pollution, and poisoning.

Finally, like the Bartrams and Wilson before him, and like George Perkins Marsh, John Wesley Powell, and Frederick Law Olmsted after him, Audubon is one of the central actors in the conservation movement. He not merely demonstrated the richness of primeval America, but preserved as much of it as possible in lasting images of its flowers, shrubs, insects, butterflies, as well as birds and mammals. At a moment when only striking landscapes—high mountains, craggy gorges, shaggy forests—were singled out for admiration, Audubon, like Thoreau, was equally sensitive to the swamp, the bayou, the prairie. And if we manage to protect any part of the primeval habitat from the bulldozers, the highway engineers, the real estate speculators, and the National Parks bureaucrats, eagerly defiling what they are supposed to preserve, it will be because Audubon stands in the way, reminding us that this birthright must not be exchanged for money or motor cars.

(1966)

CHAPTER SIX

Eakins: Painter and Moralist

Some half century ago the grand exhibition of Thomas Eakins's paintings at the Metropolitan Museum in November, 1917, gave America its first opportunity to take the measure of his art. Though William C. Brownell in an earlier report in 'Scribner's Magazine' had opened the way, this belated showing of his work, prompted by his death the year before, came after thirty years of ostracism and all but total neglect.

On a superficial view, Eakins's paintings belong to the solid but more conventional art of the nineteenth century, at a time when Henry James confessed that as a young man he was equally taken by Delacroix and Paul Delaroche. If one sees Eakins's paintings in a wider perspective, his art lies in the line of Velásquez, Ribera, and the Dutch masters of the seventeenth century. Certainly by 1917 the odds were against a fresh appreciation of his achievement. Were his paintings anything but the autumnal flowers of a vanishing tradition? Anyone who had gone drunk on the colors of the impressionists, who had responded to Cézanne, Van Gogh, Matisse, or had been jarred by the electronic music of the cubists, could hardly regard Eakins's somber realism as anything but a well-preserved memento of a past that held no conceivable future. Had not the futurists begun to proclaim that art itself was dead? And if not, would not the photograph prove a sufficient substitute for Eakins's kind of painting?

But history, happily for our descendants, plays tricks on the futurologists. Already the younger generation has gone back yearningly to Ruskin and Carlyle, to Mozart and Tchaikovsky, to the Pre-Raphaelites and to more trivial sentimental art. Overnight the adjective 'romantic' has changed from an epithet of abuse to one of admiration. Sometimes these upsets turn out perversely: witness the nervously fashionable museum directors who have been hauling out of dead storage the more massive mediocrities of the Victorian age, whose wall-filling canvases put them on a par with the equally empty wall-fillers lately favored by Madison Avenue.

Eakins can make no appeal to this kind of revivalism; and the fact that he studied the movements of horses more systematically than did Rosa Bonheur or Meissonnier does not give him a place in the same gallery. Eakins's animated, highly disciplined intelligence unites him to an older line of artists that stems back to Leonardo da Vinci, Albrecht Dürer, Giovanni della Porta: the tradition they helped establish in the exploration of the visible world still belongs as much to the future as to the past. With a few exceptions like Ryder and Emily Dickinson, our most orginal American artists—John and Washington Roebling, Herman Melville, Walt Whitman —shared Eakins's resolute faith in "science" and "democracy." They used the materials and the techniques of their 'materialistic' age to express something that transcended the values of that age. "There is no more need for romances," Whitman declared, "let facts and history be properly told." Those words might have been uttered by Eakins.

This collection of 'The Photographs of Thomas Eakins,' assembled by Gordon Hendricks, has come out at the same time as a compendious survey of 'The Painter and the Photograph' by Professor Van Deren Coke; and taken together these two books bring up for further examination not only the special metaphysical and scientific problems related to nineteenth-century art but even older aesthetic problems, many, perhaps, never to be finally resolved by reference to any single period or culture, about the relation of art to life. If Eakins has often been too glibly dismissed as a photographic realist, those who do so have plainly thought of photography as a chance by-product of optical and chemical experiments and have forgotten that these experiments were first made by painters working in their traditional media long before the necessary scientific information and mechanical contrivances were invented. One need not wonder, as Professor Coke demonstrates, that so many artists from Delacroix onward took to photography as a source of information and graphic suggestion—but as an efficient helper, not a dangerous rival. Photography was from the beginning the painters' baby.

The artists who were emotionally in tune with the new world of science were quite as fertile in mechanical invention as their more utilitarian brothers in the workshop or the factory, for art and technics had still not split apart. It was a successful portrait painter who invented the steamboat, and another who invented the electric telegraph, while one of the greatest exponents of photographic portraiture, David Octavius Hill, first took to photography to facilitate his painting of a huge group assemblage of theologians, to produce a painting that now has no value except as an historic document. Eakins's photographic realism was well established in 'Dr. Gross's Clinic' (1874), three years before he began to make photographs. (That was the year, incidentally, when he met Hannah Susan MacDowell, who was to become his wife.) Eakins's photographs, placed alongside his oils, disclose the specific qualities and limitations of both arts, as well as the common ideology to which in the nineteenth century they both conformed.

The pictures in Hendricks's book, mostly taken by Eakins, form an almost random collection, and part of its usefulness as history comes from the fact that it is nonselective, a product of domestic accident—just those plates and prints that once captured his interest and that somehow escaped the rubbish heap. The aesthetic value of these pictures is often extremely limited, hardly worth a second glance; even the subject matter is often without any more interest to an outsider than similar prints in ten thousand other collections of family photographs. If we are defining photography as an art, this end of the realist spectrum comes close to non-art: the results belong to the camera, not to the artist. And one cannot fix the blame for this on the old-fashioned camera and plates, for from the beginning masterpieces were occasionally created by the same imperfect means.

During the decade when Eakins explored photography he did, however, produce a few remarkable prints, particularly portraits, so close in quality to his best pictures that one almost wonders in what museum the original oil now exists, or why one has never seen it before. Perhaps the outstanding example here is No. 20, a picture of his mother-in-law. In its strong natural lighting, its unusually tactile background, its tender gravity, it has the true Eakins touch. Yet sometimes the photograph presented an image that Eakins, alas! did not care to carry further in oil. In quite another Eakins vein is the print of a row of sailboats beached on the sands of the Delaware River, with softly ominous clouds in the right-hand corner providing a contrast that only an artist would have juxtaposed to the sharp white sails. This powerful abstraction reproaches Eakins for not having turned it into a painting.

At the other extreme, less because of their aesthetic than their human quality, are the photos of Walt Whitman taken shortly before his death: no longer the genial but softly overripe face Eakins had painted only a little while before in an uncharacteristically impressionist manner, but now pathetically weak, bewildered, indrawn. Here in these final moments Eakins touched the tragic sense of life, as he might have if King Lear had sat for him. Those sad images disclose, as if in anticipation, a similar transformation that Eakins's own face would reveal in the series of photographs that other people, including one of his closest students, would make of him.

Not the least interesting aspect of this whole collection are the hints and unconscious disclosures about Eakins's own life; alike about his intellectual background, his unswerving devotion to art, and his own emotional and erotic relations, in or out of marriage. There are few happy faces in Eakins's own gallery of portraits; even the young, even the students horsing about naked before the camera, are singularly without joy. But there are no grimacing candid camera shots either; every portrait, whether of himself or some other character, is a chapter in Eakins's autobiography, a kind of double exposure of his mind.

Yet as soon as one places Eakins's photographs alongside some of his lesser paintings of the same subject—say, 'The Swimming Hole'—one has to ask aesthetic questions that do not admit of an easy answer. Apart from color and the subtleties of tone derived from color, do Eakins's paintings convey anything that a photograph does not? Is the value of the painting reduced by its photographic realism or are the photographs enhanced by their resemblance to formalized painting?

It is easier to say no to the second question than to the first. One might give a more confident answer if one could forget that the Greeks of the fourth century, whose creativity is attested by their buildings and sculptures, praised a painting by Apelles because the grapes looked so real that the birds pecked at them. Yet in Eakins's best photographs his mind was at work in the same fashion as in his paintings; no doubt of that. The resemblances are not accidental. In both cases whatever sprang ultimately from his subjective reactions was expressed through the visible contents alone. But if Eakins had been wholly satisfied with photography, he would not have abandoned this mode of representing nature: he would rather have carried it further, as his younger contemporary Alfred Stieglitz resolutely did in singling out 'unpaintable' images. Instead, many of Eakins's greatest paintings were done in the last dozen years of his life, and they testify to something that cannot be recorded by purely mechanical means: his integrity, his composure, his moral resolution.

There is however one point where Eakins's photographs give hints about his life which are unanswered as yet in any surviving account, and possibly will never be satisfactorily answered at all. Perhaps the most enigmatic of Eakins's pictures—this is equally true of the photographs and the oils—are those in the 'Arcadia' series. Besides the naked athletes and pseudo fauns blowing Panpipes this series includes photographs of feminine models in flowing Greek costumes, sometimes posed alongside Greek plaster casts, though Eakins despised such casts. Nothing indeed could seem more remote from Eakins's principles than this fake classic costume art. Was Eakins saying in these pictures that he wanted most the sort of freedom in presenting the human body that the Greeks enjoyed in Plato's time when even girls stripped for taking part in public games? Or was he attempting to release his imagination from the fetters of scientific exactitude and 'objective' representation in order to give his own repressed emotional impulses fuller play?

Something besides the conventions of his day seems to have held Eakins in check. Master that he was of his craft, swift and sure as a limner, there were subjective realms that he dared not enter, except by the back door, though they were open to near contemporaries like Delacroix who were less under the spell of the 'objective' world that advanced minds in the nineteenth century still mistook, in its seeming solidity and its public accessibility, for authentic reality. It is no accident that Eakins felt close to the surgeons and physicists of his generation; but he forgot, unfortunately, that the displacement of feeling and emotion is the proper psychology only for an operating table or a physics laboratory; yet even in the latter milieu it may rob the mind of necessary energies.

In seeking an answer to this enigma one is haunted by Eakins's own sober face, from early manhood to the brink of death: grave, self-contained, desperate, increasingly tragic; but whether from disappointment in his professional career or from some deeper miscarriage in his life one dare not, without some further evidence, even guess. That Eakins had faith enough to keep on with his painting despite lack of public response demonstrates his great vital reserves; in some degree this offset his emotional inhibitions. Whatever these portrait studies meant to Eakins himself, they come before us as teasingly disjointed fragments of an Eakins biography, which unfortunately may never be satisfactorily put together. Lloyd Goodrich made a beginning of that biography in his introduction to the exhibition of 1933, mainly from the evidence of Eakins's written lectures, his letters, the testimony of his pupils; and the compiler of this book of photographs has added a few touches that tell about the workings of Eakins's mind.

Possibly the main clue to Eakins comes from the central place occupied by the human body in his teaching. Nakedness for Eakins embodied a moral principle: in art as in science, nothing was ugly, nothing obscene, nothing was insignificant that came under the discipline of truth. Like Whitman, Eakins celebrated the body, if not the "body electric." There was nothing soft, still less lyrical, in this celebration. Eakins took on the ordeal of anatomical dissection as a necessary part of the painter's craft, in order to know what went on from the inside to mold any posture he might paint, and indicate the pressures and tensions.

In his life classes, Eakins used both male and female nudes as models. But one of his innovations, which helped cause his dismissal from the Pennsylvania Academy, came from his revolt against the practice of employing only prostitutes as models. Since Eakins properly regarded this association of nudity with purchasable sex as disgraceful, he persuaded a few of his girl students, with the consent of their mothers, to shuck their clothes and serve as models. But one day when a girl emerged in the nude with a bracelet still on her arm, Eakins was so furious that he tore it off and threw it on the floor. That incident delighted Whitman. "It was just like Eakins," Whitman said, "and oh! a great point in it, too."

In 1886 came Eakins's final break with respectability. In a female life class, in order to illustrate the muscular attachment to the pelvis, Eakins stripped off the male model's G-string and exposed his genitals. For a sexually hair-raising generation like the present one, the shudder and shock of that single act upon Eakins's contemporaries are almost unimaginable; yet the fact that he committed such a defiant act can hardly be attributed solely to absent-minded absorption in his anatomical demonstration. For Eakins this was not a meaningless exposure: it was, I feel sure, a morally significant act in the service of scientific verity. At all events, this was the final offense that brought about his departure from the teaching staff of the Pennsylvania Academy and put him permanently out of favor with the Philadelphia Establishment.

That confrontation with the whited sepulchers of conventional morality was disturbing enough to Eakins to prompt him to restore his inner balance and peace by a vacation on a Dakota ranch; but it had no effect on his work. Though one can hardly suppose that Eakins did not recognize his own interest in the nude as an integral expression of sex, he kept in his painting all too strictly to the inhibiting Victorian *mores*. Unlike Turner, he seems to have left behind no erotic sketches for a latter-day Ruskin to destroy. Yet one cannot forget that he had fallen from grace by his own standards in the Arcadian series, for what was a Panpipe but a more odious kind of bracelet? And it was only at the end of his life, when he depicted a naked girl posing for Benjamin Rush, that for the first time he showed his model from a frontal view. Part of Eakins's own power as a painter may derive from this pent-up reservoir of eroticism. Had he found an outlet he might have vied with Rubens, Goya, or Renoir.

Perhaps the most telling impression left by Eakins's photographs and his paintings is that there is more in them than meets the eye. Eager though he was to follow through the experiments of Marey or Muybridge that led to the motion picture, these pictures of animal motion did not lead to any new dynamism in Eakins's designs. For all that he learned about the kinetics of the body, he made far less of this knowledge than did Tintoretto, whose superb intuitive representations of motion and flight anticipated the technical achievements of the nineteenth century. The portraits that crowned Eakins's life as a painter have the composure of an Egyptian statue. So much for his 'photographic realism.'

What comes out of Eakins's work is what comes out of his life: a sense of his inviolable integrity. If his paintings had no fresh aesthetic value in themselves, they would still give him a special place as a moral guide, teaching those lost in paranoid obsessions and vacuous fantasies the human dignities of craftsmanship, responsibility, self-respect. Like Cézanne, Eakins had a small private income and a house to live in: sufficient for a sparse, thrifty life, no more. By this happy accident Eakins was entirely free from the current obsession with money, power, and immediate fame. The series of portraits he produced beginning with 'Dr. Gross's Clinic' were not done on commission and were not sold. By their unflinching honesty of characterization they did not tempt the subject to offer even a modest sum for their private acquisition. With one of the few portraits he painted on commission, for a millionaire, the unscrupulous sitter, when he saw the result, sought to crawl out of paying for it. So Eakins's paintings piled up in his studio, unpublicized, largely unvisisted.

Eakins's value for the emerging generation comes not so much from his aesthetic achievements as from his moral qualities, though the two are inseparable, since his paintings constitute a graphic biography. With unshakable resolution, Eakins painted his unsellable pictures for the honor of medicine, science, religion, art—or as people used to say, for the glory of God. Though his subjective life was so different from Ryder's, Eakins's work had the same integrity, the same indifference to pecuniary rewards. He seems to have been as deeply committed to his work as the medieval sculptors who finished their carved figures even in obscure corners where the human eye would never see them. Eakins had no need for publicity or the adulatory patter and chatter of critics who now provide an elaborate literary camouflage to conceal the artist's autistic withdrawal from reality. Whatever the restrictions of the scientific and aesthetic conventions that dominated Eakins's art, his life and work have now a special contribution to make to a generation that, morally speaking, has reached the end of its rope.

(1972)

CHAPTER SEVEN

The Brown Decades

The commonest axiom of history is that every generation revolts against its fathers and makes friends with its grandfathers. This reason alone might perhaps account for the fact that the generation which struggled or flourished after the Civil War now has a claim upon our interest. In the paintings of Burchfield and Hopper, the very buildings of the Awkward Age come to us with a certain sentimental charm: those mansard roofs, those tall, ill-proportioned windows, those dingy façades which concealed the dreadful contortions of walnut furniture, in fact, the worst emblems of the period no longer afflict us like an inappropriate joke told too frequently by a tiresome uncle. If we are lenient to the worst the Gilded Age can show, are we not perhaps ready to receive the best?

Beneath the foreign trappings of the seventies and eighties we have become conscious of a life not unlike our own: that is the first claim to our sympathy. Like our grandfathers, we face the aftermath of a war which has undermined Western Civilization as completely as the Civil War undermined the more hopeful institutions of our country. The dilemmas, the hopes, the mistakes of the earlier period are so near to our own that it would be a wonder if we did not see its achievements clearly, too. But we need a fresh name for this period, if we are to see it freshly. Shall we call the years between 1865 and 1895 the Brown Decades? If the title sounds vague, it is, as I shall show, not inappropriate.

There are occasional years when, after spring has leafed and blossomed, a long series of storms and rains destroys one's sense of the summer. Suddenly one raises one's eyes to the trees and discovers that autumn has arrived: the leaves are sere, the goldenrod stands brown and threadbare in the fields, the branches of the maples are stripped, and only the red berries of the black alder, or the dull persistent greens of the buttonwoods and poplars, remind one of the summer that never came.

There was such a violent stormy summer, and such a sudden push of autumn, in the period of American history that began with the Civil

War. The long winter of the seventeenth century, a sturdy battle with the
elements, had given way to the slow spring of the eighteenth: it was then
that the ground was ploughed and the country made ready for a new
political system and a new relationship to the institutions and customs
of the past. Then, in the few warm weeks that elapsed between 1830
and 1860, there had come a quick leafing and efflorescence. In the literary works of Emerson, Whitman, Thoreau, Melville, Hawthorne, new
modes of thought and a fresh sense of the human adventure became apparent. If there were few early fruits, the flowers were delectable and
their promise abundant.

The Civil War shook down the blossoms and blasted the promise
of spring. The colors of American civilization abruptly changed. By the
time the war was over, browns had spread everywhere: mediocre drabs,
dingy chocolate browns, sooty browns that merged into black. Autumn
had come.

The people who had fought through the Civil War were chiefly conscious of the political issues that were decided, or temporarily silenced,
by the conflict. Our recent histories have shown in detail all the industrial
and financial transformations that were either brought on or hastened
by the war: the growth of steel mills, the mechanization of agriculture, the
substitution of petroleum for whale oil, the development of the trade union
movement, and the concentration of great fortunes, built up by graft,
speculation, war profits, or the outright donation of priceless lands to
great railway corporations, acquisitions which were not called theft, and
doles which were not denounced as inimical to manhood and independence,
only because the sums involved were so huge and the recipients so rich.

While these changes were no doubt as important in their total consequences as the abolition of human slavery, the most visible transformation of all has been forgotten. The nation not merely worked differently
after the Civil War: the country *looked* different—darker, sadder, soberer.
The Brown Decades had begun. Dead men were everywhere. They were
present in memory: their portraits stoically gathered dust in empty par-
lors; they even retained possession of their bodies and walked about the
streets; they spoiled gaiety, or rather, they drove it to fevers of license and
distraction. In the years that followed the war, three American translations of the 'Divine Comedy' appeared: that terrible, rapturous celebration
of the dead was keyed to the best temper of the Brown Decades.

The change was dramatically signalled by the death of Lincoln: it
made the deep note of mourning universal, touching even those who had
stood outside the conflict. Edmund Clarence Stedman, the poet who was
to emerge from the war as a Wall Street broker, has left a memorable description of the event. "You know that a *vulgar* woman appears a lady
in mourning; and that a lady is never so elegant as when in black. Something of the same effect has been produced on our superb but bizarre and
inharmonious city. It looks like an immense black and white flower, with

leaves and petals spreading grandly and in perfect keeping, to every point of the compass. Such an effect I never saw, or dreamed of. It is overwhelming, sombre, sublime."

That note did not die out; though the white of the original decoration was soon, in effect, spattered and muddied. In part, the change lay on the outside. Society was adapting its coloration to the visible smut of early industrialism: in the new coal towns, the national banner itself, after a few days' exposure to the air, changed its red, white, and blue to brown, grey, and black. But even more the Brown Decades were created by the brown spectacles that every sensitive mind wore, the sign of renounced ambitions, defeated hopes. The inner world colored the outer world. The mood was sometimes less than tragic; but at bottom, it was not happy.

Like all such historical changes, the color had manifested itself, as a leaf turns here and there on a maple early in July, before the causes of the change itself had become dramatically apparent. Brownstone began to be used in New York on public buildings in the early fifties, and just on the eve of the war it was first used as a facing for brick houses. With this alteration came dark walnut furniture, instead of rosewood and mahogany, sombre wall papers and interiors whose dark tones swallowed up the light introduced slightly later by the fashionable bay window. By 1880 brown was the predominant note. Mary Cassatt escaped these colors and tones in her painting by living in Paris; but Ryder, lyricist that he was, worked within the prevailing palette, and Eakins, inspired partly by Rembrandt, as well as by the contemporary mood, ran most easily through the gamut from yellow brown to dark sienna. In the best work of the period these sober autumnal colors took on a new loveliness: a warm russet brown, touched off by a lichen green and the red of red oak leaves marked Richardson's treatment of the shingled house: at the very end of his career he produced cottages that, for the first time in America, brought the landscape and the architecture into the mood of the time.

No period, of course, is uniform in its color any more than in its morals or manners; there are always gradations; there are likewise always leftovers and intrusions, reminders of a dead past that is not yet dead or promises of a venture into a future still unborn. But the Brown Decades mark a period, a period we have yet to explore intimately and reckon with. If it began with the mourning note of Lincoln's funeral, it ended, like a sun thrusting through the clouds, in the golden portal of Sullivan's Transportation Building at the Chicago World's Fair in 1893. Between the first black and the final brilliance, a whole range of colors and tones was explored and embodied in permanent works of art and thought.

It is impossible to see one's own period in perspective; but on the surface, the points of resemblance between our own post-war difficulties and those which followed the Civil War are so numerous that, in going through the records and memoirs of the earlier period, one has the sense of following our own history, told in a slightly foreign language.

There was, to begin with, the sudden absence of youth that one felt keenly in Europe after the last war; the loss of youthfulness was a necessary consequence of this fact. Even those who were left after the conflict, even those who had in one way or another run away from the war, had a doubled sense of responsibility: one sees their grave anguished faces, their bleak troubled eyes, in the portraits of the time and one reads with astonishment the subject's age: it is not fifty but thirty. The younger generation had aged; and during the decade that followed the war, cynicism and disillusion were uppermost. Sometimes these qualities were consciously present; but they were equally revealing when they were unconsciously expressed, as one finds them in the diary of a contemporary poet:

Nov. 8, 1864. Stood two hours in the rain and voted for Old Abe. Realized on stocks and made $1375.

Nov. 9. Yesterday a great triumph for the National Cause. Thank God! The future of America is now secure.

Nov. 10. Fall in gold. I make on everything I manage for myself and lose on the operations of my agents.

The dual motives that ran through the period could not be better expressed.

"When Johnny came marching home," wrote one of his feminine contemporaries, Mrs. Rebecca Harding Davis, "he was a very disorganized member of society, and hard to deal with. You cannot take a man away from his work in life . . . and set him to march and fight for five years, without turning his ideas and himself topsy-turvy. The older men fell back into the grooves more rapidly than the lads who had been fighting."

All the hopes that had underlain the gallantry and heroism of the war had been suddenly punctured, partly by their fulfillment and partly by their denial. No abstract ideal can be translated into an actual condition or institution without seeming to undergo a blight: this does not prove that abstract ideals are either unnecessary or delusive: it merely means that one should be acquainted with their natural history and not expect perfection to arise in a situation where, to achieve perfection, all the necessary details and qualifications of history would have to be left out. The preservation of the Union, the freeing of the slaves, were slogans used by the community to rationalize its tragic difficulties: but such shibboleths could not serve, once they had passed into action, instead of humane and intelligent plans. These plans were frustrated after Lincoln's death; and those who had been lured into the conflict by such easy verbal promises felt cheated and abused. The slaves were freed; the union was preserved —what of it?

Moreover, as Mrs. Davis suggests, there was a wide gap between the patriotic fulfillment of a high duty, which so warmed the hearts of Emerson and Alcott, and the actual conditions of the battlefield she herself had observed in Virginia. Under the mere stress of changed conditions, some of the loyal adventurous fellows turned into thieves and rascals: the very method of warfare upset, as it always does, the ideals and rational purposes for which it was fought, leaving greed, arrogance, and vindictiveness piled up behind the bodies of the dead heroes who often enough did not get even their due six feet of earth. Occasionally, some high purpose, conceived on sentry post under the stars, like Professor Burgess's scheme for an Institute of Politics, to probe into the causes of war and learn to remove them, might eventually find a place; but Emerson discovered speedily enough how badly most of his hopes had foundered in the backwash of war.

"We hoped," he wrote, "that in the peace, after such a war, a great expansion would follow in the mind of the country; grand views in every direction—true freedom in politics, in religion, in social science, in thought. But the energy of the nation seems to have expended itself in the war." That was an old story: in fact, war leaves no other. How often can we ignore it? Some day the fatal inertia and forgetfulness of Western Civilization may occur once too often, and all its potentialities will be exhausted in some fantastic crusade to "save" civilization—even the possibility of material gain will vanish. War does not bring the martial virtues into the subsequent peace: it merely prepares a richer soil for the civilian's vices. One might as well expect a high sense of tragedy in an undertaker, as heroism in the generation that follows a war: meeting death is one thing, and disposing of the remains is another.

No sooner had the Civil War come to a close than, as a writer in 'Harper's Weekly' promptly remarked, the reaction from the tension of war showed itself "in a certain public frenzy. Enormous speculations, losses, and consequent frauds; an increase of crime, a curious and tragical recklessness in the management of railroads and steamers; a fury of extravagance in public watering places are all observable." These results were not temporary: the dinners became richer and longer, the gambling stakes higher, and the general spiritual torpor more profound. The social life of the country became a swamp. The decade that saw the Centennial Exhibition, bravely arrayed in cast-iron façades crowned with cast-iron statuary, crowing over the triumphs of the Hoe press and the Corliss engine, saw also the corruption of Grant's administration and the exposure of the Tweed Ring in New York.

In their negative and disheartening manifestations one might, indeed, work out a pretty close comparison between the two post-war generations. There was the same open public corruption, in a community that shared so many of the vices of its false officials that even the pretense of honesty was absent: those who were caught red-handed showed shame and indignation, not over their peculations, but over the fact that they were caught. There was the same faith in the Machine Age and the same interest in Adult Education we are now so aware of: in the seventies the first took the form of using iron instead of stone for the columns and cornices of buildings, and even of offering for sale—I have no definite proof that they were ever bought or used—collars and cuffs, to be worn by men, made of painted sheet-iron. As for adult education, it was promoted in the Mechanics' Institutes, now so often empty melancholy shells, that sprang up over the country in imitation of the workingman's colleges in England. Do we look askance at the use of prominent names for the advertisement of sundry wares from cigarettes to bed sheets? The habit was already gaining headway in 1867 when an advertisement proclaimed that Mrs. Henry Ward Beecher of Brooklyn, after using the Ivory Eye Cups, ordered a pair for the wife of the Reverend Charles Beecher of Georgetown, Massachusetts.

It was in the seventies, too, that Colonial architecture, which had been neglected and contemptuously set aside in the various fashionable adaptations of Gothic churches and Swiss chalets, was first reappraised, and then reinstated as a movement: going out as a habit in the older parts of the country, it slowly re-entered as a fashion, although it never really took on until the nineties. The methods of James Gordon Bennett's newspapers foreshadowed the larger abuses of our tabloids. If Stuart Chase, contemplating the last war, has depicted for us a nightmarish but tangible future in his 'Two Hour War,' a cartoonist in 1866 showed the progress of the art of war from primitive arms to the needle gun, which reduced the thirty years' war to thirty days, and from then on to the "electric organ gun" of 1880, the steam gun of 1890, and finally the "surprise bomb" (asphyxiating gases) of 1900, with its promise of a three minutes' war, both armies annihilated—and universal peace. If Mr. Chase's prediction approximates reality as closely as that of the Harper cartoonist, the world may well tremble.

The expansion that Emerson had hoped for had indeed taken place; but its dominant effect was on the utilitarian plane. Charles Francis Adams, who had served in the battlefields, now took command of railroads and stockyards: in him, the old Adams tradition of public service was limited to the little town of Quincy, and to such work as he did in later years on the Metropolitan Park Board of Boston. Mark Twain wasted endless time and energy that should have gone into his own education, trying to make a fortune out of various inventions that took his fancy; while Henry Adams, typical of those who could make no connections with the crass outward scene, after surveying the politics of Washington at close range, took refuge in the South Seas, in Japan, in Europe, in the Middle Ages, one of that large group of disoriented and bewildered Americans, Henry James, Raphael Pumpelly, William Story, Ambrose Bierce, Bret Harte, who could find no sufficient nourishment in the soil where their roots spread, and who had even before the Civil War begun to wander uneasily about Europe—grateful for the contemplative mood it promoted, the one luxury that reckless kings of commerce could not buy, could not afford to cultivate, could not import.

Ten years ago Harold Stearns wrote an article in 'The Freeman,' "What Shall a Young Man Do?" in which the doubts and dilemmas of this generation were curiously re-echoed. Living itself in post-Civil War America was an uphill job; living well, living with integrity, living for the sake of ideas—these things required exceptional stamina and intellectual hardihood.

Make no doubt of it: those who stayed behind needed either a double thickness of skin, or they needed the narrow convictions and the faith in the immediate activities of the country that the industrialist exhibited. Failing such toughness, most of them were forced to retreat into a private world that received little sustenance from the community immediately around them. How could they do otherwise? Conjure up the sordid parade of cut-throats, business gamblers, political mercenaries, short-sighted industrialists, sporting dandies, and demagogic religious preachers who claimed the spotlight during this period. It is impossible to caricature these dreadful figures; pure description sounds like abusive satire. The picture Vernon Parrington draws of these days, in the third volume of his history, is particularly good in its grasp of physiognomy: the obese and bloated masters of this post-bellum America, who shared honors with a handful of shrivelled, neurotic creatures, were beyond even the caricatures of Nash: they would almost have escaped Rowlandson. Even the best men conformed to the mold. Richardson's bulky figure, to say nothing of his huge traveling companions, attracted the attention of European gamins, who thought they belonged to a circus: once they asked outright —When is the dwarf coming?

What triumph of a morbid imagination conceived or remembered— it had been worn by Catholic priests in procession to avert the plague— the costume of the Ku Klux Klan, and turned an idle practical joke into an imposing terroristic organization? What triumphant confusion of values could have persuaded two government clerks in Washington to conceive of dignifying farming, rehabilitating agricultural life, and fostering co-operation by creating a secret order, surrounded with hocus-pocus and called the Patrons of Husbandry—a movement which was as successful at its inception as Terence Powderly's Knights of Labor, both institutions being halfway, as it were, between sound economic strategy and a tawdry adolescent dream. These movements belonged to the Brown Decades, reached their heyday then, and as national influences came to an end before the period itself was over: they made credible the popular art and decoration, the work of the scroll-saw and the lathe, the beauty of the Rogers group and the reality of the dime novel.

There was, without doubt, something pitifully inadequate, indeed grotesque, in the post-bellum scene; and the epithets that have been applied to it, the Gilded Age, the Tragic Era, the Dreadful Decade, the Pragmatic Acquiescence, are too full of truth ever to disappear. But neither epithet nor description, however accurately documented, tells the whole story. Beneath the crass surface, a new life was stirring in departments of American thought and culture that had hitherto been barren, or entirely colonial and derivative; and it is to these growths that we now turn with a feeling of kinship and understanding. For the Brown Decades are not merely a mirror of our vices and infirmities; they are also a source of some of the most important elements in our contemporary culture. If we cannot accept as a whole, with any feeling of affection, a period that so meanly caricatured human decencies and cut short so many fine potentialities, we need not overlook its happier parts, even if these aspects of the age suffered neglect in their own day.

It is time that we ceased to be dominated by the negative aspects of the Brown Decades. To dwell upon their ailments, infirmities, mischances, is to show, as in the invalid's preoccupation with his disease, that the remains of the poison are still operating in our own systems. I half-fell into this pitfall myself in treating this generation in 'The Golden Day,' even though I was aware of its positive achievements; for in interpreting the experience of the time one is tempted, even when face to face with individual talents of high merit, to read into their story the history of American society's failure and frustration, and so to belittle aspects of their work that did not reflect the miserable background.

How easy it is to appreciate the weakness of William Dean Howells in literature, his reluctance to deal with human life in its totality, and to forget both his craftsmanship and his patent understanding of the characters that came within his range! How easy it is to see in William James the father of the lower sort of American pragmatist, and to forget the richly endowed mind that wrote the classic treatise on psychology! The mere failure to publish the greater part of Charles Peirce's thought has obscured the fact that, in the very dregs of the Gilded Age, a large and universal mind quietly fulfilled itself, a mind whose depth and impact has still to be felt—and fathomed. If one is to condemn the Gilded Age for Peirce's lack of influence, one must equally condemn the glorious thirteenth century for the comparative obscurity of Roger Bacon, or the sixteenth century for not publishing the notes of Leonardo da Vinci. Doubtless the condemnation would be deserved: but the glory of their positive achievements still remains.

The creative manifestations of the Brown Decades have been overlooked, partly because we habitually seek such impulses in literature: what we cannot read we cannot see. In literature, too, we have judged the age by its roster of popular names; and in reacting against the mediocrity and feeble gentility of Thomas Bailey Aldrich, against the timid conception of life and letters that supported Howells, against the complaisant low-brow-ism of Mark Twain, we have forgotten the few significant men and women whose work is profoundly important to us—to say nothing of the presence of Melville and Whitman—the Melville whose comments on the close of the Civil War should have gained him, if nothing else did, a wide hearing from his countrymen, or the Whitman whose 'Democratic Vistas' is still the most fundamental piece of literary and social criticism that has been written in America.

Almost every account of the Gilded Age has suffered from one of two insidious forms of deflation. On one hand, its material advances, its inventions, its technical achievements, have been overpraised, or their contributions to the good life have been brashly taken for granted, without any qualifying sense of their deficiencies, as if material success could atone for an impoverished life; or—and this is just as bad—the contemporary estimates of its literature, art, and philosophy have been accepted at the Gilded Age's own value, and its fruitful contributions have therefore been ignored.

One does not quarrel with the literary mediocrities of the Brown Decades in themselves: every period has such people as Stoddard and Aldrich in plenty, and they often do meritorious work. Unfortunately, they take it as their duty not only to perform their own task, but to keep work with higher standards, surer perceptions, deeper intuitions of value, larger and more capacious experiences, from getting into circulation: jealously assuming to guard the portals of literature, they are actually supporting their own egos. Now, many of the popular writers and prophets of the period have turned out to be charlatans: the metaphysical booster psychology of Mrs. Mary Baker Eddy seems to us a little less than the inspiration of divinity; the poems of Stoddard, Aldrich, and Bayard Taylor have but a minor claim to our respect; even the generous volatile Mark Twain does not seem to us to be the great universal satirist that Howells honestly proclaimed him to be. But must we condemn the period because its arbiter in letters was Thomas Bailey Aldrich, the author of the now-forgotten 'Ponkapog Papers,' equally minor as critic and poet? To do that would be to forget the fact that those apparently sterile years are redeemed for us by the silent presence of Emily Dickinson.

Granted that the brightest successes of the Brown Decades seem to us, for the most part, to be only muddy failures, it is much more important to realize that many works which were then pushed aside as inept, ludicrous, or eccentric were in actuality genuine successes, emergent elements in a growing American tradition.

The more commonplace minds of the Brown Decades were not affected by the activities of the period that preceded them: they scorned the transcendental doctrines and hopes, in favor of "securities" which, as Black

Friday was perhaps to teach them, were as baseless as a passing dream. But almost all the vital and important workers of the period bore the mark of Emerson, Whitman, or Thoreau; and though seemingly neglected, or honored only as quaint effigies and survivals, these men brooded over the Brown Decades.

Their influence was perhaps smallest in literature, if one except the impression that Emerson made upon Emily Dickinson, or Whitman upon Burroughs; but their doctrines had brought a new confidence to all the other arts: Emerson's gospel of self-reliance and his belief in a fresh start, Whitman's hearty affirmation of the vulgarities and commonplaces of life, and Thoreau's deep sense of the landscape and its influences—all these beliefs were to have their effect upon the painter and the architect and the engineer.

Almost hidden by the dead leaves, the compost, the sour soil of the Brown Decades, a spring flower grew: its tiny bud scarcely peeped through the matted heap above it, and before it had been recognized, before it was given light and air, it had died. Does it belong to the soil or not? Surely it does. This shy flower was Emily Dickinson, whose life and words were known only to a handful of people during the Brown Decades, although the span of her working life almost defines the period. She was a rare flower, and none the worse for being so secluded, so completely overwhelmed by the coarser plants and the earthier foundations of her time: in any age, this sensitive woman would have needed some protection, for within her fine sensorium a breath was as the sound of thunder in the mountains, and the ripple of a trout in the pool might be as powerful as the breaking of the sea.

Emily Dickinson has been treated, even by some of those who admire her, as a victim of her time: if only, they say, she had had the courage and ability to run away with the lover who claimed her, if only she had prospered in the normal life of passion, physical intercourse, children, the fuller domestic cares and joys, if only—sometimes these vain words are used humorlessly—she had been "better adjusted." Let us put aside this misconception. The test of any mode of life is its outcome: how strong and sane and balanced and wise one ultimately becomes by following it. A lover and a baby might have given Emily Dickinson the same fulfillment and satisfaction as her poems: but they would hardly have increased her poise, even if they had earned it more easily. Her ecstasy, her torture, her sorrow, her hope all sprang out of the tensions of renunciation. What Melville had discovered in 'Pierre,' Emily Dickinson was to reveal in the more perfect, fragile medium of her poems: the subtle ironic tragedy that underlies human relationships. If her No was tragic, her Yes would have been tragic, too.

In one sense, Emily Dickinson, secluded behind her high hedge in Amherst, was out of touch with her age; and in another, no one had expressed its deeper experience more completely. Was her dismissal of her lover in essence different from the spirit in which many another girl had resigned her mate to the battlefield, never to see him again? In Emily Dickinson's poems, even more than in Bierce's stories of the war, even more than in Whitman's 'Drum Taps,' was the marrow of American experience during the Civil War. Just as Henry James, abroad, felt and expressed the dilemmas of the cultivated American more completely than those who immersed themselves in the local colors of their immediate environment, so Emily Dickinson, silent and unknown, insulated against all the gross contacts with her milieu, felt and expressed the tragic heart of life during the Brown Decades. That it was hidden, that only a few men dared to face the depths of their anguish, does not make the emotion less real, or prove that it was not commonly shared. No one is insulated: plagues and blessings are both blown on the wind, and one can gather the history of a period from the meditations of a recluse almost as fully as one can from a man of the world—more so, perhaps, for the first has time for reflection and sometimes records his experience. What Emily Dickinson was, that also the Brown Decades was in a measure, beneath the fuss and show and tawdriness of its daily life.

Above Emily Dickinson, overshadowing her, lush and rank as the first leaf that opens to the April sun in the swamps, was Walt Whitman. In the years immediately following the Civil War, which terminated with his paralysis in 1872, he carried the conception first revealed in 'Leaves of Grass' a little nearer to completion.

It was Whitman's task to confront the hopes and ambitions of his youth for America with the actual fulfillments of maturity. He did not shrink from this work. 'Democratic Vistas' was published at one of the lowest moments in the country's life; and no one has presented a more appalling picture of its bottomless corruption and misery than Whitman did in those pages. He found that society "in these States, is canker'd, crude, superstitious, and rotten. Political or law-made society is, and private, or voluntary society is also. In any vigour, the element of the moral conscience, the most important, the verteber to State or man, seems to me either entirely lacking, or seriously enfeebled and ungrown."

The business before the poet was not only, as he at first thought, to crown republican institutions and material prosperity with authentic and original works of art: by now the task was a matter of setting society moving in a direction opposite to that which it had taken, offering counterpoises to the mischievous and ill-fated institutions that had arisen. Whitman's original faith, though always buoyant, had proved naïve: democracy and the new world, which seemed ready for great consummations, had by 1870 acquired threatening resemblances to the feudalism which the younger Whitman had taken for granted would be left behind. Democracy no longer ensured a new literature: rather "a new literature, perhaps a new metaphysics, certainly a new poetry," were necessary as "the only sure and worthy supports and expressions of the American democracy." Throughout the 'Democratic Vistas' one is conscious of an heroic struggle going on in Whitman, a struggle to define and embrace reality, and not to shrink, in any pusillanimous hopefulness, into a private world of his own.

This seasoned and mature Whitman should displace in our minds the feeble, garrulous, sweet, somewhat sly old man of the final Camden days: every mind has a right to be known by its soundest and maturest expression. (Do we judge Plato by 'The Laws'?) Whitman had little immediate effect in literature: with the exception of John Burroughs, this was not to happen until our own generation; but in the other arts the Brown Decades harbored a number of men who understood the implications of Whitman's message and resolutely carried it on.

Whitman's 'Song of the Exposition,' poor though it was, was perhaps the most stimulating work of native art that the Centennial could show. If no poet was able to grasp or use Whitman's meaning, Thomas Eakins was equal to it in painting: there was a rapport between the two men that made Whitman Eakins' chief defender, against the poet's own disciples. William James, too, was influenced by Whitman and quoted him frequently: indeed, it is almost a tribute to Whitman's efficacy, and a re-enforcement of his point of view, to see that his effect was not confined to literature, but spread widely into other channels. Louis Sullivan came profoundly under Whitman's influence: in fact, he carried on into architectural theory and practice even the clichés of Whitman's thought, like the distrust of "feudalism." Emerson supplemented Hegel in the mind of John Roebling, the designer of the Brooklyn Bridge; and Thoreau not merely served as literary godfather to Burroughs, but, what is more important, provided a rational basis in thought for the subsequent efforts to recapture the wild domain and keep the primitive sources of American life from drying up. Neglected by their contemporaries in the Brown Decades for their interest in an earlier America—it was typical that Howells, who had read Walden in his youth, confessed forty years later that he had never looked at the book afterward —they were equally neglected by the muckraking generation that followed, because their interests, though at bottom so different, were somehow lumped together with the sordid activities of the post-Civil War decades. Ours is the first generation that can look upon these bedraggled years with a free mind and catch, amid the materialism, the mean ostentation, the barbarous waste of human life, the gleam of an active culture which neither the Civil War nor its consequent activities could overthrow.

It was the contemporary obscurity and neglect of what was best in the literature of the Brown Decades that has made us impatient of the period: that, and the fact that the emphasis of the whole society shifted to the industrial and plastic arts. What caused this shift? Literature can flourish early in a society because of its limited physical demands: even painting, although the physical utilities are slight, requires the stimulus of other paintings and the professional aid of painters—conditions difficult to meet in a new country. Books travel easily; and with only small means, one can still have command of the best: Hebrew literature was available in one volume in the most wretched settlement, and Shakespeare and Milton were not unobtainable. Indeed, where the presses are few and the supply of books scanty, the finest works of literature have perhaps a readier chance of acceptance than they have in a state where books pour forth in great quantities, and bulk conceals quality. So it happened that the first consummation of American life in our culture came through literature in the writers of the Golden Day: it was only after the Civil War that a similar process took place in the domain of the other arts.

The means of life were changing rapidly from the fifties onward: there was a necessity for inventive adaptation which turned men from the inner life to the outer one, and to such manifestations of the inner life as had a plastic or structural equivalent. For lack of an harmonious system of concepts and feelings, this necessary change did not lead to an intelligent adaptation of the environment: in the planning of cities and the layout of railroads, highroads, farms, in the exploitation of mineral resources and the utilization of the land, a good part of our soils and cities were ruined: indeed, the new industrial towns were ruins from the beginning. But the necessity for invention was present, and if it was passed over by the vulgar profiteers in all walks of life and industry, it was nevertheless a challenge and a stimulus to the best minds. It turned farmers like Andrew Jackson Downing and Frederick Law Olmsted into landscape architects; it turned agricultural colonists like John Roebling into engineers, and men with strong musical talents like John Root into architects.

Added to this was the direct stimulus of new inventions; for in the beginning they were still almost toys, and before their potentialities had been transformed into slick routines, they had a power to stir the mind, out of all proportion to any of their later effects. The telephone, the electric light, the phonograph, the improved camera, the gas engine, the typewriter, all belonged in their inception, if not their full development, to the Brown Decades: they had something of the profound fascination that the Leyden jar had in an earlier century: they were wonders of nature, before they became utilities.

A good part of all this manipulation and invention came to no good end: let us confess that. The influence of the scroll-saw or the sheet-iron cornice on architecture was no better than the application of the lathe to the decoration of furniture in the seventeenth century; and the reproductive processes which produced the cheaper chromo-lithograph only increased the amount of futile work in the world, helping printers to flourish whilst it encouraged the original artists to starve. Mark Twain praised the typewriter because it promised to save paper; but it would be quite as just to condemn it because it increased the temptation to waste it: no one has yet fully balanced up the gains and losses that came in with this exuberant technology, and possibly no one ever will. But though the common products of industry were pretty generally bad—it is hard to conceive anything lower than the architecture of the Centennial Exposition or the fashionable New-port villas of the same period—the impulse to manipulate materials, the atmosphere of work, the interest in technique, were all helpful to the serious artist: if they did little for literature, these interests had a legitimate con-tribution to make to the other arts. The Brooklyn Bridge, for example, could scarcely have been built before the Civil War—if only because the iron foundries were hardly capable of supplying sufficient iron to build New York's Crystal Palace on schedule in 1853. The steel-framed or skele-ton skyscraper, too, could not have been devised before the Brown Dec-ades: it needed the invention of the elevator in the fifties and its improve-ment in the seventies, together with the cheapening of steel through the Bessemer process. The architect, the engineer, the landscape architect, the painter, all rode in together on the rising tide of industrialism: the very disorder it produced was a challenge.

The challenge would perhaps have been disastrous, were it not for the feeling of confidence that advances in scholarship and science made during the Brown Decades: this gave an impetus to the arts, and put solid ground under them; and one would scarcely understand the vigor of creative effort in both dominant personalities, like Richardson, and obscure, somewhat lonely pioneers, like Ryder and Eakins, if one left out of account the schol-ars and the prophets.

The chief works of scholarship before the Civil War, like the histories of Motley and Prescott, were the achievements of talented individuals, operating in what was almost an intellectual vacuum: the importation of books, to say nothing of finding and getting access to documents, was some-thing of a feat. After the Civil War scholarship ceased to be the hand-maiden of Christian apologetics or the rag-tag-and-bobtail of ancient classi-cal interests; and in every department young Americans began to have firsthand relations with the whole province they sought to explore.

Raphael Pumpelly had gone abroad before the war to learn mining en-gineering; he returned and became, like Clarence King, an exploratory geologist. Stanley Hall studied in Germany to become, after William James, America's foremost psychologist, and one of its foremost educators. In Cam-bridge Chauncy Wright, who unfortunately died in the seventies, and Charles Peirce were concerned with mathematics, the physical sciences, and philosophy, treated as a unity; Lester Ward was studying Comte, and William Graham Sumner received in 1875 the post in which he was to make his classic study of Folkways; Fiske left his derivative scientific studies to make his more important explorations of American colonial history; while Henry Adams, modestly disclaiming his competence to teach medieval history, not merely acquired a position of authority in that field, to top his work on the Federal period in America, but he sought to lay the foundations for a scientific concept of history. Adams at least succeeded as a dramatist of the Middle Ages, even if he failed in his more ambitious project to carry past sequences into future probabilities. In the same period, Willard Gibbs wrote some of the most memorable pages in the history of physical science in America, buried in the transactions of the Connecticut Academy, even as Peirce's papers were buried in early numbers of 'The Open Court'; while in 1877 Lewis Morgan made the first important American contribution to ethnology in his 'Ancient Society.'

It was the decade after the Civil War that saw the renewal of our universities, with the appointment of Charles Eliot to Harvard, Andrew White to the newly founded Cornell University, and Daniel Coit Gilman to Johns Hopkins, conceived in 1867 and opened in a few improvised dwelling houses, like the more ill-fated Brookings School in our own post-war period, in 1876. Through the leadership of such men the American university was transformed from a higher type of secondary school to an institution that had some pretensions to ranking with its European equivalent. The complete *Lernfreiheit* which Eliot introduced through the elective system was, we can see now, better adapted to mature students, well grounded in the fundamentals of thought and culture, than it was to the ordinary American lad who came to it enfeebled in will through the shackles of an empty formal education, but with only a little of the toughness and disciplined application that this system at its best gives. But any one who does not appreciate the drastic necessity of Eliot's elective system in its own time does not realize the sterility of the old type of American college, nor the importance of completely transforming a system devised to cultivate gentlemen and clericals in a period that needed a more comprehensive type of education than the old humanities offered.

We have still to build up a satisfactory equivalent for the old classic curriculum: that is a task for the philosopher, not alone for the educator, and men like Patrick Geddes have laid down more than a hint for the way in which this problem must be approached. But the point to remember is that the new synthesis was impossible until the old one had been effectually broken down. It was better to suffer from the bias of specialism, unrelated interests, and incomplete development, than it was to tolerate the gentlemanly inanition of the old type of curriculum, a curriculum that had been established in substance before Descartes. No doubt we suffered even more than Germany in our monkeylike imitation of German methods, for their overemphasis on the specialty was in part compensated for by their rich communal life and their cultivation of music; but the gains outweighed the losses—or would have done so if fixation on a low level of specialization had not been demanded by our later business institutions. It needed a man of principle and conviction, like President Eliot, to see such a complete transformation through. If the student became dispersed, the curriculum was enriched; and the efforts toward synthesis that are now being made have provinces of life and knowledge to draw upon that did not exist in the seventies, when Professor Sumner conducted the first course on

Sociology to be given at Yale, and Norton took over the first chair in Art at Harvard.

The powerful group of men that Harper later drew together at the new University of Chicago, or the smaller but equally significant group that Stanley Hall called around him at a post-graduate institution like Clark, would have been inconceivable had it not been for the pioneer work of Eliot and Gilman in promoting disinterested scholarship. One grants this freely, even while one realizes that the old type of college had a definite end in view, a certain type of mind and man, certain disciplines and modes of character, and that in abandoning this system, the leaders of education have often lost sight of any ends at all, and have succumbed to the pressure of external institutions, as Thorstein Veblen sardonically pictured in 'The Higher Learning.' What is now called optimistically and euphemistically "adaptation to changing conditions" is often an excuse for subservience to money, or complete lack of intellectual integration. The servile specialist, eloquently ignorant of any department of thought but his own, and therefore fundamentally ignorant of essential relationships in his own field, was undoubtedly a product of the Brown Decades: but it is our fault, not that of the earlier period, that he has become a chronic malady of our intellectual life, instead of a passing maladjustment. The work of the Brown Decades in education was necessarily destructive. Not to recognize the beneficence of that effort is to overlook the very conditions of growth. It is better to face chaos courageously than to cherish the dream of returning to an outworn synthesis.

In dealing with all these tangible products of the Brown Decades, intellectual and material, one must not forget the immensely stirring work of its major prophets, diffuse and difficult to estimate though their influence was.

Let us put to one side the figure of Mrs. Mary Baker Eddy, though in some ways she was the most influential prophet of all: she represents the shoddier part of the period, the part symbolized by the stock prospectus and the booster and the growth of credit operations in finance with no tangible assets to confirm the values that were produced and inflated. Her own particular combination of astute financial practice and lofty spiritual pretensions, her mixture of the psychology of suggestion and Berkeleyan metaphysics and Emersonian transcendentalism and faith healing and Christian theology into a working system makes her a unique figure in both religion and finance. Incidentally, her first successful classes date from the worst period of post-Civil War depression and deflation, and she exploited the tendency to ignore inconvenient realities to an extent which should make her the patron saint of our leading financiers and politicians today. But Mrs. Eddy, for all her influence, for all her perfect congruity with the worst aspects of the Gilded Age, does not belong to the positive side of our picture: she was, after all, only a more refined type of "pain-killer." The two prophets who count most for us were Henry George and Edward Bellamy.

In dealing with the American landscape and with landscape art, I shall have occasion to discuss the change that took place during the Brown Decades in our attitude toward the land. Henry George gave this change a political and economic underpinning. Rediscovering the physiocrat's notion that all wealth comes ultimately from the land—and whoever denies this denies the solar and chemical and organic basis of life—Henry George was struck by the contrast between the free lands of California, where he had settled, and the misery that attended the individual pre-emption of the land in the East. There was no lack of timeliness in Henry George's observations. In 'Our Land and Land Policy, National and State,' he said: "We are giving away our lands in immense bodies, permitting, even encouraging, a comparatively few individuals to monopolize the land to which the coming millions of our people must look for their support. In a few years, the public domain will all be gone; in a few years more the homestead law and the pre-emption law will serve but the purpose of reminding the poor man of the good time past. We shall find ourselves embarrassed by all the difficulties which beset the statesmen of Europe—the social disease of England and the seething discontent of France." His first pamphlet on this subject was published in 1871. George argued that control of the land by individual monopolizers meant ultimately a burden upon all subsidiary activities and processes, and he held up the logical alternative to this condition, in the form of land nationalization or the single tax. Without such a revolutionary change, George pointed out that further "progress" meant a more and more demoralizing poverty, possibly a catastrophe.

The general argument against the individual appropriation of rent for the use of common utilities does not apply only to water power or coal or rentable space: it applies equally to other common factors like the social heritage itself, and is therefore true of monopolies in the form of patents for inventions. Perhaps George's chief defect was that he wished to slip in a revolutionary proposal without touching any of the other dominant activities of American society; whereas, once his principal was admitted, many other institutions and ways of life besides the rent of land and its appropriation would have been affected. He wished to produce by political sleight-of-hand what was in fact a moral conversion. But George's awareness of the political importance of the land, his perception in 1870 of dangers that were to be fully demonstrated by 1890, and the stir that he made in the torpid political and economic thought of his day by introducing into it a vital idea—all this cannot be discounted. Henry George challenged the complacencies of bourgeois economics in terms that the bourgeois economist could partly understand. Less than fifteen years after George's 'Progress and Poverty' (1879) was published, Professor Frederick Turner pointed out some of the social and economic implications of the passing of the frontier. From this point on, any one who ignored the role of the land either in American history or in our current institutional life was guilty of convenient forgetfulness: the fact was established.

More popular even than Henry George, in the closing years of the Brown Decades, was Edward Bellamy, the author of 'Looking Backward,' the best of a series of strange utopias that those uncertain days brought forth. In Bellamy, who was born in Chicopee Falls, Mass., in 1850, the New England strain was running out, perhaps, but it was still active: his literary affiliations were with Hawthorne and Emerson. His chief work, 'Looking Backward,' came after he had served as a newspaper editorial writer and written a few novels. In writing it, he had, on his own confession, no idea of attempting a serious contribution to social reform: the idea was a "mere literary fantasy, a fairy tale of social felicity. There was no thought of contriving a house which practical men might live in, but merely of hanging in midair, far out of reach of the sordid and material world of the present, a cloud palace for ideal humanity."

'Looking Backward' became, almost in spite of itself, one of the most important political pamphlets of the Brown Decades: its successor, 'Equality,' is little more than an economic and social treatise, which amplified the points left undeveloped in the first book. This was one of the first attempts to think out a logical conclusion for the processes of mechanical organization and monopoly, for the national expansion of great industries like steel and the stockyards, which were taking place under men's noses. Bellamy's picture was naturally derided by the hard-boiled Marxians of his time as an unimportant piece of utopianism: had not Engels demolished that sort of thing? The curious fact remains that Bellamy's society reminds one, not of an impossibly abstract and ideal humanity, but of the United States during its late period of "prosperity" combined with Soviet Russia as it operates and envisages itself today. Bellamy prophesied telephonic broadcasting and the abolition of the corset: he pictured a nation conscripted for work, as in Soviet Russia today, and he had a foreboding of at least the physical outlines of the modern woman: if one is amazed by Bellamy's utopia now it is not because he was so wild but because he was so practical, so close to actuality.

In short, Bellamy's utopia was a real looking forward: it showed both the promise and the threat of actual conditions. More realistically than Henry George, Bellamy saw that one could not have land nationalization or its equivalent without a similar planned and resourceful use of all the other instrumentalities of production and consumption; or rather, that socialization in one department was incompatible with unlimited individualism in every other. 'Progress and Poverty' and 'Looking Backward,' both realistic, both forward-looking, were part of the essential atmosphere of the Brown Decades. After one has reckoned with the actual depression and sordidness, one must not forget the measure of intellectual hope that these men stirred in their more generous-minded contemporaries. Riots, strikes, lockouts, assassinations, brutalities, exploitations, marked the eco-

nomic life of this period: at no period in American history has the working class in America been more desperately enslaved. The conditions that
exist today in the mill towns of New England and the South, or in the
steel towns and coal fields, were during the Brown Decades almost universal. But ideas were stirring; and if the dawn itself proved false, the hope
it offered nevertheless was real.

Now that we begin to appraise the Brown Decades as a whole we can
see why what was positive and creative in this period usually worked
against the grain of its major activities. Its best works were often produced in obscurity, like the paintings of Albert Pinkham Ryder and
Robert Loftin Newman, like the poems of Emily Dickinson, or the philosophic reflections of Charles Peirce. For this reason, I originally called this
era in American culture the Buried Renaissance: the laval flow of industrialism after the war had swept over all the cities of the spirit, leaving here
and there only an ashen ruin, standing erect in the crumbled landscape.
The notion that there was anything of value buried beneath this debris
came tardily, for what our elders pointed to with generous delight was
obviously not very valuable.

In our haste to remove the debris, unfortunately, we have already
destroyed much that was precious in the Brown Decades; and unless we
rapidly recover a little common sense we shall doubtless destroy much
more. Every work in the period, even the magnificent productions of Richardson, has been treated as an out-and-out monstrosity—a habit which
points to the fact that the desecrators are aware of epithets but impervious to
realities. The houses that Richardson built for John Hay and Henry Adams
in Washington and his even more important Marshall Field building in
Chicago have all been torn down during the last five years: his best residence in Chicago, probably his best anywhere, the Glessner house, will be
saved only by the generous bequest which will turn it into an architects'
club.

The shingle houses that Richardson first established on such sound
lines are in even greater danger, for they are built of wood: yet they
brought an indigenous comeliness into the suburbs of the eighties, and
nothing we have done since, with the exception of Frank Lloyd Wright's
prairie houses, has touched so authentically the very color and atmosphere
of the landscape: incidentally, they represent the peak of spaciousness and
comfort in our American domestic facilities. Beside these houses the best
formal "colonial" work, which we think of as our own only because we
ignore similar buildings as far apart as England and South Africa, is manifestly a foreign and unassimilated style. Just as factory buildings were once
automatically called ugly, so a snobbish fashion of thought automatically
called the architecture Richardson instituted "monstrous," and it was condemned as a social error without being examined as an aesthetic object.
One trembles in Cambridge, for example, over the fate of Austin and

Seaver halls, in the face of the growing popularity of such heavy caricatures of colonial architecture as the Chemistry Building and the Widener Library, or such pasteboard imitations as the Business School—all of which inept productions are supposed to have added to the architectural harmony of Harvard.

In other fields, however, a great deal of material remains, preserved by the inertia of attics and libraries; and our main concern must be to see that it is not permanently neglected; for the complete history of the times, on its social and cultural and intellectual side, has hardly been approached by even the best of the current accounts. Some of the finest wood engravings of the seventies and eighties are buried in American magazines like 'The Century' and 'Harper's Weekly'; and if the residue of Eakins' paintings were preserved by his widow until the taste of critics and picture-buyers again caught up with him, we owe that splendid treasure to luck and piety as much as to popular understanding: many of his subjects could not bear to have his portraits around the house.

The manuscripts of Emily Dickinson have been guarded with a jealous but not intelligent care. The principal custodian of them has even alluded to the possibility of destroying some of them, and has not greatly increased one's optimism by dismissing it—as if it were ethically within the province of any individual or family to exercise such discretion over the work of a writer who belongs, we now definitely know, to the world. The legend of Emily Dickinson's love affair has been allowed to grow like a fungus, for lack of a little decent directness in revealing it: but for the suspicious air of concealment, no legend could have grown. The same holds true of some of the letters, if not the manuscripts, of Charles Peirce, an unconventional soul, who followed his own track, and whose reflections on life and the moralities were not merely out of harmony with those of his own generation but are equally remote, apparently, from the notions held by some of the present possessors of his letters. Even the publication of Peirce's collected papers has lagged for lack of a few thousand dollars to guarantee the initial expenses of publication.

The Brown Decades did better than this by their own: Richardson's biography, a compendious description and criticism of his buildings, appeared within a few years of his death: another sumptuous monograph followed Fuller's death in the eighties, and a similar biography, by Harriet Monroe, capped Root's untimely end. Unfortunately, the existence of these works perhaps discouraged others from going over the same ground; and it is now doubtful if a satisfactory first-hand account of Richardson's life can be pieced together, so few are the survivors who could have known him. And how much has already disappeared! The possibility of recovering a complete account of the life and personality of John A. Roebling seems to grow more and more remote. If an engineer whose main life is lived in public can so easily disappear, the obscure inner existence of a Ryder must be even more inaccessible to us—unless one boldly gather the story from his paintings. When the shallow fashion of debunking comes to an end, here is obviously a whole gallery of interesting personalities to work upon—if only the necessary material itself is available. Louis Sullivan's life was only partly told by himself: it leaves off at the critical moment of the World's Fair; and a complete monograph on the man and his work would be a precious key to the Brown Decades and the subsequent years.

There is a danger that both the works and days of the principal figures of this period will vanish before either has been properly evaluated or fully assimilated. This would be a grave gap in the story of American culture, and a real loss. If these artists and poets and thinkers are imperfectly remembered, our own generation may perhaps pride itself a little more completely on its "uniqueness"; but it will lose the sense of solidity that a continuous tradition, actively passed on from master to pupil or disciple, supplies. Enough perhaps if we at last realize that the Brown Decades, with all their sordidness, their weaknesses, their monstrosities, are not without their contribution to our "usable past." Through all the dun colors of that period the work of its creative minds gleams—vivid, complex, harmonious, contradicting or enriching the sober prevalent browns. The treasure has long been buried. It is time to open it up.

(1931)

CHAPTER EIGHT

Emerson's Journals

Almost sixty years ago, in 1909 in fact, the first volume of a ten-volume edition of Ralph Waldo Emerson's 'Journals' was published; and the final volume came out in 1914. In 1883, the twelve-volume collected edition of Emerson's works had been published, with an introductory memoir by James Elliot Cabot, the editor. To bring out Emerson's 'Journals' a generation after his death was, then, a final act of piety, performed by those who had been close to Emerson. But unfortunately for Emerson's reputation this publication was somewhat belated, for the robust Emerson one finds in the 'Journals' is a far more attractive figure than the transcendental ghost lingering in the popular imagination, whose "paleness" and remoteness led Henry James, the novelist, to speak of the "white tint" of Emerson's career.

Though Cabot was too old to participate in the editing of the 'Journals,' Emerson's son, Dr. Edward Waldo Emerson, the physician, with the help of Emerson's grandson, Waldo Emerson Forbes, waded through Emerson's notebooks and selected, out of the formidable welter, what they judged to be readable, representative, and memorable, with due consideration on occasion for the feelings of contemporaries still alive. This work was severely selective. Whatever the defects in their judgment from the standpoint of a less squeamish generation, they had the editorial courage and skill to put together a coherent series of books that not only sounded the ringing metal of Emerson's mind, but exposed the mine pit and the ore from which so much of the final product had come.

I must confess to a personal fondness for this original edition of Emerson's 'Journals.' In the days when I haunted the South Reading Room of the Central Building of the New York Public Library, those 'Journals' were on the open shelves near the call desk, and I used to dip into them while waiting for my books. The format was liberal, indeed the margins were over-generous; and the typography lived up to the fine tradition of the Riverside Press—one of the first American printers to break away from the cluttered pages and the illegible print of commercial Victorian design. These widely leaded type pages had some of the spaciousness and luminosity of Emerson's own mind; and the footnotes and summaries of books read were so unobtrusive, so easily skippable, that nothing stood in the way of intimate intercourse with Emerson's mind. (But I must add that, alas! this edition, though limited, was printed on a poor paper that has now become prematurely yellowed and brittle.)

The full-fleshed Emerson was already visible in these 'Journals,' though the editors, through an understandable effort to avoid duplication and to economize space, left out those parts of the 'Journals' that had been transferred by Emerson, often without change, to his essays. Yet if all Emerson's other work had been destroyed, he might have staked his claim as a writer on the complete 'Journals' alone. In later life, I acquired these volumes for myself; and so far from their losing the interest they had for me in my youth, they had just the contrary effect, for my numerous pencil notes show that they provoked a continuous dialogue between Emerson and myself which, it happens, is still going on. When recently I had the task of selecting passages from the 'Journals' for a new edition of Emerson's essays, I had only to turn these already marked journals over to the typist. Precious though Emerson's essays and lectures are, even as biographic revelations, no one can fully fathom his mind and character without becoming familiar with these 'Journals.'

With this background, it was natural that I should have hailed with unqualified anticipatory pleasure the announcement that the Belknap Press of Harvard was going to publish the complete Emerson 'Journals,' printing much that had been omitted and restoring to the original state significant passages that had been bowdlerized or otherwise altered by Emerson's editors. This anticipatory pleasure kept on increasing, like any natural appetite, until in 1960 the first volume appeared. Then it suddenly vanished.

Typographically, the new edition has the excellences of the older one, without the extravagant margins; and the paper itself will, I suspect, prove more durable. The great difference between the two editions is the difference between their contents and their editorial aims, for the new volumes, which include various miscellaneous notebooks as well as the 'Journals' proper, have the psychological idiosyncrasy known as total recall. If these editors have any sins to confess, the sin of omission would not be among them. The first edition of the 'Journals' was a memorable contribution to American letters; the present edition is an exhibition of current standards of American scholarship at its meticulous best *by* scholars and strictly *for* scholars. This means, if I may anticipate my eventual judgment, that it has nothing whatever to do, except by sheer coincidence, with literary values and humanistic aims. The last person who would have approved the new edition is Emerson himself. It reflects his spirit about as closely as the architecture of the new William James Hall at Harvard honors that of

William James. To be fair, then, I must attempt to penetrate further the editors' intention and describe what they have actually done.

This new edition of his grandfather's 'Journals' is properly dedicated to Edward Emerson Forbes, though the writers of the Introduction to the series, after making this courteous acknowledgment to one of their worthy predecessors, cannot refrain from politely reproaching Mr. Forbes and Dr. Emerson for their genteel habit of having referred to their ancestor as Mr. Emerson. But one must not forget that even later than 1909 historic figures were often still referred to in this fashion. Did not Henry James, in using the family letters, perversely alter William's Old Abe into President Lincoln? As late as 1924, Albert Jay Nock, the editor of 'The Freeman,' could still refer to Jefferson as Mr. Jefferson. This usage was partly an indication of a more general attitude which the present editors properly challenge and correct—that of seeking to magnify the positive virtues of a great figure by minimizing the defects, the discrepancies, or the contradictions. The unity so achieved is lifeless and the total effect false. In this respect the first editors were, as is the wont of near relatives with family papers, too tender of Emerson's reputation. So it was important that their discreet suppressions should be corrected. That alone would be sufficient justification for an unexpurgated edition of the 'Journals.'

With propriety the new edition boasts the essential scholarly virtues of unsparing honesty, accuracy, thoroughness; and for this everyone concerned to come closer to Emerson must be duly grateful. Some of Emerson's early characterizations of the Negro race, for example, were doubtless so repugnant to the moral sense of his first editors half a century later that they deleted them, as Emerson himself, whose views matured, doubtless would have done had he performed the same task. But now that another half century has passed, it was obligatory for the present editors to give us Emerson's original words, painful though it is to read them; for the fact that he, who became a passionate abolitionist, could have uttered them as a young man, should give us a little more understanding of the hold similar atavistic sentiments still have over a large number of our countrymen, North as well as South, even today.

What this edition does, then, is to faithfully restore to us the entire manuscript collection, unedited except by Emerson himself. Limited to the 'Journals' that effort deserves only applause. Emerson was wont to use in his lectures little anecdotes and local allusions that he firmly removed from the printed versions; and part of the value of this new version is that it reinstates these homely allusions, and presents a more vivid colorful Emerson than the somewhat etherealized and orphic figure one finds in the 'Essays,' particularly in the First and Second Series. In replacing these passages, the editors again have performed an admirable service; for they not merely disclose further Emerson's fragrant earthiness, already permeating the earlier edition, but they likewise bring out his unflinching realism and his racy humor, though some of these qualities were present in later essays like those on Fate and Wealth and Power. The complete 'Journals' even give a hint of inner conflicts not entirely glazed over by Emerson's habitual decorum. Thus the editors have discovered omissions of references to shadowy figures like Caroline Sturgis, which might indicate, even more than his letters to her, that the elder Henry James's portrait of Emerson as an angelic soul, immune to fleshly temptations or divided feelings, could have been mistaken—though doubtless Emerson had a more cavalier way of dealing with these inner promptings than the impetuous James did.

Such accretions of fresh data, however minute, are welcome, though the picture of Emerson is sharpened rather than radically altered by the restorations and the fresh exposures of the unvarnished wood that the editors have so far made. Through it all, Emerson remains in essence what he always intended to be, a true descendant of Montaigne, in other words, a great gentleman, one incapable of doing violence to himself or to anyone else. The impression is all the deeper because now one can see under what tensions and at what price the final result was achieved.

But in doing justice to the parts of Emerson's 'Journals' the editors have deliberately disrupted the whole. This immense body of material has been arranged, not to produce a consecutive, readable journal, as in the first edition, but to regurgitate the undigested contents of Emerson's mind, year by year, as revealed in all the surviving documents, not just the 'Journals.' Whereas Volume I of the 1909 edition, covering 1820–1824, contains less than 65,000 words, Volume I of the 1960 edition, covering only two years, boasts some 185,000 words. To realize fully all that this implies, one would have to go through the six volumes so far published section by section; but it will suffice to look at Volume I. Here is Emerson's college theme book, forty-four pages; here are thirty-six pages of quotations from Emerson's readings; here, too, as in the first edition of the 'Journals,' is every book that Emerson set down as having read. Altogether, some 130 pages of juvenilia, conceivably of interest to the specialist, but irrelevant to those concerned with Emerson's living mind. Nothing has been omitted, though Emerson himself, according to Ralph Rusk, felt that all the early manuscript books should be burned. At whatever cost, this edition leaves the major task of editing to the reader. What the editors have in fact done is to throw open the entire mass of raw material for future generations of scholarly research, knowing in advance, surely, that its very rawness will incite the production of endless Ph.D. theses, with all the trivia and minutiae duly refined and painstakingly sophisticated.

The cost of this scholarly donation is painfully dear, even if one puts aside the price in dollars of this heavy make-weight of unreadable print. For the editors have chosen to satisfy their standard of exactitude in transcription by a process of ruthless typographic mutilation. As it turns out, the damage done to the text by this method is no less serious from the standpoint of humane letters than the worst bowdlerization was from that of scholarly rigor. Though nothing in the manuscripts has been omitted, something has unfortunately been added. To present the written text in printed facsimile the editors have used twenty different diacritical marks. These marks, treated as an integral part of the printed line, spit and sputter at the reader, not only to indicate cancellations, insertions, or variants, but also unrecovered matter, unrecovered canceled matter, accidentally mutilated manuscript, even erasures. What the phrase "nothing has been omitted" means on the printed page may not easily be visualized by the reader unused to academic ways: so let me give an example, one of hundreds that could be drawn on, since hardly a page lacks some evidence. I quote at random a sentence, Volume I, page 193:

The best visions of the Christian <are> ↑correspond↓ cold↑ly↓ & imperfect↑ly↓ to the promise of infinite reward<s> which the scripture|contains|reveals|.

Let me stress that I have not out of malice chosen a particularly spotted passage; just a typical one. The effect of these notations is to make the reader feel as if he were Demosthenes, practicing oratory with his mouth full of pebbles. The scholarly reason for inflicting this torture is to present in print, solely for other scholars, the manuscript journals *"wie sie eigentlich geschrieben waren."* This is as near as print can get to a photographic copy of the original; and because type is easier to read than the handwriting of most authors, these volumes are an immense gift to specialists in American literature who may at last assiduously cultivate this once neglected domain on the strict lines prescribed for the mass production of scholarly papers and books.

The editors, despite their occasional modest disclaimers, have done their work so competently that no later scholar will have to microfilm another page of Emerson's notebooks, nor need he travel to Cambridge to gain permission to view the manuscripts in the Houghton Library, so long as he has access to this new edition. But apparently it did not occur to the editors, or even to the all-too-acquiescent publisher, that these journals might have genuine value for those not committed to professional scholarship.

This, then, it turns out, is a high fidelity version of Emerson's 'Journals,' with all the virtues of mechanically exact reproduction offset by a blunt indifference to any other human aims. As is the way of many hi-fi enthusiasts, the editors show more concern to reproduce the original scratches and squeaks than the music; for instead of relegating the noise to an appendix, or even, as has often been done, to separate volumes, they have made the scratches an integral part of the very sentences from which Emerson himself had already eliminated them, reinstating the slips, the false starts, the rejected ideas, as of equal importance to the final expression. This is not only a maddening practice in itself, but it surely has an

ominous bearing on the appreciation and teaching of literature. Such technological extravagance and human destitution is of course the fashionable
mode of our day. In the present case, nothing has been lost by this process
—except Emerson: Emerson and the many potential readers who have
been prevented by this automated editing from having direct access to his
mind.

Oh! but Emerson is there! One sees his figure at a distance, through
a barbed wire entanglement of diacritical marks; the searchlight from the
control tower, meant to keep Emerson from escaping, or even making a
movement without being noticed by the guards, keeps on sweeping into
the reader's eyes and blinding him: the voice in which Emerson faintly
calls out to one is drowned by the whirring of the critical helicopter, hov-
ering over the scene; while, with sympathetic anguish, one sees Emerson
himself, sentenced to fatigue duty, laboriously picking up and reassorting
the rejected scraps he had once thrown away. Yes: Emerson is there. But
after an hour or two of trying to find an unguarded place in the scholarly
enclosure where one may get near enough to him for a little uninterrupted
conversation, one gives up in despair, and departs, as one might from a
futile visit to a friend in a concentration camp. Thus these 'Journals' have
now performed current American scholarship's ultimate homage to a writer
of genius: they have made him unreadable. And the editors have done so
by a wholly gratuitous misplacement of the typographic devices they have
employed to ensure an accurate transcription.

These, I realize, are harsh words, for what I am saying is that the
editors committed two monumental errors of judgment, impossible to rectify without a complete reprinting of the whole work. The first one was
to print all the available material *seriatim*, mingling the important with the
inconsequential, the living and maturing mind of Emerson with the debris
of his daily existence; and the other was to magnify this original error by
transcribing their accurate notations to the very pages that the potential
readers of Emerson might wish to read freely, without stumbling over
scholarly roadblocks and barricades. When I first expressed these critical
misgivings to an eminent academic friend of mine, he advised me rather
peremptorily to lay off reviewing the 'Journals': begging me, indeed, not
to make a gratuitous nuisance of myself, since I am not an 'accredited'
Emerson scholar.

True: but I am a faithful Emerson reader; and, as it turns out, that
academic disability is perhaps my chief qualification for writing this criticism. For who is to question such an authoritative enterprise, if indeed it be
questionable, except those whose reputations and promotions could not
possibly be jeopardized by passing an unfavorable verdict upon it? Happily,
such a judgment must fall most heavily, not upon the editors as individuals,
but upon a greater culprit, the Academic Establishment of which they are
a part. For it is the preconceptions and the mock-scientific assumptions
governing the pursuit of the humanities today that so adroitly ensured the

miscarriage of this great effort, and turned it into a repulsive caricature of the sober scholarly virtues it sought to exemply.

The question ultimately to be decided, in the face of my learned and venerable friend's irritated *caveat,* is whether my description of this work is exaggerated and distorted, or whether it is the editing of the 'Journals and Notebooks' that exhibits, to an appalling degree, such wanton distortion and exaggeration, disguised though it be by a passion for close historic and biographic reproduction. Viewed as an abstract feat of scholarly notation, meant solely for the limited use of specialized scholars, the result gives the layman no reason to quarrel except possibly on the purely economic ground that, like moon-rocketing, it represents a colossal expenditure of human effort, money, and time, that might have been addressed to matters of greater consequence. What is puzzling though is the obvious fact that the editors did not apparently conceive that Emerson's 'Journals' might fulfill any other purpose than that of the scholarship industry. For if the editors had considered Emerson's experience and reflections as having a value in themselves, they might, without foregoing a single exact notation of their own, have equally served the interests of humane letters.

Strangely, indeed astonishingly, this dual solution had already appeared in a book published by the same press. For in 1959, a year before the first volume of the 'Journals and Notebooks' was published, Robert Spiller and the late Stephen Whicher published the first volume of the early lectures of Emerson, composed mainly of fragments that called for detailed editing, in the same fashion as the journals. But in this edition, in almost the same format, the purposes of the general reader and those of the scholar were both respectfully heeded by relegating the entire critical apparatus to the Appendix, leaving the lectures themselves unencumbered. In the case of the Emerson 'Journals' the readable text could easily have been confined to half the number of books, presumably at half the price of the final set.

More frightening, however, than the costly error itself is the state of mind of those who decided on this systematic maltreatment of Emerson's 'Journals': namely, their belief that the exact representation of the original text is a far more important undertaking than the sympathetic selection and arrangement of that text in a fashion that might invite and encourage those who wish to have intimate intercourse with Emerson's mind. That pseudo-scientific non-selective canon of judgment has become now the hallmark of American literary scholarship on the eve of its surrender to the computer and to those limited problems that computers so deftly and swiftly handle. Unfortunately, the issues that must be opened up here are too large to be treated casually at the end of a review. But until they are faced, and until American literary scholarship itself radically overhauls its present values and purposes, such expensive errors as the present edition of Emerson's 'Journals' will continue to be made.

(1968)

CHAPTER NINE

Prelude to the Present

When the women of America have gathered together all the culture in the world and the men have collected all the money there is—who knows?—perhaps the dry old Yankee stalk will begin to stir and send forth shoots and burst into a storm of blossoms.

—VAN WYCK BROOKS

It is absurd to think that the rhythm of life can be caught in decades or centuries. Rather, it would be absurd were it not for the fact that the rhythm itself is a product of human conditions and human institutions, and as the measure of our breath accounts in part for the meters of poetry, so does the calendar give a certain contour to our lives. One can use these divisions with impunity, provided that one does not ignore the significant anticipations and the quite as significant halts and lags that lie outside our stated period. So the decade from 1910 to 1920 had, in literature, a definition of its own; yet its most characteristic marks did not appear until 1914; and its theme was first set, in a musical sense, by a little book, almost a pamphlet, very young in its statements and hopes, 'The Wine of the Puritans,' which was written by Van Wyck Brooks in 1908.

American literature, after a lush spring in the Golden Day, had entered into a period of drought, and except for a few important survivors, William Dean Howells and Henry James in particular, had turned sere and yellow, and the fruit that it bore was parched even before it was ripe. It needs something of an effort to grasp the overwhelming desiccation of those days —to understand how a really fresh and important talent like that of Henry Adams could have hesitated to publish his memoirs and historical reflections, except in the whispered sanctity of a private edition.

As late as 1914, the author of a work on 'Literature and Insurgency' could devote most of his attention to such empty popular writers as David Graham Phillips, Stewart Edward White, Winston Churchill, and Robert Chambers, under the impression that he was dealing with important literary figures. During this curious interregnum the dead were very dead indeed, and as for the living, they were scarcely alive. Whitman had vanished from the scene, his spirit preserved by a handful of generous fanatics headed by Horace Traubel, the editor of 'The Conservator'; Emerson was little more than a memory of platitude and absent-minded benignity; Thoreau was forgotten, except as a predecessor of John Burroughs; and the typical histories of American literature published before 1910 were naive, deprecating, completely colonialized and scandalously attentive to mediocrity in all the canonized attitudes. When Frank Jewett Mather declared his desire to write a life of Melville, his interest was treated as an amiable aberration, unworthy of a New Humanist in the making. Is it any wonder that some of the letters George Woodberry wrote after his retirement from Columbia show a bitter appraisal of human cowardice and rascality unmatched anywhere except in the pages of Swift?

What was lacking in this scene, from a literary point of view? Van Wyck Brooks had an answer to that. In the course of three hundred years something restless and rootless in our lives had pushed us away from Europe without bringing us closer to our own soil. We lacked a sense of our living past, and had no feeling of continuity, no firmness of tradition, no established boundaries within which a talent might discover itself at an early stage and work steadily without inner distraction or fear of external disturbance. Anything might happen to us in America; and as a result, nothing did. Our poets turned aside both from their own past and from those robust elements in their own day they were too weak to absorb; they were weakly sententious or exotic in the style of Thomas Moore and Byron; in general, Emerson, Whitman, Emily Dickinson had left no mark upon them; and the series of experiments in style and technique, begun by Wordsworth and Blake and carried over into the shadowy realms of the unconscious by the Symbolists, had little effect upon them and served neither as a criterion nor a point of departure. The past was dead for us; our sources had dried up; and when we sought to become cultivated we achieved little more than good manners and elegant reminiscence.

Suddenly into this world of tepid preferences and anemic loyalties and pale traditions a new spirit began to pour. At the beginning of the second decade there was a murmur of suppressed excitement in the air, like that which hovers over a silent crowd before the appearance of a great procession. As outriders of this procession came a group of critics, who cleared the way and heightened the consciousness of what was to come. The two older leaders of this group were H. L. Mencken and J. E. Spingarn. Mr. Mencken's reputation at present is founded on his intense, if somewhat inverted, nativism: he is for us the author of 'The American Language,' a creative inventor of colloquialisms and happy turns of slang, an editor who eagerly publishes reflections on every aspect of the Amercian scene. But in the beginning he was just the opposite of this, and his prime contribution was the fact that he imported a European standard of values into American criticism and ceased to ask of a work if it upheld our typical American gentilities.

James Huneker had done this before Mr. Mencken: it was Mencken's peculiar office to turn his appreciation of Europe into a polemical weapon for aiding the new writers, the Dreisers and Cabells, in America. Despite later efforts to restrict American literature to more parochial literary standards, the Ku-Klux Kriticism that Ernest Boyd described in the twenties, Mr. Mencken effectually demolished the illusion that our literary heritage could limit itself to British sources and examples. His work here was strictly parallel to Professor Irving Babbitt's interest in comparative literature; it paved the way not merely for a flood of foreign translations, but for the appreciation of foreign cultures on our own soil, both in their direct expression, as in Rolvaag's novels, or in such secondary manifestations as Willa Cather's 'My Antonia.'

What Mr. Mencken did for the subject matter of literature, the author of 'Creative Criticism' did for its technique and method. Under the Crocean conception of art as expression, Mr. Spingarn sought to release criticism from irrelevant preoccupations and standards. He bade the critic examine the author's inherent spirit and to judge the work first of all as an esthetic whole instead of summarily bringing it to the bar of the critic's private moral and methodological judgments. He showed that the rhetorical canons of the academy were more concerned with the practical side of expression than with the essential spirit and function of the work of art. Mr. Spingarn, almost singlehanded, changed the attitude of the academic world from that of hostility to new forms into one of at least benevolent neutrality. When, toward the end of the decade, John Livingston Lowes's excellent 'Convention and Revolt in Modern Poetry' came out, it was apparent that a real victory had been won.

Hard on the heels of the critics came the poets themselves, first gathering together in 1912 in Harriet Monroe's magazine, 'Poetry,' and then forming and reforming in various new phalanxes and battalions—'Others,' 'The Seven Arts,' 'The Little Review' and later 'Broom,' 'The Dial,' and 'transition' and a score of lesser magazines. What a clamor there was when the procession started, and how difficult it was to sort out the various members and to discover which were marching forward and which were still obstinately facing in the other direction. There was a time when the author of 'Frankincense and Myrrh' could be referred to in the same breath as the creator of 'The Man Against the Sky'; when 'Ethan Frome' could be dismissed in favor of Mrs. Wharton's documentary pictures of moneyed society. Alfred Kreymborg has told the more adventurous part of the story in 'Troubadour,' and here I am concerned not with the particular details but with the general effects.

Two attitudes emerged between 1910 and 1920. One was a sense of self-confidence and adventure, a belief in a cultural America not identified with Colonial spinsterhood, with the antiquarian possessions of the museum, nor overallured by the sordid promiscuous jangle of Broadway or the Loop, and the other, which owed something to the honest muckraking of the previous decade, must be called, in its own words, the social conscience. It was the social conscience that made all the beginners in the decade turn automatically to Europe and to contemporary socialism as a source of value and form. Wells, Bennett, Shaw, Galsworthy were the chief models, although Gorki and Rolland were not without influence.

What unequal talents the English galaxy proved! Wells and Bennett will survive probably, in single books—'Tono-Bungay' and 'The Old Wives' Tale'; Shaw may even go for a whole generation into the shadow before his satiric melodramas restore him to a place beside Congreve and Molière, while Galsworthy remains an insular possession, sanctified by usage, like some inadequate monument which still remains in the street picture because it is less objectionable than the vacancy its absence would create. But this quadrumvirate represented the social conscience, and so for a while they played an emphatic part in American thought and feeling.

To be aware of poverty and chicane and the labor movement and the obduracies of caste; these were the sigmata of the social conscience. It might be dull and timid and merely respectable; but it was earnest, even if at times its earnestness mounted to the funny pitch of singing 'Armageddon' as if the fate of nations were to be decided by the initiative, the referendum, and the recall. So 'The Masses' came. So the social settlement flourished. So one or two minor documents emerged, 'The Harbor' and 'Comrade Yetta'; and so, finally, out of that same drift and turmoil, came directly a minor but significant literary monument: Michael Gold's 'Jews Without Money.' Some of the best of Vachel Lindsay's poems, like his noble tribute to Altgeld, had the same roots.

To prepare for the good life was the very essence of this social effort; but to realize the good life, to conceive and adequately carry out, day by day, the necessary elements of such a life was still not to be thought of: the future, so dazzling in its promise, was in fact empty. When the reform was carried out, as so many reforms were indeed carried, all the glory and the delight suddenly vanished: it was the fellowship of fighting that satisfied the social conscience rather than a coherent notion of what was worth fighting for. Was it any wonder that the social conscience almost dropped out of literature during the next decade, surviving in such lusty but naïve pamphlets as 'Jimmy Higgins' and 'Oil' and 'The Goose-step,' and in the more respectable middle-class costumes of Charles Norris and Dorothy Canfield Fisher. What the conscience lacked was a deep revolutionary élan which would touch every aspect of the spirit: during the twenties it seemed for a while as if this might appear, when John Howard Lawson's 'Processional' was first produced, and the scattered but impressive panorama, John Dos Passos's 'Forty-second Parallel,' is a possible indication of its revival. But it needs more than a perception of disorder or a sense of wrong to create a fresh social synthesis—and the necessary creative travail was as lacking in literature as in politics.

The book that heralded the deflation of social hopes was Walter Weyl's 'Tired Radicals'; but the turn had already been called by Randolph Bourne, a pure spirit, one of the great unfulfilled talents that the decade produced. Bourne, indeed, symbolized in his own work the beginning and the end of that decade. It was he, following Van Wyck Brooks and John Macy, who declared war on colonialism; it was he who stood as John Dewey's most acute and gracious disciple; it was he who examined, with tact and sympathy, the new movements in education and town planning which promised to bring the nebulous utopias of nineteenth century politics down to some concrete manifestation; he, again, confronted the Power-state, when he found all his hopes and solicitudes about to be shattered in the diabolical mob-mindedness of war—and how sane, how well justified by the event were all his predictions!—and he, finally, sounded the retreat from special programs that were divorced from valuable ends and goals and had no principles capable of guiding them to more appropriate destinations, other than those suggested merely by the current go of things. In Randolph Bourne's work the decade had fully expressed itself, both in the white blossom of spring and the astringent black berry of autumn.

But, meanwhile, the sense of spiritual adventure had called a different tune. In London a raucous American voice, with something of the flatness of the prairie in its prose utterances, had begun to issue a series of defiances and challenges in 'The New Age,' directed equally against the new country he had turned his back upon and the old one to which he had come. It was Ezra Pound, a poet of diverse parts and manifold excellences, bound to be, not so much the leader of a school, as the founder of a succession of schools. What poet could escape his debt to Ezra Pound? In each fresh woodland trail he opened Mr. Pound's footprints or his hatchet marks were there before him. Mr. Aiken might be tempted, by one of those curious blindnesses that fine poets who are also critics are capable of, to leave him out of an American anthology; but the fact remained that Pound slipped in on almost every page.

The narrow program of the imagists was one of those contemporary works of purification which are important, less because of their achievements than because of their rejections. To see exactly and freshly, to escape windy metaphors and trite rhythms, such declarations as these were as important in the work of a Frost, in his psychological dialogues, as they were in the poems of H. D. And what fine, glass-blown, crystalline beauties emerged, sometimes whitely chaste, as in H. D., sometimes filled with oblique, warm, wine-tumbler reflections, as in Wallace Stevens and Alfred Kreymborg, sometimes so delicately maculate, as in William Carlos Williams. A narrow range these poems have, narrow as the flute or clavichord: the need of imagism made it necessary to disdain themes that required the full support of an orchestra; so inevitably the movement was a temporary one. Carl Sandburg joined the procession, one foot hobbling in Whitman's vast boots, the other trimly mincing in the slippers of imagism; and Amy Lowell came, terrible as an army with banners, seeking to compose out of a thousand little images a massive picture which somehow persisted in remaining what it was—a thousand little images, placed within a frame.

Was it all a belated impressionism? Were John Gould Fletcher's 'Green Symphonies' and 'White Symphonies' only Whistler retarded by the backwardness of American literature? No: it was much more than that; but the anxiety that Amy Lowell and Mary Austin showed, as critics, to disclaim the influence or importance of Whitman was a mark of a certain residual provincialism that lingered in our letters. Whitman and Stephen Crane had been there before: how feeble, how silly it was to deny it! One must again salute the essential honesty of Mr. Pound's genius for recognizing the inescapableness of Whitman, who had taken imagism and polyphonic prose in his stride and had not been limited to little themes, strained of drama, ideas, emotional intensity.

But the genteel tradition in American poetry had at last died: it had died, simply enough, for lack of the more waxen and tailor-made kind of gentleman, the literary ideal of the eighties and nineties. That was a good sign, for the virtues of this species of 'gentlemen,' his tact, his pliability, his good form, his perpetual sense of others, are hostile to the more arcane and belligerent individuality of the creative artist: 'polite letters' is a misnomer. Instead of 'gentlemen' we were face to face, once again, with authentic, fully-fleshed personalities; sardonic tongues like Bodenheim's, inviolate hermits like E. A. Robinson, shrill nobilities like William Ellery Leonard, delicate brassy hoydenisms like Edna St. Vincent Millay.

The most important of all these personalities during this decade was Robert Frost, the very image of integrity and steady growth, who created in himself an antidote to the poisons that were prevalent in our American life: a man rooted in the countryside, indifferent to fashion, unhurried and imperturbable, yet sensitive and a-quiver to every fresh stimulus, without permitting himself to be either diverted or overwhelmed by it. Frost's life was a creative act that existed in its own right; his poems were merely an inevitable rounding out of the consciousness, the insight, the beliefs that arose out of the life. No one so completely undefiled had appeared in American letters since Emily Dickinson; or rather, such immaculacy of purpose had been purchased, hitherto, at too high a price—like virtue in a nunnery. Criticisms, exhortations, social consciences, esthetic experiment, all this plowing and harrowing of our soil had been necessary; but what was even more necessary at last was a living example; and Robert Frost provided it. Van Wyck Brooks had pleaded for an aristocratic creative life in America: Robert Frost made it visible.

I have still to note another literary figure who accomplished his major work during this decade. Uncanonized in literary circles, pushed aside by new doctrines in academic quarters, he rests for the moment in proud, unhonored isolation: Thorstein Veblen. With the exception of such badly wrought and undecisive efforts as Melville's 'The Confidence Man,' Doestick's 'Plu-ri-bus-tah,' and Mark Twain's 'A Yankee at King Arthur's Court,' 'The Theory of the Leisure Class' was the first fully molded satire that this country produced; when Veblen followed it by 'Imperial Germany,' 'The Nature of Peace,' and 'The Higher Learning' his literary position was established. Veblen was not simply an economist with a turn for irony and obscure allusion; he was essentially a philosopher and a man of letters, well at home in the literature of the world, who utilized a rigorous technical method and a specific *métier* to riddle with a sharp spray of bullets the whole fabric of caste and baseless distinction that forms not merely the superstructure of our economic order, but the foundation of our whole culture. Veblen had his brief moment of popularity at the end of the war; that was, as it were, the last flicker of the social conscience. At the moment I drag him forth out of the night. He belonged to the generation of Mr. Chapman, Mr. More, Mr. Dewey; and the very fact that one can add his name to that strange concatenation proves what a grotesque fictitious entity a 'generation' is.

The decade ended, spiritually speaking, with Mr. Waldo Frank's sanguine canvass of 'Our America'—a climax to the movement heralded by 'The Wine of the Puritans.' Then darkness fell; the sense of unbounded opportunity and joyous adventure for a while disappeared. At the edge of the sky, in both the east and the west, there was a rift of light; but it was impossible to tell whether it was a dreary sundown or an even drearier dawn.

The last decade began with a collapse of ideas. Henry Adams, with great intuitive insight, if with dubious mathematics and an unwarranted translation of physical concepts, had predicted a "change of phase" in 1917— and his prediction, if not his language, was justified. The doctrines of the new physicists changed the whole aspect of the cosmos, while the work of Haldane, Thomson, Wheeler, and Jennings in biology, of Köhler and Koffka and Jung in psychology, of Geddes and Branford in sociology, of Whitehead in metaphysics, all converged toward the presentation of a more related and integrated world than the science of the nineteenth century had dared picture. Concepts like organism, pattern, configuration, supplemented and modified such older abstractions as matter, motion, the struggle for existence; it had become apparent that the vast, hasty conquests of mechanistic science had been due to its willing superficiality, and if a deeper knowledge threatened perhaps to retard the pace of invention and technology it would by the same token result in a less jerrybuilt and shaky civilization. The war in Europe might look like the accidental collision of a blind concourse of atoms, as the universe itself was so often pictured in nineteenth century thinking; its outcome might be temporarily moral chaos, but the war was, among other things, an exhibition of this abstract atomistic philosophy which had infected every type of human activity. However debauched and depressed the post-war world was, within the mind a logical and esthetic order had begun to reign again.

With the disappearance of the ancient landmarks and still more ancient foundations a few observers, like Joseph Wood Krutch, were tempted to read into the situation the death of love and morality and tragedy and all high human imaginings, but the slightest recollection of many similar periods in history should have made it plain that civilization was molting a dead skin, not going into dissolution. 'The Modern Temper' was partly the dregs of Victorian agnosticism and partly the unconscious backwash of war and revolution. To turn it into a philosophy of life was to dignify a historic accident with reasons. The myth of Ragnarok, the extinction of the gods themselves, is indeed an old one in the northern European tradition; its most imposing modern version was that of Oswald Spengler in his profound historical poem on 'The Decline of the West.' If Spengler was right, the slackening grip, the despondency over the animal basis of life itself, was a symptom of the last phase of a cold megalopolitan civilization. Perhaps this was true; but, matching metaphor for metaphor, one might point out that in deepest winter, the buds of spring have already emerged and await only the first warm sun. Life must go on, even if the engineer and the business man, as well as the poet, have quite forgotten the reason. Spengler was driven contemptuously to deny the manifestations of genuine vitality today, and to dismiss the possibility of emergent elements not comprehended in any past system: his prophecy belonged to the past as much as his history.

With the whole world of ideas in ruins, it was plain that the day of the wreckers and excavators was over: the time had come for the architect, the plan, the organized corps of workers. Who was capable of directing those forces in America? That was a question which bore directly both upon literature and upon social life.

The one significant philosophic mind the country had produced since the Civil War—James, Peirce, and Dewey were all born before—was George Santayana. He had long before 1920 retreated abroad, leaving behind the memory of an urbane, slightly sardonic personality and a series of literary and philosophic masterpieces whose chief fault was an excellence so general and well distributed that no special part stood out before the whole. With a thousand pithy sentences dotting 'The Life of Reason,' no single sentence escaped the context sufficiently to become a catchword. Those five important volumes, having been published as a unit, were at once treated to respectful silence, as a classic no one need bother to read; whereas, had they been published separately at intervals of a few years, they might possibly have enlarged Mr. Santayana's influence and sunk deep into American thought.

Mr. Santayana had originally one serious defect as a critic: a readiness to dismiss as barbarism a tendency of mind antithetical to his own native bias. One has only to compare his criticism of Whitman with Paul Elmer More's to see how Mr. More's mere Anglicism and Protestantism enabled him to accept in Whitman elements which Mr. Santayana rejected as uncouth and barbarous—that is, un-Latin.

But for more than one reason, Mr. Santayana was unfit to exercise an *intimate* effect upon this disorderly and prostrate decade. Though he could easily rise above it, he had not temperamentally sufficient experience of the disease to produce, from his own physiological reaction, the necessary anti-body that should combat it. He had, if I may use the medical figure for my own purposes, a high degree of immunity in his own right; but only one who had succumbed in some degree himself could produce an immunizing culture against it.

In America and Europe there was one school of thought that was dogmatically certain of its diagnosis and its remedy: it sought to escape the exhausting task of a fresh integration of thought and life by retreating to a set of ideas that antedated our present experience and dilemma. The New Humanists sought a fixed body of doctrine, a moral absolute, which would serve as a reference for all thought and experience—in Europe, the Catholic Church, in America a canon of eclectic humanist ideas which should include the works of Confucius and Buddha and Aristotle and organized Christianity. Such a combination of diverse and conflicting elements was made possible only by a system of arbitrary definitions whose symbols would automatically exclude all that was contradictory in the doctrine symbolized. The "expansion" of romanticism, the imputed absence of values in naturalism, the emotional outflowing of humanitarianism—against these phases in the thought of the last few centuries the New Humanists waged war.

The raising of the New Humanism into a public issue in the closing years of the decade did not establish the intellectual validity of the doctrine: as a fashion it had only the sanction of fashion. There were, one hastens to admit, salutary virtues in the scholarly work of the leaders, and a belated recognition of their importance was more reassuring than the cool silence that had greeted Mr. Woodberry and Mr. Chapman twenty or thirty years before; but behind the vigorous intellectual efforts of the leaders one detected the panicky spinsterdom of the universities, a mere undisciplined mob, sniping from the rooftops with catchwords and labels at ideas they had neither the capacity to understand, the courage to experience, nor the intellectual hardihood openly to demolish.

The notions of balance and symmetry and proportion, which the New Humanists revived, were necessary corrections to our lopsided society with its complete lack of any norm except that of material activity and business success: this, and not the middle ground or the inner check was perhaps the one positive contribution of the New Humanist creed. But, like all other ideals, balance must be translated into life in dynamic, not static, terms. Milk is a balanced human ration, containing every ingredient necessary for bodily growth; and there are works of literature and art which correspond to milk, and are useful and admirable, particularly for the nurture of the young.

But to restrict the normal human diet to milk would be a medical ineptitude; and it is no less so in the realms of the mind: not merely are "balanced" writers like Dante and Goethe a resolution of incompatible and conflicting elements, but, at any given moment in one's spiritual development, some one article of diet—the unrelieved pessimism of Koheleth, or the untrammeled naturalism of Zola, or the untempered bawdiness of Petronius—may be more wholesome than the most complete ration. To exclude such writings from a humanist canon is to abandon faith in moral choice. The moral effect of a work of art has no proportion to the conscious moral sentiment it contains. While the New Humanists talked of the excellence of the great classics of literature and religion, they were apparently thinking inwardly of the virtues of John Halifax, Gentleman.

There remained in America, outside the belligerent camp of the humanists, a handful of writers who were in the act of achieving a coherent philosophical position, and who were not committed to caging experience in some narrow cell, from whose confines they could count the rest of the world well and happily lost. What these writings sought was not a closed system, but an open synthesis, capable of bringing together and resolving and working out toward concrete issues the warring elements in our social and spiritual heritage.

One of these was Walter Lippmann, whose originally brilliant beginnings, as a pupil of Santayana, and as a writer of such intelligent political pamphlets as 'A Preface to Politics' had been partly obscured by a career in journalism. Half a generation separated that book from 'A Preface to Morals,' and those two titles put in briefest compass the vast change that had taken place. In 1913, the ends of life seemed well fixed; it was the means that required adjustment. In 1929 the means themselves were obviously, if not rudderless, still floating on an uncharted ocean; it was the elementary positions of north and south that had somehow to be re-established. I do not feel that Mr. Lippmann did more than broach the problem; but that itself was no little achievement.

An even more significant book was published in 1929, marking equally a new turn of the tide: Waldo Frank's 'The Rediscovery of America.' Mr. Frank is one of the most fully orchestrated writers of our generation and, unlike the older critics, he is young enough to have lived through the debacle and to have felt within himself the necessity for creating a new order. From Spinoza and Hegel, still more from his own mystic intuitions, he conceives the possibility of re-forming into ordered wholes the dispersed, disintegrative forces of modern life, instead of living in a world of fragments, rejections, partisanships, partialities. As in Jan Smuts's 'Holism,' the mystic concept of the whole sometimes in Mr. Frank's thought blurs the outlines of reality: the Whole is for him an antecedent cosmic fact to be attained by immediate illumination, as well as an emergent possibility to be discovered by concrete experiment and to be created in society. But setting aside criticism of detail, the main thing to be noted about Mr. Frank's affirmations is the complete absence of the intellectual nausea found in 'The Modern Temper' and in so many lesser expressions that characterize the decade.

Equally significant, perhaps, was the change in mood that came from the work of younger writers who were separated from Frank by a difference of five or ten years; such men as John Dos Passos, Malcolm Cowley, Matthew Josephson, Archibald MacLeish and Kenneth Burke. The transformation of some of these writers took the form of an increasing productiveness; and this was not merely to be attributed to maturity, since it was equally marked in the work of even younger writers who had altogether escaped the spiritual eclipse of the twenties. What bottomed it was the sense that life again had solidity, something to dig into, something to build upon.

No single work of this group as yet stands out as a whole; but the Cape Hatteras portion in Hart Crane's 'The Bridge,' certain memorable passages in Isidor Schneider's 'The Temptation of Anthony,' in Phelps Putnam's 'Daughters of the Sun,' and in Babette Deutsch's 'Epistle to Prometheus' —to mention only the most ambitious efforts—give promise of even more sustained power. Epics, even bad epics like Ossian, are written only when the energies are beginning to run high.

The new synthesis in our social and spiritual life will not come easily; it is not to be expected; nor will the effects of such a synthesis become apparent at once in our literature. Any self-conscious attempts to hasten the process will probably only delay the results by bringing too quickly to the surface ideas and desires that must penetrate every pore and fold of the unconscious. Our main duty at present is to clarify our sources, to discover what elements in the traditions of the Renaissance, of Romanticism, the Revolution, Naturalism and Mechanism are permanent ingredients of a culture that is still to emerge, and to project a basis upon which they can be integrated with the new elements in our life and thought. We cannot cast the burden of this creation upon either an obsolescent Church, a future Revolution, or a contemporary Machine, whose iron destiny we must fulfill.

Actually, this destiny, whether it be called the Mob or the Machine, or the Winter of Faustian Civilization, is just as much inside the artist as outside: that which is opposed to it has all the opportunity for projecting itself that it ever had. The position of the artist has not been altered by the Machine: the court of Louis XIV was a machine, and a devilish burdensome one, too; but that did not persuade Racine and Molière to give up the ghost. It is the very existence of repression and obdurate circumstance, as Nietzsche urged, that rouses the spirit to heroic encounter.

If the arts fulfill natural and salutary human functions, they will disappear from society only when society produces monsters. Every new baby is a check upon that mishap; for life, by its natural processes, eventually modifies its useless conventions and rectifies its mistakes; if the method is costly it is at all events certain. The Machine will rust away quicker than the instincts it throttles; or, rather, the Machine is part of man's natural history, and it will create compensatory functions and interests. The age of mechanical specialization may give rise to the age of the amateur; and the gospel of work, pushed with irrational zeal, may drive us into a leisured society.

Looking back on the last two decades, seeing how much has been usefully destroyed and how much, in the midst of this destruction has been accomplished, one has a sense far removed from futility. Those who possessed a social conscience did not scheme generously enough: a part of their program has been put into effect, and Eutopia is still at a distance. They have dulled the thorns of injustice and poverty, but they have not removed the roots. Those who sought to achieve a revolution did not lay their foundations wide enough: they carried into the promised land the customs appropriate to their older bondage. Their social anticipations must be dynamically projected toward a fresh reality; for the ideas appropriate to our revolution are still to be formulated, and are not in Marx or Bellamy. Those who climbed up the steps of an Ivory Tower discovered that they could not live without air and water and food not supplied by the Tower itself; their esthetic isolation was an illusion. We turn our backs on these false starts, these weak withdrawals.

A new world must come to birth; and there is no birth without pain, as there is no nurture without sacrifice. But the mood of defeat is dead. We have not hauled down our flag because, like Whitman's Little Captain, we can still say collectedly *We have not yet begun to fight*.

(1931)

PART TWO

Personality and History

CHAPTER TEN

Jesus: Primacy of the Person

Modern man in the West first took shape in a period of cultural disintegration: a slow, painful, largely unconscious process whose meaning did not become plain to him until all hope of arresting it had disappeared.

Some of the best traits in our character are the product of a grand retreat that took place within the very heart of classic civilization, at a time when all its values seemed secure. If pity and love have had a larger part to play in our life than they did in the ancient world, it is mainly because they nourished man during a period when he was dying of starvation while sitting at a feast. To understand our present selves, we must understand the central core which formed the primitive Christian: not because we can live again within that archaic mold, but because we can then see into the nature of our own plight and direct our efforts toward an even more positive renewal.

For more than fifteen hundred years, our Western World has been dominated by the personality and the myth of Jesus of Nazareth. The prophecies that announced him, the words attributed to him, the rites that enthroned him, the myths that magnified him, the institutions that supplanted him, have all left their imprint even on seemingly remote parts of Western man's existence. Any interpretation of contemporary events which neglects the parallel between the Roman order and the modern world, and which fails to understand the path taken by the Christian communities, lacks a possible guide to the future. If we are to find a straighter path, we must at least recognize the historic reasons for Christianity's success.

The life of Jesus of Nazareth has been both magnified and diminished by the growth of the Christian Church. His message was swallowed up in his myth: his personality was enveloped by the special claims of divinity that were attached to it: his human presence was lost in a miraculous Annunciation and a divine Transfiguration. But the myth was plainly a collective projection of the peoples who formulated it and embellished

125

it, and from what remains in the New Testament of Jesus's unmistakable insights, one must assume that much of his actual doctrine, perhaps part of the kernel, was misunderstood or rejected by his more simple-minded recorders. Too often we see the form of Jesus and hear only the words of Paul. The pale but more visible satellite partly eclipses the sun.

What was the reason for Jesus's unique triumph? The explanation of Christian theology is a simple one: he was the Son of God, and his incarnation, his suffering, and his death were part of a divine plan in which he, by taking man's sins upon himself, began a new dispensation for mankind. Why omnipotence left such an imperfect record of this event, shrouded it in such obscurity, and performed it at such a late point in history are minor problems beside the vaster mystery which faith accepts.

But the historic mystery is increased, rather than diminished, if one regards Jesus solely in his human aspect. On such terms, his power is like that of the tiny grain of mustard seed: an evidence of the absolute weight of the human personality in the face of institutions and material circumstances that would seem destined to overwhelm it and blot it out. "Whosoever will be great among you, let him be your minister; and whosoever will be chief among you, let him be your servant."

The classic world had long been waiting to hear Jesus's challenging words. Year by year its emptiness had been growing heavier; year by year the chains that bound men to their imperious burdens and their played-out pleasures had become more galling: the calluses deepened on the spirits of the proud and the raw blisters multiplied on the bodies of the lowly. In a few decades, in a few centuries, everyone would be ready for the new dispensation: not only the slaves but the centurions: not alone miserable Lazarus, but the Ethiopian Royal Treasurer.

The prophet who uttered these words was brought up in the land of Galilee, the Boeotia of Palestine, among farmers and fishermen who mingled with the busy, prosperous patricians from Jerusalem. Like Hesiod, whose 'Works and Days' reformulated the Hellenic religious consciousness and established a higher concept of justice, Jesus was alienated by humble birth from the dominant society of his time. Though he argued with the learned rabbis in the synagogue, there is no indication in his teaching that he was burdened by any weight of abstruse learning, or that he even had such acquaintance with the philosophers and poets of Graeco-Judaic civilization as Paul probably had. The carpenter, the shepherd, the fisherman, the husbandman, the worker in the vineyard, were the familiar types he knew: their ancient occupations provided him with homely images of the common life; and he shared some of their distrust for the proud merchants and the sharp moneylenders who made life hard for the poor. At home with his neighbors, he had words for simple men.

Jesus's contemporaries were more than ready for him—indeed for anyone who was certain of his inner light, and set to lift their trouble and confusion. They would read portents in the sky, even as the contemporaries of Augustus read into the approach of a comet the beginning of a new age: they would not be surprised to find the Messiah, one of the House of David, sitting by a well in the middle of their village. In the recurrent poverty of the war-torn countrysides there was an underlying connection, the connection of want and pain and fear, with the proletariat of the cities: so that once the prophet came forth, his doctrine would prosper most swiftly in the crowded, world-weary metropolises of Africa and Asia Minor. John the Baptist had come among the Jews purifying people by baptism and predicting a new day at hand. When Jesus came to John, the latter promptly recognized his qualities: he declared he was not fit to tie Jesus's shoelaces. That act of recognition and homage started the young prophet on his way.

Presently, Jesus retired to the barren hills, where he fasted and nourished his visions. Alone in the desert, he was tempted by dreams of power: the power to control the physical world, common to magic and to science, the power to rule the political destinies of the masses of men, the vulgar ambition of emperors and tyrants: all these avenues of worldly achievement he put behind him. Jesus's interest was in the redemption of man's very humanity, in the perpetual renewal and re-dedication of the living to the task of self-transformation: he sought to bring the inner and the outer aspects of the personality into organic balance by throwing off compulsions, constraints, automatisms. No one else has spoken of the moral life with fewer negations or with so many positive expressions of power and joy. His mission was not to govern men but to release them. The new doctrine would round out and fulfill the work of the law and the prophets, not leave it completely behind. This connection with the past did not save Christianity from the perils of mere apocalyptic futurism, but it showed that Jesus rejected the current impulse to break loose entirely.

There was work to do, and Jesus set about it. Inevitably he drew to him a band of disciples, for the most part plain, unlearned men; people incapable of protecting themselves by book-learning from the shock of fresh ideas and from the emotional impact of a great example. What they were capable of assimilating, mankind itself would be ripe for. Unlike the philosophers who taught initiates and students they had brought to a certain intellectual level, Jesus addressed the poor and the ignorant: he thus overcame the class limitations that had narrowed the province of philosophy and limited the political effectiveness of a Socrates, a Plato, a Zeno.

Like a guide to the hill passes, Jesus took shortcuts across the untraversible mountains of class pride, intellectual arrogance, and professional specialization. In his philosophy, the dialectical wisdom of Aristotle might not lead one as close to the core of life as the innocence of a little child. He devalued the inflated currency of the intellect. Faith in the realities of life and spirit made the great and the humble stand on the same level. This was a shocking assumption to those who had paid dearly for wealth, knowledge, position: Were all their efforts then worthless? Were the poor and the ignorant their equals?

Jesus's most venomous opposition came from conservative groups in the synagogue: not from the indifferent, but from the strict, not from the backsliders, but from those who knew the law and fulfilled it to the letter, proud that they were more virtuous than their neighbors: men who clung to the moral laws and sanitary regulations of Moses, who followed the noble duties of the Pharisees. These opponents of Jesus were proud, justly proud, of their great heritage. Jewish morals, Jewish hygiene, were both close to the order of nature: Judaism had long been uncontaminated by supernaturalism, and until it was infected by the death of neighboring cultures, it harbored few phantoms: its God operated in history, and its invisible world was truly invisible, the kingdom of the ideal, continuous with the domain of nature and inherent in the plan of nature.

Now, in Jesus, a rival to Moses appeared. With a sure instinct for attack, Jesus singled out the strong elements in Jewish culture as a point for his radical departures: he broke the Sabbath openly to stay his hunger: man did not exist for the Sabbath but the Sabbath for man. The periodic day of rest was the very citadel of the Jewish vital economy: perhaps, as Sudhoff, the medical historian, remarks, its greatest contribution to health. When Jesus challenged the sacredness of this good custom, the currents of life were indeed rising: the day of fossilized virtue was over. For Jesus, the Pharisees were "actors": that was the word he used. Such people played a part: their actions were therefore never adapted to life's surprising demands. They treated life as a set piece, and so denied it.

If Moses was the moralist, the hygienist, the organizer, Jesus was the mystic and the psychologist. The first worked on the mind through the body, and on the person through the community. The second reversed this process: the divine in man must be nourished if every other law and duty be pushed aside; and the divine was that which furthered the processes of growth and made it possible for man to slough off his dead selves, as the snake sloughs off its skin. Jesus saw that no wider, stricter observance of law could recover for life the freedom and energy it had lost in the very perfection of human institutions: in his view, goodness could obstruct life no less than wickedness, and without a perpetual challenge would undoubtedly do so. Among modern poets and philosophers, Emerson, Whitman, and Bergson come closest to sharing this philosophy.

What was needed was a radical change in attitude: an assertion of the primacy of the person, and a shift from outer circumstances to inner values. Adultery, therefore, did not consist simply in going to bed with another man's wife: that was only its most obvious form. He that looked on a woman to lust after her had already committed adultery in his heart; and a sensitive judgment would be more concerned with the concealed impulse than the open accomplishment, for it might be more obstructive to growth. Though comfort for the poor and the lowly was an essential part of Jesus's creed, he outraged his disciples by sweetly accepting the perfumed oil that was poured upon his head: oil that was bought with money which, they indignantly urged, might have been spent upon the poor. But Jesus pointed out that the woman who had anointed him had been prompted by love: her impulse was sacred. To obey that impulse was more important than to be concerned with food or clothes— even the food and clothes of the poor. For love was the highest manifestation of life. Why should the poor be fed if love were allowed to disappear from the world?

With Jesus, the possibilities of love were no longer confined to friends and lovers, to members of one's family or one's tribe: the love of God and the love of one's neighbor were equally imperative. To love well was to participate in a life that went beyond one's immediate animal need for self-preservation: for he who lost his self would find it, and he who gave up everything, as passionate lovers do for the beloved or as parents do for their children, would find himself the member of a wider society which would offset his abnegations and renunciations.

The great empires of the ancient world, Babylonia, Persia, Macedonia, Rome, had tried to build a universal state on the basis of power and law alone: Jesus sought to found a wider community on the basis of love and grace. Power meant the capacity to appropriate, to possess, to dominate; love meant the capacity to share, to renounce, to sacrifice. Jesus was indifferent to the need to bring these two efforts together; and he bequeathed the problem to the Christian Church, which failed at the height of its own powers by losing sight of Jesus's example.

There is more than one fashion of interpreting Jesus's doctrine of Eternal Life, which runs through the Gospels. A hopeless society, blocked in every effort at worldly security and satisfaction, would emphasize immortality and eternity as the most important promise of the Christian faith: life *eternal*. But it is equally consistent to interpret Jesus's words in a humanistic and naturalistic sense: *life* eternal: "Thy will be done on *earth*." In this fashion, Jesus renewed the vision of Isaiah.

The Greek philosophers had praised temperance, courage, prudence, and wisdom: they had sought to discipline the flesh and fortify rational judgment: but even when, in the doctrines of Plato, love sought beauty and perfection, no longer mere physical possession, its province remained limited: it was never strong enough to unite the Greek and the Barbarian even so that the polis itself might be saved, still less was it capable of uniting them for the Barbarian's benefit. Jesus gave love a social mission and a political province. Who was one's neighbor? Anyone who needed one's help. The parable of the Good Samaritan is a condemnation of every form of isolationism.

This was a simple doctrine, backed by simple demonstrations. While

the accounts of some of Jesus's miracles are incredible if one judges them
by their actual contents, most of them are consistent with his whole vision
of life if one judges them by their direction and intention. The restoration
of sight to the blind, of speech to the dumb, of the use of their legs to
the crippled: the casting out of neurotic 'devils' and the return to sanity
—always the end of the miracle is normal health, and the ability to go on
living. Those whom Jesus converted to his faith did not receive any superhuman powers: they were not endowed with an insight into the future or
with a detailed remembrance of the past: the feats of astrology or clairvoyance were not for them. Nor were they gifted with a special knowledge of
the physical world which would mock the science of Alexandria: they
cannot make the sun stand still or behold the beauty of Helen of Troy.
Dr. Faust would have turned away from Jesus unsatisfied—to conclude
his bargain with Mephistopheles.

The upshot of Jesus's typical miracles is that the patient becomes
whole again: *life goes on*. The return to life was not postponed until the
Resurrection Day. The very simplicity of Jesus's performances as a whole
carries conviction: indeed, it is fairly easy to distinguish miracles that
are consistent with his own vision and our own knowledge of psychotherapy from those that plainly reflect the cheap magic understood by
Jesus's too credulous followers, who sought to turn a prophet into a mere
wonder-working charlatan. Jesus's healing of the sick showed a vital insight into the unconscious: the possessor of those powers did indeed
know something about the mystery of the soul that even Socrates' *daimon*
never plumbed.

When one turns from Jesus's demonstrations to his words, the trans-
parent meaning of his acts disappears. One is confronted by paradoxical
truths, gnomic insights, homely parables that sometimes shock one by
their crass acceptance of unjust conventions, figures that lend themselves
to either a natural or a supernatural explanation, mysteries that seem
like mystifications. But Jesus is hardly responsible for the confused state
of the record: the tale of his life was long carried by word of mouth,
probably for more than a generation, before the first written record was
made. Some of those closest to him, like Paul, deliberately turned away
from the image of Jesus, the man, in order to worship with unrestricted
abandon the crucified God, a being born of the worshiper's own desperate
needs and ambivalent desires. In the course of time, much that was
precious would disappear, and not a little that was rubbish would be
added. But above the confused murmurs of the witnesses, Mark, Matthew,
and Luke, rises Jesus's life itself: it reveals a consistent purpose and an
inner unity: the mark of a real personality and not, as Mani later asserted,
of a wraith.

The very heart of Jesus's faith, Matthew Arnold pointed out, is in-
communicable in words: his "secret." To unlock this secret fully, one
must have beheld the light in the master's eyes; one must have interpreted

the enigmatic smile that surely hovered on his lips; for there is both an agility and a power of penetration in Jesus's sayings that were, one feels, but lamely passed on by his disciples. Is it any wonder that, all too soon, they sought to turn him into a more familiar figure: a magician, a sacrificial scapegoat, an Orphic initiator, a redeemer, a Messiah: that step by step they interpreted his vision of eternal life, life forever self-renewing and self-transcending, as a mere promise of golden glitter in a changeless heaven: that they transformed into a God a prophet who, on their own testimony, said he was not God. ("Why call ye me good? Only God is good.")

Jesus's acts all affirm natural life; and for him the Kingdom of Heaven did not await death and eternity but might open before the awakened soul at any moment. He declared that natural life might rise above its animal foundations: that man indeed must pass beyond his creaturely limitations if he is to enter into *his* natural kingdom. He aimed at simplicity, spontaneity, integrity, freedom: these were the conditions for man's growth and his perpetual rejuvenation, conditions which Goethe was to declare the special property of the man of genius, but which the Son of Man sought to pass on to all the Sons of Men. The civic obligations of Rome, the moral code of Jerusalem, the astronomical lore of the Chaldeans, and the art of the Greeks were all as nothing to him: his mission was to cut under every institution, every habit, every purpose, even those that were avowedly good. Was it not a failure of love that was responsible for man's self-love, out of which grew his indifference to the welfare of the poor and humble, that is, to the mass of humanity? On all minor reforms, he had nothing to say.

"John," Jesus sardonically observed, "came neither eating nor drinking, and they say, He hath a devil. The Son of Man came eating and drinking, and they say, Behold a man gluttonous and a wine-bibber, a friend of publicans and sinners. But wisdom is justified of her children."

Wisdom was indeed justified. Jesus undermined the knowledge of the learned, the pride of the powerful, the morals of the virtuous: he saw that sin and imperfection, with their self-humiliation and self-criticism, were far less dangerous to life than complacency; for sin might pave the way for an inward change which raised life to a higher pitch than unblemished virtue was capable of reaching. This inward change, the grace of the holy spirit as it was to be called, was all important: repentance must precede regeneration. Mere willing, mere rational efforts in themselves, could not bring about such a change: it needed the encouraging example of a living image, and that image was the personality of Jesus himself.

The effect of Jesus's doctrine, boldly set forth in the Sermon on the Mount, was to give strength to the humble and the weak, and to make the principle of yielding stronger than the principle of domination: a complete reversal of values. Man's weakness, for the fifth century Greeks, came from his ignorance. Jesus's position was just the opposite of this;

but he did not make the fatal error of dissolving the very idea of virtue, like the Skeptics. In the scribes and the Pharisees Jesus beheld the danger of a premature crystallization: the personality might be handicapped by the very qualities it had sought so painfully to achieve. To know oneself, from his standpoint, was to realize the miserable failure of one's successes and the redeeming success of one's failures. The capacity to recognize one's inevitable shortcomings, to profit by every occasion of disintegration, was the only guarantee of continued self-development. That was a salutary doctrine for the heirs of a disintegrating civilization.

Jesus's transvaluations were a permanent contribution to all moral doctrine. Naturally, this challenge affronted the more respectable members of the community: for the very condition of the proletariat gave them a better chance of entering the Kingdom of Heaven than the rich.

In sum, virtue could not be accumulated: the prudent investor of moral capital might find himself bankrupt overnight and the spendthrift might by a last moment's repentance find himself possessed of riches. This seems a perversion of both psychological experience and natural justice: but there is an aspect of both personality and community for which it has real meaning. Jesus came into a society encrusted with venerable superstitions and slavish usages: afflicted with pieties that had become profanities, with knowledge that stifled curiosity: a society choked by the debris of ancient cultures, threatened by those very processes of accumulation which ordered production and government make possible. The simplification of life was the very essence of salvation in such a society: the first and the last, the poor and the rich, the earlier and the later, the wise and the foolish, the saint and the sinner must all start from scratch: were they not all Sons of Men?

Every word and act of Jesus can be interpreted as an attempt to disinter the corpse of man: to raise the dead. Ceremonies, books, forms, rituals, prayers, duties, administrative regulations, laws, might all seem good in themselves, because goodness had once passed that way; but nothing was good for Jesus unless it furthered life in its perpetual process of self-transcendence and self-liberation. Or as Emerson put it: "Life only avails, not the having lived." So the Child, with its multiple potentialities for growth, is the true symbol of this doctrine. One must throw away one's accumulation of riches and learning and become poor again, poor as a beggar, innocent as a child. Old, indeed, is the belief that the good man must disencumber himself of material possessions; but Jesus, like Lao-tse, applied this injunction equally to immaterial possessions. For him it was necessary to redeem knowledge from limitations no less deadly than stubborn ignorance, and to chastise the law-abiding, no less than the more obvious criminals. The price of life was a willingness to wipe out all one's precious accumulations and begin all over again, whenever they got in the way. The virtue of the pioneer.

When Jesus's followers came to interpret his message in the patristic age, they sought a too-easy shortcut. If one must become as a little child again, was not ignorance itself then a virtue, almost a passport to heaven? If mercy and love stand above political justice, why go through the forms of political justice or bother about whether they are good or bad? And why cultivate mathematical or astronomical knowledge, if it leads to pride of learning and hardness of heart? To hold to such simplism is to mistake the true provenance of Jesus's ideas. His truths were *especially* valid for those who gave themselves to the study of science or the execution of justice: they provided a corrective to institutions Jesus otherwise did not care to challenge. In time, unfortunately, Christian virtue became a cloak for political irresponsibility, for scientific know-nothingness, and for self-righteous indifference to the humane pursuit of literature, philosophy, and art.

Jesus himself cannot perhaps escape some blame for this miscarriage: he left a gap which the Church took many centuries to close up. What was lacking in his creed was what was lacking in his native environment, the back country, far from the big cities with their art and learning; when Jesus entered Jerusalem he entered it as an enemy, deliberately scorning its ways. He did not say: I was ignorant and ye taught me, or I was cast down in spirit and ye revived me with the sound of the harp and the tabor: the joy of Solomon and the joy of David find no echo in his spirit. The great prophet of the soul left out of his mission the traditional food of the soul. Music, poesy, painting, philosophy, science, counted nought for the salvation of man. It was to life at the humblest level that Jesus appealed; and he cast out of his reckoning the great sin of all class cultures, that they deny the common man the economic support and the leisure needed to partake of man's highest goods. His was a gospel not so much of renunciation as of etherealization. When the spirit was truly alive, it could throw away all canes and crutches, and dance.

The same judgment applies to Jesus's indifference to political improvements. The easy explanation in both cases is that the current apocalyptic conviction of doom was shared by Jesus himself: if the heavens were soon to fall, what difference did it make if the arts prospered or if justice prevailed? On this matter, Renan's criticism is certainly well-taken: "To establish as a principle that we must recognize the legitimacy of power by the inscription on its coins, to proclaim that the perfect man pays tribute with scorn and without question, was to destroy republicanism in the ancient form and to favor all tyranny. Christianity, in this sense, has contributed much to weaken the sense of duty of the citizen, and to deliver the world into the absolute power of existing circumstances."

So much must be said in negation; but there is another side to the matter. The essential originality of Jesus's example can be better grasped if one realizes that the person is an emergent from society, in the same fashion that the human species is an emergent from the animal world. The expression of personality both includes the facts of community and transcends them. While the person is dependent upon the community, in the same fashion that the organism itself is dependent upon the material it absorbs from nature, one cannot fully describe the person merely in terms of its social relationships: a radical qualitative change takes place at each ascending grade in emergence. The very concept of the person was once the exclusive property of the ruler and his intimate circle: in Egypt immortality was first reserved for them alone. The gradual building up of personality and its extension in theory to every member of the community was the great contribution of the Axial prophets and redeemers: a process that reached a new plateau in Christianity. Lloyd Morgan's doctrine of emergent evolution has sociological as well as metaphysical significance.

Jesus's insights apply only to the higher realm. In his new dispensation, for example, "to him that hath shall be given and from him that hath not shall be taken even that which he hath." Applied to political society such a conception would be monstrous: a vicious miscarriage of justice. But it was not meant for society: that should be equally plain. In the realm of personality it reveals a truth in the very order of nature: it is the truth of habit, that every good act makes goodness easier and every bad act makes badness more incorrigible; it is the truth of knowledge, that those who have labored diligently acquire more than they have bargained for, while those who shirk become the victims of their own lack; it is the truth lovers know: that he who gives most receives most, and that he who withholds becomes empty.

Social equity is based on another principle, the principle of even interchange and common advantage: self-interest, not self-abandoned love. But in the personality this higher law cannot be evaded; and Jesus's special insights are applicable to all persons, even in the most perfect human societies, working under the most exemplary conditions. Hence the difficulty of applying the moral truths of Jesus to a community: so difficult that the wise Mary Boole once suggested that no officer of the State should ever countenance the belief that, as officer, he was or could be a Christian.

Actually, Jesus's truths seek to transcend the inevitable limitations of even the best corporate order: the new dispensation does not deny the need for the old dispensation, but applies to a realm it does not touch, the realm of the person. The failure to understand this fact is the great limitation of Quakerism, otherwise so close to the spirit of Jesus: in their attitude toward the Nazis, for example, many members of the Society of Friends have failed to see that Christian charity is a corrective of justice, not a substitute for it.

The social message of Jesus therefore remains ambiguous; but the personal injunctions are clear. "Do good and lend, hoping for nothing; and your reward shall be great." That sentence of Jesus, which parallels a similar one in the Bhagavad-Gita, placed conduct on a superior level. Its ultimate word was a paradox: he that loseth his life shall find it. When Jesus's transpositions were finished all the negative elements in life were on the positive side of the equation and had changed their sign: death in all its forms, vice, disease, ignorance, paralysis, had been used as a condition for a fuller and richer life. No part of existence was indifferent to spirit or untouched by it. Not merely water but poison was transmuted into wine.

Jesus's life was a brief one, consummated in loneliness, betrayal, and torture. His personality moves across the stage of history in a few swift gleams and flashes, tantalizing in their incompleteness; and his figure is muffled by the opaque bodies that surrounded him. He is fated to be betrayed for a few pieces of silver by Judas and to be denounced by the people he came to save: he sees that fate as his end approaches and the acceptance of it exalts him. The man who is nailed to the cross on the Mount of Calvary is the incarnation of humility, love, and sacrifice: humility proudly worn, love lifted into a kinship with all humanity, death made the willing utterance of life itself: a complete affirmation of man's condition, his freedom and his end.

The tragedy of Jesus rises to a swift climax. The epilogue, as told in the Gospels, lacks the austerity, the white illumination, the decisive gesture and the telling word, that mark the more visible acts of this personality. The breath has scarcely left Jesus's body before he becomes enshrouded in myth. Jesus, the man, passes out of the picture: in his place is the God foretold in prophecy and celebrated in a score of pagan cults. Karl Marx once said of himself that he was not a Marxist; and of Jesus one may say, without irreverence, that he was not a Christian. For little men, who guarded Jesus' memory, took him, drained off the precious life blood of his spirit, mummified his body, and wrapped what was left in many foreign wrappings: over these remains they proceeded to erect a gigantic tomb. That tomb was the Christian Church. The figure it holds is both greater and less than the man who walked and talked by the shores of Galilee: more indisputably a traditional god, more doubtfully an illumined man. But which figure points to the more miraculous historic fulfillment? I have no hesitation in saying—the man.

(1944)

CHAPTER ELEVEN

Augustine: Salvation
by Retreat

Toward the end of the fourth century A.D. the Roman world lay dying. Death was in the air: never more visible than when the old Roman families painfully pretended to keep alive their ancient ways, as though by rouging the face of a corpse they could bring it back to life. The letters that these families exchanged, their pious excursions into archaeology, their allusions to Cicero and even Plato, had become purely decorative: a senile grimace before a cracked mirror. Death was in the air, though the Column of Trajan still towered upward in the sunlight of the Forum and the crowds in the Hippodrome still roared with pleasure.

The specters people fancied they witnessed with their eyes were only too real: they were the projections of their tortured souls. But those whose souls were dead still saw nothing, and therefore had no premonition of the terrible changes that were in store.

Between Tertullian at the beginning of the third century and Cyprian scarcely more than a generation later, there had come a sharp change in the political climate. Tertullian still boasted of the increase of Rome's population and wealth; Cyprian asserted, on the contrary, that Rome was dying of iniquity and the disorders of old age. Events presently confirmed the darker intuition. After all, a predatory economy cannot last forever. The very success of the *Pax Romana* actually cut down the number of slaves who came to market. Meanwhile the forests around the Mediterranean and the Adriatic had been mined, because wood was used for fuel on a large scale as well as for building: long ago George Perkins Marsh, in 'Man and Nature,' pointed out the effect of the ensuing soil erosion on classic agriculture. Swamps, no longer drained, formed a breeding ground for the mosquito, carrier of malaria.

Overburdened by their debts, the independent farmers who had once made Rome great turned their bodies over to their creditors, or sought relief by serving as colonni or serfs on the big estates: they bartered freedom for security. Desperate peasants, hopeless of getting a living off the soil, wandered around Gaul in the fourth century, Spain in the fifth century. Roman manorialism, brutal as ever, over-reached itself: Salvianus mentions that many poor peasants preferred to migrate to the domains of a Gothic chief, rather than stay on those of a Roman proprietor: the outlander was more humane.

The predatory economy of Rome no longer had either the self-confidence or the discipline to extend its conquests. Parasitism had continued steadily to eat into the Roman vitals: the blind vulture could neither seize new prey nor remove the maggots that battened on its own body. The very people who profited most from this culture were the first to evade its obligations: the patricians turned over to the conquered peoples the task of guarding the Empire; and their private affairs, particularly their private amusements, engrossed them more than their public duties. In an attempt to maintain some sort of order and public discipline, the late Empire fell back on the hereditary principle: every son must follow the calling of his father: no man might desert his hereditary post. All in vain, the very class that promoted these laws was the worst offender against them.

As early as the third century the new barbarian incursions had produced a marked effect on the character of the towns. In the days of the *Pax Romana* they were built in the open, without the protection of walls, except perhaps in the border districts. Now they were surrounded by ramparts; each town became a fortress, capable of isolated self-defense even if the army failed them. When the population crowded in for protection, space was lacking and over-building took place. Up to this time the aristocracy had enjoyed both their urban homes and their rural villas. Now the patricians retreated permanently to the country. When Arcadius, in 396, sought to forbid "the impious exodus to the country" he was talking to the empty air. The exodus had taken place. Eventually the cities began to suffer from depopulation; and one of the first signs of this, on the testimony of Libanius, was the cutting down of the salaries of professors at the municipal universities.

As life worsened, people deserted their posts and slipped out of their remaining duties: every man for himself: *Sauve qui peut!* In the years between 396 and 412, Honorius issued nine edicts on desertion and concealment of deserters from the army, according to Dill. Even the guilds that supplied food to Rome tried to escape their hereditary tasks. Everyone aimed at security: no one accepted responsibility.

Mark the fact that there was at first no lapse in technical facilities. The great engineering works were of a stable nature, with small need for repair and replacement; indeed, there were large-scale expenditures for public works in the fourth century, and the visible show of temples, baths, municipal universities, and monuments was never grander than in the early period of the decline. Even the Roman state postal organization, according to Dopsch, was still operating in the Kingdom of Toulouse as late as the seventh century. What was plainly lacking, long before the barbarian invasions had done their work, long before economic dislocations became serious, was an inner go. Rome's life was now an imitation of life: a mere holding on. Security was the watchword—as if life knew any other stability than through constant change, or any form of security except through a constant willingness to take risks.

In the face of this steady deterioration and regression, the Roman's belief in the "Roman way of life," the optimism of the self-centered upper classes, remained incorrigible. There would always be a Rome and the patricians would always be on top. So they said and so they thought. Rutilius Namatianus, who had witnessed the sack of Rome in 410, observed that the disaster might have been worse; at all events, the Empire would recover. Orosius, a contemporary Christian apologist, was no less sanguine: were not the plundering Goths after all fellow Christians? Indeed, the rumor that the barbarians had spared Christians in Rome accounted for a large-scale conversion of the indifferent to Christianity.

Meanwhile, at short intervals, the old landmarks fell. The blows of the barbarian conquerors only hastened the inner decay. The last Olympic Games—first instituted in 776 B.C.—were held in 394 A.D. Soon after 404 the Flavian amphitheater in Rome was closed to gladiatorial combats. Water ceased to flow in the baths of Caracalla after 537; and the last cartload of wood for heating the water had made its way into the city many years before. Even in the Eastern Empire, where the fossilization of Graeco-Roman culture checked for almost a thousand years the final processes of decay, the School of Athens was closed in 529 and the remaining philosophers were driven to Persia. One by one the old classic lamps went out; one by one the new tapers of the Church were lighted.

Naturally, a pinched, day-to-day existence continued. Patches of the old culture still survived in Gaul or the toe of Italy for many centuries. In the country manors there were even signs that might be taken for a genuine revival: Venantius Fortunatus, describing the smoke of villas arising among the pine woods and the olives, observed that, as in the century before, the great lords were restoring their country estates with new baths, stately porticoes, and fountains.

Four centuries of political tyranny, military negligence, economic rapine, and helpless ideological dissolution had preceded the symbolic Fall of Rome: four centuries more were necessary before its institutions had definitely changed their sign. These were not the dark but the dwindling ages. The scattered fragments of the Western Empire were like a needy genteel family trying to live on its capital. No matter how it scrimps, every year finds it poorer.

In Byzantium, the old life held its own in a fantastic combination with the new Christian forms. One can tell from the sensual melancholy of the faces in the Byzantine mosaics that one is witnessing an exquisite corruption in which extreme sophistication blends with extreme naïveté. But the great Code of Justinian and the Greek Anthology were the monuments of a non-renewing creativity. For the life of man, the continuation of the Eastern Empire proved less rewarding than the disruption of the Western Empire.

In Arabia, the Judaeo-Hellenistic-Syriac culture escaped the perils of retreat and fossilization: indeed in the seventh century it underwent a sudden renascence. The formative ideas of Magian culture, incarnated in Mahomet, made available fresh energies in art, politics, and thought: proof that the actual Christian avenue of escape was not the only exit available from this dying society. At first, the religion of Islam seemed so similar to the Christian that many contemporaries regarded it merely as a new heresy: it was here that the composite world culture of the earlier epoch finally took positive form. If one judged the relative merits of Islam and Christianity solely by their immediate political and cultural results, it should be plain that Islam proved far more effective in saving and re-invigorating this corrupt society than did Christianity. But in the long run, the Christian idolum covered a larger area of human life.

By the fifth century, life had become a swamp; through its oozy bottom a few springs gurgled into the mud. Christianity dammed the outlets and created a lake: the water no longer flowed but it deepened. In time, the reservoir rose sufficiently to create a head at the dam, which could be used for power and irrigation.

Some such figure was not indeed remote from Christian minds. "We often see water," observed Gregory of Nyssa, "contained in a pipe, bursting upward through this constraining force, which will not let it leak, and this in spite of its natural gravitation: in the same way the mind of man, enclosed in the compact channel of an habitual continence, and not having any side issues, will be raised by virtue of its natural powers of motion to an exalted love." *Not having any side issues:* there lay the secret. In this restraint, in this concentration of purpose, lay the motive power eventually for a new life. We have now to watch the cleansing waters at work, pouring through the Augean stable of classic civilization.

This transformation is most compactly symbolized by the life of Paulinus of Nola, a Roman born to the patriciate, possessing immense wealth, a senator and a cultivated poet, a governor of a province and Consul before he was thirty. Such a man inherited all that the surviving classic world could offer anyone. Suddenly he disappeared, and his friends' anxious letters to him remained unanswered. After four years of silence he at length replied to the entreaties of his old friend, Ausonius, the Bordeaux professor and poet. The letter came from Spain; but the voice it carried rose from the grave. Rome was already dead for Paulinus, as it was presently to become for the world. In his monastic refuge in Spain, Paulinus had found a different light, a higher glory: the light of eternity, the glory of God. Living on scanty fare, serving as parish priest, Paulinus devoted his great fortune to ransoming prisoners. When his fortune was gone, he sold himself into slavery to ransom a widow's son.

In that story, a whole epoch is reduced to a lifetime. There is only one way now to breast the incoming tide of misfortune, and that is to dive into the threatening wave before it breaks. In this mood, patricians became Christians and Christians became hermits and monks. We can witness the general transformation of life in two great Fathers of the Church: Jerome and Augustine: the older man, the translator of the Bible into Latin, the younger one, a diligent and voluminous author, known best for his 'Confessions' and for 'The City of God.' Augustine's personality left an impression on the Christian mind second only to Paul's; and because of the nature of his times and his personal crisis, he left behind a turbid sediment in both dogma and conduct: predestination and puritanism both acquired from Augustine a special impetus.

Augustine, a son of Numidia, was born in Tagaste: his mother, Monica, a Christian, his father a pagan. Like any other North African boy in the second half of the fourth century, he grew up in a world that was nominally Christian, but in which Christianity was still under a pagan sign, molded by the civilization it despised and opposed, every move on the chessboard determined by its opponent's original gambit. When Augustine came to write his 'Confessions,' he was shocked by the paganism of his boyhood: he recalled his father's easygoing attitude toward the human body and remembered with disapproval the older man's delight that day at the Baths when he first noticed the new growth of hair about the adolescent's genitals. Even in Rome girls married at fourteen at this period; and in the sultry atmosphere of an African town, sexual passion and carnal knowledge had every opportunity. Augustine's body ripened early; and despite his balkiness over learning Greek, his mind quickly followed.

In Augustine's works one still feels the tempered edge of almost a thousand years of Greek dialectic. But classic learning had now ceased to be organic and vivid: all its original perceptions had become dim, embellished with glosses that made it even dimmer. After Augustine became a lecturer and a teacher of rhetoric, he reached the high point in his secular career when he was called upon, in Milan, to deliver a public eulogy of the reigning emperor. Once an honest piece of Latin eloquence, in celebration of the great deeds of great men, the oration had now become as hollow as anything else in the Empire: Augustine's fulsome words sang the praises of a mere boy, a nincompoop, who had done nothing. On reflection, the clever young professor became nauseated over his self-betrayal.

Intellectual curiosity drew Augustine toward Manicheeism: perhaps its flagrant metaphysical dualism made it specially attractive to a young man whose mind flew to the ethereal realms of the neoplatonists while his body still inconveniently hankered after the flesh. Even when he had become a full-fledged Christian, Augustine continued, on his own sad admission, to be haunted in his dreams by unchaste delights. But Augustine was too healthy ever to share bat-eyed Plotinus's contempt for physical needs; and no one could have expressed himself in the hot, vibrant words that Augustine used to address God in his 'Confessions,' who had not known the yearning, the madness, the ecstasy of full-blown sexual love. Augustine's whole theology bears the visible scars of his battles with himself: he was no Paul. And the vein of morbid over-scrupulousness whicn Augustine reinforced in Christianity had its origin in his own self-chastisement: he never dared relax his grip, nor could he sit at ease in the company of publicans and sinners.

Augustine's conversion to Christianity had devious personal roots: not merely did it answer all his spiritual demands, but it enabled him to regain his mother: by embracing Christianity he became fully restored to her own aching bosom. In turn, he transferred his mother-fixation to the Church. But his conversion, for all that, was an heroic step for a man to take at the height of his sexual and intellectual powers: it called for a double renunciation. His ruthlessness toward his mistress, who was mother of his children, reveals the force demanded by the conquest: this separation was a black episode in his life which reveals both a lack of sympathy for her who had shared his life and a lack of self-understanding. No wonder that the books Augustine wrote in late maturity still throb with his earlier passions: even in translation one cannot help feeling the violence and tumult of his heart, pounding through the strong rhythms and transmuted into majestic rhetoric: the wild eye and the snorting nostril of the stallion in heat, on the other side of the fence that will forever separate him from his mare. Is it altogether an accident that evil, for Augustine, was no positive force, but a deprivation or absence of the good?

As one might uncharitably anticipate in a believer who began his life as a heretic, Augustine became the arch-opponent of heresy: the Donatists, the Pelagians, above all the Manichees, his own original tribe, were to fall before his impetuous attacks. Much of what we know about the doctrines of the Manichees comes from the treatise in which Augustine attacked them. From the end of the third century the Manichees stood forth as formidable rivals to the Christians. Their founder, Mani, accepted Christianity but considered Christ only a phantasm whose mission had been to proclaim the arrival of the real God, Mani himself: a Persian prophet who, daring too much, was finally executed.

Mani carried Persian dualism to its logical conclusion: he separated heaven completely from the world and the soul completely from the body. Everything that belonged to the earth was by that fact evil. Hence, according to Alexander of Nycopolis, "because (they believe) it is the divine will and decree that matter should perish, they abstain from those things which have life and feed on vegetation and everything which is void of sense. They abstain also from marriage and the rites of Venus, and the procreation of children."

At every point, the Manichees outbid the Christians in their contempt for the world, the flesh, and the devil: their standards of purity, at least for the elect, were absolute ones, and their habits of observance seem to have been steadier. What little evidence remains gives us ground for believing that many Manichees actually practiced what the Christians preached. But this is not to justify Augustine's original faith. For the Christians were saved by that part of their doctrine the Manichees most despised, the Old Testament, with its earthiness, dominated by a God whom the Manichees regarded as a devil. There was still enough of the organic Jewish vision left in Christianity for the most ascetic saint to remember that the earth is the Lord's and the fullness thereof. So Christianity remained on the side of natural existence: its Pauline rejection of the world was never complete, because through Jesus it had kept its connection, so to say, with the joyous House of David. When Augustine demonstrated that the sun, the very embodiment of light, was sometimes helpful to man and sometimes baneful, he triumphed over his Manicheean opponents by plain good sense: for he demonstrated that goodness and badness are not contrasting properties of the physical world, like light and dark, sky and earth, but become so by their relation to the human spirit. In itself, the body was not bad; in itself, the soul was not good; indeed, it might be devilish.

Augustine's theology had little of the mild epicene humanitarianism of Origen, who thought that all men would finally be saved: little of the intellectual hospitality of Clement of Alexandria. It was only by a steel bit that Augustine could control his own unbridled spirit; and he fashioned a similar bit to curb the laxer spirits in the Church. Not by accident did Augustine lead the fight against British Pelagius, who had declared it was possible for Christians to live without sin. Augustine had found life otherwise. Doubtless he was right; but only one who had been violently prompted to pride and lust would have recognized it so easily in the "innocent" behavior of an infant who had scarcely left its mother's breast. Augustine's interpretation of childhood was a different one from Jesus's: but Augustine was essentially, when one allows for differences of terminology, a forerunner of Freud—or to put it more correctly, Freud was an unwitting Augustinian.

For Augustine, man was a "rational soul with a mortal and earthly body in its service. Therefore he who loves his neighbor does good partly to the man's body and partly to his soul. What benefits the body is called medicine; what benefits the soul, discipline. Medicine here includes everything that either preserves or restores bodily health. It includes, therefore, not only what belongs to the art of medical men, properly so-called, but also food and drink, clothing and shelter, and every means of covering and protection to guard our bodies against injuries and mishaps from without as well as from within." In this fine passage, Augustine ably translated the classic Greek doctrines into Christian terms. And from this time on medicine was destined to play an increasing part in the ministrations of the Christian Church: hospitals for long remained exclusively under its wing, and the merciful care of the sick, particularly those afflicted with the most loathsome infections, like leprosy, remained one of the special acts of Christian zeal. The last great expansion of Christianity, fourteen hundred years later, came through Christian missionaries carrying medicine, surgery, hygiene into the jungles of Africa and the plague-ridden villages of the East.

Apart from such ministrations, Augustine despised knowledge about the physical world; for, he said, it led its devotees to think only under material images and to have no belief but that which the bodily senses imposed: moreover they were puffed up over their little learning, and failed to acknowledge the fullness of the universe, known only to divine wisdom. The main task of the Christian, therefore, was not to deal with science, politics, the worldly life: his task was to prepare for citizenship in the City of God.

Careless writers sometimes refer to 'The City of God' as if it were a utopia; but in fact, this book is just the opposite: an attempt to establish the proposition that, for the Christian, there is no hope for salvation in the State or in temporal society, because of the inherent character of the human condition. Augustine dwells at length on the histories of Greece and Rome to confirm his renunciation of the polis and his interest in an otherworldly state. What is hurtful, imperfect, unattainable, must be rejected if man is to find happiness; and all earthly things partake of these weaknesses, even the wisdom of the wise, which is lost by their death. Note Augustine's emphasis: it tells much about the actual state of life. "The chief good . . . must be something which cannot be lost against the will. For no one can feel confident regarding a good which he knows can be taken from him, although he wishes to keep it and cherish it. . . . How can he be happy while in such fear of losing it?" ('De Moribus Ecclesiae Catholicae.') That which alone can be loved and possessed must be above all earthly corruption: perfect, immutable, all-embracing, in short—God, "absolute being, that which is." To seek God is the only fair goal for an earthly life. Thus Augustine.

By one mode of emphasis, Augustine's doctrines would lead Christianity toward a mysticism that had no need for the Church: a direct communion, a flashing encounter with Deity, was possible for the truly chaste and regenerate soul. No intermediary could effect this grace of the Holy Spirit. That emphasis laid the groundwork for Luther.

But if man will never by mere political measures achieve a City of God on earth, there nevertheless remains on earth an institution that claims to transcend the limits of earthly existence through the very condition of its foundation: the Christian Church itself. Not only does the Church's history connect it directly with God, but its sacred offices identify it with God: in the sacrament of the Mass the priest actually makes God manifest in the transubstantiation of the bread and wine; and the representatives of God, the clergy, become the visible hands of the invisible Superior whose instructions they alone can properly interpret and carry out. That emphasis leads to unqualified authoritarianism. It puts the highest officers of the Church beyond human criticism and human judgment.

Pope and priest, bishop and saint, might be creatures liable to sin; but the Church, through its powers of absolution, was above sin: it possessed the keys to heaven. This was a dangerous doctrine to put into the hands of finite and fallible men. It still holds almost unlimited capacities for mischief.

There is one passage in 'The City of God' where Augustine distinguishes between the three possible kinds of life, the active, the contemplative and the mean between. In the spirit of the Greeks, Augustine insists on the mean: "One may not be so given to contemplation that he neglects the good of his neighbor; nor so far in love with action that he forgets divine speculation." But it followed from his doctrine of the highest good that the contemplative life was, after all, the ultimate choice for man: how else could one behold God? Augustine contrasts the lot of Martha and Mary: the first clings to the present, the second to the future: the first to the laborious, the second to the quiet: the first to the troublous, the second to the happy: Martha to the temporal, Mary to the eternal.

The *future,* the *quiet,* the *happy,* the *eternal*—these states had come to represent the highest condition of man. They were the final goals of human existence, for the sake of which people would gladly forfeit every other opening or opportunity. The past was a bucket of ashes; the present was the groan of a woman in travail bringing forth a dead baby. Augustine spoke of peace, repeatedly, as if it were an unconditioned and absolute good. In that error he recorded the exacerbated nerves of his generation and age. They wanted peace as a sick man driven frantic by the sound of a vacuum cleaner wants silence.

In treating peace as an absolute, Augustine went back on his own better judgment. For in a healthier mood, he had described the world's course as "like a fair poem, more gracious by antithetic figures": a dim reflection of Heraclitus's philosophy. But by now strife had become intolerable and world-weariness had become universal. Peace, even at the expense of truth and justice, was the indispensable attribute of salvation and its greatest reward. Augustine sounded the final retreat.

The days of the early Christian martyrs and saints were over. Now the persecuted would become the persecutors: woe to the heretic! woe to the unbeliever! But meanwhile a new type of martyrdom appeared, self-inflicted, chosen so as to make the mood of withdrawal prevail. Already the new life had carved a shape for itself at the edge of the Egyptian desert, beyond Thebes and Alexandria. Once man had demanded an Empire to give scope to his ambitions; now his confidence shrivels, and he is content to hollow a cradle in the sand. From that point in space the perimeter of his vision widens to infinity: from the pattern of those vacant days, he can draw a picture of eternity. Seeking holiness, above all seeking peace, the Christian finally built a self-contained life around the themes of rejection and death.

No longer does the eye focus on the middle distance: one sees either the dirt beneath one's feet, the offal, the worms, the crawling scorpions, or one beholds a heavenly radiance in the sky. All that lies between becomes unreal, or at least delusive. The avenues of the senses must be closed. Even indirect passages to worldly existence must be barred: it is only a little while before Gregory the Great will reproach Desiderius, Bishop of Vienne, because he has expounded grammar to certain friends. "Regard everything as poison," warns Jerome, "which bears within it the seed of sensual pleasure."

Fear and grief have their outlets in flight, withdrawal, cowering. In most animals these emotions lead the creature to take refuge in a hole, a cave, a thicket; frequently to reject food or animal comfort. Darkness and grief go together; for sunlight is a last affliction to those who mourn. One shuts one's eyes, one buries one's head in one's hands, draws curtains, goes abroad only at night, eats little and talks less. By making a purposive discipline of these instinctive reactions, the Christian gave them a social context and meaning. Is it strange that in the modern world those who have rejected strong emotions and fancied that life holds no humanly irreparable evils, have also lost all the primitive gestures of grief and have even thrown off the formal costume of mourning?

In withdrawing to a psychological tomb, the Christian treated himself to a second burial, reproducing a condition like that in the mother's womb, when life was in complete equilibrium and held nought beyond bare animation: silence, protection, and peace all recall that primal state of animal unity. If one is not strong enough to fight, one must be discreet enough to pass unnoticed: to lie still and sham death. Grief filled men's hearts everywhere during the long period of violence that broke out in the third century and reached its height, perhaps, in the ninth: grief at parting, grief at the brevity of life, grief over injuries to one's beloved ones, grief at the most terrible memory that haunts the refugee—the memory of happier days. It was Boëthius, himself a victim of arbitrary barbarian power, who first pronounced this kind of sorrow the worst of all, and later exiled Dante echoed him.

Algasia, a Christian lady living in Gaul, anxiously wrote to Jerome to find out what Christ meant by the terrible predictions reported in the Gospel according to Matthew: "Woe to them that are with child. . . . Pray that your flight be not in winter." She had reason to suspect that the day announced in the scripture was at hand. From the end of the fourth century on the odds against security and peace worsened; therefore security and peace were all that men desired, and they would cheerfully barter all the sweet vanities of the world to ensure the existence of even a patch of normal civil life. That would be heaven. Out of this situation issued monasticism.

Like almost everything else that came to a head then, monasticism had long been under way. What everyone felt in the fifth century the persecuted Jew had already experienced before Christ's coming: witness the Therapeutae, a Jewish sect described by Philo. "They divest themselves of their property, giving it to their relatives; then, laying aside all the cares of life, they abandon the city and take up their abode in the solitary fields and gardens, well-knowing that intercourse with persons of different character is not only unprofitable but injurious." As early as 250 A.D. the Decian persecutions had caused thousands of African Christians to seek refuge in the nearby deserts. The most famous of these early hermits was Anthony, who began to live alone on the outskirts of his village, and who kept moving further and further into the desert in order to remain alone till in 305 he reached the edge of the Red Sea.

With Pachomius, who was born in 297, an ordered routine for these withdrawn people began; and when in 386, Jerome retired to the monastery of Bethlehem, this way of life had already achieved a certain communal form and discipline. The new monastery was a House of Refuge, or, if you will, a prison. Did not Tertullian say: "The prison does the same service for the Christian which the desert did for the prophet"? The terms and the conditions were almost interchangeable: in either case, you not merely "are free from causes of offense, from temptation, from unholy reminiscence, but you are free from persecution, too."

Jerome has left us an excellent description of the primitive organization of the coenobites or monastic communities. They were divided like an army into squads of ten, with one member having authority over the other nine; and ten squads formed a hundred presided over by a single authority. They lived apart in cells, but met "after the ninth hour" to sing psalms and to read the scriptures. Inevitably there entered into this life a strain of selfish preoccupation. Jerome knew well both the outward and the inward difficulties of withdrawal.

"How often," he exclaimed, "when I was living in the desert . . . did I fancy myself among the pleasures of Rome. . . . Now, although in my fear of Hell I had consigned myself to this prison, where I had no companions but scorpions and wild beasts, I often found myself among bevies of girls. My face was pale and my frame chilled from fasting, yet my mind was throbbing with desire and the fires of lust kept bubbling before me when my flesh was as good as dead." The lion that was so often pictured at Saint Jerome's side in later paintings and drawings served as a symbol of his passions, seemingly tamed, but ready to spring.

Meanwhile, Jerome gave rational justification to another side of monasticism: its withdrawal from cities. For the new monastery developed as an essentially rural retreat. Once more Western man sought in a bucolic

Eden a foundation for a satisfactory life. Jerome's description is admirable.

"Seeing that we have journeyed much of our life through a troubled sea, and that our vessel has been in turn shaken by raging blasts and shattered upon treacherous reefs, let us, as soon as may be, make for the haven of rural quietude. There such country dainties as milk and household bread, and greens watered by our own hands, will supply us with coarse but harmless fare. So living, sleep will not call us away from prayer, nor satiety from reading. In summer, the shade of a tree will afford us privacy. In autumn, the quality of the air and the leaves strewn underfoot will invite us to stop and rest. In the springtime, the fields will be brightened with flowers, and our psalms will sound the sweeter for the twittering of the birds. When winter comes with its frost and snow, I shall not have to buy fuel, and whether I sleep or keep vigil, I shall be warmer than in town. . . . Let Rome keep to itself its noise and bustle, let the cruel shows of the arena go on, let the playgoers revel in the theaters."

Jerome wrote those words of parting in Rome in 385. Already, in anticipation, he had outlined the life of the early Middle Ages; he had painted a series of scenes for a Book of Hours, or a medieval calendar, following the routine of pious life through the seasons. In this little idyll he recalled Theocritus and leaped ahead to anticipate Rousseau. Much must be renounced before this life will be possible: "How can Horace go with the Psalter, Virgil with the Gospels, Cicero with the Apostle?" How, indeed, Saint Jerome? But if there is any rational form for living during the next six centuries, it is mainly in the monastery that one will find it. This walled retreat would rise from the landscape, as isolated as a fortified villa or a rock-dominating castle, those symbols and agents of a rising feudalism. Here the shattered armies of civilization nursed their wounds and gathered strength.

(1944)

CHAPTER TWELVE

Aquinas: Cathedrals and Scholasticism

The thirteenth century was an age of high energies and great constructive activities. Its two greatest collective products—the Gothic cathedral and scholastic philosophy—stand in strong opposition. The cathedral was an image of medieval society as a whole and expressed its utmost vitality. Scholastic philosophy was a reflection of the new super-ego. The first risked security for the sake of its own audacious self-fulfillment: the second courted stultification for the sake of finality.

The new type of church building actually flaunted its daring constructional logic: punctuated by thinning walls, made more spectacular by widening windows, the gigantic cathedrals of Notre Dame or Chartres thrust their weight into the upper air: their great towers or spires were lances thrown into the infinite. In the moment of breaking away from the stolid securities of Romanesque architecture, the builders of these cathedrals showed their confidence in the self-sustaining energies of their own community, using thrust and counter-thrust to raise higher the fanning vaults of the nave, sometimes enclosing and leaving untouched portions of the old building they lacked the patience to tear down or the respect to carry through to completion. The whole structure was in a state of dynamic tension. These builders weakened the dogma of the wall in order to lift it higher with the flying buttress of reason.

Sometimes the builder's faith over-reached itself and the whole structure would collapse before it was finished, like a pyramid of acrobats that tumbles to the ground before the last man succeeds in balancing himself on the topmost shoulders. Proverbially, these cathedrals remained unfinished in the generation that conceived them. Unique among architectural forms, the Gothic cathedral allowed for and incorporated the changes wrought by history: successive layers of time and culture were worked into the fabric without destroying the living unity: the towers of Westminster Abbey were raised by Wren only in the seventeenth century and great parts of Cologne and Ulm Cathedrals were not built until the nineteenth century. So the audacity of the medieval builder was mixed with humility: he left something to time, chance, fate.

In conception and in constructional daring, the Cathedral was the crystallization of a new spirit: its symbolism went much further than the formulated dogmas and the conscious reason of its age, for it embodied the conflicts, even the heresies, that were an integral part of the real community. By the fourteenth century the Romanesque catacomb had turned into a brilliant lantern: light poured into it by day through the wine-red and sapphire-blue windows, and every change in the sky, from morning to night, was recorded in altered light and color within. Fantastic shapes that brooded batlike in the upper air competed for the eye with stone sculptures nearer at hand: nestling birds, sprays of hawthorn and twining grape leaves, that seemed like nature trapped unawares in the rock, gave way to the attenuated shapes of noble men and women, saints and kings, symbols of wisdom, piety, or honor, gravely arrayed about the portals. The dream of the Middle Ages now became palpable in stone and glass and wood and iron.

Gargoyle and Virgin, flying buttress and glass wall, utilitarian organ loft and decorated choir stall, earth and sky, were thus wrought into a living unity. The Gothic cathedral was a true epitome of medieval life, inner and outer; for it possessed qualities that went far beyond the greatest rational formulations: above all, in its originality, its gift for improvisation, its readiness to accept tension and to welcome change. The Gothic cathedral came to sudden life in the thirteenth century and already, by the fifteenth, it was singing its swan song. But when one recalls the feeble mechanical energies commanded by medieval Europe, an age of limited manpower and even more limited horsepower, the Cathedral bears witness to a concentration of vitality and power that ranks with the greatest epochs in history.

In sum, the Cathedral was more than the stone Bible of mankind, as Victor Hugo was finally to call it; for it was likewise the Grand Encyclopedia: the sum of medieval knowledge as well as medieval faith. Indeed, this building became the solid core around which the acts and ceremonies of life were wound, as around an iron armature, in order to raise to higher tension the current of daily living. Polyphonic music now translated into sound the complicated visual music of the stones themselves. Each man had his part; each order, each class, had its part; every member of corporate society, from beggar to king, realized his own existence within an audible, visible, rational whole. Here medieval beauty, strength, sanctity, and science found their ultimate embodiment.

Scholastic philosophy was closely tied to cathedral-building; but it presented a direct contrast and sought to formulate a different kind of order: it was an attempt to find a comprehensive resolution of the intellectual conflicts of its day, and to give the unqualified dogmas of the Church the same kind of support that the physician, the lawyer, or the working artisan had in the practice of his profession or trade. This philosophy arose with the university: a guild of masters and students devoted to the orderly acquisition and extension of professional knowledge, in jurisprudence, medicine, theology. Differentiating itself from the Cathedral School, the university perfected its students in the technical arts of formulating ideas and establishing verbal proof. By its command of books and texts, the university established its intellectual authority, but it lost the discipline of active working life that the other forms of the guild retained. Even in medicine, Lanfranc complained, the masters of book knowledge would have nothing to do with operative surgery: a great loss. Nevertheless, the new corporate form of the university proved indispensable to the codification and transmission of the existing body of knowledge, and to its eventual extension.

In scholastic philosophy, the bold constructional logic of the Cathedral builders gave way to a formal logic which aimed above all at certainty and order. The scholastic philosophers quarried their stones from widely separated outcrops, from the Fathers of the Church, from the Arab philosophers, Avicenna and Averroës, from the broken stonepile of Greek philosophy, above all, from the dilapidated Alexandrian museum whose ground plan had been laid out by Aristotle. But in this new philosophy it was not faith and sheer animal vitality and rational experiment that created the great structure: the active element was predominantly reason, represented by Aristotelian dialectic and logic.

Scholasticism, if one may prolong the architectural figure, was not so much the finished Cathedral as the scantling of wood by means of which the actual work of building is made possible. It created little new knowledge; but it sought to make existing knowledge form an orderly and intelligible whole. Scholasticism soared to no heights of its own, but it endeavored to support those who were capable of soaring: Aquinas made Dante possible. In short, this philosophy was mainly a constructional device: hence its deliberate lack of beauty and outward grace, its harsh utilitarian outlines, its pedestrian pace. Scholasticism was a machine for sifting evidence, for collating authorities, for manufacturing proof. It attempted to make faith reasonable and reason faithful: thus it recorded the moment of conflict within the Christian Church when it was no longer enough to quiet reason by shutting one's eyes, or dispose of doubt by appealing to the very authority that was in fact doubted.

Like the work of the great Cathedral builders, scholastic philosophy was a new style of thought. Though in the ninth century it had an important precursor in John Scotus Erigena, it arose as a body in the twelfth century; and among the first of its great exponents was Abelard, whose faith in the divinity of logic brought him into a head-on collision with Bernard of Clairvaux, who sensed the danger of bringing revelation before the bar of formal proof. Abelard's treatise, 'Sic et Non,' placed side by side the contradictory statements contained in the Bible and the writings of the Church Fathers: if all these statements were revelation, which revelation should be chosen, since in reason they were conflicting and contradictory? Scholasticism was an ingenious attempt to reconcile these Yeses and Noes.

In the shabby boarding houses and garrets where the new university at first flourished, scores of ingenious minds worked to produce a stable synthesis out of these impossible contradictions. Within a century the schoolmen became one of the great props of the Church: the university with its wide international connections and presently even its traveling scholarships, did for the intellectual life what the preaching friars did for the emotional life of the community: it created a framework of belief and dogma in which coherence and intelligibility, founded on arbitrary postulates, temporarily did service for truth. Scholasticism stretched the Church's dogmas to their extreme limit, to make them do justice to the complexities of life. When the last gaping seam was sewed together, it became apparent that the fabric itself was threadbare and weak. . . .

Among the scholastic philosophers, great doctors arose: Duns Scotus, William of Occam, John of Salisbury, Hugo of Saint Victor, Vincent of Beauvais, Albertus Magnus, "the master of those that know," and his even greater pupil Thomas Aquinas. Logicians, moralists, political philosophers, these men sought to create a formal ideology that would include the reports of revelation, of authority, and of experience.

Let us examine Thomas Aquinas. It would not be true to suggest that scholastic philosophy, with its many divergent minds, realist and nominalist, platonist and aristotelian, could be characterized by the work of this single mind, any more than it would be fair to say that the Gothic cathedral is Salisbury or Bamberg or Rheims. But it would be true to say that if one possessed only the works of Thomas Aquinas one would have the soundest and best contribution of scholastic philosophy. While Aristotle was known as The Philosopher in the medieval schools, Aquinas has a better right to the title.

This resolute monk, nicknamed the Dumb Ox because he was slow and heavy, massive in bulk and no less massive in act, was one of the great formal thinkers of all time. But his greatness lies in his accomplishment as a whole, not in any single part of it. Certainly no one else could hold such a title with as little originality as Thomas Aquinas possessed. He was not a discoverer of new paths: not a daring mind that flew from peak to peak: his very value, on the contrary, lies in his resolute pedestrianism, in his refusal to admit any truth that has not been reached in a series of formal logical steps. His faithfulness to logic was like that of a prudent modern scientist to experimental demonstration. The mechanism of his proofs, in the 'Summa Theologica,' was undeviating: First, statement of the negative case: objections, 1, 2, 3; contrary statement, counter argument, answers to objections, 1, 2, 3—and final resolution. No step was omitted; no different apparatus of proof was erected in order to break the monotony.

Thomas Aquinas could have boasted with honesty that he had never ventured to utter a truth not long sanctified by reason, by experience, by the common sense of other men. In no derogatory sense, one may call him a master of platitude, provided one adds that in medieval culture some of the platitudes of Greece and Rome came forth from their ancient graves as breathless discoveries. Aquinas's thought was so impersonally conceived that it might have been a collective product: he was most himself when he was anonymous. His greatest gift was a gift of reasonable discrimination. He took the mixed-up, disordered, unevenly shaped fragments of human experience, and, as methodically as if he were putting together a jig-saw puzzle, he fitted the bits together so neatly that one might have thought he was reproducing the original picture and that he himself was the painter of it.

Aquinas's strength is that he seems to know all the answers, or at least knows where to look for them: his weakness lies in the fact that his questions do not bring under rational scrutiny either the method of his logic or the postulates of Christian theology. He trusts reason entirely, but only so long as reason remains in the natural world. Under his spell, one mistakes a plausible formal coherence for verified truth.

Yet when this great Dominican's work is taken as a whole, one cannot dispute the power of his mind or the sheer aggregate wealth of its operations: no one, except perhaps Aristotle, had ever taken in so much or had ordered his results with such thoroughness. Here is an astounding grasp of both the grand outlines and the minute details of human existence: of life divine and human, eternal and transitory, life domestic and life political, life actual and possible, life as the mystics behold it in rare moments of visionary ecstasy and life as men and women in every walk of life experience it, day by day. Here, perhaps, the secrets of the confessional, never before available to philosophers, were utilized with astonishing skill and unshakable poise: never again to be equaled till the Jesuits in the sixteenth century, or the Freudians in the twentieth, devote themselves to the further cure of souls. Here was a new kind of saint: one who took all knowledge for his province. In this mind, one measures the height of the Church's accomplishment; and in the 'Summa Theologica' one sees that mind at its fullest mastery.

The 'Summa Theologica' is not a book; it is not even an encyclopedia. One cannot treat it as a literary achievement in the degree that one might refer in this fashion to the work of Aristotle, who is a model for academic exposition: the 'Summa' is rather to be considered as a work of engineering, conceived on a cyclopean scale, by one of the ablest technical minds of any age. Roger Bacon, in the thirteenth century, dreamed of motor-driven carriages and airships; but Thomas Aquinas erected a fabric that had nothing to equal it in technical organization until the great textile mills of the nineteenth century were designed and built. Even works of engineering may show imagination and esthetic command; but those are the last qualities to look for in the 'Summa.' An immense textile factory, with a thousand looms, each bringing forth a uniform product—that is the closest image.

In the 'Summa,' one loom is like another: each uses the same warp, the same thread, the same shuttle: it is only the color and the pattern that differ. God, the angels, the principalities, the demons, the Holy Ghost, the saints, the Church, men and women, the secular and the theological virtues, the forms of law and government, the ordering of the economic life—each has a special loom, each loom its product, each bolt unrolls as part of an orderly plan. There are no surprises, once one understands the organization of the factory. An unexpected result would imply a defect in the machinery. Every part of this work is directed toward a single goal: life perfected in the sight of God, consummated in Eternity. This is man's last end; and the best words for it are perhaps to be found in a passage in Aquinas's 'Summa Contra Gentiles':

"Man's last end is the term of his natural appetite, or that when he has obtained it, he desires nothing more: because if he still has a movement toward something, he has not yet reached an end wherein to be at rest. Now this cannot happen in this life: since the more man understands the more is the desire to understand increased in him,—this being natural to man,—unless perhaps someone there is who understands all things, and in this life this never did nor can happen to anyone that was a mere man. . . . Happiness is the last end which man desires naturally. Consequently unless together with happiness he acquires a state of immobility, he is not yet happy, since his natural desire is not yet at rest. . . . Now in this life there is no sure stability. . . . Therefore man's ultimate happiness cannot be in this life."

In Thomism, the Catholic Church found a logical doctrine of evolution from nature to supernature: from the potentialities of this world of flux and change and imperfection to the actualities of complete realization in a state of rest and immobility in another world. This philosophy allowed for the fact of change within the temporal process: it accepted the imperfections and shortcomings of biography and history. But it transferred the ultimate meaning of life to an eternal realm in which the historic process was both consummated and rationally justified in terms that transcended mere human reason. Perhaps the best modern discussion of this essential Christian position is that in Dr. Reinhold Niebuhr's 'The Nature and Destiny of Man.'

Each part of the mechanism of argument and proof in the 'Summa' is devised for supporting the belief that the ultimate meaning of life lies not in any temporal process but in its eternal consummation: the realm where time, history, change, come to an end: where virtue is immobilized in bliss and where sin is finally also immobilized in damnation. Theology supplied the pre-designed end for this proof: Aristotelian logic furnished the method. One follows the argument in a series of articulated steps: if one accepts any particular chain of demonstration, it will be easy to follow with equal conviction all the rest, for they are established in the same fashion.

Only one proof is missing. Unfortunately, it is that on which every other part depends for both its function and its end: the proof of God's existence. Life is too short, Thomas observes, to make that possible. Lacking this ultimate authority, the philosopher contents himself with limited authorities, backed by divine revelation—a logical error since the truth of revelation remains that which is to be proved. This is a serious weakness in one who trusts logic itself so unreservedly. All Thomas Aquinas's care is devoted to the superstructure, and that, accordingly, is solid and tight: it is the foundations that remain shaky. When reason must appeal to authority, authority should remain open to reason. By accepting its special revelation as final, Christian dogma provided no means for revising its postulates and replacing its crumbled underpinnings.

Nevertheless, the weaving itself is a prodigious achievement: however monotonous the process of thought in this doctrinal textile mill, however dull the surface texture of the goods, the fabric itself, when it comes within the province of actual human experience, could hardly be sounder. What rests upon observation and common sense is truly seen and wisely pondered. For Thomas Aquinas had a supremely healthy mind; nothing daunted it; nothing surprised it; nothing could shake it from faith; nothing could upset its superb equilibrium.

Let us try out Thomas Aquinas at the point where the Church's original doctrines had been most opposite to man's common needs and his biological destiny: marriage in all its aspects. And to begin with, the status of the body. "Happiness," Thomas said properly, "does not consist in bodily good as its object, but bodily good can add a certain charm and perfection to happiness." That is not an isolated expression: Thomas's supernaturalism was based on an acceptance of nature itself and of man's place in the realm of nature, even as his acceptance of revelation was based on the use of reason wherever it did not contradict revelation. His understanding of nature made him quietly oppose the holy doctrine of denial. "Now just as in respect of his corporeal nature man naturally desires the pleasures of food and sex, so in respect of his soul, he desires to know something." Both desires, in Thomas Aquinas's eyes, are rational as long as they do not actively impede the practice of a holy life: being natural, frivolity and relaxation, in due measure, at the right time, can also be justified.

Berthold of Regensburg might condemn women's preoccupation with finery and their growing love of pleasure, but the Neapolitan philosopher uttered no unconditional reproof. "If a married woman adorn herself in order to please her husband, she can do this without sin" since this may be a way of keeping him from falling into adultery. Or again: "Whatever is contrary to the natural order is vicious. Now nature has introduced pleasure into the operations that are necessary for man's life. Wherefore the natural order requires that man should make use of these pleasures, in so far as they are necessary to man's well-being, as regards the preservation of either the individual or the species. Accordingly, if anyone were to reject pleasure to the extent of omitting things that are necessary for nature's preservation he would sin, as acting contrary to the order of nature. And this applies to the vice of insensibility."

Take a critical question in Christian marriage: "Whether it is a mortal sin for a man to have knowledge of his wife, with the intention not of a marriage good but merely of pleasure." In contrast to the present opinion of Rome, Thomas Aquinas boldly replies: "On the contrary . . . carnal intercourse of this kind is one of the daily sins for which we say Our Father. Now these are not mortal sins. Therefore, etc. . . . Further, it is no mortal sin to take food for mere pleasure. Therefore in like manner it is not a mortal sin for a man to use his wife merely to satisfy desire." By the same token, what is called in Thomas's quaint terminology the payment of the marital debt, that is, sexual intercourse, he treats as a remedy against "the wife's concupiscence. Now a physician who has the care of a sick person is bound to remedy the disease without being asked. Therefore the husband is bound to pay the debt to his wife although she ask not for it"—provided she give unmistakable indications of her desire. The analogy, like so many analogies that seemed plausible to the medieval mind, is plainly specious; but the common sense is excellent.

In Thomas Aquinas's very abundance of common sense, in his cool, straightforward logic, in his naturalistic open-mindedness, the Church plainly came to terms with the vitality it had once so severely opposed and thwarted: it no longer sought to dam up life altogether, but was content to direct it and to do so was willing to carve a wider channel for it. There lay a profound wisdom, which has enabled the Catholic Church to keep its benign grip on a vast body of believers down to our own time. But in that change, plainly, one fact stood out: the period of rejection was over and a period of dangerous consummations was at hand.

It would be a pleasure to watch Aquinas's great mind confront a thousand other problems and difficulties. While his feet trudged painfully over every foot of the ground, his eye never lost sight of the horizon and his path never deviated. Such a combination of powers is too rare to miss: his inclusiveness, his balance, his strong sense of justice, his wide variety of genuine interests, are to the last degree admirable.

As for his central vision of life, I cannot withhold here a passage that sums it up. "Now if we wish to assign an end to any whole, and to the parts of that whole, we shall find, firstly, that each and every part exists for the sake of its proper act, as the eye for the act of seeing; secondly, that less honorable parts exist for the more honorable, as the senses for the intellect, the lungs for the heart; and thirdly, that all parts are for the perfection of the whole, as the matter for the form, for the parts are, as it were, the matter of the whole. Furthermore, the whole man is on account of an extrinsic end, that end being the function of God. So, therefore, in the parts of the universe also every creature exists for its own proper act and perfection, and the less noble for the nobler, as those creatures that are less noble than man exist for the sake of man, whilst each and every creature exists for the perfection of the entire universe. Furthermore, the entire universe, with all its parts, is ordained toward God as the end, inasmuch as it imitates, as it were, and shadows forth the divine goodness, to the glory of God. Reasonable creatures, however, have in some special and higher manner God as their end, since they can attain to him by their own operations of knowing and loving him. Thus it is plain that the Divine Goodness is the end of all corporeal things." That philosophy wrought every part of life into a meaningful whole: an etherealized image of feudal gradations and papal unity.

Accordingly, it is the logician, not the man, who disappoints one: it is his theory of knowledge, his theory of meaning, his theory of the relation of symbols to experiences that are gravely at fault. His logical and grammatical order are very partial contributions to objective proof. Granted that postulates must be finally tested, not by any immediate self-verification, but by their adequacy in providing a basis for experimental and empirical proofs, there is such a thing as an economy of faith as well as an economy of hypotheses: if faith is incontinent, it will spawn figments and chimeras—and reason will then be impotent. Without faith in his senses and his symbolisms man cannot create a reasonable world: but one must not tax faith with camels when gnats are easier to swallow.

Thomas Aquinas sought to unite naturalistic observation with a supernatural cosmos that was on the point of disintegration. Hence it was not reason, but false prudence, that caused him to assert that "it is unlawful to hold that any false assertion is contained in the Gospel or in any canonical scripture." Could the truth itself be unlawful? Must revelation protect itself by the aid of the Father of Lies? Actually, a great part of Thomas Aquinas's work consisted in adroitly getting around the falsehoods and errors in canonical scriptures that were in contradiction to experience and reason. Therein lay many of his most substantial contributions: for he repaired the mischief wrought by Paul and rehabilitated the very philosophers to whom Christianity would indeed have been a stumbling block. To refuse to challenge the authority of Holy Writ because faith would be deprived of its absolute certitude was to pitch faith at the level of obstinate irrationality and to dishonor all true authority.

Faced with the need for choosing between experimental evidence and rational demonstration on one hand, and arbitrary authority on the other, Aquinas chose authority for purely pragmatic reasons: it greatly simplified his task and guaranteed his orthodoxy. He still needed the protecting walls of the Church, and in contrast to the Cathedral builders, he was unwilling to weaken the piers of dogma. Had he been altogether easy in this decision he might have spared himself much of his pains; but his uneasiness led to an elaborate comparison and selection of authorities. By intelligent acts of discrimination, by testing the Bible against Plato, the Church Fathers against Aristotle, the philosopher lessened the dangers of clinging to a single text and giving that finality. Unlike Augustine, he was far enough away from the Greek philosophers no longer to feel that they might pollute his faith. Aquinas's fresh contribution to Christian doctrine came through this deliberate introduction of rejected sources: above all, Aristotle. He thus escaped the error of later Protestants who again narrowed their intellectual heritage. Within its self-imposed limits, the 'Summa Theologica' was an effective synthesis of rational knowledge.

But note one curious neglect: the words of Jesus himself were relativly seldom invoked as authority. It is almost as if the Angelic Doctor understood that Jesus's doctrine of life as the manifestation and exaltation of love was the grain of radium that might disintegrate this complex scholastic structure. Perhaps his understanding of Jesus's simplifications came to him in the very course of writing his great 'Summa,' for he left it unfinished. According to legend, Thomas had had a vision, and from that time forth he wrote no more. Did he suddenly understand Jesus's secret? Did he remember that the only words Jesus wrote were written in the sand?

One final weakness. Like most other philosophers, Aquinas understood everything except the limits of philosophy: deeply though he accepted Christian faith, he did not realize that knowledge is not enough. What can be reasoned about, what can be ordered or fabricated, was here: what must be dumbly felt, passively experienced, intuitively revealed, what must be told in hints and parables, the truths that Plato himself would not commit to writing despite his command of language, truths that escape through the finest logical filter and are deformed if caught in the gauziest of philosophic nets—all that is left outside the 'Summa.' That itself only deepens the parallels with the textile mill: there are some Dacca cottons so fine that they must be spun by hand on the human knee and woven on the most primitive of handlooms. . . . Only Dante's vision can add the colors of life to Thomas Aquinas's severe fabric.

Wherever one may put the 'Summa,' its doctrines belong to the World as well as to Heaven. As such, it was an organic expression of medieval society, not merely as it meant to be but as it actually was. But this philosophy belongs to the world in its highest sense: it is an endeavor to re-think and rationalize all human experience, omitting nothing that is important for man's development, stressing everything that worked toward ultimate human happiness and human perfection. Who better than Aquinas had a firm sense of the structure of the community: who but he dared place justice and fortitude above temperance, for the reason that the good of man is more godlike than the good of the individual, wherefore the more a virtue regards the good of man, the better it is? (That was a long way from the concern for purely individual salvation, the *sauve qui peut* mood, of early Christianity.)

Aquinas was a realist in both the medieval and the modern sense of the word. In him, the urban-minded friars espoused the cause of corporate order and human solidarity against the individualism of the more rural monks. But if Thomas Aquinas set the social virtues high, he inevitably put prudence and the theological virtues, faith, hope, and charity, even higher. The entire structure mounts logically upward to God: at the topmost point, matter reaches into the immaterial, the natural world into the supernatural, and man's mastery into God's mystery.

At some critical points, I have already noted, the fabric of Aquinas's philosophy is composed of whole cloth, like the garment woven by the clever tailors in Hans Andersen's fairy story: the proof of the existence of angels can satisfy one no better than the proof that the body, when resurrected, will be thirty years old, because that is the most perfect stage in human life. But despite the gaps that are now so plainly visible in the cloth, the very will-to-unity was life-sustaining. By sheer technical ability, Aquinas accomplished a task that his nearest equals, Aristotle before him, Leibnitz, Kant, and Spencer after him, could not surpass. With good reason, Pope Leo XIII proclaimed it in 1879 the official philosophy of the Roman Catholic Church.

So closely, however, was Aquinas's synthesis an expression of his culture that, unlike the Cathedral, it did not point beyond itself or allow for further passages of time, thought, and experience. It was a closed synthesis: if it opened avenues to the past, it made the future a dead end. No further intellectual or spiritual development was possible within this tightly mortared structure. Medieval man was thus caught between a conceptual world that remained fixed, that seemed completed for eternity, and a practical world that was continually expanding the field of action and challenging the integrity of the synthesis by which he chose to live. His idolum had originally been fabricated to give him protection in a time of decay: it was now called upon to perform the contradictory task of providing a rational basis for action in a time of constructive change. The stout piles that had been used as a breakwater against the winter storms were of no use to those bent on building ships and traversing distant seas.

(1944)

CHAPTER THIRTEEN

Bacon: Science as Technology*

The title of this paper, 'Science as Technology,' would not have surprised or shocked Francis Bacon, for perhaps his most original contribution to the enlargement of the province of science was his understanding of its great future role in transforming the physical conditions of life. But I am sure that the conclusions that I shall finally present—conclusions in the form of doubts, challenges, and questions—would have shocked him quite as much as it will, I fear, shock many of those who are here this morning, for his faith in science as a source of technology, and in technology itself as the final justification of science must now, after four centuries, be submitted to an historic evaluation and the pragmatic test. When Bacon's assumptions are rigorously examined, this should, I submit, lead to a modification of Bacon's original hopes and even a radical change in our own attitude toward many Baconian beliefs we have, somewhat blindly, taken to be axiomatic.

Doubtless it is natural, in celebrating Bacon's anniversary, that we should out of piety overemphasize those aspects of modern civilization that have confirmed his predictions and surpassed his none-too-cautious expectations. This is particularly true when we consider science as technology, for it is precisely in this department that his most extravagant intuitions have been realized. Three centuries before Jules Verne and H. G. Wells, to say nothing of later writers of science fiction, Bacon anticipated the multifold uses that technology would make of science.

Though Bacon was undoubtedly expressing, as a sensitive artist often does, the changing temper of his age, long before it was visible in the streets, his very predictions gave confidence in the new orientation toward

---

* Read January 24, 1961, in the Conference on the Influence of Science upon Modern Culture, Commemorating the 400th Anniversary of the Birth of Francis Bacon, sponsored jointly by the American Philosophical Society and the University of Pennsylvania. For a fuller account of Bacon's philosophy—and his predictions in 'The New Atlantis'—see 'The Pentagon of Power.'

the physical world as the only area in life sufficiently detached from subjective fantasies and emotional urges to serve as a common meeting ground
for minds otherwise ideologically separated. Men who could not agree
upon the nature of God, could come to terms by making a god out of nature, once they had hit upon a method that ruled out all experience that
could not be experimentally repeated or independently verified. By following through the practical consequences of science, Bacon sought to show
even those who were engaged in the most abstract calculations and experiments that they might ultimately confer greater benefits upon the race than
those who were laboring to improve it by law, by morals, or by government, or who sought to change the environment solely by manual labor
and art.

Now the notion that the scientific observation of air, earth, water, and
fire might lead to fruitful applications in technology, must have occurred
to many minds, Archimedes for one, Hero of Alexandria for another, and
Bacon's medieval namesake for a third, before Francis Bacon himself
elaborated the idea. But Bacon helped mightily to close the gap between the
spheres of science and technology, one long considered liberal but exquisitely useless, except perhaps in medicine, the other, however useful, cursed
by its servile and debasing nature. Bacon held that the advancement of
knowledge depended upon more than the abstract, logic-disciplined exercises of mind. He felt that science in future would rest increasingly on a
collective organization, not just on the work of individuals of ability, operating under their own power; and he held, further, that instruments and
apparatus were as necessary in the technology of systematic thought as
they were in mining or bridge-building.

"The unassisted hand," observed Bacon, "and the understanding left to
itself possess little power." This was an even more revolutionary conception
than Leonardo da Vinci's aphorism: "Science is the captain, practice the
soldiers"; for it implied that the captain himself had something to learn
from the men in the ranks. And it was no less revolutionary, no less effective, because, from the standpoint of a mature scientific method it was, by
overcompensation, too one-sided. Bacon's very overemphasis on the collective apparatus of science, his close concern for the operational and instrumental aspects of scientific thought, were probably needed to overcome the
bias of traditional leisure-class culture, theological and humanistic, operating by choice in a social vacuum. That was a necessary contribution in his
own day—as necessary as the opposite position may become in our own
time.

The timeliness and significance of Bacon's contribution here should have
saved him from a little of the patronizing deflation that he has been subject
to in recent years. Without doubt, he was blandly indifferent to the actual
procedures of successful scientists in his own time, like Gilbert and Galileo;
and, further, it is no doubt true that Bacon grossly overestimated the fruit-

fulness of mere fact-collecting and fumbling empirical observation, though there are still areas where this kind of systematic preparatory effort yields a certain reward. By the same token, Bacon seriously underestimated, one might almost say he entirely ignored, the immense liberation that would be effected in both science and technics through the audacities of pure mathematics, dealing with possibilities and probabilities that are, until experimentally verified, outside the field of direct observation and sensory experience.

On his own terms Bacon could not and did not anticipate the sweeping transformations of the entire framework of thought effected by single minds, almost destitute of apparatus, like Newton, Clerk Maxwell, or Einstein. Even Galileo's scientific world, a world conceived solely in terms of primary qualities and measurable quantities, was almost unthinkable to Bacon. But to offset these disabilities, which plainly reduced Bacon's importance as a philosopher of science, he had a strong sense of the sociological context of science, and of the appeal that this would make to scientists, to inventors, to engineers, and to their countless human beneficiaries. He foresaw that science would become a corporate enterprise, subject to deliberate organization; and that the social goal of science, as he phrased it in the 'New Atlantis,' would be "the enlargement of the bounds of humane empire, to the effecting of all things possible."

Curiously, what is most fresh and original in Bacon, his conception of the role of science as the spiritual arm, so to speak, of technology, is the hardest part for our contemporaries to appreciate fully today. Partly they are put off by the fact that he absurdly arrayed these new conceptions in an elaborate metaphorical court dress; but even more they are alienated, or to speak more frankly, bored, because the ideas themselves have become so engrained in our life that most of us can hardly realize that they had a specific point of origin. But if Bacon failed miserably in interpreting the methodology of science, as it was actually taking shape in his own time, he leaped ahead four centuries to the mode and milieu in which science and technics both flourish, in their peculiar fashion, today. When Benjamin Franklin founded the American Philosophical Society, he felt it necessary to stress its aim of promoting "useful knowledge": but if he had been even closer to Bacon's spirit he would have realized that usefulness is implicit in every kind of scientific knowledge, almost it would seem in proportion to its degree of abstraction and its isolation from the immediate practical concerns. The singular mission of science, as a technological agent, is to suggest uses and outlets, issuing from purely theoretic and experimental discoveries, that could not have been conceived until the scientific work itself was done.

In the past, certain branches of science, like geometry, had developed out of practical needs, like the Egyptian need for surveying anew the boundaries that had been effaced in flooded fields; and some of that interplay between practical needs and scientific investigation of course still goes on, as in the classic instance of Pasteur's researches on ferments in response to the pleas of French wine growers. But the enormous advances of science in every field have not waited for such direct stimuli, though it may very well be that they are indirect responses organically connected with the needs and purposes of our society at a hundred different points. Thus, it is quite probably not by accident that the electronics of radar location have coincided with coordinate advances in the physics and technology of high-speed flight. Increasingly, however, it is the advance of science that suggests a new technological application: indeed the technological by-products seem to multiply in direct relation to the scope and freedom of scientific research.

Bacon's interest in the practical applications of science naturally endeared him to Macaulay and the other utilitarians of the nineteenth century, for in his 'Novum Organum' Bacon boldly asserted that the "legitimate goal of the sciences is the endowment of human life with new inventions and riches." This is a more questionable goal than Bacon thought: but it is because of the accelerated fulfillment of these promises by the sciences, especially during the last half-century, that national governments and great industrial corporations have vastly augmented their financial contributions to scientific research. Bacon's merit was to make plain that there was no aspect of nature that would not lend itself to transformation and improvement through the unrestricted application of the experimental method. Necessity had always been the most reluctant mother of invention: Bacon understood that curiosity was a far more fertile parent, and that the inventions so promoted would become the mother of new necessities.

But Bacon went further: he saw that curiosity, to be fully effective, must enlist, not solitary and occasional minds, but a corps of well-organized workers, each exercising a specialized function and operating in a restricted area. By the technological organization of science as he portrayed it in the 'New Atlantis,' he proposed to fabricate an engine capable of turning out useful knowledge in the same fashion that a well-organized factory would, shortly after Bacon's prediction, turn out textiles or shoes. Bacon's description of this division of labor strikes us as quaint and finicking, because of its static, ritualistic assignment of tasks; but those who would dismiss it altogether are wider of the mark than Bacon; for part of the immense quantitative output of contemporary science is surely due to its ability to make use, not only of a few great directive minds, but of a multitude of specialized piece workers, narrowly trained for their tasks, deliberately denied any individual opportunity to explore a wider field; whose part in the whole process increasingly resembles that of a factory worker on an assembly line. The corporate personality has taken over the attributes of the individual thinker; and as science comes more and more to rely for its results upon complicated and extremely expensive apparatus, like electronic computers and cyclotrons, no work along present lines can be done without close attachment to a corporate organization. The dangers that this technological advance offers to science have not yet been sufficiently canvassed; but they will perhaps nullify no small part of its rewards.

Bacon's conception of the organization of science as a technology did not altogether overlook the part played by individual creative minds: he even had a name for such seminal investigators, for he called them "Lamps," and indicated that their function was to "direct new experiments of a Higher Light, more penetrating into nature." But his peculiar contribution was to sense that, if the illuminations and insights of creative minds were to have the widest kind of application, they would need abundant collective support: state aid, corporate organization, systematic conferences and publications, liberal rewards and honors, and finally, public exhibition and celebration in museums of science and industry. It was these features of collective organization and state regimentation, not perhaps entirely unknown in pre-Christian Alexandria, that Bacon so presciently recognized, advocated, and exalted. So it was not only the Royal Society or the American Philosophical Society that Bacon anticipated: his quaint account of the future in the 'New Atlantis' did ample justice to the new functions of our foundations for scientific research, and our specialized institutes and laboratories that utilize hundreds and even thousands of workers in what has increasingly become—with great rapidity since the national state itself became the main patron—factories for the mass production of knowledge, technologically exploitable and financially profitable.

In looking back over the fulfillment of Bacon's anticipations, it is plain that there were two critical points. The first occurred in the first half of the nineteenth century, when for the first time purely theoretic researches in physics, by Volta, Ohm, Henry, and Faraday, resulted, almost within a generation, in the invention of the electric telegraph, the dynamo, the electric motor; and within two generations in the invention of the telephone, the electric lamp, the x-ray, and the wireless telegraph: all of these being inventions that were not merely impracticable but technically inconceivable until pure scientific research made them live possibilities. The methods that were so fruitful in mechanics and electronics were then applied, with growing success, in organic chemistry and biology; though significantly enough the parts of technology with the longest accumulation of purely empiric knowledge, like mining and metallurgy, remained almost impervious to the advances of science.

The second critical point came during the first half of the twentieth century, along with a change of scale and magnitude partly brought about, almost automatically, by the expansion of the facilities for communication and the exploitation of new sources of power. This change lifted hitherto inviolable limits on human activities: a shot could be heard around the world by means of radio more than eleven times faster than it could be heard by the unaided ear a mile away. At this point, science itself became the technology of technologies; and as the mass production of scientific knowledge went hand in hand with the mass production of inventions and products derived from science, the scientist came to have a new status in society, equivalent to that earlier occupied by the captains of industry. He, too, was engaged in mass production.

The old image of the self-directed scientist still remains popular, particularly among scientists; but as science expands as a mass technology, the scientist himself becomes a servant of corporate organizations intent on enlarging the bounds of empire—by no means always "humane empire!" —and endowing themselves by means of invention with power and riches and worldly prestige. By this transformation the scientist has forfeited the qualities that were exalted, in the seventeenth century, as the very hallmark of the scientist—his detachment from worldly gains and his disinterested pursuit of truth. To the extent that his capacity for pursuing truth depends upon costly apparatus, collective collaboration, and heavy financial contributions from government or industry, he has lost, as Sir Charles Snow pointed out the other day, the capacity to stand alone and to say No—even on matters like the mal-exploitation of nuclear energy that threatens the future of the human race.

Not merely have the sciences, then, become technologies, but the scientist himself, caught in the corporate process, is fast becoming the model of a docile, standardized, organization man, imprisoned by his own obsolete premises, incapable of making his escape without altering those premises. I hope I need not underline the moral that Snow properly drew from this. But there is a corollary that I would stress. Since science as technology has already submitted, often with great eagerness, to political and economic pressures, for the sake of the immense scientific opportunities offered, it cannot escape facing the consequences of this submission, and actively helping to rectify them. The scientist now has the obligation of erecting intellectual and social safeguards against the frequently malign consequences of scientific discoveries, even if the creation of these internal checks and balances slow up, or occasionally bring to a halt, the process of scientific investigation or technological application. As an agent of technology, science no longer has the immunities or the irresponsibilities that it claimed for itself during its great quarrels with the Church. Today, the greatest danger to science comes not from the hostility of traditional institutions but from the patronage of contemporary ones.

Now if the fulfillment of Bacon's dream deserves our respectful recognition of his prophetic insights, it also imposes upon us a special duty— that of dissociating ourselves from the mythology he so largely helped to promote, so as to appraise, in the light of historic experience, his unexamined premises. These premises are now so thoroughly institutionalized that most of our contemporaries continue to act upon them without even a quiver of doubt. But observe: science as technology presents a series of problems that science, as the disinterested examination of nature in search of rational understanding, never confronted; for already it shows the same deep irrationalities and absurdities that mass production in other fields has brought about. The chief premise common to both technology and science is the notion that there are no desirable limits to the increase of knowledge, of material goods, of environmental control; that quantitative productivity is an end in itself, and that every means should be used to expand the facilities for quantitative expansion and production.

This was a defensible position in the seventeenth century when an economy of scarcity still prevailed everywhere. Then, each new facility for production, each fresh increment of energy and goods, each new scientific observation or experiment, was needed to make up the terrible deficiencies in consumable goods and verifiable knowledge. But today our situation is precisely the opposite of this. Because of the magnificent, awe-inspiring success of the sciences in widening the domain of prediction and control, in penetrating the hitherto inviolable mysteries of nature, in augmenting human power on every plane, we face a new predicament derived from this very economy of abundance: that of starvation in the midst of plenty. The quantitative overproduction of both material and intellectual goods poses, immediately for the Western World, ultimately for all mankind, a new problem: the problem of regulation, distribution, assimilation, integration, teleological direction. As science approximates more closely the condition of technology, it must concern itself with the machine technology's great weakness: the defects of a system that, unlike organic systems, has no built-in method of controlling its growth or modulating the enormous energy it commands in order to maintain, as any living organism must, a dynamic equilibrium favorable to life. No one questions the immense benefits already conferred in many departments by science's efficient methodology: but what one must challenge is the value of a system so detached from other human needs and human purposes that the process itself goes on automatically without any visible goal except that of keeping the corporate apparatus itself in a state of productivity.

In science as well as in industry huge stockpiles have been accumulating which, on our present terms, cannot be adequately distributed or effectively used. There are even signs of a kind of crude valorization, with the destruction of older accumulations, through indifference or relegation to dead storage, in order to make room for current production and ensure its marketability. Our society has already reached the paradoxical state wherein our massive additions to the corpus of scientific knowledge have, through mere quantitative excess, lowered our capacity to make rational use of any part of it. In the exploding universe of science, the scattered parts are traveling at an accelerated rate ever farther from the human center. Because of our concentration on speed and productivity, we have ignored the need for integration and assimiliation, and continuity. The dubious morals of an acquisitive society have caught the once-disinterested promoters of science, along with their strange irrational compulsions. In practice this results in an inability to use more than a small fragment of the existing corpus of knowledge—namely that which is fashionable or immediately available, because it is being commercially exploited. This has already worked havoc in medicine, as any honest physician will tell you, and the results are visible in every other professional activity.

We are now faced, accordingly, as both Norbert Wiener and I have pointed out more than once, with the situation Goethe foresaw in the fable of the Sorcerer's Apprentice: we have achieved the magic formula for automatically increasing the supply of scientific knowledge; but we have forgotten the Master Magician's formula for regulating or halting the flood, and so are on the point of drowning in it. Science as technology gets its main financial support, and therefore its overall direction, from the national government, or from great industrial corporations like those engaged in exploiting new pharmaceutical preparations, chemical pest controls, or atomic energy, and from quasi-public philanthropic foundations exerting almost equally large powers. Though the professed aim of these organizations is truth and human welfare, they are governed in perhaps an ever greater degree by the Baconian goals of riches and power. On these premises they have no concern with ordering science in accordance with some human measure, toward the fulfillment of broader human goals: for this means altering the method of mass production and slowing down the whole process. Our schools and universities are helpless to restore an organic balance, because they themselves have accepted the same ideology and rely for a large part of their activities upon endowments that are scaled to the prospects of continued expansion and quick turnover: indeed the very possibilities for professional promotion depend more upon the number of scientific papers published than upon long-term results that may not be visible for a generation or more.

Is it not time, then, that we began to ask ourselves certain questions about science as technology that Bacon, by reason of his historic position, was too uninformed to put to himself? Are we sure that the control of all natural processes by science and technics is by itself an effective way of relieving or improving man's estate? Is it not possible to have a surfeit of knowledge no less that a surfeit of food—with similar distress to and derangement of the organism? Have we not already evidence to show that science as technology may, through its inordinate growth, become increasingly irrelevant to any human concerns whatever, except that of the technologist or the corporate enterprise: that, indeed, as in the form of nuclear or bacterial weapons, it may be not merely coldly indifferent but positively hostile to human welfare?

Just because science as technology has begun to dominate every other aspect of science, we are bound, if only in self-preservation, to correct the mistakes Bacon unwittingly fostered or sanctioned. Science now makes all things possible, as Bacon believed: but it does not thereby make all possible things desirable. A good technology, firmly related to human needs, cannot be one that has a maximum productivity as its supreme goal: it must rather, as in an organic system, seek to provide the right quantity of the right quality at the right time and the right place for the right purpose. To this end deliberate regulation and self direction, in order to ensure continued growth and creativity, must govern our plans in the future, as indefinite expansion and multiplication have done during the last few centuries. The center of gravity is not the corporate organization, but the human personality, utilizing knowledge, not for the increase of power and riches, or even for the further increase of knowledge, but using it, like power and riches, for the enhancement of life. On these terms it may be that all the work that has been turned out by Solomon's Houses these last four hundred years will have to be done over again, or at least be revised and amplified and integrated and made humanly more adequate in order to do justice to all the dimensions of life.

The greatest contribution of science, the most desirable of all its many gifts, far surpassing its purely material benefits, has been its transformation of the human consciousness, through its widening illumination of the entire cosmic and historic process, and its transfer to man of the power to participate, with his whole being, in that process. Has the time not come, then—in technology as in every other aspect of the common life—to reexamine our accepted axioms and practical imperatives and to release science itself from the humanly impoverished and underdimensioned mythology of power that Francis Bacon helped to promote?

(1961)

CHAPTER FOURTEEN

Kepler: Space-Explorer

One of the reasons for the general failure to understand the radical weaknesses of both aspects of the new exploration of earth and sky is that their subjective side has been neglected, indeed not even recognized as existing: chiefly because scientists, in overcoming the subjectivism of earlier systems, resolutely denied the many evidences of science's own subjectivity. Yet at the very outset, this subjectivism was expressed with classic clarity in Kepler's 'Dream,' for this work anticipated by more than three centuries the world in which we are now actually living: its empirical knowledge, its practical devices, its compulsive drives, its mystic aspirations—and finally, most remarkably now, its rising disillusion.*

Kepler, born a century after Copernicus, but only a few years after Galileo, embodied in his own person the three great aspects of the New World transformation: the scientific side, in his classic discovery of the unexpectedly ellipsoid course taken by the planets around the sun: the religious side, in his open adoration of the sun itself and the starry sky as a substantial visible equivalent of the fading Christian Heaven: and finally, his untrammeled technical imagination; since in a day of sailing ships and short-range, inaccurate cannon he dared to depict in vividly realistic terms the first power-driven journey to the moon.

If Kepler was a sun-worshipper, he was also as moon-mad as any of the contemporary technicians in the National Aeronautics and Space Administration (NASA). As a student he devoted one of his required dissertations at Tübingen University to the question: "How would the phenomena occurring in the heavens appear to an observer stationed on the moon?" He already saw in his mind what the first astronauts beheld with hardly greater vividness from their space capsule; and Plutarch's work, 'The Face of the Moon,' so fascinated him that in 1604, in his 'Optics,' he drew from it fourteen quotations.

* For complementary studies of Galileo, Francis Bacon, and Descartes see 'The Pentagon of Power,' New York, 1971.

For three centuries Kepler's 'Somnium' (Dream), published only after his death, remained a literary curiosity, largely unread; partly because it existed only in its original Latin, supplemented in 1898 by an equally obscure German translation, but even more because it seemed too fanciful to be taken seriously. Kepler himself, however, had no hesitation in putting his projected moon flight before Galileo, for he wrote out his plan for a moon landing as early as the summer of 1609, and justified his interest in exploring that satellite on the same grounds that justified similar explorations by sea. "Who could have believed [before Columbus]" he wrote, "that a huge ocean could be crossed more peacefully and safely than the narrow expanse of the Adriatic or the Baltic Sea, or the English Channel? . . . Provide ships or sails adapted to the heavenly breezes, and there will be some who will not fear even that void [of interplanetary space]. So for those who will come shortly to attempt this journey, let us establish the astronomy."

Note the word "shortly." In 'Typee,' Herman Melville predicted, in 1846, that by the end of the nineteenth century people on the West Coast would, thanks to air travel, be spending their weekends in Honolulu. But Kepler's impatient prediction was even more audacious. Those who have seen in scientific and technical advance only a cautious hardheaded series of steps from one solid tuft of observed facts to another, have not reckoned with these hot subjective pressures. The quick leap in Kepler's mind from purely scientific astronomical exploration to this staggering practical exploit surely helps explain the vulgar engulfment in space fantasies today, now that their realization has proved feasible.

The fact that these fantasies should have appeared, fully fleshed, in Kepler's mind at the very moment when the first halting theoretic advances were being made, would seem to indicate that they issued from deep common sources in the collective psyche. The same self-confidence, the same ambitious or aggressive impulse that sustained a Cortez in the subjugation of Mexico, was also working in the leading minds in astronomy and mechanics, though in a more subtle and sublimated form.

Kepler was far from being alone. These space-centered adventurers felt the future in their bones, as people used to say—that is, in their unconscious; and to the extent that their own work helped to bring that future nearer, their predictions became self-fulfilling. This animus was far more widespread than most scholars have until recently recognized, awakened largely by Marjorie Nicolson. A century and a half before Edgar Allan Poe's description of Hans Pfaall's trip to the moon in a balloon, a report of an airship's journey from Vienna to Lisbon appeared in a current newspaper without greatly outraging popular credulity. And in the eighteenth century Dr. Samuel Johnson, in 'Rasselas,' giving a reasonable account of the possibility of aerial navigation, even coupled it with the possibility of space flight, once the aeronaut reached a point beyond the earth's gravitational field, so that he might behold the rolling earth passing beneath him.

Now the remarkable fact about Kepler's moon exploration, apart from the audacity of the conception itself, was his keen grasp of the embarrassing details. He had already canvassed in his mind some of the most serious obstacles to its accomplishment, though he knew quite well that the solution of these problems was beyond the technical equipment of his age. "On such a headlong dash," he pointed out, "we can take few human companions. . . . The first getting into motion is very hard on him, for he is twisted and turned just as if, shot from a cannon, he were sailing across mountains and seas. Therefore he must be put to sleep beforehand with narcotics and opiates, and he must be arranged, limb by limb, so that the shock will be distributed over the individual members, lest the upper part of his body be carried away from the fundament, or his head be torn from his shoulder. Then comes a new difficulty: terrific cold and difficulty in breathing. . . . Many further difficulties arise, which would be too numerous to recount. Absolutely no harm befalls us."

This last bit of reassurance was again premature; but Kepler was obviously moved by interior compulsions that would not be daunted by seemingly insuperable difficulties, still less, possible failures. Like the artist in 'Rasselas,' he might have said: "Nothing will ever be attempted, if all possible objections must be first overcome."

That this extravagant dream was not so easily translated into the practical world as Kepler impatiently anticipated, is far less surprising than the fact that it took possession of Kepler's mind at such an early date. Kepler, steeped in sun worship, seems to have realized that powers derived from the Sun God would open new possibilities and would have no difficulty in imposing the huge sacrifices necessary to make a lunar journey possible. All the forces that had been set in motion by the exploration of our own planet were eventually transferred, with no loss of momentum and no great change of method or goal, to interplanetary exploration—but accompanied likewise by the same defects: the same exorbitant pride, the same aggressiveness, the same disregard for more significant human concerns, and the same insistence upon scientific discovery, technical ingenuity, and rapid locomotion as the chief end of man. What we also know now, as Kepler could not know, is that space exploration would require a megamachine of far larger dimensions than any previous one to ensure its success; and this megamachine would take centuries to assemble.

Kepler's 'Dream' passed beyond the borderline of prudent speculation; yet by that very fact it draws attention to another characteristic of his age: the science-stimulated fantasies of the seventeenth century have often proved closer to our own twentieth-century realities than the more humanly fruitful but relatively pedestrian enterprises of eighteenth- and nineteenth-century industry; for their boasted mechanical improvements in general only applied new sources of energy and a more militarized type of organization to the most ancient neolithic industries: spinning, weaving, pot-making, or to the later Bronze and Iron Age industries of mining and smelting.

In the seventeenth century Joseph Glanvill, who still believed enough in witchcraft to write a book denouncing it, also looked forward to such other practical consequences of science as the phonograph, and instantaneous communication at a distance. Even more remarkable, an English bishop, Dr. John Wilkins, sometime Master of Trinity College, Cambridge, wrote a book in 1638 proposing travel to the moon; while in a work entitled 'Mercury or the Swift Messenger' (1641) he predicted a series of new inventions, such as the phonograph and the flying chariot. A year later, in 'A Discourse Concerning a New World,' he suggested that "as soon as the art of flying is found out some of [our] nation will make one of the first colonies that shall transplant into that other world."

What is perhaps just as important as Kepler's realistically fanciful description of a moon flight, which he hopefully thought would be a mere matter of hours, is his description of the kind of organisms that might, under the permanent conditions of extreme cold and extreme heat on the opposite sides of our satellite, have developed on the moon. For he rounds out that journey with a nightmare of no little psychological significance. With marvellous ecological insight Kepler translated the physical conditions of life on the moon into appropriate biological adaptations. He imagined that 'Prevolvan' creatures would inhabit the cold side of the moon, and 'Subvolvans' the hot side, where plants would grow visibly before one's eyes, and likewise decay in a single day; where the infra-human inhabitants would have no fixed and safe habitation, where they would traverse, in a single day, the whole of their world, following the receding waters on legs that are longer than those of our camels, or on wings, or in ships; where those that remain on the surface would be boiled by the midday sun and serve as nourishment for the approaching nomadic hordes of Prevolvans rising up from cavernous interiors.

Kepler, be it noted, had no romantic illusions such as legend attributes to Ponce de León, exploring America to find the Fountain of Youth: Kepler presents nothing less than a painful phantasmagoria of organic deformation and degradation, of grotesque creatures in a fever of insensate activity and purposeless travel: the ultimate lunar 'Jet Set.' In contradiction to his hypothetical one-day limit of maturation and death, Kepler allows the Subvolvans to build cities—but mainly, be it noted, for a characteristically technocratic reason: *to solve the problem of how they could construct them!*

One must grant Kepler not merely truly remarkable powers of scientific deduction, but an equally realistic imagination in dealing with biological conditions: for he did not for a moment suppose that any organic forms comparable to those that exist on earth could flourish in such a hostile environment. Unfortunately, this fact opens up a serious question that it is impossible to answer and fruitless to speculate upon: *Why did Kepler suppose that a journey to such a planet was worth the effort?* Why did the utmost achievements of technology, which are symbolized even today by a journey to distant planets, terminate in fantasies of shapeless monsters and cruel deaths, such as often haunt the cribs of little children? If we had an answer to this question, many other manifestations of the life-negating irrationalities that now threaten man's very survival would perhaps be sufficiently intelligible to be overcome.

Kepler's 'Somnium' has only to be translated into rational contemporary terms to serve as an urgent warning signal. What did Kepler's sky-searching mind foresee in the new world created by science and technics? It saw a world that had escaped organic limits, a world in which the processes of growth and decay had been reduced to a single day, and in which its ephemeral creatures existed only to be promptly devoured. In this world the only protection against a savage environment would be retreat into deep underground shelters; and the chief occupation of its unfortunate inhabitants would be continuous motion. A monstrous habitat, in short, in which only monsters could be at home. In cutting loose from the earth, Kepler had left behind two billion years of organic existence, with all the immensely creative activities and partnerships of living species, culminating in the mindfulness of man. As far as life values are concerned, one might trade all the planets of the solar system for a square mile of inhabited earth.

If this nightmarish conclusion were peculiar to Kepler, it might be treated as a personal aberration; but as it happens, it has been a recurrent theme of later technological kakotopias. In H. G. Wells' 'The Time Machine' the narrator realizes that the technological progress toward leisure and luxury had proved self-destructive: and he travels farther into time only to find all life gradually waning on the planet. He sees in the growing pile of civilization only a "foolish heaping that must inevitably fall back upon and destroy its makers in the end." This premonition was so deeply at odds with Wells' conscious commitment to scientific progress that he came to a startling conclusion: *"If that is so, it remains for us to live as though it were not so."* In other words, we had better close our eyes and shut our minds. A fine terminus for the scientific pursuit of celestial truth that Copernicus and Kepler had instituted!

(1970)

CHAPTER FIFTEEN

Loyola:
The Gentleman as Saint

The warring impulses of baroque man found their ultimate resolution in religion: they were incarnated in a personality who could have taken form only in this epoch: a man who was a soldier, a courtier, and a saint. On the path from military service to Holy Orders, Ignatius Loyola conceived the possibility of creating within the Roman Church itself a power capable of ruling and governing the world. Within one formidable organism he united the medieval idea of unity with the baroque idea of uniformity.

This dream of Ignatius Loyola was an ambitious one; but so far from being a fragile theatrical creation in staff and gilt, imitating marble and gold, it came close to solid fulfillment: even down to our own day it continues to play a part in the political calculations of the Vatican and partly accounts for the various shifts and stratagems Rome employed to make smooth the path of totalitarian conquest during the last generation. Perhaps only one thing kept Loyola's disciples from ultimately wielding absolute power both within and without the Church: the fact that power became their goal. If they used the resources of baroque culture, its command of machines and its love of theater, they also shared its critical weakness.

The transformation of the Spanish caballero, Ignatius Loyola, into a soldier of Christ took place when he was recovering from a wound received on the battlefield of Pampeluna. On asking for a knightly romance, 'Amadis of Gaul,' to while away his time, he was given a Bible. The reading of that book, by this unlettered and undereducated young soldier, had such a profound effect that he withdrew from the army and his family, to meditate in a cave in the mountains. There he began a process of reorientation and self-education that led to the writing of his 'Spiritual Exercises.' Still feeling inadequate to the task he set before himself, Loyola went as a full-grown man to the University of Paris. At Paris he gathered together a few fellow students by whose help he founded a new order, the Society of Jesus: an order almost as different from that of the Carthusians or the Dominicans as was Rabelais' jocose institution. He sought to save the medieval Christian synthesis by giving it the tools and weapons of the modern mind: the discipline of the new scientist, the imagination of the new artist, the psychological penetration of the new dramatist.

To understand the boldness and greatness of Loyola's conception one must realize that he was a profound Christian, and in the act of establishing his faith, an austere one. Like his contemporary, Calvin, he had a sense of his own unworthiness and regarded this as the very beginning of Christian faith: "to behold myself as an ulcer and an abscess whence have issued so many sins and iniquities and such vile poison" is almost the starting point of his 'Spiritual Exercises.' But to regenerate the personality, Christianity now required a more subtle method than it had used at a time when hardship and violence had lessened the seductiveness of worldly life: it was necessary to re-dramatize Christ's mission by the very latest contrivances of art.

Instead of attempting an artificial separation of the Christian soul from society, Loyola boldly employed the new mechanisms, the new symbols, the new forms of thought and feeling that were the special expressions of his own age. If the Jesuits did not indeed conceive baroque architecture, they made it their own, just as they turned to their own account the new mechanical discipline of the army. There was nothing archaic or backward-looking in his conception of the Christian mission: he took his faith at the point where he found it and went on from there. For Loyola, as for Shakespeare, all the world was a stage; and he saw that the drama could not be effectively produced unless the time and the setting were taken into account. By putting at the service of the Church the new gifts of dramatic visualization, as in painting, and the art of visual dramatization, as in the theater, Loyola took Christian theology out of the Schoolman's shell.

In the 'Spiritual Exercises' Loyola showed himself a true man of his time, in his insight into the theater and in his virtuosity in playing upon the human soul: Shakespeare is possibly his only rival in both departments. It is not for their contents but for their novel technique that these Exercises have remained a powerful instrument of renovation among Catholics. At every point in these Exercises, the first requirement is to recall the history: to place the drama in time. And the second procedure also belongs to the theater: to *see the place*. The third step is to behold and consider what the actors are doing: to understand the drama itself. Instead of emptying the mind of its normal imagery in an effort to achieve purity of purpose, Loyola rather directs these images. Step by step, the practitioner of the Spiritual Exercises contemplates his relation to Adam, to Christ, to the Last Judgment. Hour by hour, day by day, his contemplation and his prayers are carefully fixed on Christ's journey; and on the seventh day the person in retreat contemplates the whole passion at once.

One may look upon the Exercises as a series of stage directions for a private drama, in which a sacred historic theme displaces a secular interest. Like a good director, Loyola did not attempt to overburden the actor with a part beyond his capacity: by experiment he learned to mitigate some of the rigors he at first thought necessary, and to vary the duration and intensity of the exercises so that they might do the most good to the persons following them. In the Constitution of the Order of Jesus itself Loyola made equally radical changes in method and attitude. He got permission from the Pope to dispense with the monastic costume and the monastic tonsure, no less than with the celebration of the canonical hours. A Jesuit brother might go everywhere, and in pursuit of his mission might even adopt a disguise. The Jesuits had in this, too, the instincts of actors: a sense that the costume changes the ego. Like actors, they doubtless sometimes overplayed their parts.

In this manner, the new order became a secret society; and the terror and hatred the Jesuits long excited among their opponents were probably founded on their gift for secrecy and the art of disguise: these servants of the Papacy were everywhere and nowhere. Just as in the new churches the Jesuits took over the luxurious fantasies of the palace and created churches as gay as ballrooms, as sensuously conceived as the setting for a carnival, a palpable heaven in plaster and gold, so in the use of disguises Jesuit theatricality sometimes over-reached itself.

Yet the very frailties that in time disclosed themselves in Loyola's order derived partly from the real solidity of his own social understanding. Probably better than any other spiritual leader of modern times, he understood the period he lived in, valued precisely those elements that were fresh and original, and grasped what was necessary in the development of the Church itself if it were to remain an active spiritual force in this society, instead of hanging on as a mummified survivor of an outworn culture. Loyola saw that something more than a negative movement was necessary: no mere tightening up of discipline, no mere return to old practices, could make the Christian Church become once more a universal institution. If the Church did not expand its mission the expansion of the world would inevitably contract the importance of Christianity.

Loyola came to the conclusion, accordingly, that the Church must fully utilize the existing organs of education, of discipline, even of entertainment: it must turn pomp and worldliness themselves to its own uses. On these matters, Loyola was far more revolutionary than Calvin and Luther; for whereas they recoiled from the New World that had opened before them, Loyola both figuratively and actually sought to embrace it. The Jesuits did not confuse holiness with poverty, or even with pain and renunciation. The problem for the Society of Jesus, in the sixteenth century, was to recover the essence of Christianity even under forms that seemed to contradict it. In a letter to G. P. Caraffa, possibly as early as 1536, Loyola defended the practice of letting those who had wealth and noble position retain these advantages after joining the society: "for it is right to yield to the needs and circumstances of the moment, and not merely consider what is absolutely the most perfect thing."

Though their opportunism often led to the undoing of the Jesuits, it derived partly from Loyola's remarkable psychological tact: a trait that perhaps owes something to his Spanish culture, but even more to his native grace and understanding. In an age of great intuitive psychologists, when people were turning from an acceptance of the outer badge to a probing of the inner man, Loyola stood on the same high level as Cervantes and Shakespeare, his nearest rivals. Despite all outward differences in career and fame, an inner similarity binds these three exquisitely self-conscious gentlemen: they probed the baseness of human nature with the swift delicate touch of the surgeon, and if they prescribed no harsh purgations, if they sometimes preferred to leave the bullet in the wound rather than risk its extraction, it was because they understood better than anyone else what a difficult business it is to interfere with the personality's balance even for the sake of improving it.

Loyola's good sense was impregnable. In the matter of diet, for example, he advised not severe abstinence but vigilant moderation in eating and drinking, so that neither the body nor the spirit would be undermined; and in order to make moderation more effective, he advised the practice of imagining how Christ looked and talked when he ate with his disciples. He was so aware of the nice inter-relationship of mind and body that when Lent came he used to summon a doctor and have him examine every member of the community before he gave permission for fasting. So with vigils, so with all the other instruments of holiness: like any other tool they needed to be carefully inspected and their indiscriminate use restrained. To serve God was the end; but the means to this end were more various for Loyola than the Church had been wont to allow. The main thing was constantly to order and re-order one's life, to achieve a mobile equilibrium of virtue, to ward off emptiness, doubt, and defeat—the mood of desolation. His dictum—never to make an important decision in a period of desolation—has indeed been rediscovered by modern psychoanalysts.

Is it too much to claim for this superb psychologist that he reunited the disciplines of medicine and theology, and that his methods of treatment were closer to the needs of the total personality than those which are even now current? Theology itself Loyola exhibited with medical vigilance: he warned that Christians must be very careful in their manner of speaking and treating of predestination, faith, and grace. Hence Loyola's general avoidance of doctrinal change; his whole emphasis was upon method, upon the *technique* of Christian living. His imitation of Christ was not a saint's soliloquy, as with Thomas à Kempis, but a dramatic and gymnastic exercise.

The chief doctrinal emphasis of the Jesuits, indeed, was on free will; and this position was something of a paradox; for it was combined with an insistence upon an obedience perhaps more absolute than that undergone by any other monastic order. The Jesuits formed a military hierarchy. Under the supreme commander of the order were the various provincial generals;

and a readiness to follow the orders of his superior, as unconditional as that of a soldier on the battlefield, was exacted of each member. This paradox runs all through the order. No Jesuit may exercise the right of private judgment, even on the smallest matters that fall within the province of his superior. Yet, in relation to the growing power of the absolute state, Jesuit writers like Bellarmine were on the side of republican government.

As early as 1562 Lainez, the second General of the Jesuits, held the view that the laws of the Church were from God; but that society had the right to choose the government itself. Divine right, accordingly, was not a possession of individuals but of society as a whole: monarchies, so far from existing by divine right, were no more sacrosanct than any other man-invented institution, and the people therefore have the right to change the forms of their government.

Unfortunately, as de Sanctis points out, the Jesuits sought to have the argument both ways. If power in the secular state rested with the citizens, why did not power in the Church rest with the whole body of Christians, or with the Council of the Church, rather than with the Pope? Why could not the faithful, indeed, depose the Pope or punish him like any other servant when he commits crimes and misuses his power? The early doctrines and practices of the Church had certainly not been on the side of ecclesiastical absolutism: that was a typical corruption that sprang from the orientalized Roman Empire.

At this point, the inconsistency of Jesuit doctrine came out. They refused to acknowledge either the logic or the historic authority of the democratic position for a simple reason: they sought to establish themselves as the political bodyguard of the Papacy; and as the power behind the Papal throne, they might hope to exercise an even greater absolutism —both prompting the Pope's commands and executing his orders. The justification for Papal absolutism could only be a pragmatic one: it provides continuity. But to match the Jesuits' psychological and sociological adaptations of ancient dogma to current circumstance, they should have carried through a political transformation, too: so that continuity should no longer impede the process of self-reform. Halting here, their transformation remained abortive, and their acts of liberation only forged heavier fetters.

Into an age of extreme contrasts, violent fanaticisms, exorbitant claims, Loyola himself nevertheless brought a moderating influence. He put before sinful men and women an ideal of life that was within their possible limits of achievement: not so high as to promote a despair that easily led to cynicism and then to outright denial. Intuitively, Loyola recognized the place of quantitative measure in the moral life. Goodness and badness were not just a matter of kind but a matter of degree. Moral judgment was a matter of gauging, at every moment of life, the size and intensity of the sin itself in relation to the occasion and the general end in view.

With this conception before him, the Jesuit confessor became no mere inquisitor: he became a subtle assessor of sins whose nature afforded a genuine play to intellectual discernment and psychological tact. Under these circumstances casuistry flourished. Instead of seven deadly sins there were now seven hundred, depending upon the time, the place, the circumstance, the intention. Moreover, to understand the true inwardness of sin no less than its coarse outward manifestations, the confessor might well follow Francis Bacon's observations: "It is not possible to join serpentine wisdom with columbine innocency, except men know exactly all the conditions of the serpent. . . . Nay, an honest man can do no good upon those that are wicked to reclaim them, without the help of the knowledge of evil." To their honor as physicians of the soul—but also of course to their peril— the Jesuits sought to make use of that knowledge: they even guarded mechanically against the intimacies of the confessional by inventing the Confessional Box. Only the Talmud rivals the Jesuit books of casuistry in knowledge of the circumstances of sin: in particular, the active temptations and deviltries of baroque society. And not until psychoanalysis renewed the endeavor, were the complexities of personal conduct so patiently, so thoroughly, so sympathetically explored.

To those who sought to live a pious life, Loyola advised the same kind of moderation and forbearance that served in elevating the sinner. Here Ignatius' self-analysis must have given him a key to the dangers of fanatical devotion. Loyola's letters to Sister Theresa Rejadilla were exemplary in pointing out the temptations and dangers of unrestrained virtue. "In two things," he wrote on June 18, 1536, "the enemy makes you err. . . . The first is that he sets before you, and persuades you, into a false humility. The second is that he suggests extreme fear of God, on which you dwell too much, and to which you pay too much attention. . . . We must then be very careful; and if the enemy lifts us up, we must lower ourselves, counting our sins and miseries; and if he lowers and depresses us, we must lift ourselves up in true faith and hope in the Lord."

One may sum up Loyola's creed by saying that he took both man and society as he found them. Upon neither did he impose a wholly ideal standard, or a principle of living derived exclusively from another epoch and another moment of culture. If men were to adapt themselves to Christianity, the Christian Church, as its vehicle, must adapt itself to men, to the time, the place, the action demanded by contemporary culture: that was the Jesuit method and doctrine. The Jesuits sought in a more than Pauline fashion to be all things to all men. In order to win others over to the Lord, Loyola counseled Fathers Broet and Salmeron to "follow the same course that the enemy follows with regard to the good soul."

Pursuing this method, Father Ricci in China, at the court of the emperor in Peking, used his knowledge of science to excite the curiosity of the ruler: the Jesuits even made clockwork automatons for the emperor's amusement, so that Christian teaching might more easily gain his favor. With consummate good sense, again, the Jesuits adapted the Gospel itself to the Chinese: instead of damning the great sages and religious leaders of the Chinese past, they sought rather to show where the universal truths of Christianity had been incorporated in the 'Analects' of Confucius. In the eighteenth century Father Noël even translated 'Les Livres Classiques de la Chine': the thought of China thus made its way into Europe, along with wallpaper, porcelain, and tea. By introducing maps, astronomical calculations, clocks, mirrors, reading glasses, oil paintings, as well as the Bible and Christian doctrine, the Jesuits succeeded in identifying their religious and metaphysical beliefs with practical ingenuities the Chinese valued more highly: an astute use of the conditioned response.

This method of spreading the faith incensed the rival orders: it seemed to them an indefensible laxity, a defiance of every otherworldly claim. But was it not a generous catholicizing of Christianity? Had it been carried further, it might have paved the way for a genuine syncretism, comparable to that out of which the doctrines of Christianity itself had grown. For lack of willingness to meet other religions on common ground, the Christian churches showed a pride that could only awaken a pride equally stubborn in those they sought to convert: they brought down on themselves an odium derived from Western man's crass belief in his own inevitable rightness, superiority, and uniqueness: his lack of perspective on his own and the world's development. The Jesuits showed a more apt humility in dealing with the ancient cultures of the East: they were careful not to antagonize their possible converts. Unlike the Franciscans, they courted no martyrdom, but sought to avoid it. In this sense, the Society of Jesus was, perhaps, closer to the spirit of Jesus than the more severely orthodox missionaries. What was such doctrinal courtesy and chivalry but an imaginative interpretation of the Christian injunction to walk two miles when one is asked to go one mile?

In short, the Jesuits exemplified the meekness of the proud and the courtesy of the powerful. Yet at times that courtesy might seem complaisance; that complaisance might be mistaken for indifference; that indifference might lead to active collaboration; that collaboration might turn into active corruption. For there is a real danger when one fights fire with fire: the direction of the wind may change and the fire escape one's neatly laid plans for control. Nevertheless the good side of Jesuit 'laxity' must not be forgotten: perhaps its greatest triumph came among the Indians of Paraguay, that beautiful communist despotism the Jesuits erected there and almost maintained in the teeth of official Spanish jealousy and opposition. In economic provisions and social arrangements the Jesuits succeeded better than any other group, possibly, up to the early Mormons in Utah. As with the Mormons, part of the opposition to the Jesuits sprang out of their indubitable virtues.

As an order their numbers were never great. Preserved Smith gives their membership as some 8975 in 1620, and in 1750, according to the Jesuit authority, Campbell, there were only 22,589 members, "of whom about half were priests." But their influence in both the educational and the political worlds was immense.

From the first, however, the Jesuits provoked hostility, even within the Church itself: an hostility not exclusively confined to the ill-disposed. The contrast that they offer with the Franciscans will bear reflection. The Franciscans, thanks to their founder, have a name for purity, the Jesuits for corruption. Francis's ideal intentions are treated by the world as if they were fulfilled facts; whereas Ignatius's well-fulfilled missions have been treated almost as a certification of his bad intentions. Yet two centuries after Loyola's death much that he had planned for had already come into existence: the principles he had established had created an institution with a martial discipline that maintained its unity and caused it to prosper.

More than once, during those two hundred years, power seemed within their grasp: a power that might have enabled them to wield ultimate authority over Christendom and perhaps over the world. But the more they plotted and planned for power, the more it eluded their grasp, for here precisely was the point at which Loyola's psychological insight came to nothing. The soldier in him kept a blind spot for the soldier's defects. By binding the order unconditionally to the Papacy, without effecting a political revolution within the Church that would have decentralized its power and opened it up to co-operative and democratic processes, the Jesuits themselves ultimately became the victims of the creature they sought to control. As Christianity weakened in the eighteenth century, the Jesuits became, not the agents of its regeneration, but a further justification for its downfall, so that finally, in order to save itself, the Papacy was forced to ban the order in 1773 and command its dismemberment.

This temporary banishment was ironical but inevitable. No one could trust the Catholic Church in the eighteenth century because it might be in the control of the Jesuits: no one could trust the Jesuits because their most innocent proposal might have as its ultimate purpose only the wider domination of the Church. The Jesuits sought power and power corrupted them: adopting the enemy's methods to advance the cause of God, they readily became identified with the devil himself.

"Altogether," Loyola had said, "I must not desire to belong to myself, but to my Creator and His representative. I must let myself be led and moved as a lump of wax lets itself be kneaded, must order myself as a dead man without will or judgment." The mischief of this admonition lay not in submission to the will of God but in the equal power accorded to His representative. No human being can be safely entrusted with such powers over another: here the Jesuit inclination to diminish the theological importance of original sin, their main point of contention with the Jansenists of Port Royal, closed their eyes to an inherent source of corruption. Human power can be used safely only when it is open to division, conflict, challenge, rational opposition. By the absolutism of its constitution, the Society of Jesus, like the Papacy itself, shared in the major sin of this period: the belief in unqualified power. Without both inner and outer curbs, those who exercise power become unprincipled, or rather, they hold to only one principle: to keep what power they have and to acquire more of it. Right and justice become what suits the convenience of the governing class and enables them to maintain themselves in office.

We have seen this corruption overtake a group in our own day that bears many resemblances to the Jesuit order: the Communist Party. Here, too, discipline was absolute: here, too, the noble purpose of the founders, to remove human exploitation, served in time as a cloak for unscrupulous deeds, selfish personal ambitions, shameless ideological transformations, and brazen political perversions. Here, again, experts in the technique of revolution used the wicked devices of the enemy and became the victims of their own adopted wickedness: here, finally, the fear of opposition, the fear of submitting to criticism and of dividing with others their dearly bought position and power, led to a ruthlessness that deformed the personalities of those who wielded it, even more than it did those who were forced to submit to it. With this came the betrayal of the fundamental idea that communism had formulated and partly incorporated in Russia's economic order.

Ends and means limit and modify each other. If unrealizable ends are empty and futile, unqualified means, whose very nature cuts them off from their legitimate human goals, are no less empty. Neither the Jesuits nor the Communists were sufficiently on guard against the perversities of self-exploitation by both individual and group, rationalized as the greater glory of God. Obedient corpses, galvanically summoned to action by their superiors, are not effective or desirable substitutes for living men. Nor is *rigor mortis* an equivalent for unity of spirit.

Loyola's doctrines might have enabled a company of saints to govern, or at least mightily to influence, the new world. In order to have fulfilled this mission, however, each member would have had to be as indifferent to power as the ideal guardians of Plato's Republic—and Christian theology was at hand to remind them that this condition could not be fulfilled. Fortunately, the world was spared from the too-limited providence of the Jesuits by their own faults of character: thanks to their corruption, virtue again was saved.

No limited order, no class of privileged men, consecrated to absolute obedience, aiming at absolute power, could perform Loyola's mission: there lay his mistake. The readiness to meet evil with understanding, the readiness to widen the scope of the experimental method in dealing with human conduct were admirable; but they can work to human advantage only when every person in the community is a candidate, an adept, a practitioner, a critic, and a stern judge. The Society of Jesus, unfortunately, was conceived under the sign of the Despot. What was valid in its intentions could be executed only under the sanative forms of democracy: the co-operative thought of science and the co-operative government of a community of equals, aiming at the best life possible.

(1944)

CHAPTER SIXTEEN

Hume: Nihilistic Atomism

If we wish to discover the profoundest tendencies of a culture, we must often seek them in their most abstract manifestations, in philosophy and art. This is perhaps especially true during this period of social upheaval and revolution, when the visible institutions are no longer representative. It was not in the bloody operations of the guillotine in 1793 that the forces of revolution and disintegration showed themselves most clearly; for behind the Reign of Terror were centuries of human anguish, the sense of old wrongs and new promises; impulses that took shape in a demand for justice as well as in a demand for revenge: indeed, even the punishment rested upon social premises, however brutally these showed themselves. No: it is in the apparently innocent lucubrations of David Hume that the real Reign of Terror began: the beginnings of a nihilism that has reached its full development only in our own times. In his 'Enquiry on Human Understanding' the assault upon historic filiations and human reason reached a pitch of cool destructiveness. Hume used the technical processes of reason to sap its very foundations. He was far more radical in his attack than Rousseau, far more devastating than d'Holbach or La Mettrie.

Hume's essential doctrine was the autonomy of raw human impulse and the absolutism of raw sensation. In analyzing cause and effect, he broke down the rational connection between human events to a bald sequence of abstract sensations in time. That, however, was a mere refinement of Locke's analysis of sensations as the building-stones of "ideas," and in terms of isolated sense experience Hume's description was the most accurate report possible of the operation of one agent upon another. But Hume went much further. A passion, for him, was an original existence: it did not derive from any sense impression or copy any other existence: impulses were primordial in a fashion that was not true for any response to the outer world. "When I am angry," Hume wrote, "I am actually possessed with passion, and in that emotion have no more reference to any other object than when I am thirsty or sick, or more than five feet high. It is impossible, therefore, that this passion can be opposed by, or be contradictory to truth or reason."

According to this principle, Hume went on to show, there are only two ways in which any affection can be called unreasonable: first, when a passion is founded on the belief in the existence of objects which do not really exist, as when fear in the dark is based upon the supposition of a non-existing brute lying in wait in the bushes, or when, in carrying out a passion, we choose means insufficient for the end. "Where a passion is neither founded on false suppositions nor chooses means insufficient for the end, the understanding can neither justify it nor condemn it. It is not contrary to reason to prefer the destruction of the whole world to the scratching of my finger."

One could not caricature this doctrine if one wanted to. In the last sentence Hume has done so beyond further challenge: it stands self-condemned. But if one pursues the implications of this philosophy, one sees that this imperturbable philosopher has arrived at a position of absolute nihilism: Turgeniev's Bazarov, in 'Fathers and Sons,' is a mere amateur in moral devastation by comparison. For Hume not merely confirms the absolutism of sensations—and completely overlooks the mediation of sensations through symbols—but he completes this work with an absolutism of brute impulse: he unites a despotism of the outer world with a despotism of the ego, or rather, of the id. Life as he pictured it was life in the raw—with a rawness the most primitive savage never exhibited. In his own plain words, the passions that possess man are above reason and beyond reason.

Hume's philosophy rejects the social background; it refuses to admit the social interpretation of events or the social (symbolic) nature of their analysis; it turns its back upon social responsibilities; it shows human beings as living in a moment-to-moment continuum in which the appetites alone have an unqualified claim to existence, and in which no impulses can be called good or bad, rational or irrational, since every impulse that is founded on the existence of real objects and is pursued with appropriate means is *ipso facto* reasonable. Raskolnikov's murder of the old woman for her money, like Hitler's wiping out of the center of Rotterdam, are both in Hume's creed entirely reasonable affairs—though Hitler's invasion of Russia would be unreasonable because it chose means that were insufficient to its end.

This erroneous conclusion necessarily overtakes every theory that excludes values from the fundamental substratum of all human experience: Hume's office was to make the error so openly that it becomes a classic clarification. Since value is integral to all human experience, a theory that eliminates value as a primary ingredient inevitably smuggles it back again by making sensations or impulses, as such, the seat of value; whereas value comes into existence through man's primordial need to distinguish between life-maintaining and life-destroying processes, and to distribute his interests and his energies accordingly. Here lies the main function of reason:

that of relating and apportioning the facts of experience into an intelligible and livable whole. Reason inter-connects events that Hume analytically tears apart: for the purest sensation, the most immediate passion, takes place in a world of values, logical order, moral duties, social institutions, by which sensation and impulse are modified, into which they are integrated. Reason is as fundamental a part of the human equipment as bones, skin, viscera, nerves: by a constant process of relation and apportionment, by suppressing this impulse and by encouraging that, it maintains man's self and his community in a state of psychic wholeness.

Reasonable conduct is conduct that holds together in history and that endures under the strain of conflict and challenge: it tends toward continuity, intelligibility, and harmony. Not merely must an impulse compose its claims with other impulses: it must be modified, in turn, within a larger social context, with respect to the needs and claims of other men, present and distant. So far from having the purely supernumerary role that reason has in Hume's analysis, impotent to affect sensation or impulse, reason performs a constant, active function in the human economy. Even the most barefaced processes of rationalization are attempts to give an appearance of harmony to irrational or self-limiting conduct.

Order, continuity, intelligibility, symbolic expression, in a word, design —all these are basic in human behavior: no less basic than sensation, impulse, irrational desire. To conceive life at the level of the id is to forget that the id is organically bound to the ego and the super-ego, and that when interplay between these portions of the personality ceases, a profound disorientation of the whole personality, tending toward destructive aggression or toward suicide, must follow. Within the narrow historic compass of the last two thousand years we have already seen this take place in three widely separated periods—and we are now living through a fourth. This, incidentally, explains why pleasure and pain, which are the body's mechanical regulators of behavior, are entirely insufficient to provide a basis for rational conduct or vital expression. If pleasure were in any sense the ultimate end of life, suicide by an inhalation of nitrous oxide, followed by a last insensible whiff of carbon monoxide, might be the last word in human bliss.

Giovanni Battista Vico, the Neapolitan, saw the implications of this nihilistic movement in both life and philosophy even before Hume had brought them to a final formulation: for Vico remarked, according to Flint, that the new philosophy tended to "dissociate men, to lose sight of humanity, nations, and families, in the contemplation of isolated individuals. This individualism or atomism in philosophy was viewed by him with a persistent aversion."

Hume's mission was simply to carry the current atomism to its logical conclusion: the world became a dissociated flux of sensations and the self became a magma of impulses that might occasionally erupt into life without following any orderly channels in descent. No society could manifestly exist

on such irrational, ultra-nominalist premises. If Hume's ideological disintegration was far more complete than the social disintegration, that was
partly because it was easier to explain away reason than to live for a day
without having some recourse to it. After all, the very society that nurtured
Hume could also raise the magnificent hulk of Dr. Samuel Johnson, who in
his piety and orthodoxy would keep hold of a truth Hume denied and his
contemporaries sought to confound. "Whatever withdraws us from the
power of our senses; whatever makes the past, the distant, or the future
predominate over the present, advances us in the dignity of thinking human
beings. Far from me or from my friends be such frigid philosophy as may
conduct us, indifferent and unmoved, over any ground that has been dignified by wisdom, bravery, or virtue." ('Journal of a Trip to the Hebrides.')
If those beliefs had been dominant in the New World philosophy, one might
better have called this period the Age of Reason.

In practice, one must add, Hume recoiled from his own strict analysis.
Having used his logic to dissolve all the connections of cause and effect,
to remove value from sensation, to dissociate impulse from purpose,
Hume cast doubt upon the very instruments he had used to accomplish
this astonishing result—and so recoiled into the world of history and social
convention. No one would have been more distressed than Hume if anyone
had taken his metaphysics seriously; actually nothing alarmed him more
than raw impulse. One remembers with a smile his discomfort over Rousseau's tearful demonstration of gratitude for being rescued from his persecutors by Hume: "My dear sir! my dear sir!"

(1944)

CHAPTER SEVENTEEN

Rousseau:
Insurgent Romanticism

Rousseau's role was a quite different one from that of the corrosive Hume. In breaking with the existing habits and conventions of society, he even broke with its typical product, the sensationist philosophy itself. Though Rousseau was at one with Hume in giving a fresh sanction to impulse, he sought to bestow even on his most singular beliefs the force of a social prescription. This radical belief in man sprang out of Rousseau's capacity for love, and it is what made his influence so much more fecund, so much more rejuvenating, than that of his great rival Voltaire.

Voltaire, the petted Lucifer of the salons, satirized, criticized, and condemned the more obvious abuses of his society, in particular those associated with the Christian Churches: he did this on one condition, namely, that their correction should not deplete his income or reform his habits of life. The most unsparing of critics, the one institution Voltaire regarded as sacrosanct was himself. Voltaire laughed at Leibnitz, whom he was incapable of understanding, because he had said that this was the best of all possible worlds, in that it provided the maximum amount of order compatible with the maximum amount of variety. But Voltaire demanded that for himself this should, in fact, be the best world possible, and he scrupled at no dodge that would make it so.

Jean-Jacques Rousseau was far more conservative than either Hume or Voltaire: what he rejected lay on the surface; what he valued and clung to were the humble things that a sophisticated age either took lightly or altogether despised: the wisdom of Jesus, the wealth of the lowly. Rousseau knew that the outer structure of society was rotten and was about to collapse. "The crisis is approaching," he proclaimed in 'Emile,' "and we are on the edge of a revolution. Who can answer for your fate? What man has made, man may destroy. . . . This farmer of the taxes, who can live only on gold, what will he do in poverty? This haughty fool who cannot use his own hands, who prides himself on what is not really his, what will he do when he is stripped of all? But he who loses his crown and lives without it, is more than a king; from the rank of a king, which may be held by a coward, a villain, or a madman, he rises to the rank of a man, a position few can fill."

Rousseau, with all his frailties and minor vanities, was a much larger figure than any of his contemporaries: he was the Lao-tse of an age that gave its homage to a Machiavellian Confucius. To Voltaire Rousseau once wrote: "You enjoy, but I hope; and hope embellishes all." Rousseau's only true rival was the less famous Vico, a sounder but no less imaginative thinker. In Rousseau the revolt against despotism, regimentation, exploitation, slavery, polite conformity, callous mechanization, stifling luxury, life-denying custom, received both its formulation and its incarnation. His words rang all over Europe and America, and his visible presence reinforced them. He not merely threw the ornate rococo costume off the figure of contemporary man: he demolished the elegant automaton he found beneath it.

At the very height of the Augustan Age, Virgil wrote his 'Eclogues.' In the most refined and polished country in Europe, at the moment when life as a whole had become an elaborate artifice, Jean-Jacques Rousseau wrote his famous essay for the Academy at Dijon, affirming that progress in the arts and sciences had depraved morals. The grounds of the argument were specious, but the impulse was salutary. Like a sick dog, Rousseau had gone out to eat grass.

Rousseau was sufficiently dependent upon polished society to hate it, and sufficiently outside it coolly to understand its workings. The young house-boy who had become Madame de Warens' lover knew the cold sexual curiosity of the stylish woman as well as the maternal warmth which, in his special case, had redeemed it. The young lackey who had blamed a fellow servant for a theft committed by himself would know something about human conduct that could not be explained away on purely mechanical or utilitarian principles: the sense of guilt, the desire for self-expiation and reparation would follow the sinner almost to his grave. Unlike the philosophes, he would not turn his back on a religion that recognized man's deep need for forgiveness. The habit of masturbation would increase Rousseau's shyness; an inflamed urethra would make him a diffident, if not an incompetent, lover; he would even rationalize his sexual weaknesses as chastity. But for these flaws he might have subsided to the plane of animal heartiness upon which his early friend, Diderot, conducted his sentimental life. But Rousseau's sins served him well. His handicaps saved the young dandy who came to Paris wearing a sword and boasting a couple of dozen fine linen shirts. The essay that brought him fame at the age of thirty-eight eventually caused him to live according to his inner convictions.

Rousseau's attempt to live a more simple, integrated life than current society offered was an entirely salutary one; but his rejection of the foolish conventions of his own culture was based upon two profound errors. One was that man in the state of nature was a solitary who stood above human conventions and human restrictions. The other followed from this:

that man in society is less in a state of nature than if he existed purely on the level of his original animal needs. Rousseau opposed to man as we find him in history, associated in space and time with his fellows, rarely out of sight, never out of mind—he opposed to historic man a 'natural' man who remained outside history. Did not development for Rousseau mean complications, compulsions, corruptions? Beholding the society around him in a state of palpable disintegration, Rousseau argued in favor of a primitive state of non-development. Out of his knowledge of good and evil, Rousseau led a retreat back to mankind's abandoned Eden, and beat in vain upon its gates.

Though Rousseau's noble savage existed chiefly in his own mind, he nevertheless was on the trail of an important notion: the notion, shared by Vico, that if one could behold the human race in its embryonic state one would know something significant about its adult form. The search for the primitive involves the idea of growth and development. His admiration for the crude, the indigenous, the barbarous, for the first time brought home the full importance of the explorations Western man was making in America, Africa, Polynesia: he crystallized as a theory, indeed as a dogma, convictions that many people had expressed more loosely in the previous two centuries: witness the pamphlet of Walter Hamond, published in London in 1640, "proving that the inhabitants of the Isle called Madagascar . . . are the happiest people in the World."

And if the real savage had little to teach about man's future, except by marking an earlier starting point, he had much to tell about the possibilities of fixation and arrest. Civilization itself had been a formidable invention: as costly, as dangerous, as the original Promethean gift of fire. Civilization was founded on the astronomical calendar, on written language, on the higher division of labor, and on the translation of habits and institutions into permanent buildings, monuments, cities: it marked a bold departure from the fossilization of tribal societies: a gain in freedom, an intensification of life, which might be paid for in a disintegration against which the primitives rigorously protected themselves. Static, tribal societies were closer to the heartwood, further from the cambium layer where growth takes place.

But primitive peoples are as deeply enmeshed in social obligations as their more cultivated brothers: there lies Rousseau's main error. If man is everywhere in chains, as Rousseau said, this is particularly true of savage society, as it is of the peasant communities that Rousseau likewise respected. The savage's chains were not forged by his subservience to nature; they were rather due to his submission to his own past selves. Fear kept primitive man close to his ancestral patterns: fear kept him chained to accidental successes to which he gave the force of law and sacred prescription. Rigidity, not spontaneity, is the mark of tribal societies: repetition, not continued growth. The resistance to change is what gives a timeless quality, among savage peoples, to even the most trivial custom. Much of this rigidity, indeed, still left its mark on earlier civilizations like those of Babylonia and

Egypt; and it has persisted in the best-preserved cultures, like those of the Chinese, the Jews, and the Hindus. Change, mobility, self-development, free adaptation of means to needs—all this demands the complex forms of civilization, and brings with it an unstable social order, whose depths of corruption are commensurate with its possible heights.

Rousseau's fanciful portrait of man in a state of nature, his glorification of primitive simplicity, was essentially false: but he was not wrong in thinking that primitive life had values which no civilization can afford permanently to forfeit. What made his philosophy suddenly carry weight was the fact that Western man found himself face to face with nature in his colonization of the New World and in those audacious explorations which Bougainville and Cook were conducting during the eighteenth century. The cult of nature was itself an old one. Petrarch had spurned the arts of the city and said: "Let the soft and luxurious men of wealth be far removed from our neighborhood. Let them enjoy their hot baths and brothels, great halls and dining places, while we delight in woods, mountains, meadows, and streams." Erasmus, in his 'Praise of Folly,' had observed that those are the most happy "that have least commerce with Science and follow the guidance of Nature." Piero di Cosimo, as Vasari describes him, would not allow his rooms to be swept, ate when he felt hungry, and would never suffer the fruit trees of his garden to be pruned or trained, leaving the vines to grow and trail along the ground, "for he loved to see everything wild, saying that nature ought to be allowed to look after itself. He would often go to see animals, herbs, or any freak of nature, and his contentment and satisfaction he enjoyed by himself." In short, Rousseau had forerunners and anticipators.

But there is a difference between idealizing the noble savage and believing in a natural order. The latter belief is a salutary corrective to human willfulness and misunderstanding; but it was easy, almost inevitable, that in the eighteenth century the two should be confused. Thus William Penn, one of the wisest of Quakers, advocated studying nature: "Let us begin where she begins and end where she ends, and we cannot miss being good naturalists." Not equally sound, however, was his praise of the Indians' life, on the ground that "they are not disquieted with bills of lading and exchange, nor perplexed with Chancery suits and Exchequer reckonings. We sweat and toil to live; their pleasure feeds them; I mean their hunting, fishing, and fowling." Penn here overlooked the main point: that if hunting was a happier artifice than a bill of lading, the life of the Indians, sufficient unto itself, left a smaller residue of truths and values for mankind.

Here Shakespeare was much wiser than the admirers of the primitive: indeed, it is hardly too much to say that in 'The Tempest' he not only anticipated Rousseau but wisely answered him. If Caliban is more foul and brutal than the worst savage, it is only because Shakespeare conceived him as a more primordial form, while the real primitive is subject to restraints, conventions, values which the idealizers of primitive life mistakenly pictured as absent. Brute power, brute impulse, brute intelligence, nurtured outside society, would produce only a race of Calibans. But Shakespeare's island has other inhabitants who personify wisdom, love, spirit: these are representations of man in his true state of nature—a state as proper to him as that in which the bison or the tiger find themselves. The theme of natural life cannot be divorced from man's dream of transcending the limitations of his own nature: the impulse toward the divine. Man dominates the other creatures of the planet because he has never been content with himself. He is indeed such stuff as dreams are made on: the dream, the wish, the ideal are organically bound to his very animal existence.

What was man, then, apart from what his institutions had made or mismade him? This question plagued many of Rousseau's contemporaries. It was prompted by various spectacular events: by the discovery of a Wild Boy in England and a Wild Girl in France: by face-to-face contact with the unhappy Eskimo whom Cartwright brought back to London from Labrador, or with the Polynesian, Oomai, whom Captain Fourneaux brought back to Europe in 1774. All these figures sharpened the problem of man's development. How did man come to be human? What turned the guttural throat noises of the wild creature into human language? Vico, too, had earlier labored to interpret this miracle of miracles, the achievement of articulate speech and significant communication; he imagined the existence of an *Ursprache*. And he, too, felt that barbarism might prove a necessary means of rejuvenation.

This fascination with the primitive was not just a literary speculation; common men shared it. Sailors going ashore in the Pacific would jump ship, with small prospect of being picked up again, lured by the spectacle of sensuous ease and wild felicity: coconuts, breadfruit, dazzling tropical landscapes, and amorous dalliance with brown maidens who were easier than coconuts to pluck. In the American woods the frontiersman, dressed in deerskin coat and "leatherstocking," with a hunting knife always in his belt, learned to live by his unbridled wits and animal courage, like his near neighbors, the Indians themselves. The oceans and the prairies were beginning to be peopled by Ishmaels such as Cooper was to describe in 'The Prairie' and Melville in 'Moby-Dick.' On the level of sensation, appetite, and impulse, on the level described metaphysically by Hume, primitive life seemed to have the better of civilized existence. Those who were in revolt against the injustices of society found an outlet for themselves on the frontier. There, subject to nature, they could have life on their own terms.

Rousseau's idealizations of natural man did not, plainly, rest on any extensive anthropological inquiry: it was not a judgment about facts, but a device of criticism, a program of reform. Rousseau himself—becoming "crude, rough, impolite out of principle"—was one of the chief models for the natural man. He properly sought to make his criticism more effective by living up to his own precepts; in that respect his thought had an organic quality not shared by many other thinkers and reformers. But Rousseau did this as a man of his own time and culture, by marrying an illiterate and un-couth girl, because she was good to him, by living in a cottage and earning a pittance copying music by hand, by steadfastly reducing his physical wants. His natural man was in fact closer to the peasant than the noble savage: his spartanism came direct from Plutarch's Sparta, not from the Five Na-tions.

To live in the country and enjoy its solitude; to be free from minor obligations of attendance and courtesy; to be in harmony with the peasant and artisan, capable of sitting down at their table and enjoying their crude food; to use the empty hours for lonely rambles through the country-side; to gather plants for a herbarium and take pleasure in watching the processes of growth—these were the new elements in life as Rousseau con-ceived it and lived it. What he meant by living according to nature was this retreat into a rural environment, this pursuit of simplicity and integrity, this sympathy with the poor and the humble. The prescription, given the time and the place, was a sane and liberating one: instead of a hard veneer of manners, feeling and spontaneous affection: instead of a mechanical ceremonial, a human response appropriate to the moment: instead of a complicated ecclesiastical scheme of salvation, based on original sin and fed by the love of power it condemned, the simple morality of the Savoy-ard Vicar, with its direct appeal to the goodness of human nature and the universal nature of goodness.

Here was the basis for a new manner of living and a new education. Thousands would read Rousseau's books and imitate his example: millions who had never heard of his books would finally be affected. From the head-waters of Rousseau, a dozen mighty streams branch out through the nine-teenth century: Chateaubriand and Hugo and George Sand, Cooper and Thoreau and Whitman and Melville, even a Goethe, a Kant, a Tolstoi, an Emerson, will bring into their conception of the personality a new sense of man's relation to nature and nature's relation to man: a sanative belief in the vital and the organic which will in large degree transcend Rousseau's errors and atone for his self-deceptions.

Without this upsurge of romanticism the forces of life might have been routed. Without its many positive contributions the processes of renewal that are now imminent might have been even longer delayed.

(1944)

CHAPTER EIGHTEEN

Darwin: Mythology and Ecology

Western man's aggressive attitude toward nature and toward primitive peoples was, in a certain sense, a diversion from the assaults he had long carried on against his immediate neighbors. It had the advantage of being definitely more one-sided: therefore it provided easier and larger rewards. But man's attitude toward the primitive was ambivalent: one side of him was ashamed of his own greed and hard ambition: it led him to turn with loving interest to the very object he attacked. And just as the development of the machine was promoted by a dispassionate interest in the behavior of matter, so the exploration of the earth was followed by a new sense of awe and delight over all the forms of life.

In Europe, the works of man are so constant, so spectacular, so stimulating that thought remained predominantly urban till the eighteenth century. But in other parts of the world nature composed cathedrals, arranged triumphal arches, erected the spires of distant mountain peaks, dwarfed to pettiness man's most pretentious handiwork; and the strangeness of the new flora and fauna helped lift all living organisms out of their conventional settings. Horticulturists, cattle-breeders, bird-fanciers were stimulated by the strange species of plants and animals explorers brought back from the wilderness: as man wandered farther away from his ancestral habitats he found a new kinship with the other migratory species, the cuckoo and the stork, the duck and the swan, the eel and the salmon; and as he turned with new zeal to the improvement of the domesticated animals and plants, he began to reflect intensely on the origin of life itself. By a score of different channels the interest in nature widened: the discovery of the reproductive system of plants enabled amateur botanists of both sexes to talk as freely about sex as the Freudian theory of the libido did a century or so later: Darwin, while studying for the Church, was the member of an eating club that sampled unusual foods: in field and wood and mountain thousands of insatiable Plinys were observing the world of life, day by day, as it had never been observed hitherto, for in the wilderness such knowledge often had survival value. This interest flowed back into the laboratory and the study.

Buffon, Erasmus Darwin, Lamarck, Goethe were all interested, not merely in the vast variety of living organisms with which man's own life is intertwined, but in their nature and development and transformation. Man began to recognize himself as the topmost shoot of a towering family tree, rather than as an upstart who had been given a divine patent of nobility some five thousand years before. The greatest lesson in the new natural history was a lesson in history itself: a lesson in life's growing dominion over the non-living, as one proceeded from the most ancient strata of rocks to those in which the most primitive worms and crustaceans left behind the evidence of their structure, and from thence through reptile and bird into the age of the mammals: finally the dominance of man and the re-ordering of the entire balance of life on this planet. Here indeed the great chain of being became visible: the interaction of the non-living and the living, the continuity of living organisms, their variety and plasticity, their unsuppressible energy in meeting the hardest challenges and their capacity for planning, beyond mere survival, toward an ever-more-purposive and self-sustaining development. On one hand, stability, dynamic equilibrium: on the other, growth, development, transformation. Geology, paleontology, phylogeny all extended man's time perspective: hence man began to see his own development as part of an historic process in which his fellow creatures, the earth itself, finally the planetary system and the universe were all involved.

This new time perspective was in such contrast to the millennial earthly periods of Biblical history and the blank eternities with which Christian theology had been concerned, that even the most daring thinkers of the early nineteenth century could hardly entertain it. Thus Hegel, who is often given credit for evolutionary views, held that change was an attribute of the spirit alone and that the world of nature was only a perpetually self-repeating cycle, so that the "multiform play of its phenomena so far induces a feeling of *ennui*." But now freedom, novelty, and purposive adaptation could be detected within the entire world of life: stability maintained itself within an unending spiral of development. Above all, time itself had a new meaning, for it could be correlated with phases of organic growth, both in the history of the individual and that of the species. The apparent fixity of organic forms was reduced to an optical illusion: life was a process of change, of development: above all for man. Carrying his dead ancestral selves in his germ plasm, he nevertheless sought through his developing cortex and his more fully integrated nervous system to pass beyond himself and establish conditions that supplemented, partly supplanted, nature's.

Give nature sufficient time, exclaimed the evolutionists after von Baer and Schwann, and nature will transform a primordial cell into a band of apes or an Academy of Platonists. The exploration of time became for the nineteenth and twentieth centuries what the exploration of space had been for the sixteenth and seventeenth. Biological time: evolution. Social time: pre-historic archaeology and history.

The discovery of man's own biological roots was the culmination of a long intermittent process of observation and thought that had entered the available written record with Aristotle. Organic evolution became one of the most important themes of human life during the nineteenth century: the recognition of man's animal origin even obscured for a time his divine destination, and led to a cynical disparagement of his ideal achievements. But fresh though this new biological stirring was, the dominant mode of the period remained a mechanical one; and even in the mind man's redoubtable achievements in observing and understanding nature were perverted by his naïve faith in the utilitarian ideology. One could multiply the instances of this miscarriage of thought; but I will confine myself to the largest, that which overtook the doctrine of organic evolution itself. Here, as in the cult of nationalism, the very reaction against the machine was transformed into its opposite.

No one was more at home in the world of life than Charles Darwin. Rebelling against a career as a doctor or a clergyman, he joined the *Beagle* on a five-year cruise as a naturalist: in that ship, he wandered over the face of the earth, observing the natural landscape and the forms of life. Chronic seasickness did not deter him from his task; and though he collected specimens of every kind, his own most systematic work as a naturalist consisted in a two-volume description of the barnacle: all that lived was grist to his mill. Like a good romantic he loved the most naturalist of romantics, Wordsworth: Darwin read and re-read 'The Excursion.' As husband and father Darwin participated in the collective insurgence of life: he became the father of ten children, nine of whom survived.

Now, Charles Darwin, the naturalist, was a model for his kind: he mingled acute habits of observation with a sympathetic insight into the impulses and needs of all organic life: when he sought to observe the behavior of babies, he was a good enough naturalist to place the baby in its natural environment, the arms of a young woman. Darwin's study of the ecological relations of the earthworm gave a formative impulse to the new science of ecology: the study of groups, associations, food-chains, in all their organic complexities, gradually took the place of the isolated analysis of dead organisms and deformed structures. Darwin's investigation of the expression of emotions in animals laid the foundation for the new science of animal psychology, so fruitful in its suggestions of the primordial contents of higher human behavior. Wherever Darwin touched life at first hand his influence was a fertilizing one. If he never had a gift for systematic experiment in the fashion of Claude Bernard or Louis Pasteur, he had the prospector's gift for opening up new veins of research. In paying tribute to Darwin the great naturalist one only humbly echoes the considered judgment of most biologists.

But Darwin was lifted to fame by his contemporaries through something other than his narrative of the *Beagle* voyage or his observations of living nature. He became known as the central exponent of the theory of biological evolution. The doctrine that all existing forms of life had developed from earlier and simpler forms, all of which could be traced back to a central stock, was familiar to the Greeks and had been restated in verse by Darwin's grandfather, Erasmus Darwin: Herbert Spencer's vast philosophic synthesis of evolution had already begun publication before the 'Origin of Species' appeared. But in the 'Origin of Species' the doctrine of evolution was given by Darwin a peculiar twist: his leading idea, the idea he fancied was original to him, was the notion that the population of all species tends under natural conditions to outstrip the food supply, that this brings about a struggle for existence between the members of the same species, and that as a result, the weaker members are driven to the wall, while those who survive reproduce their kind and hand on to their descendants precisely those more favorable variations that enabled them to survive. Extermination became the key to development.

This theory, developed amid a wealth of naturalist observations, put together many widely drawn facts on modifications, fluctuations, and variations which took place within species: Darwin established the prime difference between bodily modifications that took place in the lifetime of the individual and the more radical kinds that were enregistered in the germ plasm and transmitted to the offspring. He linked up observations of the succession of the species, established by paleontology, with evidences of an organic succession found by comparative embryology. Many live fish were caught in this evolutionary net: but the main fish was a fake that had been unconsciously placed there by Darwin himself—the notion that natural selection accounted for organic development. Darwin sought to draw forth a purposive result from the facts of accidental variation: the mechanism of this purpose was the struggle for existence and the 'survival of the fittest.'

On this central thesis, Darwin's contribution remained confused and contradictory. Indeed one has only to state it clearly to see that it is a negative principle, which explains survival, if it indeed explains anything, but does not give an account of the actual processes of variation and transformation themselves: on the latter point Darwin, when pushed to a conclusion, alternated between Lamarckian striving and mechanical changes in the germ-plasm. As for natural selection itself, Hans Driesch properly characterized Darwin's hypothesis of a gradual accumulation of *accidental* variations as one that would equally well create the structure of a house by the method of throwing bricks at random on the site. What, then, was Darwin's contribution? What made the 'Origin of Species' a turning point of thought in the nineteenth century?

Darwin's 'original' contribution had been anticipated by Alfred Russel Wallace; and the imminence of Wallace's publication not merely gave him acute pain but made him hasten to finish his own work. Now the answer to this question does not lie in biology. The very theory of natural selection had been partly stated by Diderot in the eighteenth century: "I maintain," he said ". . . that the monsters annihilated one another in succession, that all faulty combinations of matter disappeared, and that only those survived whose mechanism implied no important misadaptation, and who had the power of supporting and perpetuating themselves." What did Darwin and Wallace add to this notion beyond the support of a vast volume of observations? Nothing more nor less than the Reverend T. S. Malthus's theory of population: the belief that population increases in geometrical ratio while the food supply increases in arithmetical ratio; so that poverty, vice, crime, and war are the only alternatives to either Christian abstinence or a voluntary decimation.

This theory of Malthus's performed a special social duty: it explained why the poor must remain poor, and why the upper classes, by getting all they have, are by a supreme law of nature entitled to have all that they can get. In its application to society, it was false; though it immediately suggested to the acute mind of Francis Place the "neo-Malthusian" expedient of introducing contraception to the poor, as a mechanical alternative to such dire extremes of vice and virtue. What Darwin did was to read back into nature the current struggle for economic success: both he and Wallace took Malthus uncritically without asking for proof of his neat generalizations. Thus Darwin came to confuse the fact of survival, which rests on many other circumstances besides individual ability and capacity, with the fact of biological development: he confused fitness with betterment, and adaptation with physical prowess. In short, he justified man's contemporary inhumanity to man by pinning the whole process on nature.

Here lay the secret of Darwin's great popular influence: his theory of natural selection sanctified the brutality of industrialism and gave a fresh impulse to the imperialism of the "superior" races that succeeded it. No matter that the over-emphasis of the struggle for existence forgot the factor of mutual aid: no matter that it overlooked the fact that within the species co-operation rather than struggle is one of the mainstays of life: no matter that commensalism is as primordial as a predatory mode of life. Darwinism, if not the gentle Darwin himself, would deliberately interpret the facts of love in terms of economic prowess. Hence it was not as a biologist but as a mythologist that Darwin triumphed: he lent to the brutal assertions of class, nation, and race the support of a holy "scientific" dogma. The industrial world was flattered to find its own reflections in this mythical black tarn of nature: it found the shabby tricks of the factory and the counting-house justified in the stratagems of field and forest: luck, force, ruthlessness, greed were what the ruling classes took to be the secret of survival. No one can dispute, of course, the existence of struggle, bloody aggression, and devouring appetite in the world of nature: what Darwin's theory did was to magnify these factors and to make them an all-sufficient explanation of the course of life.

Though Darwin got his lead from Malthus, he in turn gave support to Marx. The latter not merely presented Darwin with a volume of 'Das Kapital' when it appeared, but he and Engels hailed Darwinism as a scientific confirmation of their theory of the class struggle. The answer to both Darwin and Marx came from many sources; and it has been steadily increasing in volume with the advance of ecological studies. One of the earliest and best answers came from the geographer and philosophic anarchist, Kropotkin, who pointed out how completely the Darwinists had overlooked the factor of mutual aid in evolution, while another came from Samuel Butler, in 'Evolution, Old and New,' and in 'Luck or Cunning?' who pointed out the strange contradictions between Darwin the naturalist and Darwin the evolutionary philosopher. And still another came from Patrick Geddes, who pointed out that the mammalian impulse to nurture and love the young, which is intensified in man through prolonged maternal dependence in infancy, has made the family the model for all larger forms of communal co-operation. But for two generations the Malthus-Darwin myth had its way, for it made every act of raw egoism an assertion of nature's fundamental law—and must not nature be respected and obeyed?

Observe the final result. Precisely at the moment when the mechanical means of communication and transport were making the world one, a subversive ideology, on the basis of a partial, falsified view of nature, sanctioned non-co-operation and erected the struggle for existence into a dogma. Men who had guns and who used them ruthlessly—the Americans robbing the Indians, the Belgians in the Congo, the Germans in Southwest Africa, the Boers and British in Transvaal, the united Western powers in Peking— were obviously destined to survive: their brutality placed the seal of virtue on their fitness. To exterminate their rivals was to improve themselves— or so the gunmen thought.

In its popularized forms, Darwinism not merely expelled value and purpose from the processes of life: it relieved humanity of its collective super-ego. The earlier utilitarians had always unconsciously assumed the existence of values: their very faith in machines, which are products of human contrivance, placed them above those who would reduce life itself to a meaningless brawl. Herbert Spencer, George Henry Lewes, James Hinton, Samuel Butler, Patrick Geddes, each of whom had a more humane philosophy, lacked ultimate influence if not immediate homage. What the militant leaders of this society took from biology were not its truths but its errors.

Thus the spreading interest in life-processes fostered barbarism and played into the hands of the unscrupulous. In reacting against the dehumanization of the machine, people identified the natural with the savage, the organic with the primitive, life-promoting organization with wholesale extermination. They trusted the laws of chance to mimic the results of purposeful selection and design.

(1944)

CHAPTER NINETEEN

Marx: Dialectic of Revolution

The utilitarian ideology had above all one serious defect: the society that committed itself to these ideals produced many ugly and evil results that were not specified in the blueprints.

The rigorous order of the machine was opposed by the sprawling chaos of the new industrial towns; the wealth of the manufacturers was denied by the poverty of the workers; the peaks of prosperity for all classes were followed by commercial crises that often bankrupted even the more fortunate groups. On the facts of the case all the leading critics of the new industrial regime were agreed: the communist Marx, the tory Disraeli, the anarchist Bakunin, the bourgeois individualist Henry George. Even Malthus and Ricardo were agreed as to the facts though they believed that the iron law of population and the iron law of wages were in substance unalterable. Progess *and* poverty marked the new industrial order.

By the middle of the nineteenth century the miscarriage of industrialism had become more conspicuous than its promises. Science and invention and organization, so far from contributing to the relief of man's estate, seemed to have widened his collective capacity for misery. Even those who, like Herbert Spencer, were originally sure that society was automatically following the inevitable path of progress, so that militarism would give way to industrialism, war to peace, and poverty to plenty, would discover before another generation was over that their beliefs stood in need of revision; for the very remedies brought forward to relieve the evils of industrialism seemed to Spencer to bring mankind nearer 'The Coming Slavery.'

The man who sought to master this situation, who planned to convert the utilitarian hell into a proletarian heaven, was Karl Marx, a German born of a Jewish family in the Rhineland, where industry had had a foothold even in Roman times. If anyone was capable of describing and resolving the contradictions of capitalist production it would be Karl Marx, whose life was a series of contradictions. A son of the bourgeoisie, married to a woman of noble family, Marx devoted his whole life to the

199

emancipation of the working classes. But in his person, Marx never achieved the status of a manual worker, nor had he any first-hand contact with the routine of the factory. Despite his efforts as a newspaper correspondent, he and his family were parasitic on the earnings of his friend Friedrich Engels, who supported the communist movement out of a salary earned in a Manchester cotton firm. Marx migrated out of his class and his country: yet his ideology never overcame the militarist and absolutist bias of his native land, and he scarcely bothered to conceal his contempt for Russia, the country in which his writings were most widely appreciated. Finally, he who thundered against the moral airs of the bourgeoisie was too squeamish to admit Engel's beloved Irish mistress, a girl of the working classes, into his family circle.

The inner contradictions of Marx's background had their equivalent in his thought. He concealed the apocalyptic vision of a Jewish prophet behind an elaborate façade of scholarly investigation; and he called his particular scheme of thought "science" in order to hide even from himself its deep emotional urge and its essentially religious attitude toward human destiny—two qualities that gave it power to gain support among masses of depressed and desperate men. And while Marx despised wealth in the form of possessions and made his whole family live a life of bitter heroic poverty, he worshipped power as much as he hated greed: he had an inner need to dominate every group he became part of, and would unhesitatingly wreck it when it threatened to escape his control.

In the 'Communist Manifesto' he and Engels sang a paean of praise to the bourgeoisie, exclaiming that "it had been the first to show what man's activity can bring about. It has accomplished wonders far surpassing the Egyptian pyramids, Roman aqueducts, and Gothic Cathedrals; it has conducted expeditions that put in the shade all former exoduses of nations and crusades." At one moment Marx hailed the new order because it had swept away all fixed, fast, frozen relations and caused man to face with his sober senses the real conditions of life: at the next moment he condemned the bourgeoisie for performing its mission so brutally, though he himself did not hesitate to urge the workers to take equally brutal revenge when their day came.

One need hardly list all the contradictions and ambivalences of Marx's attitude toward the world around him; for he organized them into a water-tight system, a dialectic of history. His first master, Hegel, had taught him that the world as a whole was in a constant process of becoming; this was no aimless ebb and flow, but a purposeful current: it was the result of a struggle between opposites, in which a positive "thesis" begot its negation or "antithesis," and in the course of the struggle created a higher unity or "synthesis." For Hegel, 'ideals' generated the material forms and institutions of actual life. Marx accepted the dialectic process as a complete description and turned it upside down: material forms, in particular, the instruments of production and exchange, brought into existence appropriate ideas in art, religion, philosophy, morals: these were mere shadows of the 'real' world, the world of economic activity, which was governed by the necessity to eat, drink, have shelter and clothes, and to produce ever-more-elaborate means of securing physical livelihood. Like his seventeenth century precursor, Charles Blount, Marx regarded the forms of piety, justice, or art essentially as "grace before meat."

If Marx had perceived that his version of history actually complemented Hegel, instead of supplanting him, he would have created a sociological synthesis of the first order, in so far as history can be comprehended in the exclusive terms of the dialectic process. But in recasting Hegel's thought in materialist categories he rejected its valid aspects; and in holding that "material relations are the basis of all relations" he proceeded to confuse "basis" with "cause" and "reason." In Engel's farewell eulogy on the dead man, he claimed that "Marx discovered the law of evolution in human history: the simple fact, previously hidden under ideological growths, that human beings must first of all eat, drink, shelter, and clothe themselves before they can turn their attention to politics, science, art, and religion."

That claim gives away the weakness of the Marxian interpretation; for in actual history the developments of language, art, and politics are as early as the technological developments that secure man's physical existence: in society, these aspects of life are organically related and neither precedes the other. Marx was correct in saying that all of man's ideal creations have a material *basis:* he was wrong in confusing "basis" with "cause," and he was doubly wrong in not realizing that all of man's material achievements have, likewise, an ideal *basis*. Hence Marx assumes that economic institutions are self-begotten and all social changes are the by-products of that automatic technological development.

Marx's final mistake was to assume, with Hegel, that all change was of a dialectical nature: he and Engels understood best those changes in which opposition and struggle manifested themselves. They were highly conscious of the drama of life: especially the bloody drama. That made them welcome Darwinism and identify Marxism with that interpretation of nature. But they had no insight into other modes of development and growth: hence they overlooked the role of co-operation and mutual aid, which Peter Kropotkin was to emphasize. Historic observation shows that there are many modes of change, other than dialectic opposition: maturation, mimesis, mutual aid are all as effective as the struggle between opposing classes. In failing to take in the diverse modes of change, Marx compelled himself to overlook a good part of human history.

While the dialectic of history dominated Marx's thought and his plans, his larger significance comes from the fact that he brought together the three dominant streams of historic experience: the British tradition of empirical science and invention, as the basis for a new social order; the French tradition of political revolution, with its image of a complete regeneration of mankind by means of an uprising and a ruthless reign of terror; finally, the German Hegelian tradition of change as an essential attribute of both the order of nature and the order of society, so that each stage of history must be regarded, not as a closed achievement, but as in process of transcending itself by means of the very contradictions and struggles it generates. Marx transformed all three notions in the conception that the "history of all hitherto existing society is the history of class struggles," which ended "either in a revolutionary reconstitution of society at large, or in the common ruin of the contending classes."

Inflated by the yeasty optimism of his period, Marx never took seriously the second possibility. From the funeral pyre of capitalism he expected the phoenix of communism surely to rise. He was certain that the workers would be victorious; he did not admit that they might be more completely enslaved, nor did he entertain for a moment the thought that precisely for lack of class understanding and class collaboration, society itself might be thrown back into barbarism. Yet the very revolution he admired so ardently, that of 1789, provided a refutation of his main tenet. The voluntary renunciation of their feudal rights by the French aristocracy, in a sudden wave of moral enthusiasm and self-abnegation, had done more to wipe the slate clean in the French revolution than the savage guillotine had done. Compared to that single act of class collaboration all that had followed by way of coercion accomplished relatively little of permanent value. Though reason alone is impotent to effect such changes, humane intentions may at the right moment produce a powerful effect: the voluntary abolition of serfdom in Russia, prompted by the bad conscience of the ruling classes, was quite as effective as the forceful emancipation of American slaves achieved in the bloody Civil War.

By his dogmatic unwillingness to admit these facts, Marx made the path of revolution harder; for, by underlining the necessity for the class struggle and the dictatorship of the proletariat, by mingling his confident prophecies with loud threats of violence and revenge, the disciples of Marx roused the determined opposition of the ruling classes: fear urged the latter to anticipate the day of reckoning and to take matters into their own hands. Thus Marx conjured up an equally ruthless tactic of defense, an attitude which the moral and humanitarian scruples of the law-abiding nations had been slowly pushing into the background. When actual revolution finally broke out at the end of World War I, both sides showed a capacity for large-scale brutality which even Czarist Russia had hardly dared to equal during the nineteenth century.

If Marx treated the dialectic process as the revelation of destiny, his detailed interpretation of events proclaimed him a philosopher of history worthy to stand beside Vico and Comte. He realized that the French revolution had divided society artificially into two spheres, the political, in which man functioned as a tolerant, liberal, egalitarian citizen, and the economic, in which he was either a grasping capitalist or an exploited worker. Marx knew that a communistic system of production, such as the factory system by its very technical constitution actually is, could not be run for the benefit of a minority of exploiting individuals without, through its sheer productivity, wrecking this class-limited basis of existence.

But Marx believed that material conditions and technical inventions were self-created entities, existing in and by themselves: prime movers, original sources of social power. If they were otherwise, if they were the products of plan, effort, imagination, choice, they would then be subject to evaluation, rejection, improvement, change by means of the human will, as the utopians believed. This Marx could not admit as possible: hence he accepted the machine process as an absolute, imagined that the proletariat would simply take up capitalist production at the point that capitalism left off, and in 1869 denounced his friend Beesly as a reactionary because he had drawn up a program for the future.

Because of his self-imposed limitations, Marx never carried his social analysis of the machine to its conclusion: he had no plan for the deliberate projection of democratic methods into industry or of communistic processes and ideals into the art and science and morals of this society. From his standpoint, both efforts would have been self-defeating. But in rejecting such efforts, he guarded an even more colossal utopian hope which he never recognized as such: after proving that the industrial worker was brutalized, stupefied, and impoverished by capitalist production, he called upon this degraded creature to take the initiative in establishing a new order: the dictatorship of the proletariat was the key to salvation. That was worse than a paradox: it was a sentimental falsehood. In practice, the dictatorship was seized by a small group, an inner circle of ardent revolutionaries, partly drawn from the bourgeoisie and even the petty bourgeoisie, so heartily despised by the true revolutionist: Lenin was the son of a minor official. Unlike the Christian, who renounced society and therefore had no need of its arts and sciences, the Marxian worker was called upon to control a highly complex and powerful machine, and he was supposed to acquire the skill and insight and moral discipline needed on the spur of the moment.

By merely turning Hegel upside down, the materialist interpretation of history proved to be as limited as the idealist interpretation; and Marx's morbid fear of utopianism actually harnessed him to a past moment in history, that of the French revolutionary uprising. His doctrine of increasing misery, which would drive the proletariat into an armed revolt, gave to a climactic external crisis a role that a more timely sense of grievance and a more alert intelligence would have played without being driven to the last stages of desperation. Since Marx's imagination was chained to the French revolution he had no use for a superior wisdom that might have averted it: he was like a surgeon who rejects a cure done by means of diet because his own training demands the final use of the knife. Both Marx and Engels worked for civil war: indeed, Engels was preoccupied by war in every phase. Without war they could not envision change: "it is precisely the wicked passions of man—greed and lust for power—which, since the emergence of class antagonisms, serve as the levers of historical development." Thus Engels in his attack on Feuerbach. This is a sort of proletarian version of The Fable of the Bees.

As a fierce humanitarian prophet, as a student of the relation of technics to production, as a leader in the attempt to focus the energies of the working classes on their own emancipation, as well as their material improvement, Marx was a mighty figure, great because the moral fervor and humane vision of countless smaller men supported his purposes and gave direction and power to his abstract ideas. Marx is usually at his best when he makes least claim to being scientific, as in the speech in 1856 in which he said: "In our days everything seems pregnant with its contrary. Machinery, gifted with the wonderful power of shortening and fructifying human labor, we behold starving and overworking it. . . . The victories of art seem bought by the loss of character. At the same pace that mankind masters nature, man seems to become enslaved to other men or to his own infamy. . . . All our conventions and progress seem to result in endowing material forces with intellectual life and in stultifying human life into a material force." Who could have stated the case better? Carlyle, Ruskin, Tolstoy have little to add to Marx the critic.

Though the immediate program originally set forth by Marx and Engels in the 'Communist Manifesto' has not been completely fulfilled, much of it has become the common property of every country, even one like the United States, in which the glib defenders of the status quo rationalize their monopolistic privileges as "rugged individualism." A heavy graduated income tax, abolition of all right of inheritance, centralization of credit in the hands of the state by means of a national bank, centralization of the means of communication and transport, extension of factories owned by the state, and the improvement of the soil in accordance with a common plan, equal obligation of all to work, with the establishment of industrial armies, especially for agriculture—all these youthfully utopian proposals of Marx and Engels have actually been achieved, or are accepted as common sense measures that are near to achievement in many countries.

Yet these changes have taken place, not by a revolutionary dictatorship, but, as it were, by a geologic process of leaching and displacement. Under pressure of war in present-day Britain most of the early Marxian program has been achieved without precipitating any struggle between the minority whose income derives from capital and the majority whose income derives from labor: in short, revolutionary changes may come about without bringing with them a titanic and ruinous struggle. On the other hand, the further developments of capitalist institutions have placed serious brakes on change: Marx could not anticipate that the enormous growth of insurance would throw an economic bridge between the classes, nor could he anticipate the extent to which all groups, and above all the capitalists themselves, would seek security, even at the expense of further development.

Apart from the utopian indiscretions of the 'Communist Manifesto,' it is only in scattered passages in Marx—in his letters as well as in his main work, 'Capital'—that the positive side of his vision appears. Then it is plain to see that he revolted against the industrial division of labor and believed the communist state would restore the wholeness of the human personality. He praised the possibilities of life on the American frontier, where the worker was not confined to a single occupation, and he looked forward to a time when a man might practice every occupation, as a man, without becoming identified with his work.

Marx's sense of the whole man, as being the necessary goal of a fully humane system of production, has far more value for us today than Marx's tortuous rationalizations of economic theory, in his attempt to make the facts contribute the necessary incentives to revolution. Though Marx was keenly aware of the difference between the biological and social constants in human life and the cultural variables brought into existence by the historical process, he himself never attempted to describe the constants in the economic process. The evils of Victorian industrialism exercised a serpentine fascination over him, and 'Capital' was an attempt to give a systematic account of the transitory relations of capital, labor, and exchange in nineteenth century society: all that belonged in technics to this phase of capitalism he regarded as beyond modification.

But if one thing should be obvious here, it is that the concept of the whole man must rest upon a theory of production which itself takes into consideration the underlying needs of the human personality. When Marx said that current capitalism was bad, he meant plainly that it was bad for man as a human being. Hence any critique of mechanized production must take into account not only the worker's need for material sustenance, but the need for variety, for fellowship, for work-interest; not merely the need for security but the need for esthetic stimulus; not merely his demand for a just share of the rewards after the work is done, but for an equal share of reward in the work itself. The tenth item of the 'Communist Manifesto' wisely advocated not merely free education for children but the eventual combination of education with industrial production. But who needs such a combination more than the mature industrial worker himself? Too easily did Marx and his followers accept the machine as an absolute: too subserviently did they believe that the replacement of craftsmanship by automatism was an inescapable if not always a benign process.

Here William Morris's salutary contrast to Karl Marx must be emphasized. For Morris was no mere reactionary medievalist: he was too fully immersed in practical activities to linger in his pre-Raphaelite rebellion:

on the contrary, he remarked to Patrick Geddes that the iron steamships that were a-building in Glasgow were the Cathedrals of the industrial age, and he exulted not only in their craftsmanship but in the working unison they brought about. Unlike the bourgeois friend of the proletariat, Marx, Morris was a manual worker in his own right. Art, for Morris, was not a precious gift for the few but the daily bread of life, or at least the salt, without which life would lose its savor and the life-blood itself would be depleted.

Morris saw that the machine had devitalized men, and that in the current struggle for money and power the worker was slavishly accepting the ideals of his masters. What the worker needed was not just shorter hours but better hours; not more money but a richer life. Morris's picture of a renovated England in 'News from Nowhere' disclosed a new order in architecture, town planning, and regional development: an idyllic picture that now turns out to be closer to a desirable reality than the vitrified cities and the sterilized personalities that once paraded as the paradise of mechanized and socialized man. Even in industry Morris stood for the primacy of the person. "Simplicity of life, even the barest," he pointed out, "is not misery but the very foundation of refinement." Hence the true reward of labor was in life-wages: self-education, self-expression, self-government: mastery and satisfaction *in* the job, not comforts and luxuries as a relief *from* the job.

Marx closed his mind to the possibility of humanizing the machine from within: he dismissed the values of craftsmanship as ruthlessly as he dismissed the values of rural life—praising capitalism because it had "rescued a considerable part of the population from the idiocy of rural life," though that rescue consisted in throwing them into the foulest slums and the most inhuman factories the world had ever seen. Here we approach the final paradox of Marx's philosophy: it rested on the conception of the continued expansion of the machine, a pushing forward of all those processes that had regimented and enslaved mankind, and yet out of this he expected not only a liberation from the existing dilemmas of society but a final cessation of the struggle. Fichte had suggested that the ultimate aim of government was to make government superfluous; but he was realist enough to put this goal myriads of years away. Marx, on the other hand, believed that as soon as the proletariat had abolished all other classes the state would wither away: with that, the millennial motive-force of history would disappear. Marx spewed out all the utopian minnows only to swallow an ideological whale.

Despite all Marx's rich historical knowledge, his theory ends in nonhistory: the proletariat, once it has thrown off its shackles, lives happily ever afterward. So he shared the Victorian love for the happy ending, though his theory of history had grasped the fact that processes, not things, are the essence of reality. At the very moment that mankind as a whole is clothed, fed, sheltered adequately, relieved from want and anxiety, there will arise new conditions, calling equally for struggle, internal if not external conditions, derived precisely from the goods that have been achieved.

Marx boldly recognized—it was an essential part of his Hegelianism—that the evils in capitalism might engender goods; but he was not realist enough to anticipate that the goods in socialism might in time engender evils: in short, that no historic achievement is perfect, none final.

Like every futurist utopia, Marxism denies the values that lie in the process of achievement: in plans and struggles and hopes, no less than in the ultimate goal. This is the commonest mistake of a detached idealism: it attributes to some final moment the value which lies in the whole process that the ideal has helped to set in motion: this overestimate of the moment of fruition forgets the fact that it is not the climactic moment, but the whole act itself that is irradiated by the ideal. This applies to social life as a whole no less surely than to some particular phase of it like love and marriage. For the last three centuries the revolutionary movement has abounded in examples of moral fervor, heroism, and self-sacrifice: it has its long roll of martyrs from John Milton to Eugene Debs, men who renounced easy careers, who accepted long imprisonment, who showed superb contempt for death, who labored for the unseen and the unattainable without faltering or turning back. All these characteristics gave the revolution the impetus of a great moral act, containing within itself the values it sought to establish: many of those who lived for socialism in the nineteenth century indeed achieved a greater measure of brotherhood and selfless love than those who, in the twentieth century, established a socialist state.

But how different were these real goods from the image of the perfect society that the futurists possessed: that society where, as Eleanor Marx wrote to Beatrice Potter, "people would live for this world and insist on having what made it pleasant for them." Compared to the reality of the revolutionary struggle, that bourgeois idyll in disguise could only be called insipid. Real life, even under capitalism, real life with struggle, pain, disappointment, fellowship, hope, love, is better than utopia. And utopia, to become real, must accept as an incentive to thought and act the dialectic role of evil. Good conditions provide for steady growth, for maturation: hence they must more widely prevail. But negative conditions cannot be glibly exorcized: the problem of evil is to reduce it to amounts that can be assimilated; for evil is like arsenic: a tonic in grains and a poison in ounces.

The paradoxes of Marx's personal life were continued and magnified in the movement he founded. Marxians, by their anti-religious bias, could have no belief in either the religious or the sociological concept of incarnation. Yet Marx's personality continued to form the leaders who took up his work: his arrogance, his contempt, his capacity for vilifying his enemies and his incapacity to learn from anyone—except perhaps Engels—his belief that his personal dogmas were the impersonal deliverances of history, all this tended to create socialist leaders who were more capable of plotting for absolute power than of welding people with different backgrounds, ideas, and purposes into a unified group. The one-party state and the one-man government were the almost inevitable fruit of Marx's character.

In short, socialism suffered from an abortive incarnation. For Marx did not live the life of a socialist: his self-hatred and his self-contempt, which grew out of his sad situation, were magnified by repression and then projected upon every institution and every person that made him conscious of his internal conflict. The poison of Marx's hate contaminated the pure, humane streams of socialist doctrine. . . .

(1944)

CHAPTER TWENTY

Morris: Polytechnic Creativity

William Morris is about the last Victorian figure, one would think, who could appeal to the present age; for the fashionable oppish and poppish forms of non-art today bear as much resemblance to the exuberant creativity of Morris's designs as the noise of a premeditated fart bears to a trumpet voluntary by Purcell. For all that, three books about Morris have come out recently, and none of them treats him in a patronizing way as if he were only a romantic arts-and-craftsy dilettante who finally turned into a sentimental socialist. He is still too big to be either patronized or dismissed.

Though Morris called himself, accurately enough, a dreamer of dreams, born out of his due time, he was also a resolute realist, who refused to take the sordid Victorian triumphs of mechanical progress as the ultimate achievements of the human spirit. Who but a realist could have ended his medieval 'Dream of John Ball' with these words: "Men fight and lose the battle, and the thing that they fought for comes about in spite of their defeat, and when it comes, turns out not to be what they meant, and other men have to fight for what they meant under another name." That sentence should be almost enough to explain why Morris's life and work hold more meaning for the present generation than they did for his actual contemporaries.

The main outlines of William Morris's life were well presented in 1897, the year after his death, in a single volume by Aylmer Vallance; and this was followed in 1899 by a two-volume biography, almost a model of its kind, done by J. W. Mackail. The latter work, unfortunately, had been commissioned by Mackail's parents-in-law, the Burne-Joneses, both lifelong friends of Morris; and Mackail was curbed at critical points by the presence of too many living people. Mackail's inevitable discretions and reticences have hampered every later study of Morris, though, had he only taken the pains, he might have left a memorandum of his omissions, to be opened, like the correspondence between Dante Gabriel Rossetti and Jane, Morris's wife, two generations later.

The many studies that have followed since have, till now, added little except by way of historic background and ideological interpretation. The most weighty of these is that of E. P. Thompson, the Marxist author of an excellent study of the English working class, who has sought to establish that Morris during the last decade of his life was no genteel revolutionary but a well-grounded follower of Karl Marx. Thompson devoted almost 600 of some 900 pages to this aspect of Morris's career: a solid, but disproportionate mass of documentation. Of the new studies before us, that of Philip Henderson, the editor of Morris's letters, is commendable for both its insight and its balance; and it is supported by an abundance of illustrations, some in color, not only of Morris's wallpapers and prints, but also of his friends and his family, whose sad faces reveal something more than mere Victorian gravity. Paul Thompson's study—not to be confused with that of the Marxist Thompson—is of slightly more modest dimensions; and it centers on Morris's career as designer, seeing him no longer as a rebellious isolated giant, but as a well-patronized professional in the mainstream of romantic Victorian design.

Ray Watkinson's book focuses even more sharply on Morris as designer. Half of it, happily, is devoted to illustrations; and indeed the illustrations of all three books, although they overlap a little, taken together form a rather comprehensive exhibition of every phase of Morris's work as artist and craftsman. For some inexplicable reason, none of these studies refers even in passing to the work for which Morris became most famous in America—the 'Morris' arm-chair, possibly because it was not Morris's personal design. But I remember coming upon an illustration of the original chair in an old number of the 'Craftsman' magazine, and marveling over its superb lines and functional convenience—so radically different from all the bastard Morris chairs that were turned out by Grand Rapids. There is not a single chair by Breuer, Eames, Le Corbusier, or van der Rohe that can compare with it in adroitness, elegance, and adaptability to the body.

Thanks to these new books, Morris has been firmly placed in his Victorian setting. But for all that, the man himself remains strangely elusive. How was it that such a backward-looking mind produced so many forward-looking disciples? On what terms did the pre-Raphaelite romantic become the successful Victorian manufacturer? Why did the aristocratic Scawen Blunt call him "the most wonderful man I have known"? For long it was difficult to fit the parts of Morris's life together and attach them to his visible personality.

In one aspect, Morris seems a Dickensian character, almost a caricature: one whose manly simplicity recalled Joe Gargery, the blacksmith in 'Great Expectations.' Gargery's "Wot larks!" was one of his household expressions; and he had a liking for healthy, hearty authors, in the same style

—not only Dickens but Scott, Borrow, Surtees, and above all Cobbett, whom he knew almost by heart—another confident, self-taught, obstinate, explosively indignant soul like himself, or at least part of himself. But this superficially bluff, busy, extroverted man, unflappable except for his sudden outbursts of childish rage—often vented against himself—was not all of one piece. Actually, he harbored three different *personae* which were never, through any single work, so completely fused that he could utilize to the full his magnificent native gifts.

The central Morris *persona* is that of the Master-Craftsman, a figure of towering competence and enormous energy. In his revolt against Victorian kitsch and shoddy, Morris mastered personally one traditional art after another: textiles, stained glass, wallpaper, embroidery, tapestry, rugs, printing type, and every manner of ornament and decoration. The Gothic revival could with propriety be called the medieval Renaissance, for it showed all the characteristic features of that early classic Renaissance which Morris detested. Just as the sixteenth-century Renaissance was an attempt, prompted by newly recovered monuments and books, to restore erotic vitalities and intellectual curiosities that had been suppressed in Christian myth and practice, so the eighteenth-century medieval Renaissance was an attempt to recover vital components of folk culture that purely upper-class groups, princes and artists, inventors and industrialists, had left out of their system. The medievalists were against classic book learning, esthetic formalism, and sophistication. Organic complexity, freedom of adaptation, respect for materials and processes, simplicity and sincerity—these were the new notes.

Though Morris became a passionate medievalist, he actually broke through the medieval rules of craft specialization, precisely as the Renaissance artists had done. He was as much a "universal man" as Leonardo or Alberti. Despite his firm's success in church decoration, Morris ceased to be a Gothic revivalist: indeed, as an opponent of 'historic restoration'—he founded an anti-restoration society—he even condemned some of his own early works. He was rather what Henry-Russell Hitchcock, in his pioneer book on modern architecture, once happily called a New Traditionalist, seeking not to revive the past but to nourish and develop what was still alive in it. He valued excellence wherever he found it—in a Persian rug, an Indian print, or a Chinese pot. Those who best understood Morris's work and caught his spirit from the 1880s onward never became medievalists.

The second *persona* was that of the Romantic poet and fiction writer, who wrote verse so spontaneously that he was at first hardly aware of his special gift, or alert enough to guard himself against his dangerous facility. Yet his earliest volume of verse, 'The Defense of Guinevere' (1858), had poems in it equal to Keats's and Tennyson's work in the same vein. Unfortunately, Morris's later popularity as a Victorian poet came through a series of long, flaccid romances, like 'The Earthly Paradise,' whose sleepy rhythms served, we now have reason to suppose, a private purpose in his life: a poultice on a grievous marital wound. In the seventies, Morris's emotional needs drew him, not to the high Middle Ages, but to the barbaric and brutal Norse past; and his translations of the Icelandic sagas sought to create a readable Northern equivalent for the Aegean epics of Homer. Possibly this retreat into primitive fantasy and archaic poesy saved Morris's life; but the roundabout method kept him from approaching the depth of psychological insight that Melville or Dostoevsky achieved under similar stresses. Though no one can doubt the richness of Morris's inner life, that innerness brought no deeper insight into his own self: significantly he would not tolerate a wall mirror in his house. Though he could produce the most intricate patterns of wallpapers and prints, he had the extrovert's reluctance to confront the darker intricacies of the human soul, even though they tied his own life in knots.

In the last decade of Morris's life, the fluent poet and the indefatigable craftsman were joined by a third *persona,* that of the revolutionary political agitator, waving the red banner of socialist idealism. This change took place during the same dark decade when the author of the 'Princess Casamassima' felt close enough to these stirrings of revolt to picture, with not a little insight, the anarchist revolutionary movement. Morris's political conscience had been roused to activity by the Russo-Turkish crisis in the late seventies, when Tory England threatened to play an ignoble part. But from his Oxford days on Morris was the natural enemy of an economic system that was reducing all work to monotonous, machine-paced drudgery, starving the workers, housing them in ugly, crowded slums, stunting the minds and bodies of children, befouling the land and poisoning the air, threatening to create a race of white, proletarian moles, like the Morlocks whom Wells was to describe in 'The Time Machine.' Once committed to socialism, Morris gave himself completely to it, tasking himself with endless lectures, soapbox harangues, and polemic articles. He even struggled to master the tortuous scholasticism of Marx's surplus value doctrine. And he might have said of Marx as he had said of Blake, that he admired "the part of him which a mortal man can understand."

Morris's climactic involvement with socialism brought forth his real greatness both as a writer and a man; but though it came too late to alter the texture of his dream life, which kept on gushing forth in archaic fairy tales, it bestowed a fuller social content and a larger human purpose on all his private achievements as an artist, and gave him the confidence to work for a future in which all men might know the joys of creative labor that he himself had experienced. In his speeches and essays on Art and Socialism, as in his 'Dream of John Ball' and his 'News from Nowhere,' Morris not merely summed up his beliefs and experiences as an artist-craftsman, who cheerfully mastered every detail of each technical process, but sought to outline the kind of life that would still be possible, if other men shared his vision and his hope. Here a mature and chastened Morris speaks to us, still hating the age he had so early turned his back to, but now appreciating the genuine contributions of its mechanical facility in collective organization.

Better than most, Morris understood the ravages of a profit-driven technology, wantonly wiping out the traditions of a thousand years, so that the Javanese or Indian craftsman could "no longer ply his craft leisurely, working a few hours a day, in producing a maze of strange beauty on a piece of cloth." But so far from wishing to abolish all machines and return to hand labor, Morris thought that it would be possible "to reduce the work of the world to a minimum till at last pretty nearly everything that is necessary to men will be performed by machinery." So perhaps the clearest and most realistic picture of the kind of life that Morris approved will be found, not in the golden tapestry of 'News from Nowhere,' but in two books by his contemporary, Peter Kropotkin: 'Mutual Aid,' and 'Fields, Factories, and Workshops.'

Since work was part of the joy of life, Morris did not propose to surrender all of it to the machine. If the forge, the potter's wheel, the handloom, the dye-vat, the turner's lathe, the garden could no longer provide a sufficient livelihood, they were still a vital mode of human activity, and what is more, a necessary underpinning for human freedom and autonomy. Looking ahead to our time almost a full century ago, he clearly saw where our exclusive preoccupation with automatic machines, quantity production, and corporate profits was leading us. "By that time," he noted, looking backward from his ideal "Nowhere," "it was as much as—or rather more than—man could do to fix an ash pole or rake by handiwork; so that it would take a machine worth a thousand pounds, a group of workmen, and half a day's travelling, to do five shilling's worth of work." That day has in fact arrived. Because we failed to foresee as clearly as Morris the consequences of automation, we now lack competent artisans or even fumbling handymen.

Instead of accepting either megatechnics or monotechnics as inevitable, Morris sought to keep alive or if necessary to restore those forms of art and craft whose continued existence would enrich human life and even keep the way open for fresh technical achievements. He realized from his own experience that only the rich could now buy hand-made products, and that the arts he himself so joyfully practiced had priced themselves out of the market. But once the machine was put in its place and used to save labor not just to create superfluity, there was no reason why everyone should not be rich—rich not mainly in material abundance alone, but better still, in opportunities for enjoyable and self-rewarding work. To put up with a colorless and monotonous working day solely for the sake of what one could buy and spend afterwards, was for him a miscarriage of human purpose.

Certainly, Morris was no friend of the Expanding Economy and the Affluent Society. He had little use for bourgeois comforts and luxuries and still less for status symbols. Despite the intricacy of arabesque in his own decorative patterns, he was all for simplicity; and he even held that a plain distempered wall was better than most wallpaper. Do you suppose, he once asked Yeats, that he prized the kind of house his own workshop helped to decorate? "I would like a house," he said, echoing Thoreau, probably quite unconsciously, "like a big barn, where one ate in one corner, cooked in another, slept in a third, and in the fourth received one's friends." It was this aspect of Morris, his demand for functional forthrightness and simplicity, that passed, along with his ornate floral patterns, into the Art Nouveau movement, and later into the concepts of a thoroughly humanized functional architecture, expressed by architects like Lethaby, Mackintosh, and Barry Parker. In typography, too, his medieval example was soon simplified and purified by Updike and Cobden-Sanderson.

By force of his own technical mastery and his passionate social concern William Morris did more than any other single worker to repair the damage to our whole technical tradition inflicted by those who, in the pride and insolence born of their control of power-driven automata, sought to destroy every rival art, particularly any art that was still supported by ancient traditions and held a warmer human appeal. Morris, a whole generation before the anthropologists began their belated work of salvage with surviving stone age and tribal communities, performed a similar task for the arts and crafts of the Old World past. And if he had been more sympathetic with the peculiar triumphs of his own age, he might not have had the copious, concentrated energies necessary to perform this important salvage operation.

Part of this energy and concentration, we can at last say with some confidence, was a desperate overcompensation for the great flaw in Morris's life: his marriage to the pre-Raphaelite beauty, Jane Burden. If until recently no one had succeeded in putting together the three *personae* of Morris into a single credible picture, it was because one of the keys to his life, though vaguely suspected and hinted at by earlier biographers, was missing. While all the cards seemed on the table, one card was hidden: the dark queen that lay concealed under an exposed king. Morris married Jane in 1859, when he was twenty-five and she eighteen. Two children were born of this marriage; but the marriage itself seems to have been still-born. Before a decade was over, Morris lost his wife to Dante Gabriel Rossetti: she became his favorite model; and to her he openly addressed many of his later love poems. Jane turned out to be, for Morris, the Snow Queen whose heart was made of ice.

Few of Jane's contemporaries had a good word to say for this exotic beauty, or, for that matter, any word at all: she is conspicuous by her absence, for even in the two-volume biography by Mackail there are precisely four references to her in the index of a book of over 700 pages. She remains a creature of fairy tale: enigmatic, impassive, withdrawn, self-absorbed, with her pursed cupid bow lips, as if anatomically arrested in a prolonged kiss. In our ignorance, it would be unfair to ascribe the failure of their marriage to Jane alone: a glacier and a volcano do not easily unite. Perhaps it was only an accident that it was Jane, not William, who fell out of love, and endured to the end what seems for both to have been a friendly but tepid relationship.

Because of Morris's personal reticence, coupled with the discreet silence of everybody in the pre-Raphaelite circle, we shall always lack sufficient positive knowledge of what caused the ice to form and how Rossetti melted it. Even Philip Henderson's fine chapter, "Queen Square: Of Utter Love Defeated Utterly," leaves one with only a keyhole peep through the locked marital door. But the trail of evidence spreads all through Morris's work, from 'The Earthly Paradise' right on to 'News from Nowhere.' For it was in the depths of depression, confronting his wife's love for Rossetti, that Morris wrote 'The Earthly Paradise.' Henderson quotes three significant lines from this poem:

> Time and again across his heart would stream
> The pain of fierce desire whose aim was gone,
> Of baffled yearning, loveless and alone.

And he notes that in the collected works of Morris, May Morris left unprinted these clinching lines, now in the manuscript in the British Museum:

> Why seem the sons of men so hopeless now?
> Thy love is gone, poor wretch, thou art alone.

Despair and death haunt Morris's poems as they haunt the Icelandic sagas to which, during the critical years of his marriage, he turned to find his own life given back to him as in a darkened mirror. His absorption in his writing, his craft work, and his public lectures were all in part efforts to drain off the poisons that his frustrated love life threatened him with; and even these might not have been enough but for his affectionate friendships with sympathetic women, especially Georgie Burne-Jones and Aglaia Coronio—friendships of which teasing glimpses are left in the admirable volume of letters Henderson published in 1950. Passionate man that he was, Morris's personal problem was to cope with both his active need for love and his choking sense of marital frustration, maddened by the lurking presence of Rossetti. Both Rossetti and Jane succumbed to a neurotic invalidism, born probably of guilty inner conflicts. Morris saved himself by sealing off his torment with strenuous activity, and canalizing the overflow of murderous or suicidal fantasy into his long poems, romances, and translations.

On this central relationship, the chapter "Concerning Love," in Morris's utopia, 'News from Nowhere,' written in the decade before his death, seems to me to offer the weightiest bit of personal evidence. In a real sense, Morris's own life had itself been up to a point a kind of full-blown personal utopia. Born to a comfortably wealthy family, spending a happy boyhood near the Epping Forest, awakened to a lifelong ecstasy over the art of the

Middle Ages by his first encounter, at the age of eight, with Canterbury Cathedral, finding himself as an Oxford undergraduate with an unusual gift for writing verses, drawing and working with his hands, soon falling in love with and marrying a beautiful girl, becoming a success at every task he set his hands to—what was all this but the most dreamlike utopia? Even Kelmscott Manor, the house on the upper Thames he acquired in 1870, was, despite its bitter marital associations, so close to his imaged ideal that when he wrote 'News from Nowhere' he could find no happier terminus for his journey through that idyllic land than this very house.

The England that Morris pictured in 'News from Nowhere' unrolls a kind of wallpaper print of pastoral happiness, too decorative and static to be convincing. W. B. Yeats properly described Morris's fantasy as the "make-believe of a child who is remaking the world, not always in the same way, but always after his heart. . . . He has but one story to tell us, how some man or woman lost and found again the happiness that is always half of the body." But significantly, love is the one thing that still goes wrong in Morris's socialist utopia. In this cloyingly amiable society, where every form of exclusiveness and possessiveness, of tension and frustration, has disappeared, the one kind of conflict Morris allows for is sexual conflict, and the only serious failure is a failure of erotic response. In this one dark corner of 'News from Nowhere' there is not only unhappiness, but rivalry, jealousy, anguish—to the point of physical violence and murder. "All this," says the witness in the story, "we could no more help than the earthquake of the year before last."

That volcanic violence must often have been close to the surface in Morris's relations with his wife and Rossetti, he who had originally been his mentor and close friend. Since many witnesses have told tales of Morris's rages on trifling provocation, even in the Oxford days, there must have been occasions when one or another of the lovers was in deadly danger from Morris's convulsive anger. The puzzling line of verse in which Morris, still courting his wife, begs for forgiveness is almost inexplicable, except in reference to some such terrible homicidal moment. Yet miraculously all three lovers remained alive. By pouring all his energies into metrical fantasy and decorative art and incessant manual work—often beginning his day with a couple of hours at the loom, with its soothing monotonous motions—Morris got the better of his dangerous impulses; while his growing concern over political and economic conditions in imperialist England helped restore his sense of realities outside his personal life—realities he had ignored so long as his private utopia remained intact. Probably no better example of sublimation and autotherapy is on record.

Given Morris's extroverted temperament, one can hardly doubt that this tragic flaw in his marital relations limited his emotional development: more than anything else, possibly, it kept the three *personae* from coming together for their mutual support and enlargement. Even after Rossetti's death, no deeper understanding seems to have brought Morris and Jane closer; for his wife barely tolerated the motley group of socialist and anarchist comrades that Morris would gather in his Hammersmith house on a Sunday afternoon. The hollow, Shelleyan optimism of Morris's hortatory socialist songs betrays a failure on his part fully to assimilate his experience or come to terms with the complexities of human character, his own above all.

"I do not," he wrote in 1874 to Mrs. George Howard, "grudge the triumphs that the modern mind finds in having made the world (or a small corner of it) quieter and less violent, but I think that this blindness to beauty will draw down a kind of revenge one day: who knows? Years ago men's minds were full of art and the dignified shows of life, and they had but little time for justice and peace; and the vengeance on them was not the increase of the violence they did not heed, but the destruction of the art they heeded. So perhaps the gods are preparing troubles and terrors for the world (or our small corner of it) again, that it may once again become beautiful and dramatic withal; for I do not believe they will have it dull and ugly forever."

The man who could contemplate this possibility in the midst of The Century of Progress—Peace and Progress!—would not have been daunted by the evils that threaten our own age; and even about the socialist future he had struggled so earnestly to establish, he was more of a realist than Marx himself, with his pathetically juvenile picture of a final dictatorial triumph in which the dialectic process that, as Marx believed, had so far moved the world would disappear, and the State, that armored paragon of collective power, would "wither away." "Socialism," Morris observed in an article in 'Commonweal' in 1890, "will not indeed enable us to get rid of the tragedy of life . . . but will enable us to meet it without fear and without shame." In that spirit, Morris had faced the frustrations and defeats of his own life, without losing his grip in maudlin self-pity. Perhaps this is why he still has something to say to the present generation.

(1968)

CHAPTER TWENTY-ONE

Spengler: Dithyramb to Doom

Barbarism had many prophets during the last century, from Houston Stewart Chamberlain to Georges Sorel, from Nietzsche to Pareto; but the man whose work most fully displays the sinister lure of barbarism was Oswald Spengler, the author of 'The Downfall of the Western World,' timidly translated into English as 'The Decline of the West.' Spengler had a free mind and a servile emotional attitude; he presented a formidable upright figure, with a domed bald head and a keen eye, but in the presence of authority, particularly military authority, his backbone crumpled. Representing the intellect he yet abased the function of intellect before the power of "blood"; elaborating the concept of the organic in history he used it to justify the acceptance of the machine.

Conceived before the First World War, published first in Vienna in 1918, before the war had ended, Spengler's treatise was something more than a philosophy of history. To begin with it was, from the German standpoint, a work of consolation. It was written to rationalize the state in which the new German found himself: he had acquired great wealth and high physical organization by repressing most of his vital impulses except those that directly or deviously served his will-to-power. But in his heart, he was not at home in this new environment. Measured by humane standards, the relatively feeble, industrially backward, politically divided country of the Enlightenment had been a better place for the spirit: Kant in Koenigsberg, Goethe and Schiller in Weimar, Mozart and Beethoven in Vienna had put the Germans on a higher cultural level than centralized Berlin had achieved.

If Germany was defeated in her attempt to gain military and economic control of Europe, all was lost; but if Germany won, how much was gained? Nothing was left except to go on with the empty conquests of the past forty years, building railroads to Baghdad, throwing steamship lines across new trade routes, manufacturing genuine Scotch marmalade in Hamburg, and above all, giving larger scope to Junker arrogance and prowess: the too easy sack of Peking had but whetted army appetites. Thought itself

218

had become technicized, indeed partly militarized: it tended toward adding-machine accuracy, but the values algebraically represented in this process came to so many zeros. Those who still felt a sentimental pull toward the older and deeper German culture were appalled by the battlefront bleak-ness of the intellectual landscape. Spengler himself was appalled: in this he was more keenly alive than that army of American scholars who had imi-tated German methods with clever facility without realizing how little they had gained or how much they were to lose.

Drawing upon world history for consoling comparisons and precedents, Spengler found them in his theory of historic development. According to him, there are two kinds of peoples in the world: those who merely live and those who enact history. The first, if they exist before the cultural cycle be-gins, are mere vegetables: their life is directionless: they endure on a time-less level of pure being. If they come at the end of the cycle they also tumble into a Spenglerian limbo: they are "fellaheen," without ambition, without creative capacity, different from the true peasant because they clothe themselves in the tattered garments of an old civilization, containing its forms even though they progressively lose all its meanings.

Opposed to this dull village chorus are the actors, the creators: the latter experience "Destiny"; they are drawn by a dominating idea from a state of culture, in which life is bound up with a common soil and a deep in-tuitive sense of the importance of blood and race and caste, to a state of civilization, in which their waking consciousness progressively transcends their more instinctive earlier life, and in which the external conquest of na-ture takes the place of the harmonious cultivation of life. In this second state, they cease to be fettered to a particular region and become, instead, cosmopolitan, highly urbanized, increasingly indifferent to all the vital proc-esses that meant so much to both townsman and peasant during the earlier period, deeply hostile to those unconscious or unformulated forces that can-not be glibly translated into word-symbols or money-symbols. Rationalism and humanitarianism devitalize their will-to-power. Pacificism gives rise to passivism. Optimistic and cowardly to the end, the denizens of this civiliza-tion are ripe for butchery.

In the phase of culture, life germinates and flourishes; in the state of civilization, the sap sinks to the roots, the stem and leaves become brittle, and the whole structure of the organism becomes incapable of further growth. The promise of culture's springtime ends in the dormant period of civilization's winter. From the organic to the inorganic, from the living to the mechanical, from the subjectively conditioned to the objectively condi-tioned—this, said Spengler, is the line of development for all societies.

By making the rise and fall of cultures an immanent, automatic process, Spengler got caught in the net of his organic metaphor: he was thus forced to treat each culture as a unified body, dominated by a specific idea, which in turn would be symbolized by its architecture, its mathematics, its paint-ing, its statecraft, its technics. Not merely is a culture incapable of receiving the ideas or contributions of other cultures; it cannot even understand them. All intercourse with outside cultures is impossible: all carryovers from the past are for Spengler an illusion. The processes of self-repair, self-renewal, self-transcendence, which are as observable in cultures as in persons, were completely overlooked by Spengler. His many vital perceptions of the historic process served only one purpose which he kept steadfastly in view: as apology for barbarism.

Applying his theory to 'Faustian' culture, that of the last thousand years, Spengler pointed out that the Western European was about to enter the frigid state of winter. Poetry, art, philosophy were no longer open possibilities; civilization meant the deliberate abdication of the organic and vital elements: the unqualified reign of the mechanical, the desiccated, the devitalized. The region was shriveling to a point: the world city or megalopolis. (The original Megalopolis in fourth century Greece had emptied out a whole countryside in order to create a single large center.) The earth itself was now being plated with stone and steel and asphalt: man dreamed of growing crops in tanks, taking food in capsules, transplanting foetuses to protoplasmic incubators, conquering the air in stratoliners by means of oxygen tanks, and burrowing into underground cities in order to have security against his wonderful conquest of the more rarefied medium. In that process, the individual shrank once more into a mechanical atom in a formless mass of humanity: the sourest satire of Aldous Huxley's 'Brave New World' or Zamiatin's 'We' scarcely did justice to the regimentation that was actually under way. To succeed in terms of such a civilization, one must be hard. What remained of life, if one could call it life, belonged to the engineer, the business man, the soldier; in short, to pure technicians, devoid of any concern for life or the values of life, except in so far as they served the machine. Was there no way for life, then, to reassert itself? Spengler answered Yes: by brutality, by brutality and conquest. The sole outlet open to the victims of civilization was to replenish their barbarism and consummate their will-to-destruction. In politics the hour of Caesarism was at hand.

This invocation to barbarism fascinated many of Spengler's more literate contemporaries. Hence it is important to realize, not so much the illegitimacy of the poetic figure Spengler used, as the even deeper unsoundness of the grand division Spengler made between culture and civilization, by putting them at opposite ends of a cycle. These two terms represent the spiritual and the material aspects of every society; and the fact is that one is never found without the other. The overdevelopment of fortifications and castles in the fourteenth century, for example, was as much a mechanical fact, an example of sheer externalization, as the overdevelopment of subways in the modern megalopolis, though the first belonged to a vernal feudalism of blood and caste, while the other belongs to finance capitalism. So, again, the building of new towns on rectangular plans was as much a characteristic of the springtide of Faustian culture as it was of the autumnal period of the nineteenth century. Spengler's theory of cultural isolationism —unfortunately a typical example of Germanic egoism—prevented him from correctly interpreting the organic inter-relations his theory pretends to demonstrate. At every point his organicism gives place to dualism: for without that dualism he could not sanction barbarism.

To follow the real drift of the 'Downfall' one must read the pamphlets which were all that Spengler published in the following years: here the hidden aim was unveiled. In 'Man and Technics,' and in 'The Hour of Decision,' Spengler divested himself completely of the forms of scholarly judgment: he beat a frenzied tattoo on the tribal drum, attempting to summon together the forces of reaction. For Spengler was no Aristotle: he was the revived Fichte of the barbarian revolution whose name was fascism in Italy, Nazism in Germany, and totalitarianism everywhere. In its very characteristics as a work of art, a poem of devilish hate and darkening fate, Spengler's 'Downfall' was an image of the fascist states that were to be erected during the next two decades: their irrationalities, their phobias, their humorless limitations, their colossal brutalities, their perverse animus against all life, except at the blindest levels of the id, were prophetically mirrored in his work. He who understood the significance of Spengler's act of prophecy had little to learn from the further course of Europe's history.

Spengler's historical thesis took possession of a defeated and war-weary world. Men had everywhere dreamed of justice, democracy, peace. But the fruits of war were shabby efforts to achieve "normalcy," that is, forgetfulness. Instead of peace, there was a continuation of military efforts on other fronts, and a solemn determination on the part of the governing classes to stave off the deep economic changes—as urgent then as today— that threatened their power. In order to avoid the harrowing possibility of further struggle, men sought peace by paring down armaments instead of establishing more firmly the organs for political justice, and by retreating into dreams of tortoiselike isolation, with schemes for Imperial Preferences, Maginot Lines, Autarchy, and Hemispheric Solidarity.

The title of Spengler's book had an even more immediate appeal than its contents, which were difficult for even the educated to understand. For the title whispered the soothing words, *downfall, doom, death.* The postwar challenge to effective, purposive action, action in the light of human ideals, action in behalf of a better life, was dissipated by Spengler's very doctrine of 'pure' action—that is, action without rational motive or ideal content: the work of expansion and aggrandizement as practiced by the masters of the machine.

The war machine, the finance machine, the industrial machine, the education machine—all these agents redoubled their interest in technique for its own sake: the *l'art pour l'art* of practice. Witness the manner in which American bankers foisted loans on German industries and municipalities without even a touch of the banker's traditional prudence about the ultimate recovery of the capital they so glibly manipulated. Capitalism, reinvigorated by war-profits, entertained itself with prospectuses of limitless expansion. Artful Dodgers in financial technique, sheer fantasts and forgers like Ivar Kreuger, were hailed as industrial statesmen. Advertisement writers, masters of propaganda and publicity, exponents of polished insincerity, desecrated truth and beauty in the interest of their commercial clients— and thus made even genuine truth suspect and even actual beauty seem meretricious and purchasable. Such truth, bent on profitable seduction, became more degrading than a brazen lie.

So far from urging men to depart from these vicious forms of action, Spengler proclaimed that no other course was possible: history only urged the strong to gird themselves for greater depredations and the weak to prepare for greater disasters.

Because Spengler respected only physical force, the pure act, he prophesied with accuracy the nature of the post-war world and he diagnosed its typical disease—the paralysis of will, on the part of humane men and women, which followed by sheer exhaustion the over-keyed energies of the war itself. Reacting against the intensified emotions of war, men avoided all emotions: shrinking from the horrors and harshness of war, they evaded all occasions for physical struggle or hardship: too feeble, too disoriented, to achieve at once the noble ideals for which millions on the Allied side had given their lives, the post-war generation debunked all ideals: that avoided the necessity for further struggle or responsibility. Even if they did not read Spengler they were his disciples in practice.

For all his breadth of vision, Spengler succeeded only in reading back into world history the limitations of his own country, his own generation. In his scheme of living he had no place for the very class he represented: the priest, the artist, the intellectual, the scientist, the maker and conserver of ideas and ideal patterns were not operative agents: he not merely asserted that no fact has ever altered a faith, but he even said that no idea had ever modified an act. If that were true, he need not have spent so much time attempting to shout down the ideas of those who opposed the acts he favored.

Every society consists of organizers, energizers, creators, and followers: in each group and association within society a similar social division of labor can be detected; and all social action is the result of their combined efforts. For Spengler, the organizers, the men of blood and will, were supreme. The work of the creators, strange to say, he associated with death: the fixed, the immobilized, the no-saying seemed to him their only attributes; and he hated the activities of the men of religion and the men of thought because it curbed the raw outbreaks of animal passion and physical prowess that his drill sergeant's mind gloried in.

The truth is that Spengler feared the deep humanness of humanity, as he feared those domestic sentiments, truly native to man, that work against the rule of his mythical "carnivore." Spengler recoiled from the fact, so obvious in history, that dehumanized power in the long run is as pitifully weak, as impotent and sterile, as a merely wishful humanitarianism. He hated the independent power of the mind, creating values, erecting standards, subduing ferine passions, laying the basis for a more universal society, precisely because he knew in his heart of hearts, for all his loud contempt, that this *was* a power: a power men obeyed, a power even the humblest could feel within himself, at least in milliamperes, as in a radio receiving set, recording the same feelings, the same hopes and dreams, that had left the original transmitting station at full strength.

What makes Spengler so significant was that he expressed in so many words the premises upon which Western society as a whole acted: the man of fact, who despised values, was the product of the New World idolum, native to that habitat, flourishing there almost without competitors like the jack-rabbit in Australia. With the rest of Western society in decay, the antivital tendencies of the mechanical ideology now could exercise themselves unrestrained. Nothing that Spengler advocated for the coming dictatorships was outside current practice: the gangsterism he preached on a large scale had already been achieved in the one-man rule of the American political boss, petty but sometimes not so petty: his contempt for the poet and the painter, his devaluation of all ideal activity, were but the working principles of the successful philistine in every land: his glorification of technique at the expense of rational content was the very principle by which men currently advanced themselves in medicine or in education, in law or business: did not advertising condition the masses to this philosophy?

Unlike his liberal and democratic opponents, Oswald Spengler drew the inevitable conclusion from this situation. If values are unreal and if humane purposes are chimerical, then even scientific technique must ultimately become subservient to brute force: the need for rational restraint and self-discipline of any kind disappears. Thus technicism leads directly to irrationality—and the cult of barbarian power salvages the technician's otherwise growing sense of frustration and futility. It is no accident that Germany produced both the most mechanized type of personality in its robot-like soldiers and civilians, and the most unrestrained reaction against humane discipline, in the form of an exultant sub-animality.

Spengler ignored all the creative tendencies in modern life, except those associated with the machine: little though he relished the thought, his essential creed favored Russia and the United States even more than it did the fascist countries. Spengler accepted as "real" only those elements which emphasized modern man's automatism, his deflation of values, his subservience to mechanical organization, and the savage irrationality which takes the place of reason in other parts of the personality. And because these forces cannot be confined within their original frontiers, Spengler predicted, far more accurately than hopeful philosophers, the disastrous downward course that modern civilization is still following, at a steadily accelerating pace. Through its emotional impact, Spengler's work as a whole constitutes a morbid Saga of Barbarism. It began as a poem of defeat; it finally became an epic justification of the fascist attack on the very humanity of man—an attack that has already gone so far that even democratic peoples have torpidly swallowed as their own, without retching, the fascist doctrine of totalitarian air warfare: one of the deepest degradations of our age.

Spengler's day is not yet over. These are ominous times and Spengler is like a black crow, hoarsely cawing, whose prophetic wings cast a shadow over our whole landscape. The democratic peoples cannot conquer their fascist enemies until they have conquered in their own hearts and minds the underlying barbarism that unites them with their foes. In the passive barbarism that the United States now boasts under the cover of technical progress, there is no promise whatever of victory or even bare survival. Without a deep regeneration and renewal, the external triumph of American machinery and arms will but hasten the downfall of the Western World. Only those who are ready for that renewal, with all its rigors, its sacrifices, its hard adventures, are entitled to celebrate even our temporary victories.

(1939–1944)

PART THREE

Myth of the Machine

CHAPTER TWENTY-TWO

Drama of the Machines

Though we call our period the Machine Age, very few people have any perspective upon the machine, or any clear notion of its origins. Popular historians date the great transformation that has taken place with the invention of Watt's steam-engine; and in the conventional text-book the application of mechanical methods to weaving is usually treated as a critical turning-point; whereas, like all great changes, the introduction of the machine was essentially a change of mind, and it no more depended upon any single invention, like the steam-engine, than it depended upon any special industry. The gains that the machine has brought have rarely been balanced up against the losses; and Stuart Chase's recent attempt to do this showed how intricate and uncertain such an estimate must be, once one drops the comfortable Victorian notion that all change is progress and all progress is beneficial.

If we wish to have any clear notion about the machine we must think about its psychological as well as its practical origins; and similarly, we must appraise its aesthetic and ethical results. For a century we have isolated the technical triumphs of the machine; we have bowed before the handiwork of the inventor and the scientist; we have alternately exalted these new instruments for their practical success, and despised them for the narrowness of their achievements. When one examines the subject freshly, however, many of these estimates are upset. We find that there are human values in machinery that we did not suspect; we also find that there are wastes, losses, perversions of energy which the ordinary economist blandly concealed. The vast material displacements the machine has made in our physical environment are perhaps in the long run less important than its spiritual contributions to our culture.

A drama could be made of the coming of the machine into modern society.

Five or six centuries before the main body of the army forms, spies have been planted among the nations of Europe. Here and there, in strategic positions, small bodies of scouts and observers appear, preparing the way for the main force: a Roger Bacon, a Leonardo da Vinci, a Paracelsus. But the army of machines could not take possession of modern society until every department had been trained; above all, it was necessary to gather a group of creative minds, a general staff, who would see a dozen moves beyond the immediate strategy and would invent a superior tactics. These are the physicists and mathematicians; without their abstract descriptions, the useful habit of isolating certain movements and sequences would not have been adopted, and invention would probably have sought to reproduce—as in fact it first did—cumbrous mechanical men or mechanical horses, instead of their abstract equivalents, namely, steam-engines, locomotives, rifles, cranes. Behind the scientific advance-guard came the shock troops, the miners, the woodmen, the soldiers proper, and their inventive leaders. Five centuries were needed to set the stage for the modern world.

At last the machines are ready. The outposts have been posted and the army trained. Between Dante and John Bunyan there are only four centuries; but between John Bunyan's Pilgrim and Defoe's Robinson Crusoe there is a whole epoch: one is interested in his soul, the other in the ingenious adaptation of his material environment. What is the order of the battle, and where does the machine claim its first victory?

The battle which led to the establishment of the machine as a central force in Western civilization was a battle in the most literal sense; for perhaps the incentive to mechanical contrivance came, as Edward Jenks observed a generation ago, from the institution of warfare. Modern Western society distinguishes itself from many savage communities, and from such high civilizations as that of ancient China, by the application of a deadly earnestness to the slaughter of men. Holsti, in his treatise on 'War and the State,' has pointed out the ritualistic and playful elements in savage warfare; but in spite of the prudence and matter-of-factness of the professional soldier, a transformation came about when the ideal of the knightly encounter was exchanged for a relentless combat in the name of "religion" or freedom. Did this animus lead to the invention of more deadly weapons, or did the cannon and the musket automatically claim more blood? Probably both. At all events, the archetypal internal combustion engine—bullets propelled by gunpowder—was a product of warfare.

The increasing deadliness of armed combat made, in addition, new demands upon the art of the smith: first in the manufacture of fine steel armor, then with the development of the musket and the cannon, and finally, in our own day, with the armored battleship and the armored tank. These demands both accelerated the increase in skill and caused rapid advances in mining and smelting; and this in turn directed skilled minds to technological processes which had hitherto been carried on in a hit-or-miss fashion. Leonardo offered his services to princes, not to utilize his skill in painting, but because of his knowledge of ballistics and fortification, because he could construct redoubts and ditches and canals. The division between the quantitative processes of production, which became the province of the engineer, and the qualitative interests, which were relegated to the pure artist, is beautifully illustrated in the conflict that perpetually agitated Leonardo himself. Roughly, up to his time these processes were united; thenceforward the practical man and the idealist, the utilitarian and the aesthete, tended to be separated. By the time the nineteenth century opened, the gulf was almost final. The engineer knew no art; the artist had few connections with practical life; and the architect, in whom the traditional state persisted, lacked the power to integrate these two elements in his designs.

Back of the soldier stand the woodman and the miner: they are the primitive forms of the modern engineer. A certain amount of harm has been done, in interpreting the industrial changes that have taken place, by confusing derivative agents, like factory production and the invention of the power-loom, with the great prime-movers, and the prime machine-tools themselves. The woodman was the chief contributor to the precise arts: a whole tradition of woodcraft lies behind the individual inventions that began to multiply around 1760 in England. As wheelwright and turner he produced the wheels and ratchets necessary for the first clocks, whose works were made of wood; in his creation of the engine lathe, in its earliest form a bent sapling attached for motive power to a shaft, he handed on the most useful perhaps of all machine tools, for without it accurate machines and instruments of measurement could not be made. The woodman and the smith produced the water-wheel and the windmill, the first attempts to transfer the burden of work from the backs of animals to the impersonal forces of nature. Directly from the mine came a contribution which, though not so fundamental, nevertheless provided the framework of nineteenth-century civilization: the railroad, first invented to facilitate the removal of ore from the pit; while likewise invented for the mine, in order to keep the shaft from flooding with water, was the primitive steam-engine.

Once these key inventions were planted, once the General Staff was ready to supply a broad stream of abstract ideas and suggestions, the time had come for the machine to take possession of Western civilization: at last the derivative products of industrialism could spawn and multiply. From the woodman's primitive distillation of tar to the thousand dyes and medicines and poisons that come from the destructive distillation of coal, from the soldier's gunpowder and cannons and pontoons to the rock-dynamiting, foundation-digging, bridge-building, and road-laying of today; from the sailor's rough steering by sun and the North Star and the magnetic needle to the accurate trigonometrical calculations and chronometer readings of modern navigation—all this is a difference of extent and accuracy but not of kind.

The machine brought with it great gains in mechanical efficiency; unfortunately, since it derived so much of its technic and animus from the destructive arts of mining and warfare, these gains were offset by a loss of human purpose. The ideology of physical science reinforced these original weaknesses: for its method was to isolate and dismember human experience, reduce every aspect of it to its quantitative relations, and remove, as a source of error, the human personality itself. In the abstract world of physical science there was no more place for the human purpose than there was a place for thoughts and dreams in the motions of pistons or a place for work-songs in the pounding of trip-hammers. The machine was more efficient than a human being, partly because of new sources of power, and partly because its functions were completely stripped of irrelevant aims or interests.

The advantages of the machine that have been most readily appreciated have been the tapping of new natural sources of power, moving air, running water, coal, petroleum, gas, and the substitution of mechanical labor for both the creative energy of the handicraft artist and the deadening routine of the servile drudge. From the first change we derive untold quantities of power; from the second, in so far as the machine has been able to replace human labor completely, we derive the possibility of freedom—although the specialized factory worker has lost something of the occupational variety and human companionship of the old-fashioned workshop.

Neither freedom nor power is an end in itself: they are conditions of human fulfillment. But it is plain that if the ends are adequate, a commensurate grasp of the forces that condition them is a great boon—and if it were a social actuality and not, as at present, a pious hope, it would justify almost every boast of the technocrat apologists. The formal contributions of the machine, on the other hand, its value for mind and culture, are apparently much more difficult to grasp than its practical success: indeed, most industrialists would feel guilty of heresy did they believe—but who in the past was bold enough to suggest it?—that the capital achievement of the machine was an ethical and imaginative one.

Yet the more one reflects upon the machine, the less important do its practical achievements seem: Stuart Chase's contrast between the life of a modern factory worker and that of a medieval villager shows how little of the sweat and blood and power and thought of the modern world is actually consumated in life and art—and this must be the final test of all practical effort. When one weighs the solid products of the machine against the wholesale destruction it has wrought in a single century, against the forests that must be replanted, the foul cities that must be razed and rebuilt, the depleted countrysides that must be restored, against all the irredeemable human misery it has brought into existence, against its constant threat of universal annihilation by mechanized warfare—when one balances these things, the blessings of the machine seem a little tainted; and at all events, we cannot take them for granted.

Potentially, the machine has removed a part of our drudgery and routine; actually, the drudgery and routine remain, only a smaller and smaller part of society participates in it. Instead of distributing leisure, our modern industrial societies are burdened with chronic unemployment, a curse and not a benefit; and when, to keep the wheels moving, it forces its ephemeral goods upon the market, it only turns the laborer into a goods-devouring mechanism, the victim of a servile system of consumption. What then remains?

What remains is the technic of co-operative thought and action, the aesthetic excellences of the machine, and the delicate logic of materials and forces it has added to the canon of human achievements. Eliminating man, the machine has nevertheless embodied two of his deepest desires: the will-to-power and the will-to-order. It has turned the first will from the domination of other men to the domination of nature, and it has created for the accomplishment of certain physical results a universal language: the language of exact science.

If the goods of industrialism are still largely evanescent, its aesthetic is a durable contribution. The practical results are often dubious; the methods are excellent. The machine has added a whole series of arts to those produced by simple tools and handicraft methods. These arts have their own proper standards and give their own peculiar satisfaction to the human spirit. What matters the fact that the ordinary individual is the master of a hundred mechanical slaves, if the master himself remain an imbecile? But if the exact arts produced by the machine have their own contribution to make to the mind, a gain in intelligence, perception, and feeling may follow; and such gains would be vital ones indeed. Let us examine the machine more carefully as an instrument of culture.

The difficulty in appreciating the cultural contribution of the machine can best be shown, perhaps, in describing the way in which the problem of machine design was first faced, then muffed, and finally solved. For mechanical problems were formulated and partly solved long before the aesthetic and human aspects were taken into consideration: the machines became a condition of our existence before they became an emotive part of our life.

In the design of the first machines, as in the organization of the first factories, the purely practical considerations were almost inevitably uppermost, and the personality was firmly shoved to one side. So universal was this characteristic that, until recent times, the only adjective that habitually modified the word factory was "ugly," just as if utilitarian structures, a castle, a bridge, a granary, had never in the past by any chance been beautiful. Nevertheless, the elimination of the human factor had to be justified and somehow compensated. Hence, over the incomplete, unrealized forms of the early machines and bridges a meretricious touch of decoration was added, a mere relic of the warm fantasies that painting and carving had once added to almost every handicraft object. The Battersea Bridge in London, the steel work in the lower part of the Eiffel Tower, the iron trusses in the oldest section of the Metropolitan Museum exhibit this incised or moulded ornament with which the early engineer sought to transform his structure into a veritable work of art: the homage of hypocrisy. One sees the identical effort on the earliest type of steam-radiator, in the floral decorations that originally graced the typewriter, and in the nondescript arabesque that still quaintly lingers on shotguns and sewing-machines.

This first stage is a compromise. The object is divided into two parts, one of which is to be precisely designed for mechanical efficiency, and the other to be decorated after the canons of an entirely different kind of art. While the utilitarian claims the structure, which must work, the aesthete is permitted slightly to modify the surface with his irrelevant patterns, his plutonic flowers, or his aimless filigree—provided that he does not alter the structure. This compromise satisfied the utilitarian longer than it did the romantic; but it produced a bastard art; a large part of our architecture and our American furniture and our machine-stamped china has long been a witness of this weak division. Mechanically produced by the aid of machinery, it shamefully conceals its origins, at the same time that it mocks the handicraft to which it claims affiliation.

The next stage in the development of machine design was the withdrawal of the the utilitarian and the romantic to their several parts of the field. The romantic, insisting with justice that the structure is integral with the decoration, began to revive by purely handicraft methods the arts of the potter and the cabinet-maker and the printer, arts which had survived, for the most part, only in "backward" parts of the world, in the isolated islands or mountain areas of Europe, untouched by the tourist and the commercial traveller. The old workshops and ateliers had almost died out by the middle of the nineteenth century in 'progressive' England and America, when new ones, like those devoted to glass under William de Morgan and John La Farge in American, or to furniture, such as that of William Morris, sprang into existence, to prove by their example that, given leadership and active patronage, the arts of the past could survive.

But the point was that neither the patronage nor the problems were the same. The world that men carried in their heads, their *idolum,* was an entirely different one from that which set the mediaeval mason to carving the history of creation or the lives of the saints above the portals of his cathedral; and an art based like handicraft upon the stratification of classes and the social differentiation of wants could not survive with any certainty in a world that had witnessed the French revolution and had been promised a rough share of equality.

Modern handicraft, which sought to rescue the poor worker from the slavery of shoddy machine production, merely enabled the rich to enjoy in their own time an art that was as completey divorced from the social milieu as that of the palaces and monasteries and churches the collector had already begun to loot. The educational aim of the arts and crafts movement was admirable; and in so far as it gave courage to the amateur worker it was partly a success. Every modern home is, no matter how unconsciously, the better for the insistence upon the simplicity and honesty that Morris and his followers made a principal item in their creed: "Possess nothing that you do not know to be useful or believe to be beautiful." But the social outcome of the arts and crafts movement was ridiculous, as Frank Lloyd Wright said in his famous speech at Hull House in the nineties; it lacked the courage to grasp the valuable instruments that the machine had put at the call of creative purpose, and being unable to attune itself to new objectives and new standards, it was almost compelled to restore a mediaeval ideology in order to provide a social backing for its ante-machine methods. In a word, the modern arts and crafts movement tended to be weakly retrospective and sentimental. Before handworking could be restored as an admirable sport and an efficacious relief from a physically inane life, it was first necessary to dispose of the machine as a social instrument. So the real contribution to art and polity was made by the industrialist who remained on the job and saw it through.

With the third stage in design an alteration takes place. The imagination is not applied to the mechanical object after its functional design has been created: it is infused into it. The spirit works through the medium of the machine and the conditions imposed by it; and not content with a crude quantitative expression, it seeks a more positive fulfillment. This must not be confused with the aesthetic dogma, so often current, that mechanical fitness necessarily produces an aesthetic result; the source of this fallacy is that in many cases our eye has been trained to recognize beauty in nature, in the shapes of fish and birds; and when an airplane becomes like a gull, it has the advantage of this long association, while we ascribe the beauty to the mechanical adequacy. When we take an object with no natural kinships, however, like the old-fashioned telephone transmitter, the theory falls down: aesthetically, it is a clumsy object and no amount of *a priori* theory can make it anything else.

Expression through the machine implies, however, the recognition of relatively new aesthetic terms: precision, calculation, flawlessness, economy, simplicity. Feeling attaches itself, in these new forms, to different qualities from those which make handicraft so jolly: the elegance of a mathematical equation, the inevitability of physical interrelations, the naked quality of the material itself. Who discovered these qualities? Many an engineer and many a machine worker must have mutely sensed them, in the act of design or operation; but only after a hundred years of blind effort were these new feelings deliberately projected by a group of sensitive painters and sculptors, during the first decade of the present century. The Cubists discovered and attached themselves to this world of abstract mathematical relationships and mechanical technics. A succession of artists, Marcel Duchamps, Duchamps Villon, Brancusi, Braque, Stieglitz, Gabo, revealed in their paintings and sculptures the new feeling toward form that the machine had developed. Looking around at our mechanical phantasmagoria, we discovered, through their eyes, a new world; and we found that our practical expedients, and our fine utilitarian dodges, had provided us with new symbols and significances.

When this discovery was made, a new attack upon all the arts became possible. Hitherto the sole influence upon machine design had been the physical sciences; now the mind had absorbed this knowledge and had produced a fresh ideology. The arts flourish when they are continually played upon by exact knowledge and practical experience on one hand, and by the intuitions and creative patterns that arise out of the personality itself on the other; this double partnership was finally established in the mechanical arts, and a decisive start was again made. While in the traditional arts the necessary transformations came slowly, in the development of entirely new instruments, such as the automobile, the airplane, the modern bathroom, it came by a series of swift innovations, almost under our very eyes.

The key to this transformation was the discovery of the guiding principle of machine aesthetics: the principle of economy. Now the ideal aim of design is to remove from the object, be it an automobile or a bedroom, every detail, every moulding, every variation of surface, every extra part except that which induces to its effective function. Le Corbusier has been very ingenious in picking out the manifold objects in which modern taste has declared itself without pretense or fumbling. The smoking pipe, for example, is no longer carved to look like a human head or to bear an heraldic emblem; it becomes exquisitely anonymous; it is nothing more than a finely shaped apparatus for supplying drafts of air from the human mouth to a slow-burning mass of dry vegetation, to be held snugly in the hand at appropriate intervals for a quiet gesture.

This stripping down to essentials has gone on in every department where the machine and its products have been touched by an appropriate imagination. We have witnessed the same improvement in design from the ill-balanced push-power airplane to the modern tractor type; we have seen it in the transformation of the gawky Tin Lizzies into the present compact Ford. The potters of Trenton no longer paint their washstands with flowers; and the makers of typewriters exhibit a similar restraint.

Where this change has gone on, the modern spirit is at home. Since this transformation is a vital one, it affects every department of life; just as the arabesque of the Renaissance painters was reproduced in sixteenth-century costume, so the severities of our mechanical design have a counterpart in dress and gesture. Where this change has been impeded, the modern spirit is uneasy and relapses too quickly into an unctuous sentimentalism. Indeed, where the principle of economy and fitness is not heeded, the touch becomes unsure. What a contrast between the tennis costume or skating costume for women today and the vague fripperies of the formal evening dress, designed according to the canons of conspicuous waste!

The third stage in design is not yet a commonplace; for it is more easy to embody its principles in the making of machines than it is to do so in creating the products that are turned out by the machine.

For a clear example of the second task, we must turn to the prophetic works of engineering that were produced during the nineteenth century. Just because of their remoteness and because of the obviousness of their imperfections, we can see a little more plainly the goal that is to be achieved. Perhaps the three greatest monuments of the age were the Crystal Palace (1851), the Brooklyn Bridge (1883), and the Eiffel Tower (1888), all of which are still standing. In each of these structures, despite residual weaknesses, such as the coping of the Brooklyn Bridge piers, or the early L'Art Nouveau ornament of the ironwork of the Eiffel Tower, the presence of a high order of intelligence and imagination is indisputable. Created with the aid of physics and mathematics and their special technologies, the bridge, the tower, the glass-hall are likewise the expression of a promethean audacity which rose to a new occasion. Indeed, the calculations which determine the system of tensions and the pattern of cables in a bridge, or the stresses and strains in a tower, are themselves a noble human product; and the results are quite as capable of stirring the imagination as the naïver fantasies and empirical common sense of the handicraft worker, who had fairies and demons instead of catenary curves and vector functions to inspire him.

Is any further proof needed that the work of a Roebling or an Eiffel arose out of the spirit? One need look no farther than the routine factory buildings, the badly tailored iron bridges that have been put together by people without imagination, to see that technology alone is not responsible for these aesthetic successes: it lays down certain conditions and means, but by itself it does not dominate them.

Nevertheless, good results have sometimes been achieved in the precise arts by a collective organization, unconscious of the fact that it was actually producing a work of art. This is not so paradoxical as it may seem. When the engineers of the excellent ventilation building of the Holland Tube were told by a friend of mine that they had created a genuine piece of modern architecture, they were surprised, and unable to attribute the design to any single person. It was this sort of almost instinctive collective unanimity that led William Morris to refer to the great shipbuilders of

Glasgow as the modern equivalent of the Cathedral builders; and where such a feeling develops, one may be confident that the third stage of machine design, which involves the complete integration of all the functions to be performed, is on the way to achievement.

Our engineers, unfortunately, are still the victims of a very narrow system of training; and they are so unconscious of the fact that they have done the right thing that they may, five minutes later, commit in entire innocence an aesthetic monstrosity. The remedy for this does not lie in superimposing a specialist in aesthetics, a designer or an architect, but in broadening and humanizing the content of the engineer's education, increasing his aesthetic sensitiveness as well as his technological skill. John Roebling, the designer of the Brooklyn Bridge, studied architecture as well as hydraulics and mathematics, and was versed in philosophy, which he studied under Hegel and continued to reflect upon throughout life. That kind of mind, which is also the kind exhibited by a Louis Sullivan, a Frank Lloyd Wright, a Walter Gropius, and a Le Corbusier, can use the machine as an instrument of expression. When this spirit becomes common, the crude plastic dogmatism of the earlier type of engineering will disappear, and we shall have a subtle dialectics of form, capable of solving every physical problem and enclosing almost every relevant human impulse.

The achievement of adequate machine forms is not an easy matter; and the cultural expression of the machine has had to fight against several refractory human impulses: dead imitativeness, snobbishness, insensitiveness to fresh experience.

What W. F. Ogburn has termed the cultural lag holds with machine design as well as with social customs: the change in form lags behind the changed conditions of technics. It is almost as easy under our modern system of production to turn out a piece of fake handicraft—a machine-carved chair-leg or a mottled antique surface—as it is to produce a thoroughly modern object—indeed, it is a little easier, since a wholly adequate machine form requires a special kind of aesthetic sensitiveness which is only partly achieved through a knowledge of handicraft forms and which cannot be developed without the aid of a proper ideology, to say nothing of a vast amount of experimental practice. The beauty of machine work rests upon formal relationships, and the designer may have to work upon a single problem as long and as patiently as the Greek builder did on the design of the temple before the inevitable proportions for a particular form are worked out. Moreover, these proportions and forms in steel and aluminum will be different from those produced by handicraft in wood; and since habitual association takes the place in untrained minds of active aesthetic appreciation, it is impossible for such persons offhand to accept the new forms that the machine produces. Hence a severe new form, like Mies van der Rohe's tubular chair, may be rejected by the man in the street, who demands weight, carvings, curlicues—although, where no old associations are present, as in the airplane, he is as ready to accept modern aesthetics as any one else.

The second obstruction to the development of machine aesthetics has been social snobbishness. Handicraft ornament has been in the past one of the obvious means of establishing caste and social position. Even dreadfully inhuman arts, like fine lace-making, which ruins eyesight, have flourished along with happier crafts because of the desire to proclaim by such fineries the power and prestige of the wearer. Now our modern science is a collective product, and the machine has tended to produce a collective economy. Whatever the politics of a country may be, the machine, as I have pointed out elsewhere, is a communist. As the machine conquers one department after another of production, it obliterates the distinctions of caste and financial status. There can be no functional difference between a good machine design for a factory-worker's home and that for a professional man's; in so far as money differences are still permitted to count for anything, they can alter only the scale of things, not the kind.

Because of a surviving desire for exclusiveness and individuality, however, a deliberate perversion of the machine frequently takes place, even after a satisfactory stage of machine design has been reached. In the treatment of motor-cars this takes the form of irrelevant mouldings and tricky shapes for the hood; in bathrooms, it results in the introduction of period styles to supplant strong modern forms, as in the conversion of admirable water-faucets into swans' necks, or some similar absurdity; in typewriters and fountain pens it comes forth as mottled color effects which break the fine surfaces of these objects, with no aesthetic gain. In short, in our present money-ridden society, where men play with poker-chips instead of with economic and aesthetic realities, we invent a thousand ways of disguising from ourselves the fact that we have potentially achieved a collective economy, in which the possession of goods is a meaningless distinction, and in any large quantity a gratuitous burden; since our characteristic goods are equally available to every person in that society, falling on the just and the unjust, the foolish and the wise, like the rain itself.

In the late Thorstein Veblen's classic book 'The Theory of the Leisure Class' these absurdities were skillfully analyzed. Until we modify our taste and our morals sufficiently to profit by the profound change the machine has made in our lives, we shall only stultify ourselves by its employment. The real social distinction of the machine is that it dissolves social distinctions. Its immediate goal is effective work; its ultimate aim is leisure. But neither the work nor the leisure can be a blessing so long as the personality that directs it is centred upon trivial and degrading ends.

The social benefits of the machine are inseparable from its canons of workmanship and its achievements in design; for it is only in academic discussions that the good and the true and the beautiful can be permanently separated.

Economically, the machine has given us the ability to transfer work from the human slave to the mechanical slave; thus fulfilling the condition that Aristotle laid down in the 'Politics' for a free society. We have made a fact out of what seemed to him a fantastic impossibility which proved the eternal nature of the institution of human slavery. This freedom is much more important to humane living than any mere plethora of goods that the machine is capable of producing. In fact, there is a real political division between those who would promote a grander scale of consumption in order to keep our mechanical apparatus working at maximum capacity, turning out hastily contrived goods to satisfy frivolous needs, and those who would use the machine to meet a stable standard of living, creating out of the surplus energy not more goods but leisure. The first conception is the enemy of art and fine living; and, needless to say, it is the dominant one in a society that has no real standard of life, and no coherent system of ideals and ends.

The business man's ideal of heaven is the continuous turnover of goods and profits; and for the sake of achieving it, he will employ armies of super-numeraries to force goods upon a market that may have no real use for them. Socially utilized, on the other hand, the function of the machine would be the swiftest organized satisfaction of necessities, and not the wanton multiplication of fake wants, or the vociferous wastes of competitive salesmanship, or the infliction of an unbalanced standard of consumption. While the animus that led to the creation of the machine economy was narrowly utilitarian, the net result of this economy is to create a state paralleled by the slave civilizations of old, endowed with an abundance of leisure which—if not vilely misused in the promotion of more work, either through the demands of inventive ingenuity or consumptive ritual—may eventuate in a largely non-utilitarian society, dedicated more fully to those forms of play and ritual and thought and social intercourse which make life significant and enjoyable.

The nineteenth century satisfied itself with the spread of machinery to new occupations and processes. During the last generation we have taken much satisfaction in the vulgarization of its products through mass production, in the heightening of automatism, and in the distribution of luxuries to classes that once slaved at a strict margin of subsistence under what was called the iron law of wages. A weak imagination may conceive all these processes as going on indefinitely, the final outcome being such a pictur-esque horror of exact contrivance as Zamiatin showed in 'We.' But the future, on the contrary, may modify this tendency, and not passively con-tinue it. We may conceive of finer machines, of more resourceful applica-tions of power, of airplanes that will not crumple or dive, motors with new sources of energy, perhaps; but we may equally look forward to a shrinkage of the total area occupied by the machine; as, for example, a proper diet and the early habitual care of the teeth will reduce the need for the marvellous technological resources of modern dentistry; or as, again, a better conception of the human body has already relegated to the scrap-heap the weight-lifting apparatus of late-Victorian gymnastics.

To conceive of engineering as the central art is to forget that the central fact of life is not mechanism but life; and the part played by mechanism in an intelligent polity is quite different from that which it now plays in our present régime. The machine has given us a noble austerity of form; its cool uninflected environment of depersonalized functions, its background of scientific concepts and abstract categories, all this has cleared away potentially the hot little vulgarities of class and caste and the childish assertive egos that went with these things. But in order to accept such a background *as* background, all the other arts must flourish too; when our creative energies have no other channels to flow into, the machine leaves a sense of emptiness, and to compensate for this we have the luxury and dull frivolity that make so much of our life to-day—a weakness symbolized by the theatrical decorations that have begun to crop out in the entrances of our gigantic American office buildings.

In short, a fine machine ideology is an aid to handling machines; and in order for the machine to benefit the other arts, they must have an integrated life of their own. Lacking an adequate ideal of life, lacking relation to all the other arts of society and the personality, the present mechanistic system tends by itself toward destruction or routine—boredom, war, death. In our wretched factory towns, our depleted villages, our overgrown financial metropolises, the great arts of life have been either paralyzed or secluded; and the mechanical age has created an environment in which the spirit, curbed in its proper expression, revenges itself by primitive compensations, by drunkenness and aimless eroticism and other forms of anaesthesia. These defects are not inherent in the machine. They exist in ourselves; and at most, the machine has emphasized our weaknesses and called our attention to them.

To fly, to talk at a distance, to overcome natural forces—these things we have achieved, thanks to exact science and the associated arts. But the myth-making functions, which produced Prometheus, not fire, and Icarus, not flight, are still left untouched by the machine: what we will to *be* is still left unanswered by our will to do, or by our success in controlling and manipulating external forces. To preserve the efficiency of the machine as an instrument and to use it further as a work of art, we must alter the centre of gravity from the external Newtonian world to that completer world which the human personality dominates and transmutes. The narrow interests, the intense practical concerns, the crudely depersonalized standards of the older utilitarians must undergo a complete transformation if the fruits of this effort are to be enjoyed. If no other forces were at work within ourselves, causing us to redeem certain tracts of experience and to revivify arts and ways of life whose understanding and command have been lost, the machine itself would furnish a sufficient impetus. It has conquered us. Now our turn has come, not to fight back, but to absorb our conqueror, as the Chinese, again and again, absorbed their foreign invaders.

(1930)

CHAPTER TWENTY-THREE

Utopia, the City,
and the Machine*

The fact that utopias from Plato to Bellamy have been visualized largely in terms of the city would seem to have a simple historical explanation. The first utopias we know were fabricated in Greece; and in spite of their repeated efforts at confederation, the Greeks were never able to conceive of a human commonwealth except in the concrete form of a city. Even Alexander had learned this lesson so well that at least part of the energies that might have gone into wider or more rapid conquests went into the building of cities. Once this tradition was established, later writers, beginning with Thomas More, found it easy to follow, all the more so because the city had the advantage of mirroring the complexities of society within a frame that respected the human scale.

Now, there is no doubt that utopian thinking was deeply influenced by Greek thought; moreover, as I shall try to show, this mode of thinking, precisely because it respected certain human capacities that the scientific method deliberately ignores, may still serve as a useful corrective for a positivism that has no place for the potential, the purposeful, or the ideal. But when one digs deeper into the utopian tradition, one finds that its foundations are buried in a much older past than that of Greece; and the question that finally arises is not, "Why are cities so often the locus of utopia?" but, "Why did so many of the characteristic institutions of utopia first come to light in the ancient city?"

Though I have long been a student of both utopias and cities, only in recent years have sufficient data come to light to suggest to me that the concept of utopia is not a Hellenic speculative fantasy, but a derivation from an historic event: that indeed the first utopia was the city itself. If I

---

* Though no single chapter of 'The Story of Utopias' (1922) could be fitted into the plan of this book, a vital residue not merely is captured in the present chapter, but pervades other portions, illuminating significant problems overlooked by the classic utopian writers. For further confirmation see 'The Pentagon of Power' (1970), particularly Chapter Eight, 'Progress as Science Fiction.'

241

can establish this relationship, more than one insight should flow from it: not least an explanation of the authoritarian nature of so many utopias.

But first let us look at utopia through the eyes of the Greeks. Strangely enough, though Plato approaches the domain of utopia in four of his dialogues, the one that had the greatest influence, the 'Republic,' is the utopia that is most lacking in any concrete image of the city, except in the provision that it should be limited in numbers in order to maintain its integrity and unity.

In Plato's reaction against the democratic Athenian polis, the model that seduced him was that of Sparta: a state whose population was dispersed in villages. In the 'Republic,' Plato retained many of the institutions of the ancient city and sought to give them an ideal dimension; and this in itself will throw an oblique light upon both the ancient city and the post-Platonic literature of utopias. But it is only in the 'Laws' that Plato came down from the heights sufficiently to give a few details, all too few, of the actual physical characteristics of the city that would incorporate his moral and legal controls.

There is no need to go into Plato's meager descriptions of the city: most of the details of the urban environment in the 'Laws' are drawn from actual cities, though in his glowing description of Atlantis his imagination seems to conjure up the bolder Hellenistic town planning of the third century B.C. What we must rather take note of in Plato are those singular limitations that his admirers—and I am still one of them—too charitably overlooked until our own day, when we suddenly found ourselves confronted by a magnified and modernized version of the kind of totalitarian state that Plato had depicted. Bertrand Russell had first made this discovery on his visit to Soviet Russia in the early nineteen-twenties, almost two decades before Richard Crossman and others pointed out that Plato's Republic, far from being a desirable model, was the prototype of the fascist state, even though neither Hitler nor Mussolini nor yet Stalin exactly qualified for the title of Philosopher-King.

In the Second Book of the 'Republic,' it is true, Plato came near to describing the normative society of Hesiod's Golden Age: essentially the pre-urban community of the Neolithic cultivator, in which even the wolf and the lion, as the Sumerian poem put it, were not dangerous, and all the members of the community shared in its goods and its gods—in which there was no ruling class to exploit the villagers, no compulsion to work for a surplus the local community was not allowed to consume, no taste for idle luxury, no jealous claim to private property, no exorbitant desire for power, no institutional war. Though scholars have long contemptuously dismissed the "myth of the Golden Age," it is their scholarship, rather than the myth, that must now be questioned.

Such a society had indeed come into existence at the end of the last Ice Age, if not before, when the long process of domestication had come to a head in the establishment of small, stable communities with an abundant and varied food supply: communities whose capacity to produce a surplus of storable grain gave security and adequate nurture to the young. This rise in vitality was enhanced by vivid biological insight and intensified sexual activities, to which the multiplication of erotic symbols bears witness, no less than a success unsurpassed in any later culture in the selection and breeding of plants and cattle. Plato recognized the humane qualities of these simpler communities: so it is significant that he made no attempt to recapture them at a higher level. (Was the institution of common meals for male citizens, as still practiced in Crete and Sparta, perhaps an exception?) Apart from this possibility, Plato's ideal community begins at the point where the early Golden Age comes to an end: with absolute rulership, totalitarian coercion, the permanent division of labor, and constant readiness for war all duly accepted in the name of justice and wisdom. So central was war to his whole conception of an ideal community that in the 'Timaeus,' when Socrates confesses a desire to behold his static Republic in action, he asks for an account of how she waged "a struggle against her neighbors."

Everyone is familiar with the foundation stones of the 'Republic.' The city that Plato pictures is a self-contained unit; and to ensure this self-sufficiency it must have enough land to feed its inhabitants and make it independent of any other community: autarchy. The population of this community is divided into three great classes: husbandmen and craftsmen, military "protectors," and a special caste of "guardians." The last have turned out to be the usual controllers and conditioners of most ideal commonwealths, either at their inception or in their daily government: Plato had rationalized kingship.

Once selected, the members of each of these classes must keep their own vocation and strictly mind their own business, taking orders from those above and not answering back. To make sure of perfect obedience, no 'dangerous thoughts' or disturbing emotions must be permitted: hence a strict censorship that extends even to music. To ensure docility, the guardians do not hesitate to feed the community with lies: they form, in fact, an archetypal Central Intelligence Agency within a Platonic Pentagon. Plato's only radical innovation in the 'Republic' is the rational control of human breeding through communal marriage. Though delayed, this practice came to fruition briefly in the Oneida Community, and today insistently haunts the dreams of more than one geneticist.

But note that the constitution and daily discipline of Plato's ideal commonwealth converge to a single end: fitness for making war. Nietzsche's observation that war is the health of the state applies in all its fullness to Plato's Republic, for only in war is such stringent authority and coercion temporarily tolerable. Let us remember this characteristic, for with one emphasis or another we shall find it in both the ancient city and in the literary myths of utopia. Even Bellamy's mechanized "nation in overalls," conscripted for twenty years labor service, is under the same discipline as a nation in arms.

If one thinks of Plato's scheme as a contribution to an ideal future, one must wonder whether justice, temperance, courage, and wisdom had ever before been addressed to such a contradictory "ideal" outcome. What Plato had actually accomplished was not to overcome the disabilities that threatened the Greek commonwealth of his day, but to establish a seemingly philosophic basis for the historic institutions that had in fact arrested human development. Though Plato was a lover of Hellenic society, he never thought it worth while to ask how the manifold values of the society that had brought both him and Socrates into existence could be preserved and developed: at most, he was honest enough to admit in the 'Laws' that good men could still be found in bad—that is, unplatonic—societies.

What Plato did, I shall try to demonstrate, was to rationalize and perfect the institutions that had come into existence as an ideal pattern long before, with the founding of the ancient city. He purposed to create a structure that, unlike the actual city in history, would be immune to challenge from within and to destruction from without. Plato knew too little history to realize where his imagination was leading him: but in turning his back on contemporary Athens he actually retreated even further back than Sparta, though he had to wait more than two thousand years before the development of a scientific technology would make his singularly inhumane ideals realizable.

One other attribute of Plato's utopia must be noted for it was not merely transmitted to later utopias, but now threatens, paradoxically, to be the final consummation of our supposedly dynamic society. To fulfill its ideal, Plato makes his Republic immune to change: once formed, the pattern of order remains static, as in the insect societies to which it bears a close resemblance. Change, as he pictured it in the 'Timaeus,' occurred as a catastrophic intrusion of natural forces. From the first, a kind of mechanical rigidity afflicts all utopias. On the most generous interpretation, this is due to the tendency of the mind, or at least of language, noted by Bergson, to fix and geometrize all forms of motion and organic change: to arrest life in order to understand it, to kill the organism in order to control it, to combat that ceaseless process of self-transformation which lies at the very origin of species.

All ideal models have this same life-arresting, if not life-denying, property: hence nothing could be more fatal to human society than to achieve its ideals. But fortunately nothing is less likely to happen, since, as Walt Whitman observed, it is provided in the nature of things that from every consummation will spring conditions that make it necessary to pass beyond it—a better statement than Marxian dialectic supplies. An ideal pattern is the ideological equivalent of a physical container: it keeps extraneous change within the bounds of human purpose. With the aid of ideals, a community may select, among a multitude of possibilities, those which are consonant with its own nature or that promise to further human development. This corresponds to the role of the entelechy in Aristotle's biology. But note that a society like our own, committed to change as its principal ideal value, may suffer arrest and fixation through its inexorable dynamism and kaleidoscopic novelty no less than a traditional society does through its rigidity.

Though it is Plato's influence that first comes to mind when we think of later utopias, it is Aristotle who considers more definitely the actual structure of an ideal city; in fact, one may say that the concept of utopia pervades every page of the 'Politics.' For Aristotle, as for any other Greek, the constitutional structure of a polity had a physical counterpart in the city; for it was in the city that men came together not only to survive military attack or to become wealthy in trade but to live the best life possible. But Aristotle's utopian bias went beyond this; for he constantly compares the actual cities whose constitutions he had studied so carefully with their ideal possible forms. Politics for him was the "science of the possible," in a quite different sense from the way that phrase is now used by those who would cover up their mediocre expectations or their weak tactics by succumbing, without any counter-effort, to probability.

Just as every living organism, for Aristotle, had the archetypal form of its species, whose fulfillment governed the whole process of growth and transformation, so the state, too, had an archetypal form; and one kind of city could be compared with another not just in terms of power, but in terms of ideal value for human development. On one hand, Aristotle considered the polis as a fact of nature, since man was a political animal who could not live alone unless he were either a brute or a god. But it was equally true that the polis was a human artifact; its inherited constitution and its physical structure could be criticized and modified by reason. In short, the polis was potentially a work of art. As with any work of art, the medium and the artist's capability limited the expression; but human evaluation, human intention, entered into its actual design. Not dissatisfaction over the shortcomings or failures of the existing polis so much as confidence in the possibility of improvement sustained Aristotle's rational interest in utopias.

The distinction that More, an inveterate punster, made when he chose the word utopia, as an ambiguous midterm between outopia, no place, and eutopia, the good place, applies equally to the difference between Plato's and Aristotle's conceptions. Plato's Republic was in Cloudcuckooland: and after his disastrous experience in Syracuse, he could hardly hope to find it anywhere else. But Aristotle, even when in the Seventh Book of the 'Politics' he outlines the requirements for an ideal city cut to his own pattern, still has his feet on the earth: he does not hesitate to retain many traditional characteristics, even such accidental ones as the narrow, crooked streets which might help confuse and impede an invading army.

In every actual situation, then, Aristotle saw one or more ideal possibilities that arose out of the nature of the community and its relations with other communities, as well as out of the constitution of the groups and classes and vocations within the polis. His purpose, he declares clearly in the first sentence of the Second Book, "is to consider what form of political community is the best of all for those who are most able to realize their ideal of life." Perhaps one should underline this statement, for in it Aristotle expressed one of the permanent contributions of the utopian mode of thought: the perception that ideals themselves belong to the natural history of man the political animal. It is on these terms that he devotes this chapter to a criticism of Socrates as interpreted by Plato and then goes on to examine other utopias, such as those of Phaleas and Hippodamus.

The association of the potential and the ideal with the rational and the necessary was an essential attribute of Hellenic thought, which took reason itself to be the definitive central characteristic of man: it was only in the social disintegration of the third century B.C. that this faith in reason gave way to a superstitious belief in chance as the ultimate god of human destiny. But when one examines Aristotle's exposition of the ideal city, one is again struck, as one is with Plato, by how restricted these original Greek ideals were. Neither Aristotle nor Plato nor even Hippodamus could conceive a society that overpassed the bounds of the city: none of them could embrace a multi-national or poly-cultured community, even if centered in the city; nor could they admit, even as a remote ideal, the possibility of breaking down permanent class divisions or doing away with the institution of war. It was easier for these Greek utopians to conceive of abolishing marriage or private property than of ridding utopia of slavery, class domination, and war.

In this brief review of Greek utopian thought one becomes conscious of limitations that were monotonously repeated in later utopian writers. Even the humane More, though tolerant and magnanimous on the subject of religious convictions, accepted slavery and war; and the very first act of King Utopus, when he invaded the land of Utopia, was to put his soldiers and the conquered inhabitants to work digging a broad canal that turns the territory into an island and cuts it off from the mainland.

Isolation, stratification, fixation, regimentation, standardization, militarization—one or more of these attributes enter into the conception of the utopian city, as expounded by the Greeks. And these same features remain, in open or disguised form, even in the supposedly more democratic utopias of the nineteenth century, such as Bellamy's 'Looking Backward.' In the end, utopia merges into the dystopia of the twentieth century; and one suddenly realizes that the distance between the positive ideal and the negative one was never so great as the advocates or admirers of utopia had professed.

So far I have discussed utopian literature in relation to the concept of the city, as if utopia were a wholly imaginary place, and as if the classic utopian writers, with the exception of Aristotle, were formulating a prescription for a quite unrealizable mode of life, one that could be achieved only under exceptional conditions or in a remote future.

In this light, every utopia, down to those of H. G. Wells, presents a real puzzle. How could the human imagination, supposedly liberated from the constraints of actual life, be so impoverished? And this limitation is all the stranger in fourth century Greece, for the Hellenic polis had in fact emancipated itself from many of the disabilities of the power-driven oriental monarchies. How is it that even the Greeks could visualize so few alternatives to customary life? And why did so many evils, long acknowledged if uncorrected, remain in every utopia, in return for its poor show of promised goods? Where did all the compulsion and regimentation that mark these supposedly ideal commonwealths come from?

One can give more than one plausible answer to these questions. Perhaps the one that would be least palatable to our present science-oriented generation is that the abstract intelligence, operating with its own conceptual apparatus, in its own self-restricted field, is actually a coercive instrument: an arrogant fragment of the full human personality, determined to make the world over in its own over-simplified terms, willfully rejecting interests and values incompatible with its own assumptions, and thereby depriving itself of any of the co-operative and generative functions of life —feeling, emotion, playfulness, exuberance, free fantasy—in short, the liberating sources of unpredictable and uncontrollable creativity.

Compared with even the simplest manifestations of spontaneous life within the teeming environment of nature, every utopia is, almost by definition, a sterile desert, unfit for human occupation. The sugared concept of scientific control, which B. F. Skinner insinuates into his 'Walden Two,' is another name for arrested development.

But there is another possible answer to these questions; and this is that the series of written utopias that came to light in Hellenic Greece were actually the belated reflections, or ideological residues, of a remote but genuine phenomenon: the archetypal ancient city. That this utopia in fact once existed can now be actually demonstrated: its real benefits, its ideal pretensions and hallucinations, and its harsh coercive discipline were transmitted, even after its negative features had become more conspicuous and formidable, to later urban communities. But in utopian literature the ancient city left, as it were, an after-image of its 'ideal' form on the human mind.

Curiously, Plato himself, though seemingly as an afterthought, took pains to give his utopia this historic foundation; for, in the 'Timaeus,' and the 'Critias,' he describes the city and the Island Empire of Atlantis in ideal terms that might well have applied to Pharaonic Egypt or Minoan Crete, even going so far as to give the Atlantean landscape, with its abundant natural resources, an ideal dimension that was lacking in the austere background of the 'Republic.' As for antediluvian Athens, the supposedly historic community that conquered Atlantis nine thousand years before Solon's time, it was 'by coincidence' a magnified embodiment of the ideal commonwealth pictured in the 'Republic.' Later, in the 'Laws,' he draws repeatedly on the historic institutions of Sparta and Crete, again closely linking his ideal future with a historic past.

While the motive for Plato's severely authoritarian utopia was doubtless his aristocratic dissatisfaction with demagogic Athenian politics which he considered responsible for the successive defeats that began with the Peloponnesian War, it is perhaps significant that his ideological withdrawal was coupled with a return to an earlier actuality which underwrote his ideals. That this idealized image came via the Egyptian priesthood at Sais, a country Plato as well as Solon had visited, provides at least a plausible thread of connection between the historic city in its originally divine dimensions and the more secular ideal commonwealths of a later period. Who can say, then, that it was only the problems of contemporary Athens and not also the actual achievements of the historic city that prompted Plato's excursions into utopia?

Though at first reading this explanation may seem far-fetched, I propose now to indicate the data mainly from Egypt and Mesopotamia that make this historic hypothesis plausible. For it is at the very beginning of urban civilization that one encounters not only the archetypal form of the city as utopia but also another co-ordinate utopian institution essential to any system of communal regimentation: the machine. In that archaic constellation the notion of a world completely under scientific and technological control, the dominant utopian fantasy of our present age, first becomes evident. My purpose is to show that at this early stage the historic explanation and the philosophic one come together. If we understand why the earliest utopia miscarried, we shall perhaps have an insight into the dangers our present civilization faces; for history is the sternest critic of utopias.

This reference to the archetypal city that greets us a little before the beginning of recorded history as "utopia" is no idle figure of speech. To make this clear, let me first paint a composite picture of the city as Egyptian, Mesopotamian, and later records reveal it to us. First of all, the city is the creation of a king (Menes, Minos, Theseus), acting in the name of a god. The king's first act, the very key to his authority and potency, is the erection of a temple within a heavily walled sacred enclosure.

And the construction of another wall to enclose the subservient community turns the whole area into a sacred place: a city.

Without this strong religious underpinning, the king's magic powers would have been lacking and his military prowess would have failed. Roland Martin's observations about the later Aegean cities, that the city is "un fait du prince," is precisely what distinguishes this new collective artifact from earlier urban structures.

By effecting a coalition between military power and religious myth, under conditions I first attempted to outline in the symposium published as 'City Invincible' (Carl Kraeling, editor), the hunter-chieftain of the later Neolithic economy transformed himself into a king; and kingship established a mode of government and a way of life radically different from that of the proto-historic village community, as described, from the Sumerian records, by Thorkild Jacobsen. In this new constitution, the king gathers to himself the privileges and functions that were once diffused in many local communities; and the king himself becomes the godlike incarnation of collective power and communal responsibilty.

Henri Frankfort's penetrating exposition of the role of kingship in early civilizations provides a clue to the utopian nature of the city: for, if it was through the king that the functions of the community were concentrated, unified, magnified, and given a sacred status, it was only in the city that the power and glory of this new institution could be fully manifested in monumental works of art. The mystique of kingship, Frankfort suggests, was supported by its immense practical contributions in distributing agricultural plentitude, handling population growth, and creating collective wealth. The king's power to make decisions, to by-pass communal deliberations, to defy or nullify custom brought about vast communal changes, far beyond the scope of village communities. Once amassed in cities, governed by a single head, regimented and controlled under military coercion, a large population could act as one, with a solidarity otherwise possible only in a small community.

If the king represents or, as in Egypt, incarnates divine power and communal life, the city visibly incorporates them: its esthetic form and conscious order testify to an immense concentration of energy no longer needed exclusively for the functions of nutrition and reproduction. The only limits to what might be accomplished in such an organization, while the myth of divine kingship remained in working order, were those of the human imagination. Up to this time, the human community had been widely dispersed in hamlets, villages, country towns: isolated, earthbound, illiterate, tied to ancestral ways. But the city was, from the beginning, related to the newly perceived cosmic order: the sun, the moon, the planets, the lightning, the storm wind. In short, as Fustel de Coulanges and Bachofen pointed out a century ago, the city was primarily a religious phenomenon: it was the home of a god, and even the city wall points to this superhuman origin; for Mircea Eliade is probably correct in inferring that its primary function was to hold chaos at bay and ward off inimical spirits.

This cosmic orientation, these mythic-religious claims, this royal pre-emption of the powers and functions of the community are what transformed the mere village or town into a city: something 'out of this world,' the home of a god. Much of the contents of the city—houses, shrines, storage bins, ditches, irrigation works—was already in existence in smaller communities: but though these utilities were necessary antecedents of the city, the city itself was transmogrified into an ideal form—a glimpse of eternal order, a visible heaven on earth, a seat of the life abundant—in other words, utopia.

The medieval Christian picture of heaven as a place where the elect find their highest fulfillment in beholding God and singing his praises is only a somewhat etherealized version of the primordial city. With such a magnificent setting as background, the king not merely played god but exercised unqualified power over every member of the community, commanding services, imposing sacrifices, above all enforcing abject obedience on penalty of death. In the city, the good life was achieved only by mystical participation in the god's life and that of his fellow deities, and by vicarious achievement through the person of the king. There lay the original compensation for giving up the petty democratic ways of the village. To inhabit the same city as a god was to be a member of a super-community: a community in which every subject had a place, a function, a duty, a goal, as part of a hierarchic structure representing the cosmos itself.

The city, then, as it emerged from more primitive urban forms, was not just a larger heap of buildings and public ways, of markets and workshops: it was primarily a symbolic representation of the universe itself. Like kingship, the city was "lowered down from heaven" and cut to a heavenly pattern; for even in the relatively late Etruscan and Roman cultures, when a new city was founded, a priest held the plow that traced the outline of the walls, while the main streets were strictly oriented to the points of the compass. In that sense, the archetypal city was what Campanella called his own utopia: a City of the Sun. Such an embodiment of esthetic magnificence, quantitative power, and divine order captivated the mind of even distant villagers who would make pilgrimages to the city on days of religious festival. This probably accounts for the fact that the punishing labors and tyrannous exactions which made this 'utopia' possible were so submissively accepted by the whole community.

But still another characteristic utopian trait marked the ancient city, if we may read the earliest records in the Near East with as much confidence as later data from the Peru of the Incas. Not only did the lowliest subject have a direct glimpse of heaven in the setting of the temple and the palace, but with this went a secure supply of food, garnered from the nearby fields, stored under guard in the granary of the citadel, distributed by the temple. The land itself belonged to the god or the king, as it still does ultimately in legal theory to their abstract counterpart, the sovereign state; and the city forecast its literary successor in treating the land and its agricultural produce as a common possession: fair shares, if not equal shares, for all. In return, every member of the community was obliged to perform sacrifices and to devote at least part of the year to laboring for the city's god.

By substituting conscription and communism for the later institutions of the market, wage labor, private property, and money, the utopias of More, Cabet, and Bellamy all reverted to the primitive condition of this aboriginal urban organization: a managed economy under the direction of the king.

This brief summary suggests, I realize, a conclusion perhaps even more unacceptable at first glance than the notion that the Neolithic community, seen from the perspective of the Iron Age, once enjoyed the veritable Golden Age that Hesiod described.

If the present interpretation be sound, the ancient city was not only "utopia," but the most impressive and the most enduring of all utopias: one that actually fulfilled at the beginning the principal ideal prescriptions of later fantasies, and in many respects indeed surpassed them. For to an extraordinary extent the archetypal city placed the stamp of divine order and human purpose on all its institutions, transforming ritual into drama, custom and caprice into formal law, and empirical knowledge spotted with superstition into exact astronomical observation and fine mathematical calculation.

While the myth remained operative, a single agent of divine power, the king, unlike a village council of elders, could by spoken command bring about hitherto impossible improvements in the environment and alter human behavior. These were the classic conditions for constructing a utopia. Even when the myth of kingship dissolved, the city passed some of that power on to its citizens.

But one relevant question remains to be asked: At what price was this utopia achieved? What institutional apparatus made it possible to organize and build these vast ideal structures? And, if the ancient city was indeed utopia, what qualities in human nature or what defects in its own constitution caused it to change, almost as soon as it had taken form, into its opposite: a negative utopia, a dystopia or kakotopia? If eutopia became a mere wraith in the mind, a symbol of unattainable desires, of futile dreams, why did its dark shadow, kakotopia or hell, erupt so often in history, in an endless series of exterminations and destructions that centered in the city—a hell that still threatens to become a universal holocaust in our own time?

The answer to the first question may, I believe, provide a clue to the second condition. For the city that first impressed the image of utopia upon the mind was made possible only by another daring invention of kingship:

the collective human machine, the platonic model of all later machines.

The machine that accompanied the rise of the city was directly a product of the new myth; but it long escaped recognition, despite a mass of direct and indirect evidence, because no specimen of it could be found in archeological diggings. The reason that this machine so long evaded detection is that, though extremely complicated, it was composed almost entirely of human parts. Fortunately the original model has been handed on intact through a historic institution that is still with us: the army.

Let me explain. In the period when the institution of kingship arose, no ordinary machine, except the bow and arrow, yet existed: even the wagon wheel had not yet been invented. With the small desultory labor force a village could command, and with the simple tools available for digging and cutting, none of the great utilities that were constructed in the Fertile Crescent could have been built. Power machinery was needed to move the vast masses of earth, to cut the huge blocks of stone, to transport heavy materials long distances, to set whole cities on an artificial mound forty feet high. These operations were performed at an incredible speed. Without a superb machine at command, no king could have built a pyramid or a ziggurat, still less a whole city, in his own lifetime.

By royal command, the necessary machine was created: a machine that concentrated energy in great assemblages of men, each unit shaped, graded, trained, regimented, articulated, to perform its particular function in a unified working whole. With such a machine, work could be conceived and executed on a scale that otherwise was impossible until the steam engine and the dynamo were invented. The assemblage and the direction of these labor machines was the prerogative of kings and an evidence of their supreme power; for it was only by exacting unflagging effort and mechanical obedience from each of the operative parts of the machine that the whole mechanism could so efficiently function. The division of tasks and the specialization of labor to which Adam Smith imputes so much of the success of the so-called industrial revolution actually were already in evidence in the Pyramid Age, with a graded bureaucracy to supervise the whole process. Every part of the machine was regimented to carry out the king's will: "The command of the palace . . . cannot be altered. The King's word is right; his utterance, like that of a God, cannot be changed."

Most of the dehumanized routines of our later machine technology were incorporated in the archetypal machine, usually in a more naked and brutal state. But the necessary suppression of all human autonomy except that of the king was likewise the imperative condition for operating this giant machine. In other words, the disciplined forces that transformed the humble human community into a gigantic collective work of art turned it into a prison in which the king's agents, his eyes and ears and hands, served as jailers.

Though the lock step discipline of the labor machine was happily alleviated by the art and ritual of the city, this power system was kept in operation by threats and penalties, rather than by rewards. Not for nothing was the king's authority represented by a scepter, for this was only a polite substitute for the mace, that fearful weapon by which the king would kill, with a single blow on the head, anyone who opposed his will. In one of the earliest representations of a king, the Narmer palette, the king holds a mace in his hand above a captive and, in the form of a bull, destroys a city. The price of utopia, if I read the record correctly, was total submission to a central authority, forced labor, lifetime specialization, inflexible regimentation, one-way communication, and readiness for war. In short, a community of frightened men, galvanized into corpselike obedience with the constant aid of the mace, the whip, and the truncheon. An ideal commonwealth indeed!

The archetypal machine, in other words, was an ambivalent triumph of human design. If it vastly widened the scope of human capability and created a visible heaven in the great city, exalting the human spirit as it had never been exalted by man's own works before, it likewise, by the very requirements of the mechanism, debased or wiped out precious human traits that even the humblest village still cherished. What proved equally damaging to the city was that the ability to command such powers produced paranoid fantasies in the rulers themselves: hostility, suspicion, murderous aggression, coupled with collective ambitions that no single city could satisfy.

Nothing is more conspicuous in the religious texts that follow upon the creation of the city and the invention of the human machine than the uncontrolled hostility that the gods display toward each other: in their hatred, their murderous aggression, their absence of moral constraint, their readiness to inflict sadistic punishments, they mirror the boasts and practices of kings. From the beginning the labor machine and the military machine performed interchangeable functions: as an offset to the regression and regimentation necessitated by the labor machine, the destruction of rival cities, the abasement of rival gods, became the chief means of manifesting royal power. If the utopia of the city did not in fact live up to its happy promise, it was because its very success promoted more exorbitant fantasies of unrestrained power. The building of cities was a creative act; but the war machine made a dystopia—total destruction and extermination—far easier to achieve. That is the dark hidden face of the ideal city that kingship had actually built.

When one puts these two archetypal forms, the city and the machine, side by side, one is finally pressed to an all-but-inescapable conclusion: utopia was once indeed a historic fact and became possible, in the first instance, through the regimentation of labor in a totalitarian mechanism, whose rigors were softened by the many captivating qualities of the city itself, which raised the sights on all possible human achievement. Through the greater part of history, it was the image of the city that lingered in the human imagination as the closest approach to paradise that one might hope for on earth—though paradise, the original Persian word reminds us, was not a city but a walled garden, a Neolithic rather than a Bronze Age image.

In their pristine historic forms both the utopian city and the royal machine had only a short career. Fortunately in both cases, beneath the myth, the diverse and divergent realities of communal life remained in operation. Within the actual city, the old co-operative life of the village found a niche for itself; and eventually the family, the neighborhood, the workshop, the guild, the market, drew back to their own province some of the powers and initiatives that the king had claimed for himself and for the dominant minority that served him—the nobles, the priests, the scribes, the officials, the "engineers." The very mixture of vocations and occupations, of languages and cultural backgrounds within the city gave each member of the urban community the advantages of the wider whole, while various material appurtenances and social privileges, once monopolized by the citadel, slowly, over the millennia if not over the centuries, filtered down to the rest of the community. Even the Pharaoh's exclusive monopoly of immortality was broken after the revolutions that ended the Pyramid Age.

Yet the great lesson of the archetypal city, the power of human design to alter natural conditions and customary practices, was never entirely lost. This early success raised the hope, expressed in later utopias—best perhaps by Fourier and William Morris—that similar results could be attained by voluntary effort and free association and mutual aid, rather than by military compulsion, royal or platonic.

In negative form, the utopian ideal of total control from above, absolute obedience below, never entirely passed out of existence. The will to exercise such control through the military machine incited the great military conquerers from Ashurbanipal to Alexander, from Genghis Kahn to Napoleon, as well as many lesser imitators. The negative military form of the invisible machine was held in check over the greater part of history by two limiting factors: first its inherent tendency to produce, in the rulers of the machine, delusions of grandeur that intensified all its destructive potentialities and led in fact to repeated collective self-destruction. The other limiting condition was the fact that this authoritarian regime was passively challenged by the archaic, democratic, life-conserving village culture that has always embraced the larger part of mankind. And during the last millennium, the growth of voluntary forms of association, in synagogue, church, guild, university, and the self-governing city, undermined the unconditional, over-riding exercise of "sovereignty" necessary to assemble the collective human machine.

Until the sixteenth century, then, when Church and State re-united, in

England, France, and Spain, and later in Prussia, as an all-embracing source of sovereign power, the chief conditions for extending the Invisible Machine were lacking. Even the political ideal of total control, as expressed by absolute monarchs like Henry VIII, Philip II, and Louis XIV, and various Italian Dukes, was for some centuries contested by vigorous democratic counter-movements. In its ancient and no longer viable form, kingship by divine right was defeated: but the idea of absolute power and absolute control re-entered the scene as soon as the other components of the Invisible Machine had been translated into more practical modern equivalents and re-assembled.

Since it took three centuries to assemble the new Invisible Machine, and since earlier forms had not yet been identified, the rise of this great mechanical collective for long escaped contemporary observation. Because of the erroneous Victorian belief, still current in history textbooks, that the "industrial revolution" began in the eighteenth century, a vastly more important technological change has been ignored. The thousands of useful mechanical and electronic inventions that have been made, at an accelerating rate, during the last two centuries still conceal the even more significant restoration, in more scientific guise, of the archaic megamachine.

But in retrospect, the sequence is clear. Beginning in the sixteenth century, with the astronomical observations of Copernicus and Kepler, the cult of the sun came back, bringing cosmic order and regularity, already prefigured in the mechanical clock, into every department of life. Though the absolute powers of individual kings were reduced, the powers claimed by their successor, the impersonal sovereign state, were steadily increased, first by reducing the authority of religion as a source of higher knowledge and moral values, then by making all other corporate entities creatures of the sovereign power. "L'état, c'est moi," proclaimed Louis XIV, Le Roi Soleil, in words that even the earliest avatar of Atum-Re would have recognized as a factual statement. But it was only with the French Revolution that the state, under a republican mask, actually achieved in its system of universal conscription the powers that Louis XIV did not dare. to exercise completely—those powers which the 'sovereign state' now everywhere commands.

With this new mechanical assemblage came the uniformed standing army, whose very uniform was, after the printing press, the first example of mechanized mass production; and that army, in turn, was freshly disciplined everywhere by the same sort of rigorous drill, introduced by William of Orange, that produced the Sumerian or the Macedonian phalanx. In the eighteenth century, this widened mechanical discipline was transferred to the factory. On these foundations the new mechanical order, based on quantitative measurements, indifferent to human qualities or purposes, took form. As outlined by Galileo and Descartes, the new ideology of science, which was finally to become the central component of the Invisible Machine, reduced reality to the calculated, the measurable, the controllable: in other words, the universal world of the machine, both visible and invisible, both utilitarian and ideal.

Long before all the components of the new megamachine were consciously assembled, Francis Bacon, in his 'New Atlantis,' was quick not merely to anticipate its benefits but to outline the conditions for its achievement: the application of science to all human affairs, "to the effecting of all things possible." What the temple and the priesthood and astronomical observation did to establish the authority of the king, Solomon's House and its new occupants would do to establish the authority of the machine. Unlike the steam engines and power looms that still engross the historian, the new machine is mainly an assemblage of human parts: scientists, technicians, administrators, physicians, soldiers. Though it has taken more than three hundred years to perfect the parts of this machine, its final organization has taken place within the last twenty years.

In the throes of the Second World War, the archetypal compact between kingship and priesthood was ratified, with a grant of virtually unlimited financial support and opportunity for science on condition that its priesthood would sanction and devote itself to magnifying vastly the powers of the sovereign entity. Within the space of less than a lustrum, the megamachine had finally been re-assembled, with all its original potentialities inordinately inflated. The atom bomb symbolized this union of putative omnipotence with putative omniscience. So effective has been the coalition between these forces, so rapid their extension beyond the field of extermination and destruction, so all-embracing the Invisible Machine's monopoly of the instruments of both production and education, that its implicit goals and its ultimate destination have not yet been subject to any critical examination.

But one thing is already plain: in its new scientific form the divine machine is no longer an agent for creating a visible heaven on earth in the form of the city. The new megamachine, in its dual role as visible universal instrument and invisible object of collective worship, itself has become utopia, and the enlargement of its province has become the final end of life, as the guardians of our contemporary New Atlantis now conceive it.

The many genuine improvements that science and technics have introduced into every aspect of existence have been so notable that it is perhaps natural that its grateful beneficiaries should have overlooked the ominous social context in which these changes have taken place, as well as the heavy price we have already paid for them, and the still more forbidding price that is in prospect. Until the last generation it was possible to think of the various components of technology as additive. This meant that each new mechanical invention, each new scientific discovery, each new application to engineering, agriculture, or medicine, could be judged separately on its own performance, estimated eventually in terms of the human good accomplished, and diminished or eliminated if it did not in fact promote human welfare.

This belief has now proved an illusion. Though each new invention or discovery may respond to some general human need, or even awaken a fresh human potentiality, it immediately becomes part of an articulated totalitarian system that, on its own premises, has turned the machine into a god whose power must be increased, whose prosperity is essential to all existence, and whose operations, however over-controlled, irrational, or destructive, cannot be challenged, still less modified.

The only group that has understood those dehumanizing, totalitarian threats are the *avant-garde* artists, who have caricatured the system by going to the opposite extreme. Their calculated destructions and "happenings" symbolize total decontrol: the rejection of order, continuity, design, significance, and a total inversion of human values which turns criminals into saints and scrambled minds into sages. In such anti-art, the dissolution of our entire civilization into randomness and entropy is prophetically symbolized. In their humorless deaf-and-dumb language, the *avant-garde* artists reach the same goal as power-demented technicians, but by a different route—both seek or at least welcome the displacement and the eventual elimination of man. In short, both the further affirmation of the mechanical utopia and its total rejection would beget dystopia. Wherever human salvation may lie, neither utopia nor dystopia, as now conceived, promises it.

A summary word. Viewed objectively, the classic literature of utopias reveals a singularly barren tract of mind: even Plato's efforts, for all their many stimulating human insights, succeed better as a study in character contrast, as for example between Socrates and Glaucon, than as an ideal revelation of natural human potentialities. Plato's utopias were by intention too close to archaic history to make history afresh in the future. As for those modern forms of utopia, which under the name of science fiction relate all ideal possibilities to technological innovations, they are so close to the working premises of modern civilization that they hardly have time to be absorbed as fiction before they become incorporated as fact.

If, with all these limitations, a learned body like ours still finds it worthwhile to discuss both myth and utopia, is this not perhaps a covert way of acknowledging that our present scientific methodology, which equates possibility only with chance, is inadequate to deal with every aspect of human experience? Through this respectably academic side-excursion into utopia are we not, with a prudence that touches on cowardice, actually approaching a much more fertile area, now weedy with neglect—the realm embracing potentiality as an aspect of all natural existence, "foreplans of action" (Lloyd Morgan) as a dynamic attribute of living organisms, and design as a necessary constituent of rational human development? These categories constitute the fringe benefits of utopian literature; but they are far more important than the books that embody them. Perhaps after our tour of utopias we shall be ready to explore and reclaim this more important territory, with Aristotle and Whitehead to guide us rather than Plato and Sir Thomas More and Bellamy.

(1965)

CHAPTER TWENTY-FOUR

The First Megamachine

Until the nineteenth century, history was largely a chronicle of the deeds and misdeeds of kings, nobles, and armies. In revolt against a general obliviousness to the daily life and affairs of ordinary people, democratic historians swung to the opposite extreme: so the part actually played by kings has, during the last half century, been grossly under-rated, even though most of the attributes of kingship are now exercised, on a larger scale than ever before, by the all-powerful sovereign state.

From the earliest records, we know that the king incarnated the whole community and by divine right arrogated to himself the functions and offices of communal life. Only one aspect of kingship has been left out of this traditional account: strangely, the king's greatest and most lasting achievement has passed unnoticed, despite the fact that all his other public activities rested upon it. For though the myth of royal power claimed divine sanction, its rise and spread would have been impossible without the invention of the human machine. That was the supreme feat of kingship: a technological exploit that was transmitted in one form or another through purely human agents for some five thousand years before it was finally embodied in an equally totalitarian but impersonal form in modern technology.

To understand the point of origin and the line of descent is to have a fresh insight into the fate and destiny of modern man: for unless our own civilization learns to control the processes and the purposes that have so long been automatically—that is unconsciously—at work, the social aberrations that have accompanied the perfection of a machine technology threaten even worse consequences than they did in the Pyramid Age.

Though the collective human machine came into existence roughly during the same period as the first industrial use of copper, it was an independent innovation, and did not at first utilize any new mechanical aids. But the royal machine, once conceived, was assembled within a short period; and it spread rapidly, not by being imitated, but by being forcefully imposed by kings, acting as only gods or the anointed representatives of gods could act. Wherever it was successfully put together the new machine commanded power and performed labor on a scale that was never even conceivable before. With this ability to concentrate immense mechanical forces, a new dynamism came into play, which overcame, by the magic of success, the sluggish routines, the petty inhibitions, the dull repetitive routines of the basic neolithic village culture, once the scene of so many fresh experiments in horticulture and breeding.

With the energies available through the royal machine—let us call it the megamachine—the very dimensions of space and time were enlarged. Operations that once could hardly be finished in centuries were now accomplished in less than a generation. If whole mountains were not moved, large portions of them were, sometimes in blocks far bigger than any ordinary motor truck could now handle; while, on the level plains, manmade mountains of stone or baked clay, pyramids and ziggurats, arose in response to royal command. No power machines at all comparable to this mechanism were utilized on any scale until watermills and windmills swept over Western Europe from the fourteenth century of our era.

From the beginning, this human machine presented two aspects: one negative and coercive, the other positive and constructive. In fact, the second factors could not function unless the first were present. Though the military machine probably came before the labor machine, it was the latter that first achieved an incomparable perfection of performance, not alone in quantity of work done, but in quality. To call these collective entities machines is no idle play on words. If a machine be defined more or less in accord with the classic definition of Reuleaux, as a combination of resistant parts, each specialized in function, operating under human control, to transmit motion and to perform work, then the labor machine was a real machine: all the more because its component parts, though composed of human bone, nerve, and muscle, were reduced to their bare mechanical elements and rigidly restricted to the performance of their mechanical tasks.

Such machines, of immense power and practical utility, had already been invented by kings in the early part of the Pyramid Age, from the end of the fourth millennium on. Just because of their detachment from any external structure, they had paradoxically much fuller capacities for change and adaptation than the more rigid metallic counterparts of a modern assembly line. In fact, it is in the building of the pyramids that we find the first indubitable evidence of the machine's existence, and the first proof of its astonishing efficiency. Wherever kingship spread, the human machine, in its destructive if not its constructive form, always went with it. This holds as true for Mesopotamia, India, China, Cambodia, Mexico, Yucatan, or Peru, as for Egypt.

Let us examine the human machine in its archetypal original form. As so often happens, there was a certain clarity in this first demonstration that was lost when the machine was diffused and worked into the more complex patterns of later societies, mingling with more familiar but humbler forms. And if it never achieved a higher peak of performance, this is perhaps not only because of the singular human talents that designed and operated these early machines, but also perhaps because the myth that held the human part of the machine together could never again exert such a massive attractive power, unstained as it was in Egypt, until the Sixth Dynasty by its letdowns and failures, exposed its inherent perversities.

The pyramid took form as a tomb to hold the embalmed body of the Pharaoh and secure his safe passage into the after-life: though he alone, at first, had the prospect of such a godlike extension of his existence, the very idea of being able to fabricate personal immortality shows an alteration in all the dimension of existence.

Between the first small pyramid, built in the step form we find later in Central America, and the mighty pyramid of Cheops at Giza, the first and the most enduring of the Seven Wonders of the Ancient World, lies the short span of three hundred years. On the ancient time-scale for inventions the most primitive form and the final one, never again to be equalled, were practically contemporary. The swiftness of this development indicates a concentration of physical power and technical imagination: for it took far more than faith to move the mountain of stone that composed this ultimate monument. That transformation is all the more striking because the Pharaohs' tombs did not stand alone: they were part of a whole city of the dead, with buildings that housed the priests who conducted the elaborate rituals deemed necessary to ensure a happy fate for the departed divinity.

The Great Pyramid is one of the most colossal and perfect examples of the engineer's art at any period or in any culture. Considering the state of all the other arts in the third millennium, no construction of our own day surpasses this in either technical virtuosity or human audacity. This great enterprise was undertaken by a culture that was just emerging from the Stone Age, and was long to continue using stone tools, though copper was available for the chisels and saws that shaped building stones for the new monuments.

The actual operations were performed by specialized handicraft workers, aided by an army of unskilled or semi-skilled laborers, drafted at quarterly intervals from agriculture. The whole job was done with no other material aids than the 'simple machines' of classical mechanics: the inclined plane and the lever, for neither wheel nor pulley nor screw had yet been invented. We know from graphic representations that large stones were hauled on sledges, by battalions of men, across the desert sands. Yet the single stone slab that covers the inner chamber of the Great Pyramid where the Pharaoh lies weighed fifty tons. An architect today would think twice before calling for such a mechanical exploit.

Now the Great Pyramid is more than a formidable mountain of stone, 755 feet square at the base, rising to a height of 481.4 feet. It is a structure with a complex interior, consisting of a series of passages at different levels that lead into the final burial chamber. Yet every part of it was built with a kind of precision that, as J. H. Breasted emphasized, belongs to the optician's art rather than that of the modern bridge builder or skyscraper constructor. Blocks of stone were set together with seams of considerable length, showing joints of one-ten-thousandth of an inch; while the dimensions of the sides at the base differ by only 7.9 inches, in a structure that covers acres. In short, what we now characterize as flawless machine precision and machine perfection first manifested itself in the building of this great tomb: at once a symbol of the mountain of creation that emerged out of the primeval waters and a visible effort, so far remarkably successful, by purely human measure, to solidify both time and the human body in an eternal form. No ordinary human hands, no ordinary human effort, no ordinary kind of human collaboration such as was available in the building of village huts and the planting of fields, could muster such a superhuman force, or achieve an almost supernatural result. Only a divine king could accomplish such an act of the human will and such a large-scale material transformation.

Was it possible to create such a structure without the aid of a machine? Emphatically not. I repeat, the product itself showed that it was not only the work of a machine, but of an instrument of precision. Though the material equipment of dynastic Egypt was still crude, the patient workmanship and disciplined method made good these shortcomings. The social organization had leaped ahead five thousand years to create the first large-scale power machine: a machine of a hundred thousand manpower, that is, the equivalent, roughly, of 10,000 horsepower: a machine composed of a multitude of uniform, specialized, interchangeable, but functionally differentiated parts, rigorously marshalled together and co-ordinated in a process centrally organized and centrally directed: each part behaving as a mechanical component of the mechanized whole: unmoved by any internal impulse that would interfere with the working of the mechanism.

In less than three centuries, this collective human machine was perfected. Once organized and set in motion by the Pharaoh through his chief architect, *the technical competence* and imagination that envisaged the entire design was passed on, by word of mouth, and written instruction, to the component parts: the skilled workers, the overseers and taskmasters, the dumb hands. The kind of mind that designed the Pyramid was a new human type, capable of abstraction of a high order, using astronomical observations for the siting of the structure, so that each side was oriented exactly in line with true points of the compass: since at inundation the Pyramid site is only one quarter of a mile from the river, a rock foundation—which demanded the removal of sand—was needed. In the Great Pyramid the perimeter of that bed deviates from true level by little more than one-half an inch.

But the workers who carried out the design also had minds of a new order: trained in obedience to the letter, limited in response to the word of command descending from the king through a bureaucratic hierarchy, forfeiting during the period of service any trace of autonomy or initiative; slavishly undeviating in performance. Their leaders could read written orders; for the men employed left their names in red ochre, Edwards tells us, on the blocks of the Meidum Pyramid: "Boat Gang," "Vigorous Gang." They themselves would have felt at home today on an assembly line. Only the naked pin-up girl was lacking.

Alike in organization, in mode of work, and in product, there is no doubt that the machines that built the pyramids, and that performed all the other great constructive works of "civilization" in other provinces and cultures, were true machines. In their basic operations, they collectively performed the equivalent of a whole corps of power shovels, bulldozers, tractors, mechanical saws, and pneumatic drills, with an exactitude of measurement, a refinement of skill, and even an output of work that would still be a theme for boasting today.

This extension of magnitude in every direction, this raising of the ceiling of human effort, this subordination of individual aptitudes and interests to the mechanical job in hand, and this unification of a multitude of subordinates to a single end that derived from the divine power exercised by the king, in turn, by the success of the result, confirmed that power.

For note: it was the king who uttered the original commands: it was the king who demanded absolute obedience and punished disobedience with torture, mutilation, or death: it was the king who alone had the godlike power of turning live men into dead mechanical objects: and finally it was the king who assembled the parts to form the machine and imposed the new discipline of mechanical organization, with the same regularity that moved the heavenly bodies on their undeviating course.

No vegetation god, no fertility myth, could produce this kind of cold abstract order, this detachment of power from life. Only one empowered by the Sun God could remove all hitherto respected norms or limits of human endeavor. The king figures, in early accounts, as a being of heroic mold: he alone slays lions singlehanded, builds great city walls, or like Menes turns the course of rivers. That straining ambition, that defiant effort belongs only to the king and the machine that he set in motion.

To understand the structure or the performance of the human machine, one must do more than center attention upon the point where it materializes. Even our present technology, with its vast reticulation of visible machines, cannot be understood on those terms alone. In order to put together a collective machine composed solely of human parts, one needed a complex transmission mechanism, to ensure that commands issued at the top would be swiftly and accurately conveyed to every member of the unit, so that the parts would interlock to form a single operating whole.

Two collective devices were essential, to make the machine work: a reliable organization of knowledge, natural and supernatural: and an elaborate structure for giving and carrying out orders. The first was incorporated in the priesthood, without whose active aid divine kingship could not have come into existence: the second in a bureaucracy: both hierarchical organizations at whose apex stood the temple and the palace. Without them the power complex could not operate. This condition remains true today, even though the existence of automated factories and computer-regulated units conceals the human components essential even to automation.

What would now be called science was an integral part of the new machine system from the beginning. This science, based on cosmic regularities, flourished with the cult of the sun: record-keeping, time-keeping, star-watching, calendar-making, coincide with and support the institution of kingship, even though no small part of the efforts of the priesthood were, in addition, devoted to interpreting the meaning of singular events, such as the appearance of comets or eclipses of the sun or moon, or natural irregularities, such as the flight of birds or the state of a sacrificed animal's entrails.

No king could move safely or effectively without the support of such organized higher knowledge, any more than the Pentagon can move today without consulting scientists, "games theorists," and computers, a new hierarchy supposedly less fallible than entrail-diviners, but to judge by their repeated miscalculations, not notably so. To be effective, this kind of knowledge must remain a priestly monopoly: if everyone had equal access to the sources of knowledge and to the system of interpretation, no one would believe in infallibility, since its errors could not be concealed. Hence the shocked protest of Ipu-wer against the revolutionaries who overthrew the Old Kingdom was that the "secrets of the temple lay unbared"; that is, they had made 'classified information' public. Secret knowledge belongs to any system of total control. Until printing was invented, this remained a class monopoly.

Not the least affiliation of kingship with the worship of the sun is the fact that the king, like the sun, exerts force at a distance. For the first time in history, power became effective outside the immediate range of hearing and vision and the arm's reach. No military weapon by itself sufficed to convey such power: what was needed was a special form of transmission gear: an army of scribes, messengers, stewards, superintendents, gang bosses, and major and minor executives, whose very existence depended upon their carrying out the king's orders, or those of his powerful ministers and generals, to the letter. In other words, a bureaucracy: a group of men, capable of transmitting and executing a command, with the ritualistic punctilio of a priest, the mindless obedience of a soldier.

To fancy that bureaucracy is a relatively recent institution is to ignore the annals of ancient history. The first documents that attest the existence of bureaucracy belong to the Pyramid Age. In a cenotaph description at Abydos, a career official under Pepi I, in the Sixth Dynasty, c. 2375 B.C., reported "His majesty sent me at the head of this army, while the counts, while the Seal-bearers of the King of Lower Egypt, while the sole companions of the Palace, while the nomarchs (governors) and *mayors* of Upper and Lower Egypt, the companions and chief dragomans, the chief prophets of Upper and Lower Egypt, and the Chief bureaucrats were (each) at the head of a troop of Upper or Lower Egypt, or of the villages and towns which they might rule."

Not merely does this text establish a bureaucracy: it shows that the division of labor and specialization of functions necessary for efficient mechanical operation, had already taken place in the organization that, as executors of the sovereign's will, already controlled the operations of both the military and the labor machine. This development had begun at least three dynasties before, not by accident, with the building of the great stone pyramid of Djoser at Sakkara. Wilson observes, in 'City Invincible,' that "we credit Djoser, not only with the beginnings of monumental architecture in stone in Egypt, but also with the setting up of a new monster, the bureaucracy." This was no mere coincidence. And W. F. Albright, commenting upon this, pointed out that "the greater number of titles found in sealings of the First Dynasty . . . certainly pre-supposes an elaborate officialdom of some kind."

Once the hierarchic structure of the human machine was established, there was no limit to the number of hands it might control or the power it might exert. The removal of human dimensions and organic limits is indeed the chief boast of the authoritarian machine. Part of its productivity is due to its use of unstinted physical coercion to overcome human laziness or bodily fatigue. Occupational specialization was a necessary step in the assemblage of the human machine: only by intense specialization at every part of the process could the superhuman accuracy and perfection of the product have been achieved. The large scale division of labor throughout industrial society begins at this point.

The Roman maxim, that the law does not concern itself with trifles, applies likewise to the human machine. The great forces that were set in motion by the king demanded collective enterprises of a commensurate order. These human machines were by nature impersonal, if not deliberately dehumanized; they had to operate on a big scale or they could not work at all; for no bureaucracy, however well organized, could govern a thousand little workshops, each with its own traditions, its own craft skills, its own willful personal pride and sense of responsibility. So the form of control imposed by kingship was confined to great collective enterprises.

The importance of this bureaucratic link between the source of power, the divine king, and the actual human machines that performed the works of construction or destruction can hardly be exaggerated: all the more because it was the bureaucracy that collected the annual taxes and tributes that supported the new social pyramid and forcibly assembled the manpower that formed the new mechanical fabric. The bureaucracy was, in fact, the third type of "invisible machine," co-existing with the military and labor machines, and an integral part of the total structure.

Now the important part about the functioning of a classic bureaucracy is that it originates nothing: its function is to transmit, without alteration or deviation, the orders that come from above. No merely local information or human considerations may alter this inflexible transmission process —except by corruption. This administrative method ideally requires a studious repression of all the autonomous functions of the personality, and a readiness to perform the daily task with ritual exactitude. Not for the first time does such ritual exactitude enter into the process of work: indeed, it is highly unlikely that submission to colorless repetition would have been possible without the millennial discipline of religious ritual.

Bureaucratic regimentation was in fact part of the larger regimentation of life, introduced by this power-centered culture. Nothing emerges more clearly from the Pyramid texts themselves, with their wearisome repetitions of formulae, than a colossal capacity for enduring monotony: a capacity that anticipates the universal boredom achieved in our own day. Even the poetry of both early Egypt and Babylonia reveal this iterative hypnosis: the same words, in the same order, with no gain in meaning, repeated a dozen times—or a hundred times. This verbal compulsiveness is the psychical side of the systematic compulsion that brought the labor machine into existence. Only those who were sufficiently docile to endure this regimen at every stage from command to execution could become an effective unit in the human machine.

Though the human machine was powerful, it was likewise extremely fragile: once the royal power was switched off, it "went dead." The royal machine reached the limit of its capabilities, without doubt, in the construction of the Great Pyramids. Soon after this came a revolt so shattering, so profound, that centuries passed before the severed regions of Egypt could be assembled once more under a single divine ruler. Never was power to be raised to such heights of absolute command again until our own day. But the institutional forces set in motion by this first effort continued to operate. Wherever the army, the bureaucracy, and the priesthood worked together under unified royal command, the technics of unqualified power would resume operation.

The marks of this new mechanical order can be easily recognized: and first, there is a change of scale. The habit of "thinking big" was introduced with the first human machines: a superhuman scale in the individual structure magnifies the sovereign authority and reduces the size and importance of all the necessary human components, except the central figure, the king himself. Both in practice and even more in fantasy, this magnification applied to time and to space. Kramer notes that in the early dynasties reigns of incredible length are attributed to legendary kings: a total of close to a quarter of a million years for the eight kings before the flood and a total of twenty-five thousand years for the first two dynasties after the flood: this tallies with similar periods that Egyptian priests were still assigning to ancient history when Herodotus and Plato visited them.

But this multiplication of years was only the secular side of the new conception of immortality: at first, in Egypt, solely the attribute of the divine king, though there, as one notes in Sumer where a whole court was massacred in the Royal Tomb at Ur to accompany the ruler to the next world, the king's servants and ministers might also participate in this imputed extension of life. In the Sumerian deluge myth Ziusudra the king (Noah's counterpart) is rewarded by the gods An and Enlil, not by a symbolic rainbow, but by being given "life like a god." The desire for life without limits was part of the general lifting of limits which the first great assemblage of power, by means of the machine, brought about.

But if death mocks at the infantile fantasy of absolute power, which the human machine promised to actualize, life mocks at it even more. The notion of eternal life, with neither conception, growth, fruition, nor decay: an existence as fixed, as sterilized, as unchanging as that of the royal mummy, is only death in another form: a return to the state of arrest and fixation exhibited by the stable chemical elements that have not yet combined in sufficiently complex molecules to promote novelty and continued creativity. The old fertility gods did not shrink from the fact of death: they sought no infantile evasion, but promised rebirth and renewal, by prolongation of power. If the gods of power had not triumphed, if kingship had not found a negative mode of increasing the scope of the human machine and therewith bolstering up the royal claim to absolute obedience, the whole further course of civilization might have been radically different.

But along with the desire for eternal life, kings and their gods nourished other ambitions that have become part of the mythology of our own age. Etana, in the Sumerian fable, mounts an eagle to go in search of a curative herb for his sheep when they are stricken with sterility. At this moment, the dream of human flight was born, or at least became visible, though that dream still seemed so presumptuous that Etana, like Daedalus, was hurled to death as he neared his goal. Soon, however, kings were represented as winged bulls; and they had at their command heavenly messengers who conquered space and time in order to bring commands to their earthly subjects. Rockets and television sets were already beginning to germinate in this royal myth. The Genii of the 'Arabian Nights' are only popular continuations of these earlier forms of power-magic.

Within the span of early civilization, 3000 to 1000 B.C., the formative impulse to exercise absolute control over both nature and man shifted back and forth between gods and kings. Joshua commanded the sun to stand still and destroyed the walls of Jericho by martial music: but Yahweh himself, at an earlier moment, anticipated the Nuclear Age by destroying Sodom and Gomorrah with a single visitation of fire and brimstone; and a while later He even resorted to germ warfare in order to demoralize the Egyptians and aid in the escape of the Jews.

In short, none of the destructive fantasies that have taken possession of leaders in our own age, from Hitler to Stalin, from the khans of the Kremlin to the Kahns of the Pentagon, were foreign to the souls of the divinely appointed founders of the first machine civilization. With every increase of effective power, extravagantly sadistic and murderous impulses emerged out of the unconscious: not radically different from those sanctioned, not only by Hitler's extermination of six million Jews and uncounted millions of other people, but the extermination by the United States Air Force of 180,000 civilians in Tokyo in a single night by roasting alive. When a distinguished Mesopotamian scholar proclaimed that "civilization begins at Sumer" he innocently overlooked how much must be forgotten before this can be looked upon as a laudable achievement. Mass production and mass destruction are the positive and negative poles, historically, of the myth of the megamachine.

The other great prerogative of this royal technics is speed; for speed itself, in any operation, is a function of power and in turn becomes one of the chief means of displaying it. So deeply has this part of the myth of the machine become one of the uncriticized basic assumptions of our own technology that most of us have lost sight of its point of origin. But royal commands, like urgent commands in the army, are performed "on the double."

Nothing better illustrates this acceleration of pace than the fact that in Egypt, and later in Persia, each new monarch in the Pyramid Age built a new capital for use in his own lifetime. (Compare this with the centuries needed to built a medieval cathedral without royal resources for assembling power.) On the practical side, road-building and canal-building, which were the chief means for hastening transportation, have been all through history the favored form of royal public works: a form that reached its technological consummation in the Iron Age, with the building of the Corinth Canal through eighty feet or so of solid rock.

Only an economy of abundance, at a time when there were at most four or five million people in the Nile Valley, could have afforded to drain off the labor of a hundred thousand men annually, and provide them with sufficient food to perform their colossal task; for on the scale these works were executed, that was the most sterile possible use of man power. Though many Egyptologists cannot bring themselves to accept the implications, John Maynard Keynes' notion of Pyramid Building, as a necessary device for coping with the surplus labor force in an affluent society without resorting to social equalization, was not an inept metaphor. This was an archetypal example of simulated productivity. Rocket-building is our modern equivalent.

But the most lasting economic contribution of the first myth of the machine was the separation between those that worked and those that lived in idleness on the surplus extracted from the worker by reducing his standard of living to penury. According to Akkadian and Babylonian scriptures, no less than those of Sumer, the gods created men in order to free themselves from the hard necessity of work. Here, as in so many other places, the gods prefigure in fantasy what kings actually do. In times of peace, kings and nobles live by the pleasure principle; eating, drinking, hunting, playing games, and copulating endlessly. So at the very period when the myth of the machine was taking place, the problems of an economy of abundance first became visible in the behavior and the exorbitant fantasies of the ruling classes.

If we watch the aberrations of the ruling classes throughout history, we shall see how far most of them were from understanding the limitations of power, or of a life centered upon conspicuous consumption: the reduced life of the parasite on a tolerant host. The boredom of satiety dogged this economy of surplus power and surplus food from the very beginning: it led to insensate personal luxury and even more insensate acts of collective delinquency and destruction.

One early example of this dilemma of affluence must suffice. An Egyptian story translated by Flinders Petrie reveals the emptiness of a Pharaoh's life, in which every desire was too easily satisfied, and time hung with unbearable heaviness on his hands. Desperate, he appeals to his councillors for some relief from his boredom; and one of them has a classic suggestion: that he fill a boat with thinly veiled, almost naked girls, who will paddle over the water and sing songs for him. For the hour, tedium, to the Pharaoh's great delight, was overcome; for, as Petrie aptly remarks, the vizier had invented the first Musical Revue: that solace of the 'tired business man.'

In short, at its earliest point of development under the myth of divine kingship, the amorality and the purposelessness of unlimited power were revealed in both religious legend and recorded history. Though the whole panoply of modern inventions lay beyond the scope of the collective machine, which could provide only partial and clumsy substitutes, the fundamental animus behind these inventions—the effort to conquer space and time, to expand human energy through the use of cosmic forces and to establish absolute human control over both nature and man, all had been planted and nurtured in the soil of fantasy.

Some of these seeds sprouted immediately: others which needed for their execution a far higher degree of technical skill, a higher capacity for logical and mathematical abstractions, required five thousand years before they were ready to sprout. When that happened, the divine king would appear again in a new form.

                                                                    (1966)

CHAPTER TWENTY-FIVE

Mechanization
of Modern Culture

Where did the 'Machine' first take form in modern civilization? There was plainly more than one point of origin. Our mechanical civilization represents the convergence of numerous habits, ideas, and modes of living, as well as technical instruments; and some of these were, in the beginning, directly opposed to the civilization they helped to create. But the first manifestation of the new order took place in the general picture of the world: during the first seven centuries of the machine's existence the categories of time and space underwent an extraordinary change, and no aspect of life was left untouched by this transformation. The application of quantitative methods of thought to the study of nature had its first manifestation in the regular measurement of time; and the new mechanical conception of time arose in part out of the routine of the monastery. Alfred Whitehead has emphasized the importance of the scholastic belief in a universe ordered by God as one of the foundations of modern physics: but behind that belief was the presence of order in the institutions of the Church itself.

The technics of the ancient world were still carried on from Constantinople and Baghdad to Sicily and Cordova: hence the early lead taken by Salerno in the scientific and medical advances of the Middle Ages. It was, however, in the monasteries of the West that the desire for order and power, other than that expressed in the military domination of weaker men, first manifested itself after the long uncertainty and bloody confusion that attended the breakdown of the Roman Empire. Within the walls of the monastery was sanctuary: under the rule of the order surprise and doubt and caprice and irregularity were put at bay. Opposed to the erratic fluctuations and pulsations of the worldly life was the iron discipline of the rule. Benedict added a seventh period to the devotions of the day, and in the seventh century, by a bull of Pope Sabinianus, it was decreed that the bells of the monastery be rung seven times in the twenty-four hours. These punctuation marks in the day were known as the canonical hours, and some means of keeping count of them and ensuring their regular repetition became necessary.

According to a now discredited legend, the first modern mechanical clock, worked by falling weights, was invented by the monk named Gerbert who afterwards became Pope Sylvester II near the close of the tenth century. This clock was probably only a water clock, one of those bequests of the ancient world either left over directly from the days of the Romans, like the water-wheel itself, or coming back again into the West through the Arabs. But the legend, as so often happens, is accurate in its implications if not in its facts. The monastery was the seat of a regular life, and an instrument for striking the hours at intervals or for reminding the bell-ringer that it was time to strike the bells was an almost inevitable product of this life. If the mechanical clock did not appear until the cities of the thirteenth century demanded an orderly routine, the habit of order itself and the earnest regulation of time-sequences had become almost second nature in the monastery. Coulton agrees with Sombart in looking upon the Benedictines, the great working order, as perhaps the original founders of modern capitalism: their rule certainly took the curse off work and their vigorous engineering enterprises may even have robbed warfare of some of its glamor. So one is not straining the facts when one suggests that the monasteries—at one time there were 40,000 under the Benedictine rule—helped to give human enterprise the regular collective beat and rhythm of the machine; for the clock is not merely a means of keeping track of the hours, but of synchronizing the actions of men.

Was it by reason of the collective Christian desire to provide for the welfare of souls in eternity by regular prayers and devotions that time-keeping and the habits of temporal order took hold of men's minds: habits that capitalist civilization presently turned to good account? One must perhaps accept the irony of this paradox. At all events, by the thirteenth century there are definite records of mechanical clocks, and by 1370 a well-designed "modern" clock had been built by Heinrich von Wyck at Paris. Meanwhile, bell towers had come into existence, and the new clocks, if they did not have, till the fourteenth century, a dial and a hand that translated the movement of time into a movement through space, at all events struck the hours. The clouds that could paralyze the sundial, the freezing that could stop the water clock on a winter night, were no longer obstacles to time-keeping: summer or winter, day or night, one was aware of the measured clank of the clock. The instrument presently spread outside the monastery; and the regular striking of the bells brought a new regularity into the life of the workman and the merchant. The bells of the clock tower almost defined urban existence. Time-keeping passed into time-serving and time-accounting and time-rationing. As this took place, Eternity ceased gradually to serve as the measure and focus of human actions.

The clock, not the steam-engine, is the key machine of the modern industrial age. For every phase of its development the clock is both the outstanding fact and the typical symbol of the machine: even today no other machine is so ubiquitous. Here, at the very beginning of modern technics, appeared prophetically the accurate automatic machine which, only after centuries of further effort, was also to prove the final consummation of this technics in every department of industrial activity. There had been power-machines, such as the water-mill, before the clock; and there had also been various kinds of automata, to awaken the wonder of the populace in the temple, or to please the idle fancy of some Moslem caliph: machines one finds illustrated in Hero and Al-Jazari. But here was a new kind of power-machine, in which the source of power and the transmission were of such a nature as to ensure the even flow of energy throughout the works and to make possible regular production and a standardized product. In its relationship to determinable quantities of energy, to standardization, to automatic action, and finally to its own special product, accurate timing, the clock has been the foremost machine in modern technics: and at each period it has remained in the lead: it marks a perfection toward which other machines aspire. The clock, moreover, served as a model for many other kinds of mechanical works, and the analysis of motion that accompanied the perfection of the clock, with the various types of gearing and transmission that were elaborated, contributed to the success of quite different kinds of machine. Smiths could have hammered thousands of suits of armor or thousands of iron cannon, wheelwrights could have shaped thousands of great water-wheels or crude gears, without inventing any of the special types of movement developed in clockwork, and without any of the accuracy of measurement and fineness of articulation that finally produced the accurate eighteenth century chronometer.

The clock, moreover, is a piece of power-machinery whose "product" is seconds and minutes: by its essential nature it dissociated time from human events and helped create the belief in an independent world of mathematically measurable sequences: the special world of science. There is relatively little foundation for this belief in common human experience: throughout the year the days are of uneven duration, and not merely does the relation between day and night steadily change, but a slight journey from East to West alters astronomical time by a certain number of minutes. In terms of the human organism itself, mechanical time is even more foreign: while human life has regularities of its own, the beat of the pulse, the breathing of the lungs, these change from hour to hour with mood and action, and in the longer span of days, time is measured not by the calendar but by the events that occupy it. The shepherd measures from the time the ewes lambed; the farmer measures back to the day of sowing or forward to the harvest: if growth has its own duration and regularities, behind it are not simply matter and motion but the facts of development: in short, history. And while mechanical time is strung out in a succession of mathematically isolated instants, organic time—what Bergson calls duration—is cumulative in its effects. Though mechanical time can, in a sense, be speeded up or run backward, like the hands of a clock or the images of a moving picture, organic time moves in only one direction—through the cycle of birth, growth, development, decay, and death—and the past that is already dead remains present in the future that has still to be born.

Around 1345, according to Thorndike, the division of hours into sixty minutes and of minutes into sixty seconds became common: it was this abstract framework of divided time that became more and more the point of reference for both action and thought, and in the effort to arrive at accuracy in this department, the astronomical exploration of the sky focussed attention further upon the regular, implacable movements of the heavenly bodies through space. Early in the sixteenth century a young Nuremberg mechanic, Peter Henlein, is supposed to have created "many-wheeled watches out of small bits of iron" and by the end of the century the small domestic clock had been introduced in England and Holland. As with the motor car and the airplane, the richer classes first took over the new mechanism and popularized it: partly because they alone could afford it, partly because the new bourgeoisie were the first to discover that, as Franklin later put it, "time is money." To become "as regular as clockwork" was the bourgeois ideal, and to own a watch was for long a definite symbol of success. The increasing tempo of civilization led to a demand for greater power: and in turn power quickened the tempo.

Now, the orderly punctual life that first took shape in the monasteries is not native to mankind, although by now Western peoples are so thoroughly regimented by the clock that it is "second nature" and they look upon its observance as a fact of nature. Many Eastern civilizations have flourished on a loose basis in time: the Hindus have in fact been so indifferent to time that they lack even an authentic chronology of the years. Only yesterday, in the midst of the industrialization of Soviet Russia, did a society come into existence to further the carrying of watches there and to propagandize the benefits of punctuality. The popularization of timekeeping, which followed the production of the cheap standardized watch, first in Geneva, then in America around the middle of the last century, was essential to a well-articulated system of transportation and production.

To keep time was once a peculiar attribute of music: it gave industrial value to the workshop song or the tattoo or the chantey of the sailors tugging at a rope. But the effect of the mechanical clock is more pervasive and strict: it presides over the day from the hour of rising to the hour of rest. When one thinks of the day as an abstract span of time, one does not go to bed with the chickens on a winter's night: one invents wicks, chimneys, lamps, gaslights, electric lamps, so as to use all the hours belonging to the day. When one thinks of time, not as a sequence of experiences, but as a collection of hours, minutes, and seconds, the habits of adding time and saving time come into existence. Time took on the character of an enclosed space: it could be divided, it could be filled up, it could even be expanded by the invention of labor-saving instruments.

Abstract time became the new medium of existence. Organic functions themselves were regulated by it: one ate, not upon feeling hungry, but when prompted by the clock: one slept, not when one was tired, but when the clock sanctioned it. A generalized time-consciousness accompanied the wider use of clocks: dissociating time from organic sequences, it became easier for the men of the Renascence to indulge the fantasy of reviving the classic past or of reliving the splendors of antique Roman civilization: the cult of history, appearing first in daily ritual, finally abstracted itself as a special discipline. In the seventeenth century journalism and periodic literature made their appearance: even in dress, following the lead of Venice as fashion-center, people altered styles every year rather than every generation.

The gain in mechanical efficiency through co-ordination and through the closer articulation of the day's events cannot be over-estimated: while this increase cannot be measured in mere horsepower, one has only to imagine its absence today to foresee the speedy disruption and eventual collapse of our entire society. The modern industrial régime could do without coal and iron and steam easier than it could do without the clock.

"A child and an adult, an Australian primitive and a European, a man of the Middle Ages and a contemporary, are distinguished not only by a difference in degree, but by a difference in kind by their methods of pictorial representation."

Dagobert Frey, whose words I have just quoted, has made a penetrating study of the difference in spatial conceptions between the early Middle Ages and the Renascence: he has re-enforced by a wealth of specific detail, the generalization that no two cultures live conceptually in the same kind of time and space. Space and time, like language itself, are works of art, and like language they help condition and direct practical action. Long before Kant announced that time and space were categories of the mind, long before the mathematicians discovered that there were conceivable and rational forms of space other than the form described by Euclid, mankind at large had acted on this premise. Like the Englishman in France who thought that bread was the right name for *le pain* each culture believes that every other kind of space and time is an approximation to or a perversion of the real space and time in which *it* lives.

During the Middle Ages spatial relations tended to be organized as symbols and values. The highest object in the city was the church spire which pointed toward heaven and dominated all the lesser buildings, as the church dominated their hopes and fears. Space was divided arbitrarily to represent the seven virtues or the twelve apostles or the Ten Commandments or the Trinity. Without constant symbolic reference to the fables and myths of Christianity the rationale of medieval space would collapse. Even the most rational minds were not exempt: Roger Bacon was a careful student of optics, but after he had described the seven coverings of the eye he added that by such means God had willed to express in our bodies an image of the seven gifts of the spirit.

Size signified importance: to represent human beings of entirely different sizes on the same plane of vision and at the same distance from the observer was entirely possible for the medieval artist. This same habit applies not only to the representation of real objects but to the organization of terrestrial experience by means of the map. In medieval cartography the water and the land masses of the earth, even when approximately known, may be represented in an arbitrary figure like a tree, with no regard for the actual relations as experienced by a traveler, and with no interest in anything except the allegorical correspondence.

One further characteristic of medieval space must be noted: space and time form two relatively independent systems. First: the medieval artist introduced other times within his own spatial world, as when he projected the events of Christ's life within a contemporary Italian city, without the slightest feeling that the passage of time has made a difference, just as in Chaucer the classical legend of Troilus and Cressida is related as if it were a contemporary story. When a medieval chronicler mentions the King, as the author of 'The Wandering Scholars' remarks, it is sometimes a little difficult to find out whether he is talking about Caesar or Alexander the Great or his own monarch: each is equally near to him. Indeed, the word anachronism is meaningless when applied to medieval art: it is only when one related events to a co-ordinated frame of time and space that being out of time or being untrue to time became disconcerting. Similarly, in Botticelli's 'The Three Miracles of St. Zenobius,' three different times are presented upon a single stage. .

Because of this separation of time and space, things could appear and disappear suddenly, unaccountably: the dropping of a ship below the horizon no more needed an explanation than the dropping of a demon down the chimney. There was no mystery about the past from which they had emerged, no speculation as to the future toward which they were bound: objects swam into vision and sank out of it with something of the same mystery in which the coming and going of adults affects the experience of young children, whose first graphic efforts so much resemble in their organization the world of the medieval artist. In this symbolic world of space and time everything was either a mystery or a miracle. The connecting link between events was the cosmic and religious order: the true order of space was Heaven, even as the true order of time was Eternity.

Between the fourteenth and the seventeenth century a revolutionary change in the conception of space took place in Western Europe. Space as a hierarchy of values was replaced by space as a system of magnitudes. One of the indications of this new orientation was the closer study of the relations of objects in space and the discovery of the laws of perspective and the systematic organization of pictures within the new frame fixed by the foreground, the horizon, and the vanishing point. Perspective turned the symbolic relation of objects into a visual relation: the visual in turn became a quantitative relation. In the new picture of the world, size meant not human or divine importance, but distance. Bodies did not exist separately as absolute magnitudes: they were co-ordinated with other bodies within the same frame of vision and must be in scale. To achieve this scale, there must be an accurate representation of the object itself, a point for point correspondence between the picture and the image: hence a fresh interest in external nature and in questions of fact. The division of the canvas into squares and the accurate observation of the world through this abstract checkerboard marked the new technique of the painter, from Paolo Uccello onward.

The new interest in perspective brought depth into the picture and distance into the mind. In the older pictures, one's eye jumpd from one part to another, picking up symbolic crumbs as taste and fancy dictated: in the new pictures, one's eye followed the lines of linear perspective along streets, buildings, tessellated pavements whose parallel lines the painter purposely introduced in order to make the eye itself travel. Even the objects in the foreground were sometimes grotesquely placed and foreshortened in order to create the same illusion. Movement became a new source of value: movement for its own sake. The measured space of the picture re-enforced the measured time of the clock.

Within this new ideal network of space and time all events now took place; and the most satisfactory event within this system was uniform motion in a straight line, for such motion lent itself to accurate representation within the system of spatial and temporal co-ordinates. One further consequence of this spatial order must be noted: to place a thing and to time it became essential to one's understanding of it. In Renascence space, the existence of objects must be accounted for: their passage through time and space is a clue to their appearance at any particular moment in any particular place. The unknown is therefore no less determinate than the known: given the roundness of the globe, the position of the Indies could be assumed and the time-distance calculated. The very existence of such an order was an incentive to explore it and to fill up the parts that were unknown.

What the painters demonstrated in their application of perspective, the cartographers established in the same century in their new maps. The Hereford Map of 1314 might have been done by a child: it was practically worthless for navigation. That of Uccello's contemporary, Andrea Banco, 1436, was conceived on rational lines, and represented a gain in conception as well as in practical accuracy. By laying down the invisible lines of latitude and longitude, the cartographers paved the way for later explorers, like Columbus: as with the later scientific method, the abstract system gave rational expectations, even if on the basis of inaccurate knowledge. No longer was it necessary for the navigator to hug the shore line: he could launch out into the unknown, set his course toward an arbitrary point, and return approximately to the place of departure. Both Eden and Heaven were outside the new space; and though they lingered on as the ostensible subjects of painting, the real subjects were Time and Space and Nature and Man.

Presently, on the basis laid down by the painter and the cartographer, an interest in space as such, in movement as such, in locomotion as such, arose. Back of this interest were of course more concrete alterations: roads had become more secure, vessels were being built more soundly, above all, new inventions—the magnetic needle, the astrolabe, the rudder —had made it possible to chart and to hold a more accurate course at sea. The gold of the Indies and the fabled fountains of youth and the happy isles of endless sensual delight doubtless beckoned too: but the presence of these tangible goals does not lessen the importance of the new schemata. The categories of time and space, once practically dissociated, had become united: and the abstractions of measured time and measured space undermined the earlier conceptions of infinity and eternity, since measurement must begin with an arbitrary here and now even if space and time be empty. The itch to *use* space and time had broken out: and once they were coordinated with movement, they could be contracted or expanded: the conquest of space and time had begun. (It is interesting, however, to note that the very concept of acceleration, which is part of our daily mechanical experience, was not formulated till the seventeenth century.)

The signs of this conquest are many: they came forth in rapid succession. In military arts the cross-bow and the ballista were revived and extended, and on their heels came more powerful weapons for annihilating distance—the cannon and later the musket. Leonardo conceived an airplane and built one. Fantastic projects for flight were canvassed. In 1420 Fontana described a velocipede: in 1589 Gilles de Bom of Antwerp apparently built a man-propelled wagon: restless preludes to the vast efforts and initiatives of the nineteenth century. As with so many elements in our culture, the original impulse was imparted to this movement by the Arabs: as early as 880 Abû l-Qâsim had attempted flight; and in 1065 Oliver of Malmesbury had killed himself in an attempt to soar from a high place: but from the fifteenth century on the desire to conquer the air became a recurrent preoccupation of inventive minds; and it was close enough to popular thought to make the report of a flight from Portugal to Vienna serve as a news hoax in 1709.

The new attitude toward time and space infected the workshop and the counting house, the army and the city. The tempo became faster: the magnitudes became greater: conceptually, modern culture launched itself into space and gave itself over to movement. What Max Weber called the "romanticism of numbers" grew naturally out of this interest. In time-keeping, in trading, in fighting, men counted numbers; and finally, as the habit grew, only numbers counted.

(1934)

CHAPTER TWENTY-SIX

Technics and the Future

If this paper had been given a hundred years ago, its title, even in that fateful year of revolutionary turmoil, 1848, would have been entirely reassuring and its contents hopeful—unless perhaps the topic had been assigned to John Ruskin, for even in that period he perceived that there was thunder on the horizon, as well as dawn. Most educated people a century ago believed that technics, as it came forth in a flood of new inventions, was almost synonymous with Western Civilization; and whether it was or not, there was a positive relation between technical progress and the advance of the human spirit.

Much of that confidence was still present in my youth: altogether naïve yet somehow lovable, like a child's absorption in a plaything he may nevertheless, a day or two later, willfully destroy. That feeling is symbolized for me by one of the lectures my old chemistry professor, Charles Baskerville, used to give on sulphuric acid. In this lecture, with only the slightest reserve of irony, he advanced the suggestion that the production and consumption of sulphuric acid could be taken as an index of civilization; and he then staged a three-cornered statistical race between Great Britain, Germany, and the United States, which began around the middle of the nineteenth century with Great Britain in the lead and finished—and at this point the class would always break into a spontaneous cheer—with the victory of the United States. In 1914 at the outbreak of World War I the human comfort of that demonstration outweighed its logical defects.

Perhaps it is too early to say that this attitude toward technics has been completely chastened. But at all events it has become plain during the present generation that dissident voices are rising, and those voices are no longer confined to the belated camp followers of Rousseau. Today it is precisely in the departments where our scientific advances have been most decisive, where our technics have been most exquisitely refined—particularly, of course, in nuclear physics—that some of the most eminent exponents of science have begun to sound a note of deep anxiety, as they contemplate the social consequences of technical progress.

The possibility that technics might be misapplied did not apparently bother our Victorian forebears. But no reasonably detached mind can view what has happened all over the world, from Liverpool to Tokyo, the dozens of cities that have been gutted, the millions of human beings who have been coldly exterminated, without questioning the simple faith that scientific knowledge applied to invention would, in Bacon's words, tend to the relief of man's estate. The first of the barbarian invasions has taken place under our eyes; and it differs from those that overcame Rome because the barbarians have sprung up wholly, not partly, from within the society that is attacked. Is it possible, we begin to ask ourselves, that our comic strip hero, Superman, has neither the intelligence nor the moral sensibility to be entrusted with the instruments science has now put at his disposal? Disturbingly enough, the age that produced atomic energy also produced the polluted mind of a Hitler, who was capable, even without the atomic bomb, of conceiving the torture and extermination of some six million Jews alone—to say nothing of the deaths and mutilations he inflicted on millions of people of other nationalities.

Part of my effort here will be to inquire whether within the development of technics itself certain conditions have prevailed which have made these miscarriages possible and in fact almost inevitable; and if so, what changes must take place in Western Civilization as a whole that will make the machine once more the servant and benefactor of life. Certainly it would be unseemly, if not unprofitable, on a genial occasion like the present centennial, to overstress the dark side of the picture. To speak at all about technics today, a certain quality of robust animal faith in the future is necessary. If our civilization were on the edge of extinction, that very fact would rob our present speculations of any lasting significance. Yet as between those who express unlimited confidence in mankind's ability to survive any conceivable series of blunders—a group that contains such wise, competent scholars as A. L. Kroeber, the dean of American anthropologists —and those who believe that without a concerted effort to recover our human balance, our civilization is, in all probability, doomed—as between these two schools I belong, let me confess, to the second group. But that fact does not commit me to more than the wary glance downward a mountain climber may give before he attempts to extricate himself from a tight position by continuing his upward climb. For it remains to those of us who believe that the danger is serious to concentrate, not on potential catastrophes, but on those timely judgments and actions which may keep us from releasing any more of them.

So I purpose to deal mainly in this paper with a group of related special problems that have been raised by the very progress and proliferation of our mechanical and scientific technology during the past century. These problems, I believe, would be serious, indeed in some ways overwhelming, even if they had not been magnified by thirty years of warfare, barbarism, and extermination; and even if we were not now possibly on the brink of racial suicide, thanks to the fact that through the knowledge of biotic and atomic energies we now command, we in the United States alone, to look no further afield, hold powers of life and death over mankind: separated from their use by only the thinnest walls of habit, taboo, intelligence, and moral enlightenment. Yet if we recognize the existence of these essential problems promptly, and if by some further stroke of intelligence we give heed to them, that fact will go a long way toward lightening the penalties and lifting the dangers which our overt instruments of mass extermination have conjured up.

Without further ado, I purpose to treat these underlying problems under three main heads: first, the problem of time, space, and power; second, deriving from this, the general problem of quantity and quantification; and finally, the problem of automatism. The solution of these internal problems of technics seems to me essential for the integration of our mechanical functions into a new over-all social design, based on a different set of human motives and purposes than those which played so large a part in creating the age of the machine. All these problems form a budget of very teasing paradoxes; and not the least paradox, I fear, will be my final conclusion, that only by a deliberate act of restrictive self-discipline on the part of science and technics, will the human agents concerned be able to concentrate sufficiently on those decisive inventions in the realm of morals, politics, and psychological self-direction which will restore the balance to our civilization as a whole. *To save technics itself we shall have to place limits on its heretofore unqualified expansion.* But I must not anticipate.

Probably the most decisive change modern technics has brought about, certainly the most pervasive, is the change it has effected in both our concepts and our experience of space, time, energy. Most of the inventions that Leonardo and Bacon and della Porta and Glanvill correctly anticipated, and a grand succession of later inventors realized, were devices for saving time, for shrinking space, for enhancing energy, for speeding motions, for accelerating natural processes: devices which equipped modern man with seven-league boots and magic carpets, releasing people from the physical constraints of here and now. But note the curious twist that actual experience has given to all these early plans and aspirations: the faster we travel, the less we actually see and experience on the way; the larger the area of our communication, other things remaining the same, the more limited the area of understanding; the greater our physical power, the more formidable become our social and moral limitations.

As soon as we achieve the theoretic goal of annihilating distance entirely—as we now do for all practical purposes even without television when we telephone overseas—we come back again precisely to where we started: to the village world of face-to-face contact with over two billion villagers for neighbors, and at that point our human weaknesses, serious enough in a village society, become magnified far more rapidly than our virtues, by reason of the technical process itself; just as a public-address system, blaring to the world from a family dinner table, would accentuate its trivialities and bickerings rather than the less visible processes of love and devotion. Thanks to technics, men have become physically neighbors to people on the other side of the earth; but we have done little to make ourselves mental neighbors or to train ourselves in habits of courtesy, in disciplines of mutual forbearance, which would keep us in amicable relations.

In their too unwary innocence, the founders of modern technics did not anticipate these difficulties; or doubtless they would have done something to head them off. When the Royal Society was founded in England, you will recollect, its members deliberately decided to reject any collaboration with those disciplines which would now be called the social sciences and the humanities. For their purposes, it was possible to leave out of account every human impulse and need, except those which were actively engaged in either the exploration or the exploitation of the physical environment. That decision, symbolic of a thousand others that accompanied the stunningly triumphant but one-sided advance of technics, has had the result of limiting the benefits we might legitimately expect from our present mastery of time and space. From Francis Bacon onward, people thought that the advance of technics would by itself automatically solve the crucial problems of civilization: with unlimited production, they thought, we could by-pass the moral problem of just distribution, with unlimited physical means of travel, we would by the mere multiplication of contacts make men brothers.

Certainly, the whole development of man himself, from small tribal units to cities and nations, from nations to leagues, unions, and empires, has been in the direction of unity and universality, and throughout history this development has been handicapped, up to modern times, by a technics so unprogressive that it had reached its premedieval plateau very largely before the Bronze Age. But precisely at the point where technics, thanks to Henry and Faraday and Morse and Watt, had caught up with the universal vision of the great religious teachers, our social facilities, so far from keeping pace with technical invention, actually went backward.

The very language, Latin, which had enabled European scholars to communicate freely beyond their national boundaries, was allowed to lapse before we had invented a simpler and more universal vehicle of communication. Here we face another bitter paradox. For what is the use of being able to speak to another person instantaneously on the other side of the planet if we have no common language and if we have no common purpose, except that of exterminating our distant brother before he seizes the initiative and exterminates us? We have left the problem of creating a universal language mainly to a few amateurs and fanatics who naturally have so far made little headway, although with our present skills in comparative philology and logical analysis, the problem of inventing such a language presents far fewer difficulties than did the original invention of the alphabet.

The point I am making here touches almost every field of technical advance. None of our marvelous technical instruments and processes can function efficiently except in a society that has provided adequate social destinations and outlets. When technical advances are not co-ordinated with social advances, the result of an overconcentration on technics may be social conflict, frustration, retrogression. The contradiction of the motorcar, capable of going seventy-five miles an hour, reduced to the ignominious crawl of a pedestrian on the crowded avenues of our cities, can be matched in almost every other department. If this fact has been slow in coming home to us, the sudden increase in the potentialities for mass destruction and mass extermination, through the invention of the atom bomb, has driven the point in; for to turn such an instrument loose on society, without erecting fresh moral safeguards and controls, in particular without creating an effective system of world government, was an act of incredible social irresponsibility; although it only brought to a climax a whole train of such acts since the beginning of the paleotechnic revolution.

Now it is precisely in the most advanced parts of our technics that the mischief of treating technical development as an end in itself becomes most plain. For neither radio nor supersonic planes make sense until we realize that all men are brothers, and that every nation and group, however isolated in appearance, is part of an infinitely complicated and involved ecological partnership of planetary dimensions. In the sixth century B.C. the group of world religions that took form were for long theoretically far in advance of technology in their universalism and in their sense of a common moral law binding mankind together. Unfortunately, the persistent cultural lag between the machine and our religious and moral concepts is now visible in quite another manner than Professor William Fielding Ogburn believed, when he first used this term: for our technics has become universal in an ideological epoch that has turned to the worship of the false tribal gods of nationalism. *We discarded the universal insights of Confucius and Buddha, of Mo Ti and St. Paul, at the very moment they were most needed to make technics a true agent of cilivilization.*

Now, if there is any one department where the fact of human interdependence should be recognized, fully and generously, it is in technics itself. For the whole fabric of modern technology rests on a foundation of world-wide collaboration: with the result that multiple discoveries and inventions, in widely separated countries, are commonplaces of our technical development. Yet in this very field nationalism of the most abysmally tribal kind has muffled the plain facts. We Western peoples, to begin with, have talked as if modern technics were wholly the work of our own culture, indeed, of the last few centuries of our culture; whereas the scientific basis of our technology goes back directly to the Arabs and the Hindus and the Greeks; our most decisive inventions, like the printing press and the internal combustion engine, come from the Orient; while without the extra lift to the food supply, given by the Amerindian culture, through the potato and maize, we might have lacked part of the physical vitality necessary to produce our modern achievements. If one removed from modern technics a single raw material, rubber, originally the product of a backward tribe of Amazonian Indians who had themselves produced rubber raincoats and syringes, our whole economy would almost come to a halt. In other words, modern technics is a product of a world-wide collaboration; and unless we extend such collaboration and make it firmer, our civilization will within a measurable time go downhill.

Even within Western Civilization itself people often talk as if some single nation had a monopoly on invention: this boast reaches a peak of error in the very common notion that the atom bomb is an exclusively American contrivance, instead of what it actually is, the product of our whole scientific culture, contemporary and historic, and even in its final stages more immediately in debt to a German, Meitner, a Dane, Bohr, a Hungarian, Szilard, and an Italian, Fermi, than to our own workers in the same field. Patent offices create national monopolies, and immigration laws and tariff acts often erect barriers against the free movement of men and goods; but an advanced technics, such as we have created during the last century, depends upon a world-wide circulation of ideas; and unless that world-wide basis is maintained, the collecting reservoirs will be so lowered that only a trickle of inventions will come forth.

Now I turn more specifically to the problem of quantity. Though this problem derives largely from our expansion of power and our mechanical conquest of space and time, it invades every department of technics where the methods of mass production have been successfully installed. In general, the advance of the machine has been accompanied by a general quantification of life. One of the reasons for this issues forth directly from the assumptions upon which our whole mechanical world picture was based: for science, following Galileo, turned its back on the so-called secondary qualities, as ephemeral, subjective, and in any scientific sense, meaningless —unless, like color, they could be translated into measurable units. From this point of view norms, patterns, ideals, were wholly unimportant: the only intelligent questions one could ask about the physical world were those relating to quantity, and the only acceptable answers those ascertainable by measurement. Hence the capitalist's interest in quantity—his belief that there are no natural limits to acquisition—was supplemented, in technology, by the notion that quantitative production had no natural limits either: norms, limits, optimum amounts, goals, were out of the picture.

Considering the precarious conditions under which the greater portion of the human race had previously lived, the miserable dearth and scarcity and near-starvation, the besetting anxiety of trying to make both ends meet, one can well understand this new preoccupation with quantity. Just as the unlimited land of the New World promised food to the hungry, so the apparently unlimited productivity of the machine promised to make all men as wealthy, and therefore presumably as happy, as kings. Here once more our lack of concern for the social destination of the machine has curbed its real promises, as John Stuart Mill mordantly observed even at the height of Victorian optimism. For this society, which had learned the mechanical art of multiplication, had neglected the ethical art of division: hence, though the condition of the worker actually improved, it did not do so sufficiently to counteract his discontents or overcome his natural anxieties.

But that familiar problem I bring up here only to lay it aside for one that has as yet gained far less recognition: the effect of uncontrolled quantitative production when the system of distribution is fully adequate. This is, perhaps, an even more difficult problem to solve; indeed impossible without ethical criteria and human restraints, and to bring it home I shall draw my concrete example from one of the oldest departments of mass production and standardization: that of printing. No single invention, probably, has had more radical effects upon the social order than printing from movable types; for at one stroke it broke the class monopoly of culture for the first time: he who learned to read progressively had access to every part of the social heritage in a society whose boundaries were in process of continued extension. That was, without doubt, a gigantic social gain; for it laid the basis not merely for a democratic system of government but for a democratic culture; just as the machine generally, by raising the burden of servile human labor, had made it possible to achieve leisure and education without slavery.

Nevertheless, this great invention has brought penalties that have, only in our own time, become fully apparent. I do not refer to the dangers of surplus production, to the gluts and overflows of the market: I refer to the fact that even under the best economic arrangements, we still have evolved no rational means for controlling, either at source or at destination, the current output of printed matter and reducing it to humanly manageable dimensions. Before the printing press was invented, the difficulty of reproducing manuscripts by hand automatically reduced the quantity of books in circulation: often probably to a much lower point than was intellectually or socially desirable. But by now just the opposite of this has happened: the mere multiplication of our mechanical facilities has so swollen the output of printed matter, that if any human being attempted to keep up with it in the most cursory way he would have no time left for any other activity.

The result is another paradox, sometimes called, as William Cobbett first called it, "starvation in the midst of plenty": one might also characterize it as the poverty of overproductivity. So far we have invented only two minor devices for lessening some of the minor defects of this plenitude: one is the useful but nevertheless dangerous habit of skimming; the other is the device of specialization. Each specialist, by agreement, pays attention to the narrow column of water that works his particular turbine, and automatically rejects contributions that flow in any other channels: even as he turns aside, perhaps more decisively, from the broad silt-laden river of human experience from which all these activities derive. This last situation is far from satisfactory, first because it assumes that interrelationships are unimportant and that an over-all view is unnecessary; and second, because in any single department of thought, no matter how specialized, the same paralyzing overproductivity is manifest. Either to explore the past or keep up with the present becomes increasingly impossible: so that our capacity for assimilation may be said to vary inversely with our capacity for production; and eventually this will have an unfortunate effect upon our creativity, indeed on our very rationality. When our frustrations finally become acute, we may be tempted, like Hitler's followers, to seek in mere charlatanism and quackery some short cut to order.

Let no one imagine that there is a mechanical cure for this mechanical disease. Only politeness would keep me from characterizing this desperate hope as wishful thinking; for the fact is that the attempt to cope with quantification by publishing compendiums, abstracts, synopses, from 'Science Abstracts' to the 'Reader's Digest' or their hundred imitations, or the alternative device of using microfilm, instead of books, are all but sorry stopgaps: indeed, they themselves merely become a further problem. The introduction of these ingenious mechanical facilities has about the same effect that results from the widening of a crowded traffic artery in a city: it actually increases the amount of traffic the avenue will have to bear and in the long run aggravates the very condition it set out to cure. No: the fact is that here, as in so many other departments, there is no purely mechanical solution for the problem of quantification: the answer must in fact be framed in qualitative terms, not by inventing a new machine, but by transforming the purposes and values of the human agent who uses it.

Why should we gratuitously assume, as we so constantly do, that the mere existence of a mechanism for manifolding or mass production carries with it an obligation to use it to the fullest capacity? If we are not to court mental obfuscation, indeed complete paralysis, we must learn to exercise, first of all, a certain continence and discipline in publication, printing nothing by way of routine, nothing because we have a schedule to meet and pages to fill, nothing merely for the doubtful luster and glory of getting our names into print a sufficient number of times each year to jog the attention of our peers and our administrative superiors. To achieve control, we shall even, I suspect, have to reconsider and perhaps abandon the whole notion of periodical publication, particularly by week or month, as a possibly needless incitement to premature or superfluous publication. I do not intend to canvass all the professional and personal devices that we might invent to meet this situation. What I do insist upon is that we cannot continue inertly to accept a burdensome technique of overproduction without inventing a social discipline for handling it; and that until we do this our situation will steadily worsen.

What applies so plainly to mass printing applies in equal or even greater degree to almost every other department of mass production. Our production levels in every field must be based, not on the physical capacities of our machines to multiply goods, but on the psychological capacities of the human organism to assimilate them and convert them ultimately into an orderly, purposive, rational, and significant life. Without such a hierarchy of life needs and values, without the constant subordination of technics to human purpose, the present tempo of mechanical production can result only in an increasing misdirection and nullification of power and effort.

The control of quantity is bound up with still another problem, likewise derived from our very success. Every technical process tends, in its perfection, to eliminate the active worker from participation and to produce an effective substitute: the automaton. The original model for all our automatic machines is the mechanical clock; and machinery approaches perfection as it takes on the regularity, the self-regulation, the uniformity in production, that a good chronometer achieves. But the notion of a self-regulating mechanism, performing its own functions, not subject to direct human intervention or control, has spread from simple machines to the whole process. The tendency in mass production is to transfer initiative and significance from the worker who once operated the machine to the machine that operates the worker. As the process becomes more highly 'rationalized,' on its own narrow terms, the worker becomes, as it were, de-rationalized; and this applies on every level of organization.

By now we have discovered that there are serious drawbacks in this process, which were not evident in its earlier stages: not the least is that increasingly the only way in which men can assert their specifically human qualities, once they are engaged by an automatic process, is by nonparticipation, by resistance, by throwing a monkey wrench into the works. This limiting of the power of rational participation, and therefore rational control, tends likewise to produce a sense of impotence: once a process is in motion, once a product is, so to say, in the works, everyone feels that nothing can be done to alter the end product or to halt the operation. While people have little doubt that human intention, human will, start the process of invention and production, they have become so deeply the victim of their own automatism that they tend blindly to deny that human intention and human effort may also bring the process to an end or change its direction, once it has been fixed. That fact is as dangerous in the present crisis as the ideological conflicts that are at work.

Do not, I beg you, misunderstand the bearings of this argument. For me, as for the most ardent apologist for the machine, the automaton is Western Civilization's decisive answer to the problem Aristotle propounded —on what terms can human slavery be brought to an end? Furthermore, our knowledge of the wisdom of the body, as Dr. Walter Cannon called it, leaves no doubt as to the benefits of automatic processes in any kind of vital economy: automatic machines and organizations are as useful to society as the system of nervous reflexes and endocrines is to the human body: both forms of automatism leave the mind free for the exercise of its higher functions. But in individual men, the condition for successful automatism is fulfilled by an over-all agency, the brain, which may intervene when necessary and resume the functions of government: evaluation and conscious direction.

Unfortunately, the tendency of automatism is to make the human purposes subordinate to the very means originally erected to serve them. Let me give you a very trivial example of this perversion: I wish I could also say that it is an uncommon one. A friend of mine went to a hospital for observation, to determine the cause of certain disturbing physical symptoms: after making a series of exhaustive tests, spinal fluid examination, blood counts, sedimentation tests, and so forth, the physicians by a chemical analysis of the blood finally hit upon the source of her strange ailment, which turned out to be simple carbon monoxide poisoning, due to a defective furnace flue in her home. Meanwhile the untainted air of the hospital had improved her condition and her complete cure could be ensured by calling in the steam fitter to repair the furnace; so she was promptly dismissed. A week later, however, she received an urgent call from the hospital: they wanted her to report without delay for another examination. A little puzzled, my friend explained that there was nothing the matter with her, her ailment had not returned; but the hospital remained insistent. "You must come back here tomorrow," the secretary patiently explained, "to have your Wassermann taken. The nurse forgot to check this, and our records are incomplete."

This tendency to overlook the human end which our automatic organizations serve has begun to pervade our whole civilization; and in the end, if it is uncorrected, it may effectually undermine our best achievements. For the fact is that standardization, organization, automatism, which are the real and special triumphs of modern technics, tend with their very perfection to produce routineers: people whose vital interests and activities lie outside the system to which they have committed themselves. The vice that dogged the regularities and automatisms of monastic life in the Middle Ages, the vice called *acedia,* or lethargic indifference, already tends to creep into the older, staler departments of our technology. For one Robert Young who tries to awaken his colleagues from their somnolent routine, there are ten anti-Youngs in the railroad system and elsewhere, whose secret motto is: "Anything for a quiet life." Unless extraneous jolts and challenges awaken such people, as war awakens an army from its paper-shuffling and button-polishing, their indifference, and their more active boredom, may in time produce an over-all loss of efficiency. Only innocents fancy that the practice of feather-bedding is confined to trade unions.

When we eliminate the active human factor in industry, in other words, we may also eliminate, with all but fatal success, the impulses, passions, drives, and aspirations that make for continued technical perfection. This possibility has been amply demonstrated by the work of many investigators, beginning in a crude way with early efficiency engineers like Gantt, and going forward in such inquiries as those Professor Elton Mayo conducted in the famous Western Electric experiment at Hawthorne. No matter how marvelous our inventions, how productive our industries, how exquisitely automatic our machines, the whole process may be brought to a standstill by its failure fully to engage the human personality or to serve its needs. During the nineteenth century technics often served as a substitute for religion and love: the machine was to some a god, commanding obedience, to others a mistress, evoking passionate pursuit and affectionate loyalty: in any case a refuge from the vexatious problems of human destiny, of life and death.

But with the exception of states like Soviet Russia, still in the throes of industrial pioneering, full of childlike delight in the mere go of machines, that innocent faith and that attitude no longer prevail. In addition to doing its daily job, technics no longer serves as a religious system of redemption and salvation. At the end of his 'Faust,' the great humanist, Goethe, preached the new doctrine of salvation by works: meaning by works, in so many words, engineering works, like the draining of marshes and the cutting through of canals: indeed, he confessed to Eckermann, toward his end, that he would like to live on another half century so that he might behold the cutting through of the Suez and Panama canals. Does that confession not seem pathetically naïve today? Would a man on the brink of the grave now wish to prolong his life, so that he might see the first full-scale use of the atom bomb? Or the first widespread trial of bacteria in unrestricted genocide? On the contrary, these very possibilities cast a doubt on the whole process to which we have so wholeheartedly committed our civilization. If once our automatism led us to such suicidal conclusions, mankind might recoil from the machine itself, precisely as Samuel Butler predicted under cover of satire in 'Erewhon.'

Is there any way of circumventing such a crisis? Is there any alternative to such a dismal backward step? Yes. The answer is to exert a mighty effort, here and now, to correct the internal weaknesses that threaten our society. Part of this answer must come from within the world of technics itself: part from our culture as a whole: in both cases it will demand a shift from mechanical criteria to biological and human criteria. As for the first, many correctives have already appeared in our technology, as a growing interest in living processes has supplemented our original concentration on the physical world. Thanks to the development of biological, sociological, and psychological science, we are often equipped with alternative ways of performing the same task, or reaching the same end: just as a psychiatrist, confronted with a neurotic patient, may in treatment of certain cases have a choice of electrical shock (a mechanical device), of insulin shock (a chemical device), of psychoanalysis (a psychological device), or vocational and sociodramatic therapy (a sociological device). Surgeons once performed elegant operations on the stomach and duodenum that are now more happily treated by a correct diet or even psychological guidance. As soon as we transfer attention, within technics, from the machine to the personality and the community, that shift will itself introduce regulative and normative standards into every operation. But as yet, unfortunately, only a small sector of our technics has escaped the narrowing influence of its original mechanical preoccupations.

Such internal changes in technics, however, will remain secondary to a larger change in our culture as a whole: for no part of our technics is self-sustaining, and no part is unaffected by decisions we make in other departments of our culture—decisions of a moral, esthetic, religious, or political nature. Our situation today calls for a development of the repressed and dwarfed functions of the human personality, on a sufficient scale to restore the ecological balance that technics has disrupted. Unlimited profit and unlimited power can no longer be the determining elements in technics, if our civilization as a whole is to be saved: social and personal development must take precedence. Not the Power Man, not the Profit Man, not the Mechanical Man, but the Whole Man, Man in Person, so to say, must be the central actor in the new drama of civilization. This means that we must reverse the order of development which first produced the machine: we must now explore the world of history, culture, organic life, human development, as we once explored the non-living world of nature. We must understand the organics and psychics of personality as we first understood the statics and mechanics of physical processes. We must center attention on quality, value, pattern, and purpose, as we once centered attention on quantity, on mechanical order, on mass and motion.

If technics is not to play a wholly destructive part in the future of Western Civilization we must now ask ourselves, for the first time, what sort of society and what kind of man are we seeking to produce? About any and every machine, above all about the technical process itself, the critical question is: How much does this instrument further life? If it does not promote human welfare, in the fullest sense, an atomic pile is as disreputable as a pinball game or a jukebox. In short: we must do justice to the whole nature of man before we can make the most of our mechanical improvements. The restoration of the organic, the human, the personal, to a central place in our economy, is essential if we are to overcome the forces that, without such over-all direction and control, are now driving our society ever closer to internal disintegration and external destruction.

The guiding principle of the last century was summed up in the title of a notable book recently published by the Swiss scholar, Dr. Sigfried Giedion: 'Mechanization Takes Command.' But if Western Civilization is to overcome the disruptive forces that have issued forth from the very processes in which it has taken most pride, from which it has looked for the relief of man's estate and indeed his personal salvation, we will have to take for our guiding principle in the future a quite different motto: Let Man Take Command. Instead of continuing to mechanize and regiment man, we must undertake just the opposite operation; we must humanize the machine, restoring lifelike attributes, the attributes of selectivity, balance, wholeness, autonomy, and freedom, in every department where work must be done. To follow that course, in all its ramifications and implications, will be to lay down the foundations for a new age: not the ultimate Age of the Machine, as pictured by the cockeyed writers of science fiction, but the first real Age of Man.

(1954)

CHAPTER TWENTY-SEVEN

Standardization and Choice

The problem that I propose to discuss is one that goes far beyond the realm of art itself; and I do not mean to let myself be unduly confined, in endeavoring to carry that problem to its conclusions. But the problem arose, perhaps earlier than anywhere else, in the domain of art, and I am grateful that the general scope of these lectures encourages me to draw most of my illustrations from the related fields of technics and the arts. As far as time allows, I shall follow the trail opened in the arts into the rest of life; and if I do not take you the full distance, you will at least have provisions of a modest kind for making the journey by yourselves. We have seen, so far, that the split between art and technics, which is such a vexing one in our life today, perhaps existed from the very beginning of their development: that Prometheus and Orpheus, if in a sense brothers, were also like Cain and Abel bitter rivals, and that only in the more fortunate epochs of civilization were the two sides of life they represented fully reconciled.

But not least among the many paradoxes that greet us in the relations of art and technics is the fact that the process of quantification was, from an early time, applied particularly to works of art. Casting and molding and stamping are all of them very old technical devices: they are devices whereby, with a standard pattern or form, one can reproduce innumerable exact copies of the original work. At a time when the sanitation system of Athens would have disgraced a second-rate American country town, at a time when wheat was ground largely in hand querns, the process of reproduction by casting was applied with great success to statues. All this is in line with what I was saying in my last lecture; namely, that the first step in modern mass production—and so ultimately in the creation of our depersonalized, quantity-minded world today—took place when the almost equally ancient stamping process was applied to the mechanical reproduction of images, by means of wood-block printing. Though the first use for this adroit invention, it would seem, was the printing of playing cards—a characteristic contribution to the new spirit of gambling that went along with the early development of capitalism—the next use was the general making of pictures for wide distribution.

Just as the typographer took over from the calligrapher or copyist the more standardized part of his art, the printed letter, so the maker of wood-cuts took over from the illuminator the freer and more imaginative part of his art, that associated with the image. This effort to multiply and cheapen the means of reproducing pictures resulted in a remarkable series of inventions during the next five centuries. First, of course, wood-block printing: this was followed by copper and steel engraving, which served so well the new map makers and cartographers, helping to produce maps of unrivaled clarity and sharpness of line: this, again, was followed by various forms of etching, using chemical as well as mechanical processes, which enabled artists like Rembrandt to produce prints qualitatively different from those that a pencil or a pen could produce. Finally, the invention of the lithograph multiplied the facilities of the pencil. Along another line, beginning with the invention of the colored woodcut in 1508, there was a parallel growth, which led eventually to color lithography and later forms of photographic color reproduction. Even though there might be no increase in the technical mastery or the esthetic exploitation of the new media, the mechanical processes of reproduction were facilitated and extended. Along with this mass production of art, people tended to become more picture-minded; or rather, perhaps, they were confirmed in their original picture-mindedness.

To understand the bearings of this change we must realize that it was at once a technical innovation, a social device, a means of popular education, and a way by which the monopoly of art by a small group was broken down. With the invention of graphic reproduction, pictures could go into circulation like any other commodity; they could be sold at markets and fairs so cheaply that all but the poorest classes could afford to own them. Sometimes these early prints were the media of popular realistic education, as in Jost Ammann's noted series on the crafts and occupations; sometimes they served as improvised newssheets to record remarkable or fantastic events; sometimes, at a later day, they would be used by Hogarth to point moral lessons or by Rowlandson to satirize the very middle class that was buying his pictures.

From the fifteenth century onward, the picture was not merely something that you saw, in the form of tapestry, on the walls of a castle, or in the form of a fresco or an oil painting in a church or palace: in the cheap medium of an engraving it could be carried home; and so, in a sense, what it lost in uniqueness it gained in intimacy and variety and wide distribution. As long as good examples still abounded on the higher levels of art, these vulgar reproductions retained many of the virtues of original painting. If they lacked pretentiousnes, they gave to the unpretentious moments, the common occupations, the daily scene, the vulgar pastimes, the dignity of being sufficiently memorable to be preserved. That was a victory for democracy, achieved in the arts long before its proposition, that all men are created equal, was put forward in politics.

This democratization of the image was one of the universal triumphs of the machine, as well as one of the earliest. So deep and widespread was its influence that it took place even in countries like Japan, where all the dominant patterns of society remained feudal and caste-limited; and, as in Europe, the method and the spectator's interest affected the content of the print, too. Long before mechanization had taken command of transportation and textile production, it freed the image for popular consumption and produced new images in large quantities.

Viewed in its beginnings, this whole process, like that of democracy itself, seems an entirely happy one. If art is good, then surely it is good for everyone. If painting and carvings are means whereby people become conscious of feelings, perceptions, interests that would otherwise be unexpressed or unformed, then why should not prints of all kinds perform the same office, in some degree to supplement the functions of collective art, as people viewed it habitually in their public buildings, civic and religious? If one does not in this minor form of art always reach the high and exalted level of public art, why should there not be a place for a less high-flown kind of esthetic response, fit to take its place, with its slippers on, before the domestic fire? In one age the Tanagra figurine; in another the woodcut. That there was something in the machine process itself that might, if people were unguarded, make this excellent development go dreadfully awry was a possibility that hardly anybody began to suspect before the nineteenth century.

Meanwhile, as the technical processes of reproduction were being invented and perfected, as mass distribution in the graphic arts was becoming ever more feasible, something had been happening of the same order within the domain of the symbol itself. The turning of interest away from the self and toward the object, we associate with the growth of realism in late medieval and renascence painting. That change manifested itself in a variety of ways. One of them was the devaluation of traditional symbols. Thus, for one thing, the austerely divine Virgin of fourteenth century painting becomes the soft-curved doting mother of sixteenth century painting, that all too human creature: the subject ostensibly remains the same, but the descent from heaven to earth is swift. Or again, take Breughel the Elder's paintings, almost any of his figure paintings, but above all his interpretation of Christ bearing his cross to Calvary. That is in a sense one of the first bugle blows of democracy: it proclaimed liberty, equality, and fraternity more loudly than the French Revolution itself: above all, equality. For at first one looks all over the painting for the principal figure, only to find that, in the artist's perspective, there *is* no principal figure: Jesus himself is lost in a swarm of other figures and can be found only after some searching in the middle distance. One must take an imaginary ruler and draw intersecting lines from the four corners of the picture to find that Jesus occupies the mathematical—though not the visual—center of this space. Breughel, in his very method of composition, repeatedly proclaims the equality of all ranks; and the painters after him carried that leveling of persons a stage further toward the now depersonalized world of science by finding that the costume was more important than the human face, or that the landscape was more significant than the figures in it.

In the end this led to the reduction of the artist's becoming a mere transcriber of nature: a register of optical sensation: a blank surface on which images left a mark. What the Dutch realists began, the painters of the nineteenth century carried to a theoretic conclusion; and the results may be summarized by two characteristic remarks. Claude Monet, Cézanne observed, was only an eye: *but what an eye!* Gustave Courbet said that he did not paint angels because he had never discovered any in nature. From these remarks one could draw two conclusions: the painter had become a specialist in sense-data; and the only world he knew was that which was external to him. Those remarks might have been enough to persuade any cultural historian that a development was about to take place in painting similar to that which had taken place in printing; and he would not have been wrong. As a matter of fact that change had already taken place even before Courbet and the other nineteenth century realists had started to paint.

As far as realism could go in search of visual matter-of-factness the seventeenth century Dutch realists had already gone. By conscientious effort they had produced the color photograph, in fact the best color photographs that have yet been made. The exquisite perfection of these handmade photographs has never been excelled, as yet, by any product of the machine. As with the manuscript copyist, their process was laborious; and in order to rival it by mechanical means, it was first necessary to simplify it, by reducing it to black and white. The original step toward this end was taken at a very early date—1558—by Daniello Barbara who invented a camera and stop for the diaphragm. The next step awaited the further development of chemistry; and it therefore could hardly have taken place till the nineteenth century. At length, in the 1830s, it occurred to two independent inventors, Talbot and Niepce, that the abstract office performed by the realist painter's eye could also be performed by a simple apparatus that would throw the light rays from the outside world upon a chemically sensitized surface. With the invention of photography the process of depersonalization came to a climax.

Now, by perfecting a mechanical method, the "taking of pictures" by a mere registration of sensations was democratized. Anyone could use a camera. Anyone could develop a picture. Indeed, as early as the 1890s the Eastman Company went one step further in the direction of automatism and mass production, by saying to the amateur photographer—this was their earliest advertising slogan—*You press the button, we do the rest.*

What had been in the seventeenth century a slow handicraft process, requiring well-trained eyes and extremely skilled hands, with all the rewards that accompany such highly organized bodily activities, now became an all-but-automatic gesture. Not entirely an automatic gesture, I hasten to add, lest any photographers in this audience should squirm in agonized silence or break forth into a loud shout of protest. For after all it turns out that even in the making of the most mechanically contrived image, something more than machines and chemicals is involved. The eye, which means taste. The interest in the subject and an insight into the moment when it—it or he or she—is ready. An understanding of just what esthetic values can be further brought out in the manipulation of the instrument and the materials. All these human contributions are essential. As in science, no matter how faithfully one excludes the subjective, it is still the subject who contrives the exclusion. All this must be freely granted. But this is only to say that in photography another machine art like printing was born; and that the standards of esthetic success in this art are not dissimilar to those in printing. If we consider those standards for a moment we shall have a clue to one of the most essential problems connected with automatism and reproduction.

As with printing, photography did not altogether do away with the possibilities of human choice; but to justify their productions as art there was some tendency on the part of the early photographers, once they had overcome the technical difficulties of the process, to attempt to ape, by means of the camera, the special forms and symbols that had been handed down traditionally by painting. Accordingly, in the nineties, American photographs became soft and misty and impressionistic, just when impressionism was attempting to dissolve form into atmosphere and light. But the real triumphs of photography depended upon the photographer's respect for his medium, his interest in the object before him, and his ability to single out of the thousands of images that pass before his eye, affected by the time of day, the quality of light, movement, the sensitivity of his plates or film, the contours of his lens, precisely that moment when these factors were in conjunction with his own purpose. At that final moment of choice—which sometimes occurred at the point when a picture was taken, sometimes only after taking and developing a hundred indifferent prints—the human person again became operative; and at that moment, but only at that moment, the machine product becomes a veritable work of art, because it reflects the human spirit.

As far as its effect upon painting went, the first result of photography, perhaps, was to increase the danger of technological unemployment; for if the painter were only an eye, the camera's eye was not merely his equal but, in many respects, his superior. While painters themselves were among the first to exploit the possibilities of the new art—Octavius Hill, the great Edinburgh photographer, for example, went into photography in order to get a record of a large group of clergymen he wished to work into a group portrait—the inevitable result of this art was to devaluate mere realism. Wealthy patrons might continue to employ the painter because his images, being handmade, were rarer and more obviously expensive. But in the end, if the artist did not have something to say that could not be recorded by mechanical means, he and his tedious handicraft process were ready for the scrap heap. On the level of mere visual abstraction—for of course a photograph, accurate and realistic, is an abstraction from the multi-dimensional object it interprets—there was nothing more for the painter to do. As against a single person who could use a brush passably, there were thousands who could take reasonably good photographs. Here the first effect of the machine process was to deliver people from the specialist and to restore the status and function of the amateur. Thanks to the camera, the eye at least was re-educated, after having been too long committed to the verbal symbols of print. People awoke to the constant miracles of the natural world, like an invalid long secluded in a dark room, able for the first time to breathe the fresh air and feel the sunshine, grateful for the simplest play of light and shade over the landscape. But though the art of taking pictures is necessarily a selective one, the very spread and progress of that art, not least with the invention of the motion picture, was in the opposite direction: it multiplied the permanent image as images had never been multiplied before, and by sheer superabundance it undermined old habits of careful evaluation and selection. And that very fact, which went along with the achievement of a democratic medium of expression, has raised a whole series of problems that we must wrestle with today, if, here as elsewhere, we are not to starve in the midst of plenty.

This brief review of the course of the reproductive processes in art, from the wood engraving to the colored lithograph, from the photographic painting to the photograph proper, capable of being manifolded cheaply, does not take into account various subsidiary efforts in the same direction in many of the other arts, such as the reproduction of sounds, by means of the phonograph and the talking film; to say nothing of the fortunately abortive efforts of James Watt to find a mechanical means of reproducing, in the semblance of sculpture, the human form, an effort on which the inventor of the steam engine curiously wasted some of the best years of his life. I have filled in this background briefly merely in order to prepare the way for discussing the results of these many efforts to multiply the symbol, and so to deal with the problem of assimilation.

What has been the result of the mass production of esthetic symbols that began in the fifteenth century? What benefits have we derived from it and what dangers do we now confront? With your permission, I shall speak only briefly about the benefits, since we are all conscious of them. By means of our various reproductive devices, a large part of our experience, which once vanished without any sort of record, has been arrested and fixed. Because of the varied processes of reproduction that are now at hand, many important experiences, difficult to transpose into words, are now visible in images; and certain aspects of art, which were once reserved for the privileged, are now an everyday experience to those who make use of the resources of printing and photography. The gains from these processes are so demonstrable that we have, unfortunately, become a little unwary as to the deficits and losses; so I purpose now to point out how our very successes with the reproductive arts present us with a problem whose dimensions have been increasing at almost geometric ratio, year by year.

The fact is that in every department of art and thought we are being overwhelmed by our symbol-creating capacity; and our very facility with the mechanical means of multifolding and reproduction has been responsible for a progressive failure in selectivity and therefore in the power of assimilation. We are overwhelmed by the rank fecundity of the machine, operating without any Malthusian checks except periodic financial depressions; and even they, it would now seem, cannot be wholly relied on. Between ourselves and the actual experience and the actual environment there now swells an ever-rising flood of images which come to us in every sort of medium—the camera and printing press, by motion picture and by television. A picture was once a rare sort of symbol, rare enough to call for attentive concentration. Now it is the actual experience that is rare, and the picture has become ubiquitous. Just as for one person who takes part in the game in a ball park a thousand people see the game by television, and see the static photograph of some incident the next day in the newspaper, and a final shot of it the next week in a magazine, so with every other event. We are rapidly dividing the world into two classes: a minority who act, increasingly, for the benefit of the reproductive process, and a majority whose entire life is spent serving as the passive appreciators or willing victims of this reproductive process. Deliberately, on every historic occasion, we piously fake events for the benefit of photographers, while the actual event often occurs in a different fashion; and we have the effrontery to call these artful dress rehearsals "authentic historic documents."

So an endless succession of images passes before the eye, offered by people who wish to exercise power, either by making us buy something for their benefit or making us agree to something that would promote their economic or political interests: images of gadgets manufacturers want us to acquire; images of seductive young ladies who are supposed, by association, to make us seek other equally desirable goods, images of people and events in the news, big people and little people, important and unimportant events; images so constant, so unremitting, so insistent that for all purposes of our own we might as well be paralyzed, so unwelcome are our inner promptings or our own self-directed actions. As the result of this whole mechanical process, we cease to live in the multi-dimensional world of reality, the world that brings into play every aspect of the human personality, from its bony structure to its tenderest emotions: we have substituted for this, largely through the mass production of graphic symbols—abetted indeed by a similar multiplication and reproduction of sounds—a second-hand world, a ghost-world, in which everyone lives a secondhand and derivative life. The Greeks had a name for this pallid simulacrum of real existence: they called it Hades, and this kingdom of shadows seems to be the ultimate destination of our mechanistic and mammonistic culture.

One more matter. The general effect of this multiplication of graphic symbols has been to lessen the impact of art itself. This result might have disheartened the early inventors of the new processes of reproduction if they could have anticipated it. In order to survive in this image-glutted world, it is necessary for us to devaluate the symbol and to reject every aspect of it but the purely sensational one. For note, the very repetition of the stimulus would make it necessary for us in self-defense to empty it of meaning if the process of repetition did not, quite automatically, produce this result. Then, by a reciprocal twist, the emptier a symbol is of meaning, the more must its user depend upon mere repetition and mere sensationalism to achieve his purpose. This is a vicious circle, if ever there was one. Because of the sheer multiplication of esthetic images, people must, to retain any degree of autonomy and self-direction, achieve a certain opacity, a certain insensitiveness, a certain protective thickening of the hide, in order not to be overwhelmed and confused by the multitude of demands that are made upon their attention. Just as many people go about their daily work, as too often students pursue their studies, with the radio turned on full blast, hearing only half the programs, so, in almost every other operation, we only half-see, half-feel, half-understand what is going on; for we should be neurotic wrecks if we tried to give all the extraneous mechanical stimuli that impinge upon us anything like our full attention. That habit perhaps protects us from an early nervous breakdown; but it also protects us from the powerful impact of geniune works of art, for such works demand our fullest attention, our fullest participation, our most individualized and re-creative response. What we settle for, since we must close our minds, are the bare sensations; and that is perhaps one of the reasons that the modern artist, defensively, has less and less to say. In order to make sensations seem more important than meanings, he is compelled to use processes of magnification and distortion, similar to the stunts used by the big advertiser to attract attention. So the doctrine of quantification, Faster and Faster, leads to the sensationalism of Louder and Louder; and that in turn, as it affects the meaning of the symbols used by the artist, means Emptier and Emptier. This is a heavy price to pay for mass production and for the artist's need to compete with mass production.

Behold, then, the so-far-final result of our magnificent technical triumphs in the reproductive arts. We diminish the contents of the image: we narrow the human response: we progressively eliminate the powers of human choice: we overwhelm by repetition, and, in order to stave off boredom, we have to intensify the purely sensational aspects of the image. In the end, the final effect of our manifold inventions for manifolding is to devaluate the symbol itself; partly because it comes to us, as in a tied-in sale, attached to some other object which we may or may not want; partly because it has multiplied to such a point that we are overwhelmed by sheer quantity and can no longer assimilate anything but a small part of the meaning it might otherwise convey. What is responsible for this perversion of the whole process of reproduction? Something we should have been aware of from the beginning. We have gratuitously assumed that the mere existence of a mechanism for manifolding or mass production carries with it an obligation to use it to the fullest capacity. *But there simply is no such necessity. Once you discover this, you are a free man.*

I speak with some feeling on this subject, and a little experience, because for the better part of a summer I was annoyed by a loud-speaker operated by a neighbor of mine who runs a small summer hotel and who had installed this formidable instrument for the entertainment of his guests. He is a thoroughly nice man, with whom I am on very neighborly terms, and he merely thought to provide all the benefits of modern science for his temporarily rusticated urban clients. Unfortunately, though I am a quarter of a mile away, the sounds of his loud-speaker blared into my small study, as insistently as a drunken man shouting in my ear. It took weeks of vexing argument and tactful persuasion to drive home to him two simple principles: first, just because a loud-speaker is called loud, it needn't be turned on at its loudest volume in order to fulfill its mission; second, just because a machine can be on duty twenty-four hours, that is no reason for keeping it operating on that schedule. The great principle here is that as soon as mechanical limitations are thrown off, human restrictions must be clamped on. I trust that this argument will prove as convincing to this audience as it did to my neighbor; for his loud-speaker is now so inaudible that I begin to fear he has gotten rid of it altogether. But that would unfortunately mean that he had not really grasped my point; for I was pleading, not for abolition of the machine, but for its effective control.

Now let me carry this general argument about the devaluation of the image back into the realm of art. One of the real achievements of technics during the last half century has been to devise means of making color reproductions of pictures with increasingly high fidelity. Where sufficient care and craftsmanship is used, in the gelatine process, it is possible, at least in the case of pen drawings and water colors and sepia washes, to reproduce pictures so faithfully that the artist himself has often mistaken the reproduction for the original work. As a result, for a small fraction of the price of an original painting—itself sometimes priceless and beyond the means of even the wealthiest bidder—the ordinary citizen may have, as his private possession, a picture that in its original form was entirely beyond his reach, physically as well as financially. On the surface this seems an unalloyed triumph for the mechanical process. Does it not, in no small degree, atone for the devaluation of the esthetic symbol in other departments? In one sense, this actually *is* a genuine triumph for popular education, for it is capable of fulfilling the otherwise demagogic promise of making every man a king, even as it in some degree reduces the king—the proud possessor of a unique object—to the level of the man in the street.

As with the entire democratic process of equalization, that process which de Tocqueville described as the essential theme of the last seven centuries, mechanization brings about a true leveling off in both directions, upward and downward: fair esthetic shares for all, as the British could say. But what, if you look closer, is the *actual* result? Thanks to our confirmed habits of *non*-selectivity the outcome is not quite so happy as one might fancy. The actual result is that already, in big cities at least, there is a whole group of great pictures, so frequently reproduced, so often hung, so insistently visible, that they have forfeited, no matter how faithful the reproduction, all the magic of the original. We all have seen these pictures, but alas, once too often. When I was a boy such a picture was Sir Luke Fildes' painting of the benign bewhiskered physician visiting a sick child, a bathetic piece of popular art, whose devaluation would now bring tears to no one's eye. But the same thing is happening again, because of the very raising of the level of popular taste, with paintings of the highest excellence. There are paintings by Van Gogh and Matisse and Picasso that are descending the swift slippery slope to oblivion by reason of the fact that they are on view at all times and everywhere. And whereas, with every great work of art, the more one returns to it the more one sees in it, once one has reached a certain point of super-saturation, the result is the rapid effacement of the image: it sinks into the background: indeed, it disappears.

Mind you, I am not speaking about the effect of poor and inadequate reproductions of paintings; though of these unfortunately there is a terrifying abundance. I have seen reproductions of great paintings on view in famous museums of art that reflect on either the sound eyesight or the elementary honesty of their curators and directors, so false was every value and color to the original. So, too, I have looked into textbooks on art, prepared for elementary schools, in which bad pictures paraded as high art, and in which good pictures were so vilely reproduced that they constituted an esthetic betrayal of both the artist and the student. Our coarseness of discrimination here, indeed our absence of decent morals, is disquieting. But the vice I am now speaking about is quite different from these misdemeanors. Even when our reproductions are adequate, even when they are marvelously good, near to being perfect, we must still confront one very significant fact that our whole civilization seems, in its preoccupation with mechanical competence, to have long lost sight of. My elders used to put it, somewhat smugly as it seemed when I was young, by saying that it was possible to have too much of a good thing. But the long experience of the race stands behind that dictum: It *is* possible to have too much of a good thing; and indeed, the more intense, the more valuable an experience is, the more rare it must be, the more brief its duration. One could perhaps sum this up by saying that a blessing, repeated once too often, becomes a curse. Now, regularity and repetition, those gifts of the machine, must be confined to those parts of life that correspond to the reflex system in the body; they are not processes that have anything to contribute, except in a strictly subordinate way, to the higher functions, to the emotions and imagination, to esthetic feelings and rational insight. The danger of an over-regulated, over-routinized life, given to excessive repetition, was long ago discovered in the monastery. It produces the special vice called *acedia*, or abysmal apathy. Any object that is too constantly present, however interesting or desirable it may be in itself, presently loses its special significance; what we look at habitually, we overlook. Gilbert Chesterton used that perception in one of his Father Brown stories, in which the murder was committed by the postman. No one suspected the postman, indeed no one *saw* him come to the house at the hour the crime was committed, precisely because that was his usual time for making his usual rounds. His very constancy put him completely out of the minds of the witnesses. So, perhaps, many a man has fallen for the lure of another woman, not his wife, not because her charms were necessarily in any way superior, but because he has actually ceased to observe, and so ceased to respond to, the charms that his mate too habitually exposed to him; and the very irregularity and unexpectedness of his new relations gave them a disproportionate attraction. This general truth about constancy and repetition has a direct application to reproduction and domestication in art. Novelty, adventure, variety, spontaneity, intensity—these are all very essential ingredients in a work of art; and a great work of art, like El Greco's 'Toledo' at the Metropolitan, is one that presents this feeling of shock and delight, of new things to be revealed, at every encounter with it. Such works are inexhaustible in their meaning. But with one proviso: one must not go to them too often. The rarity of the experience is an essential preparation for the delight. Without rhythm and interval there is only satiation and ennui.

But all this is in opposition to the tendency of mass production. Mass production imposes on the community a terrible new burden: the duty to constantly consume. In the arts, at the very moment the extension of the reproductive processes promised to widen the area of freedom, this new necessity, the necessity to keep the plant going, has served to undermine habits of choice, discrimination, selectivity that are essential to both creation and enjoyment. Quantity now counts for more than quality. There used to be an old popular song with the words, "I'll try anything once, if I like it I'll try it again." But under the machine system, you'll not only try it again, you'll try it a thousand times, whether you like it or not, and a vast apparatus of propaganda and persuasion, of boasting and bullying, will coerce you into performing this new duty.

You know the old fable of the Sorcerer's Apprentice, which Goethe thought it worth while to put into verse, and which has even, in our time, gotten into the animated cartoon: the clever apprentice who repeated the old sorcerer's spell and got the pail and the broom to do his work for him, when the master was away, while he stayed idle. Unfortunately, though he knew how to bring into existence a whole regiment of pails and brooms, which went about their work with unflagging automatic energy, he had never mastered the formula for bringing their activities to an end: so presently he found himself floundering in a flood of water that these self-willed pails were pouring into his master's house. So with the apprentices to the machine. We not merely encourage people to share the new-found powers that the machine has opened up: we *insist* that they do so, with increasingly less respect for their needs and tastes and preferences, simply because we have found no spell for turning the machine off. The grim fable of the Sorcerer's Apprentice applies to all our activities, from photographs to reproduction of works of art, from motor cars to atom bombs. It is as if we had invented an automobile that had neither a brake nor a steering wheel, but only an accelerator, so that our sole form of control consisted in making the machine go faster. For a little while, on a straight road, we might feel safe, and even, as we increased our speed, gloriously free; but as soon as we wanted to reduce our speed or to change our direction or to back up, we should find that no provision had been made for this degree of human control—the only open possibility was *Faster, faster!* As our mass-production system is now set up, a slowing down of consumption, in any department, produces a crisis if not a catastrophe. That is why only under the pressure of war or preparation for war, in which wholesale waste and destruction come to its aid, does the machine, as now conceived, operate effectively on its own terms.

The tendencies I have been describing are, you will recognize, universal ones; but in no realm have they been more fatal than in the realm of art. As long as a work of art was an individual product, produced by individual workmen using their own feeble powers with such little extra help as they could get from fire or wind or water, there was a strict limit to the number of works of art that could be produced in a whole lifetime, whether they were paintings or statues, woodcuts or printed cottons. Under such a system of production there was no problem of quantity; or, rather, the problem was that of too little, not too much. Natural and organic limitations took the place of rational selectivity. Only those who exercised some special political or economic monopoly were ever even temporarily in a position of being threatened by a surfeit; and so the appetites remained keen, because only rarely could they be sated. Under such conditions, there was little reason to exercise a vigilant control over quantity, for fostering a discipline of restraint and a habit of studious selection; such discrimination as was necessary was that exercised on a basis of quality alone.

What has happened during the last century has brought about just the opposite kind of condition. As a result of our mechanical reproductive processes, we are now creating a special race of people: people whom one may call art-consumers. From earliest youth they are trained to conduct the normal activities of living within the sound of the radio and the sight of the television screen; and to make the fullest use of our other facilities for reproduction, they are taken, in all big cities at least, in troops and legions through the art galleries and museums, so that they may be conditioned, with equal passivity, to the sight of pictures. The intimate experiences, the firsthand activities, upon which all the arts must be based are thrust out of consciousness: the docile victims of this system are never given enough time alone to be aware of their own impulses or their inner promptings, to indulge in even so much as a daydream without the aid of a radio program or a motion picture; so, too, they lack even the skill of the amateur to attune them more closely to the work of art.

Those who have pushed the reproductive processes to their limit forget the essential nature of art: its uniqueness. While a certain kind of order and form should prevail in the background of all activities, esthetic interests that promote any intensity of stimulus and meaning must necessarily be of short duration. The fact is that our reproductive facilities in the arts will be of human value only when we learn to curb the flood of images and sounds that now overwhelm us, until we control the occasion, the quantity, the duration, the frequency of repetition, in accordance with *our* needs, with *our* capacity for assimilation. These are the saving imperatives of an age that has made the fatal error of the Sorcerer's Apprentice. Expressive art, just in proportion to its value and significance, must be precious, difficult, occasional, in a word aristocratic. It is better to look at a real work of art once a year, or even once in a lifetime, and really see it, really feel it, really assimilate it, than to have a reproduction of it hanging before one continually. I may never, for example, see the Ajanta cave paintings. From reproductions, as well as from travelers who have been in India, I well know that these paintings are worth seeing; and if ever I make the journey I expect to carry away a unique impression, reinforced by the strange faces, the different languages and customs, I shall meet on my pilgrimage. But better a few short hours in the cave, in direct contact with the work of art itself, than a lifetime in looking at the most admirable reproductions. Though here, as in many other places, I remain grateful for the mechanical reproduction, I shall never deceive myself by fancying that it is more than a hint and a promise of the original work.

Or take, for another example, the intense enjoyment of solitude in nature, in a noble grove of trees or on a high mountain top. No small part of that particular experience comes from the fact that only a few human souls are present at any moment. This is what adds the last edge of esthetic significance and emotional stimulus to the experience. If you cut a three-lane highway to the top of that mountain and bring five thousand people to enjoy the solitude, the very essence of the experience is gone: it is replaced by something else, the gregarious good nature, the commonplace sociability, of five thousand people, meeting on a mountain top instead of a city park, but with little sense of nature and with no sense of cosmic isolation.

Thus I come to the final point and moral of this lecture. The quantitative reproduction of art, through the advance of technics, from the woodblock print to the high-fidelity phonograph, has increased the need for qualitative understanding and qualitative choice. At the same time it has imposed upon us, in opposition to the duty to participate in mass consumption, the duty to control quantity: to erect rational measures and criteria of value, now that we are no longer disciplined by natural scarcity. The very expansion of the machine during the last few centuries has taught mankind a lesson that was otherwise, perhaps, too obvious to be learned: the value of the singular, the unique, the precious, the deeply personal.

There are certain occasions in life when the aristocratic principle must balance the democratic one, when the personalism of art, fully entered into, must counteract the impersonalism and therefore the superficiality of technics. We do no one any service, with our reproductive processes, if we limitlessly water the wine in order to have enough to give every member of the community a drop of it, under the illusion that he is draining an honest glass. Unless we can turn the water itself into wine, so that everyone may partake of the real thing, there is in fact no miracle, and nothing worth celebrating in the marriage of art and technics. On the other hand, if we establish this personal discipline, this purposeful selectivity, then nothing that the machine offers us, in any department, need embarrass us.

This conclusion should go some distance in repairing the breach that has so long existed between art and morals, between goodness and truth. The fact is that to enjoy the perfections and delights of art, above all in a day of mass production, the whole organism must be keyed up to its highest level of vigor, sensitive and responsive as only healthy beings are sensitive and responsive; and to achieve this state requires not only hygiene and gymnastic, as the incomparable Athenians knew, but a high state of moral alertness and conscious control. This means, finally, a readiness to reject many inferior goods in favor of the supreme good offered by a genuine work of art, which is like the blessing of friendship, when offered by a person who gives you his best without reserves.

To control the quantitative flood that our mischievous Sorcerer's Apprentices have turned loose, we need to develop habits of inhibition on which we too glibly have bestowed, in the recent past, the epithet puritanic. You will not accuse me, if you have heard these earlier lectures, of being anything but a fervent admirer of William Blake; but for all that I would amplify one of his aphorisms—Damn Braces, Bless Relaxes—and would say that there is no chance of coping with the evils of mass production unless we are likewise ready to bless braces and to exercise, whenever needed, the most strenuous control of mere quantity. To have the right amount of the right quality in the right time and the right place for the right purpose is the essence of morality; and as it turns out, it is perhaps the most important condition for the enjoyment of art. Here if anywhere, Nietzsche's words, as uttered by Zarathustra, actually hold: "Choosing is creating." Yes: choosing is creating. "Hear that, ye creating ones!"

(1952)

CHAPTER TWENTY-EIGHT

Social Consequences
of Atomic Energy

The period in which we live is characterized by strange inner contradictions. While the advance of science has placed energies of cosmic magnitude at human disposal many institutions have regressed to the lower levels of barbarism. The most rational procedures of science now have as their end product in the human economy wholly irrational goals. While the venerable sage, Albert Schweitzer, receives a Nobel peace prize in recognition of his urgent summons to practice reverence for all life, the scientific laboratories of the world are busy with researches whose full-scale application in war might put every living species in peril. On one hand, our national government withholds from its citizens the knowledge needful to make sound judgments on military policy; but at the next moment the same authorities warn us that with the instruments now available, the price of victory in another war might be the extermination of the human race: a curious conception of military success. By the automatic advance in scientific knowledge, we are now committed to processes whose tempo we do not dare to retard, whose direction we do not govern, and whose ultimate results we do not stop to evaluate. Under such conditions every permission becomes a compulsion. And as long as our present knowledge continues to expand the sphere of the irrational and the pathologically automatic, the survival of man, to say nothing of his development, is plainly threatened.

The dangers of our present situation would not be so great had our responses to it been alert and timely. Even now, we should probably be able to mobilize enough political wisdom to provide a minimal basis for the necessary co-operations and safeguards, if only we could throw off the sleepwalker's insulation from reality that characterizes our collective conduct. There are doubtless many causes and reasons for this feebleness of response, and I would not pretend, within the compass of this paper, to give even a sketchy account of them. I purpose rather to confine attention to a single aspect of our present lapse in rational judgment and responsible action: that to which the sciences themselves have contributed by the very terms of their own development. And I do this, not to throw any blame on our colleagues in the natural sciences, but to open the way for a discussion of the means by which scientists themselves might rectify past procedures by setting an example in social responsibility and sanity.

The immediate failure to evaluate and exercise a timely control over the forces whose very existence now threatens us, has its origins, at least in part, in a fatal choice that was made in the name of scientific freedom in the seventeenth century. This decision may be symbolized for us by the resolution of the Royal Society of London, at its very inception, to confine its discussions and experiments to the field of the natural sciences, and to omit all concern with matters that traditionally belonged to theology and history. The necessity to escape the limitations of purely subjective inquiry was obvious; but in defining scientific truth, in the terms Galileo and Descartes defined it, as a truth detached from all considerations of purpose, value, or practical application, science cut itself off from all human concerns except those of science itself. The new absolute for the scientist parodied the old Roman legal maxim: Let scientific truth be discovered, though the heavens fall. The unstated assumption in this maxim was the confidence that the heavens would not in fact fall.

Happily for the health of scientists as human beings, their general conduct did not always live up to the strict isolationism of their creed. Some of the greatest minds in science, indeed, from Pascal to Clerk Maxwell, never lost touch with the ultimate questions of human destiny, while still others, like Joseph Henry and Louis Pasteur, took seriously their obligations as citizens. Nevertheless, for the last three centuries, the whole weight of the scientific tradition has been on the side of detachment, of social irresponsibility, of non-concern for the uses other men might make of scientific knowledge, even though with the growth of biology and medicine strictly human interests—like those of Pasteur's wine growers—insistently invaded the laboratories. To evaluate the human results of their work, to anticipate its possible applications, to correlate the advance of science with the development of man no more occurred to scientists in pursuit of their isolated system of truths than it occurred to the capitalist enterpriser of the nineteenth century, in his equally abstract and one-sided pursuit of financial gain. Plainly, in the seventeenth century, the causal and the teleological had parted company: if one were free to analyze causes one could, so to say, damn the consequences. Beneath that belief there was another unstated assumption, implicit in the very conception of progress, namely that knowledge was, as Bacon had said, power, and that power, power over the forces of nature especially, was an unqualified good. In leaving out the prophetic concerns of Jewish and Christian theology, science had also lost insight into the dangerous liaison between power and pride: the power that lays traps for vanity and the pride that cometh before a fall.

So successful was this new methodology of science that every other scholarly discipline, even in the humanities, tended to ape science's procedures and to proclaim a similar indifference to social results. When in 1910 Henry Adams sought with almost clairvoyant anxiety to enlist his fellow-historians in an assessment of the new physical forces that were so swiftly transforming Western Civilization, they turned a deaf ear to his remarkable paper because it was concerned not with past certainties, but with potentialities and future probabilities.* As a result of these widespread habits of thought, mankind entered the atomic age without looking before or after, and therefore without the faintest preparation for the drastic changes in human institutions that must result, changes that might even affect the speed and direction of scientific effort itself. Yet the outlines of this age, the dimensions of its problems, were visible at least a generation before the first atomic bomb was detonated. Ever since Becquerel's discovery of radio-activity the old stabilities and securities had been visibly threatened. Sensitive observers were at hand who saw that without a radical readaptation of human institutions, these new forces might be ungovernable, and prove in the end perhaps fatal. As early as 1905 Henry Adams, writing to Henry Osborn Taylor, had observed: "At the present rate of progress since 1600, it will not need another century or half century to turn thought upside down. Law in that case would disappear as *a priori* principle and give place to force. Morality would become police. Explosives would reach cosmic violence. Disintegration would overcome integration."

By 1913 the novelist H. G. Wells, under the spell of the physicist, Frederick Soddy, went further: in his novel, 'The World Set Free,' he depicted the use of the atom bomb in warfare, with the total demolition of the first city attacked. Finally, in 1919, Rutherford's critical demonstrations had transformed these timely anticipations into a well grounded probability. If these fitful prophecies had been backed by systematic speculation and inquiry, undertaken by men of science, we should have had a whole generation to prepare mankind for the coming transformation. Instead, we fell into the atomic age with as little anticipation as an abstracted walker, looking for pennies on the pavement, might fall into an open manhole. The manhole was visible; but we regarded the scientific pennies as more important.

One further result must be noted in our failure to anticipate the social consequences of scientific progress and to direct it to humanly valid goals; and this is the fact that the last feverish efforts to place the inordinate powers of nuclear fission under human control took place under the restraints and compulsions of war, when small men were prompted to large decisions under the pressure of the moment, without anything like a careful canvass of alternative policies and means. Had the whole situation been examined in time, the atomic crisis might have been averted. There were two variables that it was imperative to bring under control, during the thirty years before the atom bomb was invented: one was the rate of scientific advance and the other was the rate of social adaptation. Neither of these

* See "A letter to American teachers of history" in Adams, Henry, *The degradation of the democratic dogma*, New York, Macmillan, 1919.

variables is an impersonal, uncontrollable force of nature. The rate of scientific advance is conditioned by policies of education and recruitment, by budgetary provisions for universities and research laboratories; by the amount of social approval accorded to science itself. If we had become as skeptical of the value of science as were St. Augustine and his contemporaries, science could have been starved out of existence in less than a generation. General social adaptation, though a more complex and laborious process, is likewise no purely automatic response to uncontrollable conditions. But because of the failure of our anticipatory reactions, which are the very core of intelligent behavior, decisions of utmost importance to human welfare were made, for purely military purposes, in the midst of a conflict that had already destroyed ancient inhibitions against the random extermination of life. Cosmic power plus moral nihilism is, as Henry Adams had vigilantly predicted, a formula for general disintegration. This was a case of negative social adaptation. The forces that should have been retarded were accelerated.

Now, to the honor of the scientists who produced the atomic bomb, the consciences of their leaders suddenly took fire as soon as man-controlled nuclear fission proved possible. If the awakening was too late to keep these distinguished minds from becoming accessories before the fact, it was also too partial to enable them to bring about a more general social awakening. On their own calculations, as set forth before the Senate Committee on Atomic Energy (1945–46) three years, at most five, was the limit for maintaining a national monopoly of the new weapon. They did their best, in this brief time, to repair the damage caused by their century-old indifference to social consequences. But their best was not good enough. To have aroused mankind fully to the extent of political invention and moral rehabilitation needed to provide even a minimal security, the actions of the scientists would have had to speak even louder than their words. They would have had to close their laboratories, give up their researches, renounce their careers, defy their governments, possibly endure martyrdom, if they were to convey to the public the full urgency of their convictions. Here the new sense of social responsibility failed to overcome the neutralist habits of many lifetimes. Even those who were most deeply disturbed by the possible misapplications of science continued to apply themselves to science. And while "science as usual" prevailed, it was fanciful to hope that "business as usual" and "politics as usual" could be shaken out of their rut.

If this diagnosis is even partly sound, one must now ask a further question. Does it still lie within the province of science to provide any correctives for the evils that its own practice of insulation—abetted by its sudden intrusion into the fields of politics and war—has contributed to? At this late moment, plainly, we must work against time, with the materials now available. Laudable as may be the new Society for Social Responsibility in Science, one cannot hope for immediate results from its efforts. Is it presumptuous, then, for a philosopher to suggest that, within the realm of science itself, there are still resources that might be brought into more active play: the tradition of free inquiry, the collective pooling of knowledge, the lifting of truth above all self-imposed privacies and official restrictions that hamper its circulation among men. Without violating any prudent military taboos against the disclosure of technical means, the scientists themselves are in a position to examine and weigh the probable consequences of utilizing, to this or that extent, the agents of destruction and extermination that are now available. Even the premature peacetime exploitation of this double-edged power, before we have found any practical means of disposing of the waste-product, must be subject to searching criticism. Our present disgraceful record in the industrial pollution of air and water should forewarn us against the grave likelihood of an irretrievable pollution by atomic wastes.

In other words, what scientists failed to prepare for through the period between 1910 and 1940, when the atomic age was just over the horizon, is at least open to them now, when potentiality has become actuality, when prophecy has become accomplished fact. The ill-fated consequences they refused to anticipate then now lie before them. These consequences await methodical inspection and assessment by the only body of men capable of performing it: the scientists themselves, acting as a comprehensive faculty, drawing on their membership in every related field, from nuclear physics to bacteriology, from chemistry to embryology and psychiatry. Why should they not meet in a World Congress, under the aegis of the United Nations, and pool their data as to the effects of utilizing atomic energy in wartime extermination. Let them gauge the prospective results in terms of millions of lives exterminated, of slow-dying cripples and embryological monsters in various species, of vegetation wiped out, ecological partnerships ruined, water supplies contaminated, soil and atmosphere permanently poisoned. Let them even consider the traumatic effects on the personality of our present preparations for these events, already observable, and the worse traumas to be anticipated from their becoming an actuality. In other words, let the scientists, duly assembled in a World Congress, make a qualitative and quantitative analysis of the probable outcome of a world war in which the opposing nations used these new weapons of genocide. No living mind possesses all these data; indeed, no single group of scientists can supply it: it is only in conference that the facts can be established and the threat to life dispassionately estimated. Possibly such a full dress rehearsal in the mind would keep the world from raising the curtain on the malign drama itself. At all events, it would be better to face the consequences in advance than attempt, at the last minute, to avert them, like the physicists who sought, too late, too naively, too ineffectually, to prevent the exploitation of the atomic bomb. Let the truth now be told, as perhaps the one means left to keep the heavens from falling.

There is, I submit, nothing in this Great Assize of scientific knowledge, undertaken, not to promote a national interest but to safeguard the human race, that is foreign to the procedures and purposes of science itself. In such a Congress, the scientists would confine themselves to observable results and statistical probabilities alone. In proposing to meet for such a purpose they would challenge the questionable practices that have broken down world-wide communication in the sciences and restricted not only international communication but cross-reference among practitioners in different fields. But their task would be the task of reasserting the integrity and moral responsibility of science itself, as accountable to mankind for correcting, within its own department, the evils that might issue from the incontinent or demoralized exploitation of scientific knowledge. This scientific congress need draw no military or political conclusions: they need suggest no practical steps. Their sole job would be to provide the data on which rational conclusions could be drawn and alternative policies formulated. If mankind actually lives under the grave perils at which our military and political leaders so grimly hint, there is probably a sufficient instinct for survival left in the human race to take the necessary measures of self-protection once the facts are known.

Admittedly, this proposal for a World Assize of scientific knowledge on the effects of atomic bombs, hydrogen bombs, and other means of effecting total genocide is not a panacea: it is at best but a first step toward stirring the fresh intellectual currents that may clear the air and prepare the way for further co-operative action. Nor is the proposal a novel one. In something like its present form, I put it forward six years ago in 'Air Affairs'; and independently it was broached again the other day by the mathematician and philosopher, Bertrand Russell. But it as yet lacks the only support that could make it effective: the resolute corporate backing of the scientists themselves. Suggestions of similar nature have been made from time to time by individual scientists, but popular ignorance of the total danger to life, governmental hostility to an open revelation of our erroneous policies, and moral neutralism among the great body of scientists have effectually nullified these efforts. Will scientists re-orient themselves in time to re-orient the world; or are they committed to a passive acceptance of the catastrophes their old tradition of social irresponsibility helped to create? That question is not for me to answer.

(1953)

CHAPTER TWENTY-NINE

Leonardo's Premonitions

In the mind of Leonardo da Vinci (1452–1519), one of the greatest intellects of a great age, a multitude of practical inventions accompanied his ideal projections. He and other contemporary artist-engineers demonstrated, as early as the sixteenth century, how many of the technical achievements of our own time had already been sampled in fantasy and even tested in actual or pictured models.

By now everyone is familiar with Leonardo's many daring but remarkably practical constructions, and his equally practical anticipations: likewise with his unsuccessful Great Bird. The latter was actually a glider, with wings which could not move, a failure for reasons that his near contemporary, Borelli, was soon to explain by his remarkable researches on the locomotion of animals, and in particular on the anatomy of birds. For even if Leonardo's wings had been feather-light, they would have required enormous pectoral muscles on the scale of a bird's breast to flap them.

Yet in doing justice to Leonardo, the inventor and engineer, scholars have tended to overlook how disturbed he was by his own mechanical fantasies. Like Roger Bacon, he too had foreseen in his usual enigmatic way (labelled a dream) that "men shall walk without moving [motorcar], they shall speak with those absent [telephone], they shall hear those who do not speak [phonograph]." But in another fantasy, written in the form of a letter, Leonardo conjures up the image of a hideous monster that would attack and destroy mankind. Though Leonardo gave the monster a tangible, gigantic, sub-human form, his actual performances come all too close to the hideous scientifically engineered exterminations our own age has witnessed. The monster's imperviousness to attack only completes resemblance to the airborne atomic, bacterial, and chemical weapons that now have it in their power to wipe out all of mankind. Leonardo's description, printed in MacCurdy's translation of the Notebooks under 'Tales,' demands direct quotation.

"Alas, how many attacks were made upon this raging fiend; to him every onslaught was as nothing. O wretched folk, for you there availed not the impregnable fortresses, nor the lofty walls of your cities, nor the being together in great numbers, nor your houses or palaces! There remained not any place unless it were the tiny holes and subterranean caves where after the manner of crabs and crickets and creatures like these you might find safety and a means of escape. Oh, how many wretched mothers and fathers were deprived of their children! How many unhappy women were deprived of their companions. In truth, my dear Benedetto, I do not believe that ever since the world was created there has been witnessed such lamentation and wailing of people, accompanied by so great terror. In truth the human species in such a plight has need to envy every other race of creatures . . . for us wretched mortals there avails not any flight, since this monster when advancing slowly far exceeds the speed of the swiftest courser.

"I know not what to say or do, for everywhere I seem to find myself swimming with bent head within the mighty throat and remaining indistinguishable in death, buried within the huge belly."

There is no way of proving that this nightmare was the reverse side of Leonardo's hopeful anticipations of the future: but those who have lived during the last half century have experienced both the mechanical triumphs and the human terror they have generated, and we know, even better than Leonardo, by what a large factor his anticipated evils have been multiplied.

Like his successors who actually promoted the myth of the machine and caused it to gain practical ascendancy, Leonardo could have had no conscious foreboding that he was both prefiguring and serving a myth. On the contrary, like them, he probably felt that he was creating a more sensible rational order, in which his acute intelligence, with more adequate methods and agents than man had ever possessed before, would bring all natural phenomena under the sway of the human mind. These technical premises seemed so simple, their aim so rational, their methods so open to general imitation, that Leonardo never saw the need to put the question we now must ask: Is the intelligence alone, however purified and decontaminated, an adequate agent for doing justice to the needs and purposes of life?

Yet some insight into this limitation had already lurked under the surface of Leonardo's conscious interests and tainted his otherwise favorable picture of what rational invention could do for man. He was, intellectually speaking, too large a personality to fit into any of the standard categories of engineer, inventor, artist, or scientist; though like his near contemporaries, Michelangelo and Dürer, and many earlier and later figures, he ranged freely over a wide territory, from geology to human anatomy. But he realized the limitations of mechanical invention alone. In one of his notes he wrote: "Would that it might please our Creator that I were able to reveal the nature of man and his customs even as I describe his figure."

Leonardo had at least a glimpse of what was missing from the mechanical world picture. He knew that the man he dissected and accurately depicted was not the whole man. What neither the eye nor the scalpel could reveal was equally essential to the description of any living creature. Without an insight into man's history, his culture, his hopes and prospects, the very essence of his being was not accounted for. Thus he knew the limitations of his own anatomical descriptions and mechanical inventions: the visible world represented in his paintings was but an eviscerated mummy; and he demonstrated in his own experience that the suppressed part of his unconscious world would at last erupt in the same nightmares that now haunt all of humanity.

Unfortunately, Leonardo's talents, as happens to so many of the best scientists and technicians today, were at war with his conscience. Seeking for fuller command of the machine, he was ready, like so many of our present-day scientists, to sell his services to the Duke of Milan, one of the leading despots of his day, provided he got an opportunity to exercise his inventive talents. Yet because the new ideological framework had not yet been put together, Leonardo retained an intellectual freedom and a moral discipline that only rarely could be achieved after the eighteenth century. Although Leonardo, for example, invented the submarine, he deliberately suppressed this invention "on account of the evil nature of men, who would practice assassination at the bottom of the sea." That reservation marks a moral sensitiveness equal to his inventive abilities: only a relative handful of scientists, like the late Norbert Wiener or Leo Szilard in our day, have shown any parallel concern and self-control.

Leonardo's consistent concern with moral problems, with the kind of human being he was himself becoming and was in turn helping to create, sets him off from those who confined their attention to observations, experiments, and equations without the faintest sense of responsibility for their consequences. In all likelihood his sensitiveness to the social outcome of invention created an inner conflict that curbed his success: but so strong were the pressures of both mechanization and war that he nevertheless was driven by his mechanical demon, not merely to invent submarines, but land tanks and rapid-firing guns, and many kindred devices. Yet if Leonardo's imaginative anticipations and internal conflicts had been general, the whole tempo of later mechanization might have been slower.

Leonardo was proud of his status as an engineer: he even listed half a dozen engineers of classical times, from Callius of Rhodes to Callimachus in Athens, he who was skilled in making great bronze castings, as if to establish his own place among his ancient peers. With a sense of history later engineers lost, he ransacked the annals of antiquity for suggestive hints from Greek or Persian engineers. He even cited the fact—to our present astonishment—that the Egyptians, the Ethiopians, and the Arabs had used the old Assyrian method of inflating wineskins to buoy up camels and soldiers in fording rivers; and he advocated building unsinkable boats for transporting troops, also after an ancient Assyrian model.

In his military preoccupations Leonardo did not stand alone: he was but one of a large group of highly inventive minds in Italy, France, and

Germany, all devoted to military engineering, finding immediate service, if not a full use for their inventive powers, in the train of absolute rulers who reproduced, in miniature, the powers and the ambitions of more ancient monarchs. They designed canals with canal-locks, and fortifications; they invented the paddle-wheel boat, the diving bell, the wind-turbine. Even before Leonardo, Fontana had invented the velocipede and the military tank (1420), and Konrad Keyeser von Eichstadt had invented both the diving suit (1405) and the infernal machine.

One need not be surprised that the demand for such inventions did not come from either agriculture or handicraft industry: the stimulus to invention, if not the immediate practical support, came from the same sociotechnical power complex that had produced the earliest megamachines: absolutism and war.

Similarly, Leonardo was familiar with the early German method of producing poison gas (from feathers, realgar, and sulphur) to asphyxiate a garrison: a grisly fifteenth-century invention that anticipated its first twentieth-century application by the same nation. Like other military engineers of his time, he played with the possibility of armored tanks, propelled by hand-operated cranks, to say nothing of revolving scythes, advancing in front of a horse-propelled vehicle, to mow down the enemy.

One begins to understand how deeply the old myth of unlimited power had begun to stir again in the modern mind, when one observes how Leonardo, a generous, humane spirit—so tender that he bought caged birds in the marketplace in order to release them—deserted his paintings and spent so much of his energies in both military inventions and fantasies of destruction. Had he concentrated his superb technical skill upon agriculture, he might have effected a mechanical revolution there comparable to that he actually began with his device of the flying shuttle for an automatic loom.

Unlike the unduly sanguine prophets of the nineteenth century, who equated mechanical invention with human improvement, Leonardo's dreams were colored by his consciousness of the spectacle of the human savagery and the murderous malice that some of his own proposed military instruments were designed to serve. These horrors mingled in his dreams with prospective marvels, as in the following prophecy: "It shall seem to men that they see new destructions in the sky, and the flames descending therefrom shall seem to have taken flight and to flee away in terror; they shall hear creatures of every kind speaking human language; they shall run in a moment, in person, to divers parts of the world without movement; amidst the darkness, they shall see the most radiant splendors. O marvel of mankind! What frenzy has thus impelled you!"

The vague, ambiguous prophecies of Leonardo's contemporary, Nostradamus, may easily be dismissed: but Leonardo himself committed to paper even more remarkable forebodings of the world that science and mechanization would eventually bring into existence. In his notes on necromancy, he unsparingly criticized people who were then proclaiming

the reality of fantastic powers possessed by "invisible beings" for transforming the modern world. Many of these fantasies were nothing but
early unconscious projections of natural forces that later took concrete form;
and no one described the consequences of such forces more incisively than
Leonardo, even in the act of denying their possibility.

Should the claim of the necromancers be established, Leonardo wrote,
"there is nothing on earth that would have so much power either to harm
or benefit man. . . . If it were true . . . that by such an art one had the
power to disturb the tranquil clearness of the air, and transform it into
the hue of night, to create corruscations and tempests with dreadful thun-
der-claps and lightning flashes rushing through the darkness, and with
impetuous storms to overthrow high buildings and uproot forests, and
with these to encounter armies and break and overthrow them, and—
more important than this—to make devastating tempests, and thereby to
rob the husbandmen of the rewards of their labors. For what method of
warfare can there be which can inflict such damage upon the enemy as the
exercise of the power to deprive him of his crops? What naval combat could
there be which should compare with that which he would wage who has
command of the winds and can create ruinous tempests that would sub-
merge every fleet whatsoever? In truth, whoever has control of such ir-
resistible forces would be lord over all nations, and no human skill will be
able to resist his destructive power. The buried treasure, the jewels that lie
in the body of the earth, will become manifest to him; no lock, no fortress,
however impregnable, will avail to save anyone against the will of such a
necromancer. He will cause himself to be carried through the air from East
to West, and through all the uttermost parts of the universe. But why do I
thus go on adding instance to instance? What is there which could not be
brought to pass by a mechanician such as this? Almost nothing, except the
escaping from death."

In the light of history, which can one say today is the more remarkable?—these pure fantasies themselves, welling forth out of the unconscious
without any check from history or current experience, or Leonardo's interpretations of what the social consequences would be, if the necromancers'
assertions actually proved true? The first response clearly anticipated in
dream what centuries later has become a formidable reality: control over the
forces of nature sufficient to bring about total destruction. To Leonardo's
credit, he realized in advance—*almost five centuries in advance*—the implications of these terrible dreams. He foresaw what total power would become
in the hands of unawakened and unregenerate men, as clearly as Henry
Adams did on the eve of its achievement.

In passing judgment upon that necromantic dream, Leonardo made only
one mistake: he believed that the dream was baseless "because there are
no such incorporeal beings as necromancy assumes." He could not anticipate as a probability what in his day seemed so remote from being even a
possibility—namely that science in a few centuries would discover these

invisible "incorporeal beings" in the heart of an equally invisible atom. Once that discovery was made, every link in Leonardo's chain of reasoning proved sound.

I am not alone in this interpretation of Leonardo's ominous prophecies; nor was Leonardo himself alone, as Sir Kenneth Clark has pointed out. Clark sees in Leonardo's drawings of deluges a foreboding of cosmic disaster, which he connects with other apocalyptic speculations that were current around the year 1500, and which led Dürer to dream of a similar cosmic disaster and record his dream in a drawing dated 1525. Those dreams have proved even more significant than the deformed images and blasted emptiness of many modern paintings: for the latter, so far from being prophetic anticipations, are little better than immediate transcriptions of observable physical ruins and disrupted mental states. Both Leonardo's projects and his anxieties throw a light on what followed.

During the next four centuries, the possibilities of terror that Leonardo exposed in his intimate notes were seemingly laid to rest: they were overlaid by the large apparent increase of orderly scientific interpretation and constructive technical achievement. It was possible, at least for the more prosperous manufacturing classes, themselves growing in number and influence, as against the old feudal and clerical estates, to believe that the benefits of science and mechanization would far outweigh their disabilities. And certainly, a thousand fresh inventions and tangible improvements confirmed many of these hopes.

When scrutinized more closely, the social results were, however, more disturbing than the prophets of mechanical progress were willing to admit: from the beginning in the fifteenth century blasted landscapes, befouled streams, polluted air, congested filthy slums, epidemics of avoidable disease, the ruthless extirpation of old crafts, the destruction of valuable monuments of architecture and history—all these losses counterbalanced the gains. Many of these evils were already noted defensively in Agricola's treatise on mining, 'De Re Metallica.' In the heyday of nineteenth-century industry, John Stuart Mill, no enemy of mechanical progress, could still declare in his 'Principles of Economics,' that it was doubtful if all the machinery then available had yet lightened the day's labor of a single human being. Even so, many of the gains were real: some of them would deservedly become part of the permanent heritage of mankind.

While the goods promised by mechanical invention and capitalist organization were naturally more easy to anticipate than the evils, there was one evil, more mountainous than all the rest put together, which for lack of sufficient historic information at that period it was impossible to perceive in advance or to forfend. This was the resurrection of the megamachine. Through the coalition of all the institutions and forces we have just been examining, the way had been prepared for the introduction of the megamachine on a scale that not even Chephren or Cheops, Naram-Sin, Assurbanipal, or Alexander could have deemed possible. For the accumulation of mechanical facilities had at last made it possible vastly to enlarge the scope of the megamachine, by progressively replacing the recalcitrant and uncertain human components with specialized mechanisms of precision made of metal, glass, or plastics, designed as no human organism had ever been designed, to perform their specialized functions with unswerving fidelity and accuracy.

At last a megamachine had become possible that needed, once organized, a minimum amount of detailed human participation and co-ordination. From the sixteenth century on the secret of the megamachine was slowly re-discovered. In a series of empirical fumblings and improvisations, with little sense of the ultimate end toward which society was moving, that great mechanical Leviathan was fished up out of the depths of history. The expansion of the megamachine—its kingdom, its power, its glory—became progressively the chief end, or at least the fixed obsession, of Western Man.

The Machine, "advanced" thinkers began to hold, not merely served as the ideal model for explaining and eventually controlling all organic activities, but its wholesale fabrication and its continued improvement were what alone could give meaning to human existence. Within a century or two, the ideological fabric that supported the ancient megamachine had been reconstructed on a new and improved model. Power, speed, motion, standardization, mass production, quantification, regimentation, precision, uniformity, astronomical regularity, control—above all external control—these became the passwords of modern society in the new Western style.

Only one thing was needed to assemble and polarize all the new components of the megamachine: the birth of the Sun God. And in the sixteenth century, with Kepler, Tycho Brahe, and Copernicus officiating as accoucheurs, the new Sun God was born.

(1967)

PART FOUR

Miscarriages of 'Civilization'

CHAPTER THIRTY

The Origins of War

At the time that the first great civilizations of the ancient world were coming into existence, the human race suffered an injury from which it has not yet recovered. If I interpret the evidence correctly, that injury still plays an active part in our lives, and caps our most hopeful dreams about human improvement with nightmares of destruction and extermination.

This injury happened at a moment when primitive man's powers, like ours today, had suddenly expanded; and it was due essentially to an aberration, or a series of aberrations, which put his most beneficent inventions at the command of his neurotic anxieties. So far from disappearing with time and being healed by the growth of law and reason, this original injury has only tightened its hold upon the collective actions of tribes and nations.

The aberration I refer to is the institution of war; and my purpose in discussing its origins is to bring into consciousness a group of events and beliefs that have long remained buried, partly through sheer neglect, partly through a repression of painful irrationalities that contradicted civilized man's belief in his own orderly and rational behavior. It is only today, after a century of prodigious research into human origins, that some of these events have come to light and been thrown open to interpretation.

That early injury had an effect upon civilized life, somewhat comparable to the kind of childhood injury that psychiatrists characterize as a trauma: an injury whose worst results may not show themselves till far on in adult life. Instead of being buried in the psyche of an individual, it became embedded in the institutional life of every succeeding city, state, and empire.

In making this analysis, I shall have to start from an assumption that is unprovable; namely, that there is a parallel between the general human situation today and that faced by the individual, unable to cope with the problems of his life, unable to make rational decisions, baffled, depressed, paralyzed, because he is still the prey of infantile fantasies he is unable to escape or control. In the case of individuals, we know that such fantasies, deeply embedded in childhood, may keep on poisoning the whole system, though the wound has seemingly healed and the scar is hardly visible. Childhood misapprehensions, animosities, and resentments, childhood misinterpretations of natural events, such as birth, death, separation—all account for the persistence of infantile patterns of conduct. Often, later in life, these patterns overcome the adult and leave him helpless. He still views present realities through the distorting glasses of his childhood fantasy.

That something unfortunate once happened to man at the very moment when an immense creativity was released was perhaps recognized in part in the Jewish and Christian myth of the Fall, which was anticipated by even earlier Egyptian lamentations over the perverse wickedness of man in going contrary to the gods. Many other peoples, from China to Greece, looked back to a golden age when war and strife were unknown, and when, as Lao-tse put it, one village might look at the smoke rising from the chimneys of another nearby, without envy or rivalry.

There is now enough anthropological and archaeological evidence to show that there is at least a partial basis for these wistful memories of a more peaceful past, when scarcity of food, violence, danger, and death were mainly the results of natural disasters, not the deliberate products of man. If civilization's first great achievements awakened new fears and anxieties, we must understand how and why this happened; for these fears and anxieties still press on us. As long as the source of our irrational acts remains hidden, the forces that are still driving us to destruction will seem uncontrollable. The worst part about civilized man's original errors and the most threatening aspect of our present situation are that we regard some of our most self-destructive acts as normal and unavoidable.

There is a close parallel between our own age, exalted yet stunned by the seemingly limitless expansion of all its powers, and the epoch that marked the emergence of the earliest civilizations in Egypt and Mesopotamia. In his pride over his present accomplishments, it is perhaps natural for modern man to think that such a vast release of physical energy and human potentiality had never taken place before. But on examination this proves a too flattering illusion: the two ages of power, modern and ancient, are bound together by many similar characteristics, both good and evil, which set them apart from other phases of human history.

Just as the prelude to the nuclear age came with the large-scale introduction of water, wind, and steam power, so the first steps toward civilization were taken in the neolithic domestication of plants and animals. This agricultural revolution gave man food, energy, security, and surplus manpower on a scale no earlier culture had known. Among the achievements that mark this transformation from barbarism to civilization were the beginnings of astronomy and mathematics, the first astronomical calendar, the sailboat, the plow, the potter's wheel, the loom, the irrigation canal, the man-powered machine. Civilized man's emotional and intellectual potentialities were raised further through the invention of writing, the elaboration of the permanent record in painting, sculpture, and monuments, and the building of walled cities.

This great leap forward came to a climax about 5000 years ago. A like mobilization and magnification of power did not again take place until our own era. For most of recorded history, mankind has lived on the usufruct of that early advance, making many piecemeal additions and widening the province held by civilization, but never essentially changing the original pattern.

There was probably an important religious side to this whole transformation. With the priestly observations that produced the measured months and years, people became conscious, as never before, of human dependence upon the cosmic forces, the sun, the moon, the planets, on whose operations all life depended. Planetary movement of "clockwork" regularity gave man his first glimpse of an orderly, repetitive, impersonal world, utterly reliable, but benignly productive only within the frame of its inflexible laws.

With this new cosmic theology there came a sudden fusion of sacred and secular power, in the person of the all-powerful king, standing at the apex of the social pyramid. The king was both a secular ruler and the chief priest or even, in the case of the Egyptians, a living god. He no longer needed to follow village tradition and customs, like the village council of elders. His will was law. Kingship by divine right claimed absolute powers and evoked piously obedient collective responses.

What kingly power could not do solely by intimidation, and what magical rites and orderly astronomical observation could not do alone by successful prediction, the two in combination actually did accomplish. Large assemblages of men moved and acted as if they were one, obedient to the royal command, fulfilling the will of the gods and rulers. People were driven to heroic physical efforts and sacrifices beyond all precedent. Throughout history, the major public works—canals, embankments, roads, walls, "pyramids" in every form—have been built with forced labor, either conscripted for part of the year or permanently enslaved. The enduring symbol of this vast expansion and regimentation of power is of course the Great Pyramid of Cheops, built without wheeled vehicles or iron tools, by relays of 100,000 men working over a limited span of years.

Should we be surprised that the achievements of our own age of nuclear power appeared first at this period as myths and fantasies associated with the gods? Absolute power, power to create and annihilate, became the attribute of a succession of deities. Out of his own substance the Egyptian sun god, Atum, created the universe. Instantaneous communication, remote control, the collective incineration of whole cities (Sodom and Gomorrah), and germ warfare (one of the plagues of Egypt) were freely practiced by a succession of inhumane deities in order to insure that their commands would be obeyed. Human rulers, who still lacked the facilities to carry out these dreams on a great scale, nevertheless sought to counterfeit them. With the growth of an efficient bureaucracy, a trained army, systematic taxation, and forced labor, this early totalitarian system showed all the depressing features that similar governments show in our own day.

An overconcentration on power as an end in itself is always suspect to the psychologist. He reads in it attempts to conceal inferiority, anxiety, and impotence. Perhaps early civilized man was justifiably frightened by the forces he himself had brought into existence, in the way that many people are frightened now by nuclear power. In neither case was the extension of physical power and political command accompanied by a complementary development of moral direction and humane control.

There were further grounds for doubt and fear among men of that early civilization. Though they had achieved a hitherto unattainable security and wealth, the very growth of population and the extension of trade made their whole economy more subject to conditions and forces they could not control.

Our age knows how difficult it is to achieve equilibrium and security in an economy of abundance. But the early fabric of civilization was far more precariously balanced, since the welfare of the whole was based on the magical identification of the king and the community in the beliefs and rites of their religion. The king personified the community; he was the indispensable connecting link between ordinary men and the cosmic powers they must propitiate and obey. While the king assumed full responsibility for the life and welfare of his subjects, the community, in turn, waxed and waned with the life of its ruler.

That magic identification produced a further occasion for anxiety, far deeper than any threat of actual floods or bad crops; for despite their claims to divine favor and immortality, kings too were subject to mortal accidents and misfortunes. So constant was this anxiety that the Egyptian Pharaoh's name could not be uttered without interjecting the prayer, "Life! Prosperity! Health!" This identification of the king's life with the community's fate produced an even more sinister perversion. To avert the wrath of the gods, indicated by any natural mischance, the king himself must be slain as a sacrifice. At this early stage, dream and fact, myth and hallucination, religion and science formed a confused welter. One lucky change in weather after a ritual sacrifice might give sanction to a long-repeated chain of ritualistic slaughters.

To save the king from this discouraging fate, which might lessen the attractions of the office, a further trick of religious magic came into play. A stand-in would be chosen and temporarily treated with all the honors and privileges of a king, in order to perform the final role of sacrificial victim on the altar. As the demand for such victims increased in times of trouble, these substitutes were sought outside the community, by violent capture. And what began as a one-sided raid for captives in time brought about the collective reprisals and counterraids that became institutionalized as war. Back of war lay this barbarous religious sanction: only by human sacrifice can the community be saved.

War, then, was a specific product of civilization—often if not always, mainly if not solely, the outcome of an organized effort to obtain captives for a magical blood sacrifice. In time, armed might itself took on a seemingly independent existence, and the extension of power became an end in itself, a manifestation of the "health" of the state. But underneath the heavy overlays of rationalization, war remained colored by the original infantile misconception that communal life and prosperity could be preserved only by sacrificial expiation. Civilized man's later efforts to impute the origin of war to some primal animal instinct toward murderous aggression against his own kind are empty rationalizing. Here the words of the anthropologist, Bronislaw Malinowski, are decisive, "If we insist that war is a fight between two independent and politically organized groups, war does not occur at a primitive level."

What is most remarkable about the spread of war as a permanent institution is that the collective anxiety that originally brought about the ritual of human sacrifice seems to have deepened with material progress. And as anxiety increased, it could no longer be appeased by a mere symbolic sacrifice at the altar, for the ritual itself produced hatred, fear, and a natural desire for revenge among the peoples victimized. In time ever greater numbers, with more effective weapons, were drawn into the brutal ceremony, so that what was at first a preliminary, one-sided raid before the sacrifice became the essential sacrifice itself. The alternative to permitting the mass slaughter of one's own people was the destruction of the enemy's city and temple and the enslavement of the population. These acts periodically eased anxiety and enhanced power. War provided a kind of self-justification in displacing neurotic anticipations by actual dangers—that return to reality seems to restore human equipoise. Psychiatrists observed during the Blitz in London that the need for facing real dangers often removed a patient's load of neurotic anxiety. But war performs this service at a ghastly price. Psychologically healthy people have no need to court dismemberment and death.

The growth of law and orderly behavior and morals, which improved the relation of men in cities, was not transferred to the collective relations of communities; for the ability to produce disorder, violence, and destruction itself remained a symbol of royal power. From the relatively peaceful Egyptians to the bloodthirsty Assyrians and Mongolians, one monument after another boasts of kings humiliated, prisoners killed, cities ruined. The solemn association of kingship, sacred power, human sacrifice, and military effectiveness formed a dominant complex that governed human behavior everywhere. But in time the search for sacrificial captives took on a utilitarian disguise—if spared as slaves, they added to the labor force. So the secondary products of military effort—slaves, booty, land, tribute—supplanted and concealed the original anxiety motive. Since a general expansion of productive power and culture had accompanied kingship and human sacrifice, people were conditioned to accept the evil as the only way of securing the good. The repeated death of civilizations from internal disintegration and outward assault underscores the fact that the evil elements in this amalgam largely canceled the goods and blessings.

This perception is not a discovery of modern historians. After the eighth century B.C. the working principles of a power-centered civilization were boldly challenged by a long series of religious prophets, from Amos and Isaiah to Lao-tse and Mo Ti. Whatever their differences the exponents of these new ideas scorned the notion of a mere increase of power and material wealth as the central purpose of life. In the name of peace and love they rejected irrational human sacrifice in every form—on the altar or on the battlefield. Christianity went even further. Alone among the religions, instead of sacrificing human beings to appease the divine wrath, it sacrificed its God, renouncing His power in behalf of love, in order to save mankind by cleansing the sinner of anxiety and guilt.

But the power complex, embedded in the routines of civilization, was not dislodged by even this challenge. Ironically, Christianity itself supplanted its pagan rivals by seizing the power of the state under Constantine (A.D. 313) and utilizing all its engines of compulsion. As in the times of Moloch and Bel, the bloodiest collective sacrifices in history were those made in wars to establish the supremacy of a state religion.

How are we to explain the persistence of war, with its victories that turn out as disastrous as its defeats, its just causes that produce unjust or contradictory consequences, and its heroic martyrdoms sullied and betrayed by the base, selfish conduct of the survivors? There seem to me two general answers. One is that the original pattern of civilization, as it took form in the walled city and in turn produced the "walled" state, has remained unaltered until modern times. War was an integral part of the constellation of civilized institutions, held in tension within the city, on the basis of a division of classes, slavery and forced labor, and religious uniformity. To remove any part of this fabric seemed, to the rulers of men, a threat to every other part. They exalted the sacrifices of war because they wanted to maintain their own power.

There was an additional mitigating factor: until recent times, only a small part of the world's population accepted the terms of civilized life and its constant involvement with war; moreover, the amount of damage any army could inflict was limited. In Christian nations the human cost of war had been further reduced by the acceptance of a military code that limited violence to armed soldiers and generally exempted civilians and even their property from capture or deliberate destruction. Finally, the greater part of the world's population, living in rural communities, immune by their feebleness and poverty from the rapacious temptations of urbanized power, constituted a reservoir of vitality and sanity.

These mitigations and compensations progressively reduced the evils of total war as practiced by the early empires; but neither the needs of commerce, nor the admonitions of religion, nor the bitter experience of bereavement and enslavement altered the basic pattern. By any reasonable standard, war should early have been classed with individual murder, as an unqualified collective crime or an insane act, but those who held power never permitted any subversive judgment on the irrationality of the method even if applied to rational ends. The fact that war has persisted and now threatens, at the very peak of our advances in science and technology, to become all-enveloping and all-destructive, points to the deep irrationality that first brought it into existence. This irrationality springs not only from the original aberration but from the unconscious depths of man, plagued with repressed guilt and anxiety over the godlike powers he presumptuously has learned to wield.

Western culture during the last four centuries has produced an explosive release of human potentialities and powers. Unfortunately the irrationalities of the past have been subjected to a similar projection and magnification.

The most formidable threat we confront, perhaps, is the fact that the fantasies that governed the ancient founders of civilization have now become fully realizable. Our most decisive recent inventions, the atom bomb and the planetary rocket, came about through a fusion of secular and "sacred" power, similar to their ancient union. Without the physical resources of an all-powerful state and the intellectual resources of an all-knowing corps of scientists, that sudden command of cosmic energy and interplanetary space would not have been possible. Powers of total destruction that ancient man dared impute only to his gods, any mere Russian or American air-force general can now command. So wide and varied are the means of extermination by blast and radiation burns, by slow contamination from radioactive food and water, to say nothing of lethal bacteria and genetic deformities, that the remotest hamlet is in as great peril as a metropolis. The old factor of safety has vanished.

As our agents of destruction have reached cosmic dimensions, both our tangible fears and our neurotic apprehensions have increased until they are so terrifying to live with that they are involuntarily repressed. This repression is particularly notable in America, where it is marked by the virtual absence of any discussion or critical challenge of either our nuclear weapons or our ultimate aims. This is perhaps an indication of the unconscious guilt we feel for developing and actually using the atom bomb. Along with an unwillingness to face our own conduct or search for alternative courses, our behavior presents an even more dangerous symptom—an almost pathological sense of compulsion to pyramid our errors. This drives us to invest ever-increasing quantities of intelligence and energy in the building of ever more dangerous absolute weapons, while devoting but an insignificant fraction of this same energy and intelligence to the development of indispensable political and moral controls. We are in fact using our new knowledge and our new powers to re-enforce ancient errors and prolong the life of obsolete institutions that should long ago have been liquidated.

During the last dozen years every responsible head of government has confessed openly that with our present readiness to use methods of atomic, bacterial, and chemical extermination, we might bring an end to civilization and permanently deform, if not destroy, the whole human race. Our failure to act on this warning, as an animal would act in the face of a comparable danger, gives the measure of our neurotic compulsions. So even the prudent thought of our own retributory, collective death offers no guarantee against the misuse of our powers so long as the engines of total annihilation remain available and the neurosis itself persists.

The two principal nuclear powers have been acting as if each was all-powerful and could dictate the terms of existence to the rest of the planet. In the name of absolute sovereignty they have actually achieved impotence. What has been called the "stalemate of terror" is in fact a deliberate checkmate of those humane gifts and adroit moves that might save us. This precarious stalemate may be ended at any moment by a careless gesture, which could upset the board itself and sweep away all the pieces. It can be effectively ended only by both sides acknowledging their paralyzing inability to move and agreeing to start a new game.

To conceive this new game, which can no longer be played under the old rules with the old pieces, both powers must take their eyes off each other and address themselves to the common task of saving the world from the threatened catastrophe they have impetuously brought within range. Instead, these governments with the connivance of their allies have been seeking to normalize their neurosis and have made participation in their infantile plans and infantile fantasies a test of political sanity. By now, a respected official in charge of Civil Defense finds it easier to envisage a whole nation of 180,000,000 people living permanently underground than to conceive of any means of delivering the world of its diabolical hatreds and collective paranoias. Strangely, such a national burial is put forward as an ingenious method for combating possible Russian blackmail. This failure to recognize when the remedy is worse than the disease is one of the score of current symptoms of mental disorder in apparently orderly minds.

If no great changes were yet visible in the general pattern of civilization, this picture would be extremely dismal; for as long as the old institutions remain operative, war will continue an integral expression of the anxieties and tensions they produce. Fortunately, this original structure has undergone a profound change during the past four centuries; and a large part of it is no longer acceptable. The old urban container has in fact exploded, leaving behind only a few citadels of absolute power on the ancient pattern, like the Kremlin and the Pentagon. What is even more important, the invisible walls between classes and castes have been breaking down steadily during the last several decades—more rapidly in the United States perhaps than in Communist countries.

What applies to the division of classes also applies to the disparity between nations. Neither knowledge nor power nor material goods can be monopolized by any privileged class or privileged country. Those Americans who fancied we had a permanent monopoly of atomic energy and technical skill recently found this out to their dismay; but the moral is not that we must "catch up with the Russians," but that we must accept the duties and demands of living in an open world among our equals. The real world of modern man has become porous and penetrable: every part of it is more closely interrelated than ever before and therefore more dependent upon the good will and sympathy and self-restraint of the rest of mankind. St. Paul's injunction to the little Christian congregations that everyone should be "members one of another," has now become a practical necessity of survival among the nations.

If so many other institutions of civilization, which held together solidly for 6000 years, have been crumbling away and are being replaced, is it likely that war will escape the same fate? The logic of history suggests it will not—if history has a logic. Our own military leaders have wryly admitted that in any large-scale war neither side can hope for a victory; indeed they have not the faintest notion of how such a war, once begun, might be ended, short of total extermination for both sides. Thus we are back at the very point at which civilization started, but at an even lower depth of savagery and irrationality. Instead of a token sacrifice to appease the gods, there would now be a total sacrifice, merely to bring an end to our neurotic anxieties.

In short, only the irrational, superstitious, magical function of war remains as a live possibility—the propitiation of gods in whom we do not believe by a sacrifice that would nullify the meaning of human history. In that surviving pocket of festering irrationality lies our chief, if not our only, enemy.

What are the possibilities of mankind's acquiring a fresh grip on reality and shedding the compulsive fantasies that are pushing us to destruction? There is little question of what measures must be taken to avoid a general nuclear catastrophe. Every intelligent observer understands the minimum precautions necessary for securing physical safety and for enabling a reconstituted United Nations to operate, not as a feeble hand brake on power politics, but as an active agent of international justice and comity. The only vital problem now is whether we can liberate ourselves from our irrational attitudes and habits, so that we may firmly take the necessary steps. It is not enough to appeal to human reason alone, as intelligent people often so earnestly do, to avert a general holocaust. We must first bring our long-buried sacrificial fantasies into the open before they erupt once more through internal pressure. Only exposure will counteract their power over us.

As with a neurotic patient, one of the conditions for resuming control and making rational decisions, free from pathological deformation, is the continued existence of large areas of conduct that are still orderly, co-operative, harmonious, life-directed. Once the patient has the courage to unburden himself of his disruptive experiences and recognize them for what they are, the sound parts of his personality can be brought into play. Fortunately, much of our life is still conducted on wholly rational and humane terms; furthermore, modern man is closer to confronting his hidden irrationalities than ever before. Scientific curiosity, which led to the discovery of the hidden structure of matter, also led to the exploration of the hidden structure of the human psyche. We now begin to understand the actual meaning of the morbid dreams, fantasies, and myths that have repeatedly undermined the highest human achievements.

With the knowledge that the biologist and the psychologist have furnished us, we must now perceive that both the original premises of civilization and those of our own so-called Nuclear, or Space, Age are humanly obsolete—and were always false. In purely physical terms, we now have possession of absolute power of cosmic dimensions, as in a thermonuclear reaction. But "absolute power" belongs to the same magico-religious scheme as the ritual of human sacrifice itself: living organisms can use only limited amounts of power. "Too much" or "too little" is equally fatal to life. Every organism, indeed, possesses a built-in system of automatic controls which governs its intake of energy, limits its excessive growth, and maintains its equilibrium. When those controls do not operate, life itself comes to an end. When we wield power extravagantly without respect to other human goals we actually upset the balance of the organism and threaten the pattern of the whole organic environment. Unqualified power diminishes the possibilities for life, growth, development. More than a century ago Emerson wrote, "Do not trust man, great God! with more power until he has learned to use his little power better."

The test of maturity, for nations as for individuals, is not the increase of power, but the increase of self-understanding, self-control, self-direction, and self-transcendence. For in a mature society, man himself, not his machines or his organizations, is the chief work of art.

The real problem of our age is to search into the depths of the human soul, both in the present generation and in the race's history, in order to bring to light the devious impulses that have deflected man for so long from his fullest development. For the human race has always lived and flourished, not by any one-sided exhibition of power, but by the constant sustenance and co-operation of the entire world of living beings. Not to seize power, but to protect and cherish life is the chief end of man; and the godlike powers that the human race now commands only add to its responsibilities for self-discipline and make more imperative a post-magical, post-mechanical, post-nuclear ideology which shall be centered, not on power, but on life.

Can such a new approach become operative in time to liberate man from war itself, as he was once liberated by his own efforts from incest, cannibalism, the blood feud and slavery? It is too early to answer this question, and it is perhaps almost too late to ask it. Admittedly it may take an all-out fatal shock treatment, close to catastrophe, to break the hold of civilized man's chronic psychosis. Even such a belated awakening would be a miracle. But with the diagnosis so grave and the prognosis so unfavorable, one must fall back on miracles—above all, the miracle of life itself, that past master of the unexpected, the unpredictable, the all-but-impossible.

(1959)

CHAPTER THIRTY-ONE

The Uprising of Caliban

We have the misfortune to live under the sign of Caliban. Hate, fear, suspicion, violence have become almost endemic. In America, abnormality is fast becoming our norm: automatism our overruling providence: irrationality itself the criterion of reason. Fantasies of wholesale extermination and annihilation no longer fill only the minds of certified paranoiacs: their studious translation into the practical devices of atomic, biological, and chemical warfare has dominated the activities of leaders in science and government for more than a decade.

These practical preoccupations, so quietly pursued, have given a deceptive air of sanity to projects that match the hallucinations of more obvious victims of mental disease, confined to hospitals for the incurably insane. At lower levels, the same methodical irrationality prevails under the sober guise of law, order, national security. Though in every period disintegrating forces tend to break through the crust of orderly life, in our age they have broken through at so many points that they have formed a second crust: indeed, they have spread so widely and hardened so solidly that they threaten to suppress every benign manifestation of life.

For the sake of brevity, and for reasons that will become plainer as I go on, I propose to personify the demoralizing forces of modern barbarism by the figure of Caliban. That fawning brute, that gibbering fool, that snarling animal, as Shakespeare pictured him in 'The Tempest,' may well stand as image of the lower powers of man—of nature untouched by nurture, to use Shakespeare's own terms—against whose uprising and domination no person, no civilization, is ever entirely safe.

In an effort to curb this creature, earlier societies had made him a prisoner and thrust him into a dungeon, treating him with a savageness that disclosed the proper fear that the ever-seductive temptation to relapse into brutishness provokes in the human breast. To make reparation for that harsh attitude, our more humanitarian age, prompted by a complacent naturalism and a misapplied egalitarianism, put Caliban on the same level as Prospero, and accorded him an equal degree of power and authority. In repayment for this kindness, Caliban now refuses to acknowledge that there is any higher power than his own: indeed, higher and lower are meaningless terms to him, along with good and bad, creative and destructive; but insofar as his behavior implies a recognition of difference, he is on the side of the destroyer. As a result, the problem of our time, the problem that holds a key to every other issue, is to bring Caliban back once more under the control of Prospero.

In contrast to Caliban, Prospero is the incarnation of man's higher powers. His is the discerning intelligence that foresees and anticipates, in a state of constant alertness against blind habit and meaningless automatism. His is the sensitive morality that weighs and evaluates, restrains and directs human conduct; his is the brooding imagination that, by means of art and love, fashions a fresh form for man's every activity, a more human mask for the face and character of man, and a higher destiny for his life.

To Prospero, finally, belongs the religious insight that seeks to unite the limited purposes of man with cosmic processes that outlast his brief existence; and through Prospero's very ability to interpret these processes, he takes over nature's responsibilities and turns them more consciously into the path of development and perfection. If Caliban is brute vitality and energy, undirected and self-destructive, Prospero is potentiality and purpose, value and meaning, power molded by form, providentially directed to the service of man's present life and toward the development of a greater life that shall transcend its limitations.

Caliban is the symbol of the primitive unconscious forces in man which, when neither controlled by morals nor expressed by art, offer a greater threat to reason and love than their more obvious enemies. My figures are as simple, indeed as old-fashioned, as that; and though they may mean more than Shakespeare himself intended, they can be translated, without too great distortion, into the terms of modern analytical psychology. If your Shakespeare fails you, Dr. Sigmund Freud will stand you in stead: for Caliban, read the id, the primitive underworld self, and for Prospero the superego, even though I shall define that superego in more generous terms than Freud used. If, again, you prefer the symbols of theology, you will be equally near my meaning if you identify Caliban with the demonic and Prospero with the divine.

Now those of you who have grown up during the past forty years may, for lack of any other kind of experience, believe that the inordinate violence and irrationality of our times have always characterized our civilization. Most of you cannot remember, as I do, the look of incredulous horror on everyone's face when they read the morning papers on a May day some thirty-nine years ago, and found that the steamer *Lusitania,* a ship loaded with many hundred passengers, had been sunk without warning by a German submarine. The shock of that event went far deeper than the first Fascist bombing of civilians in Madrid during the Franco uprising against the constitutional Spanish republic; and that, in turn, was greater than the horror evoked by the wiping out by the Nazis of thirty thousand Dutch civilians in the center of Rotterdam. Again, that event seemed more dreadful, at least to Americans, than our own extermination of one hundred thousand civilians (along with fifty thousand soldiers) in Hiroshima, by our dropping of the first atomic bomb in 1945.

Note that in thirty brief years, violence and slaughter had increased at geometric ratio, while the human reaction to it had altered inversely. Yet the obnoxious principle in all these cases—the ruthless killing of helpless noncombatants under the guise of military necessity—remained the same. Mankind's long sustained effort to limit the area of slaughter and rapine even in warfare has been halted in our own age: indeed, its direction has been reversed. Modern war, pursued to its logical end, means not the defeat of the enemy but his total extermination: not the resolution of the conflict but the liquidation of the opposition. This is the characteristic Caliban note of our time: one that is coming more and more to dominate both domestic and foreign politics.

The import of this fact apparently has not penetrated the armor of habit that protects sensitive persons: even professed pacifists fail to make any distinction between the limited violence of warfare, brutal though that is, and the unlimited violence of mass extermination. Few of you, perhaps, can remember the time when it was taken for granted that the poisoning of the enemy's water supply, for the purpose of embarrassing his army, was no longer permissible, indeed no longer thinkable, as an act of war. In those days our current preparations for wholesale extermination—extermination by poisoning water and atmosphere, by utilizing nerve gases and lethal bacteria lest any vestige of life by chance escape the hydrogen bombs —would have been regarded, even by coarse, unfeeling people, as the proposals, not of men, but of demented brutes. Such measures violate the principle that Immanuel Kant laid down in his essay 'On the Nature of Peace': "Confidence in the principles of an enemy must remain even during war, otherwise peace could never be concluded." When hostilities "degenerate into a war of extermination" the means befoul and blacken every justifiable human end.

One final story, trivial but no less significant, will give the measure of the change in the moral climate that began in 1914. Early in World War I, when German Zeppelins had begun to raid London by night, Bernard Shaw wrote to the 'Times' of London to suggest that the London County Council build air-raid shelters for their school children, in anticipation of Germany's widening the method of attack. The editors of the 'Times' were so indignant over Shaw's suggestion that they barely consented to print the letter; and in an editorial they reproved Shaw for being so irresponsible as to hint even in jest that a civilized government, like that of Germany, would ever stoop so low as to bomb civilians from the air. There was no need for Shaw to defend himself against that reproof: the Germans themselves supplied the answer.

I cite these facts, a handful from among a score I could draw on, to show that the violence and irrationality to which we have become calloused differ both in kind and in amount from that which one discovers in happier periods of history. Even if a growing part of the population has made Caliban their god, we have no reason to think that the kingdom and power have always been his. What, indeed, is the history of the last five thousand years of civilization, but the continued attempt, often halted, sometimes set back, but never permanently defeated, to restrict the powers of Caliban and to elevate those of Prospero?

But if we must not make the error of thinking that violence and irrationality, in their present quantities, are normal, we must equally be on guard against another illusion, more flattering to our egos, more soothing to our patriotic pride: the notion that these moments of disintegration are peculiar to peoples who, like the Germans, the Russians, or the Japanese, have long been subjected to a repressive, authoritarian government, and have not been moralized, as we have been, by the more reasonable and co-operative practices of democracy. That illusion perhaps seemed plausible in the thirties, when the contrasts between the practices of American democracy and totalitarian absolutism were more sharp than (to our shame) they now are. During that decade the democratic forces in our country had proved their capacity to meet any emergency under the Constitution, even the most paralyzing of economic depressions, without forfeiting liberty or even impairing the rights of property, despite the confident proselytism and active intervention of both Communism and Fascism. But by now we must realize that we have no natural immunity against either spontaneous or organized Calibanism. We have still some distance to go before we sink to the Russian level of political intimidation and repression; but in relation to our own conceptions of human decency and freedom, we have already sunk far too low.

Too easily, indeed, during the past decade, we have attempted to cover up our own uneasiness by redoubling our outrage over the conduct of our enemies: the familiar Freudian device of the transferred reproach. We continue to be indignant over the Iron Curtain that the Communist-dominated countries have lowered, to prevent easy travel and spontaneous social intercourse; but we forget that even under the administration of President Truman, the State Department and the Congress had erected an Iron Curtain of our own, somewhat more open-meshed, but just as arbitrary in its prohibitions. Restrictions upon free movement and social intercourse, normal, indeed indispensable, in wartime, have hardened into daily routine: people who have no criminal record and no official secrets have been confined to this country by administrative act—the withholding of a passport—as if it were a prison, and candidates for high public office are now subjected to the gratuitous humiliation of security investigations, as if the unedited dossiers of our secret police, filled with anonymous scurrilities, were a reputable means of bolstering public confidence in a loyalty that should, in a normal society not ridden by pathological suspicion and fear, be taken for granted. If the fathers of our country had been as frenetically alarmed by Benedict Arnold's treason, and loyalism generally, as our present-day governments have been by the threat of Communist subversion, they would have anticipated the French Revolution by instituting a Reign of Terror in the name of Public Safety, and thrown our young republic behind the bars of a Police State. Instead, they deliberately extended the protection of the Bill of Rights to all suspected criminals, even traitors.

Next to disregarding entirely the threat of Caliban to our civilization, the worst folly would be to identify him solely with Nazism or totalitarian communism, and to disregard the many evil features and gestures that can already be detected in our own country.

Even if by some providential exhibition of prudence and forbearance we were insured against any major outbreak of international genocide for the next century, that is no guarantee that the forces of Caliban, if otherwise unchecked, might not be dominant at the end of that time. Our children might indeed escape wholesale incineration; and yet find that what had begun as a tentative cold war against Soviet Russia had turned into a permanent cold war, a deepfreeze war, against every human faculty that did not lend itself to mechanical standardization or governmental control: a war against all those people, native or foreign, who differed in thought or attitude from our self-imposed totalitarian orthodoxy. In the act of closing ranks to face the worst we might, in fact, produce the worst.

George Orwell's nightmare world of 1984 is already uncomfortably near. The verbal rewriting of American history, in close imitation of the Russian precedent, has already begun; and if Presidents Truman and Roosevelt have been publicly referred to as traitors or the accomplices of traitors, it will not be long, if this state of mind solidifies, before Woodrow Wilson and Thomas Jefferson will be included in the same category. Whitman, Melville, Thoreau, and Emerson, to say nothing of Lowell and Howells, will vanish from our libraries for the same reason, in an effort to convert the freedom that characterized our past into the inquisitorial authoritarianism that threatens our present and may doom our future.

So much for the outward signs of Caliban. But if we would be wrong to impute all these symptoms to our present national enemies alone, we would be equally wrong if we imagined that a few malign or honestly mistaken men, in official positions, could by themselves bring about this general lowering of public morality, or that a mere weapon of destruction could by itself produce the other characteristic symptoms of this self-induced illness —baseless suspicion, hostility, random violence, non-cooperation, and non-communication. In diagnosing the collective psychosis that now threatens to break out on an even wider scale, we must not make the mistake, which medicine once made with regard to disease, of attempting to isolate only the individual germ and to locate the particular areas of infection. That kind of analysis is important; but it is equally necessary to understand the general state of the whole organism and to identify the factors that have lowered its immunity. If we are forthright in our analysis, we shall have to admit, I believe, that the inroads Caliban has already made indicate more fundamental weaknesses in our philosophy and faith. Perceptive observers, like Delacroix the painter and Burckhardt the historian, had ominous premonitions of the coming barbarism a full century ago. For this reason, an adequate diagnosis may keep us from spending too much time dealing with mere symptoms: it should rather be general enough to open the way for a more radical correction of our whole regimen.

Our delay in understanding the processes of distintegration at work in our time has, perhaps, been due to the fact that, both in Soviet Russia and in the United States, Caliban has crept into our homes, not as a marauding beast, but in the guise of a friend, bringing special gifts. In Russia he promised justice and equality, the removal of the power of property over the humble and helpless: a life centered on public service, rather than private profit. In the United States, he brought the promise of power and abundance that would transform life from a painful struggle into a picnic: everywhere he stood for a release from all constrictions, religious, moral, legal, sexual. The disguise was all the more effective because Caliban had appropriated, from Prospero, the magical spells of science: for every occasion he could quote a scientific authority, as the Devil himself reputedly can quote Scripture. Only recently has it become plain that some of the institutions we have valued most, some of the changes in the human personality we have regarded as most beneficent, have actually abetted the rise of Caliban. Following up this clue, I purpose therefore to center attention upon two changes that have come about in the last half-century: the overthrow of the superego and the domination of the automaton. Either of these transformations would have been dangerous by itself: the two together now constitute a serious threat to our whole society.

The other designation for the "overthrow of the superego" would be the "unchaining of the id." By an unusual coincidence, the practical effort was accompanied by a theoretic explanation; and this explanation first demands our attention, since it both interprets what has actually happened and indicates what measures we must take to overcome the forces of disintegration.

Both the concepts of the id and of the superego, as essential components of the human personality, were the outcome of a profound analysis of the human psyche that has taken place during the last seventy-five years, and very rapidly during the last fifty. The two men who did most to define this change, who added the dimensions of depth and height to the post-theological description of the personality, were two men of contrasting talents and purposes: one of them, Frederic W. H. Myers, known to his own generation as an investigator of extrasensory phenomena, has been practically forgotten in our time. The other, Dr. Sigmund Freud, stands out as one of the most courageous and original minds that has ever attempted to understand man's nature. The result of these investigations, if I may dare to make such a swift summary, was to establish that the human self is not, to begin with, a simple unity, but a federation of selves, old and new, latent and active, buried and budding.

At bottom, usually below the level of consciousness, is the body and its members and all the processes that go on at an organic level: the instinctual urges and reflex acts, the impulses and promptings and wishes that well up from even deeper strata and reveal themselves enigmatically to us in dreams, or more practically, in proposals and projects that lead to works of art and invention. This primitive underlayer of the self Freud called the id, which is Latin for the aboriginal "it," that which has not yet become "I" or "you" or "we." The id is that part of the spiritual anatomy which Christian theology habitually refers to as the Old Adam; and it is, perhaps, significant that the Old Adam was rediscovered at the end of a century when men blandly supposed that the primitive elements in life had been wiped out by the advance of science and mechanical industry, just as the primitive races were being wiped out—or what was almost the same thing, 'civilized'—by the spread of colonial empires. Like his contemporary, Joseph Conrad, Freud discovered the Heart of Darkness, not just in the African aborigine, but in the soul of modern man himself.

By definition, the id is basic to every other part of the personality. So long as it is attached to the whole personality, as a co-operative member of a federated constitutional government, the id is neither good nor bad. Its undifferentiated and undirected vitality, however, seems as incapable as Caliban's of choosing goals that will even insure its own survival: as Freud pointed out, the id, being the helpless victim of the pleasure principle, has no hold on reality. Indeed, the id in its unmodified state, before it has accepted the discipline of constitutional government, shows many infantile, irrational, even criminal characteristics. We behold the id in its unmodified state in the juvenile delinquent who murders a passing stranger for the pleasure of the experience. Like a little child, it is capable of saying, "I am going to kill you!" when it only means, "Stop bothering me and go away!" Or Caliban will shout, "You are a traitor!" when all he means is that the hated creature holds a different opinion about matters whereon the id, with its feeble grip on reality, sees no possibility of difference. When it breaks loose from the whole personality the id actually carries out these imbecile threats.

Above the id, Freud uncovered two other layers of the self, both later than the id, for they are products of nurture and culture, not just raw nature. One of these is the ego, the commonplace, conscious, daylight creature, the official presentable self, disciplined by experience to admit that fire burns and ice freezes, no longer under the infantile illusion of boundless power. The ego learns to walk warily among other egos, conforming and compromising, striving for security and status, for recognition and approval, accepting the taboos and customs and goals of the tribe, performing its appointed social roles: yet often prompted by the Five Lusts, as the Chinese call the libido, into seeking channels and expressions of its own, sometimes regressing into the id, yet sometimes transcending its limitations by creating an ideal self, masked by a different costume and cosmetic than that of the tribe. Above the ego Freud detected another aspect of the self, which he called the superego: the voice of duty and conscience, which seeks to bring unity into man's often conflicting claims and activities, and to direct them to a purpose beyond his immediate needs and satisfactions.

For Freud, this superego was a sort of universal Mrs. Grundy, and a male Mrs. Grundy at that, for he tended to identify its authority with that of the repressive father, who constantly stood in the way of the male child's incestuous impulses toward his mother; and so deep was his hostility toward his own father, once his eyes had been opened, that he extended to the superego his long-buried resentments. Freud's understanding of this part of the personality was, I regret to say, something less than perfect; for the most patent manifestations of this superego, in its creative aspects, come from the realms of art and religion; and since Freud regarded religion as an outmoded superstition, the product of illusion, he was not in a favorable state to appraise one of its chief characteristics: the fact that, from the age of the pyramid builders onward, it sought to turn man from the limited goal of animal survival to the endless task of self-development, self-transformation, and self-perfection. Though Freud's early disciple, Jung, presently disclosed the mechanism of this development, in his analysis of the prophetic and anticipatory function of the dream, Freud was so obsessed with the notion of the superego as a censor that he actually announced that the object of psychoanalysis was to "strengthen the ego, to make it more independent of the superego." That injunction was dangerous, for it both broke down the unity of the self and challenged the authority of the higher functions.

The reason for Freud's failure of insight here should by now be plain: in his analysis of the development of the self, he left out of account the positive influence of the other member of the family, the mother. Overemphasizing, if anything, the rule of the father, the Jovean, power-seeking, repressive, organizing element in the personality, he played down the function of the mother, with her life-bestowing gifts, her relaxing and yielding attitudes, her life-transmitting and life-nurturing functions: the mother's sympathy and responsiveness, her giving of the breast to her infant, her special effort to establish an I-and-thou intimacy through language, her endless ways of expressing love. If one necessary part of the superego is inhibitive and withholding, the other is persuasive and affirmative, expressive and life-enhancing.

Alone either agent, paternal or maternal, may be harmful to the normal development of the personality; for too much mothering, if it lead to over-attachment and overprotection, may produce weakness, and that may be as fatal as the harsh commands of an overauthoritarian father. The principle of dynamic balance, so important in all organic functions, holds with particular force here. The superego, to be effective, must draw constantly on the energies of the id at the very moment that, through art, philosophy, and religion, it gives them a creative outlet and a superpersonal goal. If, as Freud thought, art is a mere mechanism of escape, philosophy a rationalization, morality an oppression, religion an outright fraud, the only fragment of the superego left, to counterbalance the id, is scientific truth. How little that leaves us will come out presently.

Now apart from Freud's brilliant theory of dreams and the resulting diagnosis and therapy there was nothing essentially new in this analysis of the self: nothing that was not in large part already familiar to Plato, down to the description of the irrational and potentially antisocial elements that Freud found latent in the id. Did not Zeno the phrenologist discover in Socrates' bumps the evidence of criminal tendencies, and was not Socrates sufficiently well acquainted with himself to admit that these were indeed traits against which he had found it necessary to struggle? But Freud's fresh insight came at a moment when, among the European middle classes, sexuality had been unduly restricted, and in treating neuroses, particularly hysterias, Freud found that the symptoms would often disappear if the patient could be made to confront his or her sexuality and ease avoidable pressures. By lightening the burden of repression, Freud helped to restore order and health in cases where a purely censorious superego had clamped down too hard.

But if sexual repression were the cause of illness, might not the unlimited expression of sexuality be a preventive? That was a tempting thought. Freud himself did not succumb to it; for his own life, as a loving husband and the father of six children, seems a model of domestic felicity, and he turned his own unconscious drive to seek a more sterile goal into an occasion to uncover hitherto hidden areas of the psyche: so that he sublimated his homosexual impulses in science as Whitman did in poetry. But ironically, the popular result of Freud's teaching was to undo the exemplary lesson of his life. The relief of sexual tension widened into a letdown in all tensions: "Be yourself" now came only to mean "Be your lower self." Once the lid was off sex, less attractive components of the id also emerged: cruelty had already found its apologist in Nietzsche, and violence presently found its philosopher in Georges Sorel. In short, the influence of Freud's teaching, as it was vulgarized, was to favor the id: one of his favorite disciples, Georg Groddeck, even wrote an apologia for the id. With the apparent blessing of science, man's primitive self now rose to the top: it was no longer the body and its members that were despised, but every aspect of the superego, the discipline of morality, the ideal fantasies of art, and above all love. What Dr. Ian Suttie eventually called "the taboo on tenderness" came to characterize both the ideology and the actions of a great part of Western society.

This change did not, of course, take place overnight: still less was it the work of a single thinker. Though Freud was trained in the exacting disciplines of the scientific laboratory, the tendency of his work was to continue the romantic assault on civilization that had been opened in the eighteenth century by Jean Jacques Rousseau. The idealization of the primitive and the spontaneous, the natural and the effortless, was in origin a salutary revolt against life-denying systems of order. The adventurous exploration and settlement of the planet provided a counterpoise to the mechanical routine introduced by capitalism. Vitalities too long held in check by archaic institutions had reason to crave a fresh outlet, if only on a desert island with Robinson Crusoe: hence romanticism had, for a time, an activating and regenerative effect. And this was true, above all, in the political community where nationalism and democracy served as correctives to outworn institutions, molded to protect a single class. But in overthrowing the artificial hierarchies of property and privilege, the twin forces Romanticism and Revolution also tended to turn their back on natural hierarchies: including those that give authority to knowledge over ignorance, to goodness over malice and evil, to the rational over the irrational, to the universal and enduring over the time-serving and particular.

The revolt against the superego, which has taken so many forms during the last century, has had the effect of reversing the true order of human development. Primitive and unconscious processes take precedence over rational and conscious ones: hardness and sadism trample on tenderness and love. In short, elements that every high religion has devoted thousands of years to restraining, canalizing, damming, or diverting into distant fields, have now overflowed every embankment. Yes: the id and the superego have reversed roles. By now it is the primitive urges that give commands, and it is the superego, art and religion, morality and law, that timidly carry out the id's orders.

Do not misunderstand the purport of this analysis. I would not for a moment have you suppose that either Rousseau or Freud, or yet the Romantic poets and novelists, by themselves brought about the condition we now face. To hold that view would in itself be to descend to the primitive level of so much current thinking. What is important to grasp is that the result of our increased knowledge of unconscious and primitive urges—the realm of the not-yet-human—has been to besmirch our specifically human qualities, and to lower our faith in human potentialities that challenge past achievements and have still to find their form in new works of art and their incarnation in living persons. The upsurge of the id, in thought and imagination, has given extra energy to a downward movement in world civilization: the forces that should be commanding Caliban are either his helpless victims, or, as so often in modern art and politics, his not unwilling accomplices.

In seeking to understand our primal urges, we have lost sight of our peculiarly human traits and our potential human destinations, not given in nature but fabricated and projected by man. How commonplace it is to reduce every higher human development to a lower term, the pages of the Kinsey reports reveal with almost disarming—or should I say alarming?—naïveté. Dr. Kinsey and his associates would regard it as a ludicrous form of moralism—as it surely would be!—if we chose to reprove a monkey or a cat for not respecting the conventions and sentiments of human marriage. But these seemingly neutral scientists do not apparently see that it is equally absurd to turn reproof into justification, in the opposite direction. If animal behavior justifies sodomy, why not also the murder of rival males in courtship? If murder, why not cannibalism and incest? Is it not characteristic of this devaluation of the human, that in this whole study of the sexual life of American men and women, seemingly so exhaustive, the word love does not appear in the index of either volume? This is the science of Mickey Spillanes. By now its one-sided methodology has been transferred to every human activity: careful of quantities, ignorant about qualities, knowing much about causes and probabilities but indifferent to purposes.

Had this change in ideas come about during some long sleepy summer afternoon of Western man's existence, one might not have noted any general transformation, corresponding to it, in human society. But the traditional manifestations of the superego were theoretically undermined just at the moment when the irrational forces that had been gathering for more than a century had begun to break loose. During this climactic period, the struggle between economic classes had sharpened, and the tension between nations had increased. The resulting conflicts, the strikes, lockouts, assaults, aggressive demonstrations, wars, genocides, broke down long-established inhibitions against violence and spread anger and fear, brutality and terror: presently otherwise normal people were prepared to perform acts against human beings that only a little while earlier they would have hesitated to perform upon live rats. Under wartime conditions, hate and fear and violence are natural responses, indeed psychological accessories to survival. Such conditions pamper and inflate the id, and starve all of man's higher functions. Need I remind you that it is under these negative conditions that mankind has lived for the last forty years: years of hot and cold wars, of ruthless domestic repressions and vengeful revolutions, of widespread municipal gangsterism and fascist sadism, of systematic torture and random extermination. The only self that has been acceptable, under such conditions, is the lower self, hardened to any violence, heavily insulated against reason and love.

During the last forty years few of us have escaped the taint of Caliban: by our passivity, if not by our active connivance, we have contributed to the overthrow of Prospero; indeed, those who should have been most concerned to forestall this debasement have in fact all too often abetted the final betrayal: the real *trahison des clercs*. Because of the set taken by our institutions, we have reached a dead end in human development; and if the infernal instruments supplied by modern science are ever put to extensive use, that may prove a dead end in the most final sense. In descending to the level of the id, we have thrown away every guide and chart wisdom produced in the past to avert this catastrophic conclusion. Our leaders and guides seem as much the victim of their obsessive fantasies of power and retaliation as was Captain Ahab in 'Moby-Dick': that mad captain who, when the moment drew near for coming to grips with his mortal enemy, turned a deaf ear to the call of love, uttered by Pip, and cast aside sextant, compass, and chart, only to bring his ship and all but one of its crew to utter destruction. How close to home that symbol now comes! With almost one voice our obsessed and driven leaders in science and government say that there can be no turning back: indeed, no halt or pause for reflection. In the name of security they go on piling up the weapons that not merely increase our own vulnerability, but that, if used at fullest strength might wipe out the larger part of mankind and perhaps make the whole planet permanently unfit for life. Unlike the physical destructions of World War II, already so largely repaired, we know those of the atomic age will be irretrievable. Yet the only meaning of such a war, if it broke out, would be to relieve the fears produced by the infernal weapons that prompted it: the very process would cancel out every human purpose.

In short, what began as a contempt for the higher functions of life now threatens to end with a contempt for all life; for once men defile their own humanity, life, even if they survive, becomes meaningless, valueless, directionless, death-seeking. By renouncing those emergent qualities that, being attached to the superego, are specifically human, man becomes a monster, finally, even to himself, and an enemy to his own species. Under the irrational and criminal pressures of the id, we have come dangerously near losing even the animal's saving instinct of self-preservation.

But now I come to the final bitter paradox. This revolt of Caliban would hardly have proved so threatening, at least on the scale we now witness, had it not been abetted by another phenomenon: the mechanization of life and the transformation of man, the creator and inventor, into a mere agent of the automaton he has created. Modern man, in revolt against earlier systems of thought, sought to emancipate himself by controlling the forces of nature: by inventing new instruments of power, water mills, gunpowder, coal-burning engines, dynamos, he finally found himself in possession of the cosmic forces locked within the atom itself.

This transformation, which met so fully the id's infantile wish for unrestrained power, was the product of an entirely different sector of the human personality: the detached intellect, freed from all other biological promptings or moral and social claims, pursuing truth with the aid of a new methodology, that of experimental science applied to the piecemeal analysis of the external world. In all matters that lent themselves to quantitative measurement or mathematical proof, this new method produced immense results: above all, a framework of order, and with it an ability to understand, to predict, and in increasing measure to control all natural phenomena. Knowledge, as Bacon had confidently said, was power; and power became the main object of knowledge.

As a result, science became increasingly the only part of the superego that seemed to have objective existence and so was capable of exercising authority. Art and religion became supernumeraries, who danced attendance on their new master in his leisure hours. Unfortunately, this concentration on power, order, knowledge was achieved, both in technics and in science, at the expense of the human personality as a whole. To practice science successfully, its adepts voluntarily submitted to a severe system of restraints and inhibitions: within their own province, they renounced every passion or sentiment or feeling that would interfere with their single end, exact knowledge. The ideal of scientific thought was to be as free from personal bias as if it were the product of a machine. This systematic self-restraint moralized a vast department of thought more effectively than any earlier code of morality: within its own domain it fortified patience, deposed vanity, elevated humility, eliminated selfish bias, enthroned reason. But the personal and social penalty for that achievement was heavy. Causal insight widened, but purposeful direction and creative audacity, in every other department of life, weakened.

With a few admirable exceptions in every period, from Pascal to Clerk Maxwell, the practitioners of science divorced themselves from social responsibility and prophetic anxiety: indeed, they prided themselves on this indifference. The words cold, detached, rigorous, unemotional, in a word, objective, are all considered laudatory words by the scientist when applied to him. What does this mean but that science, by its method, disengaged the scientists from life, from the real world and the real self in which emotion, imagination, and dreams are as real as instruments of measurement? —that in order to concentrate effectively on his own limited object, the scientist has deliberately fabricated for himself a defective personality? There is much biographical evidence to suggest that this very suppression may itself be the outcome of anxiety, an inability to face life as a whole, particularly that part of it related to the scientist's emotional or sexual nature.

But the mischievous results long remained hidden for the reason that science approaches infallibility in every department where mathematical analysis, quantitative measurement, and experimental verification can be applied: thus, in compensation, it gives the devotees a quiet sense of god-like power. By identifying themselves with the infallibility and omniscience of science they escape any sense of their own all-too-human limitations. Power, order, and knowledge under these circumstances become absolutes;

not human instruments under human control. Though the belief in these absolutes is itself the most dangerous kind of subjectivism, it escapes the otherwise self-corrective methodology of science. So the automatic increase of scientific knowledge, technical invention, and physical power, has taken on in our time the character of a dangerous neurosis. We have now ruefully to acknowledge that a highly rationalized, scientifically disembodied super-ego is just as incapable of dealing with reality as the primitive id.

The scientist's detachment from life as a whole, his indifference as scientist to any other human values and purposes but his own, explains an otherwise strange phenomenon: the fact that the physical sciences have flourished, the last thirty years, under tyrannous systems of government. Give the scientist freedom to pursue his method, let him preserve his vocational integrity, and he will pursue his researches under social conditions that would be crippling to an artist or a poet or a philosopher. The artist usually cannot work at all under insistent restraint, because he must be a whole man to command his creative processes; if he remains creative it is by heroically pitting all his forces against the regime that thwarts him. But the scientist, who, as a matter of method and principle, turns his back upon the whole man, does not labor under such a handicap: his isolated superego, so highly moralized within its special province, has no need to rebel against less benign forms of repression. If he enjoys the freedom to follow up his researches, the scientist is all too easily lured into serving tyranny, no matter for what base ends his discoveries may be used. Superbly moralized and responsible in his own sphere, he refuses as scientist to acknowledge moral responsibilities outside it.

By our overvaluation of physical power and scientific truth, aloof from other human needs, we have paid the same price Faust had to pay when he made his compact with Mephistopheles: we have lost our souls, or to speak in more psychological terms, we have depersonalized ourselves and have turned our conscious, thinking selves into automatons. Is it any wonder that our whole cvilization goes on repeating processes it has once started, even when they have lost both their original meaning and any valuable humane end? Behold the way in which we continue to produce butter and wheat we neither eat nor share, goods that we do not have the social providence to distribute, knowledge we do not have the intellectual capacity to assimilate, instruments of mass extermination whose use might put an end to the human race.

The scientific superego, so far from helping us to control this relentless automatism, is itself a part of the same process and has no internal means of resisting it. Even the atomic scientists who have been most aware of the dangers issuing from their own discoveries, have never had the insight to question the rationale of their own vocation: rather, with antlike persistence, they have gone on with their researches, consoling their uneasy consciences, perhaps, with the thought that their duty to scientific truth is higher than any other duty to humanity. In repressing the mothering and nurturing impulses in the personality, the scientist has also lost the normal parental concern for the future of the life it cherishes. One hardly knows whether to characterize this attitude as innocence or infantilism; it certainly indicates a failure to reach maturity.

This abdication of responsibility, this failure of forethought, this detachment from all other needs and values than those of knowledge and power, has been one of the contributing factors in the resurgence of barbarism. The only part of the superego to which Freud and his contemporaries unreservedly paid homage—the passion for exact truth—has by its very divorce from the whole personality played back into the hands of Caliban. Detached from the rest of life, the scientific ego becomes automatic; and automatons cannot give provident directions to other automatons. This perhaps explains why, though one part of our culture, that dominated by science and technics, has reached the highest point ever attained in human history, the rest of our existence is falling into planless confusion, directed toward life-negating and irrational goals. These conditions stem from our failure to nurture every part of the human personality, and to match every paternal increase of power with a maternal increase of love, and with a common parental increase of moral control.

Modern man, therefore, now approaches the last act of his tragedy, and I could not, even if I would, conceal its finality or its horror. We have lived to witness the joining, in intimate partnership, of the automaton and the id, the id rising from the lower depths of the unconscious, and the automaton, the machine-like thinker and the man-like machine, wholly detached from other life-maintaining functions and human reactions, descending from the heights of conscious thought. The first force has proved more brutal, when released from the whole personality, than the most savage of beasts; the other force, so impervious to human emotions, human anxieties, human purposes, so committed to answering only the limited range of questions for which its apparatus was originally loaded, that it lacks the saving intelligence to turn off its own compulsive mechanism, even though it is pushing science as well as civilization to its own doom.

It is this last act that we are now beholding in our own time. Those of us who have strong stomachs know the evidential proofs of that union in the records of the Nazi doctors, correctly called Doctors of Infamy, who added a final horror to the Nazi extermination camps. These were men trained in the rigorous impersonal methods of science, who obediently carried through the orders of their superiors in the German government, to perform revolting tortures upon human victims under conditions that counterfeited and hideously caricatured scientific experiments. The detachment of these doctors was admirably 'scientific': their observations were coldly objective: their indifference to social results was in the best tradition of science—yet their total behavior was depraved. Though that was a classic juncture, revealing depths of evil deeper than any Dante could imagine in his candidates for the Inferno, it is by now a commonplace. But already this partnership has spread far beyond Nazi Germany and Soviet Russia. Is the final purpose of the Nazi crematories in essence different, by any other facts than distance in space and swiftness of operation, from the meaningless extermination of life that would take place in what we now politely call ABC war—a large-scale effort to liquidate the enemy population? Except for omitting the sadistic pleasures of torture, the end that is sought, complete annihilation of the hated object, is precisely the same.

As things are going now, unless a strong countermovement restores our humanity and our sanity, the union of the automaton and the id will probably bring about the catastrophic destruction of our civilization. The godlike powers that scientific thought has opened up to man are now at the service of progressively diabolical means, which have automatically sanctioned equally diabolical purposes. Once set in motion, there is no halting point in that downward descent. The only destination of such a union is the final victory of the irrational: collective genocide and suicide, on a scale that would reduce to meaninglessness the whole process of life's evolution and man's own ascent from brutishness to civilization: leaving that ultimate nothingness out of which only nothing can come.

If I thought that this last act of the tragedy was inevitable, I would not, you may be sure, have consented to give this paper. When a ship is doomed, it is wiser to strike up the band and speak cheerfully to one's fellow passengers than to hold an inquiry over the villains who sabotaged the machinery and planted a time bomb in the hold. But while there is life there is, proverbially, hope. The cries of anger and anxiety that have at last broken through the wall of silence, prompted by the hideous devastations of the hydrogen bomb, were not confined solely to our European and Asiatic friends: the instinct for self-preservation, which could be quieted among us at home when we thought that it was only the Russians who might be endangered by our lethal devices, has at last asserted itself, now that we realize that ourselves and the rest of mankind would be equally stricken, if not completely wiped out, in another large-scale war. What once mistakenly seemed a prudent method of offsetting Russian man power with American atomic power has patently become a gross mockery, now that we ourselves are in even greater jeopardy. This deep anxiety, so much more realistic than the childish assurances with which our leaders have attempted to cover over their radical miscalculations and errors, gives ground for hope: we may yet overcome this coupling of the unrestrained id and the automaton, and redress the balance in favor of life.

Admittedly, the mischief that has already been done will not easily be undone: the genii we have unloosed, as in the 'Arabian Nights' fable, cannot so easily be put back into their bottle. Generations and even centuries may pass before the nightmare that now hangs over man will be finally dissipated; for there remains the possibility that even the peacetime exploitation of atomic energy may bring grave dangers to organic life, before we exercise sufficient restraint. To go forward, we must partly retrace our steps: to overcome the misapplications of power we may be forced, as Christianity was once forced, to give up many desirable applications of technics, in order to have sufficient vitality to nourish other parts of the human personality. Fortunately those in whom the streams of life continue to run freely have still to be heard from. Prospero may yet arise and take command.

(1954)

CHAPTER THIRTY-TWO

Apology to Henry Adams

The title of this essay does not indicate that I propose to re-examine Henry Adams' contributions as an orthodox historian, and perhaps rescue his reputation from those who would cover up their own shortcomings by revealing those disclosed by Henry Adams' scholarship, in his later work like 'Mont-Saint-Michel and Chartres.' This is far from my purpose; or at most, it is but an incidental by-product of a more difficult effort. What I seek to explain, and belatedly help perhaps to overcome, is the fatal inertness of Adams' contemporaries, when confronted with his most challenging and penetrating insights into the prospects of our civilization. I shall try to show that if the plight of the human race is now a desperate one, without any earlier historic or prehistoric parallel, this is because we ignored Henry Adams' timely prognosis, and speeded the very processes that have now produced calamitous possibilities, without making the faintest effort to invent the political and moral instruments imperative for their effective control.

Today mankind, in consequence, totters like sleepwalkers above the abyss of wholesale nuclear extermination; still too enthralled by the dream of "conquering nature" to face the incredible nightmare of reality, with its threat that this very conquest may, unless mankind suddenly awakens and overcomes the paranoid obsessions of its present political leaders, bring human history itself to an end and turn the whole planet into a radioactive, almost lifeless wasteland. What I plan to examine and explain—if possible eventually to correct—is the persistent failure of our generation, even now, to observe the same facts that caused Henry Adams to utter his timely warnings, and to face in advance the problems that were dramatized, but by no means alone caused, by the successful invention of the atomic bomb. My ultimate purpose is to indicate what must be done, at least within the world of thought, if we finally are to meet this challenge.

Now I invoke the name of Henry Adams as a preface to this examination, because he stands alone among all the thinkers of his generation, in having made a timely effort to understand the forces of science, technology, and politics that have brought us to the verge of a gigantic and irretrievable disaster. His eminence as a historian only emphasizes his loneliness as a social diagnostician. Adams' contemporaries, in the words of John Bigelow in 1899, regarded Adams as either "an inspired prophet or crazy," but they were no more disposed to heed his inspiration than to believe that his madness would, fifty years later, become the very criterion of sanity. What could they make of a man who said, again I quote Bigelow, that "Russia and Germany must be regarded as one in casting a horoscope of the future, that all Latin states, France included, are going out with the tide . . . that the only first class powers that will survive as such are Russia, including Germany, and the United States." Even in 1905, few people saw with Adams that the previous nine years had "swept away men and empires and upset science," or that "another such ten years will set us on our heads and knock all our social systems silly," although that is precisely what happened.

These intuitions of Henry Adams drove him into a searching examination of the forces at work in his society; and during the first decade of the twentieth century, he summoned up all the intellectual aid he could command from physicists and fellow-historians in order to place his grave prognosis within a scientific framework that would be acceptable to them. The outcome of that effort was two papers: 'The Rule of Phase Applied to History,' written in 1909, and his 'Letter to the Teachers of History,' circulated for criticism among his colleagues in the American Historical Association in 1910. These two papers brought to a conclusion an examination of the contemporary situation he had tentatively made in another paper, on 'The Tendency of History,' which he had published as early as 1894, before the final phase he predicted, marked by the discovery of radioactivity and the possibility of directing nuclear fission, had opened. If any mind exhibited sensitive intellectual tentacles capable of probing the future, as radar probes space for signs of an oncoming body, it was the mind of Adams.

Henry Adams' prognosis met neither acceptance nor active resistance. Though his fellow-historians were full of respect for the Adams who had executed a classic work on American history in the best nineteenth-century manner—his heavily documented nine-volume study of the politics and diplomacy of the early republic—they were baffled to the point of boredom by his routine-shaking proposals. They recoiled from his suggestion that they set their investigations against a cosmic background that made mock of their habits of minute documentation and that they acknowledge contemporary forces that were almost as inaccessible to their favored methods of research.

As for the majority of Adams' other contemporaries, they took refuge in the asylum—or should one call it the underground disaster shelter?—of their own favored field of specialization; and they smiled with idiot complacency when Adams opened the gates and bade them explore the real

world that lay outside their heavily barricaded refuge. Even the advocates of
what was then called the New History, supposedly more interested in the
whole range of contemporary affairs than the exponents of the old history,
who were at home only in past wars and past politics, were equally reluctant to assess Henry Adams' contribution, equally apathetic in assessing the
new forces themselves. Adams found that he was talking to himself. So
stubborn were the emotional and intellectual defenses against his ideas, so
unready were Adams' contemporaries for a re-examination of their basic
premises, that he did not even provoke overt hostility or counter-attack,
which are often more helpful in breaking the ice of frozen error than quick
agreement.

That silence and that irresponsiveness still remain, even though events
have magnificently vindicated Adams' interpretations. Hence my deliberate
attempt to lift the cataract that has produced this fatal blindness and apply
shock treatment to this even more fatal inertia, by making public apology to
the shade of Henry Adams. Today the proverbial schoolboy can easily
show up the weaknesses of Adams' pseudo-scientific attempt to summarize
history under the second law of thermo-dynamics, the law of entropy: indeed more than one schoolboy, in the disguise of a professor, has done so
under the impression that he has removed the entire groundwork of Adams'
argument. Even I, before becoming a professor myself, ranged myself with
these opponents; though happily I lived long enough to expose my shame
and repent it in a new preface to 'The Golden Day.' One of Adams' ablest
recent critics, Professor W. H. Jordy, who has written the most detailed and
exacting appraisal of Adams' central ideas, has so exuberantly wiped out
any intellectual grounds for taking Adams' prophetic injunctions seriously
that he has even destroyed his own case against Adams. "With the advent
of the atomic bomb," observes Jordy, "the American Nostradamus has attained new stature not only for his *Rule,* but quite as much for his letters,
with their perception of future events. Despite a record more impressive
than that of most prophets, Adams scarcely predicted the atom bomb as
such." This is disparagement with a vengeance, but the kind of vengeance
that recoils on him who practices it. For to make his criticism stick, Jordy
was forced to leave out any reference to the letter in which Adams predicted the atomic bomb a generation before its invention; and he made his
case against Adams even weaker by saying that Adams did not interest himself in atomic research in physics.

The evidence contradicts this strange assertion. For the whole movement
of Adams' thought was powered by the fact that he almost alone among his
contemporaries, alone not merely among historians but among physicists,
immediately understood the revolutionary social potentialities of radium
and radioactivity. He foresaw clearly that the control of atomic fission would
soon be in human hands, and that this multiplication of human power by
an incalculably large factor would bring on societal changes of an entirely
new order, with which man was not capable of coping with the aid of any

of the political agents or moral codes he had, for some five thousand years, habitually, if ineffectually, used to control much feebler concentrations of power. Because Adams' statement of these possibilities was both scientifically and logically not without serious flaws, Adams' critics dismissed him as a "Nostradamus," an obscure mutterer of ambiguous oracles. Adams' unforgiveable weakness, on Professor Jordy's showing, was that he merely "sensed" the events he forecast half a century before they occurred, events that more prudent scholars, proud of their concentration upon immediately verifiable evidence, had the "sense" to ignore.

Now, in playing tennis, there is nothing more irritating than a novice opponent, who, by blind swings and lucky lunges, makes points that a better trained player would either never try for, or at least lose with good form; and I suppose that some such feeling irked Adams' professional colleagues when they found that his predictions had actually, for all their lack of solid scholarly apparatus, come true. But the point is that Adams, on his fellow historians' own testimony, was not a duffer but a champion player; and his extraordinary predictions were not lucky guesses, but better interpretations of data that he was alert enough to sense and respond to, but that they all-too-sleepily ignored. Did not Adams remark, in 1904: "Prosperity never before imagined, power never wielded by man, speed never reached by anything but a meteor, had made the world nervous, querulous, unreasonable, and afraid"? The man who uttered those words shocked his contemporaries, and now, in quite another fashion, shocks us, because he was already describing, half a century ago, the world in which *we* now live. This was not prophecy, but the sharpest kind of observation; and it revealed the weakness of a retrospective conception of history that confined itself to a past dead enough to be disemboweled and mummified, and deliberately ignored the embryo already kicking in the womb.

Even at the time Professor Jordy published his criticism (1952) most other historians did not realize that there might be something deficient in a method of historical analysis and exact investigation that provides its exponents with no "mere sense" of what is going to happen, and that persuades them, even when such a shattering event as a nuclear catastrophe of planetary dimensions becomes imminent, that nothing really *has* happened that calls for any revision of their method or their outlook. Though in 1894 Henry Adams had told his colleagues that "we have reached a point where we ought to face the possibility of a great and perhaps sudden change in our profession," even today, more than two generations later, that seems to most scholars a presumptuous, indeed quite impossible, demand.

Admittedly, Adams' working philosophy was not impeccable. I would not deny that he himself was largely a victim of the very conceptual framework and empiric method he sought to challenge, so that those who would now follow the master must first overthrow him. Like many social scientists today, he had taken over uncritically a notion that serves admirably only in the physical sciences: the belief that precise observation and accurate description, of a mathematical order, are the main requisites for achieving adequate truths; and to arrive at such objectivity, the human equation must, as far as possible, be eliminated, except as a still inescapable residual agent in the process itself. These have proved to be stultifying requirements in historic interpretation; for in history, only a small portion of the totality of events is open to observation, an infinitely smaller portion is ever committed to record, and of that recorded portion, a still smaller portion, not necessarily the most significant part, survives or is open to statistical treatment. One can fill this gap only by drawing on seemingly nebulous subjective impressions, not immediately open to public verification. The observer who meticulously leaves himself out of the picture leaves out the most sensitive instrument available for registering distant social tremors beyond the horizon of direct observation.

In dealing with organic and historic complexities, as Adams himself observed, the most important thing is not the correctness of isolated details, where a certain degree of error must be taken for granted and tolerated, but a sufficiently wide focus to take in all the processes at work. Without this wide focus, which keeps every part under equally close and constant observation, the very sharpness of detail in one sector may throw the whole field out of focus and thus become a major source of error. The constant danger in interpreting human behavior is to overvalue exact methods, and measurable data, separated from their historic context. The relevant data are often too complex for even verbal formulation; for the very things that the conscientious historian is tempted to leave out, because of their obscurity, their purely analogical suggestiveness, their subjective involvement, are needed to bring any richness of insight into our judgments.

In Adams' case, it is true, some of his seemingly precise formulations, like that for the geometric progression in the invention of prime movers and the release of energy, from A.D. 1300 to the year 1917, have proved uncannily accurate. But the fact that the final change of phase, which he foresaw, came just a year before Rutherford formulated the conditions for breaking up the nucleus of the atom, was at best a happy accident, since it was derived from rough estimates of the length of earlier periods which were necessarily loose and approximate. What was important, rather, was the fact that Adams, despite his commitment to the prevailing nineteenth-century mode of objectivity, had made the bold step of dealing with complexities too obscure and too subjective to be handled by the refined methods that the physical sciences had so successfully used: instead of confining himself to isolated particulars, put together at random, or often not put together at all, he had addressed himself to historic wholes and attempted to describe a large-scale cultural transformation at work on many levels.

Henry Adams' departure was even more radical than he realized. By his very stress on the future, he had moved from the world of causality to the world of organic events: a world where purpose often controls process, and where the succession of events is determined, not just by external forces working on passive objects, as temperature and pressure work to modify the behavior of a gas, but by the organism's inherited nature, by its lifetime accumulations of experience, by its own counter-proposals and demands, by its feats of resistance and resurgence. Every organism has a characteristic cycle of growth from birth to death; and even the feeblest of human communities constantly makes changes in its environment and in its own nature and culture in conformity with self-directed purposes and goals not given by purely physical stimuli or external pressures. Unfortunately Adams was so committed to the deterministic premises of pre-Einsteinian science that he cast his own thoughts in a Calvinistic strait-jacket which committed everyone, even the elect, to damnation. In any event, the problem that Adams so wisely propounded could not be answered within the ideological framework he himself brought to its solution.

But Adams' very impotence to frame an answer should have called the attention of his contemporaries to what was lacking—as A. N. Whitehead was soon to point out—in the entire conceptual scheme on which their expanding universe of exact knowledge had been based. This conceptual scheme had admirably facilitated investigation into the so-called physical world precisely because it was unimpeded by considerations that were essential for the understanding or control of organic functions or human activities: thus raw sense-data served as substitutes for meanings, chance for purpose, quantitative measurement for qualitative appraisal. This one-sided methodology operated like a bulldozer clearing the ground of organic and historic realities and leaving an open area denuded of any significant values except those promoted by physical inquiry or technological manipulation.

I regret that I have not the space to examine at length the source of Henry Adams' radical failure in analyzing the problem before him, and overcoming the contradictions in his own position, which partly nullified the impact of his admirable intuitions. Enough to say here that if we are finally to master the forces that now threaten us, and escape the catastrophic conclusions that Adams properly feared, we shall, in the long run, have to create an ideological fabric capable of doing justice to every dimension of experience: not alone to causality and chance and statistical probability, but also to historic continuity and organic purpose, to creative choice and conscious design. Some of the best minds in physics and biology are already advancing in this direction. Adams, we shall see presently, had at least a negative perception of this necessity: he saw how effectively the lack of purposeful control and valid human goals would demoralize even our practical judgment.

The historians and the other scholars to whom Adams hopefully sent his papers were stonily unreceptive to the emerging realities Adams pointed to, and they made no effort to re-examine their own work within the larger context of the approaching human transformation. Yet there were a few exceptions. Though Adams has the honor of being the first to grapple with the crisis of our time, he was not altogether alone: my own master, Patrick Geddes, wrote a memorandum in 1911 forecasting the approaching crisis in civilization and calling for collaborators to interpret it in a whole series of books. As early as 1913, H. G. Wells had published a novel, called 'The World Set Free,' in which he pictured an atomic war in the nineteen forties, with the destruction of a whole city by a single atom bomb: a 1945 weapon quaintly dropped by hand from the open cockpit of a 1913 monoplane. The scientific data on which Wells based this remarkable fantasy had come, incidentally, from Frederick Soddy, one of Rutherford's assistants, whose own work on nuclear energy, published between 1911 and 1914, reached the same conclusion as Adams had reached half a generation before; namely, that once a method of producing fission had been devised, the whole structure of society would have to be altered to bring this power under control. Though Wells' remedies, like Adams' prognosis, were cast in the stultifying conceptual framework that had helped to bring about the approaching crisis of uncontrolled expansions and explosions, he described the situation, correctly, as a race between education and catastrophe.

Unfortunately, people like Geddes, Soddy, Wells, and Adams, who were already actually living in a real world invisible to their contemporaries, had no influence on the compact majority, who continued to live in the largely unreal but palpable and visible world of solid matter, inert institutions, limited energies, and even more smugly limited men, preoccupied with their increasingly obsolete affairs of state and finance and scholarship, and attentive only to the immediate demands of profit, prestige, and political power. Instead of getting ready to control and direct the approaching transformation from coal and electricity to boundless nuclear power, scientists devoted themselves, unreservedly rather, to hastening these changes, without any thought for the possibly catastrophic consequences. Those who were dubious or apprehensive were tempted to deny the possibility of nuclear fission, as the distinguished physicist Robert Millikan did almost up to the moment it was accomplished. Otherwise, they made a virtue of their indifference and tacitly turned these broader issues over to their colleagues in the fields of political and social science, equally specialized minds, professionally proud of their incompetence to handle interrelated wholes— minds incapable of overcoming the social inertia of their period, or of plotting a new destination for forces that, if left to themselves, promised only to bring about disintegration.

But this blindness was too widespread, this refusal too absolute, this error too generally committed to admit any nice apportionment of blame. How many of my own generation, brought up in the world of Curie and Einstein, are free from reproach? Do I not remember my own high school physics teacher, in 1911, holding up his lead pencil and telling the class: "If we knew how to unlock the energy in each atom of this pencil, we would have enough power right here to run the subways of New York"? Even as late as 1934, when I wrote 'Technics and Civilization,' I shrank from dealing with the release of atomic energy, certainly not from ignorance of its possibility, but out of a cowardly hope that it might not come about and make the "impossible" demands that its release has actually imposed. That confession carries with it no absolution. Yet if we were lacking in brave foresight, even the hindsight of most of our contemporaries has so far been equally deficient.

The most striking and significant of Adams' letters, curiously overlooked by those who continue to dismiss Adams' admonitions and proposals, was not published as part of a collection till 1947, when Harold Dean Cater brought it out in a book called 'Henry Adams and His Friends,' though I myself had publicly quoted significant parts of this letter from 1942 onward, before the atom bomb was invented. Let me bring forth this passage once again, for the rest of this paper will be mainly an exegesis of the separate items in that letter. It was written from Washington, on the 17th of January, 1905; and it was addressed to the historian, Henry Osborn Taylor. Adams' words in part are as follows: "The assumption of unity, which was the mark of human thought in the Middle Ages, has yielded very slowly to the proofs of complexity. The stupor of science before radium is a proof of it. Yet it is quite sure, according to my score of ratios and curves, that, at the accelerated rate of progression since 1600, it will not need another century or half century to turn thought upside down. Law, in that case, would disappear as theory or *a priori* principle and give place to force. Morality would become police. Explosives would reach cosmic violence. Disintegration would overcome integration."

If these words had been the dim gropings of a Nostradamus, the scholar might still be pardoned for treating them with indifference, not to say patronizing contempt. Or if Adams had hit on only a single aspect of this transformation, that alone might have been attributed to luck, rather than to adequate insight into the complexities of historic change. But Adams foresaw, not merely the atom bomb itself, but even more significantly, the release from moral inhibitions and life-conserving taboos that made its use possible in the first instance, and now multiplies the dangers of nuclear fission even in its peaceful applications. The historian who, however belatedly, would take Adams' formulations seriously can no longer confine himself to his traditional presentation of past events in an orderly time-sequence: he has the much more vital task of interpretation, prognosis, and constructive proposal, particularly in re-examining those institutions whose continued existence, unchanged, now enormously increases the problems atomic energy has raised. One of these institutions—war—which for five thousand years had been the principal disrupter of man's cumulative advances in culture, broke out on a world scale in the very next decade, and is now threatening the human race with an even more ominous outbreak of purposeless violence and large-scale extermination.

Even Adams' errors, I submit, would have been fruitful, if they had been taken seriously. Though he had given undue universality to the constant acceleration of quantitative energies and the degradation of social institutions since the medieval period, he had actually stumbled upon a new factor whose tremendous and fatal significance has not yet been grasped. This was the fact that the processes of mechanical invention and scientific investigation had, during the last five centuries, become increasingly automatic, just to the extent that they had overthrown the laws and the norms, the social inhibitions and the religious restraints, in short, the dense cultural and historic tissue, that earlier societies had prudently erected in self-protection, out of fear of bringing down the wrath of the gods. Not merely the increased acceleration in the production of energy, but the increased automatism of the process itself, was what added to the final dangers when bombs of "cosmic violence" were invented. As a result every permission has become a compulsion: every new mechanical possibility has become, without respect to its actual value, a supposedly inescapable social necessity. It is not our concern for reaching the moon that produced the interplanetary rocket, but the invention of the rocket that has produced a factitious interest in the moon as a military base for more extensive violence. This applies all along the line.

That quantitative expansion, based on a detachment from organic norms, human purposes, and historic continuities, and the elimination of all other purposes except those proper to science and technology alone, was the radically new factor in modern civilization; and this is what Adams, despite his own erroneous interpretation of it, called attention to. This uncontrolled pressure to quantitative expansion—the expansion of territory, the expansion of inventions, the expansion of energy, the expansion of population, the expansion of mechanical facilities and consumable wealth, the expansion of knowledge—was what most people regarded as an indefeasible sign of progress. But Adams was the first person to follow the process to its menacing negative conclusion: explosions of cosmic violence and therewith the imminent possibility of wholesale human regression. The ultimate gains in nuclear energy, he saw with a clarity most of our own contemporaries still lack, would be canceled out by the translation of law into force, morality into police, life-enhancing processes into life-destroying ones, purposeful development into limitless disintegration. Only a radical transformation in our whole culture could halt this process, or direct it once more in channels favorable to life.

If the historians of the past two generations failed to rally to Adams' challenge, many had the excuse that they were even more ignorant of the physical sciences than Adams himself. But what shall we say of the physical scientists? Some of them were doubtless handicapped, not so much by ignorance as by knowledge that had become outmoded by the new discoveries that radioactivity had opened up. But they were even more paralyzed by their curious assumption that their sterile lifeless world of dissociated physical events, built up symbolically upon equally isolated sense-data, was a true image of the real world: and that, as scientists, they had no obligation to take account of human affairs except in pursuit of their particular order of truths, no matter what use or misuse their society might make of them. Most scientists behaved suspiciously and defensively as if they were still threatened by arbitrary curbs imposed by Church or State; and in their innocence, they refused to believe that their own methods and their new discoveries might pose a graver threat to the very existence of the human race. But their tacit doctrine, "Let the truth be pursued though the heavens fall," is a sound one only if one is quite sure that the heavens will not fall. Who can entertain that belief now? What I have interpreted so far as the automatism of post-Newtonian science and technics recognizes no goals except those identified with their own methodically curtailed interests and processes. The practitioners of science confused the kind of temporary detachment and impersonality necessary for exact observation with a quite other kind of moral code: the refusal to accept social responsibility or to anticipate social consequences within a broader context than their science.

Our colleagues in science, remembering earlier institutional curbs, naturally insist that there should be no arbitrary external control over science: but they overlook the possibility that they themselves might exercise rational *internal* control, and that, if Henry Adams was right, they have a duty to exercise it. That internal control might take many forms. The best would doubtless be a more integrated method and a larger frame of reference, which would in itself reduce the tempo of research and give equal attention to interpretation and assimilation. Not merely is it important to restore concern for qualities and patterns and ecological relationships which had been cast out by Galileo and Descartes: but it is important to recognize the part played by purpose, at every level of human activity, even though the concept of finality and purpose in the cosmos at large had been misstated by Aristotle and dogmatically thrown out by Spinoza.

Time has in fact made an ironic commentary upon the scientists who rejected the concept of purpose and defied the imposition of external control by the Church: for as a result of their nuclear triumphs they have now meekly accepted wholesale control by the state, the authority that gave them the facilities for making these discoveries and provided them with a factitious purpose for surrendering their freedom. By vast grants-in-aid from governments and affiliated financial organizations—or should I say, more accurately, by huge bribes?—scientific investigation has gone ahead voluminously in the departments favored by the Armed Forces of the State; and the scientists who have easily accepted these subsidies have also accepted the forfeiture of civic responsibility and autonomy that attends such patronage. They are in fact "kept men" and even their scientific judgments are no longer disinterested or above suspicion.

The processes of scientific investigation have now become more automatic and compulsory than ever because of this inner betrayal. Science has now lost its one great original basis for social respect: the scientists' proud commitment to an organization for discovering verifiable truths that recognized no national boundaries and no obstacles to free circulation except ignorance of its methods. To talk of disinterested science today in any of the great nations is to talk only of the work of a dwindling number. In many laboratories and research organizations the terms "objective" and "disinterested" are open only to disrespectful jeers. In order to extend their facilities and powers, scientists have consented to place large areas of investigation in physics, chemistry, and biology under a seal of official secrecy, at the service of purposes that derive neither from love of truth nor respect for humanity: without compunction they serve a perverse mythology, no more reputable than the ostentatious collective sadism of ancient monarchs.

These favored scientists have unlimited freedom of investigation within their chosen field provided that they do not examine the basic premises on which the research enterprise is founded, or question the purposes for which it will be used. In a guilty effort, indeed, to justify their own conduct, they become all too often the fanatical exponents of the policy their researches support, using their authority as scientists to bolster up the political and military errors they themselves have helped to commit. Thus purpose, extruded at the highest level as a category of thought and a principle of life, has now come back at the lowest level, as an agent for unimpeded technological expansion, and ultimately for destruction and extermination. The fact that this collapse of science's own high moral code is not openly recognized and vigorously challenged in every seat of learning is but another sign of the general moral disintegration that Adams forecast.

Yet one must correct this black picture with a few redeeming highlights. Once the change of phase predicted by Adams had become visible, a valiant group of scientists whose consciences had not been anesthetized by their intelligence sought to redeem, as citizens, their shortsighted views and narrow interests as investigators. One must honor these belated efforts, from those of Albert Einstein down; but one must also point out that they were not accompanied by the one kind of unconditional commitment that would have made them effective: that of martyrdom. Many scientists were eager to persuade their governments to renounce the use of the weapons they had helped to create: but to effect this end, only a few were willing, even temporarily, to renounce their own occupation, to say nothing of forcing a reconsideration of public policy by a stoppage of their own investigations: a collective scientific "strike." Even those who were most aware of mankind's desperate situation were not ready to invoke such a desperate remedy, though it needed an act of this order to bring about a sufficient public awakening. Within the field of science, there have been many heroic martyrs *for* science, particularly in medicine and radiology; but there have been few, if any, martyrs *against* the public misuse of science for debased purposes.

Adams foresaw that the American who lived in the year 2000 would—and I now quote him—"think in complexities unimaginable to an earlier mind. He would deal with problems altogether beyond the range of earlier society." What Adams also foresaw by inference, though he never clearly put it in so many words, was that this same American would live his life on a basis of feelings and moral evaluations infinitely cruder and more infantile than that of neolithic village communities, without sufficient human reverence for life, his own or any other being's, to pass on to the next generation even Stone-Age inhibitions against random extermination of life, or even Stone-Age respect for human continuity. This cold indifference to the moral consequences of our power-obsessed behavior accounts for the strange passiveness of our contemporaries.

As a nation we are now under the control of under-dimensioned minds with five-year perspectives, immune to human concerns: indifferent alike to the rich historic past they would nullify or the endless potentialities of the future they would abort or sterilize. Such de-moralized minds are capable in fantasy of wiping out sixty million of their fellow-countrymen, and congratulating themselves on contriving shelters that might save, also largely in fantasy, the bodies of some fraction of those that would remain. These Genghis Khans of strategy have conditioned their countrymen to ignore the fact that this unseemly massacre may still be avoided by adroit changes in military and political policy which a more humane intelligence could bring about. But in a world like ours, empty of historic values or purposes, the crassly optimistic reassurances of scientific fortune-Tellers are treated as oracles, while the well-grounded warnings of its humane Einsteins and Schweitzers and Russells are disregarded.

On Adams' terms, all these reactions were to be expected: disintegration has become our deity, as chance became the deity of a dissolving Hellenistic order. But to leave the matter here would be to give Adams' pessimism a greater justification than it deserved: for Adams never allowed for the ultimate possibility which even Oswald Spengler, equally pessimistic, allowed for in his 'Decline of the West,' that the human spirit might, if once fully conscious of its situation, escape from the death trap it had set for itself, even if forced to retreat into what Spengler called the "second religiousness."

Already a small body of scientists has arisen who are earnestly wrestling with the moral and social responsibilities of science. If their little society had existed in 1910, they might have given Adams help, and even saved him from his Calvinistic depression. These people already recognize that alternatives to our dominant ideology and policy do exist: that, as Robinson Jeffers said in one of his poems, corruption never was compulsory. Just the other day I received a letter from a microbiologist at one of Europe's famous laboratories, saying that she had just forsworn her position and her career as a scientist; and that she had been moved to this grave step by her awareness that current researches in her field, addressed to physical means for altering the genes in lower organisms, were leading in a direction that she considered potentially inimical to the human race. For this scientist, life itself was more sacred than science.

Henry Adams would not have been surprised to find that this simple but radical insight came from a woman: for in his address to the Virgin he declared:

> . . . I feel the energy of faith,
> Not in the future science but in you.

This sensitivity on the part of a working biologist, this perception of the remoter consequences of her investigations, this heroic act of renunciation in mid-career, reminds one of the kind of transformation that took place at the end of Roman civilization, when a great patrician like Paulinus of Nola gave up his career as a governor and Consul to enter a monastic retreat. Such a reaction may well be working under the surface of many lives today, still as invisible to most of us as the consequences of radioactivity were to Adams' contemporaries. And if this prove true, these renunciations and this change in the direction of interest might alter the whole pattern of our life even more swiftly than Christianity changed the sordid routines and daily defilements of the Roman Empire.

Henry Adams' sterile determinist philosophy was inadequate to plot a new direction. But fortunately his intuitions again saved him, and made him once more the prophet of our age. He saw that the males of his society, who had transferred so many of their once autonomous activities to machines and automatons, did not have sufficient life-sense to save the race. In their blind pride over their scientific facilities, they would cling to the insensate mechanisms they had created, making them go ever faster and faster, though incapable of applying the brakes, changing the direction, or choosing the destination. Anticipating that desperate strait, Henry Adams, at the end of his own career, turned to another countervailing form of energy, the energy of life, the energy of erotic love, reproduction, and creation; he sought a counterpoise to chaos by invoking woman's faith in her own creativity, in all the ramifying, formative processes of life, above all those of sex, love, motherhood. In Adams' appeal to the Virgin, all awakened souls today, quite regardless of ideology or religious faith, can unreservedly join; and perhaps, in the depths of their unconscious, this prayer is now being repeated and enacted by awakened people in millions of homes. To match the insane devices and insolent agents that threaten the human race, we now witness an outpouring of fecundity in every country, advanced or backward, with or without the means of birth control, in a manner that still puzzles and vexes the sociologist and the statistician whose predictions of a dwindling population, as late as twenty years ago, have been mocked and flouted.

Help me to feel! [cried Henry Adams to the Virgin,]
Help me to feel, not with my insect sense, with yours,
That felt all life alive in you.

This was Henry Adams' final heresy and his final offense against those committed to the dehumanized ideology and methodology of our time. That ideology has held, as its most sacred obligation, that feelings and emotions must be strictly disregarded, and that only the specialized, detached intelligence, without any other human dimensions, may be trusted. Henry Adams, who sensed so many important transformations he could not prove, was wise enough to seek, as a corrective to the large-scale perversion of life that was already taking place, the help of woman. He saw that we needed, not more information, more statistical data, more scientific research, more exact knowledge: our society was already burdened with larger quantities of power, under these heads, than we could ever make use of, without a profound change in our whole attitude toward human existence. Adams saw that we needed more feeling, feeling and gentling such as infants first get at their mother's breasts: such feeling as woman symbolically embodied and projected, from the paleolithic Venus of Wilmersdorf to the Venus of Milo, from Egyptian Isis to the Virgin of the thirteenth century: feeling that has poured into a thousand benign cultural forms, pictorial, musical, architectural, and expressed itself in every sustaining mode of embrace and envelopment and tender expression, from the kiss of greeting to the hot tears with which we take our leave from the dead. The overgrowth of the instruments of intelligence had anesthetized feeling and thereby paralyzed our capacity to respond as whole human beings to life's many-sided demands. To restore a human balance upset by our pathologically dehumanized technology, we must foster human feeling, feeling as disciplined and as refined, by constant application and correction, as our highest intellectual processes. To overcome the widespread sterilization of mind, we must unite a higher capacity for feeling with our higher capacity for thought, to produce acts that will be worthy progeny of both parents. This perhaps, at the end, was the lesson Henry Adams taught in his apostrophe to the Virgin.

To assimilate that lesson will be a harder task for our world, especially for our intellectual world, than almost any other: for with feeling will come back the organism as a whole, and with the organism will come purposes—human purposes and human goals—that have been ejected from the sacred confines of the seemingly detached scientific mind, operating in its self-sealed conceptual sphere. The alternative, unfortunately, will be to permit the present automatic forces to expand limitlessly along their present lines, without political intervention, without moral inhibitions, without a change of purpose, without a life-sustaining goal, until they either debase or destroy our human heritage beyond any possible redemption. If we cling to the dehumanized ideology and destructive myths that now threaten us with a final series of catastrophes, Henry Adams' original prediction will in all probability come true. The bombs of cosmic violence will go off, almost by themselves, and disintegration will overcome integration. In that case, our apology to Henry Adams will be as vain as our regrets; and even woman's healing love and nurture will not save us.

(1962)

CHAPTER THIRTY-THREE

The American Way of Death

As so often happens, when the minds of many people have been silently brooding over the same subject, there has recently been an outbreak of books, articles, and legislative investigations, all devoted to assessing the mechanical defects, the bodily hazards, and the mounting social disadvantages of the motor car. The tone of this discussion has been critical, not to say sacrilegious. Some of the critics have dared to say that the Sacred Cow of the American Way of Life is overfed and bloated; that the daily milk she supplies is poisonous; that the pasturage this species requires wastes acres of land that could be used for more significant human purposes; and that the vast herds of sacred cows, allowed to roam everywhere, like their Hindu counterparts, are trampling down the vegetation, depleting wild life, and turning both urban and rural areas into a single smudgy wasteland, whose fancy sociological name is Megalopolis.

The priesthood of the Sacred Cow, very sensitive to the mildest heresy, now shows definite signs of alarm, alternating plaintive moos with savage bellows; for in their religion, the cult of the Sacred Cow is closely affiliated with an older object of worship, the Golden Calf. With justified trepidation, the priestly establishment feels Religion itself (capitalized) is being challenged—that religion for whose evidences of power and glory the American people, with eyes devoutly closed, are prepared to sacrifice some 59,000 lives every year, and to maim, often irreparably, some three million more. Only war can claim so many premature deaths; for the death rate from motor cars is greater than the combined death rate from falls, burnings, drownings, railroads, firearms, and poisonous gases, plus some two thousand other deaths from unidentifiable causes. And though only roughly half as many Americans were killed outright by autos in the last four-year period as were killed in our armed forces during a similar term in the Second World War, nearly three times as many were injured.

The current uprising against the miscarriage of the horseless carriage has long been brewing; John Keats's 'The Insolent Chariots' broke the painful silence as far back as 1958. Only childish petulance on the part of the car manufacturers and their allies makes them attribute this spreading dissatisfaction with their product to the outspoken criticisms of a few mischievous critics, since the latter, till now a sorry few, have had none of the auto industry's facilities for commanding public attention and suppressing debate. The roots of the current revolt spread over a wide area, and they go much deeper than even the most impassioned advocates of safer motor car design yet realize.

If the temple of the Sacred Cow is crumbling, it is because the whole mode of existence for which it is the prime mover has become antagonistic to the genuine human needs it was once supposed to serve and enhance. The fact is that the great American dream of a nation on wheels, which began with the covered wagon, has come to a dreary terminus. The very success of the auto industry in fulfilling the mechanical conditions for that dream has turned it, ironically, into a nightmare. An essential part of the American's delight over the auto was a happy leftover from pioneer days: the ingratiating idea of private freedom, in the sense of being able to go anywhere one willed, at any time one willed, at any speed one willed, up hill and down dale exploring the great open spaces, and at least getting away from the familiar habitat, the daily round, the mechanical grind. In what has belatedly been called "automobility," now that we are losing it, the personal "auto" was even more essential than the mechanical "mobility."

Until about 1930, this dream bore more than a faint resemblance to actuality. Even such a fastidious soul as Henry James hailed the aristocratic joys of travel by motor car, which opened up the landscape and refreshed the spirit; so much so, that such usual interruptions as a leaky tire or a boggy road, if not too frequent, only added an extra spice to the adventure. Unfortunately, one of the conditions for enjoying this freedom was the existence of other possible modes of transportation, to handle mass demands, such as the wonderful transportation network of railroads, electric trolleys, and steamboats, which once spanned the country and not only took up much of the travel load but met different human needs at different speeds. By now people have fallen into the habit of characterizing the pre-motor-car era as the "horse-and-buggy" age, as if fast transportation were unknown till the auto came. Actually, electric trolleys, in New England and the Middle West, travelled over their own rights of ways at speeds of fifty miles an hour: I cherish a picture post-card, c. 1910, showing such a trolley-car, sensibly streamlined, that served Indianapolis. As with the mass movement into suburbia, which coincided with the mass production of motor cars, the desired freedom depended upon creating a more complex pattern of both movement and settlement, maintaining and improving a balanced transportation system, and maintaining and improving old cities. Had those two essential factors been understood and respected, the motor car could have made an invaluable contribution in creating a regional distribution of population. As in the Netherlands, today, this would give the countryside the social advantages of the city, and multiply the number of cities with easy access to the countryside, without the compulsive and wasteful routines that have now been developed to cope with the uncontrolled explosion of motor cars.

The huge success of the auto industry, not merely in multiplying the number of cars, but in utilizing its quasi-monopolistic resources and public monies to elbow out competing forms of locomotion and transportation, has turned the dream of automobility into the anxiety nightmare it has become today. From that nightmare Americans are now at last struggling to awake: the nightmare of the air becoming toxic with poisonous exhausts, including the highly lethal carbon monoxide; of the water supply polluted with deadly lead from gasoline exhausts already half way to the danger point even in the Arctic wastes; the nightmare of diurnal mass commutation by car, along freeways where speed is compulsory, where the constant tensions demonstrably produce higher blood pressure, where a single car, stopping in time to avert an accident, may trigger a succession of more serious accidents in the tail-gating cars behind, even when traveling at the usual drugged crawl of rush hours.

The motor car, it goes without saying, has brought many pleasant and desirable benefits; and certain by-products, like the beautiful Taconic Parkway in New York, remain permanent contributions to amenity and esthetic delight.* But the whole picture has become increasingly dismal, and the most attractive feature of the American dream, freedom of movement and settlement, is turning into a system of choiceless compulsion. Just as old Henry Ford graciously said the consumer could have a car of any color he wanted as long as it was black, so motor travel is reaching a point where the driver can go anywhere he wants to, at a high speed, so long as he demands no change in either the environment or the destination. G. K. Chesterton's epigram "Nothing fails like success" may yet prove the epitaph of the motor industry. Though danger and death have played a part in the awakening, frustration and boredom have perhaps played a greater part—if only because courting danger has unfortunately proved one of the chronic modes of faking real life and finding momentary relief from its emptiness and its desperate routines.

The signs of this revolt are multiplying. Just a few years ago the motor car owners of the San Francisco Bay region voted $750 million to rebuild the fast public transportation system which the worshippers of the Sacred Cow had cleverly scrapped only twenty years before. But even more significantly, at the moment I write, news comes from San Francisco that "an overflow crowd of spectators cheered wildly at the City Hall here . . . as the Board of Supervisors voted down two proposed freeways on which the Federal Government was willing to put up two hundred and eighty million dollars." Even worse, these delirious iconoclasts are demand-

* Now progressively robbed of its spacious curves and slow vistas for the sake of speed.

ing that the Embarcadero Freeway, whose construction, half-way through, was brought to an end by public demand, should be torn down. Is it not indeed time that Detroit began to pay a little attention to the feedback? If the current disillusion with the motor car keeps on growing, auto industry investments may not remain so profitable, unless Detroit's current representative in the Defense Department manages to involve the country in even more extensive military aggressions than Vietnam.

But to go back to the American dream. In the 1920s when a score of small corporations still gave the color of "free enterprise" to the auto industry, the automobile was a crude but relatively honest machine: clumsy in its transmission system and gear shift, capricious in its starting devices, unreliable in its braking capability, decidedly old-fashioned in its reliance upon the gas engine, but still, for all its adolescent gawkiness, a functional machine, designed for transportation and recreation. Around 1930, just when the "new capitalism" suddenly slumped down to earth, the motor car industry picked itself up by exchanging economy for style. General Motors led the way here, and even Ford was compelled to follow. In the new hierarchy of values, recreation, reliability, safety, efficiency, economy all took a lower place. Style and speed were what counted. At this point, the automotive engineer took his orders from beauty specialists, whose job was to give the car a new look every year, in order to make last year's model unfashionable, that is, prematurely obsolete. The pioneer's dream wagon entered Madison Avenue's fairyland.

Within the next two decades, the motor car became a status symbol, a religious icon, an erotic fetish: in short, "something out of this world," increasingly swollen and tumescent, as if on the verge of an orgasm. What words other than Madison Avenue's can adequately describe these exciting confections, glittering with chrome, pillowed in comfort, sleepy-soft to ride in, equipped with mirrors, cigarette lighters, radios, telephones, floor carpeting; (liquor bars and tape-recorders are still optional). But in achieving these delights the designers so far turned their backs on the sordid realities of life as to increase the dangers through accidents by displaying jutting knobs, projecting, often knife-edged, instrument panels, murderous wings, confusing shift levers, soft suspension coils, undersized wheels, flimsy hardtops, utterly inadequate front and rear fenders, such broad, barge-like hoods as to give the driver minimum visibility in passing or parking, not to mention sun-reflecting chrome on windshield wipers and window frames to blind either the driver or an approaching car.

In the process of styling the motor car for flashy sales appeal, the designers not only increased the dangers but gratuitously cancelled out good features that earlier cars had had. By lowering its center of gravity, they made the car impossible to enter except by acrobatic maneuvers—this in an age that boasts more elderly people and more arthritic limbs than ever before. Likewise they reduced the six-person capacity that had been happily achieved by eliminating the running board, to a four-person size. To speak plainly, the present motor car has been the result of a secret collaboration between the beautician and the mortician; and according to sales and accident statistics both have reason to be satisfied.

With all the vast resources available for fundamental engineering research, the American motor car industry has not succeeded in producing a single original over-all design since 1930, except the Army Jeep, an honest job unfortunately built with no attention to passenger comfort. In neither shapes nor sizes has it pioneered any car as sensible as the small Volkswagen or the VW autobus. While many able engineers doubtless remain in the automotive industry, they might stop the fashion parade if they came up with a car as rugged as a Rover; and if they sought to make even bolder departures, they would be rated as unemployable. But fortunately there are still honest men in the industry, even at the upper levels, such as a vice-president of Ford who publicly admitted as late as 1964 that "the automatic transmission"—adopted on a mass production basis in 1939—"was the last major improvement." This changeover from working machines to beauty salon dummies bears the hallmark of the affluent society and its expanding economy: compulsive spending and conspicuous waste. Unfortunately, the waste extends to human lives.

The motor car industry's studious indifference to safety, as a possible deterrent to marketability, has at last produced a public reaction; and a still greater one will possibly follow. The damning evidence against motordom, particularly against General Motors, has been marshalled together by two lawyers, Ralph Nader, who was an adviser to the Senate sub-committee investigating automobile hazards, and Jeffrey O'Connell, a professor of law at the University of Illinois, and erstwhile associate Director of the Automobile Claims Study at the Harvard Law School. Much of this evidence comes from public spirited physicians, faced with the dire human consequences of engineering negligence; and it is to the activity of a handful of zealous legislators, like New York State Senator Edward J. Speno and United States Senators Ribicoff and Gaylord Nelson, that we are indebted for the public airing of the auto industry's shocking behavior.

Now to assault the integrity of the great motor car producers is almost as audacious an enterprise as challenging the military judgment of the Pentagon; and incidentally, if we value our lives, quite as essential. The three great corporations—General Motors, Ford, and Chrysler—have a virtual monopoly of the American market as pace-setters and tastemakers, so that Studebaker, American Motors, and Willis-Overland had to follow their bad examples or go under. These three corporations do not stand alone, but reach out into a whole series of ancillary industries, beginning with steel, rubber, cement, and oil, which depend upon them for their existence. Likewise these giant enterprises spread their devastating glamor through go-go Highway Departments heavy with Federal Subsidies, and through all the current media of publicity and advertisement; while by judicious grants for "research" the auto industry does not a little to seduce the judgment and sully the objectivity of the research institutes and universities that accept their dubiously philanthropic support.

In the face of this massive vested interest, it says something for the tough original fabric of American life, and not least for the Fathers of the Constitution, that any open discussion of this seemingly all-powerful mega-machine can still take place. Yet, despite many early warning signals, the motor industry was so deeply entrenched, so assured of popular approval by its mounting profits that the present criticism of its aims and its methods has caught it off guard. If motordom knew how to silence this discussion, it would do so. General Motors has already demonstrated, with a stupidity that amounts to genius, that it is prepared to go to any lengths to prevent a rational public assessment of the changes that must be made in the American motor car to ensure its safety on the road. If General Motors' position were not so vulnerable and damnable they would not have hired detectives in the hope of digging up something unsavory about the character of the young lawyer who wrote 'Unsafe at Any Speed.' By this action, they not merely made a public confession of guilt, but added an extra count to the indictment: attempted character assassination with intent to kill.

The reaction of the motor industry to criticism of its product shows that those in control exhibit the same weaknesses that General Matthew Ridgway, that gallant and intelligent officer, has pointed out in relation to the Vietnam-Chinese policy of the Pentagon: their judgments are devoid of human understanding. And no wonder; for they issue from the same type of mind, the computer mind, programmed strictly for money and power. But since the subject of the motor car's deficiencies has been opened up there is no telling where the assault will stop: even computers may come in for a ribbing.

Now it is both the strength and the weakness of the two sober books under review that they are mainly concerned with a narrow segment of the motor car problem: the defects and dangers of bad mechanical design. Their positive value lies in their bringing together various suggestions, from engineers and physicians, for reducing the accident rate from mechanical defects, and for lessening the injuries that come from normal human error and from incalculable, uncontrollable incidents, such as a bee suddenly stinging the driver. These are indeed life-and-death matters; and the authors' common approach to the subject is probably the shortest and quickest way to open up the much larger problems that must sooner or later be faced.

On the whole matter of safety, the evidence that both books summarize is both appalling and incontrovertible. Every device for increasing the safety of the motor car has been resisted by the manufacturers, even when, like the safety door catch, it has been finally accepted; while the most dangerous part of the car in a serious accident, the chief cause of fatalities, is the steering assemblage, which still has serious defects besides the tight squeeze that most cars inflict upon the driver. What is worse than the mere failure to take urgent safety measures, is the fact that even when the automotive engineers have provided them at an early stage of the design, they have been removed, either to reduce costs, give emphasis to some meretricious selling point, or just to eliminate any concern for danger from the prospective buyer's mind.

What both books reveal is that the great motor car corporations, with all the insolence born of their supreme financial position in the economy, have not merely been careless about essential safety features in design: they have been criminally negligent, to the point of being homicidal. If these facts were not solidly established, no publisher in his senses would dare to publish these books; for every chapter would give ground for libel.

Both books are driven by the evidence to point to the ultimate source of the motor car's structural defects, namely, that the cars are built with a single thought uppermost in the mind of the manufacturers: What will make them sell? And by what pinching and paring on essentials can more money be spent on styling and on advertising the non-essentials, those glossy features that will catch the eye, flatter the ego, coddle a neurosis—and open the purse.

What these books demonstrate is that most American motor cars, even of the latest vintage, are still unfit vehicles for coping with the normal mischances of the road. When one considers the wide range of competence in licensed drivers, at different ages with different road experience, and the wide daily fluctuations in their general health, their eyesight, their inner tensions and pressures, it is obvious that the one factor that can and should be standardized and normalized rigorously, and raised to the highest degree of mechanical efficiency and structural safety, is the vehicle itself. That is the responsibility of the motor car companies, not of the motorist. And if the fulfillment of that responsibility means that the profits of General Motors must be cut down from a billion and a half dollars a year to as little as a third of that amount, this is still no reason why this responsibility should not be imposed—by legislation if necessary—as a mandatory condition for earning any profits whatever.

In stressing the need for introducing every possible mechanical dodge to make the car and its occupants less vulnerable to accidents, both books carry their stern indictments to various sensible conclusions; and I would not, by what follows, lessen the sting of their indictment, qualify their arguments, or minimize the value of their recommendations: quite the contrary. Most of the structural changes they suggest are desirable; and some, like seatbelts, are so cheap and simple that one wonders why so much effort had to go into making them standard equipment.

As if to show their open contempt for the whole safety argument, the manufacturers have lately souped up their cars and their advertising slogans in order to appeal to the least safe group of motor car drivers, the newly licensed adolescents and the perpetual adolescents; and they have underlined their incitement to calculated recklessness by giving the cars appropriate names, Thunderbirds, Wildcats, Tempests, Furies, to emphasize hell-bent power and aggressiveness, while their allies in the oil industry, for good measure, offer to place a "tiger in the tank." Speed is the pep pill that the motor car manufacturers are now cannily offering to adolescents like any dope peddler; and since power and speed are both regarded as absolute goods by the worshippers of the Sacred Cow, both as good in themselves and as the surest way to expand the industry and maximize the profits, why should anyone suppose that any other human considerations will modify their homicidal incitements? Speed, marijuana, heroin, and lysergic acid, are all attempts to use a scientific technology to overcome the existential nausea that the lopsided development of this very technology is the main cause of. Have Messrs. Nader, O'Connell, and Myers sufficiently reckoned with the vast irrational opposition that their sound and rational arguments will encounter? Will safety alone appeal to a public that, in the face of indisputable cancer statistics, now consumes more cigarettes than ever before?

But suppose the rational argument for safer cars nevertheless wins out. I don't think that the writers of these books fully realize where their proposals will ultimately lead them unless they place these essential changes within a much wider framework. Both the desire for safety and for the enjoyment of the motor car demand a broader restatement of the whole problem. What is the place of the motor car in a rational scheme of transportation? By what system of control at source can we handle the motor car explosion, which is as badly in need of birth control as the population explosion? And what measures are needed to restore to both transportation and travel—including air travel—some of the humanly desirable qualities that an exclusive concern with speed has already robbed them of?

As to the enjoyment of the motor car, some of the safety devices that have been suggested, crash helmets, shoulder straps as well as a seat belt, padded leg protection, may have unfortunate results in opposite directions; either by reducing the pleasurable sense of freedom, or by prompting those who submit to these constraints to seek a compensatory release in aiming at higher speeds with greater impunity—despite the fact that this in turn will raise the accident rate. Nothing could be worse in the long run for the auto industry than to eliminate the very things that made the automobile, at the beginning, so attractive: the sense of freedom and variety that motor travel once gave. In the interests of speed, the highway designers have steadily been taking away the visual pleasure and environmental stimulus of a long journey, and every other "improvement" conspires to the same end. The same compulsory high speed, the same wide monotonous road, producing the same hypnotic drowsiness, the same air-conditioned climate in the car, the same Howard Johnsons, the same clutter of parking lots, the same motels. No matter how fast he travels or how far he goes, the motorist never actually leaves home: indeed no effort is spared to eliminate variety in the landscape, and to make famous beauty spots by mountain or sea into as close a counterpart of the familiar shopping center as the original landscape will permit. In short, automobility has turned out to be the most static form of mobility that the mind of man has yet devised.

If speed and safety were the only considerations, there is no reason why the auto industry, once it awakened from its self-induced narcosis, should not "go with" this movement and make greater profits than ever. For it is easy to foresee the theoretic ideal limit toward which both the automotive engineer and the highway engineer have begun to move: to make the surface of this planet no better for any form of organic life than the surface of the moon. To minimize road accidents, the highway engineers have already advocated cutting down all trees and telegraph poles within a hundred feet of each side of the road. But that is only a beginning. To provide maximum safety at high speed, the car will either have to be taken out of the motorist's hands and placed under automatic control, as M.I.T. researchers have, on purely mechanical assumptions, worked out; or else turned into an armored vehicle, windowless, completely padded on the inside, with front and rear vision provided on a screen, and a television set installed to amuse the non-drivers, just as if they were in a jet plane. Along those lines, the motor car in a not-too-distant future would become a space capsule, a mobile prison, and the earth itself a featureless asteroid. Meanwhile, a further consolidation of the megamachine, with autos, jet planes, and rockets forming a single industry; the profits of that ultimate conglomerate should exceed the wildest expectations of even General Motors.

But who wants speed at that price or safety at that price? one is tempted to ask. Buckminster Fuller and Jacques Ellul will doubtless answer, Everyone: or at all events, that is what is coming, whether anyone wants it or not. This answer is naive, but not disarming. For these backward assumptions which are really the leftovers of the Victorian avant garde are precisely what must now be questioned. Beyond the area of safety and freedom of movement lies the need for a conception of what constitutes a valid human life, and how much of life will be left if we go on ever more rapidly in the present direction. What has to be challenged is an economy that is based not on organic needs, historic experience, human aptitudes, ecological complexity and variety, but upon a system of empty abstractions: money, power, speed, quantity, progress, vanguardism, expansion. The over-valuation of these abstractions, taken as goods in themselves, has produced the unbalanced, purposeless, sick-making, and ultimately suicidal existence we now confront.

In short, the crimes and the misdemeanors of the motor car manufacturers are significant, not because they are exceptional but because they are typical. These indictments of the auto industry pin down the same evils as were exposed by Rachel Carson's survey of the chemical industry's proliferation of pesticides and herbicides, and by Senator Kefauver's exposure of the pharmaceutical industry. The insolence of the Detroit chariotmakers

and the masochistic submissiveness of the American consumer are symptoms of a larger disorder: a society that is no longer rooted in the complex
realities of an organic and personal world; a society made in the image
of machines, by machines, for machines; a society in which any form
of delinquency or criminality may be practiced, from meretriciously designed motor cars or insufficiently tested wonder drugs to the wholesale
distribution of narcotics and printed pornography, provided that the profits
sufficiently justify their exploitation. If those remain the premises of the
Great Society we shall never be out of danger—and never really alive.

(1966)

CHAPTER THIRTY-FOUR

Post-Historic Man

When we reach the present and seek to move forward, we are in the realm of myth and projection. Even those who see no alternatives to the dire prospects that the present seems to offer are possibly loading their "objective" observations with their unconscious wishes and drives, by treating transient social conventions as if they were ingrained natural necessities. For many alternatives do in fact exist; and the very act of assuming that one particular possibility will prevail also implies that the knowledge such observers command is adequate to interpret the situation. This attitude, for all its ostentatious objectivity, is naïve: it fails to allow for the latent forces of life and for the surprises that characterize all emergent processes—forgetting, too, that one of the functions of intelligence is to take account of the dangers that come from trusting solely to the intelligence. Entropy can be predicted, but not creative processes and emergents.

The possible line of development I shall now attempt speculatively to follow rests on the supposition that our civilization will continue along anti-organic, anti-historic lines ever more exclusively: that it will give increasing emphasis to the practices originally brought in by capitalism, machine technics, the physical sciences, bureaucratic administration, and totalitarian government. These in turn will unite to form a more complete and watertight system, governed by a deliberately depersonalized intelligence. With this, of course, would go a corresponding neglect or suppression of older human traits and institutions, associated with the earlier transformations of man. Under these conditions all human purposes would be swallowed up in a mechanical process immune to any human desire that diverged from it. With that a new creature, post-historic man, would come into existence.

The epithet, "post-historic man," was first coined by Roderick Seidenberg, in his perspicuous book published under that title. His thesis, reduced to its barest outline, is that the instinctual life of man, dominant all through man's long animal past, has been losing its grip in the course of history, as his conscious intelligence has gained firmer control over one activity after another. In achieving that control, man has transferred authority from the organism itself to the process that intelligence analyzes and serves, that is, the causal process, in which human actors are given the same status as nonhuman agents. By detachment from the instinctual, the purposeful, and the organic and by attachment to the causal and the mechanical, the intelligence has gained firmer control over one activity after another: it now steadily pushes from the realm of the "physical" activities to those that are biological and social; and that part of man's nature which does not willingly submit to intelligence will in time be subverted or extirpated.

During the present era, on this assumption, man's nature has begun to undergo a decisive final change. With the invention of the scientific method and the depersonalized procedures of modern technics, cold intelligence, which has succeeded as never before in commanding the energies of nature, already largely dominates every human activity. To survive in this world, man himself must adapt himself completely to the machine. Nonadaptable types, like the artist and the poet, the saint and the peasant, will either be made over or be eliminated by social selection. All the creativities associated with Old World religion and culture will disappear. To become more human, to explore further into the depth of man's nature, to pursue the divine, are no longer proper goals for machine-made man.

Let us follow this hypothesis through. With intelligence uppermost, thanks to the methods of science, man would apply to all living organisms, above all to himself, the same canons he has applied to the physical world. In the pursuit of economy and power, he would create a society that would have no other attributes than those which could be incorporated in a machine. The machine in fact is precisely that part of the organism which can be projected and controlled by intelligence alone. In establishing its fixed organization and predictable behavior, intelligence will produce a society similar to that of certain insect societies, which have remained stable for sixty millions years: for once intelligence has reached a final form, it does not permit any deviation from its perfected solution.

At this point, it is not possible to distinguish between the automatism of instinct and that of intelligence: neither is open to change, and in the end intelligence, too, will become unconscious for lack of opposition and alternatives. If intelligence dictates that there is only one right response to a given situation, only one correct answer to a question, any departure, indeed, any hesitation or uncertainty, must be regarded as a failure of the mechanism or a perversity of the agent. "The party line" must be obeyed; and once scientific intelligence is supreme, even the party line will not change. In the end life, with its almost infinite potentialities, will be frozen into a single mold cast by intelligence alone.

Post-historic man has long been familiar to the modern imagination. In a series of scientific romances, picturing possible future worlds, Jules Verne and his successor, H. G. Wells, portrayed the attributes of a society created and operated by such a mechanically overwrought creature. In one of his later works, 'The Shape of Things to Come' (1933), Wells expressed something akin to worship for that race of flying technocrats who would produce order out of the chaos left by a final atomic war. One might say, indeed, that in the whole lopsided theory of mechanical progress as conceived by its leading exponents in the nineteenth century, post-historic man was the goal to which their most favored institutional improvements tended. In their notion that mechanical inventions were both the main agents of progress and the ultimate reward—a notion that dates back to Francis Bacon but hardly earlier—they also suggested that the nonmechanical improvements introduced by the arts and humanities belonged only to the childhood of the race.

Post-historic man's existence, on his own premises, will be focused on the external world and its incessant manipulation: both man's aboriginal propensities and his historic self will be finally eliminated, as "unthinkable." In more than one passage, H. G. Wells, himself, a sensitive and sensual, "all-too-human" man, by profession one of the ancient sect of seers and dreamers, speaks impatiently of any kind of introversion or subjectivity, disparaging the very gifts of emotion, feeling, and fantasy that turned him to literature. The command of natural energies, and the command of human life through the possession of these energies, is the theme of post-historic man. That cerebral direction is only a specialized expression of man's essential autonomy, and is itself the servant of some larger purpose than its own expansion, does not occur to him. Otherwise Wells and his latter-day disciples would have to put the old Roman question: *Quis custodiet ipsos custodes?* Who is to control the controller? Lacking an answer, post-historic man turns out to have no other conception of life than the extensive display of the powers of "natural magic": instantaneous communication over great distances, swift movement through space, pushbutton commands that produce automatic responses: finally, as the supreme achievement, the reduction of organic capacities and appetites in their infinitely varied manifestations to their more uniform mechanical equivalents.

What indeed is the climactic dream that haunts all the projectors of post-historic man? There is no doubt of the answer: it is that of reviving the obsolete New World motif of terrestrial exploration by creating projectiles for exploring outer space. From Jules Verne's 'Trip to the Moon,' through Wells's picture of the Martian invasion of our planet, and from these early sketches to the voluminous outpourings of science fiction, that dream is the dominating one. Even the fantasies of C. S. Lewis, supposedly humanistic or even religious in their bias, picture life as a state of war between planetary creatures who have expanded their territory astronomically but not changed their minds, except in the direction of making them more implacably intelligent.

Coming from fantasy to actual projects now under way, we find scientific ideation and technical skill of no mean order at the mercy of an infantile scheme of life, seeking extravagant supermechanisms of escape from the problems that mature men and a mature society must face. Early escapist dreams of distant exploration and colonization had at least the saving grace of enabling the adventurers to open up realms actually favorable to life. The wealth of Cathay that Marco Polo reported was no idle dream, and the undiscovered fountain of youth promised less than the real wonders that the Americas disclosed. But no one can pretend, without falsifying every fact, that existence on a space satellite or on the barren face of the moon would bear any resemblance to human life. Those who suppose that there is no meaning to living, except in continued movement through space, themselves reveal the limits of depersonalized intelligence. They show that a highly complicated technique may be the product of what is, humanly speaking, an all-too-simple mind, capable of dealing only by pointer readings with encapsulated realities, divorced from the organic complexities of life.

In our time, these post-historic fantasies, erupting out of the unconscious, have ceased to be merely prophetic: they have already taken command of mechanization and have been channeled into the most destructive and the most pitifully obsolete of human institutions, war. Meanwhile, in response to the existential nihilism of post-historic man, war itself has been transformed from a limited order of destruction and violence, directed toward limited ends, into systematic and unrestricted extermination: in other words, genocide. Is it an accident indeed that all the triumphs that point to the emergence of post-historic man are triumphs of death? The will to deny the activities of life, above all, to deny the possibility of its development, dominates this ideology; so that collective genocide or suicide is the goal of this effort: unformulated and implicit, yet not always concealed. The post-historic process began innocently by eliminating fallible human impulses from science: it will end by eliminating human nature itself from the whole world of reality. In post-historic culture life itself is reduced to predictable, mechanically conditioned and controlled motion, with every incalculable—that is, every creative—element removed.

Now the supreme achievement of mathematical and physical science in our time was, without doubt, the succession of discoveries that led to the modern conception of the atom and the equation that identified mass and energy: only mind and method of the highest order could have unlocked these cosmic secrets. But to what end was this consummate feat of the intelligence directed? What in fact prompted the final decision that enabled man to start the process of atomic fission? We all know the answer too well: its object was the production of an instrument of large-scale destruction and extermination.

In the course of a decade's wholesale development of this new source of energy, the governments of Soviet Russia and the United States have now produced enough atomic and thermonuclear weapons to make it possible, even on the most conservative estimate, to wipe out all life on this planet.

While these lethal powers were being multiplied, with all the resources available, the amount of thought spent on creating the moral and political agents that would be capable of directing such energies to a truly human destination was, by comparison, of pinheaded dimensions.

Thus detached and depersonalized scientific intelligence, which boasted its nonconcern with morals or politics or personal responsibility, embarked on a course that must ultimately undermine even its own limited existence. The scientists, who were trained to regard systematic investigation as an absolute, ignored repeated warnings from vigilant observers like Jacob Burckhardt and Henry Adams, warnings that anticipated or accompanied the earliest experiments with radioactive elements. And today, in spite of the threat of universal annihilation that exists, through the possible use of nuclear explosives in war, the nations of the world are hastily embarking on the widest possible exploitation of nuclear energy for peacetime uses—though no practical means for the disposal of nuclear waste products has yet been found, and though the handful of experimental plants that already exist have produced serious pollution. These compulsive acts resolutely ignore the fact that errors committed through miscalculation or ignorance in the overproduction of atomic radiation cannot be corrected. We may well say of post-historic man, driving himself and all about him to destruction, what Captain Ahab says to himself, in a sudden moment of illumination, in Melville's prophetic 'Moby-Dick': "All my means are sane: my motives and object mad."

For in the end, there is little doubt, post-historic man's animus against life is self-limiting. As a result of his own deep-seated maladaptation, arising possibly out of his conscious self-devaluation and the unconscious self-hatred it begets, he is likely to cut short his own career almost before it has begun. That matter I shall consider more fully, after examining further the present manifestations of his philosophy and practice.

To understand how close post-historic man already is, one must realize that he only carries to their logical extremes tendencies already well enthroned in New World culture. In his attitude toward nature, the sense of oneness and affectionate harmony, which induced primitive man to bestow his own vitality on sticks and stones, disappears: nature becomes so much dead material, to be broken down, resynthesized, and replaced by a machine-made equivalent. So, too, with the human personality: one part of it, the rational intelligence, is inflated to superhuman dimensions: every other part is deflated or displaced.

What remains of life for man is the residue that is necessary to keep intelligence, and therewith the machine, in operation. True: ambitious inventions of synthetic substitutes for life sometimes rest on illusions and encounter defeats, when applied even to the simpler phenomena of life. For all science's ability to analyze the chemical components of sea water, laboratory attempts to reproduce it have not yet created a medium in which marine creatures can survive. Despite such setbacks, post-historic man not merely expects to build up complicated protein molecules but eventually to reproduce the phenomena of life within a test tube. Meanwhile, his success in fabricating artificial fibres has led him to predict similar triumphs in converting nonorganic materials into foods. If he succeeds here, he will doubtless ratify that success by breeding a new race that will enjoy such pabulum, or rather will not even know that eating food was once an enjoyment. In time, the human beings necessary to run post-historic culture will be provided at birth with built-in responses, subject solely to external controls: a more economic alternative to the wasteful methods now applied by the political commissar and the commercial advertiser. Under post-historic incentives, frontal lobotomy may be as widely performed on children, to ensure docility and discourage autonomy, as tonsillectomy now is.

In this shift to a world directed solely by intelligence for the exploitation of power, all of post-historic man's efforts tend toward uniformity. In contrast to the organic diversities, produced originally in nature and multiplied by a large part of man's historic efforts, the environment as a whole becomes as uniform and as undeviating as a concrete superhighway, in order to subserve the uniform functioning of a uniform mass of human units. Even today, the faster one moves, the more uniform is the environment that mechanically accompanies movement and the less difference does one meet when one reaches one's destination: so that change for the sake of change, and swiftness for the sake of swiftness, create the highest degree of monotony.

If the goal is uniformity there is no aspect of nature or man that may not be assaulted. Why should post-historic man seek to preserve any of the richness of environmental individuality that still exists on earth and in turn widens the range of human choice: the grasslands, the fenlands, the woodlands, the parklands, the vinelands, desert and mountain, waterfall and lake? Why should he not, on sound post-historic grounds, grind down the mountains, either to obtain granite for uranium, and so provide a limitless supply of energy, or just for the sheer pleasure of bulldozing and grinding, till the whole round earth becomes planed down to one level platform? Why should he not, on the same terms, create a single climate, uniform from the pole to the equator, without either diurnal changes or changes of seasons: so that man's days should be free from such disturbing stimuli? If post-historic man cannot create a mechanical substitute for trees, let him reduce them to a few standardized, marketable varieties, as we have already reduced to a few dozen samples the varieties of pear tree—well over nine hundred according to U. P. Hedrick—that were cultivated in the United States only a century ago.

For his own security, as well as to ensure the proper worship of his god, the machine, post-historic man must remove any memory of things that are wild and untamable, pied and dappled, unique and precious: mountains one might be tempted to climb, deserts where one might seek solitude and inner peace, jungles whose living creatures would remind some sur-viving, unaltered human explorer of nature's original prodigality in creating a grand diversity of habitats and habits of life out of the primeval rock and protoplasm with which she began.

Already, in the great metropolises and spreading conurbations of the Western world, the foundations of the post-historic environment have been laid down: the life of an automatic-elevator operator in a great office build-ing is almost as blank and empty as life as a whole will become once post-historic culture effectually removes every memory of a richer past. At the present rate of urbanization, the destruction of all natural living spaces, or rather their transformation into low-grade urban tissue, will scarcely require a century before any alternatives to post-historic life will cease to exist. If the goal of human history is a uniform type of man, reproducing at a uni-form rate, in a uniform environment, kept at constant temperature, pres-sure, and humidity, living a uniformly lifeless existence, with his uniform physical needs satisfied by uniform goods, all inner waywardness brought into conformity by hypnotics and sedatives, or by surgical extirpations, a creature under constant mechanical pressure from incubator to incinerator, most of the problems of human development would disappear. Only one problem would remain: Why should anyone, even a computer, bother to keep this kind of creature alive?

The uniform, which was itself, like drill, the product of the oldest sys-tem of severe regimentation, that of the army, is fast becoming the invisible costume of an entire society. In the interest of uniformity, every manner of choice is eliminated, even down to the trivial detail of deciding whether one would like a thin or a thick slice of bread. Once the collective decision is made, no individual departure from it, no modification on the basis of per-sonal preference or personal judgment, becomes possible. With the further development of post-historic man, this principle of uniformity must apply to thoughts as well as to things. It is cheaper and more efficient to repress human individuality than to introduce the incalculable factors of life into a mechanical collective. One of the self-limiting facts, indeed, about the de-velopment of post-historic culture is that on its own principles it must create slot-machine minds, which admit only the prescribed coin before they eject the uniform, collectively approved product. In the long run, as certain great corporate enterprises already begin to suspect, such uniform organizations no longer create the kind of mind capable of directing them, since cowed con-formists and routineers are unable to make the sort of creative decision that originally built the organization up.

Post-historic man reduces all specifically human activity to a form of work: a transformation of energy, or an intellectual process that furthers the transformation of energy. But under this dispensation, the reward of work is not in the process but the product: instead of elaborating the proc-ess of work for the sake of animating it more fully with the human person-ality in ways that are immediately rewarding by their very exercise, machine

technics, in agreement with the whole post-historic ideology, seeks to eliminate the human element. In the case of all servile and repulsive work this
is an important human gain: the transfer of such work to automatons is, as
Aristotle long ago observed, the main condition for doing away with slavery
and giving all men the leisure citizens need for their civic duties and for
the direct cultivation of their personal lives.

But post-historic culture goes further: it tends to make all activities
automatic, whether they are sterile and servile or creative and liberal. Even
play or sport, indeed, must be regularized, and brought under the principle
of least effort. Instead of considering work a valuable means of molding a
more highly individualized personality, post-historic man seeks rather to
depersonalize the worker, conditioning and adjusting him so as to fit into
the impersonal processes of production and administration. Totalitarian
conformity springs from the machine, in fact, in every department it
touches: the standardized agent exacts a standardized response. This fact
is not confined to officially totalitarian states.

In the post-historic scheme, then, man becomes a machine, reduced as
far as possible to a bundle of reflexes: rebuilt at the educational factory
to conform to the needs of other machines. For this purpose, his original
animal nature, to say nothing of the propensities that made him more definitely human, must be made over. All his past achievements and memories,
all his urges and hopes, all his anxieties and ideals, stand in the way of this
transformation. Only those, therefore, who have been successful in eliminating their more human attributes are candidates for the highest offices
in post-historic society: those of the Conditioners and Controllers.

Sympathy and empathy, the ability to participate with imagination and
love in the lives of other men, have no place in the post-historic methodology; for post-historic culture demands that all men should be treated as
things. Humanly speaking, post-historic man is a defective, if not an active
delinquent, in the end a potential monster. The pathological nature of his
defect has been concealed by his high intelligence quotient. Disguised in
comonplace ready-made clothes, seeming to express equally commonplace,
matter-of-fact opinions, these monsters are already at work in present-day
society. Their characteristic activities—such as their preparations for
"ABC" warfare—are as irrational as their actions are compulsive and
automatic. The fact that the moral insanity if not the practical futility of
these preparations has not produced a general human recoil is a sign of how
far the development of post-historic society has already gone.

None of the characteristic activities of post-historic man, except perhaps
the exercise of scientific intelligence, has to do with the service of life
or the culture of what is veritably human. Post-historic man has already,
theoretically, left the human behind him. What survives of that birthright
is an embarrassment, which his growing control over the processes of reproduction will in time eliminate, as he now eliminates undesirable qualities
from pigs or cattle. One way or another, by psychological conditioning and

biological breeding, or by resorting to unrestrained collective exterminations, he will efface what is left of humanity.

Already, these paranoid dreams command the lives of millions of human
beings and actively threaten their future. In the current plans for mass genocide, in a "war" that would inaugurate and close the post-historic period,
man's very humanity is the object of attack. By proposing to treat the
"enemy" as if they were vermin, so many million rats or bedbugs, post-
historic man would debase both the violator and the victim before bringing
about their common annihilation.

Modern man has already depersonalized himself so effectively that he
is no longer man enough to stand up to his machines. A primitive man, in
alliance with magical powers, has confidence in his ability to control natural
forces and bring them to heel. Post-historic man, backed by all the mighty
resources of science, has so little confidence that he consents in advance to
his own replacement, to his own extinction, if the price of survival is to stop
the machinery or even lessen the amount of power fed into it. By treating
scientific knowledge and technical inventions as absolutes, he has turned
physical power into human impotence: he had rather commit universal
suicide by accelerating the process of scientific discovery than preserve the
human race by even temporarily slowing them down.

Never before was man so free from nature's restrictions; but never before was he more the victim of his own failure to develop, in any fullness,
his own specifically human traits: in some degree, as I have already suggested, he has lost the secret of how to make himself human. The extreme
state of post-historic rationalism will, we may confidently expect, carry to a
further degree the paradox already visible: not merely that the more automatic the means of living become the less life itself will be under human
control, but the more rationalized become the processes of production, the
more irrational will finally become the end product, man himself.

In short, power and order, pushed to their final limit, lead to their self-
destructive inversion: disorganization, violence, mental aberration, subjective chaos. This tendency is already expressed in America through the motion picture, the television screen, and children's comic books. These forms
of amusement are all increasingly committed to enactments of cold-blooded
brutality and physical violence: pedagogical preparations for the practical
use of homicide and genocide, just as Robinson Crusoe was a preparation
for surviving, barehanded, in a strange uninhabited land. Such evil fantasies
forecast grim realities that are already all too close at hand.

Yet this is where another factor, unforeseen by the utopians, comes in:
the compensating function of mischievous destruction. Just because man is
born with the potentialities of being fully human, he must sooner or later
revolt against the post-historic plan of life. If man must take his orders from
the machine, he still has one form of resistance left. Since he cannot rein-
sert himself, as a fully autonomous being, into the mechanical process, he

may become the sand in the works: if necessary, he will use the machine to destroy the society that has produced it. That prophecy in Dostoevsky's 'Letters from the Underworld'—repeated independently by Jakob Burckhardt—is already on the brink of fulfillment. The sniveling hero of those underworld letters, rejecting the order and comfort that the nineteenth century boasted, remembers that one form of freedom is left: that of the criminal, if not the citizen. Dostoevsky predicted the coming of a new character (oddly like Hitler) who will survey all this putative progress, and decide to "kick it to smithereens."

If no creative outlet is possible, man is so constituted that he will take pleasure in negative creation: that is, destruction. He will resume the human initiative by utilizing violence, committing acts of sadism, exulting in his power to maim and mutilate, finally to exterminate. Was it not in the country most disciplined by militarism, absolutism, and physical science that systematic torture in the form of "scientific experiments" was undertaken? Did not Germany produce the nauseating horrors of the extermination camps? In the combination of cold scientific rationalism with criminal irrationalism the fatal poison produced its equally fatal antidote.

The further we push along the post-historic path, the more ironic confirmations we have of the stupidity and villainy of its human proposals. Already the effect of two centuries of invention and mechanical organization is to create organizations that work automatically with a minimum amount of active human intervention. Instead of the indispensable leader as a driving force, as in the original ordering of civilization, this automatic system works best with anonymous people, without singular merit, who are in fact interchangeable and removable parts: technicians and bureaucrats, experts in their own narrow departments, but incompetent muddlers in the arts of life, which demand the very aptitudes they have skillfully suppressed. With the further development of cybernetic controllers, to make decisions on matters beyond the range of human patience or conscious human calculation, because of their complication or the astronomical range of numbers involved, post-historic man is on the verge of displacing the only organ of the human anatomy he fully values: the frontal lobe of the brain.

In creating the thinking machine, man has made the last step in submission to mechanization; and his final abdication before this product of his own ingenuity has given him a new object of worship: a cybernetic god. This new religion, it is true, demands an act of faith even greater than in axial man's God: the faith that this mechanical demiurge, whose calculations cannot be humanly checked, will give only the correct answers.

Let us generalize this result and see it clearly for what it is. By the perfection of the automaton man will become completely alienated from his world and reduced to nullity—the kingdom and the power and the glory now belong to the machine. Instead of participating in a meaningful intercourse with nature to get his daily bread, he has condemned himself to a life of effortless ease, provided he will content himself solely with the products and the substitutes offered by the machine. Or rather, the ease would be effortless if it did not impose the duty of consuming only the goods that the machine now insistently offers him, no matter how surfeited he may be. The incentive to think, the incentive to feel and act, in fact the incentive to live, will soon disappear.

Already, in America, man has begun to lose the use of his legs, as a result of overdependence upon the motor car. Presently, only a visceral existence, centered around the stomach and the genitals will be left, though there is reason to think that the principle of least effort will also be applied to this department. Are not American mothers actually encouraged by many physicians to make no attempt to nurse their newborn infants? From a post-historic point of view, a "formula" is far more satisfactory than the psychosomatic experience of maternal tenderness provided by breast feeding. Will not science also provide an effortless mechanical orgasm, thus doing away with the uncertainties of human affection and the need for bodily contact: a necessary aid to artificial insemination? The contempt for organic processes, the willful effort to replace them, at a price, with mechanical equivalents, have only begun to show their hand.

To understand the final goal of the post-historic system, let us examine the best existing specimen of the new incarnation: not a nightmare, like a creature from '1984,' but a visible reality. Consider an aviator whose vocation is to pilot a plane at supersonic speeds. Here is the new mechanical man, fully accoutered, completely insulated, with his electrically heated suit, his oxygen helmet, his parachute seat that can be catapulted into the stratosphere. Equipped for duty, he is a monstrous scaly animal, more like a magnified ant than a primate: certainly not a naked god. While hurtling through the lonely reaches of the sky, the life of this pilot is purely a function of mass and motion: for all his steely courage, his existence is narrowed down to a pinpoint of sentience by the necessity of co-ordinating his reactions with the whole physical mechanism upon which his survival depends. Loss of consciousness, asphyxiation, freezing, blast, all threaten him more perilously than saber-toothed tigers and hairy mammoths threatened his paleolithic ancestors. Apart from this shuttered moment-to-moment existence, dependent on retaining by artificial means a sufficient modicum of his faculties to control the machine, his working life has no other dimension.

Can one call this life? No: it is a mechanically engineered coma. This is but a specimen, small but precise, of the total change in human behavior that the successful transformation into post-historic man would bring about. The next step in forming post-historic man is to mold all his other activities to the same pattern. We already provide mechanical daydreams and mechanical thoughts, via radio and television, so ubiquitous as to be almost unevadable. We have only to put the still unfettered portions of life under similar control.

Post-historic man's starvation of life would reach its culminating point in interplanetary travel by rocket ship, or in the erection and utilization of a satellite space station. Characteristically, the purpose of such an expedition would be to collect further data about the physical universe or—and this is what now sanctions the costly research devoted to the subject—it would establish a vantage point from which to work violence upon a possible human enemy: superhuman powers for subhuman purposes. (What man truly needs is enough insight into his nature to explain why he thinks such data important, at a moment when his own immaturity and pathological unbalance need his concentrated attention.) Under such conditions, life would again narrow down to the physiological functions of breathing, eating, and excretion: even these functions would be performed on a space ship under conditions that would minimize their efficacy. Yet this is the final goal of post-historic man: the farthest reach of anything that could be called desire, the justification of his every sacrifice. His end is to turn himself into an artificial homunculus in a self-propelling capsule, traveling at maximum speed, and depressing to the point of extinction his natural gifts, above all, eliminating any spontaneous trace of spirit.

The triumph of post-historic man would, one may confidently say, do away with any serious reason for remaining alive. Only those who had lost their minds already could contemplate, without horror, such mindless experience: only those who had forfeited the attributes of life could contemplate, without despair, such a lifeless existence. By comparison, the Egyptian cult of the dead was overflowing with vitality: from a mummy in his tomb one can still gather more of the attributes of a full human being than from a spaceman.

Already, in his ideal projects for flight, as in his subhuman plans for war, post-historic man has lost hold on every living reality: he is the self-appointed victim of inner compulsions leading to death. Even if he should momentarily succeed in his self-transformation, his success would bring on the last act in the human tragedy. For that which is post-historic is also post-human.

(1956)

CHAPTER THIRTY-FIVE

Revolt of the Demons

As the nineteenth century drew to an end, most people believed that the demons that had plagued mankind all through history were at last disposed of. If they were not mere phantoms, they were at least safely locked up and so would never trouble man again, though they might still on occasion torment individuals. Disease would be wiped out through inoculation, pain would be banished by anesthesia, poverty would be overcome by machine-made plenitude, and no personal problems would exist that the rational mind, aided only by the scientific method, could not handle. Herodotus boasted of the ancient Greeks that they were emancipated from silly nonsense; that is, from belief in astrology, magic, transmigration, divine kings, and perverse, mischief-making gods. But this claim seemed even more applicable to the modern mind. Nor was it entirely an illusion; the thin, icy crust of rational behavior actually grew thicker in many areas and concealed the turbid black water beneath. Yet there were cracks in the crust even so, and before our century had well begun, the demons broke out again, precisely as Dostoevski had predicted in his 'Letters from the Underworld.'

What has happened to mankind this last half century is inexplicable in terms of either the sanguine ideology of the eighteenth-century Enlightenment or the nineteenth-century doctrine of Progress, the main props of this hope. We should still perhaps lack sufficient clues to the condition of man today had it not been for the daring discoveries made during the last decade of the nineteenth century, mainly by a middle-aged Viennese doctor named Sigmund Freud. His 'The Interpretation of Dreams,' published in 1899, exposed the devious mechanisms of human irrationality, and though it took eight years to sell the six hundred copies of the first edition, the book has had an impact on the modern mind similar to that of Galileo's 'Dialogues' and Darwin's 'The Origin of Species.' From our present vantage point, it is easy to see that, symbolically, this book marked a turning point in history.

It took a little time to realize what was happening to our innocent hopes of automatic perfection, but it is obvious that nothing has been quite the same ever since. Freud did not intentionally release the demons that now claim dominion over us; his great distinction was that he made them visible, and in a sense, by sheer familiarity, made them respectable. For he alone, by his fresh interpretation of dreams, had found a passage to the catacombs where the demons lurked.

Though Freud was a happily married man, with a large, well-beloved family, he had been going through a severe neurosis, marked by a quasi-intellectual but deeply emotional attachment to another physician, Wilhelm Fliess. It was in the analysis of his own dreams during this ecstatic but tormenting period that Freud came face to face with a long-unvisited territory of the mind. With an audacity born perhaps of desperation, he risked his reputation as a scientist to expose the irrational elements that—as Plato long ago pointed out in his parable of the black and white horses—have always been ready to invade the human psyche. These forces are so ambivalent in their manifestations that their victims in the past were regarded with awe, as the favored possessors of higher powers, or thrown into cells, as if they were criminals. Because Freud dared so greatly, twentieth-century man has an insight into the worst disorders of human behavior such as only great poets or religious teachers like Shakespeare and St. Augustine ever had before.

Freud's exploration of the hidden sources of human behavior, with the aid of the long-discredited key he had found in dreams, encountered severe disapproval from the medical fraternity for the next generation. He could hardly have succeeded in making his ideas known, still less in getting them accepted, if he had not had the help of a closely knit band of disciples, all grounded in medical science but unusually open-minded about his astonishing discoveries, partly because they—Ferenczi, Rank, Jung—were in the throes of their own psychoneuroses. Through their own experience they had come, like Freud, to suspect that neurotic difficulties were a normal phenomenon, an acute manifestation of "the psychopathology of everyday life," whose cure lay in bringing the repressed portions of the psyche into the light and air. That proved only a partly effective therapy, but it came as both a revelation and a promise of blessed relief.

Of all these followers, the one whose figure now stands out most sharply, as nearest to Freud in stature and total achievement, is Carl Gustav Jung. Jung's recent book, 'Memories, Dreams, Reflections,' (Pantheon), dictated and written mainly at the very end of his life, rounds out the picture, of the whole development that began with Freud's classic interpretation of dreams. Jung, junior to Freud by nineteen years, was predisposed by his own unruly fantasies to make the most of Freud's new approach to mental disturbances, but perhaps his greatest contributions, if we can trust his own account, came after he had broken with his Viennese master and plunged into the severe neurosis that marked his own middle life just as Freud's had been marked.

"What would we give for such an autobiography of Shakespeare?" Carlyle wrote in 1828, two decades after the word "autobiography" had entered the English language. Jung's work, with its copious disclosures of his inner life, is perhaps as near as one can get to such a literary confession—profuse in subjective materials, dreams, premonitions, projections, but relatively bare of data about more commonplace external events. For all that, his narrative tells us much about his boyhood and invites us into the lonely cell of his old age, even if it barely touches—in an account of his travels and his dealings with his patients—upon the busy, productive, yet secretly devastating years that lay between. The very title of the book, 'Memories, Dreams, Reflections,' mirrors its subjective emphasis, for a good many of the memories are concerned with dreams, often admonitory or prophetic ones, whose description and interpretation became his life work. Yet the travel letters that Jung wrote to his wife, Emma, during his famous trip to America in the company of Freud to attend the conference President Stanley Hall, of Clark University, had arranged, show that he had a sharp eye and a healthy appetite for the outer world. As Jung grew older, however, it would seem, his inner world enveloped him to such an extent that the most commonplace reports from that domain often engrossed him more than far more significant external events. While he accepted many social responsibilities and duties—treatment of patients, participation in psychoanalytic conferences—it was the hidden domain of his life that he valued, and this is what, in his final backward glance, he chose mainly to expose.

Twice during the past year I have slowly gone through Jung's autobiography in an attempt to get a rounded view of this teasing, many-faceted personality, and at almost every point I have found Jung's figure accompanied by the huge shadow of Freud. Each of these men was to establish a special school of psychoanalysis, dominated by the strong personality at the center, but the view of Freud's most faithful followers—that these men's characters and careers were utterly unlike, that Freud was the rigorous scientist and Jung the unreliable mystic—are belied both by the evidence of Dr. Ernest Jones's three-volume biography of Freud, published during the last decade, and by Jung's present self-revelation. Such antagonisms as existed between the two men were due as much to their likenesses as to their many residual differences.

Both these psychologists were the sons of fathers unsuccessful in worldly affairs; both grew up in comparative poverty; both were favored children; and if Jung was disturbed by the patently unhappy relations of his parents, seemingly a result of their sexual incompatibility, Freud was equally upset by the private intimacies of his parents. Both men loved the rural scene, but Freud was torn away from it at the age of three, while Jung remained a country boy at heart, at home in the forest and the barnyard, accustomed to the superstitions and smut of this environment, with its cruelty, its open sexuality, even its occasional incest and sodomy. Both physicians were trained in the rigorous, confidently determinist science of the late nineteenth century, and disciplined in objective observation and respect for the impersonal criteria of truth. Yet they were in varying degrees fascinated by dubious occult phenomena—poltergeists, ghosts, thought transference, clairvoyance, and prophecy—as well as by non-scientific systems of interpretation, like numerology (Freud) and alchemy and astrology (Jung). If these are sins, Freud was nearly as great a sinner as Jung. Though usually Freud took care to conceal his intellectual temptations and peccadilloes, he at one point considered proclaiming an open alliance between psychoanalysis and occultism.

To honor these physicians of the soul sufficiently, one must remember the intellectual atmosphere in which they worked, with its dogamtic mechanistic doctrines. One of William James's austerely scientific colleagues told him that if psychic research brought forth indisputable evidence of the existence of ghosts and an afterlife, he would suppress that truth in the interests of science. Similarly, orthodox medicine in the eighteen-forties had flatly rejected as fraudulent John Elliotson's demonstrations of painless surgery under hypnotism. The great contributions psychoanalysis has made to the understanding of human behavior could have been achieved only by such recklessly open-minded—indeed, often overcredulous—men as were Freud and Jung. Both of them had the courage to realize, as in Freud's rephrasing of his favorite Shakespearean quotation—borrowed from his master, the psychiatrist Charcot—that there were more things in heaven and on earth than were dreamed of in current scientific philosophy or were discoverable by its one-sidedly "objective" methods. The two men's readiness to deal with psychic leftovers, seemingly the rubbish and garbage of conscious life, was responsible for their most original contributions to psychology. (Many of our contemporaries, following in some measure Jung, have been tempted to regard the leavings and dribblings of the unconscious as a form of human sustenance superior to food, but that is another story.) At one in their basic understanding, Freud and Jung nevertheless developed along different lines, for Freud overvalued the ego, Jung the unconscious. It turns out that Jung was a sufficiently open-minded and contradictory personality to part company even with himself at the end of his autobiography.

Both men had minds and characters of extraordinary complexity; both used the austere protective covering of science to enter realms too private and subjective to be handled by the ordinary methods of science; both clung to their authority as physicians to escape the odium of seeming a new kind of medicine man, performing lengthy incantations and magic ceremonies to exorcise demons and to lift curses. Both anticipated—correctly, I believe—that the unconscious world they dared to explore would lead them far back to the very origins of human culture, and so both manifested, at a quite early date, an interest in archeology and prehistory. Indeed, Jung remembers that when he was a student he played with the thought of becoming a philologist in order to learn Egyptian and Babylonian, while Freud's desk was covered with an array of little statues that bore witness to his lifelong attachment to archaic images.

Goaded as he was into his exploration by his own unconscious, Freud was quite as tempted as Jung to treat occultism as a co-ordinate branch of "metapsychology." But he anchored himself for safety in the matter-of-fact science of the nineteenth century. In 1921, in discussing telepathy, he approvingly declared, "Analysts are fundamentally incorrigible mechanists and materialists." This was perhaps true of their conscious intentions but false as related to their unconscious preoccupations. Freud's touchiness over Havelock Ellis's calling him an artist rather than a scientist reveals the weak spot his early faith in mechanism made him wish to cover, for his conscious philosophy had not been modified by his own new discoveries, which should have made the mechanistic universe of his youth as old-fashioned to him and his followers as it is to the disciples of Rutherford, Planck, and Bohr. Jung came later, with the better grounding in philosophy and history, if not in languages, that a student in Basel, the home of the great historian Jakob Burckhardt, could get, so he moved with greater freedom over the whole field of human culture. Jung's skepticism, unlike Freud's, extended even to the exact sciences, though it did not prevent him from entertaining the truths of religion, which came by quite another route.

Curiously, even in the matter of the dominant dogma of Freudian analysis—the central role played by sex from infancy on—these men were closer together than is usually realized. True, Jung broke with Freud over this very point by strongly denying the Master's insistence that sexual repression was the sole source of neurotic symptoms (a belief Freud stubbornly equated with psychoanalysis itself), for he was far more ready than Freud to admit that unbearable burdens and misfortunes having nothing to do with sex might be responsible for many mental disorders. Instead of holding, as Freud so long did, that the disclosure of an infantile traumatic experience was the only means of cauterizing the festering neurotic wound, as a physician Jung was ready to enlist the troubled patient's philosophy or religion to bring about the cure. "We need a different language for every patient," he observes in his chapter on his psychiatric activities. "In one analysis I can be heard talking the Adlerian dialect, in another the Freudian. . . . What matters most to me is that the patient should reach his own view of things. Under my treatment a pagan becomes a pagan and a Christian a Christian, a Jew a Jew, according to what his destiny prescribes for him."

In method, Freud would allow no departure from *the* psychoanalytic procedure of seeking with limitless patience for the infantile sexual basis of a neurosis. In the act of giving sex its rightful place in the human economy, he created a dogmatic theology of sex and sought to excommunicate as heretics those who did not accept every item of his doctrine. (This notion fostered the almost comic annunciation, by Dr. Wilhelm Reich, of the orgasm as the sole vehicle of human salvation.) Such a curious departure from the ways of science inevitably calls attention to Freud's own sexual repressions, as well as to the compulsive substitute gratification—his smoking twenty cigars a day—that possibly caused and certainly aggravated the cancer of the jaw that poisoned his last sixteen years.

If the facts were not extremely painful, the contrast here between the two great analysts would be amusing. For Jung was visited by overpowering sexual impulses whose open expression shook his whole life to the roots, and these impulses were visible, just as Freud held, in his earliest childhood reactions. When he was a child of four, Jung discloses, he had a dream—a singularly Freudian dream—dominated by a towering phallus, twelve to fifteen feet high and two feet thick, with a hairless head and a single eye at the top. This vision was followed by a confrontation with evil, in which he dreamed that God defecated upon his own altar. In the dream, Jung says, the gigantic phallus did not move, but he had a feeling that at any moment it might crawl off the throne like a huge worm and move toward him. And he heard his mother's voice cry, "That is the man-eater!"

Jung relates this dream, as he does all his later dreams, with graphic exactitude and bland, if not almost blind, naïveté, but he confesses that he had never communicated it to anyone until he was in his sixties. This would seem a significant repression, though the fact that his admission came only in old age leaves doubt as to when, in his increasingly dream-ridden world, this particular image actually appeared to him. Was it a projection or an elaboration of maturity, protectively relegated to infancy? "When I die," Jung smilingly told a friend of mine, "probably no one will realize that the old man in the coffin was once a great lover." Jung's sexuality, in short, was no less overwhelming than Freud's, but it seems, since he fully enacted it, to have been far less obsessional, while Freud, apart from his fond marital relations, apparently sublimated his ambivalent sexual impulses by making them both the center of his therapeutic method and the dominant theme of his writing. In the final phase of Freud's life, the Eros theme was supplemented by the death theme, the power of Thanatos (both Eros and Thanatos conceived of as deities), yet in almost his last words on the subject he held forth the hope that a resurrection of Eros might save the world from the forces of destruction.

Unlike Jung, Freud refused to commit his intimate life to paper, save for a few details, and he rejected and disparaged the efforts of anyone else to write about it. For all his immense physical courage in facing pain, he quailed at such an exposure. As far as he could, he destroyed the data he had set down for an account of his inner life, and we would lack the most significant clue to this development had it not been for the precautions taken by Dr. Fliess's wife to preserve Freud's letters to him. Freud's words on the subject demand to be quoted: "Whoever undertakes to write a biography binds himself to lying, to concealment, to flummery, and even to hiding his own lack of understanding, since biographical material is not to be had, and if it were it could not be used. Truth is not accessible; mankind does not deserve it, and wasn't Prince Hamlet right when he asked who would escape a whipping if he had his deserts?"

These are strange words to come from the father of psychoanalysis, for the method he fabricated is nothing less than the art of autobiography carried to such exhaustive lengths in the interest of self-understanding that no painful event, whether relevant or seemingly irrelevant, remains unexposed. Freud's rejection of biography is, in his own vocabulary, a classic example of "over-determination." If lies and concealment are inevitable, if it is indeed impossible to obtain material, what becomes of psychoanalytic purgation? To clinch his objection, Freud insisted that even if one could get hold of material, one could not use it, for it would reveal the subject's weaknesses. Freud openly feared, in his own case (if Jung quotes him accurately), that the truth about his inner life would destroy his authority. As to this judgment, Freud was surely wrong. His struggle to get at the dismaying truth about his own psyche, as revealed by his dreams when he was under Fliess's influence, must count as one of the heroic episodes of science; it gave him authority to do unto others as he had done unto himself. But when his life was nearly lived out, he was wrong to suppress the record of it, for only he, with his sharp intellectual scalpel and marvellously deft touch, could have examined the morbid psychal organs without injuring the patient or cutting short his life. Such an act would have confirmed Freud's authority, much as Augustine's 'Confessions' add their weight to his philosophy and theology.

Jung, on the other hand, though almost equally reluctant, was persuaded by his publisher, the late Kurt Wolff, and by Dr. Jolande Jacobi, one of Jung's associates, to assist a younger colleague, Aniela Jaffé, in the preparation of a biography. And he did his part so well that the result is an invaluable document, though it is unsystematic, spotty, and far from complete, exactly as one would expect of an old man—now relapsing into dream, now flashing unexpected illuminations, sometimes cannily concealing what everyone else knows, sometimes revealing intimacies that tell far more. In 'Memories, Dreams, Reflections' Jung appears to have maintained a rigid reserve about parts of his life one would legitimately like to learn more of, though, if rumor can be credited, certain relevant passages about his sexual and marital relations have been omitted at the request of the surviving family. This omission—or deletion—is unfortunate in the case of a man whose personal experiment in open erotic relationships influenced the marriage of more than one patient who came to him for advice. One would like to know his final judgment in maturity upon his efforts to maintain a continuing bipolar relationship between two psychologically contrasting types, a Griselda and an Iseult. In this respect, Jung's confession goes no further than Freud's own minute autobiographical notations. In fact, the sum of his wisdom at one point seems to be that he can make no judgment about his own life. That is a singular confession. Did his life not bear further reflection, or did it teach him nothing?

If Freud opened the door to the dream world, it was Jung who took possession of it, to such a degree that the demons and angels, the tormentors and redeemers, of the unconscious increasingly displaced in his mind the everyday figures of existence. The territory of the unconscious had long been suspected, and even sporadically visited, as the unknown continent of America was occasionally visited before anyone identified it or sought to colonize it. Every artist and thinker realizes that more goes on within his mind than he is aware of, sometimes with astonishing results, such as the famous dream of the University of Pennsylvania archeologist H. V. Hilprecht, in which a Babylonian priest showed him how to put together in a meaningful sequence the widely separated fragments of an inscription that had baffled him. In the nineteenth century, Karl Eduard von Hartmann, in Germany, and Samuel Butler, in England, had indicated some of the scope of the unconscious processes. Even before that, the quick, probing mind of Emerson had more than once, like a divining rod, dipped sharply to point out these functionings. Emerson not only observed, in his 'Journal,' that by way of "beasts and dreams"—read "evolution" and "psychoanalysis"— man would "find out the secrets" of his own nature but elaborated on the second intuition in his essay on 'Demonology.' "Sleep," he said, "takes off the costume of circumstance, arms us with terrible freedom, so that every will rushes to a deed. A skillful man reads his dreams for his self-knowledge. . . . My dreams are not me; they are not Nature or the Not-me: they are both. They have a double consciousness, at once sub- and objective. We call the phantoms that rise the creation of our fancy, but they act like mutineers and fire on their commander; showing that every act, every thought, every cause is bipolar, and in the act is contained the counter-action."

It was in dealing with those who were the victims of unconscious repressions and unconscious psychic replacements that in the eighteen-eighties a new school of psychologists—Charcot, Janet, and Breuer—opened the way for the explorations of Freud and Jung. Nor were these intrepid investigators alone; a group of physicians—Ivan Bloch, Krafft-Ebing, Havelock Ellis—were exploring all the devious byways of sexuality, gradually closing in upon the basic expression of sex, while psychologists like William James and F. W. H. Myers were delving into a whole variety of possibly related phenomena indicating the working of an unknown psychal factor that failed to behave in terms of the known properties of mass and motion.

The common source from which, seemingly, these erratic manifestations arose came to be called the unconscious—seemingly the same source from which the conscious mind draws the memories, hints, images, ideas, anticipations, that are in time convertible into poems, dramas, philosophies, scientific theories, aesthetic monuments. Both Freud and Jung made themselves at home in the unconscious realm, but Freud put higher value on the potency of his conscious mind and he was reluctant to accept the testimony of his senses when upon one occasion Jung, in his presence, apparently became the catalytic agent of two unidentifiable explosions in a nearby bookcase; on the other hand, Jung from his youth on was quite apt to surrender to the unconscious and immersed himself in all its fantastic presentations, including such poltergeist phenomena as those explosions.

For Jung, the world of dreams became—to a degree matched only in adolescents or in neurotics—the supreme reality; nothing else fascinated him so much, nowhere else did he find such major values and such rewarding themes. For a long time, however, he concealed this attachment. Instead of openly challenging current medical practice, as Freud did, only to become resentful over the inevitable rebuffs, Jung affected an air of scientific detachment and non-involvement, though his doctoral thesis was in fact an examination of a youthful psychic "medium." But from the time he equated Freud's discoveries with his own observations of neurotics and psychotics in a mental hospital, Jung committed himself to the unconscious and treated its sane and insane manifestations as equally "normal" and equally real. He also found there "the matrix of a mythopoeic imagination that has vanished from our rational age." By that discovery he made meaningful and in some degree usable a vast treasury of seemingly confused religious and poetic intuitions other ages had accumulated—material that the nineteenth-century mind had patronizingly dismissed as unscientific, as of course it was.

Freud's concern with sexuality and Jung's with the unconscious were, in fact, complementary, and they restored to modern man two important provinces he had, at his peril, ignored. This restoration was a precious gift, but—as happens in the fairy stories—the implications of it were ambivalent and the consequences have proved unexpectedly disastrous. For it turns out that the unconscious is as full of double-talk as the Delphic oracle, and that if Socrates' commanding demon was a blessing, Hitler's was a curse. In the end, Jung himself, in his final self-revelation in his old age, after sinking more deeply into the unconscious than sanity usually permits, was forced to admit that consciousness is the transcendent gift of life.

Jung's lifelong devotion to the unconscious was prefigured in his youth in the form of a special ritual, which oddly paralleled mankind's own prehistoric expressions. He attached significance to a stone he had found and a small manikin he had carved; he hid them in a secret place in the attic, to which he made furtive visits. With the knowledge of symbolic ritual his own teachings now help to elucidate, we today can see that both the fetishes and the ceremony announced as plainly as any verbal declaration his future career. But Jung, like Freud, had another qualification for investigating the unconscious; he had an exceptional—indeed, an incredible—capacity for remembering his dreams in the minutest detail. So exact are Jung's descriptions of his earliest dreams that one is tempted to mistrust them as possibly much later inventions till one remembers Goethe's minute descriptions of his own juvenile feelings and fantasies in his 'Poetry and Truth.' (This similarity is perhaps the only plausible reason for believing the legend Jung mentions that Goethe begot an illegitimate ancestor of Jung's, though the symbolism of 'Faust, Part II' is Jung's veritable spiritual ancestor.)

After having some difficulty—again like Freud—in choosing a career, Jung settled for medicine, but at the last moment switched from internal medicine to psychiatry. Both men seem to have been prompted by their own as yet unformulated needs to move from the safely scientific domains that treated the diseases of the body to those shadowy areas where the same rigid system of classification and diagnosis was being applied to the disorders of the mind. Jung had already separated these two aspects of life in his recognition of his own two personalities; the conventional, extroverted personality who studied science, prepared for a career, got ready for marriage, and the daring private personality, who had confronted God in his fantasies and who felt that God was terrible as well as benign and could lead him into temptation as well as deliver him from evil—indeed, would offer him grace only if he dared to sin.

For Jung, dreams were more gripping than wakeful life; he often felt he was living simultaneously in two different ages and being two different persons. This feeling of living a double life persisted to the very end, even in the dwelling he built for himself at Bollingen—a tower that was by intention an ancestral home, a refuge for his family "ghosts," where he continued that dual existence. Though in the course of time this rural refuge became by various reconstructions a whole, many-chambered house, he kept it in the homely mode of the seventeenth century, and except for the matches with which he lighted his fire, it belonged in style to his forebears. Here he lived life as they had lived it, feeling that he was actually seeking answers to problems they had been unable to cope with or come to conclusions about. Jung denies that these were split personalities in the neurotic sense, but his diagnosis is not beyond challenge. As his life lengthened and his thought developed, Jung No. 2 (the Jung who was absorbed in the exploration of the unconscious) tended to suppress No. 1. As with two eyes that do not focus, one eye became virtually blind.

Jung's decision to concentrate upon No. 2 seems to have been made, though secretly, even before 1900, the year 'The Interpretation of Dreams' appeared, for he early became interested in spiritualistic phenomena. But when he was appointed assistant at the Burghölzli Mental Hospital, in Zürich, at the age of twenty-five, he was on the surface obeying No. 1. "With my work at Burghölzli," he observes, "life took on an undivided reality—all intention, consciousness, duty, responsibility. It was an entry into the monastery of the world, a submission to the vow to believe only in what was probable, average, commonplace, barren of meaning, to renounce everything strange and significant, and reduce anything extraordinary to the banal."

In rejecting the ordinary standards of common sense, Jung, like Freud, divested himself of every impediment to the exploration of the unconscious, as a cave explorer does when he leaves all his outdoor gear at the mouth of the cave and begins his dangerous crawl through its dark passages. This required not only hardihood but self-confidence, and both men possessed these qualities to an unusual degree. Both, too, stumbled on magnificent finds, for, once at home in the darkness, they discovered images and symbols far more wonderful, and possibly more ancient, than those of Altamira or Lascaux. These two explorers opened to view an inner world that had never been so fully exposed and explored before. For a while, Freud and Jung travelled through those caverns together. Even after the tensions that were always developing in Freud's circle caused Jung to go his own way (was not Freud himself the tyrannous, jealously possessive "Old Man of the horde" whom he projected into the dim human past?), their common commitment to the unconscious remained absolute. They had discovered an inner space whose richness made all outer space seem empty of meaning.

In Jung's mythology, the unconscious becomes an entirely independent realm, eternal rather than transitory, containing the residue of man's entire collective past, and in the act of receiving reports from the unconscious, by way of dream, Jung ushers us into the presence of mythological figures, for him the eternal archetypes—the nurturing Mother, the Wise Old Man, Hierosgamos (the Sacred Marriage), the Hero. Even his curious interest in alchemy was engendered by his belief that the alchemists, for all their use of chemical retorts and crucibles in seemingly materialistic experiments, were in fact manipulating and playing with the symbols of the unconscious. Unlike Freud, Jung examined the unconscious not merely for an oblique insight into his own propulsive drives and projections but for the wise guidance of his life, and it is by his illustrative examples here that he involuntarily reveals the inadequacy of such untutored guidance, with its obscure hints and archaic instructions—often as banal as those he rejected in the everyday life of the No. 1 personality. Among the prophetic revelations of his unconscious, by which Jung set great store, was an overpowering vision he had had in October of 1913—the vision of a catastrophic flood sweeping over Europe, with mighty yellow waves full of drowned bodies and the "floating rubble of civilization." This dream, uncanny in retrospect because it was soon verified by events, may be placed in the same category as Mme. Blavatsky's much earlier and even more realistic vision of the destruction of whole cities by nuclear blasts. But neither dream was more timely or more prophetic than Henry Adams's conscious, rational anticipation, in 1905, of civilization's approach to a world catastrophe within half a century, with explosions of "cosmic violence," or Patrick Geddes's prediction, in 1911, of the breaking out of a general war by 1915 unless strenuous efforts were made to prevent it. The unconscious no doubt played its part in these latter prophecies, too, yet in no way were the reports of the unconscious superior to those in which an acute intelligence was also at work.

Jung was not unaware of the dangers he ran because of his overcommitment to his own dream world. He makes this plain in the chapter on 'Confrontation with the Unconscious.' "It is of course ironical," he notes, "that I, a psychiatrist, should at almost every step of my experiment have run into the same psychic material which is the stuff of psychosis and is found in the insane. This is the fund of unconscious images which fatally confuse the mental patient. But it is also the matrix of a mythopoeic imagination which has vanished from our rational age. Though such imagination is present everywhere, it is both tabooed and dreaded, so that it even appears to be a risky experiment or a questionable adventure to entrust oneself to the uncertain path that leads into the depths of the unconscious." Risky it was. What warded off a dire outcome for Jung was a group of factors in their outer world that both Freud and Jung seem to have underrated in their psychotherapy. Jung deals with it only in a brief paragraph, which I shall cite in a moment, for it has a manifest bearing upon the rehabilitation of our own disordered world—a world that is once more increasingly open to the invasion of the demons, now that most of our traditional guards have been disarmed and expelled.

Whereas Freud was for the most part concerned with the morbid effects of unconscious *re*pression, Jung was more interested in the manifestations of unconscious *ex*pression, first in the dream and eventually in all the more orderly products of religion and art and morals. In interpreting flying saucers, for example, he made perhaps a more realistic appraisal of these unidentified objects than did people who expected them to contain visitors from another planet: he saw them as unconscious projections of modern man's need for the intervention of higher powers in a world menaced by its own scientific-mechanical ingenuities—typical hallucinations of an age that could conceive of Heaven only in the very mechanical terms in which it had conceived the forces that threatened it. Even Jung's much-debated interpretation of what was happening in Hitler's Germany in the thirties was not without insight, though his conduct justifies the suspicion that he himself, like all too many equally intelligent contemporaries in Europe, had momentarily turned to the same demonic powers for salvation and let himself be carried away by them. (How otherwise could he have stooped to co-operate with the *Gleichschaltung* of the psychoanalysts by assuming the presidency of the Nazi-controlled German psychological society, and how else could he have remained in that post after the blood purges and the sadistic attacks on the Jews had begun?) Though Jung's co-operative attitude has been justly criticized, here again there is a hardly less reprehensible Freudian parallel. On Dr. Ernest Jones's own lame confession in his biography of Freud, the Freudian group, with the Master's consent, allowed their Jewish members to resign in order to preserve the integrity of psychoanalysis in Nazi Germany.

All in all, a close reading of Jung's memories and dreams brings up problems quite as vexing as any in Freud's biography; above everything else, one wonders how is it that a man with his acute intelligence could place such weight on dreams as to remember them more accurately than most people can remember actual events—especially on dreams that often, even after he interprets them, seem so thin, so vapid, so tediously circuitous and unrewarding in comparison with their maturer manifestations in works of art, achieved partly by conscious effort. Does a father have to appear in dream, as Jung's did, after his death to make the son brood for the first time over the problem of life and death? Is not the death itself a sufficient reason? Or does one have to be "psychically infected" by contact with the primitive in Africa to succumb to infectious enteritis? Like so many familiar manifestations of the "occult," the product itself often seems mockingly trivial and disappointing, not worth the effort needed to dredge it up from sleep.

This overweighting of the raw stuff of the unconscious appears to be as one-sided as the total neglect of it by a dogmatic "scientific" materialism. At one point, it leads Jung to say, "Knowledge does not enrich us; it removes us more and more from the mythic world in which we were once at home by right of birth." He is partly right, of course, for much of our accurate but sterile knowledge, while useful for contriving power mechanisms, does little to nurture what is properly human. But the knowledge that led man eventually to leave his mythic world was the knowledge of good and evil, the perception that the heavenly paradise of the unconscious was actually filled with both demons and angels, and that it was not a safe guide for earthly waking life until consciousness had selectively transformed it and shaped it in order to give the angels the upper hand.

There is a baffling contradiction between the overpoweringly demonic psyche that concerns Jung himself and the poised, equable figure that Jung presented to his patients and his readers. Though by their own confession both Freud and Jung were neurotically vulnerable, their outward existence was almost a model of normality and impeccable professional respectability, for both, living out long spans of life, were rewarded by grateful patients, by contemporary honors, and by a popular acclaim such as few living prophets have ever received. The one time I beheld Jung, on his visit to this country in the thirties, he gave a quite commonplace lecture, yet he redeemed it by his presence, which seemed that of a shrewd old peasant, his own archetypal Wise Old Man, a man whom one would go to for advice in the barn if not in the clinic. Those who were his patients during what appears to have been an emotionally seething—indeed, almost shattering—period of his life felt the same reassuring touch and were healed by it. If his final testament and his collective works often happily produce the same response, it is not merely because he gives the reader such easy access to his unconscious domain but also because he discloses a vivid intelligence and a many-sided personality, at home in literature and religious mythology, and equally at home in science, though his mind was open to experiences that science on its present postulates rejects. It is Jung the whole man whose presence was reassuring, whose therapy was so often salutary. If one knew only the solitary explorer of the unconscious, one might have little faith in his unverifiable reports.

But just at the moment one begins to be impatient with Jung's habit of introducing his privately minted ideological coins from astrology and alchemy as if they were the common currency of the realm, some wisdom derived from his total experience, not from his unconscious alone, will break through. Most remarkably, this comes about at the end of the book, in his unexpected appreciation of consciousness itself. Here, against the commitments of a lifetime, he makes a magnificent about-face. Earlier, in his commentary on the Book of Job, in which he sides with Job and gibes at God's arbitrary ways, as Captain Ahab defied and taunted the inscrutable powers, he asserts that "the statements of the conscious mind may easily be snares and delusions, lies, or arbitrary opinions, but this is certainly not true of statements of the soul." Yet in his final testament Jung reverses that faulty judgment. "If the Creator were conscious of Himself," he notes, "He would not need conscious creatures; nor is it probable that the extremely indirect methods of creation, which squander millions of years upon the development of countless species and creatures, are the outcome of purposeful intention. Natural history tells us of a haphazard and casual transformation of species over hundreds of millions of years of devouring and being devoured. . . . But the history of the mind offers a different picture. Here the miracle of reflecting consciousness intervenes—the second cosmogony. The importance of consciousness is so great that one cannot help suspecting the element of *meaning* to be concealed somewhere within all the monstrous, apparently senseless biological turmoil, and that the road to its manifestation was ultimately found on the level of warm-blooded vertebrates possessed of a differentiated brain—found as if by chance, unintended and unforeseen, and yet somehow sensed, felt, and groped for out of some dark urge." This is not, naturally, a new wisdom; what is important is the fact that it came from a mind that had lingered so long in the darkest caverns of the unconscious and had been so fascinated by the images thrown on the walls that one might well have feared for his safe return.

In handling their own lives, both Freud and Jung, it becomes apparent, practiced two kinds of therapy—the one they used on their patients, which brought their repressed impulses to light and loosed the secret grip of the unconscious on the rest of the personality; and, for themselves, an even more ancient system of therapy, which was collectively developed by mankind in a spontaneous effort to cope with the irrational outpourings of the unconscious. The secret of the second mode of therapy is such an open one that neither psychologist seems to have given it sufficient weight in his system, though later physicians, when baffled, have fallen back on one or another aspect of it. Yet Jung, as I have already hinted, had more than a glimpse of the factors that in the past had given men enough stability and sanity to keep the demons under some sort of control.

Jung's testimony about the group of facts that brought about his emergence from his own neurosis, if all too brief, is emphatic. "Particularly at this time, when I was working on the fantasies, I needed a point of support in 'this world,' and I may say that my family and my professional work were that to me. It was most essential for me to have a normal life in the real world as a counterpoise to that strange inner world. My family and my profession remained the base to which I could always return, assuring me that I was an actually existing, ordinary person. The unconscious content could have driven me out of my wits. But my family, and the knowledge: I have a medical diploma from a Swiss university, I must help my patients, I have a wife and five children, I live at 228 Seestrasse in Küsnacht—these were actualities which made demands upon me and proved to me again and again that I really existed, that I was not a blank page whirling about in the winds of the spirit."

Here again the lives of Freud and Jung bear the same testimony. Each of them had a stable center of erotic interest and domestic responsibility, in a lifelong marriage that included the rearing of many children. The sexual discipline and order that family life imposes, with its integral gratifications, sacrifices, abstentions, sublimations, kept their libidos fastened to biological and social realities. However loose sexual ties may be in premarital relations among primitive peoples, every culture has recognized that erotic maturity involves a basic commitment to reproduction or to some direct sublimation of the reproductive functions, in vicarious fatherhood and motherhood. Freud and Jung, fortunately, experienced both modes of commitment; not merely as family men but as teachers and physicians, they perfected themselves in the parental role.

In addition, each of these physicians, day after day, year after year, spent no small part of his energies in the exhausting auditions of psychoanalysis, treating a long procession of patients. Even after Freud was riddled by the pain of his cancerous jaw, he maintained this discipline for sixteen years with exemplary fortitude, almost until his death, at the age of eighty-three. As with primitive man, work for them was at once a personal function, an economic necessity, and a compulsive ritual whose daily repetition served, like the prayers of the faithful, to alleviate anxiety; above all, this life-nurturing routine was a means of keeping in check, for a large part of the day—in his prime Freud often received patients till nine in the evening —the inordinate, crazily destructive impulses that they might have found it impossible to control had they been "free"; that is, open to the demonic incursions of the unconscious. Through their devotion to reproduction and breadwinning, the nurturing parental functions, Jung and Freud kept their hold on reality. But they had still another anchor: stability of residence in an identifiable historic city, maintaining an orderly pattern of social relations that included many affectionate personal ties. No matter how far they might wander in their travels or in their minds, the continuity of their personalities was supported by the continuity of their homely urban environments. Such changes as Zürich and Vienna underwent physically in the lifetimes of these men were neither cataclysmic nor spiritually disturbing. In short, the conditions that maintained their psychological balance were precisely those that our fantastically dynamic ideology and technology have for the last century been heedlessly overthrowing.

From this general interpretation of Jung's 'Memories, Reflections, Dreams' many valid conclusions might be drawn. But the most obvious of them recalls one to a principle that mankind at large took for granted until seventeenth-century science, following Galileo's lead, discarded it. And this is to give as much weight to inner subjective experience, issuing forth in dreams, proposals, feelings, memories, anxieties, prophetic anticipations, mythopoeic projections, moral values, works of art, as to the "external" world of actions, inventions, controlled observations, lawful obligations, mechanized production, quantitative measurements of every kind. Though we call these last "the world," it is only a half world, and often a poor half at that. If man had not developed his subjective life sufficiently to produce articulate language and its derivative arts of symbolic interpretation, all the present attributes of the "objective" world would have remained dormant and unconscious, waiting for the midwifery of the human mind.

In the inner life, Freud and Jung discovered, non-repeatable events and singular moments may exert a greater force on a person's development than his habitual day-to-day tasks; similarly, manifestations of care and sympathy and love, such as the good analyst gives his patient, may be as essential to human health and balance as mother love is to the infant, who—experiments on both monkeys and human beings have shown—would be ill-nourished on food alone, even in sufficient quantity. Both the outer world and the inner world are real, but each needs the correction of the other, and if one is deformed or suppressed, the other loses an essential link with reality and to that extent becomes irrational and uncontrollable. Most contemporaries would grant that wanton subjective fantasies and wishes need to be corrected by what Freud called the reality principle, but they fight shy of the notion that our mechanically conditioned minds and our implacable, overordered external world need the correction of variegated memories and dreams, of aesthetic expressions, traditional values, historical meanings, and ideal purposes not derivable from the immediate environment or even from man's original biological constitution.

In one respect, unfortunately, Freud's analysis of the psyche was onesided and Jung's was incomplete. Because they derived their most original insights from dealing with mental illness, both men tended to magnify the negative, "sinful," self-absorbed, often self-destructive aspects of the unconscious mind and to forget the important positive functions that it furthers. In a word, they overplayed the role of the disruptive demons and forgot the healing offices of the Nine Muses. Freud has made everyone aware of injuries in infancy that might induce permanent morbid effects, but he needed Adler's reminder that defects and weaknesses were often a stimulus to compensatory efforts that more than made good the loss. And the possibility that blessings, reversing traumas, might leave a permanently benign imprint on the personality seems never to have occurred to Freud, though even passing expressions of interest, love, loyalty, and praise (as in Emerson's first talk with Thoreau) may actually keep on reverberating through a lifetime.

Jung remained more amenable to such integrating experiences, especially whenever he found them confirmed by appropriate "archetypal" dreams. Unlike Freud, he did not look upon primitive rites and customs as absurd misinterpretations of natural events, nor did he despise religion as a childish illusion. What both men did was to open the passage for two-way traffic between the inner and the outer world. That all by itself was a lasting contribution. But they necessarily left to others the task of replenishing and fortifying the inner life. Neither stressed sufficiently that the fuller understanding of the dynamic potentialities of the unconscious would bring with it a demand for a firmer discipline and a more sedulous conscious direction, though Freud, in an early paper on psychotherapy, pointed this out when he observed that "it is only by the application of our highest mental functions, which are bound up with consciousness, that we can control all our impulses."

Our generation, far from accepting this challenge, has acted on the contrary principle; the more rational minds have utilized their intellectual functions to further the automatisms of the Space Age, while those who reject the kind of half-life that is now left have re-entered the aboriginal world of the unconscious, returning to a level lower than that of any primitive tribe—the frustrating, inarticulate, demon-haunted inner state that may well have existed before graphic symbols or words had yet been formed. When Jung directed his patients to their traditional religions in an effort to apply discipline and order to the outpourings of the unconscious, he at least built on a solid historical foundation, though one now badly dilapidated. But only those who are still firmly attached to traditional values and historic continuities can guess what sort of effort is actually needed to transcend the limitations of both worlds in their present extreme forms.

Once we read the lessons of Jung's life and teaching correctly, we shall perhaps understand why the advances of science and technics have cheated us of their original promise, for they have led to the increase of predictable, mechanically perfect order, automatically spreading over and dominating —for a price—every aspect of our existence. Not only that, but they have brought on devastating eruptions of the unconscious, along with wholesale collective regressions into more infantile modes of life. The more objective and efficient the control on one side, the greater the subjective disruption on the other. The demons that seventeenth-century science promised to exorcise have returned even in exact science, all the more dangerous because they are concealed under the sterile garments and surgeon's mask of science itself. In any detached appraisal, the rocket with which we propose to shoot a man to the moon has the same degree of rational utility—or, rather, irrational futility—as the Great Pyramid, an equally superb technical achievement, by which an Egyptian Pharaoh proposed to secure his passage to heaven. As for the current dreams of "human improvement" prompted in biological circles by suspiciously hypermanic excitement over DNA, who but a Nobel Prize winner would now be so innocent as to trust a Nobel Prize winner with their execution? The very readiness to spring such proposals at the first hint of the possibility of direct genetic control over human breeding indicates severe psychological disqualifications—including a crass lack of historical awareness and objective self-knowledge.

Our Victorian ancestors overlooked the possibility that their lopsided technological rationalism would produce an increasingly purposeless and irrational world, to which only machines, with no internally transmitted history and no spontaneous inner promptings, could be permanently adjusted. Today, to counterbalance this unilateral commitment, a correspondingly savage rebellion has taken place in the unconscious. From the normally creative minds of poets and artists has come an explosion of anti-life in images that correspond to the outbursts of delinquency and criminality that haunt our daily affairs and that, collectively, actually threaten the existence of mankind.

By a total inversion of human values, the favored leaders and mentors of our age prefer disease to health, destruction to creativity, pornography to potent sexual experience, debasement to development. It is not by accident that the French writer Jean Genet who has lately been hailed by a shallow but popular Existentialist philosopher as the saint of our time, is a hardened criminal who establishes his claim to our pious appreciation by publishing the memories and fantasies of homosexual experiences with which he accompanied his solitary exercises in masturbation. Jung's youthful God, who defecated on his own altar, is now worshipped by all those who equate the creative act solely with defecation. This obvious infantilism may be the ultimate revenge of the unconscious upon an increasingly overorganized and overmechanized existence in which there is no way of consciously intervening in the automatic processes or expressing human intentions except by disgusting acts of defilement and by rabid destruction.

The first effect of the discovery of the role of the unconscious was to release the demons—and even to give them temporary authority—but Jung's mature reflections point to something of greater importance. He believed that the unconscious is not merely the hiding place of the demons but the province of angels and ministers of grace, which he called the "archetypes." These last are symbols of all the inner forces that work toward unity, health, fullness of life, and purposeful conscious development. But while the destructive impulses can act promptly and undo in a few seconds what it has taken a lifetime to put together, the superior functions of the mind require continuous delicate care, for they draw upon the deepest layers of human experience, and they develop fully only when there is free and easy intercourse between the conscious and the unconscious, between the values, meanings, purposes derived from man's infinitely varied past and the new potentialities that the conscious mind continually brings into existence. No system of education that rests mainly, as ours increasingly does, on one-generation knowledge can replace that experience, even if it is the product, as ours is, of a vaster assemblage of scientists than, all told, existed before from the beginning of time.

Our age has been creating a system of intellectual and practical organization that favors mechanical automatism and abolishes human autonomy. But if we read further in the story that Freud and Jung were the first to unfold, we shall perhaps be ready to question many of the demoralizing "advances" we now meekly take to be unchallengeable. Too much of our labor-saving now turns out to be life-eliminating. If we feed our essential organic and human activities into the machine, what meaning or value will remain in the residue? Many of us are proud of our having devised a computer that can play chess with a man, but what will become of our pride when computers deign to play only with computers? Will psychiatric care restore our mental balance if the "point of support in 'this world,' " of which Jung speaks, that sustained both him and Freud disintegrates any further or disappears? Will any quantity of tranquillizers, sedatives, and aphrodisiacs make up for the demoralizing absence of meaningful, life-sustaining daily activities? "Our cult of progress," Jung remarks, "is in danger of imposing on us even more childish dreams of the future, the harder it presses us to escape from the past." In that sense, the reputed "avant-garde" in science, art, and technics turns out to be the rear guard—so many defeated and bewildered stragglers concealing their pathetic rout by counting every loss a victory. What a great number of our contemporaries still mistake for unconditionally desirable advances in modern civilization looks like an excellent prescription for sending mankind to the loony bin.

(1964)

PART FIVE

Transformations of Man

CHAPTER THIRTY-SIX

Animal into Human

When we go back to the origins of man, we go back to a time before he left any records except his own bones; and all too few of them. Some day, at the bottom of a sunken ocean bed, or in caves yet unexplored, we may discover richer human relics. But it is doubtful whether material objects, bones, stones, shards, can reveal what we want most to know—by what cunning and daring, by what dreaming and searching, man discovered the germs of his own humanness and nurtured them. What matters most about man's past will remain in the realm of speculation and fantasy. Teased by this obscurity, almost every people has fashioned a myth about its origin, nature, and destiny, though too often the mythmakers ask themselves only how their kind became Babylonians, Greeks, Jews, Romans, Japanese, and not when and how they became men.

Since none of these old myths does justice to our present knowledge, I purpose to fashion a myth that will be more in keeping with the science of our time, yet more ready to venture into factual quicksand than the scientist, if true to his prudent code, can let himself step. This myth does not, it goes without saying, profess to come from divine revelation; nor yet can the earlier parts of it be called, even by the most generous stretching of the words, verifiable truth. But in its speculative vagueness, as in its dubious flashes of illumination, it reflects the actual mystery with which it deals. Where the facts are beyond recall, our myth will seek to reconstruct them by reading back from the known into the unknown, since the historic transformation of man is repeated, in effect, with the birth and nurture of every new human being.

In significant ways, the terms of the present myth of man have changed. We no longer ask for some dramatic moment of creation that calls for an external and all-powerful creator. The extension of astronomic and geologic time lessens the need for sudden power: our creative agent is inseparable from the long process of creation itself, slowly gathering purpose and direction over the aeons, gradually "making up its mind" and at last, in man, beginning to achieve the first glimmer of self-consciousness.

Something that may later be identified as life and mind perhaps is present at every stage of the cosmic process, though visible only when one looks backward. Certainly, long before man came on the scene, a multitude of organisms had taken form and invented ways of perpetuating that form and altering it, each after their own kind, within the life cycle of their own species, in relation to environments and organic partnerships that sustained it. Out of this cosmic web of life stepped man: the creature that dared consciously to be a creator, and that found another path to creation than that of biological metamorphosis.

Man seems to have descended from a group of apelike primates that lived in trees, when a large part of the earth boasted a tropical climate. In one or more places, at one or more times, this creature took the first steps toward becoming human. Some alteration in his metabolism, some mutation in his genes—yes, perhaps some inner impetus and need—endowed him with a bigger brain, relatively, than any creature except the mouse possesses; and man's sustained urge to make something of it started him on his long career. That change made it possible for man to live in a more complex world, or rather, to take in more of the complexities and possibilities of the real world: it brought with it the development of greater manual skills, finer co-ordinations, greater sensitiveness to both outer stimuli and inner promptings, a greater aptitude for learning, a more retentive memory and a more wary foresight than any of his ancestors could boast.

The overgrowth of human brain may signify a more general condition that sets man off from his nearest animal colleagues: an abundance of unused energy not marked for nutrition, reproduction, or defense. In other animals, excess vitality runs off mainly in muscular play. In man, it produces a constant undercurrent of sounds, images, exploratory actions. His infantile interest in his own body and its products includes other expressions, though his tendency to blow and bubble and babble and hum has no purpose or direction at the beginning except sheer organic activity. Arnold Gesell has shown that in early infancy a baby will turn to constructive acts, putting one block on another, before anyone instructs him in these possibilities.

In short, the undifferentiated material for symbols and fabrications rises out of man, not waiting for any external challenge, but prompted by his own maturation. And it is surely no accident that the least controllable part of this flow—but eventually the most significant, indeed the very source of significance—wells up from the unconscious, in spontaneous daytime fantasies and nocturnal dreams. What was uniquely serviceable for man's development was his ability to fix and formalize these spontaneous images and symbols, and to attach them to objects provided by the external world.

By developing his mind, man lessened the need for other forms of organic specialization. When Karl Pearson compared man's brain to a telephone exchange, handling incoming and outgoing calls, he took in only a small part of its activity: it is a power station, a storage warehouse, a library, a theater, a museum, a hall of archives, a court of justice, a seat of government. The instinctive equipment of most species is sufficient to ensure their survival. By transferring authority to a controlling intelligence, sensitized by feeling, enlarged by imagination, man sometimes endangered his survival, but he opened the possibility of further development.

Nature, Dr. Walter Cannon demonstrated, has practiced the "economy of abundance" in fashioning man and many of his ancestors: hence the excess of energy that is stored up, ready for emergencies, the provision of paired organs, the ears, the eyes, the lungs, the kidneys, the breasts, the testicles, so that even if one member is injured the other can take over the burden and keep the organism alive. But this same generosity applies even more magnificently to man's central nervous system: long before man could count on ten fingers, he had enough neurons at his disposal to make possible the learning of an Aristotle or an Ibn-Khaldun, the wisdom of a Confucius or an Isaiah, the imagination of a Plato or a Dante. Let us not forget this generosity. The wisdom of the body has further applications to the life of man in our time: for an economy of abundance brings with it, not the duty to consume, but the readiness to create.

Man's immediate ancestors possibly went halfway on this path of development: man completed it. But the ability to walk on two feet was so lately acquired that it never became part of man's organic inheritance: he must still be taught how to walk, around the beginning of his second year, and about the same time he adds to his animal vocabulary of signals, gestures, uncouth sounds, another distinctly human trait: the imitation of formalized sounds and presently the use of words to express feelings and meanings. Words pin down man's associations and multiply them. Without words he could react to environmental pressures and stimuli; but he could not enlarge this milieu into a world that stretches far beyond his immediate sight or reach.

Along with these two outstanding achievements, goes a fact that John Fiske was perhaps the first observer to rate at its full importance: man's prolonged infancy, sanctioned if not promoted by maternal indulgence. In a sense, man is a retarded animal, for the span between his birth and his maturity, when he is ready to mate, is relatively longer than in most other species. By the time man is old enough to reproduce his kind, the horse is ready to be put to pasture in his old age. This freedom from adult tasks encouraged growth: thanks to his long childhood man found time to play and experiment, time to learn, time to take in not merely the immediate environment but the remembered experience of his kind, time to grope in dream toward a distant future. Escaping in youth the pressure to survive, he had leisure for self-development. This fact sets even primitive man apart from his animal neighbors.

With the utter helplessness of the newborn infant went a prolonged period of breast feeding: this reinforced the common mammalian trait of tenderness. In addition, the shedding of the hairy garment of the apes, particularly in the female, brought about a more intimate and pleasurable contact between mother and babe, to say nothing of her mate. Breasts and lips became instruments of erotic love, and out of that happy association spread more general habits of protection, nurture, and loving attachment. The extension of the period of parental care and childish irresponsibility promoted playfulness; and play was perhaps the earliest realm of human freedom.

In sheer play and make-believe man may have made the first great advances in culture, beginning with human speech: more significant than any acts that could be described as practical invention or work. Man's use of tools, with their sharpening of his practical intelligence, came early; but the passage from the animal to the human may have been furthered even more by his rich emotional life, colored by love, hate, fear, anxiety, laughter, tears, demanding outlets of expression and communication. Many insect orders long surpassed man in constructive facility and social organization; but no other creature shows the faintest capacity for creating durable works of art. It was not alone the Promethean theft of fire but the Orphic gift of music that turned man into a creature so different from his primordial self.

One other trait came to mark man off from his animal neighbors besides his playfulness and his artfulness: his propensity to imitate and emulate those around him: to smile when they smile, to be doleful when they are sad, to reproduce their gestures, to articulate the same sounds. Even when the immediate occasion is absent, man's retentive memory may prompt him to recall a valued moment and repeat it in play; for repetition itself gives him a certain satisfaction and security, as we see in a child's love of ritual and his insistence upon having a familiar story repeated with every detail in order.

The impulse of imitation, the disposition to make-believe, the habit of lingering over a satisfactory response in memory and working it into a meaningful pattern—these seem to me fundamental contributions to truly human development. They were means by which man detached himself from his organic limitations and from the all-too-slow process of biological change. By daily nurture, he produced a "second nature," which we now call culture, transmitted by imitation and habit. This culture became more natural and proper to him than his original make-up because it included not merely what he was and is, but what he loves and admires and purposes to be. Of all the labor-saving devices that man has invented, this earliest invention, that of detachment from the organic, seems beyond any doubt the most important. This achievement paved the way for the free development of mind long before intelligence devised further tools for its own advancement.

In achieving culture, man's first steps were doubtless the hardest, like the first pennies that lay the foundation for a fortune. By now, man's culture has become visible in the outward world, in buildings and cities, in institutions and printed records: but for long the greater part of it was carried in the mind and transmitted only by gesture and word of mouth. Poverty of numbers, poverty of material equipment, poverty of symbols, held back further development: for long his difficulty was to hold fast to the little that he had acquired. Even after the first steps had been taken, man's achievement of the specifically human must have been upset by frequent relapses into his naïvely animal past. Even today violent rage temporarily brings on this result. Would man, with his new potentialities and prospects, manage to retain his adventurous ways—or would he fall back into sleepy animalhood? At the beginning of his ascent, that question may have stirred man's deepest anxiety.

Our present age, beyond any other, should understand the urgency of this question. For man's humanity is now threatened by the possibility of relapsing into a barbarism more elemental than has ever been encountered in historic times. Though culture itself tends to be cumulative, in the process of taking it over each generation starts from scratch. Without parental love, without filial veneration, without a secure sense of the future, the very effort to become human may miscarry. Through overreliance upon mechanism and automatism our generation has begun to lose the secret of nurturing man's humanness, since he gives too little care to the conditions that make each member of the community sensitive, tender, imaginative, morally responsible, self-governing, disposed to imitate human ideals and to emulate ideal examples of humanity.

Fortunately for primitive man, he was not, like us, intimidated by the cold perfection of the machine, nor did the universe seem to him a machine. And even more fortunately, perhaps, one of the first objects of his love was himself: indeed, without his excessive vanity and self-love early man might never have explored the principal paths that carried beyond his original animal concern with survival and reproduction. It is not perhaps by accident that narcissism—preoccupation with one's bodily image and absorption in one's own capacities and desires—still marks the passage from adolescence to maturity. If in maturity overweening pride often comes before a fall, at the beginning pride and vanity came before man's rise and prompted him to greater efforts. When man loses this deep self-respect, the world itself seems corrupt and loathsome.

But was there perhaps some more devious path that led to man's emergence from his purely animal state? His sociability, his industry, his constructive propensities, his amorous excitements, his domestic partnerships and solicitudes—all these he shares with various other species. But there are two traits that, even if they are shared in some dim way by other species, leave no mark on their behavior, but color every aspect of man's existence: they function throughout human history and probably through prehistory, for the greater part unrecorded and unrecordable. One is the capacity to dream and, above all, to transform imagined projections into actual projects. The other is the sense of awe and veneration, not unmixed with anxiety, in the presence of forces that lie beyond the range of man's intelligence.

Man lives no small part of his life in the presence of the unconscious and the unknown: he is apparently the only creature who ever had the intuition that there is more in nature than meets the eye. In opening up his specific human capacities, the unknown, indeed, the unknowable, has proved an even greater stimulus than the known, while his peculiar fore-consciousness of death has added an enigmatic dimension to his life that has carried him beyond dumb animal acceptance of that terminal event. Infinity, eternity, immortality, potentiality, omniscience, omnipotence, divinity, to say nothing of zero and the square root of minus one, have no counterparts in animal experience.

If the constructive use of dreams differentiates man from other animals, this faculty may have occupied an even greater proportion of early man's attention and interest than overrational interpretations ordinarily allow. In the depths of the human personality, the unconscious and the supernatural are united in the form of dynamic images transcending any actual human experience: demons, monsters, dragons, angels, gods take possession of the dreamer and become more obsessively real than the actual world of here and now, to which he confusedly returns. With these overpowering images, independent and autonomous, sometimes as vivid in daylight as in sleep, man went farther in the direction of detachment and projection: detachment from the animal, projection of the superhuman and the divine.

The feeling of his cosmic loneliness may have separated dawnman from the manlike ape, long before he found words to express that feeling; but with it, out of the strange commanding symbols of the unconscious, may have come a sense of being favored by powers and agents seemingly not his own: powers attached, through his sexuality, to the deepest sources of life. These happy hallucinations may have touched every conscious act with an obsessive insistence. So man's self-transcending nature prospered in the climate of the supernatural; these fantasies confirmed his own tendency to overvalue his dearest object of love, himself.

All this must have antedated anything that can be called religion. In the beginning was the *mysterium tremendum,* unfathomable, uncontrollable, indescribable: the source of light and darkness, warmth and cold, delight and dejection, life and death, not yet divided out into nature, man, and God. Man learned to live with this mystery and in time to project it, interpreting the unknown by symbols equally incapable of rational explanation. True, other animals seem at times to have cosmic responses: wolves bay at the moon: elephants perform secret nocturnal ceremonies: chimpanzees have shown something like awe in the presence of the uncanny, be it only the image of a donkey, made of rags and buttons. But in man the sense of wonder and mystery may have been stirred in the first gropings of self-consciousness and even more than his practical intelligence may have helped lift him out of his animal state.

At a later stage, one finds these mysterious promptings surrounded by rationalizations and conceptual supports, translated into rituals, expressed in concrete forms of art; but in the beginning they must have antedated dogma and moral code, probably even speech. Out of this cosmic anxiety and awe, in which self-abasement and exaltation both played a part, came the sense of the sacred, which has no animal equivalent: the sacredness of blood and the birth rite, the sacredness of sex, the sacredness of the word: finally the sacredness of death, and with it the impulse to solemnly care for the bodies of the dead, and to dwell in the imagination on their future existence.

This quickening to the unknown, this widening of man's effective environment to include vistas of time and space beyond any animal need or capacity, this imputation of some more permanent value and significance to the passing moment—all this is, from the standpoint of survival or practical utility, an aberration. Yet in man's early departures from sensible animal accommodation to his visible environment we may hold a key—perhaps one of the main keys—to what is veritably human. In these reactions, man exposes himself to fearful illusions and self-deceptions that sometimes carry him beyond the borderland of sanity. But precisely because of his readiness for fantasy untouched by the here and now, he penetrates levels of existence and meaning that no other creature seems to approach.

The other source of man's unique humanness was his capacity to dream; for this is the forward-moving counterpart to memory. In origin derived perhaps from man's anxiety, the dream took on a positive function—it became the great instrument of anticipation, invention, projection, creative transformation. Sensitive to outside impressions, which keep reverberating in him long after the stimulus has ceased, man's hours of sleep, when he is detached from practical needs, are flooded with images. While the outer world supplies the material for these images, under pressure from within they undergo extravagant transformations, which his waking intelligence would reject. Man's manipulativeness and curiosity, his trial-and-error discoveries, certainly furthered his command over the external world: but the dream has the special sign of art: it expresses the nature of the dreamer and gives him further insight into his own potentialities. This self-expression was an important element in man's transformation.

Living phenomena differ from the nonliving not only in the fact that they originate in the organism and are in keeping with its general plan of life which brings about successive modifications and transformations in time—growth, maturation, reproduction, death. They likewise differ in that they are directional, anticipatory, preparatory, goal-seeking, though at the organic level the end-in-view has become so completely structured that it cannot be separated from the creature's own nature. In man, his anticipatory reactions become detached and externalized as conscious purpose; and in his awareness of his desires, he intensifies their expression or by detaching them he may divert them to ends that partly contradict his own original nature. This is one of the functions of dream. Possibility and purposiveness, along with anxiety and prudent anticipation, all seem to cluster around man's capacity to dream, and to carry this function from the unconscious of sleep to the whole field of his waking life. By detaching purpose from organic structures and functions man both brought it into consciousness and gave it a special human destination.

In following this line, man breaks away from the purely adaptive behavior of other species: he turns upon nature with counterproposals of his own, which move toward obscure goals he can never fully understand until he has given them form. In this respect, one can explain the development of human culture in general only by understanding the process of creating a work of art. This act, when it is not purely imitative, transcends the knowledge of the creator and often seems to outrun his powers: it draws on capacities that could not be known till they were summoned forth and externalized. The wish, then, is not merely father to the thought: it is the parent of all man's creative acts and functions. And because the erotic impulses themselves play a larger part in man's dreams than sex itself can satisfy, the dream carries into every act and occupation an image of some further fulfillment, open to his own creation.

With the word and the dream man was able to pass from the limited animal vocabulary of signals and signs to the almost unlimited human vocabulary of symbols. But he did not reach this goal directly: in all probability, he moved toward it by a roundabout route, by way of love and play. Before sounds took shape and became repeated often enough to be identified, man possibly had a larger repertory of expression than any other creature, if only because of his mobile facial muscles. The ancient dialogue between mother and child, which begins in gesture and facial expression, turned gurgles and babbles into formed sounds and sounds into recognizable words. As with dream images, it seems likely that man playfully cultivated his organs of speech before he turned language to the more practical uses of communication or command. Here again one can only tell plausible fairy stories. But one can watch part of the process once more in every newborn baby.

In babyhood, certainly, language begins as pure expression, as a mode of emotional communion, long before it becomes otherwise useful. Beneath its many other functions, which make for social unison and enlarge the field of common knowledge and shared behavior, language promotes emotional solidarity: it is a bond of identification and recognition. Those who speak the language with the right tone and inflection, using the familiar vocabulary, are kinsmen, neighbors, fellows: people to trust. Those who do not are outsiders and enemies: at best, ridiculous creatures, not quite "people," as the ancient Egyptians openly felt. So the deepest of bonds became in time one of the greatest of barriers between the tribes and races of man; and man's most universal artifact, the spoken word, because it is so deeply steeped in the individuality of experience, became an obstacle to the union of mankind.

There is still another function of language that so far, perhaps because it is so obvious, seems to have escaped attention. Language, the most important agent of directed thought, has the special trick of inhibiting autonomous images. Once language is achieved words may indeed summon events or images into consciousness: but when they function actively they may also, as the busy, efficient agents of directed thought, halt the self-induced hypnosis of sleep. This fact is well known to those who have been sleepless. If primitive man was at first almost a neurotic victim of his own excessive image-making power, the invention and elaboration of language may have acted as a helpful inhibiting agent, which kept him from being overwhelmed. By displacing autonomous images that welled up from the unconscious with verbal symbols attached to conscious processes, he may have brought his whole life under greater control. Much primitive thinking would still remain dreamlike, infantile, magical. But by the very nature of the word, thinking itself would become centrally directed, and in time, by its very detachment from the unconscious, it would serve to enlarge the realm of the rational, the intelligible, the practical.

Once man achieved the beginnings of verbal and graphic symbolism, he acquired a formal organ of detachment and projection: he could take in a large area of experience and keep it unified in his consciousness, bringing past and future, near and far, into a common field. So, too, he could, with the materials so brought together, express his own innerness in forms that were themselves permanent enough to recapture his original intuition even after the immediate occasion had passed. The wonder of the word, above all, must once have filled man's life as a whole far more enchantingly than the wonder of the atom does today; for the act of naming was a godlike process, a second creation: when one had gotten possession of a name, one seemed to exercise command over the object it identified. No other animal possessed such powers. This was not just the ability to think: it was the power to create, the magic breath of life. With its help the inevitabilities of nature were supplemented with possibilities divined only by man. No wonder primitive man thought, even after he had achieved civilized order, that the name was the essence of even divine identity, and that naming and creating were one.

So marvellous was his achievement that, down to our own day, man has persistently sought to apply the magic of words to realms where it is worthless. Since words often do bring about changes in human conduct, acting as a trigger if not as a bludgeon, primitive man sought to apply this power to non-human objects as well: were not clouds and trees alive? By word magic, he would invoke rain or fertility, health or energy. Yet even if recent experiments in telekinesis should be fully verified, there is little doubt that this method is the least profitable way of effecting a change in the raw physical environment: so this magic was doomed.

But it has not been for nothing that the word has remained man's principal toy and tool: without the meanings and values it sustains, all man's other tools would be worthless. Man's greatest concrete achievements rest on these abstractions. By means of symbols, man was able to escape enclosure by physical circumstance and his own biological nature. What was symbolized could sooner or later be realized, either in art or in life.

Let us examine more closely the formation of the human self, for it presents problems no other animal faces, and discloses aptitudes no other animal reveals. Over a generation ago the French sociologist, Gabriel Tarde, sought to explain human society by the Laws of Imitation. By pushing that key into holes where it did not fit he brought discredit to the concept. But man is in fact a highly imitative animal: his "consciousness of kind" brings with it a desire to impress, to please, to gain a response from his kind; and emulation, based on mutual admiration, is one of the paths to this social solidarity.

But imitation cannot be reduced to mechanical mimesis; and only at its lowest levels can it be confounded with drill. In man it involves admiration and love, an effort to identify the self with its beloved object in order to draw more closely to it; and distance and inaccessibility seem to intensify the effort. At a certain point in man's development, it is not the actual person, but an ideal pattern, that brings forth this propensity. This effort to achieve an imagined good or an ideal goal goes along with another human tendency, equally ingrained: that of lingering over and elaborating every natural act, so that it will have a special meaning and value detached from its immediate function, though often closely dependent upon it.

Thus the snatching of food becomes the ceremony of dining: the need for sexual companionship creates the forms of courtship and marriage; and a thousand other occasions of life are given a form that makes the original stimulus the least significant part of them. Man is born into a world of sensations and motor impulses: he matures into a world of meanings and values: indeed, his culture rests ultimately upon his ability to convert the raw materials of existence into forms that independently sustain social life and nurture the development of the person.

This tendency toward elaboration and efflorescence is not unknown on a purely biological level. There it is associated chiefly with sexual activity: the growing of ornate excrescences in the mating season or the turning of the simple mechanism of fertilization into the aesthetic splendors of flowers. Possibly the impulse to prolong transitory acts had its origin in man's year-round openness to sexual excitation: by formal elaboration he saved himself from exhaustion and found himself in a far more meaningful world. At all events, the long circuit of art and contemplative thought replaced the short circuit of direct action. *"Verweile doch, du bist so schön!"* may have been one of man's earliest demands.

Thus man does not simply live his life from day to day, in a sober, matter-of-fact way: he dramatizes and enacts it. For every phase in his development, he creates a plot and a dialogue, a sequence of actions, an appropriate costume, and a special stage. In time, as with an actor who has spent his life in tragic roles, his natural face may take on the features of the mask. What is culture itself but an elaborate masquerade for confirming man's original bit of make-believe, that he was not in fact a mere animal? By losing himself in role after role, drama after drama, man explores passages that the fixed parts assigned by nature would never have opened up. As a result his performance lacks the sureness and perfection of other animals, who have had to learn only one role. But in compensation, the continued shifting of parts has made him able to master new situations that would have baffled any other creature.

These characteristics must, from the beginning, have aided in man's delivery from his "given" self. For he is the only creature who does not without effort know what he is. His being is always involved in a becoming, and that becoming involves a self-transformation. He learns to "be himself" only by the process of working over his original nature. Once upon a time I knew a little boy, aged three, who became a baby bird: he no longer wore clothes but had feathers: his feet were claws: his arms were wings: his nose was a beak: his home was a tree: his bed was a nest; and all his acts, for a time, were involved in this dramatic replacement of himself. This autodrama required, too, that those around him should play appropriate supporting roles. Since we often see these impulses at work in a young child, without any promptings from the outside, we may hazard the guess that they were also present in the childhood of the race; in fact, many survivals, like totemism, indicate a similar make-believe. What is important is not the animal form but the make-believe itself.

On this interpretation, then, man became man by formalizing, ritualizing, symbolizing, dramatizing every natural act he performed; and in time this faculty permitted him to transform his entire environment, bring it closer to his self by giving it the same attributes. This capacity for symbolic projection brought forth a second self, a more truly human self, one in accord with man's still unstated and unfathomed possibilities. Only at the highest stages of his culture, when he has passed through these transformations, when he is confident that the "human" has been solidly won, does man feel as free as the Greeks did to return to his natural self in its idealized wholeness. At that moment the naked body, unblemished by decoration, appears with sudden glory in sculpture. If one accepts the conventions of make-believe, and recognizes the essential part they played in man's development, many of his strangest historic acts become logical and meaningful. But if one stands outside, even many of his most rational acts seem absurd.

Today we have largely forgotten how much of man's life was fashioned in definitely human form before his technical facilities were much better than a beaver's, and long before his social organization had begun to approach the complexities and the functional divisions of the social insects. While man was still a mere food gatherer, hardly yet a well-armed hunter, he had probably invented most of the decisive instruments of culture and above all projected a new image of himself. And if man's own body was the first object of his loving care, we should not be surprised to find that the most ancient of his arts was probably cosmetic and body decoration: an art known to the lowliest Australian Bushman and still the subject of more lavish expense than any other art in present-day society. Perhaps, by dabbing his face with red clay or ochre primitive man sought to establish his new personality, visibly different from his untouched animal self: the sudden transformation of the mask. The very word personality derives from this formal covering for the face.

These acts of self-identification happily did not stop with body painting, scarification, and tattooing: man's artful masquerade, in time, touched every part of his society and his environment, not least his inner self. By means of his culture, he wrought changes in himself within a few thousand years that nature would have needed millions of years to accomplish by the tedious process of organic evolution. And unlike biological changes, such cultural transformations could, when they proved a handicap to human development, be modified or replaced within a similar span of time.

Now the art of becoming human by gesture and word and formal act was man's earliest and greatest art. But for a long time, I would suppose, man's sense of his new identity must have been insecure and vulnerable. The possibility of losing hold of his new self—of forgetting the key to language, for instance, and lapsing into mere gibberish—may have haunted him. In our time, we are confronted with problem children who have a "reading block": they find it difficult to identify printed sentences with a meaningful flow of sounds. There may well have been a time in human development when the translation of sound into meaning was even more precarious; and the possibility of not being able to make this passage may have deepened the fear of being transformed by magic back into an animal, as in the ancient fairy tales. Hence the emphasis on repetition and ritual: the exact words in the exact order and no other. The fear of relapsing into animalhood is recorded in the adventure of Odysseus with Circe in the 'Odyssey'; and it comes out in many other forms, including severe prohibitions against sexual congress with animals. Yet with it went perhaps a sense that, in partly cutting loose from his animal roots, man had lost a source of strength. Like the plant, he needed not only the air and light above him, but the soil beneath.

Despite the fact that man became man by creating a new world, a meaningful world of symbolic and cultural forms, which had no existence for the animal, the ancient spiritual tie with his animal past could not be lightly severed. The feeling of identification lingered in primitive societies in the cult of totem animal, and was carried over into the religions of civilization, in the lion-headed or hawk-headed gods of Egypt, in the sacred bulls of Assyria, Crete, Persia. And if the temptation to sink back into the securities of his animal state long remained with him—indeed still lingers—at the beginning he perhaps put it behind him only by energetic repression.

"Dreams and beasts," Emerson noted in an early 'Journal,' "are the two keys by which we are to find out the secrets of our own nature." That has proved an even more penetrating intuition than he could have guessed. If the domestication of plants and animals was one of the upward stages in man's development, his own self-domestication was of even greater critical importance, beginning with the process of penning in his own animal self. From the beginning he knew that the vigorous animal core of him needed no special encouragement: it was rather the faint tremulous stirrings of an embryonic new self, as yet unborn, to which he must give heed.

Every new generation must repeat dawnman's original effort. But today our very consciousness of our animal origins has in some quarters given rise to the curious belief that this part of man's original nature alone is real, valid, integral, and that the forms of morality and social discipline are only superstitious impositions upon the true nature of man. Sophisticated modern man is therefore in danger of succumbing to a degradation that primitive man must have learned, after many lapses, to guard against; the threat of losing his humanity by giving precedence to his animal self and his non-human character over the social ego and the ideal superego that have transmuted this original inheritance.

Yet, however far man goes in his self-dramatization and self-transformation, he can never leave the animal behind. The blind surge and push of all organic creation bottoms his unique creative activities: his most ideal aspirations still rest on his eating and mating and seeking food and fending off dangers, as other animals do; and some measure of animal activity and animal delight belongs to his deepest humanity. Even at the Day of Judgment, Thomas Aquinas reasoned, the body would be necesary; and there is no detachment, no transcendence, that does not rest on the use of man's animal resources in ways no other animal has dreamed of.

Now that man understands these primordial connections, he must acknowledge his old debt to his partners throughout the whole range of organic creation, his constant dependence upon their activities, and not least his link with his own original nature. Though he is now the dominant species, his fate is still bound up with the prosperity of all forms of life; and he carries his own animal organs and his natural history into every ideal future that he projects. They, too, partake of the divine impetus and approach the unnameable goal.

(1956)

CHAPTER THIRTY-SEVEN

The Mindfulness of Man

The development of the central nervous system liberated man in large degree from the automatism of his instinctual patterns and his reflexes, and from confinement to the immediate environment in time and space. Instead of merely reacting to outer challenges or internal hormonal promptings, he had forethoughts and afterthoughts: more than that, he became a master of self-stimulation and self-direction, for his emergence from animalhood was marked by his ability to make proposals and plans other than those programmed in the genes for his species.

So far, purely for convenience, one may describe man's special advantages solely in terms of his big brain and complex neural organization, as if these were the ultimate realities. But this is only a portion of the story, because the most radical step in man's evolution was not just the growth of the brain itself, a private organ with a limited span of life, but the emergence of mind, which superimposed upon purely electro-chemical changes a durable mode of symbolic organization. This created a sharable public world of organized sense impressions and supersensible meanings: and eventually a coherent domain of significance. These emergents from the brain's activities cannot be described in terms of mass and motion, electro-chemical changes, or DNA and RNA messages, for they exist on another plane.

If the big brain was an organ for maintaining a dynamic balance between the organism and the environment under unusual challenges and stresses, the mind became effective as an organizing center for bringing about counter-adaptations and reconstructions both in man's own self and in his habitat; for the mind found means of outlasting the brain that first brought it into existence. At the animal level, brain and mind are virtually one, and over a large portion of man's own existence they remain almost undistinguishable—though, be it noted, much was known about the mind, through its external activities and communal products, long before the brain was even identified as the prime organ of mind, rather than the pineal gland or the heart.

In speaking of man's nervous responses, I use brain and mind as closely connected but not interchangeable terms, whose full nature cannot be adequately described in terms of either aspect alone. But I purpose to avoid both the traditional error of making mind or soul into an impalpable entity unrelated to the brain, and the modern error of disregarding as subjective— that is, beyond trustworthy scientific investigation—all typical manifestations of mind: that is, the larger part of man's cultural history. Nothing that happens in the brain can be described except by means of symbols supplied by the mind, which is a cultural emergent, not by the brain, which is a biological organ.

The difference between brain and mind is surely as great as that between a phonograph and the music that comes forth from it. There is no hint of music in the disc's microgroove or the amplifier, except through the vibrations induced via the needle by the record's rotation: but these physical agents and events do not become music until a human ear hears the sounds and a human mind interprets them. For that final purposeful act, the whole apparatus, physical and neural, is indispensable: yet the most minute analysis of the brain tissue, along with the phonograph's mechanical paraphernalia, would still throw no light upon the emotional stimulation, the esthetic form, and the purpose and meaning of the music. An electroencephalograph of the brain's response to music is void of anything that even slightly resembles musical sounds and phrases—as void as the physical disc that helps produce the sound.

When the reference is to meaning and the symbolic agents of meaning, I shall accordingly use the word mind. When the reference is to the cerebral organization that first receives and records and combines and conveys and stores up meanings, I shall refer to the brain. The mind could not come into existence without the active assistance of the brain, or indeed, without the whole organism and the environing world. Yet once the mind created, out of its overflow of images and sounds, a system of detachable and storable symbols, it gained a certain independence that other related animals possess only in a minor degree, and that most organisms, to judge by outward results, do not possess at all.

Evidence has accumulated to show that both sensory impressions and symbols leave imprints on the brain; and that without a constant flow of mental activity the nerves themselves shrink and deteriorate. This dynamic relation contrasts with the static impression of musical symbols on a phonograph record, which, rather, becomes worn-out through use. But the interrelation of mind and brain is a two-way process: for direct electronic stimulation of certain areas of the brain can, as Dr. Penfield Wilder has shown, 'bring to mind' past experiences, in a way that suggests how similar electric currents self-induced may cause irrelevant images to pop up unexpectedly into consciousness, how new combinations of symbols may be effected without deliberate effort, or how breaks in the internal electric circuit may cause forgetfulness or oblivion.

The relation between psyche and soma, mind and brain, are peculiarly intimate; but, as in marriage, the partners are not inseparable: indeed their divorce was one of the conditions for the mind's independent history and its cumulative achievements.

But the human mind possesses a special advantage over the brain: for once it has created impressive symbols and has stored significant memories, it can transfer its characteristic activities to materials like stone and paper that outlast the original brain's brief life-span. When the organism dies, the brain dies, too, with all its lifetime accumulations. But the mind reproduces itself by transmitting its symbols to other intermediaries, human and mechanical, than the particular brain that first assembled them. Thus in the very act of making life more meaningful, minds have learned to prolong their own existence, and influence other human beings remote in time and space, animating and vitalizing ever larger portions of experience. All living organisms die: through the mind alone man in some degree survives and continues to function.

As a physical organ, the brain is seemingly no bigger and little better today than it was when the first cave art appeared some thirty or forty thousand years ago—unless symbolic impressions have indeed been genetically enregistered and have made the brain more predisposed to mindfulness. But the human mind has enormously increased in size, extension, scope, and effectiveness; for it now has command of a vast and growing accumulation of symbolized experience, diffused through large populations. This experience was transmitted originally by impressive example and imitation and word-of-mouth from generation to generation. But during the last five thousand years, the mind has left its mark on buildings, monuments, books, paintings, towns, cultivated landscapes, and, of late, likewise upon photographs, phonograph records, motion pictures and computers. By these means, the human mind has in an increasing degree overcome the biological limitations of the brain: its frailty, its isolation, its privacy, its brief life-span.

This is by way of clarifying in advance the approach I shall soon make to the whole development of human culture. But one further point needs to be emphasized lest the reader overlook the basic assumption I have made: that brain and mind are non-comparable aspects of a single organic process. Though mind can exist and endure through many other vehicles than the brain, mind still needs to pass once more through a living brain to change from potential to actual expression or communication. In giving to the computer, for example, some of the functions of the brain, we do not dispense with the human brain or mind, but transfer their respective functions to the design of the computer, to its programming, and to the interpretation of the results. For the computer is a big brain in its almost elementary state: a gigantic octopus, fed with symbols instead of crabs. No computer can make a new symbol out of its own internal resources alone.

At some stage, suddenly or gradually, man must have awakened from the complacent routines that characterize other species, escaping from the long night of instinctual groping and fumbling, with its slow, purely organic adaptations, its too well memorized genetic "messages," to greet the faint dawn of consciousness. This brought an increasing awareness of past experience, along with fresh expectations of future possibility. Since evidence of fire has been found with the ancient bones of Peking man, the first steps man took beyond animalhood may have been partly due to his courageous reaction to fire, which all other animals warily avoid or flee from.

This playing with fire was both a human and a technological turning point: all the more because fire has a threefold aspect—light, power, heat. The first artificially overcame the dark, in an environment filled with nocturnal predators; the second enabled man to change the face of nature, for the first time in a decisive way, by burning over the forest; while the third maintained his internal body temperature and transformed animal flesh and starchy plants into easily digestible food.

Let there be light! With those words, the story of man properly begins. All organic existence, not least man's, depends upon the sun and fluctuates with the sun's flares and spots, and with the earth's cyclical relations to the sun, with all the changes of the weather and the seasons that accompany these events. Without his timely command of fire, man could hardly have survived the vicissitudes of the Ice Ages. His ability to think under these trying conditions may have depended, like Descartes's first insights in philosophy, upon his ability to remain quiet for long periods in a warm, enclosed space. The cave was man's first cloister.

But it is not by the light of burning wood that one must seek ancestral man's source of power: the illumination that specifically identifies him came from within. The ant was a more industrious worker than early man, with a more articulate social organization. But no other creature has man's capacity for creating in his own image a symbolic world that both cloudily mirrors and yet transcends his immediate environment. Through his first awareness of himself man began the long process of enlarging the boundaries of the universe and giving to the dumb cosmic show the one attribute it lacked: a knowledge of what for billions of years had been going on.

The light of human consciousness is, so far, the ultimate wonder of life, and the main justification for all the suffering and misery that have accompanied human development. In the tending of that fire, in the building of that world, in the intensification of that light, in the widening of man's open-eyed and sympathetic fellowship with all created being, lies the meaning of human history.

Let us pause to consider how different the entire universe looks, once we take the light of human consciousness, rather than mass and energy, to be the central fact of existence.

When the theological concept of an eternity without beginning or end was translated into astronomical time, it became apparent than man was but a newcomer on the earth, and that the earth was only a particle in a solar system that had existed for many billions of years. As our telescopes probed further into space, it became plain, too, that our own sun was but a speck in the Milky Way, which in turn was part of far vaster galaxies and stellar clouds. With this extension of space and time, man, as a physical object, with his limited span of existence, seemed ridiculously insignificant. On first reading, this colossal magnification of space and time seemed to destroy, as mere empty brag and vanity, man's claim to being of central importance; and even his mightiest Gods shriveled before this cosmic spectacle.

Yet this whole picture of cosmic evolution in terms of quantitative physical existence, with its immeasurable time and immeasurable space, reads quite differently if one returns to the center, where the scientific picture has been put together: the mind of man. When one observes cosmic evolution, not in terms of time and space, but in terms of mindful consciousness, with man in the central role as measurer and interpreter, the whole story reads quite differently.

Sentient creatures of any order, even the lowly amoeba, seem to be extremely rare and precious culminations of the whole cosmic process: so much so that the organism of a tiny ant, arrested in its development some sixty million years ago, still embodies in its mental organization and in its autonomous activities a higher mode of being than the whole earth afforded before life appeared. When we view organic change, not as mere motion, but as the increase of sentience and self-directed activity, as the lengthening of memory, the expansion of consciousness, and the exploration of organic potentialities in patterns of increasing significance, man's relation to the cosmos is reversed.

In the light of human consciousness, it is not man, but the whole universe of still "lifeless" matter that turns out to be impotent and insignificant. That physical universe is unable to behold itself except through the eyes of man, unable to speak for itself, except through the human voice, unable to know itself, except through human intelligence: unable in fact to realize the potentialities of its own earlier development until man, or sentient creatures with similar mental capabilities, finally emerged from the utter darkness and dumbness of pre-organic existence.

Note that in the last paragraph I put 'lifeless' in quotation marks. What we call lifeless matter is an illusion, or rather, a now-obsolete description based on insufficient knowledge. For among the basic properties of 'matter,' we know now, is one that for long was ignored by the physicist: the propensity for forming more complex atoms out of the primordial hydrogen atom, and more complex molecules out of these atoms, until finally organized protoplasm, capable of growth, reproduction, memory, and purposeful behavior appeared: in other words, living organisms. At every meal, we transform 'lifeless' molecules into living tissue; and with that transformation come sensations, perceptions, feelings, emotions, dreams, bodily responses, proposals, self-directed activities: more abundant manifestations of life.

All these capacities were potentially present, as Leibnitz pointed out, in the constitution of the primordial monad, along with the many other possibilities that have still to be plumbed. Man's own development and self-discovery is part of a universal process: he may be described as that minute, rare, but infinitely precious part of the universe which has, through the invention of language, become aware of its own existence. Beside that achievement of consciousness in a single being, the hugest star counts for less than a cretinous dwarf.

Physicists now estimate the age of the earth as between four and five billion years; and the earliest possible evidence of life comes about two billion years later, though living or semi-living proto-organisms that were not preserved surely must have come earlier. On that abstract time-scale man's whole existence seems almost too brief and ephemeral to be noted. But to accept this scale would betray a false humility. Time-scales are themselves human devices: the universe outside man neither constructs them nor interprets them nor is governed by them.

In terms of the development of consciousness, those first three billion years in all their repetitive blankness can be condensed into a brief moment or two of preparation. With the evolution of lower organisms during the next two billion years, those imperceptible seconds lengthened, psychologically speaking, into minutes: the first manifestations of organic sensitivity and autonomous direction. Once the mobile explorations of the backboned animals began, favored increasingly by their specialized nervous apparatus, the brain made its first groping steps toward consciousness. After that, as one species after another followed the same track, despite many branchings out, arrests, and regressions, the seconds and minutes of mindfulness lengthened into hours.

There is no need here to detail the anatomical changes and the constructive activities that accompanied the growth of consciousness in other species, from the bees and the birds to the dolphins and the elephants, or the ancestral species from which both apes and hominids evolved. But the final break-through came with the appearance of the creature we now identify as man, some five hundred thousand years ago, on our present tentative estimates.

With man's extraordinary development of expressive feeling, impressive sensitivity, and selective intelligence, which gave rise ultimately to language and transmissable learning, the hours of consciousness were prolonged into days. At first this change rested mainly on neural improvements; but as man invented special devices for remembering the past, for recording new experience, for teaching the young, for scanning the future, consciousness lengthened into centuries and millennia: no longer confined to a single life-time.

In the late paleolithic period, certain "Aurignacian" and "Magdalenian" hunting peoples made another leap upward by transfixing conscious images in painted and sculptured objects. This left a trail that can now be followed into the later arts of architecture, painting, sculpture, and writing, the arts for intensifying and preserving consciousness in a sharable and communicable form. Finally, with the invention of writing some five thousand years or more ago, the domain of consciousness was further widened and lengthened.

When at last it emerges into recorded history, organic duration reverses the mechanical, externalized time that is measured by calendars and clocks. Not how long you live, but how much you have lived, how much meaning your life has absorbed and passed on, is what matters. The humblest human mind encompasses and transfigures more conscious experience in a single day than our entire solar system embraced in its first three billion years, before life appeared.

For man to feel belittled, as so many now do, by the vastness of the universe or the interminable corridors of time is precisely like his being frightened by his own shadow. It is only through the light of consciousness that the universe becomes visible, and should that light disappear, only nothingness would remain. Except on the lighted stage of human consciousness, the mighty cosmos is but a mindless nonentity. Only through human words and symbols, registering human thought, can the universe disclosed by astronomy be rescued from its everlasting vacuity. Without that lighted stage, without the human drama played upon it, the whole theater of the heavens, which so deeply moves the human soul, exalting and dismaying it, would dissolve again into its own existential nothingness, like Prospero's dream world.

The immensities of space and time which now daunt us when with the aid of science we confront them, are, it turns out, quite empty conceits except as related to man. The word "year" is meaningless as applied to a physical system by itself: it is not the stars or the planets that experience years, still less measure them, but man. This very observation is the result of man's attention to recurrent movements, seasonable events, biological rhythms, measurable sequences. When the idea of a year is projected back upon the physical universe, it tells something further that is important to man: otherwise, it is a poetic fiction.

Every attempt to give objective reality to the billions of years the cosmos supposedly passed through before man appeared, secretly smuggles a human observer into the statement, for it is man's ability to think backwards and forwards that creates and counts and reckons with those years. Without man's time-keeping activities, the universe is yearless, as without his spatial conceptions, without his discovery of forms, patterns, rhythms, it is an insensate, formless, timeless, meaningless void. Meaning lives and dies with man, or rather, with the creative process that brought him into existence and gave him a mind.

Though human consciousness plays such a central part, and is the basis of all his creative and constructive activities, man is nevertheless no God: for his spiritual illumination and self-discovery only carry through and enlarge nature's creativity. Man's reason now informs him that even in his most inspired moments he is but a participating agent in a larger cosmic process he did not originate and can only in the most limited fashion control. Except through the expansion of his consciousness, his littleness and his loneliness remain real. Slowly, man has found out that, wonderful though his mind is, he must curb the egoistic elations and delusions it promotes; for his highest capacities are dependent upon the co-operation of a multitude of other forces and organisms, whose life-courses and life-needs must be respected.

The physical conditions that govern all life hem man in: his internal temperature must be kept within limits of a few degrees, and the acid-alkaline balance of his blood is even more delicate; while different hours of the day affect his ability to use his energies or rally against a disease, and the phases of the moon or changes in the weather willy-nilly have physiological or mental repercussions. In only one sense have man's powers become godlike: he has fabricated a symbolic universe of meaning that reveals his original nature and his slow cultural emergence; and up to a point this enables him to transcend in thought his many creaturely limitations. All his daily activities, feeding, working, mating, are necessary and therefore important: but only to the extent that they vivify his conscious participation in the creative process—that process which every religion recognizes as both immanent and transcendent, and calls divine.

Theoretically the present conquest of time and space might make it possible for a few hardy astronauts to circumnavigate every planet in the solar system, or still more improbably, to travel to one of the nearest stars, four or five light years away. Let us grant both projects as within the realm of mechanical if not biological possibility. But even if miraculously successful, these feats would be nothing compared to the deepening of consciousness and the widening of purpose that the history of a single primitive tribe has brought into existence.

Comets travel as fast as man can probably ever hope to travel, and make longer journeys: but their endless space voyages alter nothing except the distribution of energy. Man's most valiant explorations in space would still be closer to a comet's restricted possibilities than to his own historic development; whereas his earliest attempts at self-exploration, which laid the foundation for symbolic interpretation of every kind, above all language, are still far from exhausted. What is more, it is these inner explorations, which date from man's first emergence from animalhood, that have made it possible to enlarge all the dimensions of being and crown mere existence with meaning. In this definite sense human history in its entirety, man's own voyage of self-discovery, is so far the climactic outcome of cosmic evolution.

We now have reason to suspect that the achievement of consciousness may have taken place at more than one point in the stellar universe, even at many points, through creatures that perhaps exploited still other potentialities, or escaped better than man from the arrests and perversions and irrationalities that have checkered human history and which now, as man's powers vastly increase, seriously threaten his future. Yet, though organic life and sentient creatures may exist elsewhere, they are still infrequent enough to make man's achievement of his mind-molded culture infinitely more important than his present conquest of natural forces or his conceivable voyages through space. The technical feat of escaping from the field of gravitation is trivial compared to man's escape from the brute unconsciousness of matter and the closed cycle of organic life.

In short, without man's cumulative capacity to give symbolic form to experience, to reflect upon it and refashion it and project it, the physical universe would be as empty of meaning as a handless clock: its ticking would tell nothing. The mindfulness of man makes the difference.

(1967)

CHAPTER THIRTY-EIGHT

Archaic Man

We have arrived at a truism that has so far been forgotten it has the air of a paradox: the need to become human is man's first need, and perhaps it remains his deepest one. Nature provides the materials for this change, but man himself must effect it. In essence, it rests on a constant effort at self-identification, self-affirmation, self-discipline, and self-development: if much of this is routinized and imposed by the inherited culture pattern, it still was the outcome, in the first place, of willful effort. By becoming human, man exchanges the stable natural self, native to each biological species, for a countless multitude of possible selves, molded for the working out of a special drama and plot he himself helps to create.

But the "human" has never so far been the generically human: the image man coins in one culture does not yet pass as human legal tender, without a heavy discount, in other cultures. Possibly the transition from animal nature to human culture was made at different places, at different times, by stocks with somewhat different anthropoid ancestors, even if stemming from some common unspecialized line. So few in numbers were these hominids at the beginning, so widely sundered by oceans and deserts and mountains, that they separated out, in the course of their long development, into five or six major continental groups, showing patent physiological differences, beginning with differences in skin color, as between black, brown, tan, ivory, pink, and running through a gamut of other differences, such as blood types, immunities to disease, and many minor differences in anatomy. But by two marks, one biological, one social, all men proclaim themselves members of a single species: they can mate and produce equally fertile offspring; and they can communicate by speech.

These separating qualities, deepened in isolation by the effects of climate, vegetation, food, and occupational specializations, laid a basis for further cultural differences. Each group tended to conceive its own type, with its own characteristic expressions and projections, as the truly human one, when it encountered the members of another race; and so, too, each community, in its isolation, looked upon its own culture as in some sense more central than other cultures. This only means that in origin man's meaningful and valuable life was attached to a small group. "Humanity," as an open group that embraces all groups, did not exist even as a concept, probably, until the coming of the great culturally intermixed empires. Stoicism was its first great philosophic expression. Up to now it is still only an idea, though that idea approaches the phase of realization.

For the greater part of human history, then, and surely for all prehistory, the differentiating and isolating elements in culture have outweighed the pressures and aspirations that made for a wider unity. Not that marginal occasions for intermingling and borrowing were lacking: migration, marriage outside the local community, trade in special commodities, eventually travel and military conquest, all brought about some measure of cultural interchange and assimilation. But on the whole, the specific processes that served as agents in man's emergence for long remained localized and particularized: all the greater as achievements because they were the product of petty communities, limited in resources and manpower.

In this respect, early human groupings probably showed the same "territorial behavior" that biologists have lately discovered in many other species: a tendency associated with mating and the nurture of offspring to establish a delimited habitat, a home base, defended against the intrusion of outsiders, particularly outsiders of their own species. Within the claimed area, a local way of life would flourish, based on a local food supply, local sexual customs, local gods, a way confirmed in all its peculiarity by means of a local dialect and language, usually as unintelligible as a family joke to outlanders in the next valley. Secure in their specific human pattern, many groups must have largely contented themselves with that feat: to pass on that achievement seemed more important than to carry it any further. There are parts of the South, in the United States, where—it used to be sardonically remarked—merely "being white" constituted a lifetime's occupation. So there were long stretches of the human past when merely being human was enough to exhaust the efforts of the group.

In regions where there were plenty of fruits and nuts, this early period of arriving at the human estate may well have been one of leisure and plenty. Hesiod, in his 'Works and Days,' pictured that golden age when men "feasted gaily, undarkened by sufferings" and "died as if falling asleep, and all good things were theirs." That haunting image of a period before the curse of organized work and systematic butchery had descended on man may be less of a fond illusion than scholars once thought. The recurrent hardships of the glacial periods, which accompanied the early development of man, doubtless brought forth every form of skill and cunning to aid his survival. But the interglacial periods may have been relatively idyllic periods of ease and abundance; and the legend of a golden age is perhaps an authentic folk memory of a breathing spell in the midst of tropical luxuriance.

From the beginning, at all events, there are two sides to man's life, the

Promethean and the Orphic, the technical and the artistic: one mainly a struggle with the environment, the other an ideal expression and enjoyment of his own nature. These may even correspond in some degree to the rhythm of change, between a hostile marginal habitat, which called for external mastery as the price of survival, and a soft environment, which permitted playful experiments and rewarded them with further self-development.

There came a moment, probably after the lower paleolithic period and almost certainly before the neolithic, when not only had the change from animal to man reached the point of no return, but when all the prime inventions necessary to human development had been made: language, the expressive arts, morality, the use of fire and edged tools, and a body of traditional knowledge, sufficient not only to ensure physical survival but social continuity. Man had transformed himself into a creature concerned, not only with the perpetuation of his species, but with development of the good, the true, the beautiful, and the useful, as the capital instruments in his own self-transformation, and as the further by-products of that transformation.

What was incoherent, confused, ferocious, irrational, regressive, was never entirely sloughed off, but it ceased, except in moments of disintegration, to threaten man: he had achieved the means of making and remaking himself. If we call this creature "primitive man," the adjective is less significant than the noun: though he had still much to learn, he had acquired something infinitely precious: the method that made learning possible, and that further made it feasible to retain and pass on to those unborn what he had learned. Even before the great neolithic revolution, man had probably, as Carl Sauer and others have shown reason to believe, achieved settled communities, living on planted tubers and shellfish, with some of the continuities and domesticities that go with such a life.

Man cannot help leaving his imprint wherever he goes; but at the beginning, the impression he made on himself was perhaps greater than that he made on his environment. This changed when he made the great technical improvement of domestication, which we associate with the selection and cultivation of plants, and presently with the planting of crops in permanently cleared and cultivated fields. The invention of agriculture wrought a further change in man's self-culture; for domestication is a process of gentling and nurturing and breeding that demands selective care and forethought. In every part of this process woman's needs, woman's solicitudes, woman's intimacy with the processes of growth, woman's capacity for tenderness and love, played a dominating part.

As long as the old roving life prevailed, her place was necessarily a subordinate one: man's hunting prowess committed the group to a life almost as wild and mobile as the great herds of buffalo or deer that supplied his food. Hunting in packs for big game, like the hairy mammoth, paleolithic hunters perhaps developed habits of disciplined co-operation and physical courage that the older, pick-me-up ways of the food gatherers had not demanded: with this went doubtless the special masculine traits, long accounted virtues, the capacity to shed blood, to commit acts of violence. Even after the last glacial period, some of these brutal necessities may have left their mark upon the community, passing from the hunter to the herdsman, whose cold-blooded butchery indeed contrasts unfavorably with the more venturesome slayings of the hunter.

But at a critical moment a technical and social revolution took place, roughly some eight or ten thousand years ago. Like most human changes, its foundations were probably laid in an earlier period of partial cultivation; and in calling this new age the neolithic period, anthropologists clung to an old habit of overweighting the importance of durable physical relics. But though there was a marked advance in technical skill, in the passage from flaked tools and weapons to the ground and polished tools of the new economy, the profounder change was in most respects independent of these mechanical improvements: it rested on an insight into living processes: the selection and cultivation of plants, in particular the pulses and the hard grains, millet, wheat, barley, rice.

This domestication of plants seems largely woman's work: instead of taking life, like the hunter, she nurtured it in the earth, as she nurtured it in her own womb. With the planting of crops, man had for the first time a secure food supply from year to year that depended upon his own efforts more than upon luck and magic. With this came hearth and home: a permanent habitation and a regular habit of life, favorable to further nurture. Though the later domestication of animals encouraged nomadry again, in search of green pastures, the domestication of plants brought human settlement. With this, human life had a visible continuity in space and time that it had hitherto lacked: such a stabilized group of families living in villages provided by their common efforts not only a more secure supply of food, but better facilities for reproduction and the protective oversight and varied nurture of the young.

Possibly domestication had side effects that were as important for man's development as more direct and visible influences. Did woman's selective knowledge in breeding plants extend, during this period of consciously directing the reproductive processes, to the human species, too? To hazard even a guess would be to plunge again into the realm of myth. But there is modern physiological evidence to indicate that improvements in nutrition hasten the state of puberty and promote fertility: so that the quantitative increase of food in early neolithic times may have acted as a double stimulus upon population increase. So, too, we know that domestication tends, in other animals, to make reproduction a year-round function instead of a sharply seasonal one associated with a spring rutting period. Man's ancient ties to organic vernal changes are of course still visible: but his susceptibility to sexual impulses at all times of the year, his desire for sexual contact out of all relation to the need for offspring, may have grown with his own domestication; and this general expansion of the erotic impulse was perhaps not the least important aspect of the neolithic revolution, energizing his imagination and expanding the realm of sublimated sexuality, in art and ritual.

From the limited nature of his food supply and his technical equipment, even after the domestication of plants had been accomplished, we know that early man first emerged in very small communities, and the total population of all these communities must have been on the same order as the population of the North American continent when Western man discovered it: sparse and scattered. Agriculture made it possible for people to live generation after generation in little hamlets or villages; and as the food supply expanded, more such settlements must have come into existence, for with the increase of the population fresh land would be put under cultivation. Thus man became not only human but domesticated in an intimate, face-to-face environment, the world of the primary community: the family, the tribe, the clan, the village, the neighborhood. The visible presence of kinsmen and neighbors, friendly, responsive people, sharing the common life: the security of a place of limited dimensions, easily explored, full of concrete satisfactions, meaningful sights and sounds and smells, familiar landmarks—all this established a common human realm, midway between man's larger natural habitat and his symbolic abstractions: a realm where nature was humanized, and man was naturalized, for the environment reflected his own intentions and purposes, even as it preserved his memories and encouraged his hopes. To preserve that balance was the better part of wisdom: hence the fear of the non-traditional, the unaccustomed, the strange, the foreign: hence, too, the love of the accepted, the conventional, the often repeated, the proved: the veneration for ancestral ways. "This is done." "That is not done." Food, marriage, child care, all the events of life, indeed, fall under these customary canons of judgment. Unless one "belongs" one does not exist.

In this domestic village culture, there is for every occasion of life a bit of proverbial wisdom that clinches decision, guides action. In that security and inward peace, the people of the village could look across the river at another community, as Lao-tse observed, and never have the impulse to cross it. This early life was not free from severe disappointments, painful ordeals, and even ordinary psychal tensions: if it were, it would be hard to account for the early invention of beer and wine, which anesthetize anxiety, lift the depressed heart, soften pain. But compared to the repressions and conflicts that were to develop presently in the next stage of man's emergence, this phase had an almost idyllic calm. The rituals of seeding and planting and harvest enveloped human growth, though often mingled with darker rites of blood sacrifice. Feasts and festivals, crop tending and lovemaking, followed the cycle of the seasons. The Corn Goddess flourished. Economically, archaic society remains contentedly at the level of subsistence, rarely willing, while true to its own principles, to make the concentrated collective effort needed to produce a higher output. All the more, then, it welcomes the seasons of plenitude that soften its habitual penury: lucky catches, wind-falls, or the occasional golden harvests that make festal leisure possible. What extra wealth he possesses archaic man reserves for the great punctua-tion marks of life: birth, marriage, death.

In stressing the role of memory, habit, and tradition in primitive life, we have tended, during the last century, to treat the sense of the future as an entirely modern contribution. But to do this is somewhat to falsify both the facts of history and the nature of man. Human society, from the very beginning, shows plenty of forethought and anticipation, which reach well beyond the widespread animal tendency to put by food to tide over the winter: the prehistoric practice of ceremonious burial certainly con-cerns the future; and all sorts of providential and forward-looking acts, the planting and guarding of trees, the planning and building of permanent stone structures, show a design, not just to meet immediate needs, but to serve future occasions. Every monument, be it only a cairn or a sacred stone, is an admonition and a pledge to one's descendants. Just as the ability to take the future into account in any immediate judgment is one of the signs, psychologists tell us, of both intelligence and moral responsibility, so a mixture of anxiety and providence has been a constant mark of human development.

In early society the long future, as distinct from the day-to-day and generation-to-generation span, was left to the gods: man lacked both the intellectual and the physical powers to project his own plans over a millen-nial period, or to ordain wholesale social transformations that would in-volve every institution of society. But the change from a mainly backward-looking attitude to a forward-looking attitude is one only of emphasis: both were present, it would seem, in the earliest cultures, and both must be active if our present culture is to endure. "Man looks before and after," and *plans* "for what is not."

We have followed man's transformation back to its sources, hidden in time, much of it open only to the imagination. But beneath the visible sur-face of history runs an underground river carried forward from neolithic times, and still bearing the silt of even earlier cultures. Following André Varagnac, I shall call this "archaic culture." This archaic tradition, for all its many primitive characteristics, is not to be confused with the cultures of primitive peoples that survive today, though they have many common features. Our surviving primitives, through their long-introverted develop-ment, have achieved a degree of complexity and sophistication that often approaches decadence—as in the tribe that has surrounded canoe building with so many lethal taboos that they no longer dare build their canoes.

Archaic man took form in the neolithic village; and the attributes of his culture, still alive in custom down to the end of the nineteenth century, are as widely distributed as agriculture itself. Until the twentieth century mankind still lived in physical conditions approximating those of a neo-lithic village.

This communal archaic life is earthbound; its gods are the gods of vegetation; its whole routine of existence is associated with the cycle of the seasons, with the planting and harvesting of crops, with the mating of animals and the marriage of men and women. Having reached the level of skill and knowledge achieved by neolithic agriculture, the main effort of archaic man is to preserve the equilibrium of that life: he works hard enough to earn his food and lay by a surplus, if possible, for the next year; but he is not consumed by the need to pour into his working life, into mere productivity, the energy that should go into sexual play or reproduction, into games and rituals, into building and decoration. Down to our day, if Ray-mond Pearl's figures are correct, even American farmers, whose life has long been divorced from archaic rituals, still engage more often in sexual intercourse than their urban contemporaries.

The social nucleus of archaic life is the family. The household hearth is its altar, and the continuity of its life, through the house, the land, the children, the bounded fields, the animals and crops, is doubly assured by the handing on of the whole store of knowledge and precept from parent to child, from master to helper, from the old to the young. No small part of this lore is, when scientifically judged, fanciful and superstitious: ancient taboos, magical practices, mythical projections go along with its soundest empirical observations. But so close is this whole culture to the demands of life and the requirements for human nurture that it has met the test of reality—at least by the criterion of survival—longer than any other culture. Where its precepts are followed, it brings forth crops, arts, crafts, and, above all, men and women, regenerating the land itself, renewing the culture, and maintaining a sound human level.

Archaic man is the conservator of life: he guards the future by holding tight to the past and, above all, to his ancestors. Both in religious cult and in the looser form of general tradition, he worships his ancestors and seeks their guidance when he is confronted by life's situations, on the sound sup-position that the same difficulties must have occurred before. He does not for a moment imagine that the wisdom of the race is embodied in the ex-perience of a single lifetime, still less that his own individual fragment of experience would be sufficient to keep him straight. Archaic man, flinching from the new and the untried, is happy to live in the fashion of his fore-bears, to maintain the level they had reached, to pass on to his children, unimpaired, the heritage his parents passed on to him. Hence his respect for age; for only the old have lived long enough to take in the whole heri-tage and to hand it on. The wisdom of the Elders binds the present to the past and so prevents the future from falling short of the past. In case of conflict or doubt, it is in the council of the Elders that the living past speaks and lays down, with the least necessary alteration, the "eternal" way. Cus-tom and law, education and work, government and morality, are not separate departments of life: they are aspects of the whole—intuitively grasped because vividly lived—and only within this whole has each separate life its significance.

All the elements in this archaic life are part of a carefully ordered collective ritual that punctuates not merely man's works and days, but the stages of life. In this existence, the competitive spirit plays hardly any part, except perhaps in games and sexual rivalry: only what can be shared, what can be handed on to one's family or neighbor, deserves to be cherished. So deeply are habit and custom internalized that they become second nature. But the repetition is not compulsive and uniform: in every act, there is some measure of freedom, some play for individuality. One sees this objectively in the archaic arts, pottery, weaving, basketmaking, carving and even metalworking. Though the work itself is repetitive, and the general form is that of a particular village or the region, there remains a place for the personal touch, for the cherished accident (as in pottery glazes) that keeps any two products of handicraft from being absolutely uniform. What holds for useful products holds even more for art. Archaic myths and fairy stories and ballads spread from one land to another; but each version is the same with variations. Without this element of spontaneity and resilience archaic culture would not perhaps have had sufficient vitality to survive.

In archaic tradition, the land and the primeval occupations take a hold on the human spirit that is still unbroken. The land itself ceases to be mere territory, staked out against the intrusion of other creatures, though it remains that, too: it becomes a repository of sentiment, swarming with memories and projects: the place where one's ancestors are buried, whose paths were worn by their feet, whose trees were planted by their hands, whose stones were formed into walls and buildings by their labors, the place whose perpetual renewal or restoration forms the best part of the present generation's labors.

If this archaic environment was limited, it was cut to man's size and within his grasp. Its very restrictions increased his own sense of adequacy. This contrasts with our own age, whose vast expansion in every direction makes the individual feel ever more insignificant.

Though the words blood and soil have been degraded in our time by degraded men, their concrete realities pervade the archaic tradition and come down to us today even in the inflated stereotypes of patriotism and nationalism. Herodotus reports that the Cimmerians, who could have saved themselves from the invading Scythians by fleeing and finding new territory, decided instead to make a stand and be buried in their fatherland. Such an honorable attitude of piety toward the place of one's birth and nurture threads through the archaic record. And note: the cult of the ancestor, by its very nature, implies a provision for—and a loving watchfulness over—the descendant.

By the same token, though the basic form of work in archaic culture is agriculture, the other primitive occupations, hunting, fishing, boating, wood-cutting, herding, mining, weave themselves into the archaic fabric, producing modifications in human character, and accenting its individuality in special occupational roles. Through these occupations, even earlier traits and rituals enter the mainstream of archaic culture: the prowess, the risk-taking, the playful gambling of the hunter, for example, or the dogged courage and skill of the miner, whose arts go back to the paleolithic period. Through these occupations a variety of environments with their multifold suggestions and promptings helped further to shape the human spirit. Underneath later sublimations all these individualized primitive types remain, like the grain of the wood under paint or varnish.

The ancestors, the burgeoning family, and the household gods, the holy ritual, the cycle of vegetation and reproduction—these constitute the realities of archaic culture. A collective routine devoted to the nourishment and enhancement of every aspect of life; so that no part of human existence grew out of proportion to the other parts. All the goods of this life, however, fell within the charmed circle of the small community; and men paid a price for this security. The enclosed community produced the enclosed personality, and vice versa. Kindness was a quality one showed to the kinsman, and then by extension to the neighbor: truth, honesty, friendliness, forbearance, abstention from rape or murder, applied only to those within the community, not to those outside. This long apprenticeship in isolation left its mark, and even now tends to thwart a wider unity. We still associate stability and security with enclosure, and before the prospect of an open world we timidly shrink back with a kind of agoraphobia. Yet so central has this archaic culture been, so successful in providing norms for human development, that it has preserved itself under successive waves of civilization, right down to the present. In other forms than those created in neolithic times, its I-and-thou relationship must be carried into every wider community, if that community is to endure.

Though it is true that archaic culture lives to itself and lives for itself, we may easily overstress this fact, and forget that by the very diversity of human needs this insulation was far from complete. Slowly, the advances made at later stages of human development infiltrated archaic culture. It is not from the neolithic village that the almanac and the laws of private property come: it is not from the cult of the household gods that the village temple or church, attached to a prophetic tradition that claims universal assent, arises. Some of the ballads that seem the immemorial possession of a folk were produced in a distant royal court, just as many of the plants in field and orchard are the exotic booty of distant conquests or explorations, undertaken by more ambitious or envious people. These additions and accretions seep in from without and slowly become assimilated by the archaic culture. If archaic cultures become somewhat "civilized" the reverse process also takes place: the intruding civilization or religion becomes "paganized" in equal degree. No foreign form is used by archaic culture until it has, as it were, rotted and become part of the organic cultural compost.

The archaic tradition has maintained its hold, with varying degrees of tenacity, in every part of the world right down to our own time: least perhaps in North America, and most, it seems likely, in India and China. All through Europe, its relics remain in pagan festivals like Midsummer Eve and Carnival, in the persistence of folklore and sympathetic magic, in superstitions about lucky days and lucky numbers, which have defied generations of rational education.

But perhaps the deepest effect of archaic tradition was the operation of taboo: a universal trait that first drew the traveler's attention in Polynesia. Taboo affixes to this or that object or act an absolute prohibition: the canoe used by men must not be entered by women, or one who has touched the dead must purify himself before having contact with the living. Few taboos, even the almost world-wide one against incest, are more than partly rational: but the absolute inhibition invoked by the taboo was one of the great safeguards man invented against mischievous self-induced images and unconscious powers that might overwhelm him. As with a well-trained army, the generalized habit of obedience, the respect for inviolate limits, was more important than the particular occasion that brought it forth.

Precisely because taboo carries no practical or reasonable sanction, it established a strict habit of self-control. Where the young have neither veneration for their elders nor respect for taboo—where in fact they have grown up completely outside the circle of archaic culture—they easily express themselves in acts of juvenile delinquency, for whatever senseless violent impulse may seize them passes directly into action. No sacred inhibition, no sense of awful limits and bounds, now stands in the way of rape, torture, murder. And what began in our time as contempt for the ancestor now widens into a contempt for posterity. Against the fatal consequence of such a change, so horrifying in its possibilities to an age that has conjured up the hydrogen bomb, the archaic culture long guarded the human race.

Archaic life, in its time-weathered, moss-covered forms, still charms us and calls to us. When we are tired of facing the complexities of civilization, when disease has lowered our vitality and mental conflicts have disrupted our social relations, we turn back to some little village, almost lost to sight under the trees or barely visible along the shore. There we feel at one both with external nature and our own deepest selves: "restored" as we say. Do we ever indeed feel more fully satisfied with the passing moment than when we go berry picking or mushroom hunting, like dawn man, or when we idly gather sandworn stones and shells and driftwood along a beach? The joy of pure being: life concentrated and consummated in the moment. Then work is play again, and living itself no longer a problem. Jean-Jacques Rousseau could not guess it; but the whole rationale of romanticism was an attempt to get back to the ancestral norms of Stone Age culture.

In the midst of this satisfying milieu, so deeply harmonious with our nature that we forget how much of it was painfully acquired before it became natural, we ask ourselves why we should ever leave it for a more complex, more unstable, more anxious, certainly less harmonious existence. The answer to that question, once we dare to ask it, is not so simple as it seems; for it summons to the bar of rational judgment the whole development of civilization. That is the question Herman Melville asked himself in the midst of his Polynesian paradise among the Typees. "Civilization does not engross all the virtues of humanity . . ." he observed. "They flourish in greater abundance and attain greater strength among many barbarous peoples." Yet at the first chance that offered Melville left this paradise behind him. So it was with man himself, if we except those scattered tribal communities that continued to exist in their separateness—more than six hundred and fifty of them—down to our own era.

At a late moment in man's emergence he left behind the securities and intimacies and solidarities of tribal existence. What remained of archaic society served as the roadbed and right of way for the more mobile forms of civilizaton. At this point an audacious minority in a handful of specially situated communities made a daring thrust in a new direction: the experiment of civilization. With that step the past ceases to be represented in our diggings by dim campsites, scattered implements, or primitive villages. Instead we find buried cities, imposing temples, all manner of works of art: presently we come upon hieroglyphs and well-preserved written records in languages close enough to modern tongues to be translated.

When we look closer at these surviving records and monuments, we make a startling discovery: in the habits and institutions, the myths and religious rites, the forms of economic and technical organization, we are looking at our own civilization. Even the irrationalities and perversions are not altered. Only one essential change has taken place. Every dimension has been magnified.

(1956)

CHAPTER THIRTY-NINE

World Culture

The development of a world culture concerns mankind at large and each individual human being. Every community and society, every association and organization, has a part to play in this transformation; and no domain of life will be unaffected by it. This effort grows naturally out of the crisis of our time: the need to redress the dangerous overdevelopment of technical organization and physical energies made infinitely more dangerous by the psychotic counter-reactions this has now brought about. In that sense, the rise of world culture comes as a measure to secure human survival. But the process would lose no small part of its meaning were it not also an effort to bring forth a more complete kind of man than history has yet disclosed. That we need leadership and participation by unified personalities is clear; but the human transformation would remain desirable and valid, even if the need were not so imperative.

Let us make one basic assumption: the destiny of mankind, after its long preparatory period of separation and differentiation, is at last to become one. At the outset, this conception rejects the continued extension of a purely extraneous, technological kind of universalism, such as would be conceived by post-historic man. The new unity we conceive lies at the other end from totalitarian uniformity: it is one that seeks to enrich and enhance, in the very transactions of world society, the human values that differentiation has brought into existence. That is why it is stultifying to conceive that the means for bringing about unity lie, willy-nilly, in the further development of mechanical collectives and conglomerates, monitored by computers, on a planetary scale. One of the positive incentives toward bringing about world unity, indeed, is the necessity for finding alternatives to an integration based on a mechanical uniformity that would nullify individuality, curb variety, and deny a sufficient measure of regional and local autonomy.

As we have seen, the need to enlarge the area of intercourse and human co-operation had its rise in the earliest civilizations. Even the crude attempts to produce unity by economic expropriation and military conquest achieved

a post-factum justification by actually subserving man's higher development: in that sense St. Augustine could even justify the military exploits
and material organization of Rome, as providing a means for disseminating
the Christian gospel. As for the axial religions and philosophies—Buddhism, Zoroastrianism, Stoicism, Christianity, Islam—they were even more
consciously dedicated to unity than the great empires. Part of their dynamism was due to their belief that, as Pascal put it, the whole history of
mankind, for all its diversity, may be treated as the biography of a single
creature, man.

In coming to a world culture, we naturally build on these earlier efforts
at universalism. But we go even farther, because we must assume, as a result of our historic analysis, that none of man's past can in fact be left behind. With this assumption, we rectify the serious error that the New World
ideology made, alike in its utopian, its utilitarian, and its romantic philosophies. Even if we deliberately chose to make no use of the funded values
of history, the living past with its goods and its evils would still be present
under the surface, deflecting seemingly autonomous decisions, holding back
fresh advances, working all the more effectively because of our failure to
be conscious of these pressures. We may with good reason, for example,
plan to wipe out the institution of war, as earlier societies wiped out the
practices of cannibalism and incest: but if we chose to forget the facts of
power, conflict, and criminal ambition, desiring to dwell only on the pleas-
anter aspects of man's record, we might usher in the day when our very
innocence might encourage a reappearance of this evil in a new guise. And
if we failed in our education for peace to include the dedication and discipline of the soldier, his readiness to undergo hardship and face death, we
would forfeit one of the most important attributes of a noble character,
essential for world culture.

But note: no part of the past can enter world culture in the form that
it took independently in an earlier situation. As with every other fresh
integration, each part must die to its old form, in order to be born anew
within a larger whole, and become viable in terms of the new self and the
new culture we are putting forward. The failure to undergo this regeneration
is what made the earlier clinging to venerable historic examples so burdensome to the Egyptians, the Jews, the Chinese, to say nothing of other peoples who idolized their dead selves. While the ability to select, to revaluate,
and to rethink the past in terms of its further development in the future
is what has given vitality to every true cultural renascence.

Now this change toward world culture parallels a change that seems
also on the point of taking place within the human personality: a change
in the direction of wholeness and balance. In the new constellation of the
person, as we shall presently see, parts of the human organism long buried
or removed from conscious control will be brought to light, recognized,
accepted, revaluated, and redirected. The ability to face one's whole self,
and to direct every part of it toward a more unified development, is one of

the promises held forth by the advance both of objective science and subjective understanding. Wholeness is impossible to achieve, in fact, without giving primacy to the integrative elements within the personality: love, reason, the impulse to perfection and transcendence.

Without a concept of development, without a hierarchy of values, the mere lifting of unconscious repressions might simply produce, as it has often done in our day, a wholesale eruption of the libido, which would turn the mind itself into an instrument for slaying the higher impulses. Perhaps the greatest difficulty today, as a result of the general hostility to values brought in by seventeenth-century science, is the failure to recognize that wholeness demands imperatively that the highest elements in the human personality should be singled out, accepted and trusted, fortified and rewarded. The integration of the person begins at the top, with an idea, and works downward till it reaches the sympathetic nervous system, where organic integration in turn probably begins and works upward, till it emerges as an impulse of love or an image of fulfillment. In this replenishment of the whole self under a formative idea lies the promise of reducing the distortions, conflicts, isolationisms, infantilisms, and obsessions that have limited human growth.

The relations between world culture and the unified self are reciprocal. The very possibility of achieving a world order by other means than totalitarian enslavement and automatism rests on the plentiful creation of unified personalities, at home with every part of themselves, and so equally at home with the whole family of man, in all its magnificent diversity. Unified man must accept the id without giving it primacy: he must foster the superego, without making it depress the energies it needs for its own fuller expression. Without fostering such self-knowledge, such balance, such creativity, a world culture might easily become a compulsive nightmare.

To be on friendly terms with every part of mankind, one must be on equally friendly terms with every part of oneself; and to do justice to the formative elements in world culture, which give it greater significance and promise than any earlier stage in man's history, one must nourish the formative elements in the human self, with even fuller energies than axial man applied to this task. In brief, one cannot create a unified world with partial, fragmentary, arrested selves which by their very nature must either produce aggressive conflict or regressive isolation. Nothing less than a concept of the whole man—and of man achieving a consciousness of the cosmic and historic whole—is capable of doing justice to every type of personality, every mode of culture, every human potential. At this point a further human transformation, so far not approached by any recorded culture, may well take place.

The kind of person called for by the present situation is one capable of stepping over the boundaries of custom and culture, which have so far limited human growth. A person not indelibly marked by the tattooings of his tribe or restricted by the taboos of his totem: not sewed up for life in the stiff clothes of his caste and calling or encased in vocational armor he cannot remove even when it endangers his life. A person not kept by his religious dietary restrictions from sharing spiritual food that men of other nations have found nourishing; and finally, not prevented by his ideological spectacles from ever getting more than a glimpse of the world as it shows itself to men with other ideological spectacles, or as it discloses itself to those who may, with increasing frequency, be able without glasses to achieve normal vision.

The immediate object of world culture is to break through the premature closures, the corrosive conflicts, and the cyclical frustrations of history. This breakthrough would enable modern man to take advantage of the peculiar circumstances today that favor a universalism that earlier periods could only dream about. But the ultimate purpose of One World culture is to widen the human prospect and open up new domains—on earth, not in interstellar space—for human development. If the chief result of a world civilization were only to provide each individual with a television set, a motor car, a social security card, and a one-way ticket on a spaceship, one might as well turn the planet over at once to post-historic man.

The resources for this human transformation have been available for only little more than a century; and many of the technical instruments and corporate agencies have still to be shaped. But for the first time in history, man now begins to know his planet as a whole and to respond to all the peoples who inhabit it: that is, he begins to see his own multiple image in a common mirror, or rather, in a moving picture that traverses backward and forward the dimension of time. Since the exploration of the earth was undertaken by Western man before he was spiritually prepared for it, the peoples and regions that were drawn together by trade, colonization, and conquest lost many of the most precious attributes of their cultures and their personalities. The New World expansion barbarized the conquerors instead of civilizing the conquered. By the same token, Western man impoverished his own future development, too, for the heritage he mangled and often extirpated was also his own, as a member of the human race. In his land hunger, in his greed for gold and silver, for coal and iron and oil, Western man overlooked or even despised far greater riches.

Though our dawning sense of interdependence and unity comes too belatedly to repair all the damage that has been done, we see that even the residue of past cultures still holds more values than any single nation has yet created or expressed. By his very consciousness of history, modern man may free himself at last from unconscious compulsions, derived from situations he has outlived, which continue to push him off the highway of development into rubbish-filled blind alleys. Yet if he achieves a fresh understanding of the potentialities he has buried through his own failure to know himself, he may repair his shattered confidence in his future and throw open new vistas.

The survey of human existence as a whole that has gone on systematically only for the last four centuries has not alone naturalized man by bringing him within the cycle of cosmic, geological, and biological processes: it has likewise humanized nature and made it more closely than ever before an integral part of human consciousness. Man's own creative works, whether they are a temple, an atomic pile, or a mathematical theorem, are themselves expressions of nature and witnesses of potentialities that were latent in the atom and in the formative process that built up, in rhythmic series, the stable elements.

Whatever the ultimate realities, that which man knows of nature is conditioned by his self, and it changes from moment to moment and age to age as his experience matures and his capacity for symbolic interpretation grows. His feelings and emotions, his drives and his devices, are as much a part of this reality as his thoughts, for his very concept of an "objective," neutral world without feelings and values was itself the product of a particular moment in his own self-development whose limitations he has now become aware of. Yet whatever man knows of himself is conditioned by nature: so that the more exact, the more self-detached, becomes his perception of natural processes, the more fully does he free himself from the delusions of arbitrary subjectivity. Brahman and Atman are indeed one, once they are conceived in dynamic interaction: the self-creating world and the world-creating self.

This exploration of nature has naturally opened up man's inner history, too. Within the individual soul man finds in symbolic form a whole universe that seems to contain the scattered debris of past cultures and the germinal nodes of future ones. Here, within himself, he finds primitive urges and civilized constraints, tribal fixations and axial liberations, animal lethargies and angelic flights. Through the agency of culture, if not through any more direct impress upon the psyche, all of man's past selves remain disconcertingly alive. Just as man's interpretation of the so-called physical world has now become multidimensional, spanning the whole distance from interstellar to intra-atomic space, and including an exact knowledge of phenomena, like ultraviolet rays, which are outside his sensory experience, so with the inner world of man: it ranges from the depths of the unconscious to the highest levels of conscious ideation, disciplined feeling, and purposeful action.

Our view of the self now includes earlier interpretations that science, it its confident externalism, had discarded. Augustine's picture of the mind is closer to Freud's than is John Locke's, and St. Paul's description of human nature seems far more adequate than Jeremy Bentham's. Heaven and hell, as the ultimate destinations of creativity or disintegration, are necessary cardinal points in any description of the human soul. It is not through scientific description, but through sympathy and empathy, through parallel acts of re-creation, that one explores this world, even after it has been opened up to other men in the symbols and forms of art.

Every culture attaches different estimates to man's nature and history; and in its creative moments, it adds new values that enlarge the human personality and give it new destinations. Though man's release from nature's conditions or his own past selves can never be complete, the effort to achieve it is what gives individuality to every historic form: this indeed is what keeps even the most repetitive movements of history from being entirely meaningless. The making of the future is an essential part of man's self-revelation.

The problem for man today is to use his widened consciousness of natural processes and of his own historic nature to promote his own further growth. Such knowledge must now be turned to fuller uses, in the projection of a fresh plan of life and a new image of the self, which shall be capable of rising above man's present limitations and disabilities. This effort, as we have seen, is an old one; for even before man achieved any degree of self-consciousness, he was actively engaged in self-fabrication. If "Be yourself" is nature's first injunction to man, "Transform yourself" was her second— even as "Transcend yourself" seems, at least up to now, to be her final imperative. What will distinguish the present effort to create world culture, if once it takes form, is the richness and variety of the resources that are now open, and the multitude of people now sufficiently released from the struggle for existence to play a part in this new drama.

The readiness to face existence in all its dimensions, cosmic and human, is the first requirement for human development today. This readiness is itself a new fact, for even scientists, whose curiosity seems boundless, for long recoiled in fear against any exploration of the subjective self that penetrated beyond the threshold of isolated stimuli, abstracted sensations, and measured responses.

Not without a certain irony, the scientific rationalism of Dr. Sigmund Freud, with its fine surgical indifference to the seemingly morbid, brought to light the areas of the personality that positivism and rationalism had dismissed as "unreal"—the wish and the dream, the sense of guilt and original sin, the elaboration of fantasy into art; and by carrying this inquiry further, into the normal healthy manifestations of these inner states, Dr. Carl Jung disclosed the integrating functions of the symbol, and thus opened a passage from self-enclosed subjectivity to those common aesthetic expressions and practical constructions that can be shared, in a spirit of love, with other people.

This opening up of every part of the psyche coincides, it would seem, with the new relationship that has begun to develop between cultures. This is symbolized by an appreciative awareness, hardly a generation old, of the aesthetic values of African or Polynesian or Aztec or Andean art, following an equally radical change in Western man's attitude toward the great arts of Egypt, Mesopotamia, Persia, India, and China, once considered too far below the absolute standard of Greek art to merit study, still less appreciation. That change might, of course, lead to an abortive cultural relativism, innocent of any principle of development, were it not attached to the emergent purposes of world culture. The partial and fragmentary selves that man historically achieved sacrificed completeness for the sake of temporary order; and in the most partial and fragmentary form of all, that now sought by post-historic man, the order would be almost absolute, because so much that was essentially human would be left out of it.

From this negative universalism the acceptance of man's whole self, disclosed only in the fullness of history, helps to rescue us; for organic wholeness itself is impossible unless the creative and integrating processes remain uppermost. Religion and art, if not science, remind us of the constant reappearance of angelic saviors and redeemers: Promethean heroes who bring fire and light, defying the tortures of the envious gods: mother images of succor and loving devotion. We have learned nothing from historic experience if we have not learned that man lives by more than his applied intelligence alone.

Out of the depths of life itself come the superego, the conscience, the idealized image and the imagined ideal, the voice of reason and the promptings of divinity: all as integral to man's present nature as breathing or digestion. For it is not just the animal past that lives on in man's unconscious: the emergent future that has not yet taken form is likewise present: all that promises to release man from fixations and regressions and to open up untested modes of being and becoming, of transfiguration and transformation. Though no small part of human history has been preoccupied with the exploration of this inner world, even to the detriment of man's control over the external world, it has yet to enlist man's fullest capabilities. And as with the discovery of the New World there is an even more difficult stage that follows the surveying and mapping of the unknown area: that is, its settlement and cultivation.

With respect to man's inner development, we have seen it go roughly through four main stages: each of these has left a mark on both his ideas and his institutions.

In the primitive stage, the stage of magic and myth, he was innocent of self-consciousness, because his self, as an entity apart from the group, was still nonexistent; and he therefore lacked the capacity for independent action and invention which became feasible only after a certain separation had taken place. Subjectively, every part of human experience held together, expressible in meaningful images and symbols; but the price of this unity was insulation from any possibly contradictory reality. Primitive man, as we piece him together from the myths and relics that remain, was relatively whole; but in transcending his animal state he had left the real world, since he no longer recognized otherness: what he saw and felt and reacted to were his own projections, his own externalized feelings and urges, into which all outward events were somehow converted.

Civilization placed external curbs on this subjectivity: it exacted external obedience to powers other than his own, to gods and kings if not to actual conditions of nature; and it provided all human activities with a mechanical basis of order. The metes and bounds so provided secured man, in some degree, against subjective dissolution. To the extent that civilization made man recognize his own limitations, and released him from purely wishful fantasy, it enlarged the human grip on reality. But in recognizing as absolute claims outside the self, civilized man ceased to live in a unified world: the fragmentary man, with his split and contradictory selves, came into existence: the innocent paranoia of primitive man gave place to the schizoid state seemingly chronic to civilization in every phase.

With the development of axial religious consciousness a new self came into existence. In a determined effort to achieve wholeness, the inner man split himself off from the outer world and its imprisoning institutions. So real became the vision of a single unifying God, omniscient and omnipotent, that the outer world seemed, in comparison, trivial and unimportant. Meaning and value were attached to the inner, the disembodied, the subjective; and such aspects of nature as were manifestly part of another system were the expression of God's will and mind, not man's. This innerness was even more audacious in its revelations than that of primitive man; and it restored man's sense of his own self-importance, after civilization had reduced him to a mere fraction, virtually a nonentity, paralyzed by power and authority external to him.

But if axial religion escaped the fragmentation of the civilized order, it did so only by creating a dualism between "this world" and the "other world." This disturbed both inner tranquillity and practical effectiveness. Every external display of human order and power or even intelligence involved a betrayal of the inner man, or seemed a threat to his existence. That inveterate, underlying dualism of the axial self was challenged by another conception, first formulated in Ionia in the sixth century B.C., which shifted meaningful experience from the inner world to the outer world. This philosophy denied, in effect, the importance of the soul as an independent entity, with its conscious values and ideal goals, and gave weight only to the external manifestations of "earth, air, fire, and water," devoid of purpose or goal, and detached from any self-consciousness except that exhibited by rational intelligence. The self was thus reduced to the knower, and reality was reduced to that which could be known.

Unfortunately this view, which came to maturity in the seventeenth century, was only a dualism in reverse: it achieved unity by suppressing or ignoring every subjective expression except its own kind of thought. The conscious inner world that was thus brought into existence was ostentatiously antiseptic, like the operating theater in a hospital: within this special room, with its refined mechanical facilities, the mind learned to operate with a deftness and precision that only the rarest spirits had mastered before. But outside in the corridors there was dirt and disorder and disease: the rejected parts of the psyche were in a worse state under this new dispensation than the rejected parts of the physical world had been under the axial self.

At all these stages in the development of the self, only a small part of man's potentialities were consciously represented in image or idea. Fortunately, the repressed or neglected aspects, even in primitive society, were not effectively excluded from living experience. However well fortified the inner world, some of the outer world is constantly breaking through, making demands that must be met, offering suggestions that, even if unheeded, produce a certain effect. So, too, however heavy the crust formed by external nature, by human institutions and habits, the pressure from the inner world would produce cracks and fissures, and even from time to time explosively erupt. By no attention to magic formulae, by no probing of the unconscious, can one shape a tool. Similarly, by no feat of mechanical organization can one write a poem. In other words, by the very act of living men have always in some degree escaped the imperfections of their knowledge and belief. Just as life itself, in its constantly unfolding creativity, is far richer than any conception we are able to form of it, so with the human self. Man not merely builds but lives better than he knows.

At the same time, it should be plain that a great measure of man's potential energy and vitality and creativity has been dissipated, because he has not been fully oriented to every aspect of reality, outward and inward. His various historic selves have served as fine meshes that rejected far more than they admitted. We can hardly yet picture the transformation that would be wrought if every part of man's experience were hospitably received; and if every part of the inner world were as accessible and as subject to conscious direction as the outer world. So far we have lived mainly in partial worlds; and they have allowed only a small share of our energies to be directly employed. Neither the loose subjective wholeness achieved by primitive man nor, at the other extreme, the accurate, piecemeal objectivity now sought by science could do justice to every dimension of human experience. If the first was limited by its caprices, which recognized no external order or causality, the latter is equally limited by its compulsions, which recognize no inner flow of purpose and make no account of free creativity or potential divinity. Living in half-worlds, it is hardly strange that we have produced only half-men, or creatures even more distorted than these homunculi, "inverted cripples," as Nietzsche called them, magnified ears, eyes, bellies, or brains, whose other parts have shrunk away.

Perhaps an even better figure for the state of man, as disclosed by history, would be that of a series of experimental plants, each fed with some of the elements necessary for full growth, but none yet supplied with all of them: here an excess of nitrogen has favored a leggy growth of stem, there the absence of water has withered the whole plant; and, to make the figure even more accurate, in addition to these natural defects, the horticulturist himself has often clipped and pruned the growing plant or pinched its buds. What the experiment shows, if we may at last draw a lesson, is that man requires a sounder diet, including minute trace elements, than any self-enclosed historic culture has supplied him. He needs both a fuller exposure to sunlight above ground and a richer soil in the unconscious.

The ideal of wholeness itself is what has been lacking in the culture of man: his specialties and particularities have gotten the better of him. But from occasional periods, like the Renascence, when the ideal of the whole man has commanded the foremost representatives of the age, we have a hint of the immense energizing that may take place when every aspect of life is open to cultivation, when the instinctual life is no longer cut off from rational development, and when order and reason are not impoverished by torpid emotions or listless routines or limited purposes.

But even in unpropitious periods, individual figures, who had reached some degree of maturity in every department of life, may have appeared from time to time, only to be rejected by the society they transcended. At more than one moment in history, indeed, the effort to achieve wholeness, balance, universality, brought a measure of fulfillment. Greek culture, from the sixth century to the fourth, was remarkably peopled by such whole men: Solon, Socrates, Sophocles, were outstanding examples, but not rare ones: indeed, the proportion of highly developed persons in relation to the total population seems to have been greater than at possibly any other place and time.

These examples of wholeness may account for the attraction that Greek culture has exercised on the best minds of the West. To a degree that few other cultures could claim, the Greek self seems to stand for the truly and fully human. The development of any individual might show flaws: witness Socrates' serious failure to connect man in the city with man in nature. But in the main, no part of life was closed to them, and no part of the self claimed such exclusive respect that it crippled other capacities or closed other avenues of experience. Sophocles' readiness to do his duty as citizen, in service as a general, did not incapacitate him as a tragic playwright: for in both roles he was first of all a man. The ultimate mysteries and irrationalities of existence—symbolized by Chance, Fate, the Furies, Eros—entered their consciousness without upsetting their composure or undermining the real values they had won.

Yet even at its fullest development, this Hellenic self, so finely poised, so admirably complete within its own cultural boundaries, its own favored habitat, lacked universality. Their best representatives did not realize that the unity and balance they sought needed the help of other cultures and other types of personality: that in fact the barbarian they despised had had experiences and had produced values that might, for example, have kept one of their most creative minds, Plato, from conceiving such static and stultifying utopias as those he pictured in 'The Republic' and 'The Laws.' From the Jews, the Greeks needed to learn about the meaningfulness of time, change, and history; from the Persians, the fact that tension and struggle are essential to human growth, so that a polity that sought only a vegetative perfection, free from dialectic oppositions of good and evil, would be founded on illusion.

The example of the Greeks shows that the ideal possibilities of our own day have historic roots: their failures show that it is only by our accepting the realities of a contemporary world society, instead of seeking a more limited province for a more limited self, that we can find a new foundation for our own further development. The self we seek, one that will have a heightened consciousness of its own still-unused resources, has still to be created. To the shaping of that self we must give no small part of the energies that we have so far recklessly squandered on our misdirected and muddled "conquest of nature." Only by a deliberate concentration on our inner world, sufficient to counterbalance our present externalism, can we hope in time to achieve the balance and wholeness which will permit a steady flow of energies back and forth between inner and outer. In the fullness of time, a unified self will bring a world culture into existence, and that world culture will in turn sustain and bring to a higher pitch of development this new self.

Every transformation of man, not least that promoted by science, has rested on a new metaphysical, religious, and ideological base; or rather, upon deeper stirrings and intuitions whose rationalized expression takes the form of a new picture of the cosmos and the nature of man. Even neolithic man may have been no exception; for who can say what images of fertility, what intuitions of the relation of seed and soil, phallus and womb, may not have been the prelude to that order? Our hope of creating one world within and without, accessible in all its reaches to all men, prompting a life more copious, vehement, and bold than any that has appeared before, rests upon a corresponding ideological change. To achieve unity between men, we must cultivate unity within ourselves: to enact that unity, we must have a vision of the whole before our eyes.

We have need, therefore, for a rational framework that will itself have the varied attributes of life: it must be capable of reconciling persistence with change, unity with variety, the internal with the external, the causal with the teleological, process with purpose. Many attempts to formulate such a philosophy during the last two centuries have been handicapped by the traditional tendency of philosophy itself to create a single watertight system, too confidently complete to admit repair or enlargement by other minds. We see this plainly in the early efforts by Comte, Marx and Spencer to frame an all-embracing synthesis. Each philosophy, in excluding every rival system, undermined its own pretence to unity. Even the sciences themselves which can modify their foundations and make additions to the superstructure without undermining the sound parts already built, have no place for any kind of experience except that which can be ratified by their methods, which exclude nonintellectual modes of understanding or creativity.

Certainly it would be presumptuous to attempt to rectify these errors by creating still another closed system; but it would be even more stultifying to follow the path taken by most contemporary philosophers and abandon the search for a dynamic synthesis and unity as beyond human power. To effect a new transformation of man, we must be informed by a philosophy capable of uniting every aspect of human experience, and directing human development through every phase. Whilst the personless and purposeless *Weltbild* of seventeenth-century physics is already partly discredited in the sciences where it originated, the great corpus of scientific knowledge was largely formed under its influence. Most of our positive knowledge has passed through a filter devised to eliminate those aspects of experience that reveal autonomous and purposeful activities, not characteristic of purely physical systems.

Even in the human sciences the same limitation holds. The reductive technique of conventional science, interpreting the complex in terms of the simple, the higher in terms of the lower, the whole in terms of the part, is useless for revealing movement in the opposite direction. It has no method for working forward toward the future, following the path of integration and development and emergence and conscious design: so it fails to understand those organic processes in which the end or goal plays a part in determining the earlier sequence of events, even though the end, as imagined or projected, is itself subject in the very act of realization to further changes in its own structure. In existence, the human person, has a position of responsibility for interpreting and directing the course of life, in so far as that now lies increasingly within his hands. Instead of devaluating the person by reducing him to his animal lusts and drives, or to his even lower physicochemical components, it attaches a fresh value to all natural events by bringing them within the purview of the person.

This new polarization of thought around the concept of the person, as the highest emergent of the cosmic process, has been going on in many different minds during the past generation; but in a different sense than that of the axial religions. One means here, not the particular illumined person, the singular incarnation of axial religion, but the generic person, the last term in the development of the physical universe, the organic world, and the human community. As such, the person is endowed with the energies and vitalities of each earlier emergence. But he transcends his creaturely limitations by his capacity to interpret natural events, to conserve forms and values, to plan and project new goals and new destinies, to hold together in consciousness a meaningful world and to transform by action ever wider reaches of life, in accordance with that meaning.

The philosophy of the person includes every aspect of experience: the reality of love no less than the reality of power, the reality of the unique and the individualized no less than the reality of the repeated and the standardized. In the person both immanence and transcendence, necessity and freedom, are facts of experience. When we begin with the person we penetrate life at every level, not merely the past and the known, but the potential and the conceivable: that which still lies beyond our knowing. This is the polarizing idea that will soon radiate into every department of thought, quickening the perception of interrelations and integrations, and giving a new value to truths that would otherwise remain inert.

A world built up conceptually from the atom might remain forever in fragments, unfinished sequences, and meaningless disorder. In such a world, if uncorrected by a theory of organic development, even the phenomena of life might seem disjointed and accidental, without direction, without ultimate value. Whereas a world penetrated downward from the person begins with the fact of integration, with values and goals already embodied and incarnated. From that beginning one may interpret otherwise dispersed and aimless events in the light of the emergent goals toward which they have moved and by which achieved conscious existence. Such a world assumes no pre-established harmony and no fixed foreordained destination. What it reveals is a multitude of organic patterns, which, in relation to further human designs, become cumulatively significant. The increase of creativity becomes accordingly the measure of man's success in life.

As man has gone on with his own development, he has become more conscious both of the general process of organic transformation and of the important role he himself has come to play. The concept of the person, associated with creativity and divinity, was originally confined to a single individual, the supreme ruler of the land, identified and worshiped as a god. Now it has become the essential mark of a common human development, in which all men share. Instead of man in person bowing himself out of the picture, as he did when he followed the old canons of the physical sciences, he now takes a central position on the stage, knowing that the performance itself, in the theater of consciousness at least, cannot go on without him. Without man's intervention it would be meaningless dumb show.

Man begins as an actor, detached from his animal colleagues, already something of a star performer, sure of his importance, but uncertain of what part he shall play. In time, he becomes a scene painter, modifying the natural background and finding his own part modified by it, too: and he is driven to be a stagehand, likewise, shifting the "properties" to make his entrances and exits more manageable. Only after much practice in all these roles, as scene painter, stagehand, costumer, make-up artist, actor, does man discover that his main function is to write and direct the drama. In composing the play itself man uses, in Shakespearean fashion, many of the old plots left by nature, but he gives them a new turn of the imagination and works the events up to a climax that Nature, without his aid, might not have blundered upon for countless million years.

In its early stages, this intensification of creativity is represented, not in man's actual acts, but in the attributes of his gods, on whom he at first fearfully bestowed the omniscience and omnipotence he secretly coveted for himself. Only late in man's development did he find it necessary to project, in his conception of divinity, an attribute that would offset the grave threat to life hidden in this all-knowingness and all-powerfulness: a divine beneficence, Love.

What is ideally desirable, at this stage of man's development, does not exist in any past form of man, either biological or social: not cerebral man, muscular man, or visceral man: not the pure Hindu, the pure Mohammedan, the pure Christian, nor yet the pure Marxist or the pure Mechanist: not Old World man or New World man. The unity we seek must do justice to all these fragments, and be ready to include them lovingly in a self that shall be capable of transcending them. Any doctrine of wholeness that does not begin with love itself as the symbol and agent of this organic creativity can hardly hope to produce either a unified self or a unified world; for it is not in the detached intellect alone that this transformation must be effected.

This radical transvaluation of values is a necessary prelude to the next phase of man's development. Up to the present the chief activity of mankind has been confined to its biological ambit—to keep alive and reproduce itself. The quantity of time and attention that man could give to art and play, to ritual and religion, to philosophy and science, in short, to the central drama of existence, was only a modicum of that which he was forced to devote to the preparatory economic processes. What was achieved in meaning and value was almost surreptitiously filched from the so-called serious business of life. But almost within the memory of living men, a radical change in the human condition has come about. This change rivals that brought in by neolithic culture, and far outstrips that produced by earlier forms of mechanical organization, for it brings with it the promise of release from compulsory labor and every form of external slavery. Thanks mainly to advances in science, almost unlimited energies are now at man's disposal; and in most of the servile modes of work, the automatic machine is capable of performing functions that heretofore were performed only at an immense sacrifice of human life.

Because the current activities of our society continued to flow into obsolete molds, this change at first produced only industrial crises and dislocations; and even now, only a small part of its benefits is available. But already, in advanced industrial countries, the number of hours in the working week has been almost halved, and the proportion of people in the professions and in the services not devoted to agriculture or industrial production has risen steadily. As this change proceeds, a fact unknown outside the most primitive cultures comes once again into existence: no longer the domination of life by work, but the possible integration of work into a more abundant and significant life.

This relief from the demand that life shall be grimly subordinated to work holds out two great promises. The first of these is that work itself, at least that which remains outside the province of the automatic machine, may itself become an educative process, evoking intelligence and feeling, giving back even to mechanical functions the freedom the old craftsman used to exercise. This kind of creativity is largely lacking in the meretricious art of the market place, but has long been prophetically visible in art, such as the sculptures of Naum Gabo or the architecture of Frank Lloyd Wright. At this point, Le Play's great dictum, that the most important product that comes out of the mine is the miner, will apply to every occupation. Even more, we must now favor certain types of products and certain systems of production, and reject others, with reference to the effect that the work has upon the human personality: we shall weigh its influence upon love, fellowship, family life, citizenship, not merely upon mechanical efficiency.

The other great benefit of the transformation of the industrial process is the fact that its outcome need not be a plethora of material goods and gadgets, nor yet of instruments of warfare and genocide. Once we revamp the institutions of the market, and distribute goods primarily on the basis of need and active contribution rather than in proportion to property or privileged status, our gains will be gains in leisure. In fact, without leisure, our expansion in industry would be almost meaningless; for we need a plenitude of time if we are to select and assimilate all the genuine goods that modern man now commands. *Schola* means leisure; and leisure makes possible the school. The promise of a life economy is to provide schooling for the fullest kind of human growth—not for the further expansion of the machine.

This does not mean simply that more of our lives will be devoted to academic education: it means rather that education will constitute the principal business of life. This change promises to be so profound that one must emphasize it by bestowing on it a new name, to indicate that the processes of infusing value and meaning into every phase of life will not stop with the formal school.

The words education, self-development, character formation, conversion all bear upon the process; but they carry with them the limited references of their original use. That of education is still tied to the bookish training that used to begin with the mastery of the ABC's and even now lasts no longer, formally, than the attainment of the highest professional degree. The concept of self-development carries with it, if not a hint of humanistic priggishness or romantic willfulness, the general axial belief that the welfare of the self can be secured in separation from that of society, or at least that its cultivation has no public concerns: thus the personal is falsely identified with the private.

As for character formation, it recalls the stern protestant discipline, with its daily assessment of weaknesses, its aesthetically repressive regimen; and that flavor of narrowness and negation remains, though in classic British education it mingled with a strong humanist influence that promoted manly athletic exercises and nourished physical beauty. Finally, conversion, the axial term for the birth of the second self, might be considered the most decisive of educational influences: yet in its formative stages it indicates only a change of attitude and direction and does not provide the social context. One needs a term to indicate not alone these traditional aspects of education, but something that world culture itself will add to the process.

The word for this larger conception of education is the Greek term paideia, which Werner Jaeger reintroduced in his brilliant and exhaustive study of Greek education. Paideia is education looked upon as a lifelong transformation of the human personality, in which every aspect of life plays a part. Unlike education in the traditional sense, paideia does not limit itself to the conscious learning processes, or to inducting the young into the social heritage of the community. Paideia is rather the task of giving form to the act of living itself: treating every occasion of life as a means of self-fabrication, and as part of a larger process of converting facts into values, processes into purposes, hopes and plans into consummations and realizations. Paideia is not merely a learning: it is a making and a shaping; and man himself is the work of art that paideia seeks to form.

We are too easily tempted today, by habits that belong to past moments of civilization, into thinking of the kind of unity that might be achieved by a formal assembly of specialists, by an organization of "interdisciplinary activities," by an intellectual synthesis based upon some logical scheme for uniting the sciences. But paideia demands far more than that kind of formal synthesis: the unity it seeks must be sought in experience, and it demands a readiness to interchange roles, even at a sacrifice of expertness, for the sake of the greater gain to learning and life. The lesson of paideia is fundamentally the prime lesson of democracy: self-government and self-transformation cannot be delegated. What is more, the achievement of the human whole—and the achievement of the wholly human—take precedence over every specialized activity, over every narrower purpose. Though this new person will still doubtless cherish and develop the skills associated with specialized vocations, he will tend to be multi-occupational as a citizen, nourishing other interests and pursuing other activities, in harmony with a larger plan of life. To exercise all the capacities of a man or woman will become more important than to wear the identifying badge of a vocation or an office; for the day will come, as Emerson predicted, "when no badge, uniform, or star will be worn."

This gives a new significance to Karl Marx's conception of the future society, which he threw out in passing in 'Capital,' despite his own strict aversion to any kind of utopian prophecy. In this society, as Marx defined it, "the 'fragmentary man' would be replaced by the 'completely developed individual,' one for whom different social functions are but alternative forms of activity. Men would fish, hunt, or engage in literary criticism without becoming professional fishermen, hunters, or critics." That moment of insight, based chiefly on his admiration for the freedom and human balance of American culture during the Golden Day, offsets, indeed nullifies, the more characteristic absolutism of Marx's dialectic. To complete it, one should perhaps add his master Hegel's admirable definition of an educated man: One who can do what any other man can do.

One may say of unified man, then, that he is no longer the incarnation of his class, his trade, his profession, or his religious faith, any more than he is the incarnation of his exclusive national group. He is, in fact, just the opposite of the competent technician—the impersonal, neutral functionary, obedient only to the science governing his métier, incurious about any process beyond his limited range: he whom Max Weber singled out as the type that would finally dominate the modern world. The bureaucrat and the technocrat are rather the ideal prototypes of post-historic man. One World man will gladly sacrifice their mechanical efficiency, along with their cocksureness and complacency, in order to enhance the quality of life itself.

The conquering hero, the suffering saint, the ardent lover, the reckless adventurer, the patient scientist, in short all the ideal types of previous cultures, took on their personalities for a whole lifetime. They were committed to their particular virtues, as soldiers, merchants, and craftsmen were dedicated to their single vocation. Each was imprisoned by his role in a cramped chamber and never had the run of the house. The saint could not remain a saint if he became a lover, nor the sage a sage if he became an adventurer. This fixation in permanent roles, vocational and moral, brought about an arrest of life itself; and its correction will be one of the happy tasks of the open personality. While he is open to any of these possible roles, when the moment demands, a unified man would no more think of playing them throughout life than a capable actor would play only Hamlet. The historic function of these ideal images was to intensify and widen the capacities of man.

Though no single life can make use of all its opportunities or reveal all its potentialities, though restriction and concentration are in fact necessary for any full creative expression, the openness of the emerging self will widen the area of its transactions and energize all its activities. It was such a widening of medieval Christian culture, by contact with the ideal world of Greece and Rome and the actual world of China, India, Africa, and America, that made possible the brilliant achievements of the Renascence. Similarly, personal acquaintance has taught me, people like Patrick Geddes and Ananda Coomaraswamy, who actively participated in both Western and Eastern cultures, brought into the common human focus all that they touched. Even reading can do much to break though the parochialism of culture, as Emerson and Thoreau proved by their early use of Hindu texts; and when travel becomes more than mere sightseeing, when it brings about an interchange of experiences, it will multiply the number of those who are capable of reaching full human stature.

This basic ideological change and personal transformation have long been under way. But the obstacles in the way of a world-wide emergence of unified man are formidable; for the energies that will make it possible cannot be brought to the surface by any purely rational means. As with the early Christians one must expectantly watch and wait, making every possible conscious preparation, yet realizing that no cold act of will can suffice. When the favorable moment comes and its challenge is accepted, thousands and tens of thousands will spontaneously respond to it, stirred by the sense of fellowship the moment will produce. In that act forces that were neutral or antagonistic to any larger plan or purpose will likewise undergo polarization and become actively helpful. Then a new self will be born.

Yet in isolated persons, like Albert Schweitzer in the present day, like Peter Kropotkin or Patrick Geddes in an earlier day, and Goethe and Emerson even earlier, the kind of self that the moment demands has actually been incarnated. Schweitzer, for example, has transcended the specializations of vocation and nationality and religious faith. In deliberately choosing an uninviting region in Africa as the seat of his lifework, and the ministry of medicine as a means of translating his Christian ethic into practice, he sacrificed the opportunities that his special talents as theologian, musician, and philosopher seemed to demand. Seemingly under the most hostile conditions, he has demonstrated the possibility of actualizing a unified personality; and the course of life he chose, which involved the heaviest of renunciations, has proved richer in its fruits than one that would have conformed to more orthodox patterns of Old World culture.

To reach full human stature, at the present stage of development, each of us must be ready, as opportunity offers, to assimilate the contributions of other cultures; and to develop, for the sake of wholeness, those parts of his personality that are weakest. Not least, he must renounce perfection in any single field for the sake of balance and continued growth. He who belongs exclusively to a single nation, a single party, a single religion, or a single vocation without any touch or admixture from the world beyond is not yet a full man, still less can he take part in this transformation. This is a fundamental lesson of human growth, always true—but now imperatively true. In its critical moment of integration, Christianity took in Persian and Egyptian myths, Greek philosophy, and Roman organization, just as Mohammedanism took in the lessons of Moses and Zoroaster and Jesus. So One World man will embrace an even wider circle; and the whole person so created will cast aside the series of masks, some weakly benign, some monstrous, that so long concealed the living features of man.

In his very completeness, unified man will seem ideologically and culturally naked, almost unidentifiable. He will be like the Jain saints of old, "clothed in space," his nakedness a sign that he does not belong exclusively to any nation, group, vocation, trade, sect, school, or community. He who has reached the level of world culture will be at home in any part of that culture: in its inner world no less than its outer world. Everything that he does or feels or makes will bear the imprint of the larger self he has made his own. Each person, no matter how poorly endowed or how humble, is eligible to take part in this effort, and his contribution, however minute, is indispensable; yet no matter how great any individual's talents may be, the results will always be incomplete; for the equilibrium we seek is a dynamic one and the balance we promote is not an end in itself but a means to further growth. "It is provided in the essence of things," as Walt Whitman said, "that from any fruition of success, no matter what, shall come forth something to make a greater struggle necessary."

(1956)

CHAPTER FORTY

The Human Prospect

The human prospect today is both brighter and darker than it has ever been in the historic ages. For the first time, mankind exists as a self-conscious collective entity, bound together by communication at the speed of light, and by transportation at the speed of sound; we command physical powers that were once locked in the depths of nature, and knowledge enough in every department of thought, if we had the good will and the social imagination to use it, not merely to free the race from the old threats of starvation and destitution, but to give to every human being on the planet the cultural resources for personal development and enjoyment that only a minority ever participated in on any scale in the past.

But at present these happy prospects are heavily overcast by well-justified fear and dismay. The method of thinking that has made these advances possible, and the very technology that has brought them to the point of realization, are at the same time working in precisely the opposite direction. As our machines become more automatic, more intelligent, more self-governing, the life that they make possible in our communities becomes humanly less interesting, partly because we have transferred so many of our activities, even thought itself, to these mechanical agents. What is just as bad, the whole apparatus of power on which we necessarily depend has gotten out of control and is running away with us. As a result we have only replaced the old slavery of production with the new servitudes and compulsions of consumption; and in comparison with the power and resources now at our disposal, the net human gain has been dismally small.

At any moment all our boasts of scientific proficiency and progress may be nullified by planetary calamities brought on by minds that have ceased to be able to deal with organic and social realities because they themselves are encased in a system of abstractions useful only for the control of machines. Thus our power threatens to collapse into impotence—our creativity into total destruction.

I shall not end on this negative note; but it is necessary to begin here;

for unless we take the full measure of the dangers that confront us, with open eyes, we shall not summon forth the human energies that will be necessary to overcome them. The threat of wholesale nuclear extermination, on a scale that might permanently mutilate even that part of the human race which escaped immediate destruction, is only the most spectacular example of the negative results produced by science and technics when they are divorced from any other human purpose than their own propensity to increase knowledge and power, and expand the use of their own special products in a fashion profitable to the producer.

But we are in the midst of other explosions, other forms of destruction, actual, not just threatened, that will be just as fatal as long as they go in the present fashion: the population explosion, the freeway explosion, the recreation explosion, the suburban explosion (or should one say the "slurban" explosion?) are all working toward the same blank goal—that of creating more and more featureless landscapes, populated by more and more featureless people. Never before has any country possessed such a surplus of wealth, energy, food, and natural resources as the United States, and in particular, the state of California. But in addressing ourselves solely to the increase of power, profit, and prestige, we have failed to develop a varied, many-sided culture, a culture based on the realities of life itself, on human growth in a biologically sound and socially stimulating environment, on sexual maturation and a good family life, on disciplined emotional expression in the arts and in daily practice, on constant citizen participation in the public affairs of the community, for the sake of human association as well as for the practical and cultural ends. Rather, all our dominant forces today now tend to cramp and dwarf our life, to automatize and increasingly dehumanize our activities, when they might be hugely increasing our actual wealth and our real enjoyment.

Now, where the machine takes precedence of the man, and where all activities and values that sustain the human spirit are subordinated to making money and privately devouring only such goods as money will buy, even the physical environment tends to become degraded and inefficient. To say that we have not made the most of our opportunities is putting the case mildly: disorder, blight, dingy mediocrity, screaming neon-lighted vulgarity are spreading everywhere, producing, as I said, an empty life, filled with false vitality expressed in occasional outbreaks of violence and lust, either in brutal action or in more frequent fantasy.

Ever since I visited the ancient Italian town of Pompeii, buried under the ashes of Vesuvius in A.D. 79, I have found myself comparing the dead city that has been brought to light there with the seemingly live cities that we are living in—or more often trying to get away from—in America. This comparison continues to haunt me. The landscape around Pompeii is not too different from that of many parts of California; the vineyards and the olive groves and wheat fields in Roman times were no more productive. Yet this little provincial town, of some twenty-five thousand inhabitants, produced such an orderly and coherent and esthetically animated life that even in its ruined state it gives a less ruinous impression than the central areas of most American cities of ten times that population. The Pompeian frescoes and mosaics are famous in the museums of Europe, and when one compares the noble Forum of Pompeii with the jumbled junk-edged surroundings of San Francisco's own Civic Center, when one considers the amount of space and fine building given to Pompeii's temples, its markets, its law courts, its public baths, its stadium, its handsome theater, all conceived and built on the human scale, with great nobility of form, one realizes that American towns far more wealthy and populous than Pompeii do not, except in very rare cases, have anything like this kind of civic equipment, even in makeshift form.

Closer comparisons make our own achievements seem even more destitute and fraudulent: the neighborhood bakeries of Pompeii still made real bread, with flour ground on the premises just before baking—not the kind of devitalized foam-rubber loaf, laden with additives and substitutes, mechanically sliced for built-in staleness, that boasts of never being touched by human hand, though if we were not so enamored of large-scale enterprise and long-distance transportation, we could all have fresh local bread, with flour ground on the spot by small, efficient, electrically driven mills, bread fully the equal of Pompeii's, without the slave labor that probably turned the Pompeian baker's mill.

Every part of Pompeii was within walking distance, just as if its inhabitants enjoyed each other and wished to profit by each other's company. And the thousands of people who gathered to watch the games, or attend the theater, could leave their seats and reach home on foot before a similar American crowd could begin to get their cars out of a parking lot. In terms of biological vitality, in terms of social life, there is no question as to which kind of community could offer the best facilities and enjoyments for its inhabitants. Now, mind you, Pompeii was not a showpiece or an ideal community; far from it: it was just an ordinary Roman provincial town, so well designed that were it not for Vesuvius it might still be doing business on the same spot, within the same general pattern of life, as is so largely true today in the old Roman colonization towns, like Piacenza and Pavia.

The moral I draw from Pompeii is that we Americans must be spending our money on the wrong things if our towns are so poverty-stricken in civic facilities, so confused, and so ugly by contrast, in spite of all their boasted wealth and energy. What Pompeii spent on the vital contents of life, we spend on wasteful processing and meretricious packaging and phony publicity. Our trouble, then, is not merely that we have fallen in love with the machine, and have treated it as a god, to be flattered with prayers and propitiated by human sacrifices—more than 59,000 dead by motor accidents every year: over three million injured, many of them maimed for life. (Latest 1972 figures).

Our trouble is that equally we have ceased to respect ourselves, just as we have ceased to love our neighbors and want to be near them; we have ceased to cherish our own history and to enlarge our own prospects, by promoting character and variety and beauty wherever we find it, whether in landscapes or in people. Because the machine, if left to its own special devices, money and power, goes in for standardization, mass production, automation, quantitative excesses, we have let our lives be governed by these same mechanical factors. So we constantly forget that all these capacities are beneficial only when they are at the disposal of a purposeful life that is itself more rich, complex, varied, individualized, stimulating, and humanly valuable: something different from a machine's existence.

In their worship of the machine, many Americans have settled for something less than a full life, something that is hardly even a tenth of a life, or a hundreth of a life. They have confused progress with mechanization, and, lacking any will or purpose of their own, having lost any real religious faith or personal pride, they have let mechanization take command. Even where choice is possible, they prefer an air-conditioning unit to the more subtle and satisfactory method of controlling insulation and temperature by proper orientation, and by using trees and gardens more copiously. They respect the steam shovel that levels down a hill more than they value the view that their houses would command if they kept the hill and used its contours. The speculative builder prides himself on the bulldozer that gouges out a stand of trees while he rejects opportunity for a more organic type of plan that would group the houses in a more adroit irregular pattern. These bad habits make it seem as if our countrymen were hostile to all manifestations of life, including their own, except in so far as they enhanced the power and glory of machines.

Some of this attitude is doubtless left over from the pioneer days, when the individual settler had to carve a place for himself barehanded in a sometimes difficult, if not inimical, environment. Under these conditions a certain ruthlessness was sometimes unavoidable in self-defense. At all events the pioneer never had to live with the damage he did, as we do now: he could always cancel out his sins, or at least forget them, by moving on to another virgin spot. Even when the pioneer didn't rape Nature, he divorced her a little too easily: he missed the great lesson that both ecology and medicine teach—that man's great mission is not to conquer Nature by main force but to co-operate with her intelligently and lovingly for his own purposes. Yet for all our careless habits, we Americans once loved the wilderness, for the free mode of life and the self-reliant men and women it bred: whatever is left of adventurous initiative and self-government in this country owes a debt to those days.

Since in our hearts we don't altogether like the kind of mechanically sterilized and spiritually stupefying existence we now live, we have begun to tell ourselves fairy stories about our present state: fooling ourselves into believing we are recovering the old pioneer spirit with barbecue grills in the

backyard, just as we call the most compulsive and tension-producing avenues of locomotion our 'freeways'—and even boast of the freedom of going
at sixty miles an hour for hundreds of miles and never having to stop for a
red light, completely forgetting how often we are stalled for ten minutes at
a bottleneck, as we creep into the city. So again in attempting to fill up the
empty hours of leisure that our mechanical achievements have brought
about, we tend to turn every great recreation area into a congested metropolitan slum, pretending to find solace in the beauties of nature, at Yosemite
or Lake Tahoe, in an actual environment that strangely resembles a parking
lot around a hamburger joint. *If the places where we live and work were
really fit for permanent human habitation, why should we spend so much of
our time getting away from them?*

Let us face the truth. The real life of a large part of the population,
even those who live in agricultural areas, is one long retreat from the vitalities and creativities of a self-sustaining environment and a stimulating and
balanced communal life. We have accepted an assembly line existence, in
which all human functions take place in an increasingly sterilized and uniform environment, cut off from every reality except that which serves the
machine. Whether he wears a white collar or a blue collar, the typical
American now serves as a baby-sitter to a machine, or is geared into a collective organization that is itself a more formidable and all-embracing machine—a machine that can be run effectively only by bureaucatic personalities, punched and coded to perform a limited set of operations. The factory
or the office, with its thousand identical windows, its uniform air conditioning, its uniform fluorescent lighting, its equally bare and uniform parking
lot, has the typical features of this age: faceless anonymity. As far as it is
mechanically feasible, this environment has insulated its occupants from
every form of reality except the machine process itself: heat and cold, day
and night, the earth and the stars, woodland, crop land, vineland, garden
land—all forms of organic partnership between the millions of species that
add to the vitality and wealth of the earth—are either suppressed entirely
from the mind or homogenized into a uniform mixture packaged for sale.

Look at the life we lead. At the end of a day our countrymen leave this
humanly insulated collective environment for an equally cribbed and cabined
mechanism on wheels, for a journey that may take anywhere from half an
hour to two hours, depending upon how filled the parking lot is and how
clogged the freeway. This piece of defective rolling stock, with its lethal,
health-vitiating exhaust, provides the fading illusion of freedom along with
the reality of constant tension and constraint: its utility decreases in direct
proportion to its mass use, and in taking over the burden of public and private transportation, both passengers and freight, the motorcar has, with the
aid of extravagant public subsidies, under pretext of "national defense,"
wrecked the balanced transportation system that existed a generation ago,
and crippled the functions that the motorcar and the freeway, if part of a

more complex and flexible network of transportation, would actually—and admirably—serve.

Physiologically the worse for wear, our American finally reaches his dwelling, where he finds a house and a wife in the midst of what is usually called ideal suburban surroundings: a green ghetto, half natural, half plastic, also cut off from human contact, where his wife has for her chief daily companions in her solitude the radio set, the soap opera, the refrigerator, the automatic mixer, the blender, the vacuum cleaner, the automatic washing machine, the dishwasher, and, if she is lucky, the second car. They and their children finally, together or by turns, immobilize themselves before a television screen, where all that has been left out of the actual world, all their unlived life, flickers before their eyes, in images that give a faked sense of the realities they have turned their backs to, and the impulses that they have been forced to repress. Even here, the machine-conditioned American has no proper life of his own: for what he sees and hears and interprets contains only so much of the real world as the great corporate organizations, military, commercial, political, which control this medium, will permit for the furtherance of their own machine-expanding, power-buttressing, or money-making ends. Freedom of selection is chiefly the freedom of choosing more of the same from another channel.

I have of course intentionally, and doubtless grossly, caricatured the life of the representative American today; and I am as well aware as you are of the many happy qualifications and modifications that make much of it bearable, and some of it positively rewarding.

For all this, that caricature is too near reality to let one feel altogether comfortable about the human prospect: especially since it is fast becoming the universal life of mankind, alike in other countries that still call themselves free, and in countries that are under a Communist Party dictatorship. In the latter countries, indeed, people are resentfully aware of the official pressures and external compulsions, and therefore, if one may judge by recent short stories and motion pictures coming out of Soviet Russia, they have reacted against their oppressive political regimentation by cultivating a warmer sense of the eternal human decencies and moralities, as between family and family, person and person. Few of our own Hollywood or Radio City productions show anything like the same human tenderness as the recent Russian 'Ballad of a Soldier.'

At all events, the ultimate pattern of gracious American living, if we continue our rigid and unqualified commitment to the machine, is already in sight. Six hours for automatic production and forced consumption in order to maintain the expanding economy: three hours for transportation as we get farther and farther away from the place where we don't want to work, to the place where we no longer have much opportunity to sleep: six hours for mechanized togetherness, sometimes called family life and recreation: and finally, at least nine hours of sleep, partly to forget that we have not

been living, partly to provide for the increasing sale of sleeping pills, hypnotics, and tranquillizers, those indispensable adjuncts of the kind of life
we offer to our highly mechanized and urbanized population. The only
element I have left out of the day's schedule is mating: but plainly, with
artificial insemination from a bank of frozen sperm cells, in accordance
with Dr. Herman Muller's formula for human improvement, this injection
can be combined with an influenza shot or an X-ray checkup. So much for
the nightmare of our 'Brave New World': we are lucky if what we see when
we move about and what we do in our day's work turns out to be sufficiently
different to reassure us that we are awake.

Isn't it about time that we took a hard second look at this life of ours
and faced the fact that if we go on acting this way, the human prospect will
be increasingly dismal? Are we creating the kind of life that anyone in his
senses would bargain for, still less regard as the sufficient consummation
and justification of civilization? Sinclair Lewis took such a look at Zenith
and Main Street a generation or more ago; but what he found there was
relatively healthy, sweet, decent, and sane compared with the kind of life
that has been thrust upon us by the automatic proliferation of scientific invention and mechanical organization during the last twenty years. The human prospect, in California or anywhere else, does not hold much promise
as long as these conditions are unrecognized for what they are, not real
signs of progress, but symptoms of human disturbance and social disintegration; or, even when they are recognized, if they are looked upon as outside
human control, and are allowed to go on uncorrected. The time has come
to understand that mechanization without a corresponding humanization is
monstrous: just as passive consumption, without selectivity and without any
ensuing creativity in other departments than science and technics, is empty;
and power without purpose—the kind of power we now have in such abundance, power enough to exterminate the human race—is immediately destructive and suicidal, and ultimately impotent.

If you ask me how California or any other region can be improved without altering our prevailing view of life, without changing our routines, without attaching ourselves to more public purposes and higher human ends
than those we now respect, I must answer with a sad smile that no serious
improvements are possible on those old terms. If we want to improve the
regional environment, we must also improve ourselves, that is, we must
change our minds and alter our objectives, advancing from a money
economy to a life economy: in many matters we must acquire new values,
new sensitivities, new interests, new goals that will ensure a self-sustaining,
many-sided life. That life must not depend as it so largely does now upon our
constantly dancing attendance upon the machine, and pursuing only such
activities as will give the makers of machines and machine products the
maximum market for their goods.

In short, it is the whole pattern of our life that must change; and the pattern of our local life will not alter significantly until the over-all pattern for a much wider area does. As long as our country spends astronomical sums for weapons of extermination, weapons which endanger our own lives —sixty million dead on the first day of a nuclear attack—and indeed the lives of all mankind, quite as much as they threaten any enemy's, we shall not have the funds needed for more rational public purposes: for our schools and hospitals, for our theaters and churches, for our recreation areas, for the old and the young who need public help.

Part of our local planning, then, must be deliberately framed to bring the local community into relations with larger associations of peoples, if only in order to safeguard the very life we are building here; and one of the most ominous items that appeared in the paper the other day was the report that a chapter on the United Nations was being excluded from an official textbook on civics in California. I hope that report was unfounded, for if California is still populated a hundred years hence, it will be because the universal forces for co-operation and mutual understanding embodied in the United Nations, not least in UNESCO, have prevailed over egoistic, nationalistic presumptions and nuclear delusions of absolute power. If the world overcomes the irrational forces that are now undermining human culture everywhere, forces long embodied in the dangerously obsolete institution of war, it will be because people everywhere realize that all the goods of life are the joint product of the human race as a whole, and that we are bound to all our neighbors by all the facts of history and by the hopes of the future, as they are bound to us.

The kind of co-operation that still exists between all nations in the world of science and scholarship—at least that part of science and scholarship that is not under the control of totalitarian military agencies operating in secret—sets a pattern for the future relations of regions and countries: so much so that the core institution in every vital city today is no longer the palace or the temple or the market, but the university, and it is to the honor of the university that such an open discussion as is going on here today is possible in contrast to the death-oriented doctrines and isolationist nonsense taken as a prescription for "national survival."

In discussing the role of planning we all too easily get lost, however, in details of political organization, economic support, population movements, transportation facilities, metropolitan or regional government; and we neglect the factor that is central to all of these things: the dimensions of the human personality. The answer to the problems of human organization and human control will not come from computers; the answers will come from men. And it will not come from the sort of men whom we have indoctrinated with the myth of the machine: the disoriented experts and specialists whose uncoordinated and lopsided efforts, uncorrected by the more humane wisdom of their peers, and untutored by historic experience, have produced the overmechanized, standardized, homogenized, bureaucratized life that now surrounds us increasingly on every side.

Our first job in controlling the forces that are now working such destruction and havoc in every regional community is to cultivate men who are capable of exercising this control: proud, confident, self-respecting, co-operative men. Not men for sale, men tailored and trimmed to fit the machine, but men capable of using all their powers, taking back to themselves the functions they too easily resigned to the machine, and projecting human goals, in the full trajectory of life, goals which they often disregarded in their eagerness to exploit some immediate opportunity. If our mode of life or our education had produced such men in sufficient numbers, we should not now be living in an increasingly denuded and life-hostile environment; and if we are ever to give to this region, or any other region, the life-sustaining richness and variety that are possible, even in areas where natural conditions are unduly uniform or climatically difficult, we will have to begin all over again at the very beginning, with the infant in its crib. That is where education starts.

Let us consider the most limited environment. If we look at it carefully, we shall perhaps have a key to what must be done in every other area. Consider the newborn baby of the last generation, my own and the generation immediately after my own. Our mechanized civilization, in the interest of a speedy delivery, at the convenience, even at the timed participation of the physician, often endangered mother and child with impatient interference in the natural process, and too often compounded this mistake by anesthetizing the mother completely. All too soon, as a result of scientific pride over inventing a formula for feeding independent of the natural source of milk, the child was parted from its mother and deprived not only of mother's milk, but of the experience of a warm, loving, commensal relationship with her, the kind we must have also with Mother Earth.

In other words, both mother and child were cut off from a basic physical and spiritual experience, an experience which is a vital model for all remoter forms of co-operation and association. When behaviorist doctrines were at their height the next point in the child's development consisted in a systematic effort to make clockwork habits take the place of organic responses timed to the organism's own needs, especially in bowel training. Thus, as one of our most able child psychologists, Erik Erikson, has pointed out, before an American child was three—this held with his patients at least up to 1950—he had been conditioned to accept an external mechanical order as absolute, and to believe that there was nothing he could do to change it, particularly if he wanted to win the approval of those who stood in authority over him. Such a training made bad citizens for a democracy; but it fitted admirably, with its mechanical punctuality and regularity, with its human docility and conformity, into larger bureaucratic and totalitarian systems.

While many of the present generation of young people are, happily, beginning to reject every part of this process, beginning with the young mothers and enlightened physicians who accept childbirth as a normal organic process—it can take place in a home, though nowadays it too often takes place in a taxicab or a car on the way to a distant hospital—not as a surgical ordeal like a major operation. In justified reaction against the mechanical regimen that prevailed a generation ago, some of the young have even reacted to the opposite extreme, quite naturally, an extreme of heedless permissiveness and irresponsibility, thus abdicating the parental role and turning the infant itself into a tyrannous monster, subject to all the psychological disorders that befall every creature that has delusions of absolute power, devoid of purpose but endowed with every attribute of freedom except the ability to select a path and follow it. If you look closely at these two patterns of child training—one too rigorous, too machine-dominated, too overstrained, the other too feckless and reckless to pay attention even to the natural rhythms of the body and natural hierarchies of power and responsibility—you will perhaps have a clue to the characteristic weaknesses of planning today.

On one hand we have the compulsiveness and arbitrariness of our highway planning, our urban renewal projects, our overcentralized and overcrowded recreational facilities, in which the demands of the administrator, the investor, the engineer ruthlessly override the human needs to be served and deform the final product, making it really unfit for human use. But against this you have the unlimited permissiveness of suburban sprawl; and along with both tendencies an attitude of hopeless passivity, based on the curious assumption that although all these mischievous and maladroit activities are the result of human actions and human plans, they are beyond human control, once they are in existence, and are doomed to get worse and worse. This is nonsense. I would challenge that assumption, even were it necessary to wait for a whole generation of new young people to emerge —a generation who have come into the world without having to submit to an overmechanized, oversterilized, deliberately anti-organic regimen that has no faith in either life or love.

We shall never succeed in dealing effectively with the complex problems of large units and differentiated groups, unless at the same time we rebuild and revitalize the small unit. We must begin at the beginning; it is here that all life, even the life of big communities and organizations, starts. The home and the neighborhood are an integral part of the region, and some of the most pressing problems in adequate land use cannot be solved, with the big population that is flooding into California, unless we handle the whole pattern of settlement, including the layout of the individual houses and apartment units. The child has a right to live in an orderly, intelligibly patterned world, scaled to his size and his capacity for movement, and designed for encouraging his activities, and for making him feel at home with his fellows and neighbors, even when he leaves his domestic nest.

If we are to recapture the initiative from our machine-centered civilization, we must establish a life-centered environment from the moment of birth. Who can pretend that a fifteen-story, high-rise apartment in an urban renewal project is such a family environment? But neither—let us not fool ourselves—is an insulated single family house, entirely cut off from its neighbors, or lined up, side by side, for the convenience of the builder and the deed of sale, on a long uniform street, one mechanically uniformed unit after another. Neither of these environments serves as a surrogate for the mother or as a proper sample of a bigger community.

Every housing development should have the virtues of both a village and a kindergarten; the houses themselves should form a protective enclosure, so that the child can move about freely, among other children, and still be under the eye of his mother, or, rather, a whole group of mothers, safe from moving traffic, not having to share his play space with a motorcar or be toted a mile or two by car to find it. Real human communities must preserve social as well as visual variety; hence the fact that we no longer attempt to house a three-generation family within a single dwelling makes it all the more imperative to restore this combination to the neighborhood. Age segregation is just as bad as income segregation or racial segregation: we need mixed age groups to sustain life even at the simplest levels. A child needs grandparents, or substitute grandparents, as well as parents; he needs to live in a normal human community with the companionship of other children—of different ages, too—as well as those of his own peer groups and family.

None of these things happens automatically nowadays on any scale: automatic processes tend to produce isolation and segregation, not the complex social pattern produced by integrating in appropriate structures and forms a whole variety of human needs and functions. Nor can the benefits of such an integrated social design be produced by private individuals, no matter how great their financial means. Public authorities must take the lead in experimenting with new urban patterns, new layouts: they must seek to establish a tradition that the individual developers—perhaps with public assistance—can themselves carry out, instead of, as now, following the line of least resistance, which always is a mechanical repeating pattern.

I have taken this simple illustration to show how many-sided the organic planning process is, even at the smallest scale, when you understand and attempt to do justice to human needs. What I have said of housing alone applies in equal degree to the neighborhood, which must be built again into an active political unit, if our democracy is to become active and invigorated once more, as it was two centuries ago in the New England village, for that was a superior political unit. The same principles apply again to the city and the interrelationship of cities in a unified urban and regional network or grid. But I have used this illustration of how to give order, variety, and protection to the growing child for still another reason; and that is because it offers a model of the chain of relations that bind the small unit to seemingly remote parts of the environment and to problems which seemingly have nothing to do with it.

Already you have let the pressure of population and of private real estate development destroy some of your best agricultural land. Even here in the broad Central Valley, you are threatened with this evil, no less than in the Santa Clara Valley and the San Bernardino Valley, valleys whose orchards and vineyards not merely gave character to their little towns, but had positive recreational value for the bigger cities like Pasadena, Los Angeles, and San Francisco. That soil was precious; that combination of agricultural production and recreative beauty were essential to the vitality of the whole urban community; and by packing these valleys with a disorganized overload of people and vehicles you have even been lowering the health levels with smog and carbon monoxide, as recent official reports show. This random scattering of population has spoiled both the urban and the rural potentialities of these valleys: whereas if you had thought of housing in direct communal terms, to begin with, the care of the child and provision for the child's healthy growth in his family and neighborhood, you might have built two- or three-story houses instead of the low sprawling ones of a single story, a type that is now eating up land all over the country, and you might have doubled, and in many cases quadrupled, the number of people per acre, with an enormous improvement in their social and domestic environment.

By proper planning alone, you could have preserved from fifty to seventy-five per cent of the land now misused and wasted. Indeed, by means of proper planning you may still save much precious land, which is now about to be misused, from such a fate. At a residential density of from fifteen to thirty families per acre—fifteen to twenty families is the usual density in the spacious, perhaps even too spacious English New Towns—you could have provided better gardens, better playgrounds, safe green walkways to school, more accessible schools for the children, and a far better life for the parents as well: a life designed deliberately to favor the neighborly interchange of services that must become, as once it was in pioneer days, our communal substitute for menial helpers that hardly anyone can now afford to hire. Not the least advantage of such organic communal neighborhood designs is that they would release the individual housewife and mother from the slavery of her present twenty-four-hour tour of duty.

This illustration has many ramifications; but its chief use today is to indicate that respect for human conditions and for development and growth will help improve every part of the regional landscape, and will make possible a complex interlacing of functions, in a pattern of mutual aid, not mechanical regularity, that will be superior to any one-sided solutions, based on single-factor analysis and compartmental thinking devoted mainly to the exploitation and profitable use of the machine.

But before the kind of thought and design I have indicated becomes popular, we shall have to overthrow the myth of the machine and replace it with a new myth of life, a myth based upon a richer understanding of all organic processes, a sharper insight into man's positive "role in changing the face of the earth," and a passionate religious faith in man's own capacity to transform and perfect his own self and his own institutions in co-operative relation with all the forces of nature, and, above all, with his fellow men. To put all our hope in the improvement of machines is the characteristic inversion and perversion of values of the present age; and that is the reason that our machines threaten us with extinction, since they are now in the hands of deplorably unimproved men. This is no moment to fight a rear-guard action, a mere delaying action, against the forces that are denuding the landscape and dehumanizing the capacities of men. The time has come for bold counterattack—and we may not have long to wait.

During the last three years I, like many of my colleagues, have noted a new generation coming into the colleges: a generation trained perhaps more lovingly than their rigid and passive predecessors. They are no longer cagey conformists, no longer bent on dodging all the adventurous possibilities of life by an overemphasis on security, measured in income, or in status, measured only by the things money will buy. These young people, sometimes at great sacrifice, put babies ahead of careers; and they find, in themselves and their family life, resources that are not found in machines and are often deplorably lacking in the bigger community itself, lacking especially in the big cities. Though they have grown up in an age of violence and totalitarian conformity, they now challenge its brutalities and reject its compulsions; and their respect for themselves is greater than their respect for anything the machine, with or without their help, has created. They are still in all probability a minority; but the seed of life has ripened in them: if their elders do not betray them by surrendering even more abjectly than they have already done to the forces of disintegration and extermination, this generation will assume responsibility that too many of us still shrink from. They will overcome our passivities, overthrow our regimentations, and place the guardians of life once more in command. This is still an uncertain promise: but at least—and at last—it opens up a human prospect.

(1962)

CHAPTER FORTY-ONE

The Opening Future*

In passing from the past to the future, we pass from memory and reflection to observation and current practice and thence to anticipation and prediction. As usually conceived, this is a movement from the known to the unknown, from the probable to the possible, from the domain of necessity to the open realm of choice. But in fact these aspects of time and experience cannot be so neatly separated. Some part of the past is always becoming present in the future; and some part of the future is already present in the past. Instead of thinking of these three segments of time in serial order, we would do well to take the view of a mathematician like A. N. Whitehead and narrow the time band to a tenth of a second before and the tenth of a second after any present event. When one does this, one understands that the past, the present, and the future are in that living moment almost one; and, if our minds were only capable of holding these three elements together in consciousness over a wider span of time, we should deal with our problems in a more organic fashion, doing justice not merely to the succession of events but to their virtual coexistence through anticipation and memory.

Now part of the future we face has already been determined, and we have no control over it. To begin at the physical level, we are limited by the forces of inertia; at the biological level, by the facts of organic inheritance. At the social level we must reckon with institutional persistences which, if not so ingrained as biological structures, cannot be suddenly altered; even at the highest level of the human personality, memory and habit tend to keep our actions in a groove. We do well to reckon with these constant factors and their sluggish ways: if they fetter our creativity, they also tend to limit the possibility of chaos. For good or bad, a part of our future is given; and, like a Christmas gift, we must accept it gracefully, before we try to exchange it for something that fits us better.

We might, for example, in view of the special role that sexuality and love

* Final address at the Wenner-Gren Conference on Man's Role in Changing the Face of the Earth.

were to play in man's life, have wished that nature—sometime about the point when the structure of the frog was under consideration—had put the reproductive organs and the organs of excretion in different parts of the body. But we cannot hope that this fatal topographical mistake will be corrected. We have many similar commitments that carry over from the past. Some of us now wish, it seems, to feed the growing population of the earth with a synthetic concentrate; but if they succeed with the concentrate—I for one do not wish them well!—they will still have to furnish people with some bulk-producing jelly, as we do a sick person who has been on a liquid diet, in order to keep their bowels functioning; and they may even find it necessary, despite man's inordinate adaptability, to create some illusion of gustatory pleasure, lest the appetite for life itself should wane.

So again the fact that man has been an active, roaming, searching, prying animal, never at ease when he feels imprisoned or involuntarily hemmed in, should make us think twice, it seems to me, before we make any estimate of possible or desirable populations for the planet. Before we convert our rocks and rills and templed hills into one spreading mass of low-grade urban tissue, under the delusion that, because we accomplish this degradation with the aid of bulldozers and atomic piles and electronic computers, we are advancing civilization, we might ask what all this implies in terms of the historic nature of man.

Already there are metropolitan bathing beaches and "wild" recreation areas, where, on a Sunday afternoon in summer, the sign "Standing Room Only" describes the facilities available. Perhaps some of the perversity and criminal mischief exhibited in our cities, particularly by the more muscular types, may be due to this very constriction of space. Are we prepared to breed legless men, satisfied in their urban pens, as we now breed almost wingless fowl? If not, should we wonder that a race that flourished for some five hundred thousand years or more with a population density of perhaps ten per square mile may not find life altogether satisfactory at a constant density of four hundred per acre?

In calling attention to these constants, I am trying to emphasize what the French philosopher Raymond Ruyer, in his book 'Neo-finalisme,' characterizes as the fibrous structure of history. Just because of the nature of time, memory, and inheritance, we cannot make sensible plans for the future without doing justice to the threads and fibers that run through every past stage of man's development and will run though the future as well. In dealing with man's history, it is convenient to cut it off into stages and periods; so we speak as though the Stone Age were represented in our society only by museum showcases of axes and arrowheads. But the fact is that about four-fifths of the planet's population are still living under conditions that approximate those of a Neolithic village, certainly far closer than they touch those of a twentieth-century metropolis. And when the other day some of our friends here said, almost a little contemptuously, "Don't let us go back to Paleolithic society," I was tempted to ask them how far they thought they could express that idea without using one of the tools of Paleolithic society, namely, language.

To sum up this point: the future is not a blank page; and neither is it an open book. The current notion that one has only to measure existing trends and to project, on a grander scale, the forces and institutions that dominate our present-day society in order to give a true picture of the future is based on another kind of illusion—the statistical illusion. This method overweights those elements in the present which are observable and measurable and seemingly powerful, and it overlooks many other elements that are hidden, unmeasured, irrational. In the third century A.D. an objective observer might well have predicted, on the basis of the imperial public works program, an increase in the number of baths, gladiatorial arenas, garrison towns, and aqueducts. But he would have had no anticipation of the real future, which was the product of a deep subjective rejection of the whole classic way of life and so moved not merely away from it but in the opposite direction. Within three centuries the frontier garrisons were withdrawn, the Roman baths were closed, and some of the great Roman buildings were either being used as Christian churches or treated as quarries for building new structures. Can anyone who remembers this historic transformation believe that the rate of scientific and technological change must accelerate indefinitely or that this technological civilization will inevitably remain dominant and will absorb all the energies of life for its own narrow purposes, profit and power?

Often the most significant factors in determining the future are the irrationals. By "irrational" I do not mean subjective or neurotic, because from the standpoint of science any small quantity or unique occasion may be considered as an irrational, since it does not lend itself to statistical treatment and repeated observation. Under this head, we must allow, when we consider the future, for the possibility of miracles, on the grounds developed by Charles Babbage in the 'Ninth Bridgewater Treatise' and by James Clerk Maxwell in his famous letter on singular points. By a miracle, we mean not something outside the order of nature but something occurring so infrequently and bringing about such a radical change that one cannot include it in any statistical prediction.

Maxwell's doctrine gives exactly the insight needed into the situation to correct our usual view of the human prospect. He pointed out that even in physical systems, no less than in life generally, there occur, at rare unpredictable intervals, moments when an infinitesimally small force, because of its character and its position in the whole constellation of events, was able to effect a very large transformation. This doctrine allows for the direct impact of the human personality in history, not only by organized movements and group actions, but by individuals who are sufficiently alert to intervene at the right time and the right place for the right purpose. At such moments —they were obviously present and were seized in the founding of Buddhism,

Christianity, and Islam—a single human personality may overcome the inertia of formidable institutions.

Even though one must realize, on further consideration, that this doctrine of singular points admits of negative miracles, too, and that, with hydrogen bombs in world-wide production, such a negative miracle is quite possible, I find that the doctrine makes an important qualification in our faith in purely statistical predictions. For, as Maxwell pointed out, the higher and more complex the system, the more often do singular points occur in it; so that there are more such points among living organisms than among crystals and more in the human personality than among animals. Our sense of the probable future of the earth, therefore, must make some allowance for extravagant improbabilities—even for changes that exist as yet only as fantasies in the minds of individual men. And note this: singular points, even when they radically change human events, are not easy to detect until they have done their work: possibly the decision that will save mankind from nuclear warfare has already been taken. Though that fact would profoundly change all our calculations, we may not be able to pin down that moment until centuries have passed.

This brings me to another doctrine that qualifies and completes that which does justice to the fibrous structure of history. I refer to the doctrine of emergence. By emergence one signifies the change that comes about when a structure or organism alters, not in this or that part, but as a whole; when the new emergent possibilities that did not exist at a lower level of existence become visible and operative. Let me illustrate this on the simplest level—the predictions made in the periodic table. Thanks to Mendelejev, it was possible to predict the atomic weight and many of the other characteristics of elements that had not yet been discovered and even to name their total number—ninety-two. What made this prediction possible was not merely their rhythmic order but their essential stability. This applied equally to radium. Everything about radium could be predicted except its emergent quality, namely, its radioactivity, its radical instability, which gave the first hint that the atom itself might have some of the characteristics of the organism. As a result, though the number of stable elements is still limited, even when allowing for isotopes, the theoretic number of unstable elements has possibly astronomical dimensions.

Now it seems to me that complex social transformations, capable of affecting every part of society, are often true emergents and are as undiscoverable in advance, on the basis of past observation, as was radium. No matter how fully we know the facts, we cannot predict the new dynamic pattern into which they will fall when they reach the moment of emergence. So the best observer of Neolithic society could not have predicted the new type of large-scale, wide-reaching urban organization that grew out of it in Egypt, Babylonia, and China. Nor yet can the most penetrating student of national organizations and mechanical collectives predict the nature of the world community that may emerge in our time and, by the very act of emergence, alter our current values and habits. Yet many of the most difficult problems we face today, like that of overpopulation, which remain insoluble so long as men face each other in competing political and religious units, may be simplified, or become non-existent, once a world culture comes into existence.

All in all, there is no simple formula for dealing with either probabilities or possibilities in human society. Even if we had full knowledge of all the constants and variables—and, of course, we are far from that—we would still be in need of something more important in order to make wise decisions: that is, a theory of human development. The lack of any common notions here has been one of the most serious handicaps to our discussion of the future. Because of our failure we tend to make false goals out of the processes that we control; so the increase of quantity, or the promotion of change for the sake of change, like the actions of a bored child turning from one toy to another, constitutes our only directive. As a result of our failure, there are anthropologists and psychologists who look upon the whole experiment of civilization as a mistake or who, even if they do not go so far, treat each culture as a confined, self-subsistent entity, with no other goal than that of continuing in its ancient "way of life." But surely we cannot make good use of the earth unless we have some notion as to what is "good" and what is "useful," what is aimless change and what is a goal-directed transformation. And how can we arrive at these concepts unless we have some definite understanding of man's nature, his development, and his goals?

The evolution theory, as set forth by the great Victorians, was an attempt to give a meaningful interpretation of organic development. You will recall that, even before the great Darwin, Herbert Spencer had begun the modest work of synthesizing all knowledge on the basis of the evolutionary formula. His synthetic philosophy posited a continuous process of change, from indefinite simple homogeneity to definite complex heterogeneity. This plausible formula turned out to be inadequate for many reasons. The process of evolution was not a straight-line movement but one full of twists and turnings, of false starts, strategic retreats, and tangential explorations. By making mere survival a test of organic development, this theory tacitly placed some of the most primitive organisms, like the amoeba, on the same plane as man, for both have survived; and, on the same terms, parasites, which have lost their heterogeneity and complexity, deserved a higher rank than highly developed creatures that did not survive.

Now, the fact is that we cannot derive direction and purpose from any random succession of events; and the attempt to superimpose evolution on the framework of seventeenth-century science, which had deliberately eliminated the attributes of life from the bare framework of mass and motion, was doomed to failure. That failure now vitiates a significant part of our thinking, even in the biological sciences. In our effort to reduce complex phenomena to the simplest terms, we inevitably end up with life in a state of organic decomposition, in a formless, purposeless, dehumanized world, with man himself nothing more than a collection of cheap chemicals.

To correct for this physically accurate but one-sided interpretation, we should, I submit, begin with the most highly developed forms and work downward; for only in a scheme dominated by the attributes of life and personality—order, direction, purpose, intelligence, selectivity, sensitiveness, autonomy, self-transformation, consciousness, art—can we find any criterion for development lower in the scale.

In dealing with the physical world, this elimination of the phenomena of life and mind pays off. We get along much more rapidly if we reduce all factors to their simplest terms, paying attention to the quantitative and repeatable elements and eliminating, as Galileo and Kepler agreed, the secondary and subjective qualities like color, form, and pattern. But, when all events are subjected to this process of reduction and isolation, the most obvious characteristics of organic life disappear from view, namely, the fact that the organism is an autonomous, self-perpetuating, self-transforming being, in dynamic equilibrium, but with a definite cycle of growth, maturation, and decomposition; and, the higher the scale of life, the more plainly does growth record itself in superorganic forms and creative activities, detached from mere survival. Instead of being a passive victim of external forces, living creatures, as Iago Galdston has wisely reminded us, have their own trajectory of growth; and, the higher the rank of organism, the more remote and the more comprehensive are its goals. It is not enough for man to live in the purely physiological sense; he must live the good life, that is, he must expand the realm of significance, value, and form. On any sound reading of biological evolution or human history, it seems to me, development is often at odds with immediate security or ultimate survival. All higher life is precarious, as the highest states of life are themselves rare, fleeting, and evanescent.

Just because man has now become the dominant species on the planet, he needs both the knowledge of the external world, independent of his wishing, that science provides him and a knowledge of his own inner life, detached from the operation of extraneous forces and institutions, directed toward goals he himself projects. What will happen to this earth depends very largely upon man's capacities as a dramatist and a creative artist, and that in turn depends in no slight measure upon the estimate he forms of himself. What he proposes to do to the earth, utilizing its soils, its mineral resources, its water, its flow of energies, depends largely upon his knowledge of his own historic nature and his plans for his own further self-transformations. As the dominant biological species, man now has a special responsibility to his fellow creatures as well as to himself. Will he turn the cosmic energies at his disposal to higher ends, or will he, wilfully or carelessly, exterminate life and bring his own existence to a premature end? If he thinks of himself as an insignificant bag of chemicals, he may wantonly reduce all forms and structures to mere dust and rubble.

If you force me to talk about probabilities, not about possibilities, still less hopes, I would say that man's future seems black, though perhaps a shade lighter than it was five years ago; for if the nations now armed with nuclear weapons agree not to exterminate each other, even though provoked by a sense of intolerable outrage, the forces still dominant in our age are moving in the direction so keenly analyzed by Roderick Seidenberg, whose picture of 'Posthistoric Man' is to me even more frightening than either Aldous Huxley's or George Orwell's somewhat melodramatized versions. The difficulty is that our machine technology and our scientific methodology have reached a high pitch of perfection at a moment when other important parts of our culture, particularly those that shape the human personality—religion, ethics, education, the arts—have become inoperative or, rather, share in the general disintegration and help to widen it. Objective order and vocational discipline have gone hand in hand with subjective disorder and formlessness. We seem to be forgetting the art of creating whole mentally balanced human beings, immunized to pathological temptations. The widening wave of neuroticism and criminality, so visible in every advanced society, indicates, it would seem, some lack in the human nutrients needed to create full human beings—a lack that no increased production of snakeroot, for use in psychotherapy, will make up for. If we are to achieve some degree of ecological balance, we must aim at human balance too.

Too much of our discussion here, I am afraid, has dealt with proposals for man's exercising control over nature without reference to the kind of control he must exercise over himself. But, plainly, the greater the quantity of energy at man's disposal, the more important becomes the old Roman question: "Who is to control the controller?" At present that is a life-and-death question; and Marston Bates has rightly brought up the deep concern we must all feel over the manner in which government agencies in every big country have gone about exploiting our new powers. Atomic energy by itself is a neutral thing, obviously. It promises nothing; it threatens nothing. It is we who do the promising; it is we who exert the threat. What makes nuclear power a danger is the fact that it has been released in a world savagely demoralized by two world wars, the last of which turned into a war of unlimited annihilation; and the moral nihilism, first preached and enacted by the Fascist powers, has now been taken over by every person and agency that subscribes to the conception of total war—or, in plain English, unlimited extermination.

By now the wartime threat of nuclear power is obvious even to those who still cling to the idea of using it. For the sake of gaining momentary victory over a transient enemy, they would be ready to bring human history and perhaps all life on this planet to an end. But in recoiling from this ultimate madness, in acknowledging that co-existence is better than non-existence, we are not necessarily out of the woods; for even the peacetime uses of atomic energy should give us grave concern. On this score, I am not at all reassured by the sedative explanations that our own Atomic Energy Commission has put out. Certainly the history of ordinary industrial pollution gives us no ground for confidence: our childish shortsightedness under the excitement of novelty, our contempt for health when profits are at stake, our lack of reverence for life, even our own life, continue to poison the atmosphere in every industrial area and to make the streams and rivers, as well as the air we breathe, unfit for organic life. The people who are now proposing to use atomic energy on a vast scale are the same people who have not yet made an effort, technologically, to dispose of the lethal carbon monoxide exhaust of the motorcar, the same people whose factories expose the inhabitants of industrial areas to air polluted with virtually the entire number of known cancer-producing substances.

For all our apparent concern to lower the death rate, we have scarcely yet begun to cope with the problems of ordinary industrial pollution. Yet, without even a prudent look over their shoulders, our governmental and industrial leaders are now proposing to manufacture atomic energy on a vast scale, before they have the slightest notion of how to dispose safely of the fissioned waste products.

This is one of those moments when it is well to remember the life-wisdom of the fairy tales before we turn the latest gift of science into a horror story. When some deep-seated human wish is gratified by magic in these stories, there is usually some fatal catch attached to the gift, which either makes it do just the opposite of what is hoped or suddenly deprives the recipient of the promised boon, as Gilgamesh, in the Babylonian epic, is robbed by the serpent of the plant that would give him immortality. This catch is already visible in atomic energy. We know how to turn nuclear fission on, but, once we have created a radioactive element, we must wait for nature to turn it off if we cannot use it in a further reaction. If once we raised the ceiling of radiation above the critical level, we could not undo that fatal mistake.

Now I am not saying that the problems presented by the peacetime exploitation of atomic energy cannot be overcome. What I am saying is that the problem of atomic pollution must be faced, not at the last possible moment, when irreparable damage has already been done, but at the earliest possible moment. Already, as John Bugher has pointed out, the indiscriminate use of radium paint for the instrument dials of a plane constitutes an occupational hazard for the pilot. We do not know yet whether a technical solution is possible or whether the solution will have to be a political one that will ban nuclear energy except in laboratory quantities. Before we can have any notion of the long-term effects of atomic radiation, even in such relatively small amounts as have been released during the last ten years, we should, in all prudence, put atomic energy under strict probation. Our haste to exploit it betrays a frivolous sense of irresponsibility, which casts doubts on the fitness of our present leaders to exercise these powers.

On this matter, the Atomic Energy Commission can speak with no authority whatever, for it lacks the only data that would be convincing, namely, that provided by time—and only by time. Our knowledge of radioactivity, if one takes it back to the discovery of the Becquerel rays, covers only some sixty years, or two generations; our large-scale production of fissioned materials covers only a decade. If in ordinary engineering calculations one multiplies by two as a factor of safety, in atomic calculations one should multiply by many times that number. We simply do not know enough about the long-term effects of atomic energy in even minor quantities to justify the risks we are already taking. But we know enough about the nature of radiation itself, beginning with the records we have of injury and death to early radiologists, to know that the risks are serious and the results often fatal. In view of that fact, we have a right to demand humility and prudence, not cockiness and indecent haste, in even the peace-time exploitation of atomic energy, no less than a total veto on its large-scale use in war. The compulsive aspect about our peaceful exploitation of atomic energy should itself put us on our guard. It seems, indeed, almost neurotically compulsive, perhaps because it is bound up with our repressed sense of guilt. What will all our atomic power profit us if it radically undermines the balance of nature or the basis of human life?

Now we come to a point where I feel obliged to put a terminal question: What has this conference disclosed to us?

I cannot presume to voice the sense of the meeting on this matter, for it has disclosed many different things to each one of us; and perhaps some of the most important things we shall carry away from our papers and discussions may not become visible until long after we have separated, though they have already seeded themselves in our minds. But to me the conference confirmed a belief that has long been growing more definite; namely, that the still dominant pattern of seventeenth-century science, with its dismembered and isolated data, with its preference for single-factor analysis, with its strict separation of quantity and quality, with its reductive technique, must be supplemented in dealing with the phenomena of life with a method that does justice to the essential nature of life: the autonomy and integrity of organisms, with their selective and purposive behavior. We must abandon the semantic hoax of reducing organic behavior to "mechanisms," for a machine is an arrangement of predetermined parts for serving a specific human end; and the conception of a machine reintroduces the very element of teleology that causal analysis attempts in vain to eliminate from the world of life.*

Now, when one deals with human beings neither Cartesian causality nor Aristotelian teleology, nor yet pure chance, no matter how we reinterpret and refine these concepts, sufficiently accounts for the transformations of man in history. For human behavior is not merely purposive and goal-

* For a more thorough critical analysis, see the chapter on Descartes in 'The Pentagon of Power.'

seeking but conscious; not merely tied to existing ecological associations but capable of projecting a whole new pattern of relations in which both man's objective knowledge of nature and his subjective projection of dream and wish and imagined purpose modify natural processes and bring them to a different destination. That which distinguishes the superorganic processes of culture from organic processes is precisely what man himself, in his cumulative acts of self-nurture, self-education, and self-transformation, has contributed to nature's original gifts. And, if this is the case, one cannot hope to find out what man can do or should do in shaping the earth without canvassing something more than his present knowledge of origins, processes, and stages.

To command the forces now at man's disposal and direct them toward organic and human development, man must be capable of directing his actions toward ideal ends, imaginatively conceived and rationally criticized. The formulation of these ends does not come within the province of science, so long as it remains faithful to its own salutary discipline; it is rather the product of the arts and the humanities, of religious visions and moral aspirations. I come back, accordingly, to the need for a common philosophy of human development that will do justice to all our partial historic formulations. Until we have that, we cannot make enlightened choices and project appropriate goals. Because truth itself is a formative influence, scientific knowledge must enter into such a formulation, to replace the sometimes inspired guesswork of early religions; but there comes a moment when knowledge must be applied to action, when action must be guided by rational plans, when plans must be laid out in terms of an ideal goal, and when the ideal goal must be chosen consciously with a view to the kind of self we are trying to produce, and therewith to the kind of facilities—geographic, economic, cultural—that self needs for carrying through its purposes and its whole life-course.

In most of our prognoses about man's relations with the earth we have tended, I am afraid, simply to carry forward processes now observable, with such acceleration as may be expected from the cumulative nature of scientific and technical changes, provided that these remain constant and undisturbed. Thus, we have taken technological civilization as a base line and have assumed that its spread to more primitive technological cultures will continue, with results similar to those now visible in highly industrialized countries. In these predictions we overlook the effects of human consciousness, of human reactions, of human purposes that would possibly project a different destination; some of us, if we do not regard human nature as fixed, treat it as a dependent variable, entirely governed by the machine. Surely, only by regarding man's own self-transformation as negligible would anyone think it worthwhile to speculate, as some of us have done, on the transformations of energy that might make the earth capable of sustaining as many as thirty billion people. That increase of population could not in fact be accomplished without a wholesale regimentation of humanity, so limiting its field of action, so curtailing its choices, so adapting it to merely physiological criteria of survival—with no thought of development—that the result would no longer be recognizable as man but as an inferior creature with an inferior planet to work and die in.

Now the facts are, I submit, quite different from those assumed to operate under this too simple description. As I suggested earlier, "within the limit of earth's resources and man's biological nature, there are as many different possible futures as there are ideals, systems of values, goals and plans, and social, political, educational, and religious organizations for bringing about their realization." To assume that there is only one possibility left, that represented by our now-dominant technological civilization, is an act of blind religious faith, committed by those who believe this civilization is the ultimate goal of human evolution. In no sense is this an objective scientific judgment. All our present statistical curves may be deflected and altered in the real future by human choice and human contrivance; and in making these choices our normative ideas and ideals—indeed, our unconscious resistances and drives—will play no less a part than our knowledge.

Let me illustrate. There are, for example, large areas of the United States in national and state parks that might have been gutted out for industrial purposes had not the ideas and values of the romantic movement, as expressed by Henry Thoreau, Frederick Law Olmsted, and George Perkins Marsh, resulted in appropriate political action. Those of us who assume that the one-sided exploitation of the machine without any regard for the quality of life, is fated to go on and become more compulsive are, consciously or covertly, casting their vote for what Roderick Seidenberg calls "post-historic man." There would be only one virtue in that kind of society, adjustment, and only one reward—security. And the only freedom left would be that extolled by Karl Marx: "the conscious acceptance of necessity."

In the United States, no less than in Russia, we are moving uncomfortably near such a society; indeed, its main outlines have already been sketched in. If the production of posthistoric man were to become the dominant purpose of our culture, not a few of the problems we have been discussing would be automatically disposed of. If the goal is uniformity, why should we seek to preserve any of the richness of environmental and cultural individuality that still exists on the earth and, in turn, widens the range of human choice? Why should we not, on these terms, create by mechanical processes one single climate, uniform from the pole to the equator? Why should we not grind down the mountains, whether to obtain granite and uranium and soil, or just for the pleasure of bulldozing and grinding, until the whole round earth becomes planed down to one level platform.

If this is not to be mankind's fate, how are we to save ourselves from it? The formal answer is simple, though it presents difficulties it may take generations of strenuous effort to overcome. We must throw overboard this childishly inadequate picture of man's nature and destiny, and resume the functions and offices of men. The greatest of these functions, capable of dominating all others, is that of conscious self-fabrication. We shall be ill prepared to meet the real challenges of the future if we imagine that our present institutions, because of the extraordinary successes of the machine economy in production, have congealed into a final mold from which man can never hope to escape. There is rather plenty of evidence at this moment to indicate that man may, as Teilhard de Chardin's paper suggested, be on the point of emerging onto a new plane. For the first time man may, as a conscious, interrelated group, take possession of the whole planet. For the last century, not merely have we been able to think of the world as a whole, in time and space, but we have been able through our manifold inventions to act in the same fashion. Yet both our thinking and our acting have been crude, not to say primitive, because we have not yet created the sort of self, freed from nationalistic and ideological obsessions, capable of acting within this global theater.

I cannot, with the brief space that remains at my disposal, begin to characterize this new self, this "one world" self, as one might be tempted to call it; for it has as yet only begun to emerge. But if one of man's main tasks in the future will be to resettle and recultivate the earth, for the sake of human education and vital enjoyment, primarily, rather than for the sake of power, some of the characteristics of this ideal self may be defined in advance. Though it will cherish the skills and talents associated with professional training, it will be multi-occupational as well as multi-environmental; it will demand, wherever it settles or moves, the largest possible variety of opportunities and choices. To exercise all the functions of a man will become more important than to wear the identifying badge of a nation or an office; for the day will come, to quote Emerson again, when no badge, uniform, or star will be worn. The members of this conference, Carl Sauer has told us, were chosen not as representatives of a discipline, an institution, or a country but for their qualities as thinking human beings. So, in our meetings we have had, in a happy degree, a foretaste of what world culture and unified man would be. On such a basis, one need not fear posthistoric uniformity. When we begin the cultivation of the earth as a whole for more deeply human purposes, we may look forward rather to an efflorescence of individuality.

Certainly we can hardly hope to block the seemingly inexorable march of posthistoric man by clinging to obsolete institutions and archaic forms of the human self, fabricated by earlier cultures. To fight against the world-wide tendency toward mechanical uniformity and human nullity by trying to reserve some small segment of our life for an individuated development would be to surrender any hope of final victory. What we need to confront the threatening omniscience and omnipotence of posthistoric man is to cultivate powers equally godlike in a quite different part of the personality. Must we not cultivate a force that came late even in man's conception of godhood—the force that Henry Adams prophetically summoned up in opposition to the dynamo? I mean the force of love. And I mean love in all its meanings: love as erotic desire and procreativeness; love as passion and aesthetic delight, lingering over its images of beauty; love as fellow-feeling and neighborly helpfulness, bestowing its gifts on all who need it; love as parental solicitude and sacrifice; love as the miraculous capacity for overvaluing its own object and, thereby, glorifying it and transfiguring it, releasing for life something that only the lover can see. We need such a redeeming and all-embracing love at this moment to rescue the earth itself and all the creatures that inhabit it from the insensate forces of hate, violence, and destruction.

The awful omniscience and omnipotence of our science and technics would turn out to be more self-destructive than ignorance and impotence if the compensating processes of life did not foster a new kind of personality, whose loving concerns will in time offset these dangerous tendencies. We are now at a point where over two billion people have become our neighbors, and we shall have to learn all over again, without going back to our Stone Age ancestors, what the love of neighbors means. We can communicate with them at the speed of light; we can co-operate with them, to our common advantage, in long-term works of dressing and keeping the earth—or we can exterminate them, if we should be so vicious or so reckless, as surely as an electrocutioner, by a press of the button, can kill a condemned man. If we approach the earth and man in a spirit of love, we shall respect their individuality and treasure the gifts to personality that organic variety itself brings with it. We shall beware of all uniformities, unless, like the animal reflexes, they are agents of a higher life. Of every invention, of every organization, of every fresh political or economic proposal, we must dare to demand: Has it been conceived in love and does it further the long-term purposes of man?

Much that we now do would not survive such a question. But much that is still open to man's creative acts of self-transformation would at last become possible. Not power but power directed by love into the forms of beauty and truth is what we need for our survival, to say nothing of our further development. Only when love takes the lead will the earth, and life on earth, be safe again. And not until then.

(1955)

CHAPTER FORTY-TWO

The Flowering
of Plants and Men*

Though I have on two or three other occasions been given the task of summarizing a conference, it always turns out that the job is beyond my powers, indeed possibly beyond anyone's powers, and that the main effect of our discussions is to point to the necessity of holding still another conference, to bring to a sharper focus the ideas we have been putting forth and probing. But since I have been listening assiduously to the many able papers that have been presented during the last two days, I could not help assembling my own general impression of the results. And with all respect to both the speakers and the audience, I must say that, although a great amount of important information has been conveyed to us, we have only been delicately nibbling at the edges of the problem—the challenge of survival, for men and plants.

If I venture to speak very frankly, without the usual degree of scientific detachment, it is because I am in fact not a scientist but a Dutchess County gardener: my sole qualification here is that I have handled plants, have assisted in a modest way in their growth, and have learned something about the nature of life, including my own, by observing how selective, how self-respecting, how wilful, indeed choosey, plants can be, in singling out the conditions necessary for their survival, and still more, for their fullest growth and flowering.

One of the things that has struck me about this conference is that so little mention has been made of the plants themselves and the great part they have played in encouraging man's own development; and further how essential it now is to reclaim and extend the dominion of plants once more, if man's own survival is to be secured. Though not a few references have been made to primeval forms, like the algae, I propose to widen our area of exploration sufficiently to take in the whole world of living plants, and to suggest that the chances of our own survival are closely bound up

* Address given at a symposium, 'Challenge for Survival,' sponsored by The New York Botanical Garden and The Rockefeller University.

with the recovery of the common territory we have too readily surrendered to an underdimensioned, organically deficient technology, now producing a multitude of environmental changes that are undermining the very existence of both plants and men.

So let me ask you, first of all, what will be left of the plant world if we allow the basically village culture, founded on a close symbiotic partnership between man and plants, to disappear? For some twelve thousand years, all the higher achievements of civilization have rested on this culture, one devoted to the constructive improvement of the habitat and the loving care of plants—their selection, their nurture, their breeding, their enjoyment. That culture, as Edgar Anderson suggested, originally made some of its best discoveries in breeding by being equally concerned with the color, the odor, the taste, the flower and leaf patterns, the sexual functions, and the nutritive qualities of plants, valuing them not only for food and medicine, but for esthetic delight. There are plenty of people working in scientific laboratories today who, though they may still call themselves biologists, have no knowledge of this culture, except by vague hearsay, and no respect for its achievements. They dream of a world composed mainly of synthetics and plastics, in which no creatures above the rank of algae or yeasts would be encouraged to grow.

In the earlier stages of human development, the relationship between man and plants had been a one-sided one, not an active partnership. Though plants, birds, and insects have always been among man's chief foods, man was able to do very little to modify natural vegetation, still less to assist in the cultivation of favored plants: man's relation to the existing botanical system was parasitic rather than symbiotic. But first by preservation and selection, and then by active cultivation, man found himself, once the last glacial period came to an end, able actively to reshape his habitat and to do something for the plant world. In doing so, he made his own environment immensely more habitable, more edible, and—what is equally important—more lovable. And in the very act of establishing a new role for plants, man both deepened his roots in the landscape and gave himself a new leisure and a new security. It was in the garden that man, thanks largely to woman's efforts, for the first time felt completely at home.

In my recent book, 'Technics and Human Development,' I pointed out that the great advances in neolithic domestication were made with hardly any mechanical aids. One of man's instruments, fire, had been in his hands for some five hundred thousand years. The other was the stone ax, with which man could chop down trees. Those who equate neolithic plant domestication with grain cultivation and plow culture have not caught up with recent archaeology; for though these last inventions were extremely important, the major advances of the neolithic revolution had been made long before through a fuller understanding of plant nurture, plant selection, plant hybridization, in the timing of cultivation to fit the seasons, and in the close watching of the relation of plant growth to soil, water, ash, and dung.

With the aid of the ax, neolithic man opened up clearings in the forests of the highlands where the plants he chose would have sufficient space, moisture, nutriment, and freedom from competition to thrive, while on the edge of the clearings in the same area the berry bushes took hold and spread about further through the co-operation of the greedy finches and cardinals. This picture of the beginnings of neolithic domestication—though of course partly hypothetic—corresponds to the growing archaeological evidence, and emphasizes something that needs emphasis, namely, that though grain cultivation capped this process, what was even more important for human development was the combination of plant variety, continuity of occupation, and the growing interdependence of man, plants, insects, and birds. Up to this point man's greatest improvements had been made with the materials of his own body: the symbols of dream, ritual, language, and art. Now he was at least sufficiently well established to enter into an active partnership with plants, and later with the animals that paleolithic hunters had venerated. With plant domestication, man's inner life and his outer life achieved a balance.

This active partnership between man and plants did something more than ensure their common survival: it provided, as never before, the conditions for their further development. Every domesticated plant and animal we use today, with a few trifling exceptions like the boysenberry and the coffee plant, was originally a product of neolithic domestication, whose clearings and tilled acres and vineyards and orchards finally engirdled the Earth. Though the period of botanical and agricultural experiment came to a climax before the Bronze Age, this culture has a record of longevity and continuity that indicates how admirably it met the conditions necessary for both ecological balance and human development in every kind of geographic environment.

The local center of this culture was the successor of the neolithic village, where the traditional rites, the traditional customs, the traditional lore of cultivation, were passed on from generation to generation, from century to century: slowly absorbing the improvements introduced by the higher cultures, being guided by the new astronomical calendar, making use of the horse and the ox and the plow, gratefully accepting the iron hoe and the iron spade, yet always stable enough to pass on the essential knowledge of plant needs and cultivation processes and human purposes to ensure the village's survival. If survival were to be our only criterion of fitness, this basic neolithic culture would hold the record. That village economy spread over the entire planet and it left everywhere the imprint of its essential features: variety, balance, controlled and limited growth. If this culture never reached the constructive heights of the urban civilization of the Bronze, the Iron, or the Nuclear Age, it never descended to their depths of destruction and extermination.

Both plants and men—even when due allowance is made for overbrowsed forests and overgrazed pastures and eroded hillsides—were safe in the hands of such backward communities: their very feebleness and lethargy were an insurance against gross human mismanagement. But all this has changed, almost within our own generation; and the ancient symbiotic relation, so helpful to both human and plant life, may be dissolved in an excess of technological dynamism, within our life-time.

Those who still talk glibly about the inevitability of further mechanization and urbanization, who look forward to an almost solid urbanoid mass sometimes called Megalopolis, reaching from Maine to Florida, or even covering the greater part of the planet, do not in the least realize the implications of their complacent predictions. With almost criminal levity, they have accepted, as if it were a fatal necessity, the ruthless destruction of the balanced environment essential to human life. On a purely physical level, that balance is dependent upon the part played by plants in maintaining the oxygen-nitrogen cycle necessary to plant, animal, and above all human existence. For twelve thousand years agriculture, as practiced by village communities, ensured human continuity. Today the villages are being wiped out, the farming population reduced in the United States to a mere tenth of the total; and precisely the richest soils and the most cultivable areas are being made into urban deserts.

I have no wish to frighten you; but it is time we realized, if all too belatedly, that this lopsided technology has little prospect, if it goes on expanding at its present rate, of surviving for even a century, much less twelve thousand years. As the cultivated areas shrink, as millions of square miles of good soils are turned into sterile expressways, concrete clover-leaves, parking lots, and airports; as the air, the water, and the soil become polluted with chemical poisons, nuclear wastes, and inorganic debris; as essential bird and insect species die off, the prospects of human survival on any terms diminish.

As long as from seventy to ninety per cent of the world's population was engaged in cultivating plants, human life as a whole was secure. In the past century this biological factor of safety has shrunk. Tomorrow it may be gone. If our leaders were sufficiently awake to these dangers they would plan not for urbanization but for ruralization.

Our present dangerous lack of ecological balance is largely due to the fact that our technology, in overcoming our organic limitations and increasing, by an enormous factor, the amount of energy at our disposal, has none of the self-limiting and self-correcting devices that organic systems have developed. Some of you perhaps remember the illustration W. H. Hudson gave in 'Far Away and Long Ago' of what happened on the pampas of the Argentine when a single plant, the Canada thistle, invaded this environment. Within a short time the herds of cattle were starving and the economy was threatened, because the thistles, freed from the restraints of their original environment, grew higher than a horse's head, and became so thick that cattle could not make their way through them.

Well, modern technology, whether under capitalist or communist exploitation, has proved to be the Canada thistle of our culture. The aim of our technology is not to enhance life and to foster the processes of growth and efflorescence, but to exploit power and bring ever larger portions of the environment, and of human life, too, under more and more rigid and regimented modes of control. Expansion, magnification, multiplication, quantification, speed, turnover, profit, "overkill"—these are the criteria of technical success. In the interests of an expanding economy, we have been settling for a contracted life in which no organic function will be tolerated unless it can be profitably attached to some corporate megamachine and made to conform to its requirements.

But why should we regard our machines as more sacred than organisms and treat their needs as superior to those of animals and plants and men? Why should our economy seek to expand every year, instead of aiming, like organic systems, at establishing a balance favorable to human needs in the order of their biological and social importance? Why should we allow ourselves to be assaulted, for example, with supersonic transportation, when the hours saved for the passengers on these planes will be offset by the days lost to millions of groundlings whose lives will be periodically shattered by the noise of their breaking the sound barrier? Does man live by transportation alone?

A colleague of mine, a professor at M.I.T., has calculated that if a superjet plane, in a single flight over a population of as little as five million people, disturbed the life of each one for only ten seconds, the amount of time lost on the ground would add up to something like 13,800 hours. In all, a total of 578 man-days would be lost in order to enable a few score high-pressured travelers to reach their destination a few hours sooner. Such fake time saving would be laughed out of existence were it not for the fact that our machine worship has become as fantastically irrational as the star worship of the Aztecs, who slaughtered thousand of lives every year as a religious sacrifice.

This same system of jet propulsion has now been applied, at least in military models, to land transportation in vehicles without wheels; and Marshall McLuhan has even proclaimed that both the wheel and the roadway have become obsolete and all transportation would be conducted on a cushion of air. Apparently Professor McLuhan has not yet learned that the exhausts of ordinary motor cars and jet engines have already risen to a dangerous level; and that anything like a universal transportation system by jets would soon reach an extermination level. Even the most vaporous mind should by now be sufficiently familiar with the scientific data to realize that such a system of transportation, operated on a large scale, would be an invitation to mass suicide.

The notion that our age has an obligation to foster such technological depredations in the name of progress must be challenged. Whose progress —man's or the machine's? Why indeed should any government subsidize jet-age travel when the net effect is to ruin every landscape and every historic site to which we bring our jet liners and motor coaches? Until now

Delphi, for instance, presented one of the most wonderful landscapes in the world: a landscape whose profound religious atmosphere remained, though the temples are ruined and the religion itself has passed away. But, speaking for myself, I don't dare go back to Delphi. I know that it has already become a parking lot, and in a few years all that made it so precious will, if our present habits continue, disappear: even the eagles will probably cease to hover in the sky, and the sea of olive trees in the Vale of Amphissa will be cut down to make way for hotel sites and golf courses.

Isn't it time for us to ask ourselves a few serious questions about the overheated technology upon which we have become so dependent, and the expanding economy that we have been so sedulously promoting and coddling, at the expense of organic balance and development, to say nothing of human health, poise, sanity? We are no longer in control of this overpowered and overpowering corporate mechanism: we are driving this supposedly up-to-date vehicle without either a steering wheel or a brake, and our only form of control is through the use of an accelerator to make it go faster, even though that greatly increases the danger.

Our Canada thistle technics has the effect of reducing all life to the level of the machine, even as it reduces all human intelligence to the level of a computer, without the feelings, emotions, purposes, desires, hopes that bring us into relation with the lives of other men and indeed with the whole cosmos of living beings. We are creating a monoculture which is becoming more standardized, more homogenized and flattened out every day. Even our recreation is no longer the sphere of spontaneity and self-expression: it too has become standardized; and in many of our overcrowded national parks in summer, the smog and the rubbish and the defacement of the landscape fully equal that produced in our cities. Is it not significant that even on the open water speed alone has become the criterion of enjoyment? The fast-moving, noisy, air-polluting motorboat has taken the place of the more adventurous sailboat, which called for muscular exercise, a weather eye, a knowledge of sea and shore, along with self-confidence, even courage.

In the course of our meetings we have been examining, in a shy, somewhat circuitous way, some of the effects of this humanly deficient monoculture, with its insidious displacement of human needs, its erosion and pollution of the natural environment, and its reduction of the area of both wild and cultivated lands. What we must realize is the fact that though science and technology have brought mankind huge benefits, which we have every right to be proud of and every reason to enjoy, they have also burdened us with painful deficits that must be liquidated, and they threaten us with serious disorders that we must promptly cope with. What is worse, these negative results are in part due to the very superabundance of their products, like the cans and bottles that now litter our roadsides, so-called disposable containers that no one has yet found an economic and decent way of disposing of.

If we are to recover both our ecological and our cultural balance, we must subject our entire economy to a rigorous examination, and deal with our difficulties at their source, instead of paying attention to them only when they have become so embedded in the whole structure of production and consumption that they cannot be removed except with heroic exertions and at extravagant cost. In other words, instead of becoming heartsick over our littered roadsides, our rubbish dumps, our auto cemeteries, we must challenge the whole economy of the disposable container. Instead of just fighting against turning our last wetlands into jet ports, we must challenge the notion that all other human needs should be sacrificed to fast transportation. In short, we must dare to question the religion of the machine, and be ready to flout the superstitious observances and taboos that have been erected to ensure the supremacy of automation, computerism, and electronic communication over more important services to human life that the wilderness areas, the cultivated farmland and parkland, vineyards and orchards produce.

If we intend to provide for the survival of plants and men, we had better become iconoclasts of this machine-centered religion: we must throw down these idols, and ask the bat-eyed priests of technology what on earth they think they are doing. Obviously, the Earth, in all its variety and complexity of environments, is the last place for which they feel any sense of responsibility: they are off on dizzy trips to outer space—"trips" in *both* present senses of the word. One of the high priests of this religion, Buckminster Fuller, has even said, seemingly with a straight face, that the space capsule is the one truly perfect environment yet invented by man; and it is increasingly plain that the chief end of this religion is to reduce the Earth itself to a space capsule: the most deadly, defunctionalized, dehumanized environment that the mind of man has yet conceived—compared to which the most backward neolithic mud village was a paradise of creativity and human autonomy.

Instead of defending our position, putting up a dreary rearguard fight against the armies that are conquering the Earth for the sake of unlimited power and profit and prestige, the time has come for man and his plants to join forces in a counterattack. Mere survival is not good enough: we must devise a strategy to ensure the further development of plants and men. The odds against our success are far from hopeless, for in fact, all life is on our side—and has been since the very beginning, slow though we have been to realize this fact. Here I return to my original theme: we have something to learn from the plants. The flowering plants, above all, have much to teach us about our own nature. Not by accident, the young, who are in revolt against our power-stricken and machine-regimented society, have seized upon the symbolism of the flower, and call themselves "flower children." In a very innocent, simpleminded, sometimes downright silly way, they have used the flower symbol to express their rejection of this automated and computerized and life-hostile technology. We, too, must learn to be flower children again, and rejoin the old procession and pageant of life.

Yes: the plants, above all the flowering plants, have something to teach us. Remember Loren Eiseley's beautiful chapter in 'The Immense Journey,' about that turning point in organic development when the Age of Reptiles gave way to the Age of Mammals, those warm-blooded beasts that suckled their young. Eiseley pointed out that the Age of Mammals was accompanied by an explosion of flowers; and that the reproductive system of the angiosperms was responsible, not merely for covering the whole earth with a green carpet composed of many different species of grass—over four thousand—but for intensifying vital activity of every kind, since the nectars and pollens and seeds and fruits and the succulent leaves dilated the senses, exhilarated the mind, and immensely increased the total food supply. Not merely was this explosion of flowers a cunning device of reproduction, but the flowers themselves assumed a variety of forms and colors that in most cases cannot possibly be accounted for as having survival value in the struggle for existence. It may add to the attraction of a lily's sexuality to have all of its sexual organs displayed amid teasingly open petals; but the huge success of so many compositae, with their insignificant florets, shows that biological prosperity might have been purchased without any such floral richness and inventiveness.

Efflorescence is an example of nature's untrammeled creativity and the fact that floral beauty cannot be explained or justified on purely utilitarian grounds is precisely what makes this explosion so wonderful—and so typical of all life processes. Biological creativity exists for its own sake: if survival were all that mattered, life might have remained in the primal ooze, or crept no further upward than the lichens. The capacity for self-transformation has not yet been expressed in any currently accepted biological doctrine, nor yet is it explained by the chemical instrumentality of DNA. But long before man himself became conscious of beauty, beauty existed in the endlessly varied forms and colors of the flowering plants. The selection and encouragement of these plants, quite apart from any utilitarian value, was what gave man his first real glimpse, perhaps, of paradise—for paradise is only the original Persian name for a walled garden. The capacity for exuberant expression symbolized by efflorescence—this is the primal gift of life; and to consciously maintain it and guard it and expand it is one of the ultimate reasons for human existence. There are no mechanical or electronic substitutes for this kind of creativity.

But observe: our present-day civilization, in allowing its neolithic foundations to crumble, now finds itself in a curious position. Thanks to man's superb intelligence and his ability to translate mathematical and physical abstractions into practical inventions, the gift of exuberance has been transferred from the world of living organisms to the world of machines, electronic apparatus, and power utilities. Here we are deliberately displacing organic variety and replacing it with a more limited mechanical variety. Ulysses Hedrick tells us that over ninety species of apples were cultivated in American before 1860, while today, to judge by the supermarkets, there are only two varieties left: Delicious and McIntosh. Yet at the same time there has been an explosion of machines, for the technological world shows immense vitality and exuberance that threatens to suppress every other manifestation of life. The most dynamic parts of this technology, so far from being devoted to the cultivation of plants or the culture of human beings, derive from our massive preparations for war; and in their actual use they display a callous indifference, indeed a stupendous and stultifying hostility, to the needs of organisms.

In 'The Myth of the Machine' I have drawn a parallel between the high-powered technology of the Pyramid Age, which produced the towered cities, the great canal systems, dams, irrigation works, and along with these, war and destruction on an unparalleled scale, and the megatechnic organizations of our own time. In both examples, the engineering was magnificent: don't think I undervalue the technical achievement. But it was the lack of ecological insight that resulted, in Sumer, not merely in the silting up of the canals but in the salinization of the fields and in the eventual ruin of agriculture. Something of the same nature is happening in the United States today.

As if the lethal smog from our multimillion cars and factory chimneys were not a sufficient threat to life, we extend the area of poisoning by spraying pesticides and herbicides recklessly over the landscape, and by pouring detergents into already heavily polluted streams. The birds and the insects now exist in ever-dwindling numbers, thanks largely to DDT—a nerve poison whose use should never have been permitted—and the vegetables and flowers and fruits dependent upon their co-operation in fertilization will, if this process goes on, be doomed. Hence the morbid interest some biologists have shown in developing sub-foods, from algae and yeasts. But the full meaning of this attack upon every mode of life by our war-directed technology has hardly yet been grasped. What it means, at bottom, is that we are regressing from the age of mammals, birds, and flowers, back to the age of the cold-blooded reptiles.

Before we let the armored reptiles and the flying reptiles reconquer the planet, we had better take a good hard look at the kind of existence that is now offered to us as the highest expression of our scientific age. Why should we offer homage to machines, as if they were superior kinds of organisms, and think so humbly and distrustfully about the human mind, with its incalculable reserves of potential creativity, provided it keeps hold of our historic nature and in touch with all its co-operating resources in the living environment. Why should we accept the notion of an expanding economy as a method of salvation, when actually what we need is a *balanced* economy, which will put the needs of life before the claims of profit, prestige, or power. Why should we waste our surplus on mechanical gadgets and inane superfluities, when we might be cultivating our gardens and bringing forth new plants—some if possible with a higher protein content!—that we never cultivated before. Why should we invest public funds in sterile highrise tenements, in all their dreary uniformity, when the environment of life demands homes, gardens, communities that express individuality and identity, as every natural species does, as a condition for normal development. Why, to put it briefly, should we value parking lots above parks, and content ourselves with plastic flowers, mockeries of both nature and art, fit only to be placed, Nazi-fashion, at the entrance to extermination camps. Every city should be a garden city, for gardens can give more intense sensory awakening and delight than any noxious halucinogen.

These are not private questions or peculiar answers. The young are already asking them. If we had not shut our minds to feedback, we should all of us have been asking them long ago. It is incredible that it was only in 1938 that Landsberg wrote about Air Pollution, and no one else had taken the subject seriously, except in terms of dirt, though as Landsberg wisely pointed out, the smoke nuisance was the subject of a constructive paper by John Evelyn three whole centuries ago. Yet it is more absurd to tolerate a technology producing high-speed changes on a world-wide scale, but with no apparatus for detecting its errors, no effective public method for correcting them, and no willingness to utilize the scientific information available if this threatens to limit its continued expansion and profit making. The Romans, in their high regard for justice, used to say "Let justice prevail, though the ceiling fall." But our technocrats are so committed to the worship of the sacred cow of technology that they say in effect: Let the machine prevail, though the earth be poisoned, the air be polluted, the food and water be contaminated, and mankind itself be condemned to a dreary and useless life, on a planet no more fit to support life than the sterile surface of the moon.

It is against this miscarriage of science and technology, this wholesale curtailment of the possibilities of life, this continued threat of collective extermination by nuclear bombardment that might wipe out all higher life on this planet, or by slower but equally deadly modes of poisoning, that the young today are in revolt. In their use of the flower as the symbol of vitality and creativity, of unashamed sexuality and love, they are reminding us of the terms upon which men and plants have not only survived but prospered together—with the aid, of course, of all the other species and orders whose combined activities have produced a living environment. Unless we change our minds, as the young are doing, and alter our whole routine of living, we shall not need a nuclear war to bring the whole evolutionary process to a halt. So my final word to you is to remember what the young are saying to us, in words that were first used by John Ruskin: *"There is no wealth but life."*—Let it flower!

(1968)

Sources

39. World Culture. From Chapters VIII and IX of *The Transformations of Man*, (1956).

40. The Human Prospect. Originally "California and the Human Horizon," address read before the Institute on Planning for the North Central Valley, at Davis, California, January 12, 1962. Published in *The Urban Prospect*, (1968).

41. The Opening Future. Originally "Summary Remarks: Prospect," final address delivered at the International Symposium on "Man's Role in Changing the Face of the Earth," June 16–21, 1955. Published in *Man's Role in Changing the Face of the Earth*, edited by William L. Thomas, (1956).

42. The Flowering of Plants and Men. From *The Myth of the Machine: II. The Pentagon of Power*, (1970). Also published in the *Garden Journal*, XVIII (May/June 1968).

Note: The publishing history of the material included in this book may be found in Elmer S. Newman, *Lewis Mumford: A Bibliography, 1914–1970* (New York, 1971).

Index

Books by Lewis Mumford
available in paperback editions
from Harcourt Brace Jovanovich, Inc.